THE LITERARY SOUTH

THE
LITERARY
SOUTH

COMPILED AND EDITED BY

Louis D. Rubin, Jr.

LOUISIANA STATE UNIVERSITY PRESS
Baton Rouge

10 9 8 7 6 5 4 3 2

Library of Congress Cataloging-in-Publication Data

The Literary South.

   1. American literature—Southern States. 2. Southern States—Literary collections. I. Rubin, Louis Decimus, 1923–
PS 551.L55 1986   810′.8′0975   86–7484
ISBN 0-8071-1359-X
Louisiana Paperback Edition, 1986

PREFACE

This anthology has been designed to provide a survey, grouped along historical lines, of the principal manifestations of the Southern literary imagination. It has two functions: one general, one particular. The book's general function is to allow the reader interested in the South to become familiar with its writers and what they have been concerned with over the past several hundred years. Its particular function is to serve as a textbook anthology for college and university courses in Southern literature.

In selecting the contents I have been guided by the following assumptions and objectives.

1. Most courses in Southern literature concentrate on the twentieth century (with a few notable exceptions). This is perhaps as it should be, but what is often fascinating and illuminating about the earlier material is the remarkable fashion in which much of it does anticipate the achievement of Faulkner, Warren, Welty, Wolfe, and other modern writers. For that reason alone it merits intensive study and I have kept that function in mind when making my selections.

2. The majority of teachers now approach Southern literature not so much as an historical artifact, paralleling the political and social history of the region, as they do critically and imaginatively, in order to show it as embodying the concerns and attitudes of the historical community. In other words, historical emphasis is now thematic and topical, not documentary. I have therefore included very few of the old "standard" historical documents. I have omitted a sample of the *Federalist,* Jackson on nullification and Calhoun on states' rights, Lee's Farewell Address (which was written by Colonel Marshall), Grady's New South speech, Booker T. Washington's Atlanta Address, and so on. There is little about the South and its people in these documents that may not be appropriately developed through literary analysis of fiction and poetry.

3. The writing of black Southerners from slavery times to the present is not only an important expression of the Southern imagination, but also an illumination of the writing of white Southerners. The South today is an integrated society, and we can now see that for the previous two hundred years it was tending in that direction even while the white population strove to resist this tendency. Thus, a sizable quantity of work by black Southerners is included in this collection.

4. More attention needs to be paid to Southern writing prior to 1789 because—although there was no self-conscious "South" as such before the rise of the sectional controversy in the 1800s—many characteristics that mark the Southern imagination were developing during colonial times.

PREFACE

5. Certain kinds of writing in the antebellum and local-color periods are important today as examples of a genre of writing, but with limited space, only representative works were selected. Thus, I have included Simms and Kennedy among the antebellum romancers, but omitted Caruthers and Cooke. For the local-color story I have included examples by Page, Cable, Murfree, Harris, and Chesnutt.

6. When the reputation of a writer is both as novelist and poet, I felt it was unnecessary to include a short story by that writer as a substitute for the novel. The space could be put to better use with a selection of the author's verse, and the teacher could supplement that with a novel if desired. (For example, I wouldn't think of teaching a course in Southern literature without Warren's *All The King's Men,* and there seemed no good reason to include one of his short stories when his importance and distinction do not lie in that genre.)

7. It is difficult to evaluate the textbook requirements for Southern writing the closer it gets to our own time; there is less agreement about its "canon." Time and taste have, in effect, sorted out most nineteenth-century writing, and although there were items I would have liked to include because of personal interest, I resisted the temptation because I was aware of the eccentricity of such preferences. With works written after 1920, however, this isn't nearly as easy to do. Others will perhaps disagree with some of my inclusions and certainly with some of my exclusions. For the most recent writers, I decided to include almost none of them, on the grounds that each person will have his and her ideas about who is and is not appropriate. Because my objective was neither to "promote" contemporary reputations nor to adjudicate on relative merit, but to provide representative selections of work that most teachers using this anthology would and should expect to find here, I have made my choices accordingly. Consequently, I have had to omit work that I think is extremely good, some of it by authors who are good friends of mine.

Finally, no one could attempt to assemble such an anthology without drawing constantly upon the insights and help of other students of the South and its literature. I am indebted to Hugh Holman, Richard Beale Davis, Lewis P. Simpson, Evans Harrington, George Core, Dan Young, James Justus, Walter Sullivan, Robert Jacobs, Blyden Jackson, Rayburn Moore, Arlin Turner, Floyd Watkins, Morris Cox, Richard Calhoun, Lee Greene, Jack Raper, Lewis Lawson, Jack Guilds, Lewis Leary, Robert Bain, William Harmon—such are the blessings of friendship that I am listing at one and the same time my personal friends and most of the leading scholars in my field. For in general, the study of Southern literature has largely involved a community of scholars and gentlemen who are friends and fellow workers, and it has been a privilege to

PREFACE

be part of this activity. I must also thank those students who have helped me in forming ideas and insights—but that list would be so lengthy that I had better not even begin to enumerate them.

LOUIS D. RUBIN, JR.

For
Walter and Jane Sullivan
and the
Red Cross Knight

CONTENTS

CONTENTS

CONTENTS

III.
AFTER THE WAR

CONTENTS

V.
AFTER THE RENASCENCE

CONTENTS

PART ONE

LITERATURE IN THE COLONIAL SOUTH

The economic, political, and cultural differences that produced, on the eastern seaboard of North America, sections identifiable as South and North were more than two hundred years in the making. To expect to find much that will be recognizable as "Southern" in the early literature of the region that ultimately became known as the American South is therefore very dubious. All we can do is look at the literature written in the seventeenth and eighteenth centuries and attempt to identify tendencies, attitudes, themes, ways of seeing, thinking, and feeling, which in the light of subsequent developments might be viewed as significant.

When we speak of "literature" in the colonial context, of course, we have to be a great deal less narrow and rigorous than in later times in our definition of it. Pioneering folk are notably without much time or inclination for reading and writing, and it was well into the eighteenth century before the Southern colonies had advanced importantly beyond the stage of an adventure in the wilderness and evolved any kind of settled, established, leisurely life that would permit much in the way of reflection and contemplation. For more than a century after the founding of Jamestown there were no newspapers, magazines, or printing presses in the Southern colonies. Thus, in any meaningful study of the incipient literary consciousness of what was to become the South, we must proceed just as we would in the instance of New England or the Middle Colonies: include in our concept of literature journals, diaries, sermons, promotional and travel accounts, and public documents, even while pouncing upon every available scrap of "imaginative" literature of the more formally belletristic type, without too much regard for actual literary merit as such.

To do so—however fascinating it might be—is not really central to the purposes of this anthology, which, after all, is concerned chiefly with *Southern* literature—works of literature that are emblematic of an identifiable region's literary imagination. Until that region becomes itself, and the adjective "Southern" becomes a significant cultural and social label instead of principally a geographical designation, there is not much point in attempting any thoroughgoing scrutiny of its writings. We have selected a very few "representative" samples of early writings, chosen because of what they reveal about the development of the body of literature that we later, and with some confidence, examine as distinctively or characteristically Southern.

In so doing let us note at the outset that we are in a very different situation from what we might have faced had we attempted to do this even as recently as a half-century ago. For during the past fifty years literary scholars have discovered and identified a vastly greater and richer body of writings in the Southern colonies than had formerly been thought to exist. It was believed—and asserted in print—that, except for a handful of political writings and one or two travel journals and other fragments, the early Southern colonies were almost totally without any literary interests or expression. Anthologies of American literature customarily allotted hundreds of pages to the poems, sermons, and political writings of the New England Puritans, while "covering" the Southern scene with an excerpt from William Byrd II's *History of the Dividing Line* and political writings by Thomas Jefferson and James Madison. The reason given for such a disparity was that Southern colonials stayed outdoors much of the time and were not too concerned with intellectual and literary matters, and consequently produced no literature.

Actually, Virginia, Maryland, and Carolina colonials often possessed large private libraries, which they consulted regularly. They wrote poems, essays, histories, pamphlets and were especially adept at satire, mock heroics, and burlesques. They penned extended and affectionate descriptions of their country and were often careful observers and recorders of the natural environment. They gathered in social clubs at Annapolis, Charleston, and elsewhere to discuss life and letters, and frequently wrote down their conclusions in polished form. These colonials were early interested in the theater and supported players and plays. They wrote lengthy and carefully composed public letters to friends in England that were intended to be read and passed along. They were also acquainted with the classics and strongly interested in history. Their ministers were as active in writing as those from other regions and circulated well-conceived, painstakingly reasoned sermons on both public and private matters, which were widely circulated and admired. And so on.

In political and social thinking they reached their finest heights. The great Virginians and Carolinians of the Revolutionary War generation proved able to articulate the guiding principles of political freedom used as the foundation of the American republic's ideals. As the twentieth-century critic H. L. Mencken declared, it was in the Southern colonies "that nearly all the political theories we still cherish and suffer under came to birth." Such men as Jefferson, Madison, Mason, Wythe, Washington, Laurens, the Pinckneys, and the Lees did not suddenly come into existence out of a mindless, intellectually sterile, pleasure-loving cultural slough. They were able to be what they were for the new nation because they thought and wrote out of a long and rich heritage of learning and intellect.

From that day in May 1607 when the colonists went ashore at Jamestown to the day in July 1776 when a Virginian's declaration of American political independence was signed by the members of the Continental Congress in Philadelphia, there was steady growth and maturation of Southern colonials to the point at which they considered themselves Americans ready for self-government. By the close of the seventeenth century such native-born Virginians as Robert Beverley had long since abandoned the habit of thinking of themselves as Englishmen residing in the New World. Beverley's *History and Present State of Virginia* (1705) was written to inform the English about life in Virginia by one who considered himself neither beyond the borders of established civilization nor under any requirement to apologize for the failure of his country to be what Englishmen thought it should be. At times he is highly censorious of the ways of his fellow Virginians, but as an American—an "Indian," Beverley expressed it—criticizing his compatriots.

Beverley's brother-in-law, Wiliam Byrd II, though also native born, tended to express more deference to what he felt his English friends might think about life in the New World, but Byrd had spent a large portion of his life in England, where he had many literary, scientific, and social acquaintances. Even with Byrd, one does not feel that the consciousness at work in his writings is that of an Englishman whom chance has expatriated from his home. The reality for Byrd is America. However much he misses the sophisticated life of London, his attitude is seldom one of unnatural deprivation.

During the 1720s, 1730s, and 1740s, as the Southern colonies grew in population and as their frontiers extended steadily westward, they developed functioning systems of self-government for internal affairs and came to expect that the mother country's role in their governance would be confined to matters of trade, commerce, and other areas involving their external relationships with England and Europe. Thus, when the English government in the mid-1740s began pointedly acting to reassert its right to approve or reject the internal laws of colonial legislatures, there was immediate resentment. The outbreak of war with France, fought to establish possession of trans-Allegheny America, temporarily suspended the vigorous assertion of colonial grievances, but once it was over the tension between England and the colonies increased markedly, and the procession of events was underway that within less than two decades led to the Stamp Act, the Townshend duties, the boycott on importation of English goods, the tax on tea, and ultimately the formation of Committees of Correspondence, and the coming of outright armed resistance and the Declaration of Independence.

The Southern colonies, Virginia in particular, were foremost in their assertions of the right to self-government, and when the time came to "dissolve the political bands which have connected them" with the mother country, the Virginians especially were ready to lead the way. And although the causes that brought about the American Revolution were complex and involved planter debts, land policy, the Navigation Acts and their impact on trade with Europe and the West Indies, and so on, the underlying "cause" of the American Revolution was that the colonies—and especially the largest, wealthiest, and most populous of them, Virginia—were politically mature and ready to govern themselves. When independence was won and the new nation set out to enact a constitution and create a permanent government, that political maturity was reflected in the authority and wisdom with which they were able to compromise their differences and agree upon a workable basis for American union.

By the time of the Revolution and the adoption of the Constitution, the Southern colonies had begun to feel a community of interest centered upon the presence in them all of a plantation economy based upon slavery. South Carolina and Georgia were zealous to guard against what they felt was economic and political domination on the part of the Northern states; Virginia and Maryland occupied something of a middle ground. At one point during the Constitutional convention the issue of slavery threatened to split the convention in two, but it was compromised. The differences that ultimately resulted in secession, however, were already present. For the divisive issues to grow and take on dangerous proportions, it would be necessary to develop a far greater divergence in economic systems and in social makeup, than that present in 1789. With the rise of manufacturing and merchandising centers in the Northeast, and the rapid expansion of cotton cultivation in the South resulting from a workable ginning process, a North–South schism became a threat to continued union. That schism—and the consciousness of it—was what made Virginians, Carolinians, Georgians, Tennesseans, and later Alabamians, Mississippians, Louisianans, and Floridians begin to think of themselves as Southerners. And it was not until then that the call went out for a distinctively Southern literature.

The following selections by residents of the several Southern colonies have been chosen to illustrate a little of the range and shapes of colonial Southern writing. The first is a work by an Englishman, John Smith, recounting his adventures in the New World. It is almost impossible to say at what point the writing that comes afterward becomes recognizably "Southern" when seen in the light of later, post-colonial developments. Yet the reader will note certain characteristics already present that in later generations would seem emblematic of the Southern imagination.

In the two poems on Bacon's Rebellion by John Cotton of Aquia Creek, written years before the close of the seventeenth century, there is a kind of anonymity, a careful avoidance of private, personal identity, that contrasts markedly with the poems written by New Englanders of the same period. The poet composes two poems, stating opposite interpretations of the conflict. Which represents his own convictions? Does either? It may not be overly fanciful to trace a line of descent from such manifestations of literary formalism to Edgar Allan Poe's insistence that a poem must constitute an achieved, carefully wrought literary effect, not a "metre-making argument" as Emerson declared. And from Poe the line goes straight on to the assertions of the twentieth-century Southern critics that poems must be read as objective entities in language, not as extensions of the poet's biography, statements of intellectual history, or for their ideological content. Note also that the imagery in the two Bacon's Rebellion poems is legal throughout, not theological. In antebellum literature we will find that almost all the Southern lyric poets were lawyers or studied law.

The account by William Byrd II of the Dividing Line expedition of 1728 —perhaps the richest of all pre-Revolutionary Southern writings—develops for humorous and satirical purposes a contrast between the crude, slothful inhabitants of a North Carolina "Lubberland" and the civilized Virginians. To achieve his humor Byrd employs a formal, literary diction that contrasts comically with the "low life" subject matter. In the nineteenth century this is the hallmark of Southern humor, and in our own time William Faulkner, Erskine Caldwell, Flannery O'Connor, Eudora Welty, and others make rich comedy out of the same approach. Almost nothing resembling this is to be found in the writings of colonials from the Northeastern centers.

Other qualities in the early, "pre-Southern" work seem to be harbingers of later Southern literary attitudes; we shall mention only one. The selection from Thomas Jefferson's *Notes on the State of Virginia* offers a powerful denunciation of the moral and social evils of human slavery. Already the "peculiar institution," as it would later be called, is seen as menacing the hopes of the just-created republic. The passage quoted is only one section of a lengthy work, and the impassioned tone plus the sense of deep apprehension of the future that characterize Jefferson's utterance clash strikingly with the hopefulness, optimism, and pride in country that otherwise fill his book. In the new nation's leading political philosopher—a Virginian born more than three decades before the American Revolution—we find an acute awareness of what would in a succeeding generation prove to be the South's great dilemma.

Jefferson thought of himself as a Virginian and an American. In the lengthy correspondence with his friend James Madison, written from abroad during the period of writing of the Constitution, his approach was almost entirely from the standpoint of the nation as a whole, rather than as a Virginian. Slavery, however, was predominantly a Virginia—and a Carolina and Georgia—problem. In Jefferson's position as an American and Virginian we find, at the very beginning of the new nation's history, what will be an abiding characteristic of the Southern imagination: the consciousness of being part of and yet separate from the nation as a whole, and the moral, ethical, and patriotic issues of individual and community identity involved in that position.

CAPTAIN JOHN SMITH

(1580–1631)

The Pocohontas story, which has played so creative a role in American mythology, grows out of the several accounts written by Captain John Smith, soldier, adventurer, and prolific author of descriptions of the New World that he helped settle. It was the doughty Smith's leadership and discipline that saved the Jamestown colony from starvation in 1608–1609, the year after its founding. Although the actual narrative of his adventures with the Indian maiden who was Powhatan's daughter does not appear until the *General Historie* of 1624 and has been dismissed as romantic invention, some contemporary historians believe it really took place, though perhaps as an initiation ceremony rather than an actual threat to Smith's life. Whether real or not, the rescue of the Captain by the Indian maiden, just as he was about to be executed, has enthralled the imaginations of later generations.

Smith, who went back to England and never returned to the Virginia colony after being wounded by a gunpowder explosion in the autumn of 1609, was an ingenious and forceful propagandist for Virginia and, in addition to his leadership at Jamestown, greatly aided in the founding of New England a little later.

From JOHN SMITH'S ACCOUNTS OF POCAHONTAS

(A) From A TRUE RELATION

Powhatan understanding we detained certaine Salvages, sent [*i.e., in May* 1608] his Daughter, a child of tenne yeares old: which, not only for feature, countenance, and proportion, much exceedeth any of the rest of his people: but for wit and spirit, [is] the only *Nonpariel* of his Country. This hee sent by his most trustie messenger, called *Rawhunt*, as much exceeding in deformitie of person; but of a subtill wit and crafty understanding.

He, with a long circumstance, told mee, how well *Powhatan* loved and respected mee; and in that I should not doubt any way of his kindnesse, he had sent his child, which he most esteemed, to see me; a Deare and bread besides, for a present: desiring me that the Boy [*Thomas Salvage*] might come againe, which he loved exceedingly. His litle Daughter hee had taught this lesson also, not taking notice at all of the Indeans that had beene prisoners three daies, till that morning that she saw their fathers and friends come quietly, and in good tearmes to entreate their libertie.

Opechankanough sent also unto us, that for his sake, we would release two that were his friends: and for a token, sent me his shooting Glove and Bracer, which the day our men was taken upon; separating himselfe from the rest a long time, intreated to speake with me, where in token of peace, he had preferred me the same. Now all of them having found their peremptorie conditions but to increase our malice; which they seeing us begin to threaten to destroy them, as familiarly as before, without suspition or feare, came amongst us, to begge libertie for their men.

In the afternoone, they being gone, we guarded them as before to the Church; and after prayer, gave them to *Pocahuntas*, the Kings Daughter, in regard of her fathers kindnesse in sending her. After having well fed them, as all the time of their imprisonment, we gave them their bowes, arrowes, or what else they had; and with [their] much content, sent them packing. *Poca-*

huntas also we requited with such trifles as contented her, to tel that we had
· used the *Paspaheyans* very kindly in so releasing them.

1608

(B) From PROCEEDINGS OF THE
ENGLISH COLONIE IN VIRGINIA

Some propheticall spirit calculated [that] hee had the Salvages in such subjection, hee would have made himselfe a king, by marrying *Pocahontas*,
Powhatans daughter. (It is true she was the very Nomparell of his kingdome,
and at most not past 13 or 14 years of age. Very oft shee came to our fort,
with what shee could get for Captaine *Smith*; that ever loved and used all
the Countrie well, but her especially he ever much respected: and she so
well requited it, that when her father intended to have surprized him, shee
by stealth in the darke night came through the wild woods and told him of
it. But her marriage could no way have intitled him by any right to the kingdome, nor was it ever suspected hee had ever such a thought; or more
regarded her, or any of them, than in honest reason and discreation he
might. If he would, he might have married her, or have done what him listed; for there was none that could have hindred his determination.)

1612

(C) From THE GENERAL HISTORIE

Then they led him to the *Youthtanunds*, the *Mattapanients*, the *Payanka-
tanks*, the *Nantaughtacunds*, and *Onawmanients* upon the rivers of
Rapahanock, and *Patawomek*; over all those rivers, and backe againe by
divers other severall Nations, to the Kings habitation at *Pamaunkee*: where
they entertained him with most strange and fearefull Conjurations;

> *As if neare led to hell,*
> *Amongst the Devils to dwell.*

Not long after, early in a morning a great fire was made in a long house,
and a mat spread on the one side, as on the other; on the one they caused
him to sit and all the guard went out of the house, and presently came skipping in a great grim fellow, all painted over with coale, mingled with oyle;
and many Snakes and Wesels skins stuffed with mosse, and all their tayles
tyed together, so as they met on the crowne of his head in a tassell; and
round about the tassell was as a Coronet of feathers, the skins hanging
round about his head, backe, and shoulders, and in a manner covered his
face; with a hellish voyce, and a rattle in his hand. With most strange gestures and passions he began his invocation, and environed the fire with a

circle of meale; which done, three more such like devils came rushing in with the like antique tricks, painted halfe blacke, halfe red: but all their eyes were painted white, and some red stroakes like Mutchato's, along their cheekes: round about him those fiends daunced a pretty while, and then came in three more as ugly as the rest; with red eyes, and white stroakes over their blacke faces, at last they all sat downe right against him; three of them on the one hand of the chiefe Priest, and three on the other. Then all with their rattles began a song, which ended, the chiefe Priest layd downe five wheat cornes: then strayning his armes and hands with such violence that he sweat, and his veynes swelled, he began a short Oration: at the conclusion they all gave a short groane; and then layd down three graines more. After that, began their song againe, and then another Oration, ever laying downe so many cornes as before, till they had twice inciruled the fire; that done, they tooke a bunch of little stickes prepared for that purpose, continuing still their devotion, and at the end of every song and Oration, they layd downe a sticke betwixt the divisions of Corne. Till night, neither he nor they did either eate or drinke; and then they feasted merrily, with the best provisions they could make. Three dayes they used this Ceremony; the meaning whereof they told him, was to know if he intended them well or no. The circle of meale signified their Country, the circles of corne the bounds of the Sea, and the stickes his Country. They imagined the world to be flat and round, like a trencher; and they in the middest. . . .

At last they brought him to *Meronocomoco* [*5 Jan. 1608*], where was *Powhatan* their Emperor. Here more than two hundred of those grim Courtiers stood wondering at him, as he had beene a monster; till *Powhatan* and his trayne had put themselves in their greatest braveries. Before a fire upon a seat like a bedsted, he sat covered with a great robe, made of *Rarowcun* skinnes, and all the tayles hanging by. On either hand did sit a young wench of 16 or 18 yeares, and along on each side the house, two rowes of men, and behind them as many women, with all their heads and shoulders painted red: many of their heads bedecked with the white downe of Birds; but every one with something: and a great chayne of white beads about their necks.

At his entrance before the King, all the people gave a great shout. The Queene of *Appamatuck* was appointed to bring him water to wash his hands, and another brought him a bunch of feathers, in stead of a Towell to dry them: having feasted him after their best barbarous manner they could, a long consultation was held, but the conclusion was, two great stones were brought before *Powhatan*: then as many as could layd hands on him, dragged him to them, and thereon laid his head, and being ready with their clubs, to beate out his braines, *Pocahontas* the Kings dearest daughter, when no intreaty could prevaile, got his head in her armes, and laid her owne upon his to save him from death: whereat the Emperour was contented he should live to make him hatchets, and her bells, beads, and copper; for they thought him as well of all occupations as themselves. For the

King himselfe will make his owne robes, shooes, bowes, arrowes, pots; plant, hunt, or doe any thing so well as the rest.

> *They say he bore a pleasant shew,*
> *But sure his heart was sad.*
> *For who can pleasant be, and rest,*
> *That lives in feare and dread:*
> *And having life suspected, doth*
> *It still suspected lead.*

1624

(D) From THE GENERALL HISTORIE

During this time, the Lady *Rebecca*, alias *Pocahontas*, daughter to *Powhatan*, by the diligent care of Master *John Rolfe* her husband and his friends, [w]as taught to speake such *English* as might well bee understood, well instructed in Christianitie, and was become very formall and civill after our *English* manner; shee had also by him a childe which she loved most dearely, and the Treasurer and Company tooke order both for the maintenance of her and it, besides there were divers persons of great ranke and qualitie had beene very kinde to her; and before she arrived at London, Captaine *Smith* to deserve her former courtesies, made her qualities knowne to the Queenes most excellent Majestie and her Court, and writ a little booke to this effect to the Queene: An abstract whereof followeth.

To the most high and vertuous
Princesse, Queene *Anne* of
Great Brittanie

Most admired Queene,

The love I beare my God, my King and Countrie, hath so oft emboldened mee in the worst of extreme dangers, that now honestie doth constraine mee [to] presume thus farre beyond my selfe, to present your Majestie this short discourse: if ingratitude be a deadly poyson to all honest vertues, I must bee guiltie of that crime if I should omit any meanes to bee thankfull.

So it is,

That some ten yeeres agoe being in *Virginia*, and taken prisoner by the power of *Powhatan* their chiefe King, I received from this great Salvage exceeding great courtesie, especially from his sonne *Nantaquaus*, the most manliest, comeliest, boldest spirit, I ever saw in a Salvage, and his sister *Pocahontas*, the Kings most deare and wel-beloved daughter, being but a childe of twelve or thirteene yeeres of age whose compassionate pitiful heart, of my desperate estate, gave me much cause to respect her: I being the first Christian this proud King and his grim attendants ever saw: and thus inthralled in their barbarous power, I cannot say I felt the least occasion of want that was in the power of those my mortall foes to prevent, notwithstanding al their threats. After some six weeks fatting amongst those Salvage Courtiers, at the minute of my execution, she hazarded the beating out of her owne braines to save mine; and not onely that, but so prevailed with her father, that I was safely conducted to *James* towne: where I found about eight and thirtie miserable poore and sick creatures, to keepe possession of all those large territories of *Virginia*; such was the weaknesse of this poore Commonwealth, as had the Salvages not fed us, we directly had starved. And this reliefe, most gracious Queene, was commonly brought us by this Lady *Pocahontas*.

Notwithstanding all these passages, when inconstant Fortune turned our peace to warre, this tender Virgin would still not spare to dare to visit us, and by her our jarres have beene oft appeased, and our wants still supplyed; were it the policie of her father thus to imploy her, or the ordinance of God thus to make her his instrument, or her extraordinarie affection to our Nation, I know not: but of this I am sure; when her father with the utmost of his policie and power, sought to surprize mee, having but eighteene with mee, the darke night could not affright her from comming through the irkesome woods, and with watered eies gave me intelligence, with her best advice to escape his furie; which had hee knowne, hee had surely slaine her.

James towne with her wild traine she as freely frequented, as her fathers habitation; and during the time of two or three yeeres, she next under God, was still the instrument to preserve this Colonie from death, famine and utter confusion; which if in those times, [it] had once beene dissolved, *Virginia* might have line [*lain*] as it was at our first arrivall to this day.

Since then, this businesse having beene turned and varied by many accidents from that I left it at: it is most certaine, after a long and troublesome warre after my departure, betwixt her father and our Colonie; all which time shee was not heard of.

About two yeeres after shee her selfe was taken prisoner, being so detained neere two yeeres longer, the Colonie by that meanes was relieved, peace concluded; and at last rejecting her barbarous condition, [she] was married to an *English* Gentleman, with whom at this present she is in *England*; the first Christian ever of that Nation, the first *Virginian* ever spake *English*, or had a childe in marriage by an

Englishman: a matter surely, if my meaning bee truly considered and well understood, worthy a Princes understanding.

Thus, most gracious Lady, I have related to your Majestie, what at your best leasure our approved Histories will account you at large, and done in the time of your Majesties life; and however this might bee presented you from a more worthy pen, it cannot from a more honest heart, as yet I never begged any thing of the state, or any: and it is my want of abilitie and her exceeding desert; your birth, meanes and authoritie; her birth, vertue, want and simplicitie, doth make mee thus bold, humbly to beseech your Majestie to take this knowledge of her, though it be from one so unworthy to be the reporter, as my selfe, her husbands estate not being able to make her fit to attend your Majestie. The most and least I can doe, is to tell you this, because none so oft hath tried it as my selfe, and the rather being of so great a spirit, how ever her low stature: if she should not be well received, seeing this Kingdome may rightly have a Kingdome by her meanes; her present love to us and Christianitie might turne to such scorne and furie, as to divert all this good to the worst of evill: where[as] finding so great a Queene should doe her some honour more than she can imagine, for being so kinde to your servants an subjects, would so ravish her with content, as endeare her dearest bloud to effect that, your Majestie and all the Kings honest subjects most earnestly desire.

And so I humbly kisse your gracious hands.

Being about this time preparing to set saile for *New–England*, I could not stay to doe her that service I desired, and she well deserved; but hearing shee was at *Branford* with divers of my friends, I went to see her. After a modest salutation, without any word, she turned about, obscured her face, as not seeming well contented; and in that humour her husband, with divers others, we all left her two or three houres, repenting my selfe to have writ she could speake *English*. But not long after, she began to talke, and remembred mee well what courtesies shee had done: saying,

You did promise *Powhatan* what was yours should bee his, and he the like to you; you called him father being in his land a stranger, and by the same reason so must I doe you:

which though I would have excused, I durst not allow of that title, because she was a Kings daughter; with a well set countenance she said,

Were you not afraid to come into my fathers Countrie, and caused feare in him and all his people (but mee), and feare you here I should call you father; I tell you then I will, and you shall call mee childe, and so I will bee for ever and ever your Countrieman. They did tell us alwaies you were dead, and I knew no other till I came to *Plimoth*; yet *Powhatan* did command *Uttamatomakkin* to seeke you, and know the truth, because your Countriemen will lie much.

This Salvage, one of *Powhatans* Councell, being amongst them held an understanding fellow; the King purposely sent him, as they say, to number the people here, and informe him well what wee were and our state. Arriving at *Plimoth*, according to his directions, he got a long sticke, whereon by notches hee did thinke to have kept the number of all the men hee could see, but he was quickly wearie of that taske.

Comming to *London*, where by chance I met him, having renewed our acquaintance, where many were desirous to heare and see his behaviour, hee told me

Powhatan did bid him to find me out, to shew him our God, the King, Queene, and Prince, I so much had told them of.

Concerning God, I told him the best I could, the King I heard he had seene, and the rest hee should see when he would; he denied ever to have seene the King, till by circumstances he was satisfied he had: Then he replyed very sadly,

You gave *Powhatan* a white Dog, which *Powhatan* fed as himselfe; but your King gave me nothing, and I am better than your white Dog.

The small time I staid in *London*, divers Courtiers and others, my acquaintances, hath gone with mee to see her, that generally concluded, they did thinke God had a great hand in her conversion, and they have seene many *English* Ladies worse favoured, proportioned, and behavioured; and as since I have heard, it pleased both the King and Queenes Majestie honourably to esteeme her, accompanied with that honourable Lady the Lady *De la Ware*, and that honourable Lord her husband, and divers other persons of good qualities, both publikely at the maskes and otherwise, to her great satisfaction and content, which doubtlesse she would have deserved, had she lived to arrive in *Virginia*.

1624

JOHN COTTON

(*fl.* 1676)

The best poem written in America in the seventeenth century—and quite possibly the best during the colonial era—is "Bacons Epitaph, Made by His Man." It is one of several poems appended to a contemporary narrative of Nathaniel Bacon's Rebellion in Virginia in 1676–1677, written by John Cotton, who lived on the Eastern Shore of Virginia. The "Epitaph" and its accompanying poem "Upon the Death of G:B." take opposite sides on the rebellion, so it is impossible to determine from them the author's own views.

Bacon's Rebellion, which erupted out of a quarrel over Indian raids and land policies along the western extremities of the Virginia colony, pitted a young aristocrat, recently from England, and his followers against Governor William Berkeley and the Council of State. It was a dispute that ultimately involved the capture and burning of Jamestown by the rebels, before Bacon died of fatigue and dysentery and the rebellion collapsed.

In later years Bacon's Rebellion came to be depicted as the first round of resistance to the British Crown by the American settlers. Historians have tended to qualify that estimate, however, and the rebellion has been ascribed to factionalism, the desire of the colonists for Indian land, and economic and social issues, as well as Berkeley's autocracy.

BACONS EPITAPH, MADE BY HIS MAN

Death why soe crewill! what, no other way
To manifest thy splleene, but thus to slay
Our hopes of safety; liberty, our all
Which, through thy tyrany, with him must fall
To its late Caoss? Had thy riged force
Bin delt by retale, and not thus in gross
Griefe had bin silent: Now wee must complaine
Since thou, in him, hast more then thousand slane
Whose lives and safetys did so much depend
On him there lif, with him there lives must end.
    If't be a sin to thinke Death brib'd can bee
Wee must be guilty; say twas bribery
Guided the fatall shaft. Verginias foes,
To whom for secrit crimes just vengance owes
Disarved plagues, dreding their just disart
Corrupted Death by Parasscellcian art
Him to destroy; whose well tride curage such,

JOHN COTTON

There heartless harts, nor arms, nor strength could touch.
　　Who now must heale those wounds, or stop that blood
The Heathen made, and drew into a flood?
Who i'st must pleade our Cause? nor Trump nor Drum
Nor Deputations; these alass are dumb,
And Cannot speake. Our Arms (though nere so strong)
Will want the aide of his Commanding tongue,
Which Conquer'd more than Ceaser: He orethrew
Onely the outward frame; this Could subdue
The ruged workes of nature. Soules repleate
With dull Child could, he'd annemate with heate
Drawne forth of reasons Lymbick. In a word
Marss and Minerva both in him Concurd
For arts, for arms, whose pen and sword alike,
As Catos did, may admireation strike
In to his foes; while they confess withall
It was there guilt stil'd him a Criminall.
Onely this differance doth from truth proceed:
They in the guilt, he in the name must bleed,
While none shall dare his Obseques to sing
In disarv'd measures, untill time shall bring
Truth Crown'd with freedom, and from danger free,
To sound his praises to posterity.
　　Here let him rest; while wee this truth report,
Hee's gon from hence unto a higher Court
To pleade his Cause: where he by this doth know
Whether to Ceaser hee was friend, or foe.

UPON THE DEATH OF G: B.

Whether to Ceaser he was Friend or Foe?
Pox take such Ignorance, do you not know?
Can he be Friend to Ceaser, that shall bring
The Arms of Hell, to fight against the King?
(Treason, Rebellion) then what reason have
Wee for to waite upon him to his Grave,
There to express our passions? Wilt not bee
Worss then his Crimes, to sing his Ellegie
In well tun'd numbers; where each Ella beares
(To his Flagitious name) a flood of teares?
A name that hath more soules with sorow fed,
Then reched Niobe single teares ere shed;

UPON THE DEATH OF G: B.

A name that fil'd all hearts, all eares, with paine,
Untill blest fate proclamed, Death had him slane.
Then how can it be counted for a sin
Though Death (nay though my selfe) had bribed bin,
To guide the fatall shaft? we honour all
That lends a hand unto a T[r]ators fall.
What though the well paide Rochit soundly ply
And box the Pulpitt in to flatterey;
Urging his Rethorick, and straind elloquence,
T'adorne incoffin'd filth and excrements;
Though the Defunct (like ours) nere tride
A well intended deed untill he dide?
'Twill be nor sin, nor shame, for us, to say
A two fould Passion checker-workes this day
Of Joy and Sorow; yet the last doth move
On feete impotent, wanting strength to prove
(Nor can the art of Logick yeild releife)
How Joy should be surmounted, by our greife.
Yet that wee Grieve it cannot be denide,
But 'tis because he was, not cause he dide.
So wep the poore destresed Ilyum Dames
Hereing those nam'd, there Citty put in flames,
And Country ruing'd; If wee thus lament
It is against our present Joyes consent.
For if the rule, in Phisick, trew doth prove,
Remove the cause, th' effects will after move,
We have outliv'd our sorows, since we see
The Causes shifting, of our miserey.
     Nor is't a single cause, that's slipt away,
That made us warble out a well-a-day.
The Braines to plot, the hands to execute
Projected ills, Death Joyntly did nonsute
At his black Bar. And what no Baile could save
He hath commited Prissoner to the Grave;
From whence there's no repreive. Death keep him close
We have too many Divells still goe loose.

1676

EBENEZER COOK(E)

(1670–c. 1732)

In 1708, there appeared in London a wickedly sarcastic poem depicting the misadventures of a sot-weed factor (a dealer in tobacco) in the colony of Maryland. *The Sot-Weed Factor* was composed in Hudibrasts, poetic lines of four iambic feet with often outrageously rhymed couplets, in imitation of the style popularized by Samuel Butler in *Hudibras,* and it presented a highly disenchanted view of social and cultural conditions in the Chesapeake Bay region.

Not too much is known about Cook. Sometime before 1722 he was practicing law in Maryland. During the 1720s and 1730s he also produced numerous other poems and a mock-heroic work on Bacon's Rebellion in Virginia. In 1730 a *Sot-Weed Redivivus* appeared in Annapolis, which he may also have written.

With its racy language and uninhibited metaphor, Cook's poem about the tobacco trade in Maryland was among the first Southern works to develop the confrontation of persons of culture and refinement with the vigorous and often semibarbaric doings of frontier Americans. William Byrd II would also draw upon this contrast, the Southwest Humorists of the nineteenth century would develop it in great detail, and in the twentieth century it is still widely practiced even though the frontier has gone. Unlike the poems of the Massachusetts Bay colony, Cook's work is secular, realistic, comic, without a trace of piety or sanctimony. When in the 1960s the Maryland novelist John Barth wrote a comic prose-epic of the early days of his native state, he called it by the same name as Cook's poem and used its author as his protagonist.

From THE SOT-WEED FACTOR OR, A VOYAGE TO MARYLAND

A SATYR

Condemn'd by Fate to way-ward Curse,
Of Friends unkind, and empty Purse;
Plagues worse than fill'd *Pandora*'s Box,
I took my leave of *Albion*'s Rocks:
With heavy Heart, concern'd that I
Was forc'd my Native Soil to fly,
And the *Old World* must bid good-buy,
But Heav'n ordain'd it should be so,

And to repine is vain we know:
Freighted with Fools, from *Plymouth* sound,
To *Mary-Land* our Ship was bound,
Where we arriv'd in dreadful Pain,
Shock'd by the Terrours of the Main;
For full three Months, our wavering Boat,
Did thro' the surley Ocean float,
And furious Storms and threat'ning Blasts,
Both tore our Sails and sprung our Masts:
Wearied, yet pleas'd, we did escape
Such Ills, we anchor'd at the *Cape*;
But weighing soon, we plough'd the *Bay*,
To Cove it in *Piscato-way*,
Intending there to open Store,
I put myself and Goods a-shore:
Where soon repair'd a numerous Crew,
In Shirts and Drawers of *Scotch-cloth* Blue.
With neither Stockings, Hat, nor Shooe.
These *Sot-weed* Planters Crowd the Shoar,
In Hue as tawny as a Moor:
Figures so strange, no God design'd,
To be a part of Humane Kind:
But wanton Nature, void of Rest,
Moulded the brittle Clay in Jest.
At last a Fancy very odd
Took me, this was the Land of *Nod*;
Planted at first, when Vagrant *Cain*,
His Brother had unjustly slain:
Then conscious of the Crime he'd done,
From Vengeance dire, he hither run;
And in a Hut supinely dwelt,
The first in *Furs* and *Sot-weed* dealt,
And ever since his Time, the Place,
Has harbour'd a detested Race;
Who when they cou'd not live at Home,
For Refuge to these Worlds did roam;
In hopes by Flight they might prevent,
The Devil and his fell intent;
Obtain from Tripple Tree repreive,
And Heav'n and Hell alike deceive:
But e're their Manners I display,
I think it fit I open lay
My Entertainment by the way;
That Strangers well may be aware on,

EBENEZER COOK(E)

What homely Diet they must fare on.
To touch that Shoar, where no good Sense is found,
But Conversation's lost, and Manners drown'd.
I crost unto the other side,
A River whose impetuous Tide,
The Savage Borders does divide;
In such a shining odd invention,
I scarce can give its due Dimention.
The *Indians* call this watry Waggon
Canoo, a Vessel none can brag on;
Cut from a *Popular-Tree*, or *Pine*,
And fashion'd like a Trough for Swine;
In this most noble Fishing-Boat,
I boldly put myself a-float;
Standing Erect, with Legs stretch'd wide,
We paddled to the other side:
Where being Landed safe by hap,
As *Sol* fell into *Thetis* Lap.
A ravenous Gang bent on the stroul,
Of Wolves for Prey, began to howl;
This put me in a pannick Fright,
Least I should be devoured quite:
But as I there a musing stood,
And quite benighted in a Wood,
A Female Voice pierc'd thro' my Ears,
Crying, *You Rogue drive home the Steers.*
I listen'd to th' attractive sound,
And straight a Herd of Cattel found
Drove by a Youth, and homewards bound:
Cheer'd with the sight, I straight thought fit,
To ask where I a Bed might get.
The surley Peasant bid me stay,
And ask'd from whom I'de run away.
Surprized at such a saucy Word,
I instantly lugg'd out my Sword;
Swearing I was no Fugitive,
But from *Great-Britain* did arrive,
In hopes I better there might Thrive.
To which he mildly made reply,
I beg your Pardon, Sir, *that I*
Should talk to you Unmannerly;
But if you please to go with me
To yonder House, you'll welcome be.
Encountring soon the smoaky Seat,

THE SOT-WEED FACTOR

The Planter old did thus me greet;
"Whether you come from Gaol or Colledge,
"You're welcome to my certain Knowledge;
"And if you please all Night to stay,
"My Son shall put you in the way."
Which offer I most kindly took,
And for a Seat did round me look;
When presently amongst the rest,
He plac'd his unknown *English* Guest,
Who found them drinking for a whet,
A Cask of Syder on the Fret,
Till Supper came upon the Table,
On which I fed whilst I was able.
So after hearty Entertainment,
Of Drink and Victuals without Payment;
For Planters Tables, you must know,
Are free for all that come and go.
While Pon and Milk, with Mush well stoar'd,
In wooden Dishes grac'd the Board;
With Homine and Syder-pap,
(Which scarce a hungry Dog wou'd lap)
Well stuff'd with Fat, from Bacon fry'd,
Or with *Molossus* dulcify'd.
Then out our Landlord pulls a Pouch,
As greasy as the Leather Couch
On which he sat, and straight begun,
To load with Weed his *Indian* Gun;
In length, scarce longer than ones Finger,
Or that for which the Ladies linger:
His Pipe smoak'd out with aweful Grace,
With aspect grave and solemn pace;
The reverend Sire walks to a Chest,
Of all his Furniture the best,
Closely confin'd within a Room,
Which seldom felt the weight of Broom;
From thence he lugs a Cag of Rum,
And nodding to me, thus begun:
I find, says he, you don't much care,
For this our *Indian* Country Fare;
But let me tell you, Friend of mine,
You may be glad of it in time,
Tho' now your Stomach is so fine;
And if within this Land you stay,
You'll find it true what I do say. . . .

EBENEZER COOK(E)

Up to *Annapolis* I went,
A City Situate on a Plain,
Where scarce a House will keep out Rain;
The Buildings fram'd with Cyprus rare,
Resembles much our *Southwark* Fair:
But Stranger here will scarcely meet
With Market-place, Exchange, or Street;
And if the Truth I may report,
'Tis not so large as *Tottenham Court.*
St. *Mary*'s once was in repute,
Now here the Judges try the Suit,
And Lawyers twice a Year dispute:
As oft the Bench most gravely meet,
Some to get Drunk, and some to eat
A swinging share of Country Treat.
But as for Justice right or wrong,
Not one amongst the numerous throng,
Knows what they mean, or has the Heart,
To give his Verdict on a Stranger's part:
Now Court being call'd by beat of Drum,
The Judges left their Punch and Rum,
When Pettifogger Docter draws,
His Paper forth; and opens Cause:
And least I shou'd the better get,
Brib'd *Quack* supprest his Knavish Wit.
So Maid upon the downy Field,
Pretends a Force, and Fights to yeild:
The Byast Court without delay,
Adjudg'd my Debt in Country Pay;
In Pipe staves, Corn, or Flesh of Boar,
Rare Cargo for the *English* Shoar:
Raging with Grief, full speed I ran,
To joyn the Fleet at *Kicketan;*
Embarqu'd and waiting for a Wind,
I left this dreadful Curse behind.
May Canniballs transported o'er the Sea
Prey on these Slaves, as they have done on me;
May never Merchant's, trading Sails explore
This Cruel, this Inhospitable Shoar;
But left abandon'd by the World to starve,
May they sustain the Fate they well deserve:
May they turn Savage, or as *Indians* Wild,
From Trade, Converse, and Happiness exil'd;
Recreant to Heaven, may they adore the Sun,

And into Pagan Superstitions run
For Veangeance ripe. . . .
May Wrath Divine then lay those Regions wast
Where no Man's Faithful, nor a Woman Chast.

15 January, 1707[8]

ROBERT BEVERLEY

(c. 1673–1722)

Robert Beverley's *History and Present State of Virginia* (1705) is the first history of the colony to be written by a native Virginian. He began it while in England when asked by a bookseller to examine a volume in preparation on the history of the British colonies in America. Appalled by the error and misinformation he found, Beverley sat down to write a history which, "in Justice to so fine a Country," would depict Virginia as it actually was.

Today the historical information in Beverley's book is considered of minor importance. It is his depiction of the locale and the society, the informed account of the organization and operation of government, and the remarkably objective descriptions of the Indians that constitute the considerable value and charm of what Richard Beale Davis has termed "the first self-consciously American history of a Southern colony."

Beverley was the son of Major Robert Beverley, a supporter of Governor Berkeley during Bacon's Rebellion. He was educated abroad, and in 1697 married Ursula Byrd, sister of William Byrd II. She died in childbirth and Beverley never remarried. Until 1705 he held the important political position of Clerk of the General Assembly, but some indiscreet letters he wrote from England, highly critical of Governor Francis Nicholson, and the attacks on Nicholson and others in the *History and Present State* ended his tenure of office. He went back to his plantation in King and Queen County and stayed there for the remainder of his life, enjoying the leisure and pleasures of a Virginia gentleman, in particular the fishing he so liked.

His account of "my country," as he called it—meaning not England but America—is by no means uncritical. The following selection reveals his love of nature and countryside. But he was also careful to enumerate and describe the "thunder, heat, and troublesome vermin" that infested the Virginia countryside during warm weather, and he worried because his countrymen were too inclined to accept nature's blessings without being sufficiently energetic to improve their lot. It is the paradox and tension between Beverley's love of Edenic nature and his belief in the value of "discipline, work, performance" that give much of the zest and excitement to what Leo Marx has termed "an ingenious, vigorous, wonderfully vivid book."

From THE HISTORY AND PRESENT STATE OF VIRGINIA

from Chap. XIX

OF THE TEMPERATURE OF THE CLIMATE, AND THE INCONVENIENCIES ATTENDING IT

The Natural Temperature of the Inha[bit]ed part of the Country, is hot and moist: tho' this Moisture I take to be occasion'd by the abundance of low Grounds, Marshes, Creeks, and Rivers, which are every where among their lower Settlements; but more backward in the Woods, where they are now Seating, and making new Plantations, they have abundance of high and dry Land, where there are only Crystal Streams of Water, which flow gently from their Springs, and divide themselves into innumerable Branches, to moisten and enrich the adjacent Lands.

The Country is in a very happy Situation, between the extreams of Heat and Cold, but inclining rather to the first. Certainly it must be a happy Climate, since it is very near of the same Latitude with the Land of Promise. Besides, As *Judæa* was full of Rivers, and Branches of Rivers; So is *Virginia*: As that was seated upon a great Bay and Sea, wherein were all the conveniences for Shipping and Trade; So is *Virginia*. Had that fertility of Soil? So has *Virginia*, equal to any Land in the known World. In fine, if any one impartially considers all the Advantages of this Country, as Nature made it; he must allow it to be as fine a Place, as any in the Universe; but I confess I am asham'd to say any thing of its Improvements, because I must at the same time reproach my Country-Men with a Laziness that is unpardonable. If there be any excuse for them in this Matter, 'tis the exceeding plenty of good things, with which Nature has blest them; for where God Almighty is so Merciful as to work for People, they never work for themselves.

All the Countries in the World, seated in or near the Latitude of *Virginia*, are esteem'd the Fruitfullest, and Pleasantest of all Clymates. As for Example, *Canaan, Syria, Persia*, great part of *India, China* and *Japan*, the *Morea, Spain, Portugal*, and the Coast of *Barbary*, none of which differ many Degrees of Latitude from *Virginia*. These are reckon'd the Gardens of the World, while *Virginia* is unjustly neglected by its own Inhabitants, and abus'd by other People.

That which makes this Country most unfortunate, is, that it must submit to receive its Character from the Mouths not only of unfit, but very unequal Judges; For, all its Reproaches happen after this manner.

Many of the Merchants and others that go thither from *England*, make no distinction between a cold, and a hot Country: but wisely go sweltering about in their thick Cloaths all the Summer, because they used to do so in their *Northern* Climate; and then unfairly complain of the heat of the Country. They greedily Surfeit with their delicious Fruits, and are guilty of great Intemperance, through the exceeding Generosity of the Inhabitants; by which means they fall Sick, and then unjustly complain of the unhealthiness of the Country. In the next place, the Sailers for want of Towns there, are put to the hardship of rowling most of the Tobacco, a Mile or more, to the Water-side; this Splinters their Hands sometimes, and provokes 'em to curse the Country. Such Exercise, and a bright Sun, makes them hot, and then they imprudently fall to drinking cold Water, or perhaps New Cyder, which in its Season, they find at every Planter's House; Or else they greedily devour all the green Fruit, and unripe Trash they can meet with, and so fall into Fluxes, Fevers, and the Belly-Ach, and then, to spare their own Indiscretion, they in their Tarpawlin Language, cry, God D——— the Country. This is the true State of the case, as to the Complaints of its being Sickly; For, by the most impartial observation I can make, if People will be perswaded to be Temperate, and take due care of themselves, I believe it is as healthy a Country, as any under Heaven: but the extraordinary pleasantness of the Weather, and the goodness of the Fruit, lead People into many Temptations. The clearness and brightness of the Sky, add new vigour to their Spirits, and perfectly remove all Splenetick and sullen Thoughts. Here they enjoy all the benefits of a warm Sun, and by their shady Groves, are protected from its Inconvenience. Here all their Senses are entertain'd with an endless Succession of Native Pleasures. Their Eyes are ravished with the Beauties of naked Nature. Their Ears are Serenaded with the perpetual murmur of Brooks, and the thorow-base which the Wind plays, when it wantons through the Trees; the merry Birds too, join their pleasing Notes to this rural Consort, especially the Mock-birds, who love Society so well, that whenever they see Mankind, they will perch upon a Twigg very near them, and sing the sweetest wild Airs in the World: But what is most remarkable in these Melodious Animals, they will frequently fly at small distances before a Traveller, warbling out their Notes several Miles an end, and by their Musick, make a Man forget the Fatigues of his Journey. Their Taste is regaled with the most delicious Fruits, which without Art, they have in great Variety and Perfection. And then their smell is refreshed with an eternal fragrancy of Flowers and Sweets, with which Nature perfumes and adorns the Woods almost the whole year round.

Have you pleasure in a Garden? All things thrive in it, most surpriseingly; you can't walk by a Bed of Flowers, but besides the entertainment of their Beauty, your Eyes will be saluted with the charming colours of the

ROBERT BEVERLEY

Humming Bird, which revels among the Flowers, and licks off the Dew and Honey from their tender Leaves, on which it only feeds. It's size is not half so large as an *English* Wren, and its colour is a glorious shining mixture of Scarlet, Green, and Gold. Colonel *Byrd*, in his Garden, which is the finest in that Country, has a Summer-House set round with the *Indian* Honey-Suckle, which all the Summer is continually full of sweet Flowers, in which these Birds delight exceedingly. Upon these Flowers, I have seen ten or a dozen of these Beautiful Creatures together, which sported about me so familiarly, that with their little Wings they often fann'd my Face.

.   .   .

Their Winters are very short, and don't continue above three or four Months, of which they have seldom thirty days of unpleasant Weather, all the rest being blest with a clear Air, and a bright Sun. However, they have very hard Frost sometimes, but it rarely lasts above three or four days, that is, till the Wind change; for if it blow not between the *North-East*, and *North-West* Points, from the cold Appellatian Mountains, they have no Frost at all. But these Frosts are attended with a Serene Sky, and are otherwise made Delightful, by the tameness of the Wild-fowl and other Game, which by their incredible Number, afford the pleasantest Shooting in the World.

Their Rains, except in the depth of Winter, are extreamly agreeable and refreshing. All the Summer long they last but a few Hours at a time, and sometimes not above half an Hour, and then immediately succeeds clear Sun-shine again: but in that short time it rains so powerfully, that it quits the debt of a long Drought, and makes every thing green and gay.

I have heard that this Country is reproacht with suddain, and dangerous changes of Weather; but that Imputation is unjust: For tho' it be true, that in the Winter, when the Wind comes over those vast Mountains to the *North-West*, which are supposed to retain mighty Magazines of Ice, and Snow, the Weather is then very rigorous; yet in Spring, Summer, and Autumn, such Winds are only cool and pleasant Breezes, which serve to refresh the Air, and correct those Excesses of Heat, which the Situation wou'd otherwise make that Country liable to.

WILLIAM BYRD II

(1674–1744)

The leading literary figure of the colonial South was William Byrd II, planter, merchant, scientist, satirist, real estate speculator, and perhaps the finest gentleman of his era. Like the other leading Virginia grandees of the so-called Golden Age of the tidewater plantations, Byrd was no scion of British aristocracy, but came from middle class origins. His grandfather was a London goldsmith, and his father, William Byrd I, as an Indian trader near the Falls of the James amassed much of the wealth that made his distinguished son's career possible. The elder Byrd built up large holdings of property, imported slaves and indentured servants, and merchandised goods from abroad. His son, educated in England, returned home to Virginia a man of distinction, with numerous important friends in British social, political, and intellectual circles. At Westover on the James he presided over his estates, bought and sold property, corresponded with social and scientific friends in England, accumulated a large library of books, and improved the family fortunes. At his death he left 179,000 acres of land, which his own son, William Byrd III, speedily dissipated.

Although William Byrd II spent almost half of his life in England, he mostly thought and wrote as a Virginian. The vast body of his writings, few of which were published in his lifetime, display his interests. In Richard Beale Davis's words, "in his letters especially he shows his curiosity about natural history, medicine, and meteorology. In his diaries, kept in shorthand and discovered only in the twentieth century, he displays his reading interests, his ability in several languages, and most of all his personal habits and everyday occupations. These day-by-day jottings are curiously detached. In his prose histories he is at once travel writer, observer of Indian life and customs and of plants and animals, shrewd analyst of character (with the obvious prejudices of his class and colony), satiric and witty raconteur, and devotee of moderation."

Of Byrd's numerous writings, by far the most interesting to modern readers are the Dividing Line histories. In 1728 Byrd headed a group of Virginia commissioners who met a similar group from North Carolina to make a survey of the disputed boundary line between the two colonies. Taking with them surveyors and a host of servants, the commissioners commenced their mapmaking at oceanside and during the spring months and the following fall carried the line well into the interior, with the Virginians continuing alone after the Carolinians had fulfilled their obligation and ultimately reaching the hills and low mountains to the north of the present-day Winston-Salem, where the coming of winter ended the expedition. Byrd wrote two accounts: a *Secret History*, apparently prepared during or shortly after the expedition itself, and a *History*, which was composed later and evidently was intended for publication. Neither account, however, was published until the nineteenth century, when an edition of the *History* was brought out. The *Secret History* remained unpublished until 1929.

There is relatively little duplication in the two accounts. The *History*, intended for formal publication, is much more detailed and judicious; its author added considerably more material drawn both from his observations and his vast reading. The *Secret History* is racy, witty, and considerably less polite in its approach. Both abound in accounts of the disputes between the commissioners and of the peculiar social, economic, and sexual habits of the inhabitants of the region being traversed, and no opportunity is lost to make fun of the promiscuous, venial, avaricious, and deceitful.

Byrd's descriptions of his adventures along the border of Lubberland, as he called North Carolina, are almost the first instance of the vein of humorous writing that would a century later become known as Southwestern Humor, in which a cultivated, genteel narrator chronicles the comic goings-on of the low life of the backwoods regions in tones that are scandalized, amused, appalled, and fascinated. As a landed Virginia grandee, wealthy, and accustomed to deference, Byrd encounters the inhabitants of the back country, many of whom have specifically moved there to find the freedom of maneuver largely denied them in the ordered, settled hiearchical plantation society of tidewater Virginia. When he perceives that his status and stature do not receive quite the deference from the North Carolina commissioners and the inhabitants of the countryside he is accustomed to getting in his own tidewater plantation society, he resorts to satire. The result is humor with rich overtones of class and caste, in a mode that would later be explored by such nineteenth-century writers as Longstreet, Baldwin, Hooper, Harris, and Thorpe, and in our own day by Caldwell, Flannery O'Connor, Faulkner, and others, who would continue the old Southern tradition of low comedy based on the peccadilloes and racy vigor of the poor whites.

THE DIVIDING LINE EXPEDITION

MARCH 6, 1728

[From THE HISTORY]

At Noon, having a Perfect Observation, we found the Latitude of Coratuck Inlet to be 36 Degrees and 31 Minutes.

Whilst we were busied about these Necessary Matters, our Skipper row'd to an Oyster Bank just by, and loaded his Periauga with Oysters as Savoury and well-tasted as those from Colchester of Walfleet, and had the advantage of them, too, by being much larger and fatter.

About 3 in the Afternoon the two lagg Commissioners arriv'd, and after a few decent excuses for making us wait, told us they were ready to enter upon Business as soon as we pleas'd. The first Step was to produce our respective Powers, and the Commission from each Governor was distinctly read, and Copies of them interchangeably deliver'd.

It was observ'd by our Carolina Friends, that the Latter Part of the Virginia Commission had something in it a little too lordly and Positive. In answer to which we told them twas necessary to make it thus peremptory, lest the present Commissioners might go upon as fruitless an Errand as their Predecessors. The former Commissioners were ty'd down to Act in Exact Conjunction with those of Carolina, and so could not advance one Step farther, or one Jot faster, than they were pleas'd to permit them.

The Memory of that disappointment, therefore, induc'd the Government of Virginia to give fuller Powers to the present Commissioners, by Authorizing them to go on with the Work by Themselves, in Case those of Carolina should prove unreasonable, and refuse to join with them in carrying the business to Execution. And all this was done lest His Majesty's gracious Intention should be frustrated a Second time.

After both Commissions were considered, the first Question was, where the Dividing Line was to begin. This begat a Warm debate; the Virginia Commissioners contending, with a great deal of Reason, to begin at the End of the Spitt of Sand, which was undoubtedly the North Shore of Corautck Inlet. But those of Carolina insisted Strenuously, that the Point of High Land ought rather to be the Place of Beginning, because that was fixt and certain, whereas the Spitt of Sand was ever Shifting, and did actually run out farther now than formerly. The Contest lasted some Hours, with great Vehemence, neither Party receding from their Opinion that Night. But next Morning, Mr. M. . . . ., to convince us he was not that Obstinate Person he had been represented, yielded to our Reasons, and found Means to bring over his Collegues.

Here we began already to reap the Benefit of those Peremptory Words in our Commission, which in truth added some Weight to our Reasons. Nevertheless, because positive proof was made by the Oaths of two Credible Witnesses, that the Spitt of Sand had advanced 200 Yards towards the Inlet since the Controversy first began, we were willing for Peace-sake to make them that allowance. Accordingly we fixed our Beginning about that Distance North of the Inlet, and there Ordered a Cedar-Post to be driven deep into the Sand for our beginning. While we continued here, we were told that on the South Shore, not far from the Inlet, dwelt a Marooner, that Modestly call'd himself a Hermit, tho' he forfeited that Name by Suffering a wanton Female to cohabit with Him.

His Habitation was a Bower, cover'd with Bark after the Indian Fashion, which in that mild Situation protected him pretty well from the Weather. Like the Ravens, he neither plow'd nor sow'd, but Subsisted chiefly upon

Oysters, which his Handmaid made a Shift to gather from the Adjacent Rocks. Sometimes, too, for Change of Dyet, he sent her to drive up the Neighbour's Cows, to moisten their Mouths with a little Milk. But as for raiment, he depended mostly upon his Length of Beard, and She upon her Length of Hair, part of which she brought decently forward, and the rest dangled behind quite down to her Rump, like one of Herodotus's East Indian Pigmies.

Thus did these Wretches live in a dirty State of Nature, and were mere Adamites, Innocence only excepted.

MARCH 7, 1728

[From THE HISTORY]

This Morning the Surveyors began to run the Dividing line from the Cedar-Post we had driven into the Sand, allowing near 3 Degrees for the Variation. Without making this Just allowance, we should not have obeyd his Majesty's order in running a Due West Line. It seems the former Commissioners had not been so exact, which gave our Friends of Carolina but too just an Exception to their Proceedings.

The Line cut Dosier's Island, consisting only of a Flat Sand, with here and there an humble Shrub growing upon it. From thence it crost over a narrow Arm of the Sound into Knot's Island, and there Split a Plantation belonging to William Harding.

The Day being far spent, we encamp in this Man's Pasture, tho' it lay very low, and the Season now inclin'd People to Aguish Distempers. He sufferd us to cut Cedar-Branches for our Enclosure, and other Wood for Firing, to correct the moist Air and drive away the Damps. Our Landlady, in the Days of her Youth, it seems, had been a Laundress in the Temple, and talkt over her Adventurers in that Station, with as much pleasure as an Old Soldier talks over his Battles and Distempers, and I believe with as many Additions to the Truth.

The Soil is good in many Places of this Island, and the Extent of it pretty large. It lyes in the form of a Wedge: the South End of it is Several Miles over, but towards the North it Sharpens into a Point. It is a Plentiful Place for Stock, by reason of the wide Marshes adjacent to it, and because of its warm Situation. But the Inhabitants pay a little dear for this Convenience, by losing as much Blood in the Summer Season by the infinite Number of Mosquetas, as all their Beef and Pork can recruit in the Winter.

The Sheep are as large as in Lincolnshire, because they are never pincht by cold or Hunger. The whole Island was hitherto reckon'd to lye in Virginia, but now our Line has given the greater Part of it to Carolina. The Principal Freeholder here is Mr. White, who keeps open House for all Travellers, that either Debt or Shipwreck happens to cast in his way.

.   .   .

MARCH 12, 1728

[From THE SECRET HISTORY]

Complaint was made to Me this Morning, that the Men belonging to the Periauga, had stole our People's Meat while they Slept. This provoked me to treat them a la Dragon, that is to swear at them furiously; & by the good Grace of my Oaths, I might have past for an Officer in his Majesty's Guards. I was the more out of Humour, because it disappointed us in our early March, it being a standing Order to boil the Pot over Night, that we might not be hinder'd in the Morning. This Accident, & Necessity of drying our Bed-Cloaths kept us from decamping til near 12 a Clock. By this delay the Surveyors found time to plot off their Work, and to observe the Course of the River. Then they past it over against Northern's Creek, the Mouth of which was very near our Line. But the Commissioners made the best of their way to the Bridge, and going ashoar walkt to Mr. Ballance's Plantation. I retir'd early to our Camp at some distance from the House, while my Collegues tarry'd within Doors, & refresh't themselves with a Cheerful Bowl. In the Gaiety of their Hearts, they invited a Tallow-faced Wench that had sprain'd her Wrist to drink with them, and when they had rais'd her in good Humour, they examined all her hidden Charms, and play'd a great many gay Pranks. While Firebrand who had the most Curiosity, was ranging over her sweet Person, he pick't off several Scabs as big as Nipples, the Consequence of eating too much Pork. The poor Damsel was disabled from making any resistance by the Lameness of her Hand; all she cou'd do, was, to sit stil, & make the Fashionable Exclamation of the Country, Flesh a live & tear it, & by what I can understand she never spake so properly in her Life. One of the Representatives of N. Carolina made a Midnight Visit to our Camp, & his Curiosity was so very clamorous that it waked Me, for which I wish't his Nose as flat as any of his Porcivorous Countrymen.

.   .   .

MARCH 25, 1728

[From THE HISTORY]

The air was chill'd this Morning with a Smart North-west Wind, which favour'd the Dismalites in their Dirty March. They return'd by the Path they had made in coming out, and with great Industry arriv'd in the Evening at the Spot where the Line had been discontinued.

After so long and laborious a Journey, they were glad to repose themselves on their couches of Cypress-bark, where their sleep was as sweet as it wou'd have been on a Bed of Finland Down.

In the mean time, we who stay'd behind had nothing to do, but to make the best observations we cou'd upon that Part of the Country. The Soil of our Landlord's Plantation, tho' none of the best, seem'd more fertile than any thereabouts, where the Ground is near as Sandy as the Desarts of Affrica, and consequently barren. The Road leading from thence to Edenton, being in distance about 27 Miles, lies upon a Ridge call'd Sandy-Ridge, which is so wretchedly Poor that it will not bring Potatoes.

The Pines in this Part of the country are of a different Species from those that grow in Virginia: their bearded Leaves are much longer and their Cones much larger. Each Cell contains a Seed of the Size and Figure of a black-ey'd Pea, which, Shedding in November, is very good Mast for Hogs, and fattens them in a Short time.

The Smallest of these Pines are full of Cones, which are 8 or 9 Inches long, and each affords commonly 60 or 70 Seeds. This Kind of Mast has the Advantage of all other, by being more constant, and less liable to be nippt by the Frost, or Eaten by the Caterpillars. The Trees also abound more with Turpentine, and consequently yield more Tarr, than either the Yellow or the White Pine; And for the same reason make more durable Timber for building. The Inhabitants hereabouts pick up Knots of Lightwood in Abundance, which they burn into tar, and then carry it to Norfolk or Nansimond for a Market. The Tar made in this method is the less Valuable, because it is said to burn the Cordage, tho' it is full as good for all other uses, as that made in Sweden and Muscovy.

Surely there is no place in the World where the Inhabitants live with less Labour than in N Carolina. It approaches nearer to the Description of Lubberland than any other, by the great felicity of the Climate, the easiness of raising Provisions, and the Slothfulness of the People.

Indian Corn is of so great increase, that a little Pains will Subsist a very large Family with Bread, and then they may have meat without any pains at all, by the Help of the Low Grounds, and the great Variety of Mast that grows on the High-land. The Men, for their Parts, just like the Indians, impose all the Work upon the poor Women. They make their Wives rise out of their Beds early in the Morning, at the same time that they lye and

Snore, till the Sun has run one third of his course, and disperst all the unwholesome Damps. Then, after Stretching and Yawning for half an Hour, they light their Pipes, and, under the Protection of a cloud of Smoak, venture out into the open Air; tho', if it happens to be never so little cold, they quickly return Shivering into the Chimney corner. When the weather is mild, they stand leaning with both their arms upon the corn-field fence, and gravely consider whether they had best go and take a Small Heat at the Hough: but generally find reasons to put it off till another time.

Thus they loiter away their Lives, like Solomon's Sluggard, with their Arms across, and at the Winding up of the Year Scarcely have Bread to Eat.

To speak the Truth, tis a thorough Aversion to Labor that makes People file off to N Carolina, where Plenty and a Warm Sun confirm them in their Disposition to Laziness for their whole Lives.

MARCH 26, 1728

[From THE HISTORY]

Since we were like to be confin'd to this place, till the People return'd out of the Dismal, twas agreed that our Chaplain might Safely take a turn to Edenton, to preach the Gospel to the Infidels there, and Christen their Children. He was accompany'd thither by Mr. Little, One of the Carolina Commissioners, who, to shew his regard for the Church, offer'd to treat Him on the Road with a Fricassee of Rum. They fry'd half a Dozen Rashers of very fat Bacon in a Pint of Rum, both which being disht up together, serv'd the Company at once for meat and Drink.

Most of the Rum they get in this Country comes from New England, and is so bad and unwholesome, that it is not improperly call'd "Kill-Devil." It is distill'd there from forreign molosses, which, if Skilfully manag'd yields near Gallon for Gallon. Their molasses comes from the same country, and has the name of "Long Sugar" in Carolina, I suppose from the Ropiness of it, and Serves all the purposes of Sugar, both in their Eating and Drinking.

When they entertain their Friends bountifully, they fail not to set before them a Capacious Bowl of Bombo, so call'd from the Admiral of that name. This is a Compound of Rum and Water in Equal Parts, made palatable with the said long Sugar. As good Humour begins to flow, and the Bowl to Ebb, they take care to replinish it with Shear Rum, of which there always is a Reserve under the Table. But such Generous doings happen only when that Balsam of life is plenty; for they have often such Melancholy times, that neither Land-graves nor Cassicks can procure one drop for their Wives, when they ly in, or are troubled with the Colick or Vapours. Very few in this

Country have the Industry to plant Orchards, which, in a Dearth of Rum, might supply them with much better Liquor.

The Truth is, there is one Inconvenience that easily discourages lazy People from making This improvement: very often, in Autumn, when the Apples begin to ripen, they are visited with Numerous Flights of paraqueets, that bite all the Fruit to Pieces in a moment, for the sake of the Kernels. The Havock they make is Sometimes so great, that whole Orchards are laid waste in Spite of all the Noises that can be made, or Mawkins that can be dresst up, to fright 'em away. These Ravenous Birds visit North Carolina only during the warm Season, and so soon as the Cold begins to come on, retire back towards the Sun. They rarely Venture so far North as Virginia, except in a very hot Summer, when they visit the most Southern Parts of it. They are very Beautiful; but like some other pretty Creatures, are apt to be loud and mischievous.

· · ·

APRIL 7, 1728

[From THE HISTORY]

The Next day being Sunday, we order'd Notice to be sent to all the Neighbourhood that there wou'd be a Sermon at this Place, and an Opportunity of Christening their Children. But the Likelihood of Rain got the better of their Devotion, and what perhaps, Might Still be a Stronger motive of their Curiosity. In the Morning we despacht a runner to the Nottoway Town, to let the Indians know we intend them a Visit that Evening, and our honest Landlord was so kind as to be our Pilot thither, being about 4 Miles from his House.

Accordingly in the Afternoon we marcht in good Order to the Town, where the Female Scouts, station'd on an Eminence for that purpose, had no sooner spy'd us, but they gave Notice of our Approach to their Fellow-Citizens by continual Whoops and Cries, which cou'd not possibly have been more dismal at the Sight of their most implacable Enemys.

This Signal Assembled all their Great Men, who receiv'd us in a Body, and conducted us into the Fort. This Fort was a Square Piece of Ground, inclos'd with Substantial Puncheons, or Strong Palisades, about ten feet high, and leaning a little outwards, to make a Scalade more difficult.

Each side of the Square might be about 100 Yards long, with Loopholes at proper Distances, through which they may fire upon the Enemy.

Within this Inclosure we found Bark Cabanes Sufficient to lodge all their people, in Case they should be obliged to retire thither. These Cabanes are no other but Close Arbours made of Saplings, arched at the top, and cover'd so well with Bark as to be proof against all Weather. The fire is made in the Middle, according to the Hibernian Fashion, the Smoak whereof finds no other Vent but at the Door, and so keeps the whole family Warm, at the Expense both of their Eyes and Complexion.

The Indians have no standing Furniture in their Cabanes but Hurdles to repose their Persons upon, which they cover with Mats or Deer-skins. We were conducted to the best Appartments in the Fort, which just before had been made ready for our Reception, and adorn'd with new Mats, that were sweet and clean.

The Young Men had Painted themselves in a Hideous Manner, not so much for Ornament as Terror. In that frightful Equipage they entertain'd us with Sundry War-Dances, wherein they endeavour'd to look as formidable as possible. The Instrument they danct to was an Indian-drum, that is, a large Gourd with a Skin bract tort over the Mouth of it. The Dancers all Sang to this Musick, keeping exact Time with their feet, while their Heads and Arms were screw'd into a thousand Menacing Postures.

Upon this occasion the Ladies had array'd themselves in all their finery. They were Wrapt in their Red and Blue Match-Coats, thrown so Negligently about them, that their Mehogony Skins appear'd in Several Parts, like the Lacedaemonian Damsels of Old. Their Hair was breeded with white and Blue Peak, and hung gracefully in a large Roll upon their Shoulders.

This peak Consists of Small Cylinders cut out of a Conque-Shell, drill'd through and Strung like Beads. It serves them both for Money and Jewels, the Blue being of much greater Value than the White, for the same reason that Ethiopian Mistresses in France are dearer than French, because they are more Scarce. The Women wear Necklaces and Bracelets of these precious Materials, when they have a mind to appear lovely. Tho' their complexions be a little Sad-Colour'd, yet their Shapes are very Strait and well porportion'd. Their Faces are Seldom handsome, yet they have an Air of Innocence and Bashfulness, that with a little less dirt wou'd not fail to make them desirable. Such Charms might have had their full Effect upon Men who had been so long deprived of female conversation, but that the whole Winter's Soil was so crusted on the Skins of those dark Angels, that it requir'd a very strong Appetite to approach them. The Bear's oyl, with which they anoint their Persons all over, makes their skins Soft, and at the Same time protects them from every Species of Vermin that use to be troublesome to other uncleanly People.

We were unluckily so many, that they cou'd not well make us the Complement of Bed-fellows, according to the Indian Rules of Hospitality, tho' a grave Matron whisper'd one of the Commissioners very civily in the Ear, that if her Daughter had been but one year Older, she should have been at his Devotion.

It is by no means a loss of Reputation among the Indians, for Damsels that are Single to have Intrigues with the Men; on the contrary, they count it an Argument of Superior Merit to be liked by a great Number of Gallants. However, like the Ladys that Game they are a little Mercenary in their Amours, and seldom bestow their Favours out of Stark Love and Kindness. But after these Women have once appropriated their Charms by Marriage, they are from thencefourth faithful to their Vows, and will hardly ever be tempted by an Agreeable Gallant, or be provokt by a Brutal or even by a fumbling Husband to go astray.

The little Work that is done among the Indians is done by the poor Women, while the men are quite idle, or at most employ'd only in the Gentlemanly Diversions of Hunting and Fishing.

In this, as well as in their Wars, they now use nothing but Fire-Arms, which they purchase of the English for Skins. Bows and Arrows are grown into disuse, except only amongst their Boys. Nor is it ill Policy, but on the contrary very prudent, thus to furnish the Indians with Fire-Arms, because it makes them depend entirely upon the English, not only for their Trade, but even for their subsistence. Besides, they were really able to do more mischief, while they made use of Arrows, of which they wou'd let Silently fly Several in a Minute with Wonderful Dexterity, whereas now they hardly ever discharge their Firelocks more than once, which they insidiously do from behind a Tree, and then retire as nimbly as the Dutch Horse us'd to do now and then formerly in Flanders.

We put the Indians to no expense, but only of a little Corn for our Horses, for which in Gratitude we cheer'd their hearts with what Rum we had left, which they love better than they do their Wives and Children.

Tho' these Indians dwell among the English, and see in what Plenty a little Industry enables them to live, yet they chuse to continue in their Stupid Idleness, and to Suffer all the Inconveniences of Dirt, Cold, and Want, rather than to disturb their hands With care, or defile their Hands with labour.

The whole Number of People belonging to the Nottoway Town, if you include Women and Children, amount to about 200. These are the only Indians of any consequence now remaining within the Limits of Virginia. The rest are either removed, or dwindled to a very inconsiderable Number, either by destroying one another, or else by the Small-Pox and other Diseases. Tho' nothing has been so fatal to them as their ungovernable Passion for Rum, with which, I am sorry to say it, they have been but too liberally supply'd by the English that live near them.

And here I must lament the bad Success Mr. Boyle's Charity has hitherto had towards converting any of these poor Heathens to Christianity. Many children of our Neighbouring Indians have been brought up in the College of William and Mary. They have been taught to read and write, and have been carefully Instructed in the Principles of the Christian Religion, till they came to be men. Yet after they return'd home, instead of civilizeing and converting the rest, they have immediately Relapt into Infidelity and Barbarism themselves.

And some of them too have made the worst use of the Knowledge they acquir'd among the English, by employing it against their Benefactors. Besides, as they unhappily forget all the good they learn, and remember the Ill, they are apt to be more vicious and disorderly than the rest of their Countrymen.

I ought not to quit this Subject without doing Justice to the great Prudence of Colo Spotswood in this Affair. That Gentleman was lieut Governor of Virginia when Carolina was engaged in a Bloody War with the Indians. At that critical Time it was thought expedient to keep a Watchful Eye upon our Tributary Savages, who we knew had nothing to keep them to their Duty but their Fears.

Then it was that he demanded of each Nation a Competent Number of their great Men's Children to be sent to the College, where they serv'd as so many Hostages for the good Behaviour of the Rest, and at the same time were themselves principled in the Christian Religion. He also Plac'd a School-Master among the Saponi Indians, at the salary of Fifty Pounds P Annum, to instruct their Children. The Person that undertook that Charitable work was Mr. Charles Griffin, a Man of good Family, who by the Innocence of his Life, and the Sweetest of his Temper, was perfectly well qualify'd for that pious undertaking. Besides, he had so much the Secret of mixing Pleasure with instruction, that he had not a Scholar, who did not love him affectionately.

Such Talents must needs have been blest with a Proportionable Success, had he not been unluckily remov'd to the College, by which he left the good work he had begun unfinisht. In short, all the Pains he had undertaken among the Infidels had no other Effect but to make them something cleanlier than other Indians are.

The Care Colo Spotswood took to tincture the Indian Children with Christianity produc'd the following Epigram, which was not publisht during his Administration, for fear it might then have lookt like flattery.

> Long has the Furious Priest assay'd in Vain,
> With Sword and Faggot, Infidels to gain,
> But now the Milder Soldier wisely tryes
> By Gentler Methods to unveil their Eyes.
> Wonders apart, he knew 'twere vain t'engage
> The fix'd Preventions of Misguided Age.
> With fairer Hopes he forms the Indian Youth
> To early Manners, Probity and Truth.
> The Lyon's whelp thus on the Lybian Shore ⎫
> Is tam'd and Gentled by the Artful Moor, ⎬
> Not the Grim Sire, inured to Blood before. ⎭

I am sorry I can't give a Better Account of the State of the Poor Indians with respect to Christianity, altho' a great deal of Pains has been and still continues to be taken with them. For my Part, I must be of Opinion, as I hinted before, that there is but one way of Converting these poor Infidels, and reclaiming them from Barbarity, and that is, Charitably to intermarry with them, according to the Modern Policy of the most Christian King in Canada and Louisiana.

Had the English done this at the first Settlement of the Colony, the Infidelity of the Indians had been worn out at this Day, with their Dark Complexions, and the Country had swarm'd with People more than it does with Insects.

It was certainly an unreasonable Nicety, that prevented their entering into so good-Natur'd an Alliance. All Nations of men have the same Natural Dignity, and we all know that very bright Talents may be lodg'd under a very dark Skin. The principal Difference between one People and another proceeds only from the Different Opportunities of Improvement.

The Indians by no means want understanding, and are in their Figure tall and well-proportion'd. Even their Copper-colour'd Complexion wou'd admit of Blanching, if not in the first, at the farthest in the Second Generation.

I may safely venture to say, the Indian Women would have made altogether as Honest Wives for the first Planters, as the Damsels they us'd to purchase from aboard the Ships. It is Strange, therefore, that any good Christian Shou'd have refused a wholesome, Straight Bed-fellow, when he might have had so fair a Portion with her, as the Merit of saving her Soul.

.   .   .

APRIL 8, 1728

[From THE SECRET HISTORY]

When we were drest, Meanwell & I visited most of the Princesses at their own Appartments, but the Smoke was so great there, the Fire being made in the middle of the Cabbins, that we were not able to see their Charms. Prince James' Princess sent my Wife a fine Basket of her own making, with the Expectation of receiving from her some present of ten times its Value. An Indian Present like those made to Princes, is only a Liberality put out to Interest, & a bribe placed to the greatest Advantage. I cou'd discern by some of our Gentlemen's Linnen, discolour'd by the Soil of the Indian Ladys, that they had been convincing themselves in the point of their having no furr. About Ten we march't out of the Town, some of the Indians giving us a Volley of small Arms at our departure. We drank our Chocolate at one Jones's about 4 Miles from the Town, & then proceeded over Black-Water Bridge to Col° Henry Harrisons, where we were very handsomely entertain'd, & congratulated one another upon our Return into Christen-dome.

A GARLAND OF COLONIAL VERSE

GEORGE ALSOP

(1638–*after* 1666)

George Alsop came to Maryland as a bonded or indentured servant, perhaps because of his Royalist views. Returning to England after 1666, he published a long work of prose and poetry entitled *A Character of the Province of Maryland*, from which the following verses are excerpted. Alsop later took holy orders and became an Anglican minister in London.

[TRAFIQUE IS EARTH'S GREAT ATLAS]

Trafique is Earth's great Atlas, that supports
The pay of Armies, and the height of Courts,
And makes Mechanicks live, that else would die
Meer starving Martyrs to their penury:
None but the Merchant of this thing can boast,
He, like the Bee, comes loaden from each Coast,
And to all Kingdoms, as within a Hive,
Stows up those Riches that doth make them thrive:
Be thrifty, Mary-Land, keep what thou hast in store,
And each years Trafique to thy self get more.

1664

['TIS SAID THE GODS LOWER DOWN THAT CHAIN ABOVE]

'Tis said the Gods lower down that Chain above,
That tyes both Prince and Subject up in Love;
And if this Fiction of the Gods be true,
Few, *Mary-Land*, in this can boast but you:
Live ever blest, and let those Clouds that do
Eclipse most States, be alwayes Lights to you;
And dwelling so, you may for ever be
The only Emblem of Tranquility.

1664

RICHARD LEWIS

(c. 1700–1734)

Very little is known about Richard Lewis of Maryland, though he wrote a considerable number of occasional poems. It is thought that he was a native of Wales and a student at Balliol College, Oxford, before coming to the New World. He taught school at Annapolis, was interested in science as well as letters, and was well enough known as poet to have his "Journey from *Patapsco* to *Annapolis*" attacked by Alexander Pope in *The Dunciad* as part of that poet's general assault upon the scientific deism of his day. In effect, Lewis was the first genuine nature poet in America.

From A JOURNEY FROM PATAPSCO TO ANNAPOLIS

Me vero primum dulces ante omnia Musae
Quarum sacra fero ingenti perculsus amore,
Accipiant; Coelique vias et Sydera *monstrent;—*
Sin bas ne possem Natura accedere partes,
Frigidus onstiterit circum praecordia Sanguis
Rura *mihi, et* rigui *placeant in Vallibus* Amnes,
Flumina *amen,* Sylvaque *inglorius.—*
Virg. Geor. 2.

At length the wintry horrors disappear;
And APRIL views with smiles the infant year:

RICHARD LEWIS

The grateful earth from frosty chains unbound,
Pours out its vernal treasures all around,
Her face bedeckt with grass, with leaves the trees are crown'd.
In this soft season, e'er the dawn of day,
I mount my horse, and lonely take my way,
From woody hills that shade Patapsko's head,
(In whose deep vales he makes his stony bed,
From whence he rushes with resistless force,
Tho' huge rough rocks retard his rapid course,)
Down to Annapolis, on that smooth stream
Which took from fair Anne-Arundel its name.

And now the star that ushers in the day,
Begins to pale her ineffectual ray.
The moon with bluted horns now shines less bright,
Her fading face eclips'd with growing light;
The fleecy clouds with streaky lustre glow,
And day quits heav'n to view the earth below;
O'er yon tall trees the sun shews half his face,
And fires their floating foliage with his rays;
Now sheds aslant on earth his lightsome beams,
That trembling shine in many-colour'd streams:
Slow-rising from the marsh, the mist recedes,
The trees, emerging, rear their dewy heads;
Their dewy heads the sun with pleasure views,
And brightens into pearls the pendent dews.

The beasts uprising quit their leafy beds,
And to the chearful sky erect their heads;
All joyful rise, except the filthy swine,
On obscene litter stretch'd they snore supine:
In vain the day awakes, sleep seals their eyes,
Till hunger breaks the bond and bids them rise.

And now the sun with more exalted ray,
From cloudless skies distributes riper day;
Thro' sylvan scenes my journey I pursue,
Ten thousand beauties rising to my view;
Which kindle in my breast poetick flame,
And bid me my CREATOR'S praise proclaim;
Tho' my low verse ill suits the noble theme.

But now th' enclosed plantation I forsake,
And onwards thro' the woods my journey take;
The level road the longsom way beguiles,
A blooming wilderness around me smiles:

A JOURNEY FROM PATAPSCO TO ANNAPOLIS

Here hardy oak, there fragrant hick'ry grows,
Their bursting buds the tender leaves disclose;
The tender leaves in downy robes appear,
Trembling they seem to move with cautious fear,
Yet new to life, and strangers to the air.
Here stately pines unite their whisp'ring heads,
And with a solemn gloom embrown the glades.
See there a green savana opens wide,
Thro' which smooth streams in wanton mazes glide;
Thick-branching shrubs o'er-hang the silver streams
Which scarcely deign t' admit the solar beams.

While with delight on this soft scene I gaze,
The cattle upward look, and cease to graze,
But into covert run thro' various ways.
And now the clouds in black assemblage rise,
And dreary darkness overspreads the skies,
Thro' which the sun strives to transmit his beams,
But sheds his sickly light in stragling streams.
Hush'd is the musick of the woodland quire,
Foreknowing of the storm, the birds retire
For shelter, and forsake the shrubby plains,
And a dumb horror thro' the forest reigns:
In that lone house which opens wide its door,
Safe—may I tarry till the storm is o'er.

Hark how the thunder rolls with solemn sound!
And see the forceful lightning darts a wound
On yon tall oak!—behold its top laid bare!
Its body rent, and scatter'd thro' the air,
The splinters fly!—now—now the winds arise,
From different quarters of the lowring skies;
Forth issuing fierce, the west and south engage,
The waving forest bends beneath their rage:
But where the winding valley checks their course,
They roar and ravage with redoubled force;
With circling sweep in dreadful whirlwinds move,
And from its roots tear up the gloomy grove;
Down-rushing fall the trees, and beat the ground,
In fragments fly the shatter'd limbs around;
Tremble the underwoods, the vales resound.

Follows with patt'ring noise the icy hail,
And rain fast falling floods the lowly vale.
Again the thunders roll, the lightnings fly,

And as they first disturb'd, now clear the sky;
For lo, the gust decreases by degrees,
The dying winds but sob amidst the trees;
With pleasing softness falls the silver rain,
Thro' which at first faint-gleaming o'er the plain,
The orb of light scarce darts a watry ray
To gild the drops that fall from ev'ry spray;
But soon the dusky Vapours are dispel'd,
And thro' the mist that late his face conceal'd,
Bursts the broad sun, triumphant in a blaze
Too keen for sight—yon cloud refracts his rays,
The mingling beams compose the ethereal bow,
How sweet, how soft its melting colours glow!
Gaily they shine, by heav'nly pencils laid,
Yet vanish swift;—how soon does beauty fade!

    The storm is past, my journey I renew,
And a new scene of pleasures greets my view:
Wash'd by the copious rain the gummy pine
Does chearful with unsully'd verdure shine;
The dogwood flowers assume a snowy white,
The maple blushing gratifies the sight:
The sassafras unfolds its fragrant bloom,
The vine affords an exquisite perfume;
These grateful scents wide-wafting thro' the air,
The smelling sense with balmy odours cheer.
And now the birds sweet singing stretch their throats,
And in one choir unite their various notes,
Nor yet unpleasing is the turtles voice,
Tho' he complains while other birds rejoyce. . . .

    The mind advis'd by this instructive sight,
Descending sudden from th' aerial height,
Obliges me to view a different scene,
Of more importance to myself, tho' mean.
These distant objects I no more pursue,
But turning inward my reflective view,
My working fancy helps me to survey,
In the just picture of this April day,
My life o'erpast,—a course of thirty years
Blest with few joys, perplex'd with num'rous cares.

    In the dim twilight of our infancy,
Scarce can the eye surrounding objects see;
Then thoughtless childhood leads us pleas'd and gay,

A JOURNEY FROM PATAPSCO TO ANNAPOLIS

In life's fair morning thro' a flowry way:
The youth in schools, inquisitive of good,
Science pursues thro' learning's mazy wood;
Whose lofty trees, he, to his grief perceives,
Are often bare of fruit, and only fill'd with leaves:
Thro' lonely wilds his tedious journey lies,
At last a brighter prospect cheers his eyes;
Now the gay fields of poetry he views,
And joyous, listens to the tuneful muse;
Now history affords him vast delight,
And opens lovely landscapes to his sight;
But ah too soon this scene of pleasure dies!
And o'er his head tempestuous troubles rise;
He hears the thunders roll, he feels the rains,
Before a friendly shelter he obtains;
And thence beholds with grief the furious storm,
The noon-tide beauties of his life deform:
He views the painted bow in distant skies;
Hence, in his heart some gleams of comfort rise;
He hopes the gust has almost spent its force,
And that he safely may pursue his course.

Thus far my life does with the day agree,
Oh may its coming stage from storms be free!
While passing thro' the worlds most private way,
With pleasure I my MAKER's works survey;
Within my heart let peace a dwelling find,
Let my goodwill extend to all mankind:
Freed from necessity, and blest with health;
Give me content, let others toil for wealth:
In busy scenes of life let me exert
A careful hand, and wear an honest heart;
And suffer me my leisure hours to spend,
With chosen books, or a well natur'd friend.
Thus journeying on, as I advance in age,
May I look back with pleasure on my stage;
And as the setting sun withdrew his light
To rise on other worlds serene and bright,
Chearful may I resign my vital breath,
Nor anxious tremble at th' approach of death;
Which shall (I hope) but strip me of my clay,
And to a better world my soul convey.

Thus musing I my silent moments spend,
'Till to the river's margin I descend,

From whence I may discern my journey's end:
Annapolis adorns its further shore,
To which the boat attends to bring me o'er.
And now the moving boat the floods divides,
While the stars tremble on the circling tides;
Pleas'd with the sight again I raise mine eye,
To the bright glories of the azure sky;
And fill'd with holy horror thus I cry.

    While I behold these wonders of thy hand;
The moon and stars that move at thy command,
Obedient thro' their circuit of the sky,
ALMIGHTY LORD! will thy dread majesty
Vouchsafe to view the wretched son of man,
Thy creature, who but yesterday began,
Thro' animated clay to draw his breath,
To-morrow doom'd a prey to ruthless death!

    TREMENDOUS GOD! may I not justly fear
That I, unworthy object of thy care,
Into this world from thy bright presence tost,
Am in the immensity of nature lost!
And that my notions of the world above,
Are but creations of my own self-love;
To feed my coward heart, afraid to die,
With fancied feasts of immortality!

    These thoughts, which thy amazing works suggest,
Oh glorious FATHER, rack my troubled breast.

    Yet, GRACIOUS GOD, reflecting that my frame
From thee deriv'd its animating flame;
And whate'er I am, however mean,
By thy command I entred on this scene
Of life,—thy wretched creature of a day,
Condemn'd to travel thro' a tiresome way;
Upon whose banks, (perhaps to cheer my toil)
I see thin verdures rise, and daisies smile:
Poor comforts these, my pains t' alleviate;
While on my head tempestuous troubles beat.
And must I, when I quit this earthly scene,
Sink total into death, and never rise again!

    No sure,—these thoughts which in my bosome roll,
Must issue from a never-dying soul;
These active thoughts that penetrate the sky,

Excursive into dark futurity;
Which hope eternal happiness to gain,
Could never be bestow'd on man in vain.

To thee, Oh FATHER, fill'd with fervent zeal,
And sunk in humble silence I appeal;
Take me my great CREATOR to thy care,
And gracious listen to my ardent prayer!

SUPREME OF BEINGS, omnipresent power,
My great preserver from my natal-hour,
Fountain of wisdom, boundless Deity,
OMNISCIENT GOD, my wants are known to thee,
With mercy look on mine infirmity!
Whatever state thou shalt for me ordain,
Whether my lot in life be joy or pain;
Patient let me sustain thy wise decree,
And learn to know myself, and honour thee.

1731

JOHN MARKLAND

(*fl.* 1730–1735)

A selection from Markland's "Typographia. An Ode, on Printing" belongs in any compendium of Southern verse if only because the author's prodigious industry and misplaced ingenuity produced a work that is comic beyond most consciously intended efforts of this nature by colonial poets. Setting out to praise the arrival of the printer William Parks in Virginia and also the benevolent administration of Governor James Gooch, Markland wrote a poem that followed the pattern of the Pindaric Ode in all but tone and meaning. The poem culminates in a final line that likens the royal governor's tenure to that of the Roman Emperor Augustus—a sure mastery of unintentional incongruity.

The poet John Markland was probably an attorney in New Kent County, Virginia, in 1733, and is believed to have attended Cambridge University in England. "Typographia" first appeared in 1730.

JOHN MARKLAND

From TYPOGRAPHIA. AN ODE

. . .

IX

Yet fair befal His Fame,
And may his Mem'ry long
In latest Annals live,
Who first contriv'd the *wondrous Frame*,
That to *dead Types* supply'd a *Tongue*,
And *Speech* to *lifeless Characters* could give.
O well was he employ'd the while,
And happy was the vent'rous Toil!
His Breast had compass'd some great Thought,
Tho' formless yet, and void,
His busy Faculties were all employ'd,
How future Ages might be surest taught,
By old Examples, long since done,
What Paths to follow, what to shun,
How Vertue ev'n in Death befriends,
And how Ambition ends,
How *Socrates* instructed, *Caesar* fought;
Long Time, his swelling Breast
The great *Idea* had opprest,
'Till, fix'd at Length, he in a Rapture bid,
Come up a *glorious, great Design*,—And so it did.

. . .

XII

Happy the *Art*, by which we learn
The Gloss of Errors to detect,
The Vice of Habits to correct,
And sacred Truths, from Falshood to discern!
By which we take a far-stretch'd View
And learn our Fathers Vertues to pursue,
Their Follies to eschew.
And may that *Art* to latest Times proclaim
Its PATRON's Honourable Name.
As some *Sybillin* Book of old,
Had *Sybils* known the Times to come,
Wrapt in *Futurity's* dark Womb,
Would thus these happy Days have told:

ANACREONTIC

"Revolving Ages hence,
"In Climates now unknown,
"A *Ruler's* gentle Influence
"Shall o'er his Land be shewn;
"*Saturnian Reigns* shall be renew'd,
"Truth, Justice, Vertue, be pursu'd,
"Arts flourish, Peace shall crown the Plains,
"Where GOOCH administers, AUGUSTUS reigns.

1730

WILLIAM DAWSON

(1704–1752)

William Dawson was a graduate of Queen's College, Oxford, and came to Virginia as a protégé of Commissary James Blair, the founder of the College of William and Mary and one of the most powerful men in Virginia. Ultimately, Dawson succeeded Blair both as president and as bishop's commissary. His *Poems on Several Occasions by a Gentleman of Virginia* was published anonymously in 1736.

ANACREONTIC

Old Poets sing the Dame, to Stone
Converted by Jove's radiant Son:
How Progne builds her clayey Cell
In Chimneys, where she once did dwell.
For me, (did Fate permit to use,
Whatever Form our Fancies choose)
I'd be my lovely Sylvia's Glass,
Still to reflect her beauteous Face;
I'd be the pure and limpid Wave,
In which my Fair delights to lave;
I'd be her Garment, still to hide
Her snowy Limbs, with decent Pride;
I'd be the Girdle, to embrace
The gradual Taper of her Waist;
I'd be her Tippet, still to press
The snowy Velvet of her Breast;
But if the rigid Fates denied

Such Ornaments of Grace and Pride,
I'd be her very Shoe, that she
With scornful Tread might Trample me.

1736

SAMUEL DAVIES

(1723–1761)

A native of Delaware, Samuel Davies came to Virginia in 1747 as an evange-list-minister of New Light Presbyterianism. Preaching in various places, he won many converts with his eloquent oratory, and his tact and presentability did much to alleviate the suspicion in which evangelical activities were held by the Established Church in the colony. A man of considerable literary talent, he wrote numerous widely admired sermons and some occasional verse. In 1753, while en route to England, he was asked to write an epitaph for the deceased sister of a friend and composed the following three so that his friend might choose one. During the French and Indian War Davies did much to rally volunteers for Colonel George Washington's Virginia troops with his inspired sermons. At one point he spoke of "that heroic youth, Col. Washington, whom I cannot but hope Providence has hitherto preserved in so signal a manner, for some important service to his country." Davies left Virginia in 1759 to become president of the College of New Jersey, later Princeton University.

[THREE EPITAPHS]

Does beauty spread her charms? Does wealth o'erflow?
Does health bloom fresh, or youthful vigour glow?
Are all earth's blessings in profusion pour'd?
And all these sweets with no affliction sour'd?
Ah! trust not these, to guard from early death
All these adorn'd the precious dust beneath.

Or,

Ye that in beauty, or in youth confide,
Come view this monument, to blast your pride;
The charms of beauty, youth in flowery bloom,
Wither'd at morn, lie mould'ring in this tomb,

And you may meet the same surprizing doom.

Or,

This monument proclaims this solemn truth,
Beauty is fading, frail the bloom of youth;
Life short, [a span,] a dream, an empty show,
And all is fleeting vanity below.
Careless spectator! learn from hence to die;
Prepare, prepare for immortality.

1753

RICHARD BLAND

(1710–1776)

Richard Bland, a graduate of the College of William and Mary and of Edinburgh University, was one of the most distinguished members of the Virginia House of Burgesses and a leader in the growing resistance to British control after the French and Indian War. He was renowned as a classical scholar and his friends sometimes referred to him as the "Virginia Antiquary" because of his knowledge of early colonial history. His poetic epistle was directed to his friend Landon Carter, the eloquently outspoken, imperious, and rather crotchety master of "Sabine Hall," who, like Bland, was active as a pamphleteer in opposition to British policies.

AN EPISTLE TO
LANDON CARTER, ESQ., UPON
HEARING
THAT HE DOES NOT INTEND TO
STAND
A CANDIDATE AT THE NEXT ELECTION
OF BURGESSES

You'l envy not, you say, Dear Sir, the great,
Their Pomp, their Luxury, their pageant state,
But bless'd with all that Heav'n below can give,
A mind contented and a taste to live,
You'l smile superior on their empty show,
Their seeming pleasure but their real woe.

RICHARD BLAND

At Sabine Hall, retir'd from public praise,
You'l spend in learned ease your future days.
Yet deign to hear a Muse, whose honest strain
Did ne'er commend the vicious nor the vain,
But sometimes in the cause of Virtue soars,
And scorns less merit for her Lay, than yours.
Whilst you, my friend! with pleasing joy survey
Your teeming flocks, as through the meads they stray,
Whilst you, in Sylvian shades and pleasant groves,
Hear Philomelas chanting to their Loves;
Whilst you, secure from all domestic strife,
Enjoy delightful scenes of rural life;
Permit me to deplore my country's fate,
The dire misfortunes of her tot'ring state.
When Power's uplifted arm was hurling down,
With spurious show of service to the CROWN,
A mighty weight, to crush our antient Laws,
And with our spoils to gorge its greedy Jaws,
You then appear'd, your Country's surest Friend,
And did her Cause with manly sense defend.
But now, alas! you do not deign to hear
Your Country's groans, involved in horrid War.
Canadian Wolves, a bloody, savage Band,
Invade with hostile arms her virgin Land,
Forsaken by her Guardian and her Friend,
Who used to her the sagest councils lend,
But now in fields and meadows spends his days
Recluse from public view, and scorns our praise;
But now the life of Tully's self is spent
Supine at Rome, and carping momers sent
With baleful nonsense, in the grandest Cause,
T' assist her Senate, and ordain her Laws.
Young pageant Elfs do now live pleas'd, and aim
By shocking common sense, at public fame.
Agelaus self would laugh to hear such Tools,
The gewgaws of the vulgar and of fools,
With Midas ears, bray out with vain pretence,
'We are the men of weight and men of sense.'
Rise then judicious Friend! step boldly forth,
And vindicate your merit and your worth;
Strike bold Pretenders, to the highest place,
Into oblivion, and a just disgrace.
Yes! all ye sons of Folly and of Vice,
From whom our present Evils take their rise,

Yes! all ye slaves of Luxury and Lust
Avant! Begone! sink into native dust.
Do not our annals with your names disgrace,
Depart to your own dul and stupid race.
The Country's Patriot once again appears
To vindicate our Laws, and calm our fears.
He'l suffer none, whilst he his Pen can wave,
To be with ease and safety Fool or Knave.
He'l always foremost be, and boldly rise
A Friend to Virtue and a Foe to Vice.
Then stand once more, aloud your country cries,
(Nor do her prayers nor her commands despise),
Stand once again, and save a sinking Land,
Which is sincerely wish'd by Yours D———k B———d.

The date of "Dick" Bland's effusion is "June 20, 1758."

1758

THOMAS BURKE

(c. 1747–1783)

Not everyone in Virginia shared Richard Bland's estimation of Landon Carter. Irish-born Thomas Burke, of Accomac County and Norfolk, circulated among friends the following considerably less laudatory poem about Carter. In 1771 Burke moved to North Carolina, where he was elected a delegate to the Continental Congress and later served as Governor.

TRANSMOGRIFICATION

Unwitting, once *Actæon* stray'd
  To that sequester'd Stream
Where, bathing, Night's resplendent Maid
  Assuag'd the sultry Beam.

More curious *Landon*, when the Queen
  Her Brother's Aid implor'd
And took Cathartics for the Spleen,
  Her secret Haunts explor'd

In Hopes the Off'rings *Cynthia* laid

On *Cloacina's* Shrine
With Clinks and Rhymes might lend some Aid
To eke his brainless Line.

Both guilty Chiefs her Vengeance share;
For straight the prudish Lass
Chang'd poor *Actæon* to a Deer
And *Carter* to an Ass.

Tho' by his Hounds *Actæon* bleeds,
Yet *Landon's* Fates surpass him:
Since none annuls another's Deeds,
No God can e'er un-ass him.

c. 1767

THOMAS JEFFERSON

(1743–1826)

In his lifetime Thomas Jefferson published only one book, the *Notes on the State of Virginia* (1785), and then only because an unauthorized edition of the work was being circulated abroad. Yet in breadth of imagination, ardor, and felicity of expository prose his writings represent an ideal for what the Virginia gentleman of the Great Age might be as man of letters. His genius was especially for politics, as befitted one who both enunciated the American dream of human freedom at the outbreak of the Revolution and then twenty years afterward directed the political movement whereby the new nation affirmed its belief in popular representative government. He was also philosopher, diplomatist, architect, scientist, musician, bibliophile, archaeologist, educator, and agriculturalist. In power and range of intellect he was foremost of those Virginians of the Revolutionary War generation who, although separated from England and Western Europe by 3000 miles of water, were not provincials but true citizens of the world.

The *Notes on the State of Virginia*, written in response to a set of queries by the French government concerning each of the several states then fighting for independence from Great Britain, was begun while Jefferson was governor and concluded several years after his retirement from that office. Jefferson addressed himself in turn to the institutions, customs, geography, economy, natural history, and population of Virginia. He set out to disprove Buffon's generalization that the conditions of the New World produced a degeneracy in its fauna and flora, by providing both statistical and logical refutation. When writing about customs and manners, however, Jefferson felt impelled to deal with the chattel slavery that played so prominent a part in his state's economy, and in words that were both admonitory and prophetic, he expressed his detestation of human servitude and his fears of what black slavery portended for the future.

Although himself a slaveholder, Jefferson could view the South's 'peculiar institution,' as it was later called, in the way he did because slavery had not yet become a political issue that importantly divided the new nation along sectional lines. A later generation of Southern leaders, faced with growing political attack from the industrial Northeast upon an economic system that had now grown increasingly profitable after the invention of the cotton gin, was unable to muster Jefferson's moral vision or his willingness to subject his own community to such disinterested self-scrutiny. Jefferson's denunciation of the evil effects of slavery upon both white and black has an eloquence and passion that are the mark of one of the great political minds in all Southern and American history.

Jefferson's ideal for his beloved America was a community of virtuous farmers—he was hostile to manufactures because he did not wish the new nation to develop large cities with urban populations detached from the land and open, as he thought, to corruption and manipulation. There seems to be an inherent contradiction in his advocacy of a republic of small farms and the existence of the plantation system of which he was an exemplar, yet it was bridged by his belief in education and democracy and his hopes for the evolution of a society that would be sufficiently free of domination by a privileged class to permit the flourishing of a genuine leadership of talent. Undoubtedly his impassioned hatred of slavery came in part from the realization that a plantation economy based upon ownership of slaves threatened his dream of agrarian virtue, as well as from his belief that blacks were inherently incapable of becoming citizens of his commonwealth. Jefferson did indeed share many of the racial assumptions of his time. What is remarkable, however, is not that Jefferson was a Virginia slaveholder, but that a Virginia slaveholder could hold Thomas Jefferson's views on slavery.

His belief in the evil and injustice of slavery was manifested in his original draft of the Declaration of Independence, in which he denounced King George III for waging "cruel war against human nature itself, violating its most sacred rights of life and liberty in the persons of a distant people who never offended him, captivating and carrying them into slavery in another hemisphere, or to incur miserable death in their transportation thither." In his account of the writing of the Declaration, part of a *Memoir* written in the last several years of his life, he attributed the deletion of the remarks on slavery to the opposition of South Carolina and Georgia and the uneasy consciences of delegates from New England because of their own citizens' role in the furtherance of the slave trade. The following version of the Declaration is reproduced from the *Memoir, Correspondence, and Miscellanies, from the Papers of Thomas Jeffer-*

son, edited by Thomas Jefferson Randolph and published in Charlottesville, Virginia, in 1829, three years after Jefferson's death.

From NOTES ON THE STATE OF VIRGINIA

THE PARTICULAR CUSTOMS AND MANNERS THAT MAY HAPPEN TO BE RECEIVED IN THAT STATE?

It is difficult to determine on the standard by which the manners of a nation may be tried, whether *catholic* or *particular.* It is more difficult for a native to bring to that standard the manners of his own nation, familiarized to him by habit. There must doubtless be an unhappy influence on the manners of our people produced by the existence of slavery among us. The whole commerce between master and slave is a perpetual exercise of the most boisterous passions, the most unremitting despotism on the one part, and degrading submissions on the other. Our children see this, and learn to imitate it; for man is an imitative animal. This quality is the germ of all education in him. From his cradle to his grave he is learning to do what he sees others do. If a parent could find no motive either in his philanthropy or his self-love, for restraining the intemperance of passion towards his slave, it should always be a sufficient one that his child is present. But generally it is not sufficient. The parent storms, the child looks on, catches the lineaments of wrath, puts on the same airs in the circle of smaller slaves, gives a loose to his worst of passions, and thus nursed, educated, and daily exercised in tyranny, cannot but be stamped by it with odious peculiarities. The man must be a prodigy who can retain his manners and morals undepraved by such circumstances. And with what execration should the statesman be loaded, who permitting one half the citizens thus to trample on the rights of the other, transforms those into despots, and these into enemies, destroys the morals of the one part, and the amor patriæ of the other. For if a slave can have a country in this world, it must be any other in preference to that in which he is born to live and labor for another: in which he must lock up the faculties of his nature, contribute as far as depends on his individual endeavors to the evanishment of the human race, or entail his own miserable condition on the endless generations proceeding from him. With the morals of the people, their industry also is destroyed. For in a warm climate, no man will labor for himself who can make another labor for him. This is so true, that of the proprietors of slaves a very small proportion indeed are ever seen to labor. And can the liberties of a nation be thought secure when we have removed their only firm basis, a conviction in the minds of the people that these liberties are of the gift of God? That they are not to be violated but with his wrath? Indeed I tremble for my country when I reflect that God is just: that his justice cannot sleep forever: that considering numbers, nature and natural means only, a revolution of the wheel of fortune, an exchange of situation, is among possible events: that it may become probable by supernatural interference! The Almighty has no attribute which can take side with us in such a contest.—But it is impossible to be temperate and to pursue this subject through the various considerations of policy, of morals, of history natural and civil. We must be contented to hope they will force their way into everyone's mind. I think a change already perceptible, since the origin of the present revolution. The spirit of the master is abating, that of the slave rising from the dust, his condition mollifying, the way I hope preparing, under the auspices of heaven, for a total emancipation, and that this is disposed, in the order of events, to be with the consent of the masters, rather than by their extirpation.

.   .   .

THE PRESENT STATE OF MANUFACTURES, COMMERCE, INTERIOR AND EXTERIOR TRADE?

We never had an interior trade of any importance. Our exterior commerce has suffered very much from the beginning of the present contest. During this time we have manufactured within our families the most necessary articles of cloathing. Those of cotton will bear some comparison with the same kinds of manufacture in Europe; but those of wool, flax and hemp are very coarse, unsightly, and unpleasant: and such is our attachment to agriculture, and such our preference for foreign manufactures, that be it wise or unwise, our people will certainly return as soon as they can, to the raising raw materials, and exchanging them for finer manufactures than they are able to execute themselves.

The political oeconomists of Europe have established it as a principle that every state should endeavour to manufacture for itself: and this principle, like many others, we transfer to America, without calculating the difference of circumstance which should often produce a difference of result. In Europe the lands are either cultivated, or locked up against the cultivator. Manufacture must therefore be resorted to of necessity not of choice, to support the surplus of their people.But we have an immensity of land courting the industry of the husbandman. Is it best then that all our citizens should be employed in its improvement, or that one half should be called off from that to exercise manufactures and handicraft arts for the other? Those who labour in the earth are the chosen people of God, if ever he had a chosen people, whose breasts he has made his peculiar deposit for substantial and genuine virtue. It is the focus in which he keeps alive that sacred fire, which otherwise might escape from the face of the earth. Corruption of morals in the mass of cultivators is a phænomenon of which no age nor nation has furnished an example. It is the mark set on those, who not looking up to heaven, to their own soil and industry, as does the husbandman, for their subsistance, depend for it on the casualties and caprice of customers. Dependance begets subservience and venality, suffocates the germ of virtue, and prepares fit tools for the designs of ambition. This, the natural progress and consequence of the arts, has sometimes perhaps been retarded by accidental circumstances: but, generally speaking, the proportion which the aggregate of the other classes of citizens bears in any state to that of its husbandmen, is the proportion of its unsound to its healthy parts, and is a good-enough barometer whereby to measure its degree of corruption. While we have land to labour then, let us never wish to see our citizens occupied at a work-bench, or twirling a distaff. Carpenters, masons, smiths, are wanting in husbandry: but, for the general operations of manufacture, let our work-shops remain in Europe. It is better to carry provisions and materials to workmen there, than bring them to the provisions and materials, and with them their manners and principles. The loss by the transportation of commodities across the Atlantic will be made up in happiness and permanence of government. The mobs of great cities add just so much to the support of pure government, as sores do to the strength of the human body. It is the manners and spirit of a people which preserve a republic in vigour. A degeneracy in these is a canker which soon eats to the heart of its laws and constitution.

From THE MEMOIR

THE DECLARATION OF INDEPENDENCE

Congress proceeded the same day to consider the Declaration of Independence, which had been reported and laid on the table the Friday preceding, and on Monday referred to a committee of the whole. The pusillanimous idea that we had friends in England worth keeping terms with, still haunted the minds of many. For this reason, those passages which conveyed censures on the people of England were struck out, lest they should give them offence. The clause too, reprobating the enslaving the inhabitants of Africa, was struck out in complaisance to South Carolina and Georgia, who had never attempted to restrain the importation of slaves, and who, on the contrary, still wished to continue it. Our northern brethren also, I believe, felt a little tender under those censures; for though their people had very few slaves themselves, yet they had been pretty considerable carriers of them to others. The debates having taken up the greater parts of the 2nd, 3rd, and 4th days of July, were, on the evening of the last, closed; the Declaration was reported by the committee, agreed to by the House, and signed by every member present, except Mr. Dickinson. As the sentiments of men are known not only by what they receive, but what they reject also, I will state the form of the Declaration as originally reported. The parts struck out by Congress shall be distinguished by a black line drawn under them;* and those inserted by them shall be placed in the margin, or in a concurrent column.

A Declaration by the Representatives of the United States of America, in *General* Congress assembled.

When, in the course of human events, it becomes necessary for one people to dissolve the political bands which have connected them with another, and to assume among the powers of the earth the separate and equal station to which the laws of nature and of nature's God entitle them, a decent respect to the opinions of mankind requires that they should declare the causes which impel them to the separation.

certain

We hold these truths to be self evident: that all men are created equal; that they are endowed by their creator with [*inherent and*] inalienable rights; that among these are life, liberty and the pursuit of happiness; that to secure these rights, governments are instituted among men, deriving their just powers from the consent of the governed; that whenever any form of government becomes destructive of these ends, it is the right of the people to alter or to abolish it, and to institute new government, laying its foundation on such principles, and organizing its powers in such form, as to them shall seem most likely to effect their safety and happiness. Prudence, indeed, will dictate that governments long established should not be changed for light and transient causes; and accordingly all experience hath shewn that mankind are more disposed to suffer while evils are sufferable, than to right themselves by abolishing the forms to which they are accustomed.

*In this publication, the parts struck out are printed in *Italics* and inclosed in brackets.

THOMAS JEFFERSON

But when a long train of abuses and usurpations [*begun at a distinguished period and*] pursuing invariably the same object, evinces a design to reduce them under absolute despotism, it is their right, it is their duty to throw off such government, and to provide new guards for their future security. Such has been the patient sufferance of these colonies; and such is now the necessity which constrains them to [*expunge*] their former systems of government. The history of the present king of Great Britain is a history of [*unremitting*] injuries and usurpations, [*among which appears no solitary fact to contradict the uniform tenor of the rest, but all have*] in direct object the establishment of an absolute tyranny over these states. To prove this, let facts be submitted to a candid world [*for the truth of which we pledge a faith yet unsullied by falsehood.*]

alter

repeated

all having

He has refused his assent to laws the most wholesome and necessary for the public good.

He has forbidden his governors to pass laws of immediate and pressing importance, unless suspended in their operation till his assent should be obtained; and, when so suspended, he has utterly neglected to attend to them.

He has refused to pass other laws for the accommodation of large districts of people, unless those people would relinquish the right of representation in the legislature, a right inestimable to them, and formidable to tyrants only.

He has called together legislative bodies at places unusual, uncomfortable, and distant from the depository of their public records, for the sole purpose of fatiguing them into compliance with his measures.

He has dissolved representative houses repeatedly [*and continually*] for opposing with manly firmness his invasions on the rights of the people.

He has refused for a long time after such dissolutions to cause others to be elected, whereby the legislative powers, incapable of annihilation, have returned to the people at large for their exercise, the state remaining, in the mean time, exposed to all the dangers of invasion from without and convulsions within.

He has endeavored to prevent the population of these states; for that purpose obstructing the laws for naturalization of foreigners, refusing to pass others to encourage their migrations hither, and raising the conditions of new appropriations of lands.

obstructed
by

He has [*suffered*] the administration of justice [*totally to cease in some of these states*] refusing his assent to laws for establishing judiciary powers.

He has made [*our*] judges dependant on his will alone for the tenure of their offices, and the amount and payment of their salaries.

He has erected a multitude of new offices, [*by a self-assumed power*] and sent hither swarms of new officers to harrass our people and eat out their substance.

He has kept among us in times of peace standing armies [*and ships of war*] without the consent of our legislatures.

He has affected to render the military independent of, and superior to, the civil power.

He has combined with others to subject us to a jurisdiction foreign to our constitutions and unacknowledged by our laws, giving his assent to their acts of pretended legislation for quartering large bodies of armed troops among us; for protecting them by a mock trial from punishment for any murders which they should commit on the inhabitants of these states; for cutting off our trade with all parts of the world; for imposing taxes on us without our consent;

in many cases

for depriving us [   ] of the benefits of trial by jury; for transporting us beyond seas to be tried for pretended offences; for abolishing the free system of English laws in a neighboring province, establishing therein an arbitrary government, and enlarging its boundaries, so as to render it at once an example and fit instrument for introducing the same absolute rule into

THOMAS JEFFERSON

colonies

these [*states*]; for taking away our charters, abolishing our most valuable laws, and altering fundamentally the forms of our governments; for suspending our own legislatures, and declaring themselves invested with power to legislate for us in all cases whatsoever.

He has abdicated government here [*withdrawing his governors, and declaring us out of his allegiance and protection.*]

by declaring us out of his protection and waging war against us.

He has plundered our seas, ravaged our coasts, burnt our towns and destroyed the lives of our people.

He is at this time transporting large armies of foreign mercenaries to complete the works of death, desolation and tyranny already begun with circumstances of cruelty and perfidy [ ] unworthy the head of a civilized nation.

scarcely paralleled in the most barbarous ages and totally

He has constrained our fellow citizens taken captive on the high seas to bear arms against their country, to become the executioners of their friends and brethren, or to fall themselves by their hands.

excited domestic insurrections among us, and has

He has [ ] endeavored to bring on the inhabitants of our frontiers the merciless Indian savages, whose known rule of warfare is an undistinguished destruction of all ages, sexes and conditions [*of existence.*]

[*He has incited treasonable insurrections of our fellow citizens, with the allurements of forfeiture and confiscation of our property.*

He has waged cruel war against human nature itself, violating its most sacred rights of life and liberty in the persons of a distant people who never offended him, captivating and carrying them into slavery in another hemisphere, or to incur miserable death in their transportation thither. This piratical warfare, the opprobium of INFIDEL *powers, is the warfare of the* CHRISTIAN *king of Great Britain. Determined to keep open a market where* MEN *should be bought and sold, he has prostituted his negative for suppressing every legislative attempt to prohibit or to restrain this execrable commerce. And that this assemblage of horrors might want no fact of distinguished die, he is now exciting those very people to rise in arms among us, and to purchase that liberty of which he has deprived them, by murdering the people on whom he also obtruded them: thus paying off former crimes committed against the* LIBERTIES *of one people, with crimes which he urges them to commit against the* LIVES *of another.*]

In every stage of these oppressions we have petitioned for redress in the most humble terms: our repeated petitions have been answered only by repeated injuries.

A prince whose character is thus marked by every act which may define a tyrant is unfit to be the ruler of a [ ] people [*who mean to be free. Future ages will scarcely believe that the hardiness of one man adventured, within the short compass of twelve years only, to lay a foundation so broad and so undisguised for tyranny over a people fostered and fixed in principles of freedom.*]

Nor have we been wanting in attentions to our British brethren. We have warned them from time to time of attempts by their legislature to extend [*a*] jurisdiction over [*these our states*]. We have reminded them of the circumstances of our emigration and settlement here, [*no one of which could warrant so strange a pretension: that these were effected at the expence of our own blood and treasure, unassisted by the wealth or the strength of Great Britain: that in constituting indeed our several forms of government, we had adopted one common king, thereby laying a foundation for perpetual league and amity with them: but that submission to their parliament was no part of our constitution, nor ever in idea, if history may be credited: and,*] we [ ] appealed to their native justice and magnanimity [*as well as to*] the ties of our common kindred to disavow these usurpations which [*were likely to*] interrupt our connection and correspondence. They too have been deaf to the voice of justice and of consanguinity, [*and when occasions have been given them, by the regular course of their laws, of removing from their councils the disturbers of our harmony, they have, by*]

free

an unwarrantable
us

have

and we have conjured them
by
would inevitably

their free election, re-established them in power. At this very time too, they are permiting their chief magistrate to send over not only soldiers of our common blood, but Scotch and foreign mercenaries to invade and destroy us. These facts have given the last stab to agonizing affection, and manly spirit bids us to renounce for ever these unfeeling brethren. We must endeavor to forget our former love for them, and hold them as we hold the rest of mankind, enemies in war, in peace friends. We might have been a free and a great people together; but a communication of grandeur and of freedom, it seems, is below their dignity. Be it so, since they will have it. The road to happiness and to glory is open to us too. We will tread it apart from them, and] acquiesce in the necessity which denounces our [*eternal*] separation[　]!

We therefore the representatives of the United States of America in General Congress assembled, appealing to the supreme judge of the world for the rectitude of our intentions, do in the name, and by the authority of the good people of these colonies, solemnly publish and declare, that these united colonies are, and of right ought to be free and independent states; that they are absolved from all allegiance to the British crown, and that all political connection between them and the state of Great Britain is, and ought to be, totally dissolved; and that as free and independent states, they have full power to levy war, conclude peace, contract alliances, establish commerce, and to do all other acts and things which independent states may of right do.

And for the support of this declaration, with a firm reliance on the protection of divine providence, we mutually pledge to each other our

[Marginal notes:] We must therefore

and hold them as we hold the rest of mankind, enemies in war, in peace friends.

We therefore the representives of the United States of America in General Congress assembled, do in the name, and by the authority of the good people of these [*states reject and renounce all allegiance and subjection to the kings of Great Britain and all others who may hereafter claim by, through or under them; we utterly dissolve all political connection which may heretofore have subsisted between us and the people or parliament of Great Britain: and finally we do assert and declare these colonies to be free and independent states*] and that as free and independent states, they have full power to levy war, conclude peace, contract alliances, establish commerce, and to do all other acts and things which independent states may of right do.

And for the support of this declaration, we mutually pledge to each other our lives, our fortunes, and our sacred honour.

lives, our fortunes, and our sacred honour.

The Declaration thus signed on the 4th, on paper, was engrossed on parchment, and signed again on the 2nd of August.

PART TWO

LITERATURE IN THE OLD SOUTH

A "SOUTHERN" LITERATURE

When in the year 1847 the poet James Mathewes Legaré, desirous of founding a Southern literary magazine, wrote to the leading statesman of the South, John C. Calhoun, enclosing a prospectus, Calhoun not only sent in his subscription but declared that "we want, above all other things, a Southern literature, from school books up to works of the highest order." Like most other lawyer-politicians of the Old South, Calhoun was not a passionate devotee of works of the literary imagination; an old Charleston pleasantry existed to the effect that he was the only man ever to have written a love poem beginning with the word "whereas." His approval of Legaré's venture, which never came to fruition, resulted not so much from his desire to encourage the belle lettres as his wish to further a self-conscious Southern nationalism. For by 1847 the North–South schism was very much in evidence, and Calhoun and his planter friends were anxious to unify the region politically and thus present a concerted defense against Northern antislavery forces.

The idea of a distinctively Southern literature was initially tied in with regional self-consciousness and sectional self-defense, for it was only when the states south of the Potomac and the Ohio began to feel their economic and political interests threatened by the growing population and commercial expansion of the Northeast that they began to think of themselves as a geographical unit and call themselves Southerners rather than Virginians, Carolinians, Georgians, Tennesseans, and so on. And since it was the slavery interest that set the Southern states apart—and which lay at the base of the Southern position of the protective tariff, nullification, states' rights, westward expansion, the rights of the states in the territories, and ultimately outright secession itself—the literature of the Old South was from the first an expression, insofar as it was concerned with its specific Southern identity, of the same impulse that produced the defense of slavery and the secession movement. This is not to say, of course, that the writers of the South thought of what they wrote principally as political literature, or that as writers they felt any strong conscious obligation to defend slavery. Indeed, most of what they wrote (and practically all of it that held or holds any importance as literature) made little reference to slavery or politics. What is important in understanding the literature of the Old South is that the milieu in which it was nurtured was charged with political energy and, especially as the sectional controversy intensified and secession began to be an issue, the area in which literature could operate without touching on politically sensitive subject matter was quite limited.

In the years immediately following the establishment of the nation and before the rise of the slavery issue, writers in the South thought of themselves principally as American writers, which indeed they were. But from the first the social, economic, and cultural situation in the Southern states hindered the growth of an important literature. There were very few cities, and these remained small. The South was rural, it remained principally rural, and its social ideal was the plantation. Even the cities had relatively little art or music, no great libraries, and almost nothing resembling literary coteries where citizens might gather to discuss books and cultivate an incipient professionalism. Such literary life as there was, therefore, remained dispersed. Moreover, those ambitious souls who sought to found literary magazines repeatedly confronted the fact that there was not much of a native reading public. And as the cultivation of cotton spread through the lower South so that it became the region's principal product, so did slavery, and with it the rise of the antislavery movement—with the result that politics was a Southern preoccupation. In C. Hugh Holman's summation, "the great profession of its citizens was law; its passion was public life; and its special genius was in politics. It delighted in open and public pleasures—the hunt, the race, the ball, the banquet—and cared little for the introspective calm of the study and could endure the odor of the midnight lamp only for short intervals." Southern authors who would support themselves, in whole or in part, from the proceeds of their writings had to look northward, to Boston, New York, and Philadelphia, for publishers to bring out their books and magazines with sufficient circulation revenues to pay decent rates to contributors.

Literature in the South remained primarily a gentleman's art, pursued as an avocation. It centered in the Tidewater cities. Most of the practitioners were lawyers, and even those who became professional writers, as did William Gilmore Simms and Henry Timrod, studied law. The law was the avenue whereby a young man of ambition without wealth and long-standing family status could elevate himself. As might be expected, the literature these men wrote—in particular the poetry—was formal, carefully wrought, and contained; it was an affair of surfaces, an adornment. These authors were very much involved in the civic life and concerns of their community and there was very little of the kind of intellectual and emotional detachment and alienation from society that one finds in New England writers. Even a dedicated professional man of letters such as Simms was intensely involved in the political and economic life of his community. He wrote prodigiously, and won a national audience for his historical romances of the Revolution and the Southern frontier. He also labored mightily to encourage and stimulate literary activity in the South and was an inveterate founder of literary magazines. But one will search through Simms' enormous body of writings in vain for any kind of penetrating critique of the basic social and moral premises of his society. If he felt alienated at times, his work does not show it. Thus, with Simms the historical romance remains the two-dimensional adventure story form that it was for James Fenimore Cooper in the North and Walter Scott in England. There is no breakthrough into scrutiny of the underlying moral and religious assumptions of the community that marks the fiction of Hawthorne and Melville; at no point does Simms develop any real conflict between individual needs and private integrity and the public values of the society. Nor does Simms or any of the other

Southern fiction writers work with the social dimensions of the great tradition of the English novel as practiced by Defoe, Richardson, Fielding, and Dickens. Despite the intense social sensibility of the region, the characterization and story line are not grounded in the life and times of the society. The antebellum Southern fiction writers provide relatively little of the way that people talked, behaved, what they thought about, how they spent their daily lives.

The single major literary artist of the Old South was Edgar Allan Poe. Others had talent; he had genius. But Poe's fiction is not set in his native Virginia; neither is his poetry. The setting and locale for his art are not geographically specific but usually contrived for the thematic effect desired by the author. It is not surprising, therefore, that only in recent years have critics made very much of Poe's Southern identity. Yet there are important links between the writer and his region. His reliance upon craftsmanship, his insistence that the imaginative writer should be concerned with literary effect, with plot and characterization, and not with political and social ideas and moral or religious instruction—all seem central to the Southern aesthetic of his own day and afterward. His basic view of human beings is of limited, fallible, recalcitrant creatures who are incapable of perfectibility, so that the institutions and arrangements of such people do not exist to achieve an ultimate perfection but to make reasonable freedom, order, subordination, and control possible. This is a way of looking at individual humanity and society quite characteristic of the Southern writers, but at a far remove from the Transcendentalists of New England. There is no Millenialism in Poe; the here and now, not a future perfection, is where the truth lies.

Another characteristic of Poe's art and thought sets him apart from most other American authors of his day yet is thoroughly characteristic of Southern writing: his view of evil is psychological, not theological. It is not that his concept of man is incompatible with religious truth—unreligious or atheistic—but rather that his imagination is thoroughly secular; in the created world of men and matter, what men must deal with exists in the form and shape of human beings and material objects—it is not transcendent or ineffable. Even when extraordinary events occur in Poe's tales of horror and grotesquerie they derive not from theological intervention but the intensity and malevolence of the occult will. In all of Poe there is no moment corresponding to that in Hawthorne's *The Scarlet Letter* when Arthur Dimmesdale stands upon the platform at night and the lightning in the sky seems to form itself into a gigantic letter A in heavenly indictment of his sin.

Poe, declares C. Hugh Holman, "was the employer of a surrealistic landscape and remote places and times to portray a world of the tortured inner soul, a kind of symbolic imagery of the inner self." This is quite true—and we might ask ourselves just why was it that he turned his imagination inward upon itself in such a way, if not because in his time and place, as a Southern author who thought of himself as a gentleman, such an inward direction was the *only possible one* for him? For if, like many European authors he admired, he had looked not inside but without, at the society around him, had striven to ground his art and focus his imagination on the moral and social delineation of his community, what direction must his remarkable perceptiveness, his acute awareness of the discrepancy between the actual and the ideal, have taken? It was not that Poe underwent any conscious struggle over whether to look around him at men on the Southern land or inside him at "the tortured inner soul," but that everything in his society, his upbringing, his social position, his relationship to his community served to guide his imagination in the direction that it took. But if we think of a story such as "The Fall of the House of Usher" and imagine what it would have been like if Poe had set it in Virginia and made a serious effort to describe the ancestral residence as a plantation house and Roderick Usher as a Virginia planter, we might gain an awareness of why, given the moral significance Poe saw in Usher's situation, he might not have felt impelled to set his art and anchor his imagination in the life and texture of the actual Southern community.

One is tempted to say that Poe wrote so far from the everyday life of his region *because* he feared where his genius might lead him; but there is no basis in fact for any such supposition. Yet there is a very real sense in which the *only way* a Southern writer of Poe's imagination and insight could have pursued his art without putting both it and himself in a highly subversive relationship to his community was by creating a literature "out of space, out of time," centered on the tortured inner soul.

LANGUAGE

Lesser Southern writers of the antebellum period did, of course, write about the life around them. Yet with certain exceptions one does not look to the formal literature of the South, which was essentially a Tidewater literature, for any realistic depiction of the way real people talked, behaved, thought, and felt; such an objective was not deemed a proper concern of literature. The language of literature was not that of everyday life, and it was not thought appropriate that it should be. Even Simms, who was as a writer far removed from the vulgarian and the iconoclast, found when he attempted a story mildly portraying lowlife seriously that his audience criticized him for his supposed crudeness, and he was impelled to retort that "too many of our critics draw their rules of judgment, not from their thoughts, but from their taste. This is a very important distinction. Such people are diseased with fastidiousness. They are always afflictingly nice. They seldom use appropriate language. They look through the dictionary for the bad words, only to blame Dr. Johnson for putting them there. The very idea of strong passions, in exercise, revolts them, overlooking the truth, that where there are no passions in exercise, there can be no trial of the virtues—no proof of their existence—no triumph over their continual foes."

The extent to which the language convention of formal literature removed the imaginative writer from the vernacular texture of his own experience—an essentially middle-class experience in all respects—can be seen, unwittingly, in a composition by the poet Paul Hamilton Hayne, who in the 1850s was a member of the Russell's Book Shop group of writers in Charleston that included Simms, Henry Timrod, and William John Grayson. Hayne had served as the editor of *Russell's Magazine.* He came from a distinguished Carolina Low-country family, but lost almost everything during the war and settled in a little wooden cottage near Augusta, Georgia, for the rest of his life. In one of a series of sketches of Charleston writers that he wrote for the *Southern Bivouac* in the 1870s, Hayne described an occasion shortly after the war when he invited his old friend Simms to pay him a visit. He put the invitation, he said, in the form of a sonnet:

> Old Friend! Come to me while our woods are grand
> With gold and crimson splendors; while our sky
> Smiles down with looks of calm regality,
> And fruitful winds breathe o'er the opulent land.
> I yearn once more to clasp thy cordial hand,
> To hear thy voice, to feel thy kindling eye
> So clear with spiritual light, that will not die
> Nor veil its luster at dull Time's command;
> We'll roam through breezy dell, o'er hill-side walk;
> Speak of lost loves, of fortune's lustier morn;
> But, lest such themes should make us too forlorn
> (Wreathing our souls with their sad cypress twine),
> In thoughtful pauses of memorial talk
> We'll quaff a Mermaid measure of rare wine!

And then, since his sketch for the *Southern Bivouac* was anecdotal and jour- nalistic, he continued in prose:

Let me modestly confess that I am just a little proud of the concluding line of this poem. It is the most imaginative line I ever wrote. "Tell it not in Gath," my good reader, "whisper it not in the streets of Askalon," but the plain truth may as well be acknowledged, the "rare wine" was rather "middling" "Monongehela," and the "Mermaid measure" a pewter cup of modest dimensions, which had seen service.

What is striking here is the utter contrast between the two language conven- tions: Poetry—that is, formal and acknowledged Literature—and ordinary Prose, which was journalistic, and by intent nonliterary. In his everyday life Paul Hayne did not walk through any dells, but in valleys and lowland bottoms. "Sad cypress twine" in the poem had nothing to do with the trees in the Low- country of South Carolina; in the poem, "cypress" denotes the black funereal cloth of European literature that in medieval times came from the island of Cyprus. The question is why Hayne considered it appropriate to refer to "a Mermaid measure of rare wine" when he was really inviting Simms to sit around and drink whiskey out of pewter cups. For Hayne and his fellow poets the answer is that ordinary life—and its language— needed to be not merely intensified but also elevated and ennobled if it was to appear in literature.

The proper language for poetry was that of the English Romantics, not everyday Southern vernacular. But Hayne, Simms, and their fellow Southern poets did not reside in the Lake Country of England. On ordinary social occasions they drank Monongahela whiskey. And a language convention that forbade them to use the words, and the attitudes and insights embodied in the words, of their daily experience had the effect of separating literature from life and making it abstract, ideal, bloodless. In Hayne's journalism, however, he could say just what he thought. To a later audience unaccustomed to the particular conventions of ideality accepted by Hayne's generation, his sonnet and a great deal of the formal literature written by Southern authors during the antebellum period seem artificial, thin, pallid. Even Simms, when he wrote fiction, instinctively moved to adopt a high-sounding, portentous, consciously elevated language whenever he had something "important" to say.

The one area of the literature of the Old South to which we may look when we want to observe antebellum Southerners as they typically acted and talked is nonfiction, and in particular the body of sketches, anecdotes, and tales that comprise the literary subgenre known as Southwestern Humor—the Southwest in question being not the trans-Mississippi but the "Old Southwest": Georgia, Alabama, Tennessee, Mississippi. Here we encounter a very different way of dealing with language and a very different way of describing and interpreting human experience. In the sketches of Augustus Baldwin Longstreet, Johnson Jones Hooper, Joseph G. Baldwin, George Washington Harris, Thomas Bangs Thorpe, and others, rural Southerners talk in the rhythms of everyday speech. They mispronounce words, use dialect forms, display accents, and are given to vivid, racy, vulgar turns and phrases of speech.

These writers were men of education and substance and they wrote for readers like themselves. Their objective, however, was to amuse, not to elevate or transport or moralize. And because humor was considered a low form on the literary scale of valuation since it typically concerned lowlife and was inferior in moral and artistic worth to more serious literature, its practitioners felt free to describe what they saw in the language ordinarily used. For they were not writing Literature; they were telling stories, commenting on the foibles of Southern rural people. They published their writings in local newspapers or in such sporting papers as William T. Porter's *Spirit of the Times* in New York—equivalent today, one might say, to writing for *Field and Stream, Outdoor Life,* or *The Sporting News.* (The one exception was Joseph G. Baldwin, whose work appeared in the *Southern Literary Messenger,* the antebellum South's longest-lived literary journal, and significantly Baldwin's work, though entirely humorous, contains far less dialect and vernacular detail than that of the others. Even so, Baldwin did not think of himself as writing Literature, but only prose sketches, and so did his readers.)

When the writings of some Southwestern humorists proved so popular that they were put into book form and published by Northeastern publishing houses, the authors were astounded and gratified. But if—as these authors did—most readers thought of the works of Longstreet, Hooper, Harris, and the others as mere humorous journalism instead of genuine literature, the South's greatest writer, Edgar Allan Poe, recognized otherwise. Although he did not use the form himself, Poe wrote a review of Longstreet's *Georgia Scenes* for the *Southern Literary Messenger*. Praising the raciness, vitality, and accuracy of Longstreet's sketches, he examined each in detail and concluded with the flat statement that the book was "a sure omen of better days for the literature of the South."

A later generation, not given to such an exclusive view of what constituted Literature, has no trouble in recognizing genuine literary achievement in the writings of the Southwest humorists. The matter-of-factness with which these writers chronicled all manner of human experience considered too indelicate, gross, or coarse to be given literary note is quite authentic and even refreshing. Yet for all its verisimilitude and inclusiveness, Southwestern humor had its limitations. Because it was designed to be comic, and dealt with lowlife in the hinterlands for the most part, it could not be shaped to treat moral and religious experience except in a very obvious and negative way. It was written to poke fun, to undercut pretense and artificiality, and it could thus depict a preacher's hypocrisy, a politician's corruptness, a rustic swain's awkwardness and ignorance, a lover's concupiscence. If the formal literature of the day was too idealistic, too concerned with heroes and heroines, ennobling virtues, and high-minded truth, and used a literary language deficient in vitality and actuality, the humor of the Southwest could not encompass such elements, for it was committed to a view of man that presented him in his unregenerate, natural, biological guise. Honesty, skepticism, and frankness are important values, but there are others that writers must deal with—a twentieth-century Southern author, William Faulkner, named them as "love and honor and pity and pride and compassion and sacrifice"—and these the humorists could not portray. Such values were "Serious," and required elevated language and lofty thought; they were the proper province of Literature, not humor.

The antebellum Southern writer faced a dilemma. In order to capture the highest human values and aspirations, it was necessary to write in a language that left out the flesh-and-blood actuality of daily life, as well as a broad spectrum of human nature. To bring the two ways of viewing human experience together, the South must produce a writer who was committed in attitude and language to the everyday patterns of Southern life, but who was not content to restrict the depiction of men and women to a least-common-denominator view of human nature for comic purposes alone. Such a writer, if sufficiently concerned with capturing the "love and honor and pity and pride and compassion and sacrifice" in the life he knew, but unwilling to do so at the expense of the everyday vernacular denotation of that life, might be able, if he tried hard enough and long enough, to discover how to *use* his own vernacular language and ways of looking at human nature to write about people who were interested in and motivated by genuine moral and religious ideals and could seek to act meaningfully upon them.

It was unlikely, however, that this writer would enter literature through the established cultural channels of the day. He would probably not be a product of the Tidewater South, for there the genteel society of city and plantation would direct him toward the formal literature of ideality so early in his career that he could never afterward discard the erudition and artificiality of its customary language. Nor would the heightened political concerns of his embattled community, and his sense of being a loyal member of it, permit him to critically examine the extent to which that community did, or did not, embody its professed ideals in its social fabric and its political and economic institutions.

It was likely, therefore, that the writer we have in mind would probably be from the Upcountry, where social and cultural forms were not yet so firmly set, and far enough away from the cities, towns, and plantation society of the Old South that were in full flower so that he would not feel their influence too crucially. He would likely begin his writing career as a journalist and not think of himself as a Literary Man at first. He would work through his journalism into deepened meanings and more complex characterizations for his prose.

This writer did indeed appear. His parents were from Virginia and Kentucky and he was born in Missouri. When the war came that destroyed the Old South, however, he was still in his twenties and not yet a journalist but a pilot on a Mississippi River steamboat.

When the War Between the States broke out, Poe had been dead for 13 years; Simms had done almost all of his best work. The achievements of Southern historical fiction, as practiced by Simms, William Alexander Carruthers, John Pendleton Kennedy, and John Esten Cooke, were mostly past. The one important antebellum writer who found sustenance for continued artistic achievement in the events and the meanings of the war was Henry Timrod. In such poems as "Ethnogenesis" and "The Cotton Boll" he voiced the aspirations of his society. His finest war poetry, however, arose not from hope but apprehension and loss. In the remarkable "Sonnet: I Know Not Why," "Spring," "Charleston," "The Unknown Dead," and the beautiful hymn to defeated valor, the Magnolia Cemetery "Ode," Timrod was able to turn the defeat and catastrophe endured by his community into his own private ordeal, and in grave, beautiful public elegy to portray the fall of the Old South.

WILLIAM WIRT

(1772–1834)

The most famous composition by the lawyer-politician-essayist William Wirt is undoubtedly Patrick Henry's "Give me Liberty or Give Me Death!" speech to the Virginia House of Burgesses in 1775. Generations of American schoolchildren memorized and recited this classic piece of patriotic oratory; at the school examination exercises in *The Adventures of Tom Sawyer* Tom "stepped forward with conceited confidence and soared into the unquenchable and indestructible" oratorical gem "with fine fury and frantic gesticulation, and broke down in the middle of it." Yet when it was first delivered, nobody wrote it down or even made notes, and while Wirt drew upon the memories of some of Henry's surviving contemporaries when he reconstructed it some forty years later, the result, except for the famous peroration, is obviously far more Wirt's than Henry's and bears only an approximate resemblance to what was actually said in 1775 at St. John's Church in Richmond.

Wirt's own bona fide writings have fared less well with posterity. He was an attorney, of German ancestry, who was born in Bladensburg, Maryland, and practiced law in Richmond. In 1803 he published, anonymously, *The Letters of the British Spy*. Other essays of Wirt's were gathered into *The Rainbow* (1804) and *The Old Bachelor* (1814). *Sketches of the Life and Character of Patrick Henry* (1817), which contains the famous speech, is the work on which his reputation primarily rests. Wirt served as attorney general of the United States from 1817 through 1829 and was the Anti-Masonic Party's reluctant Presidential candidate in 1832. He moved to Washington in 1817 when he joined the cabinet of James Monroe, and afterwards settled in Baltimore.

From SKETCHES OF THE LIFE AND CHARACTER OF PATRICK HENRY

[From Section IV]

Mr. President: It is natural for man to indulge in the illusions of hope. We are apt to shut our eyes against a painful truth, and listen to the song of that siren till she transforms us into beasts. Is this the part of wise men, engaged in a great and arduous struggle for liberty? Are we disposed to be of the number of those who, having eyes, see not, and having ears, hear not, the things which so nearly concern their temporal salvation? For my part, whatever anguish of spirit it may cost, I am willing to know the whole truth; to know the worst, and to provide for it.

I have but one lamp by which my feet are guided, and that is the lamp of experience. I know of no way of judging of the future but by the past. And, judging by the past, I wish to know what there has been in the conduct of the British ministry for the last ten years to justify those hopes with which the gentlemen have been pleased to solace themselves and the House? Is it that insidious smile with which our petition has been lately received? Trust it not, sir; it will prove a snare to your feet. Suffer not yourselves to be betrayed with a kiss. Ask yourselves how this gracious reception of our petition comports with those warlike preparations which cover our waters and darken our land. Are fleets and armies necessary to a work of love and reconciliation? Have we shown ourselves so unwilling to be reconciled that force must be called in to win back our love? Let us not deceive ourselves, sir. These are the implements of war and subjugation, the last arguments to which kings resort.

I ask the gentlemen, sir, what means this martial array, if its purpose be not to force us to submission? Can the gentlemen assign any other possible motive for it? Has Great Britain any enemy in this quarter of the world, to call for all this accumulation of navies and armies? No, sir, she has none. They are meant for us; they can be meant for no other. They are sent over to bind and rivet upon us those chains which the British ministry has been so long forging. And what have we to oppose to them? Shall we try argument? Sir, we have been trying that for the last ten years. Have we anything new to offer upon the subject? Nothing. We have held the subject up in every light of which it is capable; but it has been all in vain.

Shall we resort to entreaty and humble supplication? What terms shall we find which have not been already exhausted? Let us not, I beseech you, sir, deceive ourselves longer. Sir, we have done everything that could be done, to avert the storm which is now coming on. We have petitioned, we have remonstrated, we have supplicated; we have prostrated ourselves before the throne, and have implored its interposition to arrest the tyrannical hands of the ministry and Parliament. Our petitions have been slighted; our remonstrances have produced additional violence and insult; our supplications have been disregarded; and we have been spurned, with contempt, from the foot of the throne. In vain, after these things, may we indulge the fond hope of peace and reconciliation. There is no longer any room for hope.

If we wish to be free; if we mean to preserve inviolate those inestimable privileges for which we have been so long contending; if we mean not basely to abandon the noble struggle in which we have been so long engaged, and which we have pledged ourselves never to abandon until the glorious object of our contest shall be obtained—we must fight! I repeat it, sir, we must fight! An appeal to arms, and to the God of hosts, is all that is left us.

They tell us, sir, that we are weak—unable to cope with so formidable an adversary. But when shall we be stronger? Will it be the next week or the next year? Will it be when we are totally disarmed, and when a British guard shall be stationed in every house? Shall we gather strength by irresolution and inaction? Shall we acquire the means of effectual resistance by lying supinely on our backs, and hugging the delusive phantom of hope, until our enemies shall have bound us hand and foot? Sir, we are not weak, if we make a proper use of those means which the God of nature hath placed in our power. Three millions of people, armed in the holy cause of Liberty, and in such a country as that which we possess, are invincible by any force which our enemy can send against us.

Besides, sir, we shall not fight our battles alone. There is a just God, who presides over the destinies of nations, and who will raise up friends to fight our battles for us. The battle, sir, is not to the strong alone; it is to the vigilant, the active, the brave. Besides, sir, we have no election. If we were base enough to desire it, it is now too late to retire from the contest. There is no retreat but in submission and slavery! Our chains are forged. Their clanking may be heard on the plains of Boston! The war is inevitable—and let it come! I repeat it, sir, let it come!

It is vain, sir, to extenuate the matter. The gentlemen may cry, Peace, peace! but there is no peace. The war has actually begun! The next gale that sweeps from the north will bring to our ears the clash of resounding arms! Our brethren are already in the field! Why stand we here idle? What is it that the gentlemen wish? What would they have? Is life so dear or peace so sweet as to be purchased at the price of chains and slavery? Forbid it, Almighty God. I know not what course others may take, but as for me, give me liberty or give me death!

JOHN PENDLETON KENNEDY

(1795–1870)

Although more a sketchbook than a novel, and written in imitation of Washington Irving's *Bracebridge Hall*, John Pendleton Kennedy's *Swallow Barn* is important for having set the fictional image of the Southern plantation in much the form it would appear for a century to come. In Francis Pendleton Gaines' summation, "he threw the glamour of romantic coloring over all: over the century-old brick mansion with its ornate approaches, its wings, its doors, its great hall, its spacious rooms, its antique furniture; over the characters, their dress, conversations, points of view; over the meals from the bowl of iced toddy an hour before dinner to the iced wine that followed the dessert; over the Negro quarters, that 'attractive landscape,' the patches for melons and 'taters; over the whole conduct of life, designed for the attainment of happiness, characterized by thriftless gaiety and by the flood of hospitality which 'knew no retiring ebb'; over quaint merrymaking and elaborate social functions, over magnificence of manor and all outward expressions of an inner grace."

By profession a lawyer, businessman, and politician, Kennedy was never a full-time writer. Literature was an uncertain affair for a young man to stake a career on in the 1830s and Kennedy declined to take such risks. Had he been willing to do so, he might ultimately have enjoyed a highly successful career, for he probably possessed more genuine talent for the writing of fiction than most of his contemporaries. His first full-fledged novel, *Horse Shoe Robinson* (1835), is a well-handled Revolutionary War romance. But he wrote only one additional novel, *Rob of the Bowl* (1838), which many think was his best work of fiction. His one other major literary production was a two-volume life of William Wirt (1849).

Kennedy's father was a Scotch-Irish merchant and his mother the daughter of an established Virginia plantation family. He grew up outside Baltimore. After his father suffered severe business losses, his mother's plantation in Jefferson County, Virginia (now West Virginia) was the family's principal source of income. Kennedy studied law, served in the militia in the War of 1812, and afterward began practicing law and writing. He served three terms in the United States Congress and in 1852 President Fillmore appointed him Secretary of the Navy. Kennedy was a Unionist during the secession crisis and strongly supported the Union cause when war broke out.

Perhaps it was Kennedy's strong mercantile ties that led him in *Swallow Barn* to depict the plantation life he had known through his mother's family as pleasant and graceful but somewhat improvident and in a state of decline. He defended slavery, but thought it would soon become extinct and felt it impeded the South's progress. The plantation life of *Swallow Barn* is touched with nostalgia and a sense of decline and fall; if it is Edenic in its order and tranquillity, the perspective is from after the Fall.

What seems especially interesting about *Horse Shoe Robinson*, Kennedy's Revolutionary War romance, is how episodes and scenes featuring middle-class characters such as Galbraith Robinson himself and the villainous Wat Adair tend to dominate the love scenes and other developments centered on upper-class characters and activities. In the episode reproduced here involving Adair's maiming of the trapped wolf, elements appear that very much anticipate the realistic folk portraiture of the Southwestern humorists. What Kennedy might have been able to do if he had devoted his energies principally to fiction can be seen in this episode. We can also glimpse what the formal literature of the Old South might have been if it had developed more in the manner of the novel rather than the romance.

From SWALLOW BARN

Chapter XLVI

THE QUARTER

Having despatched these important matters at the stable, we left our horses in charge of the servants, and walked towards the cabins, which were not more than a few hundred paces distant. These hovels, with their appurtenances, formed an exceedingly picturesque landscape. They were scattered, without order, over the slope of a gentle hill; and many of them were embowered under old and majestic trees. The rudeness of their construction rather enhanced the attractiveness of the scene. Some few were built after the fashion of the better sort of cottages; but age had stamped its heavy traces upon their exterior: the green moss had gathered upon the roofs, and the coarse weatherboarding had broken, here and there, into chinks. But the more lowly of these structures, and the most numerous, were nothing more than plain log-cabins, compacted pretty much on the model by which boys build partridge-traps; being composed of the trunks of trees, still clothed with their bark, and knit together at the corners with so little regard to neatness that the timbers, being of unequal lengths, jutted beyond each other, sometimes to the length of a foot. Perhaps, none of these latter sort were more than twelve feet square, and not above seven in height. A door swung upon wooden hinges, and a small window of two narrow panes of glass were, in general, the only openings in the front. The intervals between the logs were filled with clay; and the roof, which was constructed of smaller timbers, laid lengthwise along it and projecting two or three feet beyond the side or gable walls, heightened, in a very marked degree, the rustic effect. The chimneys communicated even a droll expression to these habitations. They were, oddly enough, built of billets of wood, having a broad foundation of stone, and growing narrower as they rose, each receding gradually from the house to which it was attached, until it reached the height of the roof. These combustible materials were saved from the access of the fire by a thick coating of mud; and the whole structure, from its tapering form, might be said to bear some resemblance to the spout of a tea kettle; indeed, this domestic implement would furnish no unapt type of the complete cabin.

JOHN PENDLETON KENNEDY

From this description, which may serve to illustrate a whole species of habitations very common in Virginia, it will be seen, that on the score of accommodation, the inmates of these dwellings were furnished according to a very primitive notion of comfort. Still, however, there were little garden-patches attached to each, where cymblings, cucumbers, sweet potatoes, water-melons and cabbages flourished in unrestrained luxuriance. Add to this, that there were abundance of poultry domesticated about the premises, and it may be perceived that, whatever might be the inconveniences of shelter, there was no want of what, in all countries, would be considered a reasonable supply of luxuries.

Nothing more attracted my observation than the swarms of little negroes that basked on the sunny sides of these cabins, and congregated to gaze at us as we surveyed their haunts. They were nearly all in that costume of the golden age which I have heretofore described; and showed their slim shanks and long heels in all varieties of their grotesque natures. Their predominant love of sunshine, and their lazy, listless postures, and apparent content to be silently looking abroad, might well afford a comparison to a set of terrapins luxuriating in the genial warmth of summer, on the logs of a mill-pond.

And there, too, were the prolific mothers of this redundant brood,—a number of stout negro-women who thronged the doors of the huts, full of idle curiosity to see us. And, when to these are added a few reverend, wrinkled, decrepit old men, with faces shortened as if with drawing-strings, noses that seemed to have run all to nostril, and with feet of the configuration of a mattock, my reader will have a tolerably correct idea of this negro-quarter, its population, buildings, external appearance, situation and extent.

Meriwether, I have said before, is a kind and considerate master. It is his custom frequently to visit his slaves, in order to inspect their condition, and, where it may be necessary, to add to their comforts or relieve their wants. His coming amongst them, therefore, is always hailed with pleasure. He has constituted himself into a high court of appeal, and makes it a rule to give all their petitions a patient hearing, and to do justice in the premises. This, he tells me, he considers as indispensably necessary;—he says, that no overseer is entirely to be trusted; that there are few men who have the temper to administer wholesome laws to any population, however small, without some omissions or irregularities; and that this is more emphatically true of those who administer them entirely at their own will. On the present occasion, in almost every house where Frank entered, there was some boon to be asked; and I observed, that in every case, the petitioner was either gratified or refused in such a tone as left no occasion or disposition to murmur. Most of the women had some bargains to offer, of fowls or eggs or other commodities of household use, and Meriwether generally referred them to his wife, who, I found, relied almost entirely on this resource, for the supply of such commodities; the negroes being regularly paid for whatever was offered in this way.

One old fellow had a special favour to ask,—a little money to get a new padding for his saddle, which, he said, "galled his cretur's back." Frank, after a few jocular passages with the veteran, gave him what he desired, and sent him off rejoicing.

"That, sir," said Meriwether, "is no less a personage than Jupiter. He is an old bachelor, and has his cabin here on the hill. He is now near seventy, and is a kind of King of the Quarter. He has a horse, which he extorted from me last Christmas; and I seldom come here without finding myself involved in some new demand, as a consequence of my donation. Now he wants a pair of spurs which, I suppose, I must give him. He is a preposterous coxcomb, and Ned has administered to his vanity by a present of a *chapeau de bras*—a relic of my military era, which he wears on Sundays with a conceit that has brought upon him as much envy as admiration—the usual condition of greatness."

The air of contentment and good humor and kind family attachment, which was apparent throughout this little community, and the familiar relations existing between them and the proprietor struck me very pleasantly. I came here a stranger, in great degree, to the negro character, knowing but little of the domestic history of these people, their duties, habits or temper, and somewhat disposed, indeed, from prepossessions, to look upon them as severely dealt with, and expecting to have my sympathies excited towards them as objects of commiseration. I have had, therefore, rather a special interest in observing them. The contrast between my preconceptions of their condition and the reality which I have witnessed, has brought me a most agreeable surprise. I will not say that, in a high state of cultivation and of such self-dependence as they might possibly attain in a separate national existence, they might not become a more respectable people; but I am quite sure they never could become a happier people than I find them here. Perhaps they are destined, ultimately, to that national existence, in the clime from which they derive their origin—that this is a transition state in which we see them in Virginia. If it be so, no tribe of people have ever passed from barbarism to civilization whose middle stage of progress has been more secure from harm, more genial to their character, or better supplied with mild and beneficent guardianship, adapted to the actual state of their intellectual feebleness, than the negroes of Swallow Barn. And, from what I can gather, it is pretty much the same on the other estates in this region. I hear of an unpleasant exception to this remark now and then; but under such conditions as warrant the opinion that the unfavorable case is not more common than that which may be found in a survey of any other department of society. The oppression of apprentices, of seamen, of soldiers, of subordinates, indeed, in every relation, may furnish elements for a bead-roll of social grievances quite as striking, if they were diligently noted and brought to view.

What the negro is finally capable of, in the way of civilization, I am not philosopher enough to determine. In the present stage of his existence, he presents himself to my mind as essentially parasitical in his nature. I mean that he is, in his moral constitution, a dependant upon the white race; dependant for guidance and direction even to the procurement of his most indispensable necessaries. Apart from this protection he has the helplessness of a child,—without foresight, without faculty of contrivance, without thrift of any kind. We have instances, in the neighborhood of this estate, of individuals of the tribe falling into the most deplorable destitution from the want of that constant supervision which the race seems to require. This helplessness may be the due and natural impression which two centuries of servitude have stamped upon the tribe. But it is not the less a present and insurmountable impediment to that most cruel of all projects—the direct, broad emancipation of these people;—an act of legislation in comparison with which the revocation of the edict of Nantes would be entitled to be ranked among political benefactions. Taking instruction from history, all organized slavery is inevitably but a temporary phase of human condition. Interest, necessity and instinct, all work to give progression to the relations of mankind, and finally to elevate each tribe or race to its maximum of refinement and power. We have no reason to suppose that the negro will be an exception to this law.

At present, I have said, he is parasitical. He grows upward, only as the vine to which nature has supplied the sturdy tree as a support. He is extravagantly imitative. The older negroes here have—with some spice of comic mixture in it—that formal, grave and ostentatious style of manners, which belonged to the gentlemen of former days; they are profuse of bows and compliments, and very aristocratic in their way. The younger ones are equally to be remarked for aping the style of the present time, and especially for such tags of dandyism in dress as come within their reach. Their fondness for music and dancing is a predominant passion. I never meet a negro man—unless he is quite old—that he is not whistling; and the women sing from morning till night. And as to dancing, the hardest day's work does not restrain their desire to indulge in such pastime. During the harvest, when their toil is pushed to its utmost—the time being one of recognized privileges—they dance almost the whole night. They are great sportsmen, too. They angle and haul the seine, and hunt and tend their traps, with a zest that never grows weary. Their gayety of heart is constitutional and perennial, and when they are together they are as voluble and noisy as so many blackbirds. In short, I think them the most good-natured, careless, lighthearted, and happily-constructed human beings I have ever seen. Having but few and simple wants, they seem to me to be provided with every comfort which falls within the ordinary compass of their wishes; and, I might say, that they find even more enjoyment,—as that word may be applied to express positive pleasures scattered through the course of daily occupation —than any other laboring people I am acquainted with.

I took occasion to express these opinions to Meriwether, and to tell him how much I was struck by the mild and kindly aspect of this society at the Quarter.

This, as I expected, brought him into a discourse.

"The world," said he, "has begun very seriously to discuss the evils of slavery, and the debate has sometimes, unfortunately, been levelled to the comprehension of our negroes, and pains have even been taken that it should reach them. I believe there are but few men who may not be persuaded that they suffer some wrong in the organization of society—for society has many wrongs, both accidental and contrived, in its structure. Extreme poverty is, perhaps, always a wrong done to the individual upon whom it is cast. Society can have no honest excuse for starving a human being. I dare say you can follow out that train of thought and find numerous evils to complain of. Ingenious men, some of them not very honest, have found in these topics themes for agitation and popular appeal in all ages. How likely are they to find, in this question of slavery, a theme for the highest excitement; and, especially, how easy is it to inflame the passions of these untutored and unreckoning people, our black population, with this subject! For slavery, as an original question, is wholly without justification or defence. It is theoretically and morally wrong—and fanatical and one-sided thinkers will call its continuance, even for a day, a wrong, under any modification of it. But, surely, if these people are consigned to our care by the accident, or, what is worse, the premeditated policy which has put them upon our commonwealth, the great duty that is left to us is, to shape our conduct, in reference to them, by a wise and beneficent consideration of the case as it exists, and to administer wholesome laws for their government, making their servitude as tolerable to them as we can consistently with our own safety and their ultimate good. We should not be justified in taking the hazard of internal convulsions to get rid of them; nor have we a right, in the desire to free ourselves, to whelm them in greater evils than their present bondage. A violent removal of them, or a general emancipation, would assuredly produce one or the other of these calamities. Has any sensible man, who takes a different view of this subject, ever reflected upon the consequences of committing two or three millions of persons, born and bred in a state so completely dependent as that of slavery—so unfurnished, so unintellectual, so utterly helpless, I may say—to all the responsibilities, cares and labors of a state of freedom? Must he not acknowledge, that the utmost we could give them would be but a nominal freedom, in doing which we should be guilty of a cruel desertion of our trust—inevitably leading them to progressive debasement, penury, oppression, and finally to extermination? I would not argue with that man whose bigotry to a sentiment was so blind and so fatal as to insist on this expedient. When the time comes, as I apprehend it will come,—and all the sooner, if it be not delayed by these efforts to arouse something like a vindictive feeling between the disputants on both sides—in which the roots of slavery will begin to lose their hold in our soil; and when we shall have the means for providing these people a proper asylum, I shall be glad to see the State devote her thoughts to that enterprise, and, if I am alive, will cheerfully and gratefully assist in it. In the mean time, we owe it to justice and humanity to treat these people with the most considerate kindness. As to what are ordinarily imagined to be the evils or sufferings of their condition, I do not believe in them. The evil is generally felt on the side of the master. Less work is exacted of them than voluntary laborers choose to perform: they have as many privileges as are compatible with the nature of their occupations: they are subsisted, in general, as comfortably—nay, in their estimation of comforts, more comfortably, than the rural population of other countries. And as to the severities that are alleged to be practised upon them, there is much more malice or invention than truth in the accusation. The slaveholders in this region are, in the main, men of kind and humane tempers—as pliant to the touch of compassion, and as sensible of its duties, as the best men in any community, and as little disposed to inflict injury upon their dependents. Indeed, the owner of slaves is less apt to be harsh in his requisitions of labor than those who toil much themselves. I suspect it is invariably characteristic of those who are in the habit of severely tasking themselves, that they are inclined to regulate their demands upon others by their own standard. Our slaves are punished for misdemeanors, pretty much as disorderly persons are punished in all societies; and I am quite of opinion that our statistics of crime and punishment will compare favorably with those of any other population. But the punishment, on our side, is remarked as the personal act of the master; whilst, elsewhere, it goes free of ill-natured comment, because it is set down to the course of justice. We, therefore, suffer a reproach which other polities escape, and the conclusion is made an item of complaint against slavery.

"It has not escaped the attention of our legislation to provide against the ill-treatment of our negro population. I heartily concur in all effective laws to punish cruelty in masters. Public opinion on that subject, however, is even stronger than law, and no man can hold up his head in this community who is chargeable with mal-treatment of his slaves.

"One thing I desire you specially to note: the question of emancipation is exclusively our own, and every intermeddling with it from abroad will but mar its chance of success. We cannot but regard such interference as an unwarrantable and mischievous design to do us injury, and, therefore, we resent it—sometimes, I am sorry to say, even to the point of involving the innocent negro in the rigor which it provokes. We think, and, indeed, we know, that we alone are able to deal properly with the subject; all others are misled by the feeling which the natural sentiment against slavery, in the abstract, excites. They act under imperfect knowledge and impulsive prejudices which are totally incompatible with wise action on any subject. We, on the contrary, have every motive to calm and prudent counsel. Our lives, fortunes, families—our commonwealth itself, are put at the hazard of this resolve. You gentlemen of the North greatly misapprehend us, if you suppose that we are in love with this slave institution—or that, for the most part, we even deem it profitable to us. There are amongst us, it is true, some persons who are inclined to be fanatical on this side of the question, and who bring themselves to adopt some bold dogmas tending to these extreme views—and it is not out of the course of events that the violence of the agitations against us may lead ultimately to a wide adoption of these dogmas amongst the slaveholding States. It is in the nature of men to recalcitrate against continual assault, and, through the zeal of such opposition, to run into ultraisms which cannot be defended. But at present, I am sure the Southern sentiment on this question is temperate and wise, and that we neither regard slavery as a good, nor account it, except in some favorable conditions, as profitable. The most we can say of it is that, as matters stand, it is the best auxiliary within our reach.

"Without troubling you with further reflections upon a dull subject, my conclusion is that the real friends of humanity should conspire to allay the ferments on this question, and, even at some cost, to endeavor to encourage the natural contentment of the slave himself, by arguments to reconcile him to a present destiny, which is, in fact, more free from sorrow and want than that of almost any other class of men occupying the same field of labor."

Meriwether was about to finish his discourse at this point, when a new vein of thought struck him:

"It has sometimes occurred to me," he continued, "that we might elevate our slave population, very advantageously to them and to us, by some reforms in our code. I think we are justly liable to reproach, for the neglect or omission of our laws to recognize and regulate marriages, and the relation of family amongst the negroes. We owe it to humanity and to the sacred obligation of Christian ordinances, to respect and secure the bonds of husband and wife, and parent and child. I am ashamed to acknowledge that I have no answer to make, in the way of justification of this neglect. We have no right to put man and wife asunder. The law should declare this, and forbid the separation under any contingency, except of crime. It should be equally peremptory in forbidding the coercive separation of children from the mother—at least during that period when the one requires the care of the other. A disregard of these attachments has brought more odium upon the conditions of servitude than all the rest of its imputed hardships; and a suitable provision for them would tend greatly to gratify the feelings of benevolent and conscientious slaveholders, whilst it would disarm all considerate and fair-minded men, of what they deem the strongest objection to the existing relations of master and slave.

"I have also another reform to propose," said Meriwether, smiling. "It is, to establish by law, an upper or privileged class of slaves—selecting them from the most deserving, above the age of forty-five years. These I would endue with something of a feudal character. They should be entitled to hold small tracts of land under their masters, rendering for it a certain rent, payable either in personal service or money. They should be elevated into this class through some order of court, founded on certificates of good conduct, and showing the assent of the master. And I think I would create legal jurisdictions, giving the masters or stewards civil and criminal judicial authority. I have some dream of a project of this kind in my head," he continued, "which I have not fully matured as yet. You will think, Mr. Littleton, that I am a man of schemes, if I go on much longer—but there is something in this notion which may be improved to advantage, and I should like, myself, to begin the experiment. Jupiter, here, shall be my first feudatory—my tenant in socage—my old villain!"

"I suspect," said I, "Jupiter considers that his dignity is not to be enhanced by any enlargement of privilege, as long as he is allowed to walk about in his military hat as King of the Quarter."

"Perhaps not," replied Meriwether, laughing; "then I shall be forced to make my commencement upon Carey."

"Carey," interrupted Hazard, "would think it small promotion to be allowed to hold land under you!"

"Faith! I shall be without a feudatory to begin with," said Meriwether. "But come with me; I have a visit to make to the cabin of old Lucy."

From HORSE SHOE ROBINSON

from CHAPTER XV

HORSE SHOE AND BUTLER
RESUME THEIR JOURNEY, WHICH IS DELAYED
BY A SAVAGE INCIDENT

Morning broke, and with the first day-streak Robinson turned out of his bed, leaving Butler so thoroughly bound in the spell of sleep, that he was not even moved by the loud and heavy tramp of the sergeant, as that weighty personage donned his clothes. Horse Shoe's first habit in the morning was to look after Captain Peter, and he accordingly directed his steps toward the rude shed which served as a stable, at the foot of the hill. Here, to his surprise, he discovered that the fence-rails which, the night before, had been set up as a barrier across the vacant doorway, had been let down, and that no horses were to be seen about the premises.

"What hocus-pocus has been here?" said he to himself, as he gazed upon the deserted stable. "Have these rummaging and thieving Tories been out marauding in the night? or is it only one of Captain Peter's old-sodger tricks, letting down the bars and leading the young geldings into mischief? That beast can snuff the scent of a corn field or a pasture ground as far as a crow smells gunpowder. He'd dislocate and corruptify any innocent stable of horses in Carolina!"

In doubt to which of these causes to assign this disappearance of their cavalry, the sergeant ascended the hill hard-by, and directed his eye over the neighboring fields, hoping to discover the deserters in some of the adjacent pastures. But he could get no sight of them. He then returned to the stable and fell to examining the ground about the door, in order to learn something of the departure of the animals by their tracks. These were sufficiently distinct to convince him that Captain Peter, whose shoes had a peculiar mark well known to the sergeant, had eloped during the night, in company with the major's gelding and two others, these being all, as Horse Shoe had observed, that were in the stable at the time he had retired to bed. He forthwith followed the foot-prints which led him into the high road, and thence along it westward for about two hundred paces, where a set of field bars, now thrown down, afforded entrance into the cornfield. At this point the sergeant traced the deviation of three of the horses into the field, whilst the fourth, it was evident, had continued upon the road.

The conclusion which Galbraith drew from this phenomenon was expressed by a wise shake of the head and a profound fit of abstraction. He took his seat upon a projecting rail at the angle of the fence, and began to sum up conjectures in the following phrase:

"The horse that travelled along that road, never travelled of his own free will: that's as clear as preaching. Well, he wa'n't rode by Wat nor by Mike Lynch, or else they are arlier men than I take them to be: but still, I'll take a book oath that creetur went with a bridle across his head, and a pair o' legs astride his back. And whoever held that bridle in his hand, did it for no good! Scampering here and scampering there, and scouring woods in the night too, when the country is as full of Tories as a beggar's coat with ———, it's a dogmatical bad sign, take it which way you will. Them three horses had the majority, and it is the nature of these beasts always to follow the majority: that's an observation I have made; and, in particular, if there's a cornfield, or an oatpatch, or a piece of fresh pasture to be got into, every individual horse is unanimous on the subject."

Whilst the sergeant was engrossed with these reflections, "he was ware," as the old ballads have it, of a man trudging past him along the road. This was no other than Wat Adair, who was striding forward with a long and rapid step, and with all the appearance of one intent upon some pressing business.

"Halloo! who goes there? where away so fast, Wat?" was Robinson's challenge.

"Horse Shoe!" exclaimed Adair, in a key that bespoke surprise, and even alarm,—"Ha, ha, ha!—By the old woman's pipe, you frightened me! I'll swear, Galbraith Robinson, I heard you snoring as I passed by your window three minutes ago."

"I'll swear that's not the truest word you ever spoke in your life, Wat; though true enough for you, mayhap. Do you see how cleverly yon light has broke across the whole sky? When I first turned out this morning it was a little ribbon of day: the burning of a block-house at night, ten miles off, would have made a broader streak. It was your own snoring you heard, Wat; you have only forgot under whose window it was."

"What old witch has been pinching you, Horse Shoe, that *you* are up so early?" asked Adair. "Get back to the house, man, I will be with you presently; I have my farm to look after, I'll see you presently."

"You seem to me to be in a very onreasonable hurry, Wat, considering that you have the day before you. But, softly, I'll walk with you, if you have no unliking to it."

"No, no, I'm busy, Galbraith; I'm going to look after my traps; I'd rather you'd go back to the house and hurry breakfast. Go! You would only get scratched with briers if you followed me."

"Ha, ha, ha! Wat! Briers, did you say? Look here, man, do you see them there legs? Do they look as if they couldn't laugh at yourn in any sort of scrambling I had a mind to set them to? Tut, I'll go with you just to larn you the march drill."

"Then I'll not budge a foot after the traps."

"You are crusty, Wat Adair; what's the matter with you?"

"Is Major Butler up yet?" asked the woodman thoughtfully.

"*Who* do you say? *Major* Butler."

"*Major!*" cried Adair, with affected surprise.

"Yes, you called him Major Butler?"

"I had some dream, I think, about him: or, didn't you call him so yourself, Horse Shoe?"

"Most ondoubtedly, I did not," replied Robinson seriously.

"Then I dreamt it, Horse Shoe: these dreams sometimes get into the head, like things we have been told. But, Galbraith, tell me the plain up-an-down truth, what brings you and Mr. Butler into these parts? What are you after in Georgia? It does seem strange to find men that are wanted below, straggling here in our woods at such a time as this."

"There are two sorts of men in this world, Wat," said the sergeant, with a smile, "them that axes questions, and them that won't answer questions.

Now, which, do you think, I belong to? Why, to the last, you tinker! Where are our horses, Wat? Tell me that. Who let them out of the stable?"

"Perhaps they let themselves out," replied Adair, "they were not haltered."

"You are either knave or fool, Wat. Come here. There are the tracks of the beast that carried the man up this road, who sot loose all the horses that were in that stable."

Mike Lynch, perhaps," said Adair, with an assumed expression of ignorance. "Where can that fellow have been so early? Oh, I remember, he told me last night that he was going this morning to the blacksmith's. He ought to be back by this time."

"And you are here to larn the news from him?" said the sergeant, eyeing Adair with a suspicious scrutiny.

"You have just hit it, Horse Shoe," returned Wat, laughing. "I did want to know if there were any more squads of troopers foraging about this district: for these cursed fellows whip in upon a man and cut him up blade and ear, without so much as thanks for their pillage, and so I told Mike to inquire of the blacksmith, for he is more like to know than anybody else, whether there was any more of these pestifarious scrummagers abroad."

"And your traps, Wat?"

"That was only a lie, Galbraith—I confess it. I was afeared to make you uneasy by telling you what I was after. But still it wasn't a broad, stark, daylight lie neither; it was only a civil fib, for I was going after my wolf trap before I got my breakfast. But here comes Mike."

At this juncture Lynch was seen emerging from the wood, mounted on a rough, untrimmed pony, which he was urging forward under repeated blows with his stick. The little animal was covered with foam; and, from his travel-worn plight, gave evidence of having been taxed to the utmost of his strength in a severe journey. At some hundred paces, distant, the rider detected the presence of Adair and his companion, and came to a sudden halt. He appeared to deliberate as if with a purpose to escape their notice; but finding that he was already observed by them, he put his horse again in motion, advancing only at a slow walk. Adair hastily quitted Robinson, and, walking forward until he met Lynch, turned about and accompanied him along the road, conversing during this interval in a key too low to be heard by the sergeant.

"Here's Horse Shoe thrusting his head into our affairs. Conjure a lie quickly about your being at the blacksmith's; I told him you were there to hear the news."

"Aye, aye! I understand."

"You saw Hugh?"

"Yes. The gang will be at their post."

"Hush! Be merry; laugh and have a joke—Horse Shoe is very suspicious."

"You have ridden the crop-ear like a stolen horse," continued Adair, as soon as he found himself within the sergeant's hearing. "See what a flurry you have put the dumb beast in. If it had been your nag, Mike Lynch, I warrant you would have been more tedious with him."

"The crop-ear is not worth the devil's fetching, Wat. He is as lazy as a land-turtle, and too obstinate for any good-tempered man's patience. Look at that stick—I have split it into a broom on the beast."

"You look more like a man at the end of the day than at the beginning of it," said Robinson. "How far had you to ride, Michael?"

"Only over here to the shop of Billy Watson, in the Buzzard's nest," replied Lynch, "which isn't above three miles at the farthest. My saw wanted setting, so I thought I'd make an early job of it, but this beast is so cursed dull I have been good three-quarters of an hour since I left the smith's,"

"What news do you bring?" inquired Adair.

"Oh, none worth telling again. That cross-grained, contrary, rough-and-tumble bear gouger, old Hide-and-Seek, went down yesterday with the last squad of Ferguson's new draughts."

"Wild Tom Eskridge," said Wat Adair. "You knowed him, Horse Shoe, a superfluous imp of Satan!" continued the woodman, laying a particular accent on the penultimate of this favorite adjective, which he was accustomed to use as expressive of strong reprobation. "So he is cleared out at last! Well, I'm glad on't, for he was the only fellow in these hills I was afeard would give you trouble, Galbraith."

"Superfluous or not," replied the sergeant, pronouncing the word in the same manner as the woodman, and equally ignorant of its meaning, "it will be a bad day for Tom Eskridge, the rank, obstropolous Tory, when he meets me, Wat Adair. I have reason to think that he tried to clap some of Tarleton's dragoons on my back over here at the Waxhaws. There's hemp growing for that scape-grace at this very time."

"You heard of no red coats about the Tiger?" asked Adair.

"Not one," replied Lynch; "the nearest post is Cruger's, in Ninety-Six."

"Then your way, Mr. Robinson, is tolerable for to-day," added Adair: "but war is war, and there is always some risk to be run when men are parading with their rifles in their hands. But see! it is hard upon sunrise. Let us go and give some directions about breakfast. I will send out some of the boys to hunt up the horses; they will be ready by the time we have had something to eat."

Without further delay, Adair strode rapidly up the hill to the dwelling-house, the sergeant and Lynch following as soon as the latter had put his jaded beast in the stable. By the time these were assembled in the porch the family began to show signs of life, and it was a little after sunrise when Butler came forth ready for the prosecution of his journey. A few words were exchanged in private between Lynch and the woodman, and after much idle talk and contrived delay, two lazy and loitering negro boys were sent off in quest of the travellers' horses. Not long after this the animals were seen coursing from one part of the distant field to another, defying all attempts to get them into corner, or to compel them to pass through the place that had been opened in order to drive them towards the stable.

There was an air of concern and silent bewilderment visible upon Butler's features, and an occasional expression of impatience escaped his lips as he watched from the porch the ineffectual efforts of the negroes to force the truant steeds towards the house.

"All in good time," said Adair, answering the thoughts and looks of Butler, rather than his words, "all in good time; they must have their play out. It is a good sign, sir, to see a traveller's horse so capersome of a morning. Wife, make haste with your preparations; Horse Shoe and his friend here mustn't be kept back from their day's journey. Stir yourself, Mary Musgrove!"

"Will the gentlemen stay for breakfast?" inquired Mary, with a doubtful look at Butler.

"Will they? To be sure they will! Would you turn off friends from the door with empty stomachs, you mink, and especially with a whole day's starvation ahead of them?" exclaimed the woodman.

"I thought they had far to ride," replied the girl, "and would choose, rather than wait, to take some cold provision to eat upon the road."

"Tush! Go about your business, niece! The horses are not caught yet, and you may have your bacon fried before they are at the door."

"It shall be ready, then, in a moment," returned Mary, and she betook herself diligently to her task of preparation. During the interval that followed, the maiden several times attempted to gain a moment's speech with Butler, but the presence of Adair or Lynch as frequently forbade even a whisper; and the morning meal was at length set smoking on the table without the arrival of the desired opportunity. The repast was speedily finished, and the horses having surrendered to the emissaries who had been despatched to bring them in, were now in waiting for their masters. Horse Shoe put into the woodman's hand a small sum of money in requital for the entertainment afforded to his comrade and himself, and having arranged their baggage upon the saddles, announced that they were ready to set forward on their journey. Whilst the travellers were passing the farewells customary on such occasions, Mary Musgrove, whose manner during the whole morning gave many indications of a painful secret concern, now threw herself in Butler's way, and as she modestly offered him her hand at parting, and heard the little effusion of gallantry and compliment with which it was natural for a well-bred man and a soldier to speak at such a moment, she took the opportunity to whisper—"The left hand road at the Fork—remember!" and instantly glided away to another part of the house.

Butler paused but for an instant, and then hurried forward with the sergeant to their horses.

"Wat, you promised to put us on the track to Grindall's Ford," said Horse Shoe, as he rose into his seat.

"I am ready to go part of the way with you," replied the woodman, "I will see you to the Fork, and after that you must make out for yourselves. Michael, fetch me my rifle."

It was not more than half past six when the party set forth on their journey. Our two travellers rode along at an easy gait, and Wat Adair, throwing his rifle carelessly across his shoulder, stepped out with a long swinging step that kept him, without difficulty, abreast of the horsemen, as they pursued their way over hill and dale.

They had not journeyed half a mile before they reached a point in the woods at which Adair called a halt.

"My trap is but a little off the road," he said, "and I must beg you to stop until I see what luck I have this morning. It's a short business and soon done. This way, Horse Shoe; it is likely I may give you sport this morning."

"Our time is pressing," said Butler. "Pray give us your directions as to the road, and we will leave you."

"You would never find it in these woods," replied Wat; "there are two or three paths leading through here, and the road is a blind one till you come to the fork; the trap is not a hundred yards out of your way."

"Rather than stop to talk about it, Wat," said the sergeant, "we will follow you, so go on."

The woodman now turned into the thickets, and opening his way through the bushes, in a few moments conducted the two soldiers to the foot of a large gum tree.

"By all the crows, I have got my lady!" exclaimed Wat Adair, with a whoop that made the woods ring. "The saucy slut! I have yoked her, Horse Shoe Robinson! There's a picture worth looking at."

"Who?" cried Butler; "of whom are you speaking?"

"Look for yourself, sir," replied the woodman. "There's the mischievous devil; an old she-wolf that I have been hunting these two years. Oh, ho, madam! Your servant!"

Upon looking near the earth, our travellers descried the object of this triumphant burst of joy, in a large wolf that was now struggling to release herself from the thraldom of her position. The trap was ingeniously contrived. It consisted of a long opening into the hollow trunk of the tree, beginning about four feet from the ground, and cut out with an axe down to the root. An aperture had been made at the upper end of the slit about a foot wide, and the wood had been hewed away downwards, in such a manner as to render the slit gradually narrower as it approached the lower extremity, until near the earth it was not more than four inches in width, thus forming a wedge-shaped loophole into the hollow body of the tree. A part of the carcase of a sheep had been placed on the bottom inside, the scent of which had attracted the wolf, and, in her eagerness to possess herself of this treasure she had risen on her hind legs high enough to find the opening sufficiently wide to allow her head to be thrust in, whence, slipping downwards the slit became so narrow as to prevent her from withdrawing her jaws. The only mode of extrication from this trap was to rear her body to the same height at which she found admission, an expedient which, it seems, required more cunning than this proverbially cunning animal was gifted with. She now stood captive pretty much in the same manner that oxen are commonly secured in their stalls.

For a few moments after the prisoner was first perceived, and during the extravagant yelling of Adair at the success of his stratagem, she made several desperate but ineffectual efforts to withdraw her head; but as soon as Butler and Robinson had dismounted, and, together with their guide, had assembled around her, she desisted from her struggles, and seemed patiently to resign herself to the will of her captor. She stood perfectly still with that passive and even cowardly submission for which, in such circumstances, this animal is remarkable: her hind legs drooped and her tail was thrust between them, whilst not a snarl nor an expression of anger or grief escaped her. Her characteristic sagacity had been completely baffled by the superior wolfish cunning of her ensnarer.

Wat laughed aloud with a coarse and almost fiendish laugh, as he cried out—

"I have cotched the old thief at last, in spite of her cunning! With a warning to boot. Here is a mark I sot upon her last winter," he added, as he raised her fore leg, which was deprived of the foot; "but she would be prowling, the superfluous devil! It is in the nature of these here blood-suckers, to keep a going at their trade, no matter how much they are watched. But I knowed I'd have her one of these days. These varmints have always got to pay, one day or another, for their villanies. Wa'n't she an old fool, Horse Shoe, to walk into this here gum for a piece of dead mutton? Ha, ha, ha! if she had had only the sense to rear up, she might have had the laugh on us! But she hadn't; ha, ha, ha!"

"Well, Wat Adair," said Robinson, "you had a mischievous head when you contrived that trap."

"Feel her ribs, Mr. Butler," cried Wat, not heeding the sergeant; "I know who packed that flesh on her. There isn't a lamb in my flock to-day that wouldn't grin if he was to hear the news."

"Well, what are you going to do with her, Adair?" inquired Butler; "remember you are losing time here."

"Do with her!" ejaculated the woodman; "that's soon told: I will skin the devil alive."

"I hope not," exclaimed Butler. "It would be an unnecessary cruelty. Despatch her on the spot with your rifle."

"I wouldn't waste powder and ball on the varmint," replied Adair. "No, no, the knife, the knife!"

"Then cut her throat and be done with it."

"You are not used to these hellish thieves, sir," said the woodman. "There is nothing that isn't too good for them. By the old sinner, I'll skin her alive! That's the sentence!"

"Once more, I pray not," said Butler imploringly.

"It is past praying for," returned Adair, as he drew forth his knife and began to whet it on a stone. "She shall die by inches, and be damned to her!" he added, as his eye sparkled with savage delight. "Now look and see a wolf punished according to her evil doings."

The woodman stood over his captive and laughed heartily, as he pointed out to his companions the quailing and subdued gestures of his victim, indulging in coarse and vulgar jests whilst he described minutely the plan of torture he was about to execute. When he had done his ribaldry, he slowly drew the point of his knife down the back-bone of the animal, from the neck to the tail, sundering the skin along the whole length. "That's the way to unbutton her jacket," he said, laughing louder than ever.

"For God's sake, desist!" ejaculated Butler. "For my sake, save the poor animal from this pain! I will pay you thrice the value of the skin."

"Money will not buy her," said Wat, looking up for an instant. "Besides, the skin is spoiled by that gash."

"Here is a guinea, if you will cut her throat," said Butler, "and destroy her at once."

"That would be murder outright," replied Adair; "I never take money to do murder; it goes agin my conscience. No, no, I will undress the old lady, and let her have the benefit of the cool air in this hot weather. And if she should take cold, you know, and fall sick and die of that, why then, Mr. Butler, you can give me the guinea. That will save my conscience," he added, with a grin that expressed a struggle between his avarice and cruelty.

"Come, Galbraith, I will not stay to witness the barbarity of this savage. Mount your horse, and let us take our chance alone through the woods. Fellow, I don't wish your further service."

"Look there now!" said Adair; "where were you born, that you are so mighty nice upon account of a blood-sucking wolf? Man, it's impossible to find your way through this country; and you might, by taking a wrong road, fall in with them that would think nothing of serving you as I serve this beast."

"Wat, curse your onnatural heart," interposed the sergeant. "Stob her at once. It's no use, Mr. Butler," he said, finding that Adair did not heed him, "we can't help ourselves. It's wolf agin wolf."

"I knowed you couldn't, Horse Shoe," cried Wat, with another laugh. "So you may as well stay to see it out."

Butler had now walked to his horse, mounted, and retired some distance into the wood to avoid further converse with the tormentor of the ensnared beast, and to withdraw himself from a sight so revolting to his feelings. In the meantime, Adair proceeded with his operation with an alacrity that showed the innate cruelty of his temper. He made a cross incision through the skin, from the point of one shoulder to the other, the devoted subject of his torture, remaining, all the time, motionless and silent. Having thus severed the skin to suit his purpose, the woodman now, with an affectation of the most dainty precision, flourished his knife over the animal's back, and then burst into a loud laugh.

"I can't help laughing," he exclaimed, "to think what a fine, dangling, holiday coat I am going to make of it. I shall strip her as low as the ribs, and then the flaps will hang handsomely. She will be considered a beauty in the sheep-folds, and then she may borrow a coat, you see, from some lamb; a wolf in sheep's clothing is no uncommon sight in this world."

"Wat Adair," said Horse Shoe, angrily, "I've a mind to take the wolf's part and give you a trouncing. You are the savagest wolf in sheep's clothing yourself that it was ever my luck to see."

"You think so, Horse Shoe!" cried Wat, tauntingly. "You might chance to miss your way to-day, so don't make a fool of yourself! Ill will would only take away from you a finger-post—and it isn't every road through this district that goes free of the Tory rangers."

"Your own day will come yet," replied Horse Shoe, afraid to provoke the woodman too far on account of the dependence of himself and his companion upon Adair's information in regard to the route of their journey. "We have to give and take quarter in this world."

"You see, Horse Shoe," said Adair, beginning to expostulate, "I don't like these varmints, no how; that's the reason why. They are cruel themselves and I like to be cruel to them. It's a downright pleasure to see them winch, for, bless your soul! they don't mind common throat-cutting, no more than a calf. Now here's the way to touch their feelings."

At this moment he applied the point of his knife to separating the hide from the flesh on either side of the spine, and then, in his eagerness to accomplish this object, he placed his knife between his teeth and began to tug at the skin with his hands, accompanying the effort with muttered expressions of delight at the involuntary but ill-suppressed agonies of the brute. The pain, at length, became too acute for the wolf, with all her characteristic habits of submission, to bear, and, in a desperate struggle that ensued between her and her tormentor, she succeeded, by a convulsive leap, in extricating herself from her place of durance. The energy of her effort of deliverance rescued her from the woodman's hand, and turning short upon her assailant, she fixed her fangs deep into the fleshy part of his thigh, where, as the foam fell from her lips, she held on firmly as if determined to sell her life dearly for the pain she suffered. Adair uttered a groan from the infliction, and, in the hurry of the instant, dropped his knife upon the ground. He was thus compelled to bear the torment of the grip, until he dragged the still pertinaciously-adhering beast a few paces forward, where grasping up his knife, he planted it, by one deeply driven blow, through and through her heart. She silently fell at his feet, without snarl or bark, releasing her hold only in the impotency of death.

"Curse her!" cried Adair, "the hard-hearted, bloody-minded devil! That's the nature of the beast—cruel and wicked to the last, damn her!" he continued, raving with pain, as he stamped his heel upon her head: "damn her in the wolf's hell to which she has gone!"

Robinson stood by, unaiding, and not displeased to see the summary vengeance thus inflicted by the victim upon the oppressor. This calmness provoked the woodman, who, with that stoicism which belongs to uncivilized life, seemed determined to take away all pretext for the sergeant's exultation, by affecting to make light of the injury he had received.

"I don't mind the scratch of the cursed creature," he said, assuming a badly counterfeited expression of mirth, "but I don't like to be cheated out of the pleasure of tormenting such mischievous varmints. It's well for her that she put me in a passion, or she should have carried a festered carcase that the buzzards might have fed upon before she died. But come—where is Mr. Butler? I want that guinea. Ho, sir!" he continued, bawling to Butler, as he tied up his wound with a strap of buckskin taken from his pouch, "my guinea! I've killed the devil to please you, seeing you would not have it."

Butler now rode up to the spot, and, in answer to this appeal, gave it an angry and indignant refusal.

"Lead us on our way, sir," he added. "We have lost too much time already with your brutal delay. Lead on, sir!"

"You will get soon enough to your journey's end," replied Adair with a smile, and then sullenly took up his rifle and led the way through the forest.

A full half hour or more was lost by the incident at the trap and Butler's impatience and displeasure continued to be manifested by the manner with which he urged the woodman forward upon their journey. After regaining the road, and traversing a piece of intricate and tangled woodland, by a bridle-patch into which their guide had conducted them, they soon reached a broader and more beaten highway, along which they rode scarce a mile before they arrived at the Fork.

"I have seen you safe as far as I promised," said the woodman, "and you must now shift for yourselves. You take the right hand road; about ten miles further you will come to another prong, there strike to the left, and if you have luck you will get to the ford before sundown. Three miles further is Christie's. Good bye t' ye! And Horse Shoe, if you should come across another wolf stuck in a tree, skin her, d' ye hear? Ha! ha! ha! Good bye!"

"Ride on!" said Butler to the sergeant, who was about making some reply to Adair; "ride on! Don't heed or answer that fellow, but take the road he directs. He is a beast and scoundrel. Faster, good sergeant, faster!"

As he spoke he set his horse to a gallop. Robinson followed at equal speed, the woodman standing still until the travellers disappeared from his view behind the thick foliage that overhung their path. Having seen them thus secure in his toil, the treacherous guide turned upon his heel, shouldered his rifle, and limped back to his dwelling.

"I have a strange misgiving of that ruffian sergeant," said Butler, after they had proceeded about a quarter of a mile. "My mind is perplexed with some unpleasant doubts. What is your opinion of him?"

"He plays on both sides," replied Horse Shoe, "and knows more of you than by rights he ought. He spoke consarning of you, this morning, as *Major* Butler. It came out of his mouth onawares."

"Ha! Is my name on any part of my baggage or dress?"

"Not that I know of," replied the sergeant; "and if it was, Wat can't read."

"Were you interrupted in your sleep last night, Galbraith? Did you hear noises in our room?"

"Nothing, Major, louder nor the gnawing of a mouse at the foot of the plank partition. Did you see a spirit that you look so solemn?"

"I did, sergeant!" said Butler, with great earnestness of manner. "I had a dream that had something more than natural in it."

"You amaze me, Major! If you saw anything, why didn't you awake me?"

"I hadn't time before it was gone, and then it was too late. I dreamed, Galbraith, that somehow—for my dream didn't explain how she came in —Mary Musgrove, the young girl we saw—"

"Ha! ha! ha! Major, that young girl's oversot you! Was that the sperit?"

"Peace, Galbraith, I am in earnest; listen to me. I dreamt Mary Musgrove came into our room and warned us that our lives were in danger; how, I forgot, or perhaps she did not tell, but she spoke of our being waylaid, and, I think, she advised that at this very fork of the road we have just passed, we should take the left hand—the right, according to my dream, she said, led to some spring."

"Perhaps the Dogwood, Major," said Robinson, laughing; "there is such a place, somewhere in these parts."

"The Dogwood! by my life," exclaimed Butler; "she called it the Dogwood spring."

"That's very strange," said Robinson gravely; "that's very strange, unless you have hearn some one talk about the spring before you went to bed last night. For, as sure as you are a gentleman, there is such a spring not far off, although I don't know exactly where."

"And what perplexes me," continued Butler, "is that, this morning, almost in the very words of my dream, Mary Musgrove cautioned me, in a whisper, to take the left road at the fork. How is she connected with my dream? Or could it have been a reality, and was it the girl herself who spoke? I have no recollection of such a word from her before I retired to bed."

"I have hearn of these sort of things before, major, and never could make them out. For my share, I believe in dreams. There is something wrong here," continued the sergeant, after pondering over the matter for a few moments, and shaking his head, "there is something wrong here, Major Butler, as sure as you are born. I wasn't idle in making my own observations: first, I didn't like the crossness of Wat's wife last night; then, the granny there, she raved more like an old witch, with something wicked in her that wouldn't let her be still, than like your decent old bodies when they get childish. What did she mean by her palaver about golden guineas in Wat's pocket, and the English officer? Such notions don't come naturally into the head, without something to go upon. And, moreover, when I turned out this morning, before it was cleverly day, who do you think I saw?"

"Indeed I cannot guess."

"First, Wat walking up the road with a face like a man that had sot a house on fire; and when I stopped him to ax what he was after, down comes Mike Lynch—that peevish bull-dog—from the woods, on a little knot of a pony, pretty nigh at full speed, and covered with lather; and there was a sort of colloguing together, and then a story made up about Mike's being at Billy Watson's, the blacksmith's. It didn't tell well, major, and it sot me to suspicions. The gray of the morning is not the time for blacksmith's work: there's the fire to make up, and what not. Besides, it don't belong to the trade, as I know, here in the country, to be at work so arly. I said nothing; but I made a sort of reckoning in my own mind that they looked like a couple of desarters trying to sham a sentry. Then again, there was our horses turned loose. There is something in these signs, you may depend upon it, Major Butler!"

"That fellow has designs against us, Galbraith," said Butler, musing, and paying but little attention to the surmises of the sergeant, "I can hardly think it was a dream. It may have been Mary Musgrove herself, but how she got there is past my conjecture. I saw nothing, I only heard the warning. And I would be sworn she addressed me as Major Butler. You say Wat Adair gave me the same title?"

"As I am a living man," replied Horse Shoe, "he wanted to deny it; and then he pretended it was a fancy of his own."

"It is very strange, and looks badly," said Butler.

"Never mind, let the worst come to the worst, we have arms and legs both," returned the sergeant.

"I will take the hint for good or for ill," said the major. "Sergeant, strike across into the left hand road; in this I will move no farther."

"That's as wise a thing as we can do," replied Robinson. "If you have doubts of a man, seem to trust him, but take care not to follow his advice.

There is another hint I will give you, let us examine our fire-arms to see that we are ready for a battle."

Butler concurring in this precaution, the sergeant dismounted, and having primed his rifle afresh, attempted to fire it into the air, but it merely flashed, without going off. Upon a second trial the result was the same. This induced a further examination, which disclosed the fact that the load which had been put in the day previous had been discharged, and a bullet was now driven home in the place of the powder. It was obvious that this was designed. The machination of an enemy became more apparent when, upon an investigation into the condition of Butler's pistols, they were also found incapable of being used.

"This is some of Michael Lynch's doing whilst we were eating our breakfast," said Horse Shoe, "and it is flat proof of treason in our camp. I should like to go back if it was only for the satisfaction of blowing out Wat's brains. But there is no use in argufying about it. We must set things to rights, and move on with a good look-out ahead."

With the utmost apparent indifference to the dangers that beset them, the sergeant now applied himself to the care of restoring his rifle to a serviceable condition. With the aid of a small tool which he carried for such a use, he opened the breach and removed the ball: Butler's pistols were likewise put in order, and our travellers, being thus restored to an attitude of defence, turned their horses' heads into the thicket upon their left, and proceeded across the space that filled up the angle made by the two branches of the road; and, having gained that branch which they sought, they pressed forward diligently upon their journey.

The path they had to travel was lonely and rugged, and it was but once or twice, during the day, that they met a casual wayfarer traversing the same wild. From such a source, however, they were informed that they were on the most direct road to Grindall's ford, and that the route they had abandoned would have conducted them to the Dogwood spring, a point much out of their proper course, and from which the ford might only have been reached by a difficult and tortuous by-way.

These disclosures opened the eyes of Butler and his companion to the imminent perils that encompassed them, and prompted them to the exercise of the strictest vigilance. Like discreet and trusty soldiers, they pursued their way with the most unwavering courage, confident that the difficulty of retreat was fully equal to that of the advance.

WILLIAM GILMORE SIMMS

(1806–1870)

William Gilmore Simms, the foremost man of letters of the antebellum South, was born in Charleston, South Carolina, the son of an Irish tradesman. His mother, who came from a middle-class Charleston family, died when he was two and his father moved west to Tennessee and then to Mississippi. Simms was reared in Charleston by his grandmother and was largely self-educated. He was married in 1826, but his wife died six years later. During the Nullification crisis Simms was a Unionist, and his support of President Jackson in the columns of the *City Gazette*, a daily newspaper he had purchased in 1830, cost him so many subscribers that he was forced to sell out and assume the paper's debts.

Simms had already published considerable poetry, so he went North to establish himself in literary circles. In 1833 his first work of fiction appeared, *Martin Faber*. The following year he brought out the first of his romances of the old colonial border, *Guy Rivers*, which was widely praised. In 1835 *The Yemassee*, a romance of the Indian war of 1715, was published, as well as the first of his Revolutionary War romances, *The Partisan*.

His literary position was now solidly established; he was one of the best-known historical novelists of his day. His second marriage, to Chevillette Roach, whose father owned two plantations in the Barnwell district of South Carolina, made him a member of the planter class, though he never received in Charleston the social recognition he thought he merited. He set up his family at a 3000-acre plantation, "Woodlands," and resided there for most of his life. Almost every year, however, he journeyed to New York, where he pursued his literary career. Throughout the 1840s he was active in the "Young America" literary group, favoring Jacksonian Democracy and literary nationalism. As the sectional controversy grew more intense, however, Simms' strong support of slavery split him from many of his Northern allies. For much of his adult life he worked tirelessly at establishing a Southern literary voice, editing magazines, writing for other Southern periodicals, and helping other writers to achieve publication. He was a central figure in the Russell's Bookstore group of writers in Charleston, whose ranks included Henry Timrod and Paul Hamilton Hayne. In the 1850s this group seemed to be developing into the first truly professional literary coterie in the South, until the growing excitement over slavery and secession brought an end to *Russell's Magazine*, which Hayne edited with Simms' assistance.

The coming of secession, which Simms supported, and the war left no place for literary activity in the South. Simms underwent a series of misfortunes. In 1862 "Woodlands" was severely damaged by fire. In 1863 his wife died. In 1865 "Woodlands" was again burned, in the wake of Sherman's march from Savannah through the Carolinas. After the war, bereft of income, he wrote unceasingly for poorly paying, second-line magazines and newspapers to provide food and clothing for his children and himself. He died in 1870.

Although Simms' most important writing was probably his seven Revolutionary War romances—*The Partisan* (1835), *Mellichampe* (1836), *The Scout* (1841), *Katherine Walton* (1851), *Woodcraft* (1852), *The Forayers* (1855), and *Eutaw* (1856)—these are only part of an incredibly prolific literary output, including many novels, plays, works of history, biographies, collections of short stories, at least fifteen books of poetry, and abundant literary criticism.

With some reason Simms always felt he was something of a prophet without honor in his own state, and in particular in Charleston, where his humble origins, he thought, were always a barrier to recognition, along with the obsession with politics that he rightly felt served to discourage interest in literature in the South. When he died, he left an epitaph that he asked be engraved on his tombstone: "Here lies one who, after a reasonably long life, distinguished chiefly by unceasing labors, has left all his better works undone."

THE LOST PLEIAD

I

Not in the sky,
Where it was seen
So long in eminence of light serene,—
Nor on the white tops of the glistering wave,
Nor down, in mansions of the hidden deep,
Though beautiful in green
And crystal, its great caves of mystery,—
Shall the bright watcher have
Her place, and, as of old, high station keep!

II

Gone! gone!
Oh! never more, to cheer
The mariner, who holds his course alone
On the Atlantic, through the weary night,
When the stars turn to watchers, and do sleep,
Shall it again appear,
With the sweet-loving certainty of light,
Down shining on the shut eyes of the deep!

WILLIAM GILMORE SIMMS

III

The upward-looking shepherd on the hills
Of Chaldea, night-returning, with his flocks,
He wonders why his beauty doth not blaze,
Gladdening his gaze,—
And, from his dreary watch along the rocks,
Guiding him homeward o'er the perilous ways!
How stands he waiting still, in a sad maze,
Much wondering, while the drowsy silence fills
The sorrowful vault!—how lingers, in the hope that night
May yet renew the expected and sweet light,
So natural to his sight!

IV

And lone,
Where, at the first, in smiling love she shone,
Brood the once happy circle of bright stars:
How should they dream, until her fate was known,
That they were ever confiscate to death?
That dark oblivion the pure beauty mars,
And, like the earth, its common bloom and breath,
That they should fall from high;
Their lights grow blasted by a touch, and die,—
All their concerted springs of harmony
Snapt rudely, and the generous music gone!

V

Ah! still the strain
Of wailing sweetness fills the saddening sky;
The sister stars, lamenting in their pain
That one of the selectest ones must die,—
Must vanish, when most lovely, from the rest!
Alas! 'tis ever thus the destiny.
Even Rapture's song hath evermore a tone
Of wailing, as for bliss too quickly gone.
The hope most precious is the soonest lost,
The flower most sweet is first to feel the frost.
Are not all short-lived things the loveliest?
And, like the pale star, shooting down the sky,
Look they not ever brightest, as they fly
From the lone sphere they blest!

1828

THE EDGE OF THE SWAMP

'Tis a wild spot, and even in summer hours,
With wondrous wealth of beauty and a charm
For the sad fancy, hath the gloomiest look,
That awes with strange repulsion. There, the bird
Sings never merrily in the sombre trees,
That seem to have never known a term of youth,
Their young leaves all being blighted. A rank growth
Spreads venomously round, with power to taint;
And blistering dews await the thoughtless hand
That rudely parts the thicket. Cypresses,
Each a great ghastly giant, eld and gray,
Stride o'er the dusk, dank tract,—with buttresses
Spread round, apart, not seeming to sustain,
Yet link'd by secret twines, that underneath,
Blend with each arching trunk. Fantastic vines,
That swing like monstrous serpents in the sun,
Bind top to top, until the encircling trees
Group all in close embrace. Vast skeletons
Of forests, that have perish'd ages gone,
Moulder, in mighty masses, on the plain;
Now buried in some dark and mystic tarn,
Or sprawl'd above it, resting on great arms,
And making, for the opossum and the fox,
Bridges, that help them as they roam by night.
Alternate stream and lake, between the banks,
Glimmer in doubtful light: smooth, silent, dark,
They tell not what they harbor; but, beware!
Lest, rising to the tree on which you stand,
You sudden see the moccasin snake heave up
His yellow shining belly and flat head
Of burnish'd copper. Stretch'd at length, behold
Where yonder Cayman, in his natural home,
The mammoth lizard, all his armor on,
Slumbers half-buried in the sedgy grass,
Beside the green ooze where he shelters him.
The place, so like the gloomiest realm of death,
Is yet the abode of thousand forms of life,—
The terrible, the beautiful, the strange,—
Winged and creeping creatures, such as make
The instinctive flesh with apprehension crawl,
When sudden we behold. Hark! at our voice
The whooping crane, gaunt fisher in these realms,

Erects his skeleton form and shrieks in flight,
On great white wings. A pair of summer ducks,
Most princely in their plumage, as they hear
His cry, with senses quickening all to fear,
Dash up from the lagoon with marvellous haste,
Following his guidance. See! aroused by these,
And startled by our progress o'er the stream,
The steel-jaw'd Cayman, from his grassy slope,
Slides silent to the slimy green abode,
Which is his province. You behold him now,
His bristling back uprising as he speeds
To safety, in the centre of the lake,
Whence his head peers alone,—a shapeless knot,
That shows no sign of life; the hooded eye,
Nathless, being ever vigilant and sharp,
Measuring the victim. See! a butterfly,
That, travelling all the day, has counted climes
Only by flowers, to rest himself a while,
And, as a wanderer in a foreign land,
To pause and look around him ere he goes,
Lights on the monster's brow. The surly mute
Straightway goes down; so suddenly, that he,
The dandy of the summer flowers and woods,
Dips his light wings, and soils his golden coat,
With the rank waters of the turbid lake.
Wondering and vex'd, the pluméd citizen
Flies with an eager terror to the banks,
Seeking more genial natures,—but in vain.
Here are no gardens such as he desires,
No innocent flowers of beauty, no delights
Of sweetness free from taint. The genial growth
He loves, finds here no harbor. Fetid shrubs,
That scent the gloomy atmosphere, offend
His pure patrician fancies. On the trees,
That look like felon spectres, he beholds
No blossoming beauties; and for smiling heavens,
That flutter his wings with breezes of pure balm,
He nothing sees but sadness—aspects dread,
That gather frowning, cloud and fiend in one,
As if in combat, fiercely to defend
Their empire from the intrusive wing and beam.
The example of the butterfly be ours.
He spreads his lacquer'd wings above the trees,
And speeds with free flight, warning us to seek

For a more genial home, and couch more sweet
Than these drear borders offer us tonight.

1840

GRAYLING; OR, "MURDER WILL OUT"

CHAPTER I

The world has become monstrous matter-of-fact in latter days. We can no longer get a ghost story, either for love or money. The materialists have it all their own way; and even the little urchin, eight years old, instead of deferring with decent reverence to the opinions of his grandmamma, now stands up stoutly for his own. He believes in every "ology" but pneumatology. "Faust" and the "Old Woman of Berkeley" move his derision only, and he would laugh incredulously, if he dared, at the Witch of Endor. The whole armoury of modern reasoning is on his side; and, however he may admit at seasons that belief can scarcely be counted a matter of will, he yet puts his veto on all sorts of credulity. That cold-blooded demon called Science has taken the place of all the other demons. He has certainly cast out innumerable devils, however he may still spare the principal. Whether we are the better for his intervention is another question. There is reason to apprehend that in disturbing our human faith in shadows, we have lost some of those wholesome moral restraints which might have kept many of us virtuous, where the laws could not.

The effect, however, is much the more seriously evil in all that concerns the romantic. Our story-tellers are so resolute to deal in the real, the actual only, that they venture on no subjects the details of which are not equally vulgar and susceptible of proof. With this end in view, indeed, they too commonly choose their subjects among convicted felons, in order that they may avail themselves of the evidence which led to their conviction; and, to prove more conclusively their devoted adherence to nature and the truth, they depict the former not only in her condition of nakedness, but long before she has found out the springs of running water. It is to be feared that some of the coarseness of modern taste arises from the too great lack of that veneration which belonged to, and elevated to dignity, even the errors of preceding ages. A love of the marvellous belongs, it appears to me, to all those who love and cultivate either of the fine arts. I very much doubt whether the poet, the painter, the sculptor, or the romancer, ever yet lived, who had not some strong bias—a leaning, at least,—to a belief in the wonders of the invisible world. Certainly, the higher orders of poets and painters, those who create and invent, must have a strong taint of the superstitious in their composition. But this is digressive, and leads us from our purpose.

It is so long since we have been suffered to see or hear of a ghost, that a visitation at this time may have the effect of novelty, and I propose to narrate a story which I heard more than once in my boyhood, from the lips of an aged relative, who succeeded, at the time, in making me believe every word of it; perhaps, for the simple reason that she convinced me she believed every word of it herself. My grandmother was an old lady who had been a resident of the seat of most frequent war in Carolina during the Revolution. She had fortunately survived the numberless atrocities which she was yet compelled to witness; and, a keen observer, with a strong memory, she had in store a thousand legends of that stirring period, which served to beguile me from sleep many and many a long winter night. The story which I propose to tell was one of these; and when I say that she not only devoutly believed it herself, but that it was believed by sundry of her contemporaries, who were themselves privy to such of the circumstances as could be known to third parties, the gravity with which I repeat the legend will not be considered very astonishing.

The revolutionary war had but a little while been concluded. The British had left the country; but peace did not imply repose. The community was still in that state of ferment which was natural enough to passions, not yet at rest, which had been brought into exercise and action during the protracted seven years' struggle through which the nation had just passed. The state was overrun by idlers, adventurers, profligates, and criminals. Disbanded soldiers, half-starved and reckless, occupied the highways, —outlaws, emerging from their hiding-places, skulked about the settlements with an equal sentiment of hate and fear in their hearts;—patriots were clamouring for justice upon the tories, and sometimes anticipating its course by judgments of their own; while the tories, those against whom the proofs were too strong for denial or evasion, buckled on their armour for a renewal of the struggle. Such being the condition of the country, it may easily be supposed that life and property lacked many of their necessary securities. Men generally travelled with weapons which were displayed on the smallest provocation: and few who could provide themselves with an escort ventured to travel any distance without one.

There was, about this time, said my grandmother, and while such was the condition of the country, a family of the name of Grayling, that lived somewhere upon the skirts of "Ninety-six" district. Old Grayling, the head of the family, was dead. He was killed in Buford's massacre. His wife was a fine woman, not so very old, who had an only son named James, and a little girl, only five years of age, named Lucy. James was but fourteen when his father was killed, and that event made a man of him. He went out with his rifle in company with Joel Sparkman, who was his mother's brother, and joined himself to Pickens's Brigade. Here he made as good a soldier as the best. He had no sort of fear. He was always the first to go forward; and his rifle was always good for his enemy's button at a long hundred yards. He was in several fights both with the British and tories; and just before the war was ended he had a famous brush with the Cherokees, when Pickens took their country from them. But though he had no fear, and never knew when to stop killing while the fight was going on, he was the most bashful of boys that I ever knew; and so kind-hearted that it was almost impossible to believe all we heard of his fierce doings when he was in battle. But they were nevertheless quite true for all his bashfulness.

Well, when the war was over, Joel Sparkman, who lived with his sister, Grayling, persuaded her that it would be better to move down into the low country. I don't know what reason he had for it, or what they proposed to do there. They had very little property, but Sparkman was a knowing man, who could turn his hand to a hundred things; and as he was a bachelor, and loved his sister and her children just as if they had been his own, it was natural that she should go with him wherever he wished. James, too, who was restless by nature—and the taste he had enjoyed of the wars had made him more so—he was full of it; and so, one sunny morning in April, their wagon started for the city. The wagon was only a small one, with two horses, scarcely larger than those that are employed to carry chickens and fruit to the market from the Wassamaws and thereabouts. It was driven by a negro fellow named Clytus, and carried Mrs. Grayling and Lucy. James and his uncle loved the saddle too well to shut themselves up in such a vehicle; and both of them were mounted on fine horses which they had won from the enemy. The saddle that James rode on,—and he was very proud of it,—was one that he had taken at the battle of Cowpens from one of Tarleton's own dragoons, after he had tumbled the owner. The roads at that season were excessively bad, for the rains of March had been frequent and heavy, the track was very much cut up, and the red clay gullies of the hills of "Ninety-six" were so washed that it required all shoulders, twenty times a day, to get the wagon-wheels out of the bog. This made them travel very slowly, —perhaps, not more than fifteen miles a day. Another cause for slow travelling was, the necessity of great caution, and a constant look-out for enemies both up and down the road. James and his uncle took it by turns to ride a-head, precisely as they did when scouting in war, but one of them always kept along with the wagon. They had gone on this way for two days, and saw nothing to trouble and alarm them. There were few persons on the high-road, and these seemed to the full as shy of them as they probably were of strangers. But just as they were about to camp, the evening of the second day, while they were splitting light-wood, and getting out the kettles and the frying-pan, a person rode up and joined them without much ceremony. He was a short thick-set man, somewhere between forty and fifty: had on very coarse and common garments, though he rode a fine black horse of remarkable strength and vigour. He was very civil of speech, though he had but little to say, and that little showed him to be a person without much education and with no refinement. He begged permission to make one of the encampment, and his manner was very respectful and even humble; but there was something dark and sullen in his face—his eyes, which were of a light gray colour, were very restless, and his nose turned up sharply, and was very red. His forehead was excessively broad, and his eye-brows thick and shaggy—white hairs being freely mingled with the dark, both in them and upon his head. Mrs. Grayling did not like this man's looks, and whispered her dislike to her son; but James, who felt himself equal to any man, said, promptly—

"What of that, mother! we can't turn the stranger off and say 'no;' and if he means any mischief, there's two of us, you know."

The man had no weapons—none, at least, which were then visible; and deported himself in so humble a manner, that the prejudice which the party had formed against him when he first appeared, if it was not dissipated while he remained, at least failed to gain any increase. He was very quiet, did not mention an unnecessary word, and seldom permitted his eyes to rest upon those of any of the party, the females not excepted. This, perhaps, was the only circumstance, that, in the mind of Mrs. Grayling, tended to confirm the hostile impression which his coming had originally occasioned. In a little while the temporary encampment was put in a state equally social and warlike. The wagon was wheeled a little way into the woods, and off the road; the horses fastened behind it in such a manner that any attempt to steal them would be difficult of success, even were the watch neglectful which was yet to be maintained upon them. Extra guns, concealed in the straw at the bottom of the wagon, were kept well loaded. In the foreground, and between the wagon and the highway, a fire was soon blazing with a wild but cheerful gleam; and the worthy dame, Mrs. Grayling, assisted by the little girl, Lucy, lost no time in setting on the frying-pan, and cutting into slices the haunch of bacon, which they had provided at leaving home. James Grayling patrolled the woods, meanwhile for a mile or two round the encampment, while his uncle, Joel Sparkman, foot to foot with the stranger, seemed—if the absence of all care constitutes the supreme of human felicity —to realize the most perfect conception of mortal happiness. But Joel was very far from being the careless person that he seemed. Like an old soldier, he simply hung out false colours, and concealed his real timidity by an extra show of confidence and courage. He did not relish the stranger from the first, any more than his sister; and having subjected him to a searching examination, such as was considered, in those days of peril and suspicion, by no means inconsistent with becoming courtesy, he came rapidly to the conclusion that he was no better than he should be.

"You are a Scotchman, stranger," said Joel, suddenly drawing up his feet, and bending forward to the other with an eye like that of a hawk stooping over a covey of partridges. It was a wonder that he had not made

the discovery before. The broad dialect of the stranger was not to be subdued; but Joel made slow stages and short progress in his mental journey-
ings. The answer was given with evident hesitation, but it was affirmative.

"Well, now, it's mighty strange that you should ha' fou't with us and not
agin us," responded Joel Sparkman. "There was a precious few of the
Scotch, and none that I knows on, saving yourself, perhaps,—that didn't go
dead agin us, and for the tories, through thick and thin. That 'Cross Creek
settlement' was a mighty ugly thorn in the sides of us whigs. It turned out a
raal bad stock of varmints. I hope,—I reckon, stranger,—you aint from that
part."

"No," said the other; "oh no! I'm from over the other quarter. I'm from
the Duncan settlement above."

"I've hearn tell of that other settlement, but I never know'd as any of the
men fou't with us. What gineral did you fight under? What Carolina
gineral?"

"I was at Gum Swamp when General Gates was defeated;" was the still
hesitating reply of the other.

"Well, I thank God, I warn't there, though I reckon things wouldn't ha'
turned out quite so bad, if there had been a leetle sprinkling of Sumter's, or
Pickens's, or Marion's men, among them two-legged critters that run that
day. They did tell that some of the regiments went off without ever once
emptying their rifles. Now, stranger, I hope you warn't among them
fellows."

"I was not," said the other with something more of promptness.

"I don't blame a chap for dodging a bullet if he can, or being too quick
for a bagnet, because, I'm thinking, a live man is always a better man than a
dead one, or he can become so; but to run without taking a single crack at
the inimy, is downright cowardice. There's no two ways about it, stranger."

This opinion, delivered with considerable emphasis, met with the ready
assent of the Scotchman, but Joel Sparkman was not to be diverted, even by
his own eloquence, from the object of his inquiry.

"But you ain't said," he continued, "who was your Carolina gineral.
Gates was from Virginny, and he stayed a mighty short time when he come.
You didn't run far at Camden, I reckon, and you joined the army ag'in, and
come in with Greene? Was that the how?"

To this the stranger assented, though with evident disinclination.

"Then, mou'tbe, we sometimes went into the same scratch together? I
was at Cowpens and Ninety-Six, and seen sarvice at other odds and eends,
where there was more fighting than fun. I reckon you must have been at
'Ninety-Six,'—perhaps at Cowpens, too, if you went with Morgan?"

The unwillingness of the stranger to respond to these questions appeared
to increase. He admitted, however, that he had been at "Ninety-Six,"
though, as Sparkman afterwards remembered, in this case, as in that of the
defeat of Gates at Gum Swamp, he had not said on which side he had

fought. Joel, as he discovered the reluctance of his guest to answer his questions, and perceived his growing doggedness, forbore to annoy him, but mentally resolved to keep a sharper look-out than ever upon his motions. His examination concluded with an inquiry, which, in the plaindealing regions of the south and south-west, is not unfrequently put first.

"And what mout be your name, stranger?"

"Macnab," was the ready response, "Sandy Macnab."

"Well, Mr. Macnab I see that my sister's got supper ready for us; so we mou't as well fall to upon the hoecake and bacon."

Sparkman rose while speaking, and led the way to the spot, near the wagon, where Mrs. Grayling had spread the feast. "We're pretty nigh on to the main road, here, but I reckon there's no great danger now. Besides, Jim Grayling keeps watch for us, and he's got two as good eyes in his head as any scout in the country, and a rifle that, after you once know how it shoots, 'twould do your heart good to hear its crack, if so be that twa'n't your heart that he drawed sight on. He's a perdigious fine shot, and as ready to shoot and fight as if he had a nateral calling that way."

"Shall we wait for him before we eat?" demanded Macnab, anxiously.

"By no sort o' reason, stranger," answered Sparkman. "He'll watch for us while we're eating, and after that I'll change shoes with him. So fall to, and don't mind what's a coming."

Sparkman had just broken the hoecake, when a distant whistle was heard.

"Ha! That's the lad now!" he exclaimed, rising to his feet. "He's on trail. He's got a sight of an inimy's fire, I reckon. 'Twon't be onreasonable, friend Macnab, to get our we'pons in readiness;" and, so speaking, Sparkman bid his sister get into the wagon, where the little Lucy had already placed herself, while he threw open the pan of his rifle, and turned the priming over with his finger. Macnab, meanwhile, had taken from his holsters, which he had before been sitting upon, a pair of horseman's pistols, richly mounted with figures in silver. These were large and long, and had evidently seen service. Unlike his companion, his proceedings occasioned no comment. What he did seemed a matter of habit, of which he himself was scarcely conscious. Having looked at his priming, he laid the instruments beside him without a word, and resumed the bit of hoecake which he had just before received from Sparkman. Meanwhile, the signal whistle, supposed to come from James Grayling, was repeated. Silence ensued then for a brief space, which Sparkman employed in perambulating the grounds immediately contiguous. At length, just as he had returned to the fire, the sound of a horse's feet was heard, and a sharp quick halloo from Grayling informed his uncle that all was right. The youth made his appearance a moment after accompanied by a stranger on horseback; a tall, fine-looking young man, with a keen flashing eye, and a voice whose lively clear tones, as he was heard approaching, sounded cheerily like those of a trumpet after victory. James

Grayling kept along on foot beside the new-comer; and his hearty laugh, and free, glib, garrulous tones, betrayed to his uncle, long ere he drew nigh enough to declare the fact, that he had met unexpectedly with a friend, or, at least, an old acquaintance.

"Why, who have you got there, James?" was the demand of Sparkman, as he dropped the butt of his rifle upon the ground.

"Why, who do you think, uncle? Who but Major Spencer—our own major?"

"You don't say so!—what!—well! Li'nel Spencer, for sartin! Lord bless you, major, who'd ha' thought to see you in these parts; and jest mounted too, for all natur, as if the war was to be fou't over ag'in. Well, I'm raal glad to see you. I am, that's sartin!"

"And I'm very glad to see you, Sparkman," said the other, as he alighted from his steed, and yielded his hand to the cordial grasp of the other.

"Well, I knows that, major, without you saying it. But you've jest come in the right time. The bacon's frying, and here's the bread;—let's down upon our haunches, in right good airnest, camp fashion, and make the most of what God gives us in the way of blessings. I reckon you don't mean to ride any further to-night, major?"

"No," said the person addressed, "not if you'll let me lay my heels at your fire. But who's in your wagon? My old friend, Mrs. Grayling, I suppose?"

"That's a true word, major," said the lady herself, making her way out of the vehicle with good-humoured agility, and coming forward with extended hand.

"Really, Mrs. Grayling, I'm very glad to see you." And the stranger, with the blandness of a gentleman and the hearty warmth of an old neighbour, expressed his satisfaction at once more finding himself in the company of an old acquaintance. Their greetings once over, Major Spencer readily joined the group about the fire, while James Grayling—though with some reluctance—disappeared to resume his toils of the scout while the supper proceeded.

"And who have you here?" demanded Spencer, as his eye rested on the dark, hard features of the Scotchman. Sparkman told him all that he himself had learned of the name and character of the stranger, in a brief whisper, and in a moment after formally introduced the parties in this fashion—

"Mr. Macnab, Major Spencer. Mr. Macnab says he's true blue, major, and fou't at Camden, when General Gates run so hard to 'bring the d—d militia back.' He also fou't at Ninety-Six, and Cowpens—so I reckon we had as good as count him one of us."

Major Spencer scrutinized the Scotchman keenly—a scrutiny which the latter seemed very ill to relish. He put a few questions to him on the subject of the war, and some of the actions in which he allowed himself to have been concerned; but his evident reluctance to unfold himself—a reluctance

so unnatural to the brave soldier who has gone through his toils honourably
—had the natural effect of discouraging the young officer, whose sense of
delicacy had not been materially impaired amid the rude jostlings of military life. But, though he forbore to propose any other questions to Macnab,
his eyes continued to survey the features of his sullen countenance with
curiosity and a strangely increasing interest. This he subsequently explained
to Sparkman, when, at the close of supper, James Grayling came in, and the
former assumed the duties of the scout.

"I have seen that Scotchman's face somewhere, Sparkman, and I'm convinced at some interesting moment; but where, when, or how, I cannot call
to mind. The sight of it is even associated in my mind with something painful and unpleasant; where could I have seen him?"

"I don't somehow like his looks myself," said Sparkman, "and I mislists
he's been rether more of a tory than a whig; but that's nothing to the purpose now; and he's at our fire, and we've broken hoecake together; so we
cannot rake up the old ashes to make a dust with."

"No, surely not," was the reply of Spencer. "Even though we knew him
to be a tory, that cause of former quarrel should occasion none now. But it
should produce watchfulness and caution. I'm glad to see that you have not
forgot your old business of scouting in the swamp."

"Kin I forget it, major?" demanded Sparkman, in tones which, though
whispered, were full of emphasis, as he laid his ear to the earth to listen.

"James has finished supper, major—that's his whistle to tell me so; and
I'll jest step back to make it cl'ar to him how we're to keep up the watch to-
night."

"Count me in your arrangements, Sparkman, as I am one of you for the
night," said the major.

"By no sort of means," was the reply. "The night must be shared
between James and myself. Ef so be you wants to keep company with one
or t'other of us, why, that's another thing, and, of course, you can do as you
please."

"We'll have no quarrel on the subject, Joel," said the officer, good-na-
turedly, as they returned to the camp together.

CHAPTER II

The arrangements of the party were soon made. Spencer renewed his offer
at the fire to take his part in the watch; and the Scotchman, Macnab, volunteered his services also; but the offer of the latter was another reason why
that of the former should be declined. Sparkman was resolute to have
everything his own way; and while James Grayling went out upon his
lonely rounds, he busied himself in cutting bushes and making a sort of tent
for the use of his late commander. Mrs. Grayling and Lucy slept in a wag-

on. The Scotchman stretched himself with little effort before the fire; while Joel Sparkman, wrapping himself up in his cloak, crouched under the wagon body, with his back resting partly against one of the wheels. From time to time he rose and thrust additional brands into the fire, looked up at the night, and round upon the little encampment, then sunk back to his perch and stole a few moments, at intervals, of uneasy sleep. The first two hours of the watch were over, and James Grayling was relieved. The youth, however, felt in no mood for sleep, and taking his seat by the fire, he drew from his pocket a little volume of Easy Reading Lessons, and by the fitful flame of the resinous light-wood, he prepared, in this rude manner, to make up for the precious time which his youth had lost of its legitimate employments, in the stirring events of the preceding seven years consumed in war. He was surprised at this employment by his late commander, who, himself sleepless, now emerged from the bushes and joined Grayling at the fire. The youth had been rather a favourite with Spencer. They had both been reared in the same neighbourhood, and the first military achievements of James had taken place under the eye, and had met the approbation of his officer. The difference of their ages was just such as to permit of the warm attachment of the lad without diminishing any of the reverence which should be felt by the inferior. Grayling was not more than seventeen, and Spencer was perhaps thirty-four—the very prime of manhood. They sat by the fire and talked of old times and told old stories with the hearty glee and good-nature of the young. Their mutual inquiries led to the revelation of their several objects in pursuing the present journey. Those of James Grayling were scarcely, indeed, to be considered his own. They were plans and purposes of his uncle, and it does not concern this narrative that we should know more of their nature than has already been revealed. But, whatever they were, they were as freely unfolded to his hearer as if the parties had been brothers, and Spencer was quite as frank in his revelations as his companion. He, too, was on his way to Charleston, from whence he was to take passage for England.

"I am rather in a hurry to reach town," he said, "as I learn that the Falmouth packet is preparing to sail for England in a few days, and I must go in her."

"For England, major!" exclaimed the youth with unaffected astonishment.

"Yes, James, for England. But why—what astonishes you?"

"Why, lord!" exclaimed the simple youth, "if they only knew there, as I do, what a cutting and slashing you did use to make among their red coats, I reckon they'd hang you to the first hickory."

"Oh, no! scarcely," said the other, with a smile.

"But I reckon you'll change your name, major?" continued the youth.

"No," responded Spencer, "if I did that, I should lose the object of my voyage. You must know, James, that an old relative has left me a good deal of money in England, and I can only get it by proving that I am Lionel Spencer; so you see I must carry my own name, whatever may be the risk."

"Well, major, you know best; but I do think if they could only have a guess of what you did among their sodgers at Hobkirk's and Cowpens, and Eutaw, and a dozen other places, they'd find some means of hanging you up, peace or no peace. But I don't see what occasion you have to be going cl'ar away to England for money, when you've got a sight of your own already."

"Not so much as you think for," replied the major, giving an involuntary and uneasy glance at the Scotchman, who was seemingly sound asleep on the opposite side of the fire. "There is, you know, but little money in the country at any time, and I must get what I want for my expenses when I reach Charleston. I have just enough to carry me there."

"Well, now, major, that's mighty strange. I always thought that you was about the best off of any man in our parts; but if you're strained so close, I'm thinking, major,—if so be you wouldn't think me too presumptuous, —you'd better let me lend you a guinea or so that I've got to spare, and you can pay me back when you get the English money."

And the youth fumbled in his bosom for a little cotton wallet, which, with its limited contents, was displayed in another instant to the eyes of the officer.

"No, no, James," said the other, putting back the generous tribute; "I have quite enough to carry me to Charleston, and when there I can easily get a supply from the merchants. But I thank you, my good fellow, for your offer. You *are* a good fellow, James, and I will remember you."

It is needless to pursue the conversation farther. The night passed away without any alarms, and at dawn of the next day the whole party was engaged in making preparation for a start. Mrs. Grayling was soon busy in getting breakfast in readiness. Major Spencer consented to remain with them until it was over; but the Scotchman, after returning thanks very civilly for his accommodation of the night, at once resumed his journey. His course seemed, like their own, to lie below; but he neither declared his route nor betrayed the least desire to know that of Spencer. The latter had no disposition to renew those inquiries from which the stranger seemed to shrink the night before, and he accordingly suffered him to depart with a quiet farewell, and the utterance of a good-natured wish, in which all the parties joined, that he might have a pleasant journey. When he was fairly out of sight, Spencer said to Sparkman,

"Had I liked that fellow's looks, nay, had I not positively disliked them, I should have gone with him. As it is, I will remain and share your breakfast."

The repast being over, all parties set forward; but Spencer, after keeping along with them for a mile, took his leave also. The slow wagon-pace at which the family travelled, did not suit the high-spirited cavalier; and it was necessary, as he assured them, that he should reach the city in two nights more. They parted with many regrets, as truly felt as they were warmly expressed; and James Grayling never felt the tedium of wagon travelling to be so severe as throughout the whole of that day when he separated from his favourite captain. But he was too stout-hearted a lad to make any complaint; and his dissatisfaction only showed itself in his unwonted silence, and an over-anxiety, which his steed seemed to feel in common with himself, to go rapidly ahead. Thus the day passed, and the wayfarers at its close had made a progress of some twenty miles from sun to sun. The same precautions marked their encampment this night as the last, and they rose in better spirits the next morning, the dawn of which was very bright and pleasant, and encouraging. A similar journey of twenty miles brought them to the place of bivouac as the sun went down; and they prepared as usual for their securities and supper. They found themselves on the edge of a very dense forest of pines and scrubby oaks, a portion of which was swallowed up in a deep bay—so called in the dialect of the country—a swamp-bottom, the growth of which consisted of mingled cypresses and bay-trees, with tupola, gum, and dense thickets of low stunted shrubbery, cane grass, and dwarf willows, which filled up every interval between the trees, and to the eye most effectually barred out every human intruder. This bay was chosen as the background for the camping party. Their wagon was wheeled into an area on a gently rising ground in front, under a pleasant shade of oaks and hickories, with a lonely pine rising loftily in occasional spots among them. Here the horses were taken out, and James Grayling prepared to kindle up a fire; but, looking for his axe, it was unaccountably missing, and after a fruitless search of half an hour, the party came to the conclusion that it had been left on the spot where they slept last night. This was a disaster, and, while they meditated in what manner to repair it, a negro boy appeared in sight, passing along the road at their feet, and driving before him a small herd of cattle. From him they learned that they were only a mile or two from a farmstead where an axe might be borrowed; and James, leaping on his horse, rode forward in the hope to obtain one. He found no difficulty in his quest; and, having obtained it from the farmer, who was also a tavern-keeper, he casually asked if Major Spencer had not stayed with him the night before. He was somewhat surprised when told that he had not.

"There was one man stayed with me last night," said the farmer, "but he didn't call himself a major, and didn't much look like one."

"He rode a fine sorrel horse,—tall, bright colour, with white fore foot, didn't he?" asked James.

"No, that he didn't! He rode a powerful black, coal black, and not a bit of white about him."

"That was the Scotchman! But I wonder the major didn't stop with you. He must have rode on. Isn't there another house near you, below?"

"Not one. There's ne'er a house either above or below for a matter of fifteen miles. I'm the only man in all that distance that's living on this road;

and I don't think your friend could have gone below, as I should have seen him pass. I've been all day out there in that field before your eyes, clearing up the brush."

CHAPTER III

Somewhat wondering that the major should have turned aside from the track, though without attaching to it any importance at that particular moment, James Grayling took up the borrowed axe and hurried back to the encampment, where the toil of cutting an extra supply of light-wood to meet the exigencies of the ensuing night, sufficiently exercised his mind as well as his body, to prevent him from meditating upon the seeming strangeness of the circumstance. But when he sat down to his supper over the fire that he had kindled, his fancies crowded thickly upon him, and he felt a confused doubt and suspicion that something was to happen, he knew not what. His conjectures and apprehensions were without form, though not altogether void; and he felt a strange sickness and a sinking at the heart which was very unusual with him. He had, in short, that lowness of spirits, that cloudy apprehensiveness of soul which takes the form of presentiment, and makes us look out for danger even when the skies are without a cloud, and the breeze is laden, equally and only, with balm and music. His moodiness found no sympathy among his companions. Joel Sparkman was in the best of humours, and his mother was so cheery and happy, that when the thoughtful boy went off into the woods to watch, he could hear her at every moment breaking out into little catches of a country ditty, which the gloomy events of the late war had not yet obliterated from her memory.

"It's very strange!" soliloquized the youth, as he wandered along the edges of the dense bay or swamp-bottom, which we have passingly referred to,—"it's very strange what troubles me so! I feel almost frightened, and yet I know I'm not to be frightened easily, and I don't see anything in the woods to frighten me. It's strange the major didn't come along this road! Maybe he took another higher up that leads by a different settlement. I wish I had asked the man at the house if there's such another road. I reckon there must be, however, for where could the major have gone?"

The unphilosophical mind of James Grayling did not, in his farther meditations, carry him much beyond this starting point; and with its continual recurrence in soliloquy, he proceeded to traverse the margin of the bay, until he came to its junction with, and termination at, the high-road. The youth turned into this, and, involuntarily departing from it a moment after, soon found himself on the opposite side of the bay thicket. He wandered on and on, as he himself described it, without any power to restrain himself. He knew not how far he went; but, instead of maintaining his watch for two hours only, he was gone more than four; and, at length, a sense of weariness which overpowered him all of a sudden, caused him to seat himself at the foot of a tree, and snatch a few moments of rest. He denied that he slept in this time. He insisted to the last moment of his life that sleep never visited his eyelids that night,—that he was conscious of fatigue and exhaustion, but not drowsiness,—and that this fatigue was so numbing as to be painful, and effectually kept him from any sleep. While he sat thus beneath the tree, with a body weak and nerveless, but a mind excited, he knew not how or why, to the most acute degree of expectation and attention, he heard his name called by the well-known voice of his friend, Major Spencer. The voice called him three times,—"James Grayling! —James!— James Grayling!" before he could muster strength enough to answer. It was not courage he wanted,—of that he was positive, for he felt sure, as he said, that something had gone wrong, and he was never more ready to fight in his life than at that moment, could he have commanded the physical capacity; but his throat seemed dry to suffocation,—his lips effectually sealed up as if with wax, and when he did answer, the sounds seemed as fine and soft as the whisper of some child just born.

"Oh! major, is it you?"

Such, he thinks, were the very words he made use of in reply; and the answer that he received was instantaneous, though the voice came from some little distance in the bay, and his own voice he did not hear. He only knows what he meant to say. The answer was to this effect.

"It is, James!—It is your own friend, Lionel Spencer, that speaks to you; do not be alarmed when you see me! I have been shockingly murdered!"

James asserts that he tried to tell him that he would not be frightened, but his own voice was still a whisper, which he himself could scarcely hear. A moment after he had spoken, he heard something like a sudden breeze that rustled through the bay bushes at his feet, and his eyes were closed without his effort, and indeed in spite of himself. When he opened them, he saw Major Spencer standing at the edge of the bay, about twenty steps from him. Though he stood in the shade of a thicket, and there was no light in the heavens save that of the stars, he was yet enabled to distinguish perfectly, and with great ease, every lineament of his friend's face.

He looked very pale, and his garments were covered with blood; and James said that he strove very much to rise from the place where he sat and approach him;—"for, in truth," said the lad, "so far from feeling any fear, I felt nothing but fury in my heart; but I could not move a limb. My feet were fastened to the ground; my hands to my sides; and I could only bend forward and gasp. I felt as if I should have died with vexation that I could not rise; but a power which I could not resist, made me motionless, and almost speechless. I could only say, 'Murdered!'—and that one word I believe I must have repeated a dozen times.

" 'Yes, murdered!—murdered by the Scotchman who slept with us at your fire the night before last. James, I look to you to have the murderer brought to justice! James!—do you hear me, James?'

"These," said James, "I think were the very words, or near about the very words, that I heard; and I tried to ask the major to tell me how it was, and how I could do what he required; but I didn't hear myself speak, though it would appear that he did, for almost immediately after I had tried to speak what I wished to say, he answered me just as if I had said it. He told me that the Scotchman had waylaid, killed, and hidden him in that very bay; that his murderer had gone to Charleston; and that if I made haste to town, I would find him in the Falmouth packet, which was then lying in the harbour and ready to sail for England. He farther said that everything depended on my making haste,—that I must reach town by to-morrow night if I wanted to be in season, and go right on board the vessel and charge the criminal with the deed. 'Do not be afraid,' said he, when he had finished; 'be afraid of nothing, James, for God will help and strengthen you to the end.' When I heard all I burst into a flood of tears, and then I felt strong. I felt that I could talk, or fight, or do almost anything; and I jumped up to my feet, and was just about to run down to where the major stood, but, with the first step which I made forward, he was gone. I stopped and looked all around me, but I could see nothing; and the bay was just as black as midnight. But I went down to it, and tried to press in where I thought the major had been standing; but I couldn't get far, the brush and bay bushes were so close and thick. I was now bold and strong enough, and I called out, loud enough to be heard half a mile. I didn't exactly know what I called for, or what I wanted to learn, or I have forgotten. But I heard nothing more. Then I remembered the camp, and began to fear that some-thing might have happened to mother and uncle, for I now felt, what I had not thought of before, that I had gone too far round the bay to be of much assistance, or indeed, to be in time for any, had they been suddenly attacked. Besides, I could not think how long I had been gone; but it seemed very late. The stars were shining their brightest, and the thin white clouds of morning were beginning to rise and run towards the west. Well, I bethought me of my course,—for I was a little bewildered and doubtful where I was; but, after a little thinking, I took the back track, and soon got a glimpse of the camp-fire, which was nearly burnt down; and by this I reckoned I was gone considerably longer than my two hours. When I got back into the camp, I looked under the wagon, and found uncle in a sweet sleep, and though my heart was full almost to bursting with what I had heard, and the cruel sight I had seen, yet I wouldn't waken him; and I beat about and mended the fire, and watched, and waited, until near daylight, when mother called to me out of the wagon, and asked who it was. This wakened my uncle, and then I up and told all that had happened, for if it had been to save my life, I couldn't have kept it in much longer. But though mother said it was very strange, Uncle Sparkman considered that I had been only dreaming; but he couldn't persuade me of it; and when I told him I intended to be off at daylight, just as the major had told me to do, and ride my best all the way to Charleston, he laughed, and said I was a fool. But I felt that I was no fool, and I was solemn certain that I hadn't been dreaming; and though both mother and he tried their hardest to make me put off going, yet I made up my mind to do it, and they had to give up. For, wouldn't I have been a pretty sort of a friend to the major, if, after what he told me, I could have stayed behind, and gone on only at a wagon-pace to look after the murderer! I dont think if I had done so that I should ever have been able to look a white man in the face again. Soon as the peep of day, I was on horseback. Mother was mighty sad, and begged me not to go, but Uncle Sparkman was mighty sulky, and kept calling me fool upon fool, until I was almost angry enough to forget that we were of blood kin. But all his talking did not stop me, and I reckon I was five miles on my way before he had his team in traces for a start. I rode as briskly as I could get on without hurting my nag. I had a smart ride of more than forty miles before me, and the road was very heavy. But it was a good two hours from sunset when I got into town, and the first question I asked of the people I met was, to show me where the ships were kept. When I got to the wharf they showed me the Falmouth packet, where she lay in the stream, ready to sail as soon as the wind should favour."

CHAPTER IV

James Grayling, with the same eager impatience which he has been suffered to describe in his own language, had already hired a boat to go on board the British packet, when he remembered that he had neglected all those means, legal and otherwise, by which alone his purpose might be properly effected. He did not know much about legal process, but he had common sense enough, the moment that he began to reflect on the subject, to know that some such process was necessary. This conviction produced another difficulty; he knew not in which quarter to turn for counsel and assistance; but here the boatman who saw his bewilderment, and knew by his dialect and dress that he was a back-countryman, came to his relief, and from him he got directions where to find the merchants with whom his uncle, Spark-man, had done business in former years. To them he went, and without circumlocution, told the whole story of his ghostly visitation. Even as a dream, which these gentlemen at once conjectured it to be, the story of James Grayling was equally clear and curious; and his intense warmth and the entire absorption, which the subject had effected, of his mind and soul, was such that they judged it not improper, at least to carry out the search of the vessel which he contemplated. It would certainly, they thought, be a curious coincidence—believing James to be a veracious youth—if the Scotchman should be found on board. But another test of his narrative was proposed by one of the firm. It so happened that the business agents of Major Spencer, who was well known in Charleston, kept their office but a few rods distant from their own; and to them all parties at once proceeded. But here the story of James was encountered by a circumstance that made somewhat against it. These gentlemen produced a letter from Major Spencer, intimating the utter impossibility of his coming to town for the space of a month, and expressing his regret that he should be unable to avail himself of the opportunity of the foreign vessel, of whose arrival in Charleston, and proposed time of departure, they had themselves advised him. They read the letter aloud to James and their brother merchants, and with difficulty suppressed their smiles at the gravity with which the former related and insisted upon the particulars of his vision.

"He has changed his mind," returned the impetuous youth; 'he was on his way down, I tell you,—a hundred miles on his way,—when he camped with us. I know him well, I tell you, and talked with him myself half the night."

"At least," remarked the gentlemen who had gone with James, "it can do no harm to look into the business. We can procure a warrant for searching the vessel after this man, Macnab; and should he be found on board the packet, it will be a sufficient circumstance to justify the magistrates in detaining him, until we can ascertain where Major Spencer really is."

The measure was accordingly adopted, and it was nearly sunset before the warrant was procured, and the proper officer in readiness. The impatience of a spirit so eager and so devoted as James Grayling, under these delays, may be imagined; and when in the boat, and on his way to the packet where the criminal was to be sought, his blood became so excited that it was with much ado he could be kept in his seat. His quick, eager action continually disturbed the trim of the boat, and one of his mercantile friends, who had accompanied him, with that interest in the affair which curiosity alone inspired, was under constant apprehension lest he would plunge overboard in his impatient desire to shorten the space which lay between. The same impatience enabled the youth, though never on shipboard before, to grasp the rope which had been flung at their approach, and to mount her sides with catlike agility. Without waiting to declare himself or his purpose, he ran from one side of the deck to the other, greedily staring, to the surprise of the officers, passengers, and seamen, in the faces of all of them, and surveying them with an almost offensive scrutiny. He turned away from the search with disappointment. There was no face like that of the suspected man among them. By this time, his friend, the merchant, with the sheriff's officer, had entered the vessel, and were in conference with the captain. Grayling drew nigh in time to hear the latter affirm that there was no man of the name of Macnab, as stated in the warrant, among his passengers or crew.

"He is—he must be!" exclaimed the impetuous youth. "The major never lied in his life, and couldn't lie after he was dead. Macnab is here—he is a Scotchman—"

The captain interrupted him—

"We have, young gentleman, several Scotchmen on board, and one of them is named Macleod—"

"Let me see him—which is he?" demanded the youth.

By this time, the passengers and a goodly portion of the crew were collected about the little party. The captain turned his eyes upon the group, and asked,

"Where is Mr. Macleod?"

"He is gone below—he is sick!" replied one of the passengers.

"That's he! That must be the man!" exclaimed the youth. "I'll lay my life that's no other than Macnab. He's only taken a false name."

It was now remembered by one of the passengers, and remarked, that Macleod had expressed himself as unwell, but a few moments before, and had gone below even while the boat was rapidly approaching the vessel. At this statement, the captain led the way into the cabin, closely followed by James Grayling and the rest.

"Mr. Macleod," he said, with a voice somewhat elevated, as he approached the berth of that person, "you are wanted on deck for a few moments."

"I am really too unwell, captain," replied a feeble voice from behind the curtain of the berth.

"It will be necessary," was the reply of the captain. "There is a warrant from the authorities of the town, to look after a fugitive from justice."

Macleod had already begun a second speech declaring his feebleness, when the fearless youth, Grayling, bounded before the captain and tore away, with a single grasp of his hand, the curtain which concealed the suspected man from their sight.

"It is he!" was the instant exclamation of the youth, as he beheld him. "It is he—Macnab, the Scotchman—the man that murdered Major Spencer!"

Macnab,—for it was he,—was deadly pale. He trembled like an aspen. His eyes were dilated with more than mortal apprehension, and his lips were perfectly livid. Still, he found strength to speak, and to deny the accusation. He knew nothing of the youth before him—nothing of Major Spencer—his name was Macleod, and he had never called himself by any other. He denied, but with great incoherence, everything which was urged against him.

"You must get up, Mr. Macleod," said the captain; "the circumstances are very much against you. You must go with the officer!"

"Will you give me up to my enemies?" demanded the culprit. "You are a countryman—a Briton. I have fought for the king, our master, against these rebels, and for this they seek my life. Do not deliver me into their bloody hands!"

"Liar!" exclaimed James Grayling—"Didn't you tell us at our own camp-fire that you were with us? that you were at Gates's defeat, and Ninety-Six?"

"But I didn't tell you," said the Scotchman, with a grin, "which side I was on!"

"Ha! remember that!" said the sheriff's officer. "He denied, just a moment ago, that he knew this young man at all; now, he confesses that he did see and camp with him."

The Scotchman was aghast at the strong point which, in his inadvertence, he had made against himself; and his efforts to excuse himself, stammering and contradictory, served only to involve him more deeply in the meshes of his difficulty. Still he continued his urgent appeals to the captain of the vessel, and his fellow-passengers, as citizens of the same country, subjects to the same monarch, to protect him from those who equally hated and would destroy them all. In order to move their national prejudices in his behalf, he boasted of the immense injury which he had done, as a tory, to the rebel cause; and still insisted that the murder was only a pretext of the youth before him, by which to gain possession of his person, and wreak upon him the revenge which his own fierce performances during the war had naturally enough provoked. One or two of the passengers, indeed, joined with him in entreating the captain to set the accusers adrift and make sail at once; but the stout Englishman who was in command, rejected instantly the unworthy counsel. Besides, he was better aware of the dangers which would follow any such rash proceeding. Fort Moultrie, on Sullivan's Island, had been already refitted and prepared for an enemy; and he was lying, at that moment, under the formidable range of grinning teeth, which would have opened upon him, at the first movement, from the jaws of Castle Pinckney.

"No, gentlemen," said he, "you mistake your man. God forbid that I should give shelter to a murderer, though he were from my own parish."

"But I am no murderer," said the Scotchman.

"You look cursedly like one, however," was the reply of the captain. "Sheriff, take your prisoner."

The base creature threw himself at the feet of the Englishman, and clung, with piteous entreaties, to his knees. The latter shook him off, and turned away in disgust.

"Steward," he cried, "bring up this man's luggage."

He was obeyed. The luggage was brought up from the cabin and delivered to the sheriff's officer, by whom it was examined in the presence of all, and an inventory made of its contents. It consisted of a small new trunk, which, it afterwards appeared, he had bought in Charleston, soon after his arrival. This contained a few changes of raiment, twenty-six guineas in money, a gold watch, not in repair, and two pistols which he had shown while at Joel Sparkman's camp fire; but, with this difference, that the stock of one was broken off short just above the grasp, and the butt was entirely gone. It was not found among his chattels. A careful examination of the articles in his trunk did not result in anything calculated to strengthen the charge of his criminality; but there was not a single person present who did not feel as morally certain of his guilt as if the jury had already declared the fact. That night he slept—if he slept at all—in the common jail of the city.

CHAPTER V

His accuser, the warm-hearted and resolute James Grayling, did not sleep. The excitement, arising from mingling and contradictory emotions, —sorrow for his brave young commander's fate, and the natural exultation of a generous spirit at the consciousness of having performed, with signal success, an arduous and painful task combined to drive all pleasant slumbers from his eyes; and with the dawn he was again up and stirring, with his mind still full of the awful business in which he had been engaged. We do not care to pursue his course in the ordinary walks of the city, nor account for his employments during the few days which ensued, until, in consequence of a legal examination into the circumstances which anticipated the regular work of the sessions, the extreme excitement of the young accuser had been renewed. Macnab or Macleod,—and it is possible that both names were fictitious,—as soon as he recovered from his first terrors, sought the aid of an attorney—one of those acute, small, chopping lawyers, to be found in almost every community, who are willing to serve with equal zeal the sinner and the saint, provided that they can pay with equal liberality. The prisoner was brought before the court under *habeas corpus*, and several grounds submitted by his counsel with the view to obtaining his discharge. It became necessary to ascertain, among the first duties of the state, whether Major Spencer, the alleged victim, was really dead. Until it could be established that a man should be imprisoned, tried, and punished for a crime, it was first necessary to show that a crime had been committed, and the attorney made himself exceedingly merry with the ghost story of young Grayling. In those days, however, the ancient Superstition was not so feeble as she has subsequently become. The venerable judge was one of those good men who had a decent respect for the faith and opinions of his ancestors; and though he certainly would not have consented to the hanging of Macleod under the sort of testimony which had been adduced, he yet saw enough, in all the circumstances, to justify his present detention. In the meantime, efforts were to be made, to ascertain the whereabouts of Major Spencer; though, were he even missing,—so the counsel for Macleod contended,—his death could be by no means assumed in consequence. To this the judge shook his head doubtfully. " 'Fore God!" said he, "I would not have you to be too sure of that." He was an Irishman, and proceeded after the fashion of his country. The reader will therefore *bear* with his *bull*. "A man may properly be hung for murdering another, though the murdered man be not dead; ay, before God, even though he be actually unhurt and uninjured, while the murderer is swinging by the neck for the bloody deed!"

The judge,—who it must be understood was a real existence, and who had no small reputation in his day in the south,—proceeded to establish the correctness of his opinions by authorities and argument, with all of which, doubtlessly, the bar were exceedingly delighted; but, to provide them in this place would only be to interfere with our own progress. James Grayling, however, was not satisfied to wait the slow processes which were suggested for coming at the truth. Even the wisdom of the judge was lost upon him, possibly, for the simple reason that he did not comprehend it. But the ridicule of the culprit's lawyer stung him to the quick, and he muttered to himself, more than once, a determination "to lick the life out of that impudent chap's leather." But this was not his only resolve. There was one which he proceeded to put into instant execution, and that was to seek the body of his murdered friend in the spot where he fancied it might be found —namely, the dark and dismal bay where the spectre had made its appearance to his eyes.

The suggestion was approved—though he did not need this to prompt his resolution—by his mother and uncle, Sparkman. The latter determined to be his companion, and he was farther accompanied by the sheriff's officer who had arrested the suspected felon. Before daylight, on the morning after the examination before the judge had taken place, and when Macleod had been remanded to prison, James Grayling started on his journey. His fiery zeal received additional force at every added moment of delay, and his eager spurring brought him at an early hour after noon, to the neighbourhood of the spot through which his search was to be made. When his companions and himself drew nigh, they were all at a loss in which direction first to proceed. The bay was one of those massed forests, whose wall of thorns, vines, and close tenacious shrubs, seemed to defy invasion. To the eye of the townsman it was so forbidding that he pronounced it absolutely impenetrable. But James was not to be baffled. He led them round it, taking the very course which he had pursued the night when the revelation was made him; he showed them the very tree at whose foot he had sunk when the supernatural torpor—as he himself esteemed it—began to fall upon him; he then pointed out the spot, some twenty steps distant, at which the spectre made his appearance. To this spot they then proceeded in a body, and essayed an entrance, but were so discouraged by the difficulties at the outset that all, James not excepted, concluded that neither the murderer nor his victim could possibly have found entrance there.

But, lo! a marvel! Such it seemed, at the first blush, to all the party.

While they stood confounded and indecisive, undetermined in which way to move, a sudden flight of wings was heard, even from the centre of the bay, at a little distance above the spot where they had striven for entrance. They looked up, and beheld about fifty buzzards—those notorious domestic vultures of the south—ascending from the interior of the bay, and perching along upon the branches of the loftier trees by which it was overhung. Even were the character of these birds less known, the particular business in which they had just then been engaged, was betrayed by huge gobbets of flesh which some of them had borne aloft in their flight, and still continued to rend with beak and bill, as they tottered upon the branches where they stood. A piercing scream issued from the lips of James Grayling as he beheld this sight, and strove to scare the offensive birds from their repast.

"The poor major! the poor major!" was the involuntary and agonized exclamation of the youth. "Did I ever think he would come to this!"

The search, thus guided and encouraged, was pressed with renewed diligence and spirit; and, at length, an opening was found through which it was evident that a body of considerable size had but recently gone. The branches were broken from the small shrub trees, and the undergrowth trodden into the earth. They followed this path, and, as is the case commonly with waste tracts of this description, the density of the growth diminished sensibly at every step they took, till they reached a little pond, which, though circumscribed in area, and full of cypresses, yet proved to be singularly deep. Indeed, it was an alligator-hole, where, in all probability, a numerous tribe of these reptiles had their dwelling. Here, on the edge of the pond, they discovered the object which had drawn the keen-sighted vultures to their feast, in the body of a horse, which James Grayling at once identified as that of Major Spencer. The carcass of the animal was already very much torn and lacerated. The eyes were plucked out, and the animal completely disembowelled. Yet, on examination, it was not difficult to discover the manner of his death. This had been effected by fire-arms. Two bullets had passed through his skull, just above the eyes, either of which must have been fatal. The murderer had led the horse to the spot, and committed the cruel deed where his body was found. The search was now continued for that of the owner, but for some time it proved ineffectual. At length, the keen eyes of James Grayling detected, amidst a heap of moss and green sedge that rested beside an overthrown tree, whose branches jutted into the pond, a whitish, but discoloured object, that did not seem native to the place. Bestriding the fallen tree, he was enabled to reach this object, which, with a burst of grief, he announced to the distant party was the hand and arm of his unfortunate friend, the wristband of the shirt being the conspicuous object which had first caught his eye. Grasping this, he drew the corse, which had been thrust beneath the branches of the tree, to the surface; and, with the assistance of his uncle, it was finally brought to the dry land. Here it underwent a careful examination. The head was very much disfigured;

the skull was fractured in several places by repeated blows of some ·hard instrument, inflicted chiefly from behind. A closer inspection revealed a bullet-hole in the abdomen, the first wound, in all probability, which the unfortunate gentleman received, and by which he was, perhaps, tumbled from his horse. The blows on the head would seem to have been unnecessary, unless the murderer—whose proceedings appeared to have been singularly deliberate,—was resolved upon making "assurance doubly sure." But, as if the watchful Providence had meant that nothing should be left doubtful which might tend to the complete conviction of the criminal, the constable stumbled upon the butt of the broken pistol which had been found in Macleod's trunk. This he picked up on the edge of the pond in which the corse had been discovered, and while James Grayling and his uncle, Sparkman, were engaged in drawing it from the water. The place where the fragment was discovered at once denoted the pistol as the instrument by which the final blows were inflicted. " 'Fore God," said the judge to the criminal, as these proofs were submitted on the trial, "you may be a very innocent man after all, as, by my faith, I do think there have been many murderers before you; but you ought, nevertheless, to be hung as an example to all other persons who suffer such strong proofs of guilt to follow their innocent misdoings. Gentlemen of the jury, if this person, Macleod or Macnab, didn't murder Major Spencer, either you or I did; and you must now decide which of us it is! I say, gentlemen of the jury, either you, or I, or the prisoner at the bar, murdered this man; and if you have any doubts which of us it was, it is but justice and mercy that you should give the prisoner the benefit of your doubts; and so find your verdict. But, before God, should you find him not guilty, Mr. Attorney there can scarcely do anything wiser than to put us all upon trial for the deed."

The jury, it may be scarcely necessary to add, perhaps under certain becoming fears of an alternative such as his honour had suggested, brought in a verdict of "Guilty," without leaving the panel; and Macnab, *alias* Macleod, was hung at White Point, Charleston, somewhere about the year 178—.

"And here," said my grandmother, devoutly, "you behold a proof of God's watchfulness to see that murder should not be hidden, and that the murderer should not escape. You see that he sent the spirit of the murdered man—since, by no other mode could the truth have been revealed—to declare the crime, and to discover the criminal. But for that ghost, Macnab would have got off to Scotland, and probably have been living to this very day on the money that he took from the person of the poor major."

As the old lady finished the ghost story, which, by the way, she had been tempted to relate for the fiftieth time in order to combat my father's ridicule of such superstitions, the latter took up the thread of the narrative.

"Now, my son," said he, "as you have heard all that your grandmother has to say on this subject, I will proceed to show you what you have to believe, and what not. It is true that Macnab murdered Spencer in the manner related; that James Grayling made the discovery and prosecuted the pursuit; found the body and brought the felon to justice; that Macnab suffered death, and confessed the crime; alleging that he was moved to do so, as well because of the money that he suspected Spencer to have in his possession, as because of the hate which he felt for a man who had been particularly bold and active in cutting up a party of Scotch loyalists to which he belonged, on the borders of North Carolina. But the appearance of the spectre was nothing more than the work of a quick imagination, added to a shrewd and correct judgment. James Grayling saw no ghost, in fact, but such as was in his own mind; and, though the instance was one of a most remarkable character, one of singular combination, and well depending circumstances, still, I think it is to be accounted for by natural and very simple laws."

The old lady was indignant.

"And how could he see the ghost just on the edge of the same bay where the murder had been committed, and where the body of the murdered man even then was lying?"

My father did not directly answer the demand, but proceeded thus:—

"James Grayling, as we know, mother, was a very ardent, impetuous, sagacious man. He had the sanguine, the race-horse temperament. He was generous, always prompt and ready, and one who never went backward. What he did, he did quickly, boldly, and thoroughly! He never shrank from trouble of any kind: nay, he rejoiced in the constant encounter with difficulty and trial; and his was the temper which commands and enthrals mankind. He felt deeply and intensely whatever occupied his mind, and when he parted from his friend he brooded over little else than their past communion and the great distance by which they were to be separated. The dull travelling wagon-gait at which he himself was compelled to go, was a source of annoyance to him; and he became sullen, all the day, after the departure of his friend. When, on the evening of the next day, he came to the house where it was natural to expect that Major Spencer would have slept the night before, and he learned the fact that no one stopped there but the Scotchman, Macnab, we see that he was struck with the circumstance. He mutters it over to himself, "Strange, where the major could have gone!" His mind then naturally reverts to the character of the Scotchman; to the opinions and suspicions which had been already expressed of him by his uncle, and felt by himself. They had all, previously, come to the full conviction that Macnab was, and had always been, a tory, in spite of his protestations. His mind next, and very naturally, reverted to the insecurity of the highways; the general dangers of travelling at that period; the frequency of crime, and the number of desperate men who were everywhere to be met with. The very employment in which he was then engaged, in scouting the woods for the protection of the camp, was calculated to bring such reflections to his mind. If these precautions were considered necessary for the safety of persons so poor, so wanting in those possessions which might prompt cupidity to crime, how much more necessary were precautions in the case of a wealthy gentleman like Major Spencer! He then remembered the conversation with the major at the camp-fire, when they fancied that the Scotchman was sleeping. How natural to think then, that he was all the while awake; and, if awake, he must have heard him speak of the wealth of his companion. True, the major, with more prudence than himself, denied that he had any money about him, more than would bear his expenses to the city; but such an assurance was natural enough to the lips of a traveller who knew the dangers of the country. That the man, Macnab, was not a person to be trusted, was the equal impression of Joel Sparkman and his nephew from the first. The probabilities were strong that he would rob and perhaps murder, if he might hope to do so with impunity; and as the youth made the circuit of the bay in the darkness and solemn stillness of the night, its gloomy depths and mournful shadows, naturally gave rise to such reflections as would be equally active in the mind of a youth, and of one somewhat familiar with the arts and usages of strife. He would see that the spot was just the one in which a practised partisan would delight to set an ambush for an unwary foe. There ran the public road, with a little sweep, around two-thirds of the extent of its dense and impenetrable thickets. The ambush could lie concealed, and at ten steps command the bosom of its victim. Here, then, you perceive that the mind of James Grayling, stimulated by an active and sagacious judgment, had by gradual and reasonable stages come to these conclusions: that Major Spencer was an object to tempt a robber; that the country was full of robbers; that Macnab was one of them; that this was the very spot in which a deed of blood could be most easily committed, and most easily concealed; and, one important fact, that gave strength and coherence to the whole, that Major Spencer had not reached a well-known point of destination, while Macnab had.

"With these thoughts, thus closely linked together, the youth forgets the limits of his watch and his circuit. This fact, alone, proves how active his imagination had become. It leads him forward, brooding more and more on the subject, until, in the very exhaustion of his body, he sinks down beneath a tree. He sinks down and falls asleep; and in his sleep, what before was plausible conjecture, becomes fact, and the creative properties of his imagination give form and vitality to all his fancies. These forms are bold, broad, and deeply coloured, in due proportion with the degree of force which they receive from probability. Here, he sees the image of his friend; but, you will remark—and this should almost conclusively satisfy any mind that all that he sees is the work of his imagination,—that, though Spencer tells him that he is murdered, and by Macnab, he does not tell him how, in what manner, or with what weapons. Though he sees him pale and ghostlike, he does not see, nor can he say, where his wounds are! He sees his pale features distinctly, and his garments are bloody. Now, had he seen the spectre in the true appearances of death, as he was subsequently found, he would not have been able to discern his features, which were battered, according to his own account, almost out of all shape of humanity, and covered with mud; while his clothes would have streamed with mud and water, rather than with blood."

"Ah!" exclaimed the old lady, my grandmother, "it's hard to make you believe anything that you don't see; you are like Saint Thomas in the Scriptures; but how do you propose to account for his knowing that the Scotchman was on board the Falmouth packet? Answer to that!"

"That is not a more difficult matter than any of the rest. You forget that in the dialogue which took place between James and Major Spencer at the camp, the latter told him that he was about to take passage for Europe in the Falmouth packet, which then lay in Charleston harbour, and was about to sail. Macnab heard all that."

"True enough, and likely enough," returned the old lady; "but, though you show that it was Major Spencer's intention to go to Europe in the Falmouth packet, that will not show that it was also the intention of the murderer."

"Yet what more probable, and how natural for James Grayling to imagine such a thing! In the first place he knew that Macnab was a Briton; he felt convinced that he was a tory; and the inference was immediate, that such a person would scarcely have remained long in a country where such characters laboured under so much odium, disfranchisement, and constant danger from popular tumults. The fact that Macnab was compelled to disguise his true sentiments, and affect those of the people against whom he fought so vindictively, shows what was his sense of the danger which he incurred. Now, it is not unlikely that Macnab was quite as well aware that the Falmouth packet was in Charleston, and about to sail, as Major Spencer. No doubt he was pursuing the same journey, with the same object, and had he not murdered Spencer, they would, very likely, have been fellow-passengers together to Europe. But, whether he knew the fact before or not, he probably heard it stated by Spencer while he seemed to be sleeping; and, even supposing that he did not then know, it was enough that he found this to be the fact on reaching the city. It was an after-thought to fly to Europe with his ill gotten spoils; and whatever may have appeared a politic course to the criminal, would be a probable conjecture in the mind of him by whom he was suspected. The whole story is one of strong probabilities which happened to be verified; and if proving anything, proves only that which we know—that James Grayling was a man of remarkably sagacious judgment, and quick, daring imagination. This quality of imagination, by the way, when possessed very strongly in connexion with shrewd common sense and well-balanced general faculties, makes that particular kind of intellect which, because of its promptness and powers of creation and combination, we call genius. It is genius only which can make ghosts, and James Grayling was a genius. He never, my son, saw any other ghosts than those of his own making!"

I heard my father with great patience to the end, though he seemed very tedious. He had taken a great deal of pains to destroy one of my greatest sources of pleasure. I need not add that I continued to believe in the ghost, and, with my grandmother, to reject the philosophy. It was more easy to believe the one than to comprehend the other.

EDGAR ALLAN POE

(1809–1849)

The one major literary artist of the Old South was Edgar Allan Poe. Little honored in his lifetime, and forced to eke out a precarious living as a magazinist, he wrote poetry and fiction that are widely read and admired, and as a critic he produced the first truly professional literary criticism written in America. Through the French Symbolists, who saw in his grotesqueries and his images of darkness and pain the emblems of a profound insight into the confusion and irrationality of the human situation, Poe played an important role in the creation of modern literary sensibility. "Poe's universal glory," wrote the French poet Paul Valery, "is weak or contested only in his native country and England. This Anglo-Saxon poet is strangely neglected by his own race."

Poe was born in Boston, Massachusetts. He was three years old when his mother died in Richmond, Virginia, and was reared by a Scots-born merchant, John Allan. For five years, 1815 to 1820, Allan lived in England, where Poe attended school. Thereafter Poe grew up in Richmond and was sent to the University of Virginia in 1826. Allan's refusal to pay Poe's gambling debts led Poe to withdraw from the University after less than a year. He enlisted in the army, soon rose to the rank of sergeant major, and in 1830 was appointed to West Point. By this time, however, his rift with Allan—who had never formally adopted him—had become irreparable.

Poe was determined to be a writer. He had already published *Tamerlane and Minor Poems* in Boston in 1827. At West Point he published another book, *Poems*, in 1831 and shortly afterward he left the Military Academy by court martial, for having deliberately missed classes and drill, after Allan had refused to help him resign.

In Baltimore, where he lived from 1831 to 1835 with an aunt, Mrs. Maria Clemm, he wrote a set of stories that impressed the judges of a literary prize sponsored by the *Baltimore Sunday Visiter*. One of them, the novelist John

Pendleton Kennedy, took him under his care, encouraging him and helping to arrange a position for him on the staff of the *Southern Literary Messenger* in Richmond.

Poe was successful as an editor, greatly increased the magazine's circulation, and, with a series of often-slashing critical reviews, attracted considerable attention to the publication. However, the magazine's publisher, T.W. White, was embarrassed by his young editor's literary tactics and that, coupled with Poe's tendency to drink to excess, brought an end to the arrangement. In 1838 Poe and his young bride, his cousin Virginia Clemm whom he married when she was only 13, left for New York. There and in Philadelphia he did editorial work, wrote for magazines, published fiction and poetry, and engaged in the literary wars of the period—incurring the lasting enmity of certain influential critics. When Virginia died in 1847 he felt the loss deeply, and his drinking increased.

He wanted most to found a new magazine, and he drew up plans and a prospectus but it never materialized. In 1849 he went to Richmond, apparently to become engaged to his childhood sweetheart, Sarah Elmira Shelton, now a widow. Stopping in Baltimore on his way back, he seems to have become involved with some political ward-heelers who got him drunk in order to march him to the polls and have him vote. He was discovered exhausted and ill on the streets, only semiconscious, and died on October 7, 1849.

The poems, stories, and criticism that Poe wrote would constitute an impressive achievement even if his circumstances had not forced him to do hack writing to make a living. Throughout his career he published books steadily: *The Narrative of Arthur Gordon Pym* in 1838, *Tales of the Grotesque and Arabesque* in 1841, *Tales* and *The Raven and Other Poems* in 1845. He more or less invented the modern detective story with his stories of the French sleuth C. Auguste Dupin. His short fiction constituted a new sharpening and focusing of fiction for magazine use; he was one of the formative forces in the development of the short story. As a literary critic Poe emphasized craftsmanship at a time when almost all American literary criticism was moralistic and idealistic. The province of the poem, he declared, was Beauty, rather than Truth.

In his essay "The Philosophy of Composition" he set out to show that craftsmanship and conscious design were central to the poetic process. Whether or not the description he gives of how he wrote "The Raven" is literal, it obviously is what he would have liked to think was his way of writing. Whether in prose or poetry, his work is filled with passion, emotion, intense feelings of all kinds; craftsmanship would seem to have been his means for confronting and disciplining a powerfully and painfully emotional sensibility. At all times in his writing the irrational, the horrible, and the fantastic appear to be held in check only by a determinedly conscious effort of technique. It is this that so appealed to the French poets, who saw in his work the delineation of the dark, sinister side of the human condition that lurked under the optimistic moralizing and fervent espousals of Progress that characterized the nineteenth century.

SONNET—TO SCIENCE

Science! true daughter of Old Time thou art!
   Who alterest all things with thy peering eyes.
Why preyest thou thus upon the poet's heart,
   Vulture, whose wings are dull realities?
How should he love thee? or how deem thee wise?
   Who wouldst not leave him in his wandering
To seek for treasure in the jewelled skies,
   Albeit he soared with an undaunted wing?
Hast thou not dragged Diana from her car?
   And driven the Hamadryad from the wood
To seek a shelter in some happier star?
   Hast thou not torn the Naiad from her flood,
The Elfin from the green grass, and from me
The summer dream beneath the tamarind tree?

1829

ROMANCE

Romance, who loves to nod and sing,
With drowsy head and folded wing,
Among the green leaves as they shake
Far down within some shadowy lake,
To me a painted paroquet
Hath been—a most familiar bird—
Taught me my alphabet to say—
To lisp my very earliest word
While in the wild wood I did lie,
A child—with a most knowing eye.
Of late, eternal Condor years
So shake the very Heaven on high
With tumult as they thunder by,
I have no time for idle cares
Through gazing on the unquiet sky.
And when an hour with calmer wings
Its down upon my spirit flings—
That little time with lyre and rhyme

To while away—forbidden things!
My heart would feel to be a crime
Unless it trembled with the strings.

1829

TO HELEN

Helen, thy beauty is to me
   Like those Nicéans barks of yore,
That gently, o'er a perfumed sea,
   The weary, way-worn wanderer bore
   To his own native shore.

On desperate seas long wont to roam,
   Thy hyacinth hair, thy classic face,
Thy Naiad airs have brought me home
   To the glory that was Greece
And the grandeur that was Rome.

Lo! in yon brilliant window-niche
   How statue-like I see thee stand!
   The agate lamp within thy hand,
Ah, Psyche, from the regions which
   Are Holy-Land!

1831

ISRAFEL*

In Heaven a spirit doth dwell
"Whose heart-strings are a lute";
None sing so wildly well
As the angel Israfel,
And the giddy stars (so legends tell)
Ceasing their hymns, attend the spell
   Of his voice, all mute.

Tottering above
   In her highest noon,
   The enamoured moon
Blushes with love,
   While, to listen, the red levin
   (With the rapid Pleiads, even,

---

*And the angel Israfel, whose heart-strings are a lute, and who has the sweetest voice of all God's creatures"—Koran [Poe's note].

EDGAR ALLAN POE

Which were seven,)
　Pauses in Heaven.

And they say (the starry choir
　And the other listening things)
That Israfeli's fire
Is owing to that lyre
　By which he sits and sings—
The trembling living wire
　Of those unusual strings.

But the skies that angel trod,
　Where deep thoughts are a duty—
Where Love's a grown up God—
　Where the Houri glances are
Imbued with all the beauty
　Which we worship in a star.

Therefore, thou are not wrong,
　Israfeli, who despisest
An unimpassioned song;
To thee the laurels belong,
　Best bard, because the wisest!
Merrily live, and long!

The ecstasies above
　With thy burning measures suit—
Thy grief, thy joy, thy hate, thy love,
　With the fervour of thy lute—
　Well may the stars be mute!
Yes, Heaven is thine; but this
　Is a world of sweets and sours;
　Our flowers are merely—flowers,
And the shadow of thy perfect bliss
　Is the sunshine of ours.

If I could dwell
Where Israfel
　Hath dwelt, and he where I,
He might not sing so wildly well
　A mortal melody,
While a bolder note than this might swell
　From my lyre within the sky.

1831

DREAM-LAND

By a route obscure and lonely,
Haunted by ill angels only,
Where an Eidolon, named NIGHT,
On a black throne reigns upright,
I have reached these lands but newly
From an ultimate dim Thule
From a wild weird clime that lieth, sublime,
    Out of SPACE—out of TIME.

Bottomless vales and boundless floods,
And chasms, and caves, and Titan woods,
With forms that no man can discover
For the dews that drip all over;
Mountains toppling evermore
Into seas without a shore;
Seas that restlessly aspire,
Surging, unto skies of fire;
Lakes that endlessly outspread
Their lone waters—lone and dead,—
Their still waters—still and chilly
With the snows of the lolling lily.

By the lakes that thus outspread
Their lone waters, lone and dead,—
Their sad waters, sad and chilly
With the snows of the lolling lily,—
By the mountains—near the river
Murmuring lowly, murmuring ever,—
By the grey woods,—by the swamp
Where the toad and the newt encamp,—
By the dismal tarns and pools
    Where dwell the Ghouls,—
By each spot the most unholy—
In each nook most melancholy,—
There the traveller meets aghast
Sheeted Memories of the Past—
Shrouded forms that start and sigh
As they pass the wanderer by—
White-robed forms of friends long given,
In agony, to the Earth—and Heaven.

For the heart whose woes are legion
'Tis a peaceful, soothing region—

EDGAR ALLAN POE

For the spirit that walks in shadow
'Tis—oh 'tis an Eldorado!
But the traveller, travelling through it,
May not—dare not openly view it;
Never its mysteries are exposed
To the weak human eye unclosed;
So wills its King, who hath forbid
The uplifting of the fringèd lid;
And thus the sad Soul that here passes
Beholds it but through darkened glasses.

By a route obscure and lonely,
Haunted by ill angels only,
Where an Eidolon, named NIGHT,
On a black throne reigns upright,
I have wandered home but newly
From this ultimate dim Thule.

1844

THE RAVEN

Once upon a midnight dreary, while I pondered, weak and weary,
Over many a quaint and curious volume of forgotten lore,
While I nodded, nearly napping, suddenly there came a tapping,
As of some one gently rapping, rapping at my chamber door.
" 'Tis some visitor," I muttered, "tapping at my chamber door—
      Only this, and nothing more."

Ah, distinctly I remember it was in the bleak December,
And each separate dying ember wrought its ghost upon the floor.
Eagerly I wished the morrow;—vainly I had sought to borrow
From my books surcease of sorrow—sorrow for the lost Lenore—
For the rare and radiant maiden whom the angels name Lenore—
      Nameless here for evermore.

And the silken sad uncertain rustling of each purple curtain
Thrilled me—filled me with fantastic terrors never felt before;
So that now, to still the beating of my heart, I stood repeating,
" 'Tis some visitor entreating entrance at my chamber door—
Some late visitor entreating entrance at my chamber door;—
      This it is, and nothing more."

Presently my soul grew stronger; hesitating then no longer,
"Sir," said I, "or Madam, truly your forgiveness I implore;
But the fact is I was napping, and so gently you came rapping,

THE RAVEN

And so faintly you came tapping, tapping at my chamber door,
That I scarce was sure I heard you"—here I opened wide the door;—
       Darkness there, and nothing more.

Deep into that darkness peering, long I stood there wondering, fearing,
Doubting, dreaming dreams no moral ever dared to dream before;
But the silence was unbroken, and the darkness gave no token,
And the only word there spoken was the whispered word, "Lenore!"
This I whispered, and an echo murmured back the word, "Lenore!"—
      Merely this, and nothing more.

Back into the chamber turning, all my soul within me burning,
Soon I heard again a tapping somewhat louder than before.
"Surely," said I, "surely that is something at my window lattice;
Let me see, then, what thereat is, and this mystery explore—
Let my heart be still a moment and this mystery explore;—
      'Tis the wind and nothing more!"

Open here I flung the shutter, when, with many a flirt and flutter,
In there stepped a stately raven of the saintly days of yore;
Not the least obeisance made he; not an instant stopped or stayed he;
But, with mien of lord or lady, perched above my chamber door—
Perched upon a bust of Pallas just above my chamber door—
      Perched, and sat, and nothing more.

Then this ebony bird beguiling my sad fancy into smiling,
By the grave and stern decorum of the countenance it wore,
"Though thy crest be shorn and shaven, thou," I said, "art sure no craven,
Ghastly grim and ancient raven wandering from the Nightly shore—
Tell me what thy lordly name is on the Night's Plutonian shore!"
      Quoth the raven, "Nevermore."

Much I marvelled this ungainly fowl to hear discourse so plainly,
Though its answer little meaning—little relevancy bore;
For we cannot help agreeing that no living human being
Ever yet was blessed with seeing bird above his chamber door—
Bird or beast upon the sculptured bust above his chamber door,
      With such name as "Nevermore."

But the raven, sitting lonely on the placid bust, spoke only
That one word, as if his soul in that one word he did outpour.
Nothing farther then he uttered—not a feather then he fluttered—
Till I scarcely more than muttered "Other friends have flown before—
On the morrow *he* will leave me, as my hopes have flown before."
      Then the bird said "Nevermore."

Startled at the stillness broken by reply so aptly spoken,

"Doubtless," said I, "what it utters is its only stock and store
Caught from some unhappy master whom unmerciful Disaster
Followed fast and followed faster till his songs one burden bore—
Till the dirges of his Hope that melancholy burden bore
        Of 'Never—nevermore.' "

But the raven still beguiling all my sad soul into smiling,
Straight I wheeled a cushioned seat in front of bird and bust and door;
Then, upon the velvet sinking, I betook myself to linking
Fancy unto fancy, thinking what this ominous bird of yore—
What this grim, ungainly, ghastly, gaunt, and ominous bird of yore
        Meant in croaking "Nevermore."

This I sat engaged in guessing, but no syllable expressing
To the fowl whose fiery eyes now burned into my bosom's core;
This and more I sat divining, with my head at ease reclining
On the cushion's velvet lining that the lamplight gloated o'er,
But whose velvet violet lining with the lamplight gloating o'er,
        She shall press, ah, nevermore!

Then, methought, the air grew denser, perfumed from an unseen censer
Swung by angels whose faint foot-falls tinkled on the tufted floor.
"Wretch," I cried, "thy God hath lent thee—by these angels he hath sent
    thee
Respite—respite and nepenthe from thy memories of Lenore!
Quaff, oh quaff this kind nepenthe and forget this lost Lenore!"
        Quoth the raven, "Nevermore."

"Prophet!" said I, "thing of evil!—prophet still, if bird or devil!—
Whether Tempter sent, or whether tempest tossed thee here ashore,
Desolate, yet all undaunted, on this desert land enchanted—
On this home by Horror haunted—tell me truly, I implore—
Is there—*is* there balm in Gilead?—tell me—tell me, I implore!"
        Quoth the raven, "Nevermore."

"Prophet!" said I, "thing of evil—prophet still, if bird or devil!
By that Heaven that bends above us—by that God we both adore—
Tell this soul with sorrow laden if, within the distant Aidenn,
It shall clasp a sainted maiden whom the angels name Lenore—
Clasp a rare and radiant maiden whom the angels name Lenore."
        Quoth the raven, "Nevermore."

"Be that word our sign of parting, bird or fiend!" I shrieked, upstarting—
"Get thee back into the tempest and the Night's Plutonian shore!
Leave no black plume as a token of that lie thy soul hath spoken!
Leave my loneliness unbroken!—quit the bust above my door!
Take thy beak from out my heart, and take thy form from off my door."

ULALUME

Quoth the raven, "Nevermore."

And the raven, never flitting, still is sitting, still is sitting
On the pallid bust of Pallas just above my chamber door;
And his eyes have all the seeming of a demon's that is dreaming,
And the lamp-light o'er him streaming throws his shadow on the floor;
And my soul from out that shadow that lies floating on the floor
        Shall be lifted—nevermore!

1845

ULALUME

The skies they were ashen and sober;
    The leaves they were crispèd and sere—
    The leaves they were withering and sere;
It was night, in the lonesome October
    Of my most immemorial year;
It was hard by the dim lake of Auber,
    In the misty mid region of Weir—
It was down by the dank tarn of Auber,
    In the ghoul-haunted woodland of Weir.

Here once, through an alley Titanic,
    Of cypress, I roamed with my Soul—
    Of cypress, with Psyche, my Soul.
These were days when my heart was volcanic
    As the scoriac rivers that roll—
    As the lavas that restlessly roll
Their sulphurous currents down Yaanek
    In the ultimate climes of the pole—
That groan as they roll down Mount Yaanek
    In the realms of the boreal pole.

Our talk had been serious and sober,
    But our thoughts they were palsied and sere—
    Our memories were treacherous and sere—
For we knew not the month was October,
And we marked not the night of the year
    (Ah, night of all nights in the year!)—
We noted not the dim lake of Auber—
    (Though once we had journeyed down here)—
Remembered not the dank tarn of Auber,
    Nor the ghoul-haunted woodland of Weir.

And now, as the night was senescent

And the star-dials pointed to morn—
   As the star-dials hinted of morn—
At the end of our path a liquescent
   And nebulous lustre was born,
Out of which a miraculous crescent
   Arose with a duplicate horn—
Astarte's bediamonded crescent
   Distinct with its duplicate horn.

And I said—"She is warmer than Dian;
   She rolls through an ether of sighs—
   She revels in a region of sighs—
She has seen that the tears are not dry on
   These cheeks, where the worm never dies,
And has come past the stars of the Lion,
   To point us the path to the skies—
   To the Lethean peace of the skies—
Come up, in despite of the Lion,
   To shine on us with her bright eyes—
Come up through the lair of the Lion,
   With love in her luminous eyes."

But Psyche, uplifting her finger,
   Said—"Sadly this star I mistrust—
   Her pallor I strangely mistrust:—
Oh, hasten!—oh, let us not linger!
   Oh, fly!—let us fly!—for we must."
In terror she spoke, letting sink her
   Wings till they trailed in the dust—
In agony sobbed, letting sink her
   Plumes till they trailed in the dust—
   Till they sorrowfully trailed in the dust.

I replied: "This is nothing but dreaming:
   Let us on by this tremulous light!
   Let us bathe in this crystalline light!
Its Sibylic splendor is beaming
   With Hope and in Beauty to-night:—
   See!—it flickers up the sky through the night!
Ah, we safely may trust to its gleaming,
   And be sure it will lead us aright—
We safely may trust to a gleaming,
   That cannot but guide us aright,
   Since it flickers up to Heaven through the night."

Thus I pacified Psyche and kissed her,

And tempted her out of her gloom—
And conquered her scruples and gloom;
And we passed to the end of the vista,
   But were stopped by the door of a tomb—
   By the door of a legended tomb;
And I said—"What is written, sweet sister,
   On the door of this legended tomb?"
She replied: "Ulalume—Ulalume—
   'Tis the vault of thy lost Ulalume!"

Then my heart it grew ashen and sober
   As the leaves that were crispèd and sere—
   As the leaves that were withering and sere.
And I cried—"It was surely October
   On *this* very night of last year
   That I journeyed—I journeyed down here—
   That I brought a dread burden down here—
   On this night of all nights of the year,
   Ah, what demon has tempted me here?
Well I know, now, this dim lake of Auber—
   This misty mid region of Weir—
Well I know, now, this dank tarn of Auber,
   This ghoul-haunted woodland of Weir."

Said we, then—the two, then: "Ah, can it
   Have been that the woodlandish ghouls—
   The pitiful, the merciful ghouls—
To bar up our way and to ban it
   From the secret that lies in these wolds—
   From the thing that lies hidden in these wolds—
Have drawn up the spectre of a planet
   From the limbo of lunary souls—
This sinfully scintillant planet
   From the Hell of the planetary souls?"

1847

THE FALL OF THE HOUSE OF USHER

Son cœur est un luth suspendu;
Sitôt qu'on le touche il résonne.

De Béranger

During the whole of a dull, dark, and soundless day in the autumn of the year, when the clouds hung oppressively low in the heavens, I had b,een passing alone, on horseback, through a singularly dreary tract of country; and at length found myself, as the shades of the evening drew on, within view of the melancholy House of Usher. I know not how it was—but, with the first glimpse of the building, a sense of insufferable gloom pervaded my spirit. I say insufferable; for the feeling was unrelieved by any of that half-pleasurable, because poetic, sentiment, with which the mind usually receives even the sternest natural images of the desolate or terrible. I looked upon the scene before me—upon the mere house, and the simple landscape features of the domain—upon the bleak walls—upon the vacant eye-like windows—upon a few rank sedges—and upon a few white trunks of decayed trees—with an utter depression of soul which I can compare to no earthly sensation more properly than to the after-dream of the reveller upon opium—the bitter lapse into everyday life—the hideous dropping off of the veil. There was an iciness, a sinking, a sickening of the heart—an unredeemed dreariness of thought which no goading of the imagination could torture into aught of the sublime. What was it—I paused to think—what was it that so unnerved me in the contemplation of the House of Usher? It was a mystery all insoluble; nor could I grapple with the shadowy fancies that crowded upon me as I pondered. I was forced to fall back upon the unsatisfactory conclusion, that while, beyond doubt, there *are* combinations of very simple natural objects which have the power of thus affecting us, still the analysis of this power lies among considerations beyond our depth. It was possible, I reflected, that a mere different arrangement of the particulars of the scene, of the details of the picture, would be sufficient to modify, or perhaps to annihilate its capacity for sorrowful impression; and, acting upon this idea, I reined my horse to the precipitous brink of a black and lurid tarn that lay in unruffled lustre by the dwelling, and gazed down—but with a shudder even more thrilling than before—upon the remodelled and inverted images of the gray sedge, and the ghastly tree-stems, and the vacant and eye-like windows.

Nevertheless, in this mansion of gloom I now proposed to myself a sojourn of some weeks. Its proprietor, Roderick Usher, had been one of my boon companions in boyhood; but many years had elapsed since our last meeting. A letter, however, had lately reached me in a distant part of the country—a letter from him—which, in its wildly importunate nature, had admitted of no other than a personal reply. The MS. gave evidence of nervous agitation. The writer spoke of acute bodily illness—of a mental disorder which oppressed him—and of an earnest desire to see me, as his best, and indeed his only personal friend, with a view of attempting, by the cheerfulness of my society, some alleviation of his malady. It was the manner in which all this, and much more, was said—it was the apparent *heart* that went with his request—which allowed me no room for hesitation; and I accordingly obeyed forthwith what I still considered a very singular summons.

Although, as boys, we had been even intimate associates, yet I really knew little of my friend. His reserve had been always excessive and habitual. I was aware, however, that his very ancient family had been noted, time out of mind, for a peculiar sensibility of temperament, displaying itself, through long ages, in many works of exalted art, and manifested, of late, in repeated deeds of munificent yet unobtrusive charity, as well as in a passionate devotion to the intricacies, perhaps even more than to the orthodox and easily recognizable beauties, of musical science. I had learned, too, the very remarkable fact, that the stem of the Usher race, all time-honored as it was, had put forth, at no period, any enduring branch; in other words, that the entire family lay in the direct line of descent, and had always, with very trifling and very temporary variation, so lain. It was this deficiency, I considered, while running over in thought the perfect keeping of the character of the premises with the accredited character of the people, and while speculating upon the possible influence which the one, in the long lapse of centuries, might have exercised upon the other—it was this deficiency, perhaps, of collateral issue, and the consequent undeviating transmission, from sire to son, of the patrimony with the name, which had, at length, so identified the two as to merge the original title of the estate in the quaint and equivocal appellation of the "House of Usher"—an appellation which seemed to include, in the minds of the peasantry who used it, both the family and the family mansion.

I have said that the sole effect of my somewhat childish experiment —that of looking down within the tarn—had been to deepen the first singular impression. There can be no doubt that the consciousness of the rapid increase of my superstition—for why should I not so term it?—served mainly to accelerate the increase itself. Such, I have long known, is the paradoxical law of all sentiments having terror as a basis. And it might have been for this reason only, that, when I again uplifted my eyes to the house itself, from its image in the pool, there grew in my mind a strange fancy—a fancy so ridiculous, indeed, that I but mention it to show the vivid force of the sensations which oppressed me. I had so worked upon my imagination as really to believe that about the whole mansion and domain there hung an atmosphere peculiar to themselves and their immediate vicinity—an atmosphere which had no affinity with the air of heaven, but which had reeked up from the decayed trees, and the gray wall, and the silent tarn—a pestilent and mystic vapor, dull, sluggish, faintly discernible, and leaden-hued.

Shaking off from my spirit what *must* have been a dream, I scanned more narrowly the real aspect of the building. Its principal feature seemed to be that of an excessive antiquity. The discoloration of ages had been great. Minute fungi overspread the whole exterior, hanging in a fine tangled web-

EDGAR ALLAN POE

work from the eaves. Yet all this was apart from any extraordinary dilapidation. No portion of the masonry had fallen; and there appeared to be a wild inconsistency between its still perfect adaptation of parts, and the crumbling condition of the individual stones. In this there was much that reminded me of the specious totality of old wood-work which has rotted for long years in some neglected vault, with no disturbance from the breath of the external air. Beyond this indication of extensive decay, however, the fabric gave little token of instability. Perhaps the eye of a scrutinizing observer might have discovered a barely perceptible fissure, which, extending from the roof of the building in front, made its way down the wall in a zigzag direction, until it became lost in the sullen waters of the tarn.

Noticing these things, I rode over a short causeway to the house. A servant in waiting took my horse, and I entered the Gothic archway of the hall. A valet, of stealthy step, thence conducted me, in silence, through many dark and intricate passages in my progress to the *studio* of his master. Much that I encountered on the way contributed, I know not how, to heighten the vague sentiments of which I have already spoken. While the objects around me—while the carvings of the ceilings, the sombre tapestries of the walls, the ebon blackness of the floors, and the phantasmagoric armorial trophies which rattled as I strode, were but matters to which, or to such as which, I had been accustomed from my infancy—while I hesitated not to acknowledge how familiar was all this—I still wondered to find how unfamiliar were the fancies which ordinary images were stirring up. On one of the staircases, I met the physician of the family. His countenance, I thought, wore a mingled expression of low cunning and perplexity. He accosted me with trepidation and passed on. The valet now threw open a door and ushered me into the presence of his master.

The room in which I found myself was very large and lofty. The windows were long, narrow, and pointed, and at so vast a distance from the black oaken floor as to be altogether inaccessible from within. Feeble gleams of encrimsoned light made their way through the trellised panes, and served to render sufficiently distinct the more prominent objects around; the eye, however, struggled in vain to reach the remoter angles of the chamber, or the recesses of the vaulted and fretted ceiling. Dark draperies hung upon the walls. The general furniture was profuse, comfortless, antique, and tattered. Many books and musical instruments lay scattered about, but failed to give any vitality to the scene. I felt that I breathed an atmosphere of sorrow. An air of stern, deep, and irredeemable gloom hung over and pervaded all.

Upon my entrance, Usher arose from a sofa on which he had been lying at full length, and greeted me with a vivacious warmth which had much in it, I at first thought, of an overdone cordiality—of the constrained effort of the *ennuyé* man of the world. A glance, however, at his countenance convinced me of his perfect sincerity. We sat down; and for some moments, while he spoke not, I gazed upon him with a feeling half of pity, half of awe. Surely, man had never before so terribly altered, in so brief a period, as had Roderick Usher! It was with difficulty that I could bring myself to admit the identity of the wan being before me with the companion of my early boyhood. Yet the character of his face had been at all times remarkable. A cadaverousness of complexion; an eye large, liquid, and luminous beyond comparison; lips somewhat thin and very pallid, but of a surpassingly beautiful curve; a nose of a delicate Hebrew model, but with a breadth of nostril unusual in similar formations; a finely moulded chin, speaking, in its want of prominence, of a want of moral energy; hair of a more than weblike softness and tenuity; these features, with an inordinate expansion above the regions of the temple, made up altogether a countenance not easily to be forgotten. And now in the mere exaggeration of the prevailing character of these features, and of the expression they were wont to convey, lay so much of change that I doubted to whom I spoke. The now ghastly pallor of the skin, and the now miraculous lustre of the eye, above all things startled and even awed me. The silken hair, too, had been suffered to grow all unheeded, and as, in its wild gossamer texture, it floated rather than fell about the face, I could not, even with effort, connect its Arabesque expression with any idea of simple humanity.

In the manner of my friend I was at once struck with an incoherence —an inconsistency; and I soon found this to arise from a series of feeble and futile struggles to overcome an habitual trepidancy—an excessive nervous agitation. For something of this nature I had indeed been prepared, no less by his letter, than by reminiscences of certain boyish traits, and by conclusions deduced from his peculiar physical conformation and temperament. His action was alternately vivacious and sullen. His voice varied rapidly from a tremulous indecision (when the animal spirits seemed utterly in abeyance) to that species of energetic concision—that abrupt, weighty, unhurried, and hollow-sounding enunciation—that leaden, self-balanced and perfectly modulated guttural utterance, which may be observed in the lost drunkard, or the irreclaimable eater of opium, during the periods of his most intense excitement.

It was thus that he spoke of the object of my visit, of his earnest desire to see me, and of the solace he expected me to afford him. He entered, at some length, into what he conceived to be the nature of his malady. It was, he said, a constitutional and a family evil, and one for which he despaired to find a remedy—a mere nervous affection, he immediately added, which would undoubtedly soon pass off. It displayed itself in a host of unnatural sensations. Some of these, as he detailed them, interested and bewildered me; although, perhaps, the terms and the general manner of their narration had their weight. He suffered much from a morbid acuteness of the senses; the most insipid food was alone endurable; he could wear only garments of certain texture; the odors of all flowers were oppressive; his eyes were tortured by even a faint light; and there were but peculiar sounds, and these from stringed instruments, which did not inspire him with horror.

To an anomalous species of terror I found him a bounden slave. "I shall perish," said he, "I *must* perish in this deplorable folly. Thus, thus, and not otherwise, shall I be lost. I dread the events of the future, not in themselves, but in their results. I shudder at the thought of any, even the most trival, incident, which may operate upon this intolerable agitation of soul. I have, indeed, no abhorrence of danger, except in its absolute effect—in terror. In this unnerved—in this pitiable, condition—I feel that the period will sooner or later arrive when I must abandon life and reason together, in some struggle with the grim phantasm, FEAR."

I learned, moreover, at intervals, and through broken and equivocal hints, another singular feature of his mental condition. He was enchained by certain superstitious impressions in regard to the dwelling which he tenanted, and whence, for many years, he had never ventured forth—in regard to an influence whose supposititious force was conveyed in terms too shadowy here to be re-stated—an influence which some peculiarities in the mere form and substance of his family mansion had, by dint of long sufferance, he said, obtained over his spirit—an effect which the *physique* of the gray walls and turrets, and of the dim tarn into which they all looked down, had, at length, brought about upon the *morale* of his existence.

He admitted, however, although with hesitation, that much of the peculiar gloom which thus afflicted him could be traced to a more natural and far more palpable origin—to the severe and long-continued illness—indeed to the evidently approaching dissolution—of a tenderly beloved sister—his sole companion for long years—his last and only relative on earth. "Her decease," he said, with a bitterness which I can never forget, "would leave him (him the hopeless and the frail) the last of the ancient race of the Ushers." While he spoke, the lady Madeline (for so was she called) passed through a remote portion of the apartment, and, without having noticed my presence, disappeared. I regarded her with an utter astonishment not unmingled with dread—and yet I found it impossible to account for such feelings. A sensation of stupor oppressed me, as my eyes followed her retreating steps. When a door, at length, closed upon her, my glance sought instinctively and eagerly the countenance of the brother—but he had buried his face in his hands, and I could only perceive that a far more than ordinary wanness had overspread the emaciated fingers through which trickled many passionate tears.

The disease of the lady Madeline had long baffled the skill of her physicians. A settled apathy, a gradual wasting away of the person, and frequent although transient affections of a partially cataleptical character were the unusual diagnosis. Hitherto she had steadily borne up against the pressure of her malady, and had not betaken herself finally to bed; but on the closing in of the evening of my arrival at the house, she succumbed (as her brother told me at night with inexpressible agitation) to the prostrating power of the destroyer; and I learned that the glimpse I had obtained of her person would thus probably be the last I should obtain—that the lady, at least while living, would be seen by me no more.

For several days ensuing, her name was unmentioned by either Usher or myself; and during this period I was busied in earnest endeavors to alleviate the melancholy of my friend. We painted and read together, or I listened, as if in a dream, to the wild improvisations of his speaking guitar. And thus, as a closer and still closer intimacy admitted me more unreservedly into the recesses of his spirit, the more bitterly did I perceive the futility of all attempt at cheering a mind from which darkness, as if an inherent positive quality, poured forth upon all objects of the moral and physical universe, in one unceasing radiation of gloom.

I shall ever bear about me a memory of the many solemn hours I thus spent alone with the master of the House of Usher. Yet I should fail in any attempt to convey an idea of the exact character of the studies, or of the occupations, in which he involved me, or led me the way. An excited and highly distempered ideality threw a sulphureous lustre over all. His long improvised dirges will ring forever in my ears. Among other things, I hold painfully in mind a certain singular perversion and amplification of the wild air of the last waltz of Von Weber. From the paintings over which his elaborate fancy brooded, and which grew, touch by touch, into vaguenesses at which I shuddered the more thrillingly, because I shuddered knowing not why;—from these paintings (vivid as their images now are before me) I would in vain endeavor to educe more than a small portion which should lie within the compass of merely written words. By the utter simplicity, by the nakedness of his designs, he arrested and overawed attention. If ever mortal painted an idea, that mortal was Roderick Usher. For me at least, in the circumstances then surrounding me, there arose out of the pure abstractions which the hypochondriac contrived to throw upon his canvas, an intensity of intolerable awe, no shadow of which felt I ever yet in the contemplation of the certainly glowing yet too concrete reveries of Fuseli.

One of the phantasmagoric conceptions of my friend, partaking not so rigidly of the spirit of abstraction, may be shadowed forth, although feebly, in words. A small picture presented the interior of an immensely long and rectangular vault or tunnel, with low walls, smooth, white, and without interruption or device. Certain accessory points of the design served well to convey the idea that this excavation lay at an exceeding depth below the surface of the earth. No outlet was observed in any portion of its vast extent, and no torch or other artificial source of light was discernible; yet a flood of intense rays rolled throughout, and bathed the whole in a ghastly and inappropriate splendor.

I have just spoken of that morbid condition of the auditory nerve which rendered all music intolerable to the sufferer, with the exception of certain

EDGAR ALLAN POE

effects of stringed instruments. It was, perhaps, the narrow limits to which he thus confined himself upon the guitar which gave birth, in great measure, to the fantastic character of his performances. But the fervid *facility* of his *impromptus* could not be so accounted for. They must have been, and were, in the notes, as well as the words of his wild fantasias (for he not unfrequently accompanied himself with rhymed verbal improvisations), the result of that intense mental collectedness and concentration to which I have previously alluded as observable only in particular moments of the highest artificial excitement. The words of one of these rhapsodies I have easily remembered. I was, perhaps, the more forcibly impressed with it as he gave it, because, in the under or mystic current of its meaning, I fancied that I perceived, and for the first time, a full consciousness on the part of Usher of the tottering of his lofty reason upon her throne. The verses, which were entitled "The Haunted Palace," ran very nearly, if not accurately, thus:—

I

In the greenest of our valleys,
    By good angels tenanted,
Once a fair and stately palace—
    Radiant palace—reared its head.
In the monarch Thought's dominion—
    It stood there!
Never seraph spread a pinion
    Over fabric half so fair.

II

Banners yellow, glorious, golden,
    On its roof did float and flow
(This—all this—was in the olden
    Time long ago);
And every gentle air that dallied,
    In that sweet day,
Along the ramparts plumed and pallid,
    A winged odor went away.

III

Wanderers in that happy valley
    Through two luminous windows saw
Spirits moving musically
    To a lute's well-tunèd law;
Round about a throne, were sitting

(Porphyrogene!)
In state his glory well befitting,
　　The ruler of the realm was seen.

IV

And all with pearl and ruby glowing
　　Was the fair palace door,
Through which came flowing, flowing, flowing
　　And sparkling evermore,
A troop of Echoes whose sweet duty
　　Was but to sing,
In voices of surpassing beauty,
　　The wit and wisdom of their king.

V

But evil things, in robes of sorrow,
　　Assailed the monarch's high estate;
(Ah, let us mourn, for never morrow
　　Shall dawn upon him, desolate!)
And, round about his home, the glory
　　That blushed and bloomed
Is but a dim-remembered story
　　Of the old time entombed.

VI

And travellers now within that valley,
　　Through the red-litten windows, see
Vast forms that move fantastically
　　To a discordant melody;
While, like a rapid ghastly river,
　　Through the pale door,
A hideous throng rush out forever,
　　And laugh—but smile no more.

I well remember that suggestions arising from this ballad led us into a train of thought wherein there became manifest an opinion of Usher's which I mention not so much on account of its novelty (for other men have thought thus), as on account of the pertinacity with which he maintained it. This opinion, in its general form, was that of the sentience of all vegetable things. But, in his disordered fancy, the idea had assumed a more daring character, and trespassed, under certain conditions, upon the kingdom of inorganization. I lack words to express the full extent, or the earnest

EDGAR ALLAN POE

abandon of his persuasion. The belief, however, was connected (as I have previously hinted) with the gray stones of the home of his forefathers. The conditions of the sentience had been here, he imagined, fulfilled in the method of collocation of these stones—in the order of their arrangement, as well as in that of the many *fungi* which overspread them, and of the decayed trees which stood around—above all, in the long undisturbed endurance of this arrangement, and in its reduplication in the still waters of the tarn. Its evidence—the evidence of the sentience—was to be seen, he said (and I here started as he spoke) in the gradual yet certain condensation of an atmosphere of their own about the waters and the walls. The result was discoverable, he added, in that silent, yet importunate and terrible influence which for centuries had moulded the destinies of his family, and which made *him* what I now saw him—what he was. Such opinions need no comment, and I will make none.

Our books—the books which, for years, had formed no small portion of the mental existence of the invalid—were, as might be supposed, in strict keeping with this character of phantasm. We pored together over such works as the Ververt et Chartreuse of Gresset; the Belphegor of Machiavelli; the Heaven and Hell of Swedenborg; the Subterranean Voyage of Nicholas Klimm of Holberg; the Chiromancy of Robert Flud, of Jean D'Indaginé, and of De la Chambre; the Journey into the Blue Distance of Tieck; and the City of the Sun of Campanella. One favorite volume was a small octavo edition of the *Directorium Inquisitorium*, by the Dominican Eymeric de Gironne; and there are passages in Pomponius Mela, about the old African Satyrs and Ægipans, over which Usher would sit dreaming for hours. His chief delight, however, was found in the perusal of an exceedingly rare and curious book in quarto Gothic—the manual of a forgotten church —the *Vigiliæ Mortuorum secundum Chorum Ecclesiæ Maguntinæ*.

I could not help thinking of the wild ritual of this work, and of its probable influence upon the hypochondriac, when, one evening, having informed me abruptly that the lady Madeline was no more, he stated his intention of preserving her corpse for a fortnight (previously to its final interment), in one of the numerous vaults within the main walls of the building. The worldly reason, however, assigned for this singular proceeding, was one which I did not feel at liberty to dispute. The brother had been led to his resolution (so he told me) by consideration of the unusual character of the malady of the deceased, of certain obtrusive and eager inquiries on the part of her medical men, and of the remote and exposed situation of the burial-ground of the family. I will not deny that when I called to mind the sinister countenance of the person whom I met upon the staircase, on the day of my arrival at the house, I had no desire to oppose what I regarded as at best but a harmless, and by no means an unnatural, precaution.

At the request of Usher, I personally aided him in the arrangements for the temporary entombment. The body having been encoffined, we two alone bore it to its rest. The vault in which we placed it (and which had been so long unopened that our torches, half smothered in its oppressive atmosphere, gave us little opportunity for investigation) was small, damp, and entirely without means of admission for light; lying, at great depth, immediately beneath that portion of the building in which was my own sleeping apartment. It had been used, apparently, in remote feudal times, for the worst purposes of a donjon-keep, and, in later days, as a place of deposit for powder, or some other highly combustible substance, as a portion of its floor, and the whole interior of a long archway through which we reached it, were carefully sheathed with copper. The door, of massive iron, had been, also, similarly protected. Its immense weight caused an unusually sharp, grating sound, as it moved upon its hinges.

Having deposited our mournful burden upon tressels within this region of horror, we partially turned aside the yet unscrewed lid of the coffin, and looked upon the face of the tenant. A striking similitude between the brother and sister now first arrested my attention; and Usher, divining, perhaps, my thoughts, murmured out some few words from which I learned that the deceased and himself had been twins, and that sympathies of a scarcely intelligible nature had always existed between them. Our glances, however, rested not long upon the dead—for we could not regard her unawed. The disease which had thus entombed the lady in the maturity of youth, had left, as usual in all maladies of a strictly cataleptical character, the mockery of a faint blush upon the bosom and the face, and that suspiciously lingering smile upon the lip which is so terrible in death. We replaced and screwed down the lid, and, having secured the door of iron, made our way, with toil, into the scarcely less gloomy apartments of the upper portion of the house.

And now, some days of bitter grief having elapsed, an observable change came over the features of the mental disorder of my friend. His ordinary manner had vanished. His ordinary occupations were neglected or forgotten. He roamed from chamber to chamber with hurried, unequal, and objectless step. The pallor of his countenance had assumed, if possible, a more ghastly hue—but the luminousness of his eye had utterly gone out. The once occasional huskiness of his tone was heard no more; and a tremulous quaver, as if of extreme terror, habitually characterized his utterance. There were times, indeed, when I thought his unceasingly agitated mind was laboring with some oppressive secret, to divulge which he struggled for the necessary courage. At times, again, I was obliged to resolve all into the mere inexplicable vagaries of madness, for I beheld him gazing upon vacancy for long hours, in an attitude of the profoundest attention, as if listening to some imaginary sound. It was no wonder that his condition terrified—that it infected me. I felt creeping upon me, by slow yet certain degrees, the wild influences of his own fantastic yet impressive superstitions.

It was, especially, upon retiring to bed late in the night of the seventh or eighth day after the placing of the lady Madeline within the donjon, that I experienced the full power of such feelings. Sleep came not near my couch —while the hours waned and waned away. I struggled to reason off the nervousness which had dominion over me. I endeavored to believe that much, if not all of what I felt, was due to the bewildering influence of the gloomy furniture of the room—of the dark and tattered draperies, which, tortured into motion by the breath of a rising tempest, swayed fitfully to and fro upon the walls, and rustled uneasily about the decorations of the bed. But my efforts were fruitless. An irrepressible tremor gradually pervaded my frame; and, at length, there sat upon my very heart an incubus of utterly causeless alarm. Shaking this off with a gasp and a struggle, I uplifted myself upon the pillows, and, peering earnestly within the intense darkness of the chamber, hearkened—I know not why, except that an instinctive spirit prompted me—to certain low and indefinite sounds which came, through the pauses of the storm, at long intervals, I knew not whence. Overpowered by an intense sentiment of horror, unaccountable yet unendurable, I threw on my clothes with haste (for I felt that I should sleep no more during the night), and endeavored to arouse myself from the pitiable condition into which I had fallen, by pacing rapidly to and fro through the apartment.

I had taken but few turns in this manner, when a light step on an adjoining staircase arrested my attention. I presently recognized it as that of Usher. In an instant afterward he rapped, with a gentle touch, at my door, and entered, bearing a lamp. His countenance was, as usual, cadaverously wan —but, moreover, there was a species of mad hilarity in his eyes—an evidently restrained *hysteria* in his whole demeanor. His air appalled me—but any thing was preferable to the solitude which I had so long endured, and I even welcomed his presence as a relief.

"And you have not seen it?" he said abruptly, after having stared about him for some moments in silence—"you have not then seen it?—but, stay! you shall." Thus speaking, and having carefully shaded his lamp he hurried to one of the casements, and threw it freely open to the storm.

The impetuous fury of the entering gust nearly lifted us from our feet. It was, indeed, a tempestuous yet sternly beautiful night, and one wildly singular in its terror and its beauty. A whirlwind had apparently collected its force in our vicinity; for there were frequent and violent alterations in the direction of the wind; and the exceeding density of the clouds (which hung so low as to press upon the turrets of the house) did not prevent our perceiving the life-like velocity with which they flew careering from all points against each other, without passing away into the distance. I say that even their exceeding density did not prevent our perceiving this—yet we had no glimpse of the moon or stars—nor was there any flashing forth of the lightning. But the under surfaces of the huge masses of agitated vapor, as well as all terrestrial objects immediately around us, were glowing in the unnatural light of a faintly luminous and distinctly visible gaseous exhalation which hung about and enshrouded the mansion.

"You must not—you shall not behold this!" said I, shudderingly, to Usher, as I led him, with a gentle violence, from the window to a seat. "These appearances, which bewilder you, are merely electrical phenomena not uncommon—or it may be that they have their ghastly origin in the rank miasma of the tarn. Let us close this casement;—the air is chilling and dangerous to your frame. Here is one of your favorite romances. I will read, and you shall listen;—and so we will pass away this terrible night together."

The antique volume which I had taken up was the "Mad Trist" of Sir Launcelot Canning; but I had called it a favorite of Usher's more in sad jest than in earnest; for, in truth, there is little in its uncouth and unimaginative prolixity which could have had interest for the lofty and spiritual ideality of my friend. It was, however, the only book immediately at hand; and I indulged a vague hope that the excitement which now agitated the hypochondriac, might find relief (for the history of mental disorder is full of similar anomalies) even in the extremeness of the folly which I should read. Could I have judged, indeed, by the wild overstrained air of vivacity with which he hearkened, or apparently hearkened, to the words of the tale, I might well have congratulated myself upon the success of my design.

I had arrived at that well-known portion of the story where Ethelred, the hero of the Trist, having sought in vain for peaceable admission into the dwelling of the hermit, proceeds to make good an entrance by force. Here, it will be remembered, the words of the narrative run thus:

"And Ethelred, who was by nature of a doughty heart, and who was now mighty withal, on account of the powerfulness of the wine which he had drunken, waited no longer to hold parley with the hermit, who, in sooth, was of an obstinate and maliceful turn, but, feeling the rain upon his shoulders, and fearing the rising of the tempest, uplifted his mace outright, and, with blows, made quickly room in the plankings of the door for his gauntleted hand; and now pulling therewith sturdily, he so cracked, and ripped, and tore all asunder, that the noise of the dry and hollow-sounding wood alarummed and reverberated throughout the forest."

At the termination of this sentence I started and, for a moment, paused; for it appeared to me (although I at once concluded that my excited fancy had deceived me)—it appeared to me that, from some very remote portion of the mansion, there came, indistinctly, to my ears, what might have been, in its exact similarity of character, the echo (but a stifled and dull one certainly) of the very cracking and ripping sound which Sir Launcelot had so particularly described. It was, beyond doubt, the coincidence alone which had arrested my attention; for, amid the rattling of the sashes of the casements, and the ordinary commingled noises of the still increasing storm, the sound, in itself, had nothing, surely, which should have interested or disturbed me. I continued the story:

"But the good champion Ethelred, now entering within the door, was sore enraged and amazed to perceive no signal of the maliceful hermit; but, in the stead thereof, a dragon of a scaly and prodigious demeanor, and of a fiery tongue, which sate in guard before a palace of gold, with a floor of silver; and upon the wall there hung a shield of shining brass with this legend enwritten—

> Who entereth herein, a conqueror hath bin;
> Who slayeth the dragon, the shield he shall win;

And Ethelred uplifted his mace, and struck upon the head of the dragon, which fell before him, and gave up his pesty breath, with a shriek so horrid and harsh, and withal so piercing, that Ethelred had fain to close his ears with his hands against the dreadful noise of it, the like whereof was never before heard."

Here again I paused abruptly, and now with a feeling of wild amazement —for there could be no doubt whatever that, in this instance, I did actually hear (although from what direction it proceeded I found it impossible to say) a low and apparently distant, but harsh, protracted, and most unusual screaming or grating sound—the exact counterpart of what my fancy had already conjured up for the dragon's unnatural shriek as described by the romancer.

Oppressed, as I certainly was, upon the occurrence of this second and most extraordinary coincidence, by a thousand conflicting sensations, in which wonder and extreme terror were predominant, I still retained sufficient presence of mind to avoid exciting, by any observation, the sensitive nervousness of my companion. I was by no means certain that he had noticed the sounds in question; although, assuredly, a strange alteration had, during the last few minutes, taken place in his demeanor. From a position fronting my own, he had gradually brought round his chair, so as to sit with his face to the door of the chamber; and thus I could but partially perceive his features, although I saw that his lips trembled as if he were murmuring inaudibly. His head had dropped upon his breast—yet I knew that he was not asleep, from the wide and rigid opening of the eye as I caught a glance of it in profile. The motion of his body, too, was at variance with this idea—for he rocked from side to side with a gentle yet constant and uniform sway. Having rapidly taken notice of all this, I resumed the narrative of Sir Launcelot, which thus proceeded:

"And now, the champion, having escaped from the terrible fury of the dragon, bethinking himself of the brazen shield, and of the breaking up of the enchantment which was upon it, removed the carcass from out of the way before him, and approached valorously over the silver pavement of the castle to where the shield was upon the wall; which in sooth tarried not for his full coming, but fell down at his feet upon the silver floor, with a mighty great and terrible ringing sound."

No sooner had these syllables passed my lips, than—as if a shield of brass had indeed, at the moment, fallen heavily upon a floor of silver—I became aware of a distinct, hollow, metallic, and clangorous, yet apparently muffled, reverberation. Completely unnerved, I leaped to my feet; but the measured rocking movement of Usher was undisturbed. I rushed to the chair in which he sat. His eyes were bent fixedly before him, and throughout his whole countenance there reigned a stony rigidity. But, as I placed my hand upon his shoulder, there came a strong shudder over his whole person; a sickly smile quivered about his lips; and I saw that he spoke in a low, hurried, and gibbering murmur, as if unconscious of my presence. Bending closely over him, I at length drank in the hideous import of his words.

"Now hear it?—yes, I hear it, and *have* heard it. Long—long—long —many minutes, many hours, many days, have I heard it—yet I dared not —oh, pity me, miserable wretch that I am!—I dared not—I *dared* not speak! *We have put her living in the tomb!* Said I not that my senses were acute? I *now* tell you that I heard her feeble first movements in the hollow coffin. I heard them—many, many days ago—yet I dared not—*I dared not speak!* And now—to-night—Ethelred—ha! ha!—the breaking of the hermit's door, and the death-cry of the dragon, and the clangor of the shield —say, rather, the rending of her coffin, and the grating of the iron hinges of her prison, and her struggles within the coppered archway of the vault! Oh! whither shall I fly? Will she not be here anon? Is she not hurrying to upbraid me for my haste? Have I not heard her footstep on the stair? Do I not distinguish that heavy and horrible beating of her heart? Madman!" —here he sprang furiously to his feet, and shrieked out his syllables, as if in the effort he were giving up his soul—"MADMAN! I TELL YOU THAT SHE NOW STANDS WITHOUT THE DOOR!"

As if in the superhuman energy of his utterance there had been found the potency of a spell, the huge antique panels to which the speaker pointed threw slowly back, upon the instant, their ponderous and ebony jaws. It was the work of the rushing gust—but then without those doors there *did* stand the lofty and enshrouded figure of the lady Madeline of Usher. There was blood upon her white robes, and the evidence of some bitter struggle upon every portion of her emaciated frame. For a moment she remained trembling and reeling to and fro upon the threshold—then, with a low moaning cry, fell heavily inward upon the person of her brother, and in her violent and now final death-agonies, bore him to the floor a corpse, and a victim to the terrors he had anticipated.

From that chamber, and from that mansion, I fled aghast. The storm was still abroad in all its wrath as I found myself crossing the old causeway. Suddenly there shot along the path a wild light, and I turned to see whence a gleam so unusual could have issued; for the vast house and its shadows were alone behind me. The radiance was that of the full, setting, and blood-red moon, which now shone vividly through that once barely discernible fissure, of which I have before spoken as extending from the roof of the building, in a zigzag direction, to the base. While I gazed, this fissure rapidly widened—there came a fierce breath of the whirlwind—the entire orb of the satellite burst at once upon my sight—my brain reeled as I saw the mighty walls rushing asunder—there was a long tumultuous shouting sound like the voice of a thousand waters—and the deep and dank tarn at my feet closed sullenly and silently over the fragments of the *"House of Usher."*

THE PHILOSOPHY OF COMPOSITION

Charles Dickens, in a note now lying before me, alluding to an examination I once made of the mechanism of "Barnaby Rudge," says—"By the way, are you aware that Godwin wrote his 'Caleb Williams' backwards? He first involved his hero in a web of difficulties, forming the second volume, and then, for the first, cast about him for some mode of accounting for what had been done."

I cannot think this the *precise* mode of procedure on the part of Godwin —and indeed what he himself acknowledges, is not altogether in accordance with Mr. Dickens's idea—but the author of "Caleb Williams" was too good an artist not to perceive the advantage derivable from at least a somewhat similar process. Nothing is more clear than that every plot, worth the name, must be elaborated to its *dénouement* before anything be attempted with the pen. It is only with the *dénouement* constantly in view that we can give a plot its indispensable air of consequence, or causation, by making the incidents, and especially the tone at all points, tend to the development of the intention.

There is a radical error, I think, in the usual mode of constructing a story. Either history affords a thesis—or one is suggested by an incident of the day—or, at best, the author sets himself to work in the combination of striking events to form merely the basis of his narrative—designing, generally, to fill in with description, dialogue, or autorial comment, whatever crevices of fact, or action, may, from page to page, render themselves apparent.

I prefer commencing with the consideration of an *effect*. Keeping originality *always* in view—for he is false to himself who ventures to dispense with so obvious and so easily attainable a source of interest—I say to myself, in the first place, "Of the innumerable effects, or impressions, of which the heart, the intellect, or (more generally) the soul is susceptible, what one shall I, on the present occasion, select?" Having chosen a novel, first, and secondly a vivid effect, I consider whether it can be best wrought by incident or tone—whether by ordinary incidents and peculiar tone, or the converse, or by peculiarity both of incident and tone—afterward look-ing about me (or rather within) for such combinations of event, or tone, as shall best aid me in the construction of the effect.

I have often thought how interesting a magazine paper might be written by any author who would—that is to say who could—detail, step by step, the processes by which any one of his compositions attained its ultimate point of completion. Why such a paper has never been given to the world, I am much at a loss to say—but, perhaps, the autorial vanity has had more to do with the omission than any one other cause. Most writers—poets in especial—prefer having it understood that they compose by a species of fine frenzy—an ecstatic intuition—and would positively shudder at letting the public take a peep behind the scenes, at the elaborate and vacillating crudi-ties of thought—at the true purposes seized only at the last moment—at the innumerable glimpses of idea that arrived not at the maturity of full view —at the fully matured fancies discarded in despair as unmanageable—at the cautious selections and rejections—at the painful erasures and interpolations—in a word, at the wheels and pinions—the tackle for scene-shifting—the step-ladders and demon-traps—the cock's feathers, the red paint, and the black patches, which, in ninety-nine cases out of the hun-dred, constitute the properties of the literary *histrio*.

I am aware, on the other hand, that the case is by no means common, in which an author is at all in condition to retrace the steps by which his con-clusions have been attained. In general, suggestions, having arisen pell-mell, are pursued and forgotten in a similar manner.

For my own part, I have neither sympathy with the repugnance alluded to, nor, at any time, the least difficulty in recalling to mind the progressive steps of any of my compositions; and, since the interest of an analysis, or reconstruction, such as I have considered a *desideratum*, is quite indepen-dent of any real or fancied interest in the thing analyzed, it will not be regarded as a breach of decorum on my part to show the *modus operandi* by which some one of my own works was put together. I select "The Raven" as most generally known. It is my design to render it manifest that no one point in its composition is referrable either to accident or intuition—that the work proceeded, step by step, to its completion with the precision and rigid consequence of a mathematical problem.

Let us dismiss, as irrelevant to the poem, *per se*, the circumstance—or say the necessity—which, in the first place, gave rise to the intention of compos-ing *a* poem that should suit at once the popular and the critical taste.

We commence, then, with this intention.

The initial consideration was that of extent. If any literary work is too long to be read at one sitting, we must be content to dispense with the immensely important effect derivable from unity of impression—for, if two sittings be required, the affairs of the world interfere, and every thing like totality is at once destroyed. But since, *ceteris paribus*, no poet can afford to dispense with *any thing* that may advance his design, it but remains to be seen whether there is, in extent, any advantage to counterbalance the loss of unity which attends it. Here I say no, at once. What we term a long poem is, in fact, merely a succession of brief ones—that is to say, of brief poetical effects. It is needless to demonstrate that a poem is such, only inasmuch as it intensely excites, by elevating, the soul; and all intense excitements are, through a psychal necessity, brief. For this reason, at least one half of the "Paradise Lost" is essentially prose—a succession of poetical excitements interspersed, *inevitably*, with corresponding depressions—the whole being deprived, through the extremeness of its length, of the vastly important artistic element, totality, or unity, of effect.

It appears evident, then, that there is a distinct limit, as regards length, to all works of literary art—the limit of a single sitting—and that, although in certain classes of prose composition, such as "Robinson Crusoe" (demanding no unity,) this limit may be advantageously overpassed, it can never properly be overpassed in a poem. Within this limit, the extent of a poem may be made to bear mathematical relation to its merit—in other words, to the excitement or elevation—again, in other words, to the degree of the true poetical effect which it is capable of inducing; for it is clear that the brevity must be in direct ratio of the intensity of the intended effect:—this, with one proviso—that a certain degree of duration is absolutely requisite for the production of any effect at all.

Holding in view these considerations, as well as that degree of excitement which I deemed not above the popular, while not below the critical, taste, I reached at once what I conceived the proper *length* for my intended poem—a length of about one hundred lines. It is, in fact, a hundred and eight.

My next thought concerned the choice of an impression, or effect, to be conveyed; and here I may as well observe that, throughout the construction, I kept steadily in view the design of rendering the work *universally* appreciable. I should be carried too far out of my immediate topic were I to demonstrate a point upon which I have repeatedly insisted, and which, with the poetical, stands not in the slightest need of demonstration—the point, I mean, that Beauty is the sole legitimate province of the poem. A few words, however, in elucidation of my real meaning, which some of my friends have evinced a disposition to misrepresent. That pleasure which is at once the most intense, the most elevating, and the most pure, is, I believe, found in the contemplation of the beautiful. When, indeed, men speak of Beauty, they mean, precisely, not a quality, as is supposed, but an effect—they refer, in short, just to that intense and pure elevation of *soul*—*not* of intellect, or of heart—upon which I have commented, and which is experienced in consequence of contemplating "the beautiful." Now I designate Beauty as the province of the poem, merely because it is an obvious rule of Art that effects should be made to spring from direct causes—that objects should be attained through means best adapted for their attainment—no one as yet having been weak enough to deny that the peculiar elevation alluded to is *most readily* attained in the poem. Now the object, Truth, or the satisfaction of the intellect, and the object Passion, or the excitement of the heart, are, although attainable, to a certain extent, in poetry, far more readily attainable in prose. Truth, in fact, demands a precision, and Passion a *homeliness* (the truly passionate will comprehend me) which are absolutely antagonistic to that Beauty which, I maintain, is the excitement, or pleasurable elevation, of the soul. It by no means follows from any thing here said, that passion, or even truth, may not be introduced, and even profitably introduced, into a poem—for they may serve in elucidation, or aid the general effect, as do discords in music, by contrast—but the true artist will always contrive, first, to tone them into proper subservience to the predominant aim, and, secondly, to enveil them, as far as possible, in that Beauty which is the atmosphere and the essence of the poem.

Regarding, then, Beauty as my province, my next question referred to the *tone* of its highest manifestation—and all experience has shown that this tone is one of *sadness*. Beauty of whatever kind, in its supreme development, invariably excites the sensitive soul to tears. Melancholy is thus the most legitimate of all the poetical tones.

The length, the province, and the tone, being thus determined, I betook myself to ordinary induction, with the view of obtaining some artistic piquancy which might serve me as a key-note in the construction of the poem—some pivot upon which the whole structure might turn. In carefully thinking over all the usual artistic effects—or more properly *points*, in the theatrical sense—I did not fail to perceive immediately that no one had been so universally employed as that of the *refrain*. The universality of its employment sufficed to assure me of its intrinsic value, and spared me the necessity of submitting it to analysis. I considered it, however, with regard to its susceptibility of improvement, and soon saw it to be in a primitive condition. As commonly used, the *refrain*, or burden, not only is limited to lyric verse, but depends for its impression upon the force of monotone —both in sound and thought. The pleasure is deduced solely from the sense of identity—of repetition. I resolved to diversify, and so heighten, the effect, by adhering, in general, to the monotone of sound, while I continually varied that of thought; that is to say, I determined to produce continuously novel effects, by the variation *of the application* of the *refrain*—the *refrain* itself remaining, for the most part, unvaried.

These points being settled, I next bethought me of the *nature* of my *refrain*. Since its application was to be repeatedly varied, it was clear that the *refrain* itself must be brief, for there would have been an insurmountable difficulty in frequent variations of application in any sentence of length. In proportion to the brevity of the sentence, would, of course, be the facility of the variation. This led me at once to a single word as the best *refrain*.

EDGAR ALLAN POE

The question now arose as to the *character* of the word. Having made up my mind to a *refrain*, the division of the poem into stanzas was, of course, a corollary: the *refrain* forming the close to each stanza. That such a close, to have force, must be sonorous and susceptible of protracted emphasis, admitted no doubt: and these considerations inevitably led me to the long *o* as the most sonorous vowel, in connection with *r* as the most producible consonant.

The sound of the *refrain* being thus determined, it became necessary to select a word embodying this sound, and at the same time in the fullest possible keeping with that melancholy which I had predetermined as the tone of the poem. In such a search it would have been absolutely impossible to overlook the word "Nevermore." In fact, it was the very first which presented itself.

The next *desideratum* was a pretext for the continuous use of the one word "nevermore." In observing the difficulty which I at once found in inventing a sufficiently plausible reason for its continuous repetition, I did not fail to perceive that this difficulty arose solely from the preassumption that the word was to be so continuously or monotonously spoken by a *human* being—I did not fail to perceive, in short, that the difficulty lay in the reconciliation of this monotony with the exercise of reason on the part of the creature repeating the word. Here, then, immediately arose the idea of a *non*-reasoning creature capable of speech; and, very naturally, a parrot, in the first instance, suggested itself, but was superseded forthwith by a Raven, as equally capable of speech, and infinitely more in keeping with the intended *tone*.

I had now gone so far as the conception of a Raven—the bird of ill omen —monotonously repeating the one word, "Nevermore," at the conclusion of each stanza, in a poem of melancholy tone, and in length about one hundred lines. Now, never losing sight of the object *supremeness*, or perfection, at all points, I asked myself—"Of all melancholy topics, what, according to the *universal* understanding of mankind, is the *most* melancholy?" Death —was the obvious reply. "And when," I said, "is this most melancholy of topics most poetical?" From what I have already explained at some length, the answer, here also, is obvious—"When it most closely allies itself to *Beauty*: the death, then, of a beautiful woman is, unquestionably, the most poetical topic in the world—and equally is it beyond doubt that the lips best suited for such a topic are those of a bereaved lover."

I had now to combine the two ideas, of a lover lamenting his deceased mistress and a Raven continuously repeating the word "Nevermore."—I had to combine these, bearing in mind my design of varying, at every turn, the *application* of the word repeated; but the only intelligible mode of such combination is that of imagining the Raven employing the word in answer to the queries of the lover. And here it was that I saw at once the opportunity afforded for the effect on which I had been depending—that is to say, the effect of the *variation of application*. I saw that I could make the first query propounded by the lover—the first query to which the Raven should reply "Nevermore"—that I could make this first query a commonplace one —the second less so—the third still less, and so on—until at length the lover, startled from his original *nonchalance* by the melancholy character of the word itself—by its frequent repetition—and by a consideration of the ominous reputation of the fowl that uttered it—is at length excited to superstition, and wildly propounds queries of a far different character—queries whose solution he has passionately at heart—propounds them half in superstition and half in that species of despair which delights in self-torture —propounds them not altogether because he believes in the prophetic or demoniac character of the bird (which, reason assures him, is merely repeating a lesson learned by rote) but because he experiences a frenzied pleasure in so modeling his questions as to receive from the *expected* "Nevermore" the most delicious because the most intolerable of sorrow. Perceiving the opportunity thus afforded me—or, more strictly, thus forced upon me in the progress of the construction—I first established in mind the climax, or concluding query—that query to which "Nevermore" should be in the last place an answer—that query in reply to which this word "Nevermore" should involve the utmost conceivable amount of sorrow and despair.

Here then the poem may be said to have its beginning—at the end, where all works of art should begin—for it was here, at this point of my preconsiderations, that I first put pen to paper in the composition of the stanza:

> "Prophet," said I, "thing of evil! prophet still if bird or devil!
> By that heaven that bends above us—by that God we both adore,
> Tell this soul with sorrow laden, if within the distant Aidenn,
> It shall clasp a sainted maiden whom the angels name Lenore—
> Clasp a rare and radiant maiden whom the angels name Lenore."
> Quoth the Raven, "Nevermore."

I composed this stanza, at this point, first that, by establishing the climax, I might the better vary and graduate, as regards seriousness and importance, the preceding queries of the lover and—secondly, that I might definitely settle the rhythm, the metre, and the length and general arrangement of the stanza,—as well as graduate the stanzas which were to precede, so that none of them might surpass this in rhythmical effect. Had I been able, in the subsequent composition, to construct more vigorous stanzas, I should, without scruple, have purposely enfeebled them, so as not to interfere with the climacteric effect.

And here I may as well say a few words of the versification. My first object (as usual) was originality. The extent to which this has been neglected, in versification, is one of the most unaccountable things in the world. Admitting that there is little possibility of variety in mere *rhythm*, it is still clear that the possible varieties of metre and stanza are absolutely infinite —and yet, *for centuries, no man, in verse, has ever done, or ever seemed to think of doing, an original thing.* The fact is, that originality (unless in minds of very unusual force) is by no means a matter, as some suppose, of impulse or intuition. In general, to be found, it must be elaborately sought, and although a positive merit of the highest class, demands in its attainment less of invention than negation.

Of course, I pretend to no originality in either the rhythm or metre of the "Raven." The former is trochaic—the latter is octameter acatalectic, alternating with heptameter catalectic repeated in the *refrain* of the fifth verse, and terminating with tetrameter catalectic. Less pedantically—the feet employed throughout (trochees) consist of a long syllable followed by a short: the first line of the stanza consists of eight of these feet—the second of seven and a half (in effect two-thirds)—the third of eight—the fourth of seven and a half—the fifth the same—the sixth three and a half. Now, each of these lines, taken individually, has been employed before, and what originality the "Raven" has, is in their *combination into stanza*; nothing even remotely approaching this combination has ever been attempted. The effect of this originality of combination is aided by other unusual, and some altogether novel effects, arising from an extension of the application of the principles of rhyme and alliteration.

The next point to be considered was the mode of bringing together the lover and the Raven—and the first branch of this consideration was the *locale.* For this the most natural suggestion might seem to be a forest, or the fields—but it has always appeared to me that a close *circumscription of space* is absolutely necessary to the effect of insulated incident:—it has the force of a frame to a picture. It has an indisputable moral power in keeping concentrated the attention, and, of course, must not be confounded with mere unity of place.

I determined, then, to place the lover in his chamber—in a chamber rendered sacred to him by memories of her who had frequented it. The room is represented as richly furnished—this in mere pursuance of the ideas I have already explained on the subject of Beauty, as the sole true poetical thesis.

The *locale* being thus determined, I had now to introduce the bird—and the thought of introducing him through the window, was inevitable. The idea of making the lover suppose, in the first instance, that the flapping of the wings of the bird against the shutter is a "tapping" at the door, originated in a wish to increase, by prolonging, the reader's curiosity, and in a desire to admit the incidental effect arising from the lover's throwing open the door, finding all dark, and thence adopting the half fancy that it was the spirit of his mistress that knocked.

I made the night tempestuous, first, to account for the Raven's seeking admission, and secondly, for the effect of the contrast with the (physical) serenity within the chamber.

I made the bird alight on the bust of Pallas, also for the effect of contrast between the marble and the plumage—it being understood that the bust was absolutely *suggested* by the bird—the bust of *Pallas* being chosen, first, as most in keeping with the scholarship of the lover, and secondly, for the sonorousness of the word, Pallas, itself.

About the middle of the poem, also, I have availed myself of the force of contrast, with a view of deepening the ultimate impression. For example, an air of the fantastic—approaching as nearly to the ludicrous as was admissable—is given to the Raven's entrance. He comes in "with many a flirt and flutter."

Not the *least obeisance made he*—not a moment stopped or stayed he,
But with mien of lord or lady, perched above my chamber door.

In the two stanzas which follow, the design is more obviously carried out:—

Then this ebony bird beguiling my sad fancy into smiling
By the *grave and stern decorum of the countenance it wore,*
"Though thy *crest be shorn and shaven* thou," I said, "art sure no craven,
Ghastly grim and ancient Raven wandering from the nightly shore—
Tell me what thy lordly name is on the Night's Plutonian shore?"
    Quoth the Raven, "Nevermore."

Much I marvelled *this ungainly fowl* to hear discourse so plainly,
Though its answer little meaning—little relevancy bore;
For we cannot help agreeing that no living human being
Ever yet was blessed with seeing bird above his chamber door—
Bird or beast upon the sculptured bust above his chamber door,
    With such name as "Nevermore."

The effect of the *dénouement* being thus provided for, I immediately drop the fantastic for a tone of the most profound seriousness:—this tone commencing in the stanza directly following the one last quoted, with the line,

But the Raven, sitting lonely on that placid bust, spoke only, etc.

From this epoch the lover no longer jests—no longer sees any thing even of the fantastic in the Raven's demeanor. He speaks of him as a "grim, ungainly, ghastly, gaunt, and ominous bird of yore," and feels the "fiery eyes" burning into his "bosom's core." This revolution of thought, or fancy, on the lover's part, is intended to induce a similar one on the part of the reader—to bring the mind into a proper frame for the *dénouement*—which is now brought about as rapidly and as *directly* as possible.

EDGAR ALLAN POE

With the *dénouement* proper—with the Raven's reply, "Nevermore," to the lover's final demand if he shall meet his mistress in another world—the poem, in its obvious phase, that of a simple narrative, may be said to have its completion. So far, every thing is within the limits of the accountable —of the real. A raven, having learned by rote the single word "Nevermore," and having escaped from the custody of its owner, is driven at midnight, through the violence of a storm, to seek admission at a window from which a light still gleams—the chamber-window of a student, occupied half in poring over a volume, half in dreaming of a beloved mistress deceased. The casement being thrown open at the fluttering of the bird's wings, the bird itself perches on the most convenient seat out of the immediate reach of the student, who, amused by the incident and the oddity of the visitor's demeanor, demands of it, in jest and without looking for a reply, its name. The raven addressed, answers with its customary word, "Nevermore"—a word which finds immediate echo in the melancholy heart of the student, who, giving utterance aloud to certain thoughts suggested by the occasion, is again startled by the fowl's repetition of "Nevermore." The student now guesses the state of the case, but is impelled, as I have before explained, by the human thirst for self-torture, and in part by superstition, to propound such queries to the bird as will bring him, the lover, the most of the luxury of sorrow, through the anticipated answer "Nevermore." With the indulgence, to the extreme, of this self-torture, the narration, in what I have termed its first or obvious phase, has a natural termination, and so far there has been no overstepping of the limits of the real.

But in subjects so handled, however skilfully, or with however vivid an array of incident, there is always a certain hardness or nakedness, which repels the artistical eye. Two things are invariably required—first, some amount of complexity, or more properly, adaptation; and, secondly, some amount of suggestiveness—some under-current, however indefinite, of meaning. It is this latter, in especial, which imparts to a work of art so much of that *richness* (to borrow from colloquy a forcible term) which we are too fond of confounding with *the ideal*. It is the *excess* of the suggested meaning —it is the rendering this the upper instead of the under-current of the theme —which turns into prose (and that of the very flattest kind) the so-called poetry of the so-called transcendentalists.

Holding these opinions, I added the two concluding stanzas of the poem —their suggestiveness being thus made to pervade all the narrative which has preceded them. The under-current of meaning is rendered first apparent in the lines—

"Take thy beak from out *my heart*, and take thy form from off my door!"
Quoth the Raven, "Nevermore!"

It will be observed that the words, "from out my heart," involve the first

metaphorical expression in the poem. They, with the answer, "Nevermore,"
dispose the mind to seek a moral in all that has been previously narrated.
The reader begins now to regard the Raven as emblematical—but it is not
until the very last line of the very last stanza, that the intention of making
him emblematical of *Mournful and Never-ending Remembrance* is permitted
distinctly to be seen:

> And the Raven, never flitting, still is sitting, still is sitting,
> On the pallid bust of Pallas, just above my chamber door;
> And his eyes have all the seeming of a demon's that is dreaming,
> And the lamplight o'er him streaming throws his shadow on the floor;
> And my soul *from out that shadow* that lies floating on the floor
> > Shall be lifted—nevermore.

SOME SOUTHERN LYRICISTS

FRANCIS SCOTT KEY

(1779–1843)

The composer of our national anthem was a native of Pipe Creek in Western Maryland. After graduation from St. John's College in Annapolis, he studied law and then settled at Frederick, Maryland, in law partnership with Roger Brooke Taney, later Chief Justice of the United States. In 1805 Key moved to Georgetown where he practiced before the Supreme Court. After he had fought in the Battle of Bladensburg in 1814, when the American troops outside Washington were routed by the British, Key was authorized by President James Madison to visit the British battle fleet in Chesapeake Bay, together with a companion, to seek the release of the aged Dr. William Beanes, who had been taken prisoner by the British. The envoys were forced to remain aboard a British ship until after the naval attack on Fort McHenry in Baltimore harbor. After an all-night bombardment, Key kept watching the fort with his field glasses, while Dr. Beanes repeatedly asked, "Can you see the flag?" Finally a rift in the clouds at dawn showed the American standard still flying over the fort. Key wrote a rough draft of his poem on the way back to Baltimore and published a revised version in the Baltimore *Patriot* on September 20, 1814. He apparently wrote it to be sung to the tune of a British drinking song, "To Anacreon in Heaven." The song became popular at once, but it was not until 1931—generations after it had won general acceptance as the national song—that Congress voted it official status as our anthem. Key's *Poems* were posthumously collected and published in 1857.

THE STAR-SPANGLED BANNER

O! say, can you see, by the dawn's early light,
  What so proudly we hailed at the twilight's last gleaming—
Whose broad stripes and bright stars, through the clouds of the fight,
  O'er the ramparts we watched were so gallantly streaming!
And the rocket's red glare, the bombs bursting in air,
Gave proof through the night that our flag was still there;
O! say, does that star-spangled banner yet wave
O'er the land of the free, and the home of the brave?

On that shore dimly seen through the mists of the deep,
  Where the foe's haughty host in dread silence reposes,
What is that which the breeze, o'er the towering steep,
  As it fitfully blows, half conceals, half discloses?
Now it catches the gleam of the morning's first beam,
In full glory reflected now shines on the stream;
'Tis the star-spangled banner; O! long may it wave
O'er the land of the free, and the home of the brave.

And where is that band who so vauntingly swore
  That the havoc of war and the battle's confusion,
A home and a country should leave us no more?
  Their blood has washed out their foul footsteps' pollution.
No refuge could save the hireling and slave
From the terror of flight, or the gloom of the grave;
And the star-spangled banner in triumph doth wave
O'er the land of the free and the home of the brave.

O! thus be it ever, when freemen shall stand
  Between their loved homes and the war's desolation!
Blest with victory and peace, may the heav'n-rescued land
  Praise the power which hath made and preserved us a nation.
Then conquer we must, when our cause it is just,
And this be our motto: "In God is our trust."
And the star-spangled banner in triumph shall wave
O'er the land of the free, and the home of the brave.

1814

RICHARD HENRY WILDE

(1789–1847)

Richard Henry Wilde was Irish-born and came to the United States with his family at the age of eight, eventually settling at Augusta, Georgia. He was almost entirely self-educated and studied law while working in his mother's general store in Augusta. His law career was highly successful, and in 1811 he was elected Attorney-General of Georgia. Wilde served as U. S. Congressman from 1815 to 1817, in 1825, and from 1827 to 1835. Defeated for reelection in 1835, he left the United States for an extended stay in Europe. In 1837, he immersed himself in Italian scholarship and translation in Florence, and produced a book on the poet Torquato Tasso and worked on one about Dante. He returned home in 1840 and in 1844 was admitted to the bar in New Orleans.

Although Wilde's own lyric poems were never collected, he was highly regarded by some of his contemporaries. "My Life Is Like a Summer Rose," which John Greenleaf Whittier called "a perfect poem," was part of a lengthy *Meditation*. "The Mocking Bird," Wilde's version of the almost obligatory poem on the South's substitute for the literary nightingale of English romantic poetry that Southern poets felt impelled to write, was first published in Griswold's *The Poets and Poetry of America*.

"MY LIFE IS LIKE THE SUMMER ROSE"

My life is like the summer rose,
   That opens to the morning sky,
But, ere the shades of evening close,
   Is scattered on the ground—to die!
Yet on the rose's humble bed
The sweetest dews of night are shed,
As if she wept the waste to see—
But none shall weep a tear for me!

My life is like the autumn leaf
   That trembles in the moon's pale ray;
Its hold is frail—its date is brief,
   Restless—and soon to pass away!

Yet, ere that leaf shall fall and fade,
The parent tree will mourn its shade,
The winds bewail the leafless tree—
But none shall breathe a sigh for me!

My life is like the prints which feet
　　Have left on Tampa's desert strand;
Soon as the rising tide shall beat,
　　All trace will vanish from the sand;
Yet, as if grieving to efface
All vestige of the human race,
On that lone shore loud moans the sea—
But none, alas! shall mourn for me!

1818

TO THE MOCKING-BIRD

Winged mimic of the woods! thou motley fool!
　　Who shall thy gay buffoonery describe?
Thine ever-ready notes of ridicule
　　Pursue thy fellows still with jest and gibe.
　　Wit, sophist, songster, Yorick of thy tribe,
Thou sportive satirist of Nature's school,
　　To thee the palm of scoffing we ascribe.
Arch-mocker and mad Abbot of Misrule!
　　For such thou art by day—but all night long
Thou pourest a soft, sweet, pensive, solemn strain,
　　As if thou didst in this thy moonlight song
Like to the melancholy Jacques complain,
　　Musing on falsehood, folly, vice, and wrong,
And sighing for thy motley coat again.

[date uncertain]

EDWARD COOTE PINKNEY

(1802–1828)

Pinkney was born in London, where his father, William Pinkney, was American ambassador to England. The young Pinkney was educated in Baltimore, then entered the United States Navy as a midshipman and saw active service in the

Mediterranean and the Atlantic. Pinkney began the study of law in Baltimore in 1822, following the death of his father, and afterward practiced it with no great success. After an abortive trip to Mexico, where he failed to obtain a position with the Mexican navy, he returned to Baltimore, worked as a newspaper editor, and died in 1828 after prolonged ill health. In 1823 he published a Byronic narrative, *Rodolph*, and in 1825 a volume of his lyric verses, *Poems*. He read widely and was much influenced by the English Romantic poets, particularly Byron.

A HEALTH

I fill this cup to one made up of loveliness alone,
A woman, of her gentle sex the seeming paragon;
To whom the better elements and kindly stars have given
A form so fair, that, like the air, 'tis less of earth than heaven.

Her every tone is music's own, like those of morning birds,
And something more than melody dwells ever in her words;
The coinage of her heart are they, and from her lips each flows
As one may see the burthened bee forth issue from the rose.

Affections are as thoughts to her, the measures of her hours;
Her feelings have the fragrancy, the freshness, of young flowers;
And lovely passions, changing oft, so fill her, she appears
The image of themselves by turns,—the idol of past years!

Of her bright face one glance will trace a picture on the brain,
And of her voice in echoing hearts a sound must long remain,
But memory such as mine of her so very much endears,
When death is nigh my latest sigh will not be life's but hers.

I fill this cup to one made up of loveliness alone,
A woman, of her gentle sex the seeming paragon—
Her health! and would on earth there stood some more of such a frame,
That life might be all poetry, and weariness a name.

1824

SONG

Day depart this upper air,
    My lively, lovely lady;
And the eve-star sparkles fair,
    And our good steeds are ready.
Leave, leave these loveless halls,

So lordly though they be;—
Come, come—affection calls—
Away at once with me!

Sweet thy words in sense as sound,
And gladly do I hear them,
Though thy kinsmen are around,
And tamer bosoms fear them.
Mount, mount,—I'll keep thee, dear,
In safety as we ride;—
On, on—my heart is here,
My sword is at my side!

1825

THOMAS HOLLEY CHIVERS

(1807–1858)

The only one of this group of antebellum lyricists who did not also study and practice law, Thomas Holley Chivers was born in Washington, Georgia, studied at Transylvania College, and received a degree in medicine in 1830. He travelled in the West, began writing poems, and published his own books regularly. In 1840 Chivers and Poe became friends. Chivers was obviously very much influenced by Poe's verse, although it would also appear that Poe drew some of his ideas from Chivers. Chivers was very much taken with the New England Transcendentalists and believed strongly in the "felicitous outpouring of that oversoul of passion." But he was also strongly committed to seeking tonal and musical effects in language, and to a greater extent even than Poe was given to overwrought patterns of sound. "If you will come to the South to live," Chivers wrote Poe in 1847, "I will take care of you as long as you live." However, Chivers resented claims that he had plagiarized or borrowed too heavily from Poe and wrote in 1850 that "Poe stole all his *Raven* from me; but was the greatest Poetical Critic that ever existed." His poetical works include *The Path of Sorrow* (1832), *Nacoochee* (1837), *Eonchs of Ruby* (1851), *Memoralia* (1853), *Virginalia* (1853), and *Atlanta* (1853).

THOMAS HOLLEY CHIVERS

APOLLO

What are stars, but hieroglyphics of God's glory writ in lightning
    On the wide-unfolded pages of the azure scroll above?
But the quenchless apotheoses of thoughts forever brightening
    In the mighty Mind immortal of the God, whose name is Love?
Diamond letters sculptured, rising, on the azure ether pages,
    That now sing to one another—unto one another shine—
God's eternal Scripture talking, through the midnight, to the Ages,
    Of the life that is immortal, of the life that is divine—
    Life that *cannot* be immortal, but the life that is divine.

Like some deep, impetuous river from the fountains everlasting,
    Down the serpentine soft valley of the vistas of all Time,
Over cataracts of adamant uplifted into mountains,
    Soared his soul to God in thunder on the wings of thought sublime.
With the rising golden glory of the sun in ministrations,
    Making oceans metropolitan of splendor for the dawn—
Piling pyramid on pyramid of music for the nations—
    Sings the Angel who sits shining everlasting in the sun,
    For the stars, which are the echoes of the shining of the sun.

Like the lightnings piled on lightnings, ever rising, never reaching,
    In one monument of glory towards the golden gates of God—
Voicing out themselves in thunder upon thunder in their preaching,
    Piled this Cyclop up his Epic where the Angels never trod.
Like the fountains everlasting that forever more are flowing
    From the throne within the centre of the City built on high,
With their genial irrigation life forever more bestowing—
    Flows his lucid, liquid river through the gardens of the sky,
    For the stars forever blooming in the gardens of the sky.

1853

PHILIP PENDLETON COOKE

(1816–1850)

A writer of considerable native ability, Philip Pendleton Cooke grew up and lived in a society admirably fitted for encouraging his nonliterary interests. Outdoor activities—hunting, fishing—and a busy social life also came naturally to him, and as he wrote to his friend Poe when asked to contribute to Burton's *Gentleman's Magazine* in 1839, "My wife enticed me off to visit her kins-people in the country, and I saw more of guns and dogs and horses than of pens and paper. Amongst dinners, barbeques, snipe-hunting and etc. I could not gain my brains into the humour for writing to you or to anybody else." When he died of pneumonia at the age of 33, it was from having waded into the icy Shenandoah River in January to retrieve a wounded duck.

Cooke was born in Martinsburg, Virginia (now West Virginia), into a well-placed and distinguished family. He graduated from Princeton University, studied law, and set up practice, though never with much success. He began writing and publishing poetry at an early age and in the mid-1830s was a steady contributor to the *Southern Literary Messenger*. In 1847 his *Froissart Ballads, and Other Poems* was published by Carey and Hart in Philadelphia. He then wrote fiction and began producing tales that showed considerable promise. Cooke also wrote some literary criticism, which is among the best produced in the South in his era. Poe considered him his most perceptive and valuable critic.

Most scholars agree that he was more talented than his younger brother John Esten Cooke, who nonetheless achieved considerably more renown for his prose romances.

FLORENCE VANE

I loved thee long and dearly
   Florence Vane;
My life's bright dream and early
   Hath come again;
I renew, in my fond vision,
   My heart's dear pain,
My hopes, and thy derision,
   Florence Vane.

PHILIP PENDLETON COOKE

The ruin lone and hoary,
   The ruin old,
Where thou didst hark my story,
   At even told,—
That spot—the hues Elysian
   Of sky and plain—
I treasure in my vision,
   Florence Vane.

Thou wast lovelier than the roses
   In their prime;
Thy voice excelled the closes
   Of sweetest rhyme;
Thy heart was as a river
   Without a main;
Would I had loved thee never,
   Florence Vane.

But fairest, coldest wonder!
   Thy glorious clay
Lieth the green sod under—
   Alas the day!
And it boots not to remember
   Thy disdain—
To quicken love's pale ember,
   Florence Vane.

The lilies of the valley
   By young graves weep,
The pansies love to dally
   Where maidens sleep;
May their bloom, in beauty vieing,
   Never wane
Where thine earthly part is lying,
   Florence Vane!

1840

LIFE IN THE AUTUMN WOODS

Summer has gone,
And fruitful Autumn has advanced so far
That there is warmth, not heat, in the broad sun,
And you may look, with naked eye, upon
   The ardors of his car;
The stealthy frosts, whom his spent looks embolden,

Are making the green leaves golden.

What a brave splendor
Is in the October air! how rich, and clear,
And bracing, and all-joyous! We must render
Love to the Spring-time, with its sproutings tender,
    As to a child quite dear;
But Autumn is a thing of perfect glory,
    A manhood not yet hoary.

I love the woods,
In this good season of the liberal year;
I love to seek their leafy solitudes,
And give myself to melancholy moods,
    With no intruder near,
And find strange lessons, as I sit and ponder,
    In every natural wonder.

But not alone,
As Shakespeare's melancholy courtier loved Ardennes,
Love I the browning forest; and I own
I would not oft have mused, as he, but flown
    To hunt with Amiens—
And little thought, as up the bold deer bounded,
    Of the sad creature wounded.

A brave and good,
But world-worn knight—soul-wearied with his part
In this vexed life—gave man for solitude,
And built a lodge, and lived in Wantley wood,
    To hear the belling hart.
It was a gentle taste, but its sweet sadness
    Yields to the hunter's madness.

What passionate
And keen delight is in the proud swift chase!
Go out what time the lark at heaven's red gate
Soars joyously singing—quite infuriate
    With the high pride of his place;
What time the unrisen sun arrays the morning
    In its first bright adorning.

Hark! the quick horn—
As sweet to hear as any clarion—
Piercing with silver call the ear of morn;
And mark the steeds, stout Curtal and Topthorne,
    And Greysteil and the Don—

PHILIP PENDLETON COOKE

Each one of them his fiery mood displaying
    With pawing and with neighing.

    Urge your swift horse
After the crying hounds in this fresh hour;
Vanquish high hills, stem perilous streams perforce,
On the free plain give free wings to your course,
    And you will know the power
Of the brave chase,—and how of griefs the sorest
    A cure is in the forest.

    Or stalk the deer;
The same red lip of dawn has kissed the hills,
The gladdest sounds are crowding on your ear,
There is a life in all the atmosphere:—
    Your very nature fills
With the fresh hour, as up the hills aspiring
    You climb with limbs untiring.

    It is a fair
And goodly sight to see the antlered stag
With the long sweep of his swift walk repair
To join his brothers; of the plethoric bear
    Lying in some high crag,
With pinky eyes half closed, but broad head shaking,
    As gadflies keep him waking.

    And these you see,
And, seeing them, you travel to their death
With a slow, stealthy step, from tree to tree,
Noting the wind, however faint it be.
    The hunter draws a breath
In times like these, which, he will say, repays him
    For all care that waylays him.

    A strong joy fills
(A joy beyond the tongue's expressive power)
My heart in Autumn weather—fills and thrills!
And I would rather stalk the breezy hills
    Descending to my bower
Nightly, by the sweet spirit of Peace attended,
    Than pine where life is splendid.

1843

JAMES MATHEWES LEGARÉ

(1823–1859)

A distant cousin of the writer-scholar-statesman Hugh Swinton Legaré, James Mathewes Legaré was born in Charleston, South Carolina. He attended the College of Charleston and St. Mary's College in Baltimore and, like Henry Timrod and Paul Hamilton Hayne, studied law in the office of James Louis Petigru. He too quickly found the law less than congenial.

Legaré sought to earn a living from his writings and produced poetry and fiction. He also wished to establish a literary magazine and secured John C. Calhoun's endorsement for the project, but no issue was ever published. Legaré was also interested in mechanical invention and hoped to invent something that would make his fortune; he did develop a process for molding cotton into plastic form for building purposes, but nothing came of it. Legaré spent most of his adult life in Aiken, South Carolina, where his father had settled. His sole book of poetry was *Orta-Undis, and Other Poems* (1848), printed by Ticknor and Company of Boston at the author's expense.

TO A LILY

Go bow thy head in gentle spite,
Thou lily white.
For she who spies thee waving here,
With thee in beauty can compare
As day with night.

Soft are thy leaves and white: Her arms
Boast whiter charms.
Thy stem prone bent with loveliness
Of maiden grace possesseth less:
Therein she charms.

Thou in thy lake dost see
Thyself: So she
Beholds her image in her eyes
Reflected. Thus did Venus rise
From out the sea.

Inconsolate, bloom not again
Thou rival vain

Of her whose charms have thine outdone:
Whose purity might spot the sun,
And make thy leaf a stain.

1845

THE REAPER

How still Earth lies!—behind the pines
The summer clouds sink slowly down.
The sunset gilds the higher hills
And distant steeples of the town.

Refreshed and moist the meadow spreads,
Birds sing from out the dripping leaves,
And standing in the breast-high corn
I see the farmer bind his sheaves.

It was when on the fallow fields
The heavy frosts of winter lay,
A rustic with unsparing hand
Strewed seed along the furrowed way.

And I too, walking through the waste
And wintry hours of the past,
Have in the furrows made by griefs
The seeds of future harvests cast.

Rewarded well, if when the world
Grows dimmer in the ebbing light,
And all the valley lies in shade,
But sunset glimmers on the height.

Down in the meadows of the heart
The birds sing out a last refrain,
And ready garnered for the mart
I see the ripe and golden grain.

1847

GEORGE MOSES HORTON

(1797?–1883?)

George Moses Horton was born into slavery in Northampton County, North Carolina. Bondage did not keep him from learning how to read and write and becoming a poet. Indeed, he was a professional poet, for he supported himself in large part by poems composed for students at the University of North Carolina in Chapel Hill, where he lived on the income from his writings, and odd jobs through an agreement whereby he paid his owner a certain sum each week for his own services. Certain members of the University community encouraged and helped him, particularly Mrs. Caroline Lee Hentz, wife of a professor and then a popular novelist. Horton published a book of his poems, *Hope of Liberty*, in Raleigh in 1829. The poet hoped he could make money to purchase his freedom, but the returns from neither that book nor a later one, *Poetical Works of George Moses Horton*, published in Hillsboro, North Carolina, in 1845 through subscription by various whites, were enough to make that dream come true. From publication by antislavery societies of *Poems by a Slave* (Philadelphia, 1837, and Boston, 1838, the latter along with Phillis Wheatley's poetry) he received no royalties and was probably not even aware of the edition's existence. Not until the Union Army moved through North Carolina in 1865 did Horton become a free man; he then went to Philadelphia. In that year he published another book, *The Naked Genius*, in Raleigh. What he did or how he lived in Philadelphia is not known.

Until very recently, most of the Horton poems included in anthologies were the rather simple hymn-metered verses the Abolitionist press reprinted. Other poems, however, such as "Division of an Estate," in the 1845 edition, are considerably more sophisticated and accomplished.

DIVISION OF AN ESTATE

It well bespeaks a man beheaded, quite
Divested of the laurel robe of life,
When every member struggles for its base,
The head; the power of order now recedes,
Unheeded efforts rise on every side,
With dull emotion rolling through the brain
Of apprehending slaves. The flocks and
　　herds,

In sad confusion, now run to and fro,
And seem to ask, distressed, the reason why
That they are thus prostrated. Howl, ye dogs!
Ye cattle, low! ye sheep, astonish'd, bleat!
Ye bristling swine, trudge squealing through
   the glades,
Void of an owner to impart your food!
Sad horses, lift your heads and neigh aloud,
And caper frantic from the dismal scene;
Mow the last food upon your grass-clad lea,
And leave a solitary home behind,
In hopeless widowhood no longer gay!
The trav'ling sun of gain his journey ends
In unavailing pain; he sets with tears;
A king sequester'd sinking from his throne,
Succeeded by a train of busy friends,
Like stars which rise with smiles, to mark the
   flight
Of awful Phoebus to another world;
Stars after stars in fleet succession rise
Into the wide empire of fortune clear,
Regardless of the donor of their lamps;
Like heirs forgetful of parental care,
Without a grateful smile or filial tear,
Redound in rev'rence to expiring age.
But soon parental benediction flies
Like vivid meteors; in a moment gone,
As though they ne'er had been. But O! the
   state,
The dark suspense in which poor vassals
   stand
Each mind upon the spire of chance hangs
   fluctuant;
The day of separation is at hand;
Imagination lifts her gloomy curtains,
Like ev'ning's mantle at the flight of day,
Thro' which the trembling pinnacle we spy,
On which we soon must stand with hopeful
   smiles,
Or apprehending frowns; to tumble on
The right or left forever.

1845

FREDERICK DOUGLASS

THE ART OF A POET

True nature first inspires the man,
But he must after learn to scan,
   And mark well every rule;
Gradual the climax then ascend,
And prove the contrast in the end,
   Between the wit and fool.

A fool tho' blind, may write a verse,
And seem from folly to emerge,
   And rime well every line;
One lucky, void of light, may guess
And safely to the point may press,
   But this does not refine.

Polish mirror, clear to shine,
And streams must run if they refine,
   And widen as they flow;
The diamond water lies concealed,
Till polished it is ne'er revealed,
   Its glory bright to show.

A bard must traverse o'er the world,
Where things concealed must rise unfurled,
   And tread the feet of yore;
Tho' he may sweetly harp and sing,
But strictly prune the mental wing,
   Before the mind can soar.

1865

FREDERICK DOUGLASS

(1817?–1895)

The dominant form of writing by black Southerners before 1865 was, not surprisingly, the slave narrative. These accounts were composed by (and often for) runaway bondsmen who had escaped to the North and published by abolitionist societies as examples of the horrors of slavery as well as of the intense desire—and by implication the intellectual competence—of black Southerners to be free. The best known narrative was that of the remarkable Frederick Douglass. He was born into slavery at Tuckahoe, Maryland, of a white father and a slave mother, and named Frederick Augustus Washington Bailey. After successfully fleeing from slavery to New York and then Massachusetts in 1838, he took the name of Frederick Douglass and soon became active in the antislavery cause. He founded a newspaper, the *North Star*, and during the 1840s and 1850s was at the forefront of antislavery activities. After the war Douglass became a champion of black enfranchisement and civil rights, writing and arguing eloquently for educational opportunities, military privileges, and the rights of blacks in labor. He was closely identified with the Republican Party and held numerous offices, including that of Minister Resident and Consul General to Haiti.

As a writer he produced three autobiographies, *Narrative of the Life of Frederick Douglass* (1845), *My Bondage and My Freedom* (1855), and *Life and Times of Frederick Douglass* (1881, enlarged in 1892). The earliest version, from which the following excerpt is taken, is particularly graphic in its vivid picture of slave experience.

From NARRATIVE OF THE LIFE OF FREDERICK DOUGLASS, AN AMERICAN SLAVE, BY HIMSELF

From CHAPTER X

But to return to Mr. Freeland, and to my experience while in his employment. He, like Mr. Covey, gave us enough to eat; but, unlike Mr. Covey, he also gave us sufficient time to take our meals. He worked us hard, but always between sunrise and sunset. He required a good deal of work to be done, but gave us good tools with which to work. His farm was large, but he employed hands enough to work it, and with ease, compared with many of his neighbors. My treatment, while in his employment, was heavenly, compared with what I experienced at the hands of Mr. Edward Covey.

Mr. Freeland was himself the owner of but two slaves. Their names were Henry Harris and John Harris. The rest of his hands he hired. These consisted of myself, Sandy Jenkins, and Handy Caldwell. Henry and John were quite intelligent, and in a very little while after I went there, I succeeded in creating in them a strong desire to learn how to read. This desire soon sprang up in the others also. They very soon mustered up some old spelling-books, and nothing would do but that I must keep a Sabbath school. I agreed to do so, and accordingly devoted my Sundays to teaching these my loved fellow-slaves how to read. Neither of them knew his letters when I went there. Some of the slaves of the neighboring farms found what was going on, and also availed themselves of this little opportunity to learn to read. It was understood, among all who came, that there must be as little display about it as possible. It was necessary to keep our religious masters at St. Michael's unacquainted with the fact, that, instead of spending the Sabbath in wrestling, boxing, and drinking whisky, we were trying to learn how to read the will of God; for they had much rather see us engaged in those degrading sports, than to see us behaving like intellectual, moral, and accountable beings. My blood boils as I think of the bloody manner in which Messrs. Wright Fairbanks and Garrison West, both class-leaders, in connection with many others, rushed in upon us with sticks and stones, and broke up our virtuous little Sabbath school, at St. Michael's—all calling themselves Christians! humble followers of the Lord Jesus Christ! But I am again digressing.

I held my Sabbath school at the house of a free colored man, whose name I deem it imprudent to mention; for should it be known, it might embarrass him greatly, though the crime of holding the school was committed ten years ago. I had at one time over forty scholars, and those of the right sort, ardently desiring to learn. They were of all ages, though mostly men and women. I look back to those Sundays with an amount of pleasure not to be expressed. They were great days to my soul. The work of instructing my dear fellow-slaves was the sweetest engagement with which I was ever blessed. We loved each other, and to leave them at the close of the Sabbath was a severe cross indeed. When I think that these precious souls are to-day shut up in the prison-house of slavery, my feelings overcome me, and I am almost ready to ask, "Does a righteous God govern the universe? and for what does he hold the thunders in his right hand, if not to smite the oppressor, and deliver the spoiled out of the hand of the spoiler?" These dear souls came not to Sabbath school because it was popular to do so, nor did I teach them because it was reputable to be thus engaged. Every moment they spent in that school, they were liable to be taken up, and given thirty-nine lashes. They came because they wished to learn. Their minds had been starved by their cruel masters. They had been shut up in mental darkness. I taught them, because it was the delight of my soul to be doing something that looked like bettering the condition of my race. I kept up my school nearly the whole year I lived with Mr. Freeland; and, beside my Sabbath school, I devoted three evenings in the week, during the winter, to teaching the slaves at home. And I have the happiness to know, that several of those who came to Sabbath school learned how to read; and that one, at least, is now free through my agency.

The year passed off smoothly. It seemed only about half as long as the year which preceded it. I went through it without receiving a single blow. I will give Mr. Freeland the credit of being the best master I ever had, *till I became my own master.* For the ease with which I passed the year, I was, however, somewhat indebted to the society of my fellow-slaves. They were noble souls; they not only possessed loving hearts, but brave ones. We were linked and interlinked with each other. I loved them with a love stronger than any thing I have experienced since. It is sometimes said that we slaves do not love and confide in each other. In answer to this assertion, I can say, I never loved any or confided in any people more than my fellow-slaves, and especially those with whom I lived at Mr. Freeland's. I believe we would have died for each other. We never undertook to do any thing, of any importance, without a mutual consultation. We never moved separately. We were one; and as much so by our tempers and dispositions, as by the mutual hardships to which we were necessarily subjected by our condition as slaves.

At the close of the year 1834, Mr. Freeland again hired me of my master, for the year 1835. But, by this time, I began to want to live *upon free land* as well as *with Freeland*; and I was no longer content, therefore, to live with him or any other slaveholder. I began, with the commencement of the year, to prepare myself for a final struggle, which should decide my fate one way or the other. My tendency was upward. I was fast approaching manhood, and year after year had passed, and I was still a slave. These thoughts roused me—I must do something. I therefore resolved that 1835 should not pass without witnessing an attempt, on my part, to secure my liberty. But I was not willing to cherish this determination alone. My fellow-slaves were dear to me. I was anxious to have them participate with me in this, my life-giving determination. I therefore, though with great prudence, commenced early to ascertain their views and feelings in regard to their condition, and to imbue their minds with thoughts of freedom. I bent myself to devising ways and means for our escape, and meanwhile strove, on all fitting occasions, to impress them with the gross fraud and inhumanity of slavery. I went first to Henry, next to John, then to the others. I found, in them all, warm hearts and noble spirits. They were ready to hear, and ready to act when a feasible plan should be proposed. This was what I wanted. I talked to them of our want of manhood, if we submitted to our enslavement without at least one noble effort to be free. We met often, and consulted frequently, and told our hopes and fears, recounted the difficulties, real and imagined, which we should be called on to meet. At times we were almost disposed to give up, and try to content ourselves with our wretched lot; at others, we were firm and unbending in our determination to go. Whenever we suggested any plan, there was shrinking—the odds were fearful. Our path was beset with the greatest obstacles; and if we succeeded in gaining the end of it, our right to be free was yet questionable—we were yet liable to be returned to bondage. We could see no spot, this side of the ocean, where we could be free. We knew nothing about Canada. Our knowledge of the north did not extend farther than New York; and to go there, and be forever harassed with the frightful liability of being returned to slavery—with the certainty of being treated tenfold worse than before—the thought was truly a horrible one, and one which it was not easy to overcome. The case sometimes stood thus: At every gate through which we were to pass, we saw a watchman—at every ferry a guard—on every bridge a sentinel—and in every wood a patrol. We were hemmed in upon every side. Here were the difficulties, real or imagined—the good to be sought, and the evil to be shunned. On the one hand, there stood slavery, a stern reality, glaring frightfully upon us,—its robes already crimsoned with the blood of millions, and even now feasting itself greedily upon our own flesh. On the other hand, away back in the dim distance, under the flickering light of the north star, behind some craggy hill or snow-covered mountain, stood a doubtful freedom—half frozen—beckoning us to come and share its hospitality. This in itself was sometimes enough to stagger us; but when we permitted ourselves to survey the road, we were frequently appalled. Upon either side we saw grim death, assuming the most horrid shapes. Now it was starvation, causing us to eat our own flesh;—now we were contending with the waves, and were drowned;—now we were overtaken, and torn to pieces by the fangs of the terrible bloodhound. We were stung by scorpions, chased by wild beasts, bitten by snakes, and finally, after having nearly reached the desired spot,—after swimming rivers, encountering wild beasts, sleeping in the woods, suffering hunger and nakedness,—we were overtaken by our pursuers, and, in our resistance, we were shot dead upon the spot! I say, this picture sometimes appalled us, and made us

> "rather bear those ills we had,
> Than fly to others, that we knew not of."

In coming to a fixed determination to run away, we did more than Patrick Henry, when he resolved upon liberty or death. With us it was a doubtful liberty at most, and almost certain death if we failed. For my part, I should prefer death to hopeless bondage.

Sandy, one of our number, gave up the notion, but still encouraged us. Our company then consisted of Henry Harris, John Harris, Henry Bailey, Charles Roberts, and myself. Henry Bailey was my uncle, and belonged to my master. Charles married my aunt: he belonged to my master's father-in-law, Mr. William Hamilton.

The plan we finally concluded upon was, to get a large canoe belonging to Mr. Hamilton, and upon the Saturday night previous to Easter holidays, paddle directly up the Chesapeake Bay. On our arrival at the head of the bay, a distance of seventy or eighty miles from where we lived, it was our purpose to turn our canoe adrift, and follow the guidance of the north star till we got beyond the limits of Maryland. Our reason for taking the water route was, that we were less liable to be suspected as runaways; we hoped to be regarded as fishermen; whereas, if we should take the land route, we should be subjected to interruptions of almost every kind. Any one having a white face, and being so disposed, could stop us, and subject us to examination.

The week before our intended start, I wrote several protections, one for each of us. As well as I can remember, they were in the following words, to wit:—

"This is to certify that I, the undersigned, have given the bearer, my servant, full liberty to go to Baltimore, and spend the Easter holidays. Written with mine own hand, &c., 1835.

"WILLIAM HAMILTON
"Near St. Michael's, in Talbot county, Maryland."

We were not going to Baltimore; but, in going up the bay, we went toward Baltimore, and these protections were only intended to protect us while on the bay.

As the time drew near for our departure, our anxiety became more and more intense. It was truly a matter of life and death with us. The strength of our determination was about to be fully tested. At this time, I was very active in explaining every difficulty, removing every doubt, dispelling every fear, and inspiring all with the firmness indispensable to success in our undertaking; assuring them that half was gained the instant we made the move; we had talked long enough; we were now ready to move; if not now, we never should be; and if we did not intend to move now, we had as well fold our arms, sit down, and acknowledge ourselves fit only to be slaves. This, none of us were prepared to acknowledge. Every man stood firm; and at our last meeting, we pledged ourselves afresh, in the most solemn manner, that, at the time appointed, we would certainly start in pursuit of freedom. This was in the middle of the week, at the end of which we were to be off. We went, as usual, to our several fields of labor, but with bosoms highly agitated with thoughts of our truly hazardous undertaking. We tried to conceal our feelings as much as possible; and I think we succeeded very well.

After a painful waiting, the Saturday morning, whose night was to witness our departure, came. I hailed it with joy, bring what sadness it might. Friday night was a sleepless one for me. I probably felt more anxious than the rest, because I was, by common consent, at the head of the whole affair. The responsibility of success or failure lay heavily upon me. The glory of the one, and the confusion of the other, were alike mine. The first two hours of that morning were such as I never experienced before, and hope never to again. Early in the morning, we went, as usual, to the field. We were spreading manure; and all at once, while thus engaged, I was overwhelmed with an indescribable feeling, in the fulness of which I turned to Sandy, who was near by, and said, "We are betrayed!" "Well," said he, "that thought has this moment struck me." We said no more. I was never more certain of any thing.

The horn was blown as usual, and we went up from the field to the house for breakfast. I went for the form, more than for want of any thing to eat that morning. Just as I got to the house, in looking out at the lane gate, I saw four white men, with two colored men. The white men were on horse-back, and the colored ones were walking behind, as if tied. I watched them a few moments till they got up to our lane gate. Here they halted, and tied the colored men to the gatepost. I was not yet certain as to what the matter was. In a few moments, in rode Mr. Hamilton, with a speed betokening great excitement. He came to the door, and inquired if Master William was in. He was told he was at the barn. Mr. Hamilton, without dismounting, rode up to the barn with extraordinary speed. In a few moments, he and Mr. Freeland returned to the house. By this time, the three constables rode up, and in great haste dismounted, tied their horses, and met Master William and Mr. Hamilton returning from the barn; and after talking awhile, they all walked up to the kitchen door. There was no one in the kitchen but myself and John. Henry and Sandy were up at the barn. Mr. Freeland put his head in at the door, and called me by name, saying, there were some gentlemen at the door who wished to see me. I stepped to the door, and inquired what they wanted. They at once seized me, and, without giving me any satisfaction, tied me—lashing my hands closely together. I insisted upon knowing what the matter was. They at length said, that they had learned I had been in a "scrape," and that I was to be examined before my master; and if their information proved false, I should not be hurt.

In a few moments, they succeeded in tying John. They then turned to Henry, who had by this time returned, and commanded him to cross his hands. "I won't!" said Henry, in a firm tone, indicating his readiness to meet the consequences of his refusal. "Won't you?" said Tom Graham, the constable. "No, I won't!" said Henry, in a still stronger tone. With this, two of the constables pulled out their shining pistols, and swore, by their Creator, that they would make him cross his hands or kill him. Each cocked his pistol, and, with fingers on the trigger, walked up to Henry, saying, at the same time, if he did not cross his hands, they would blow his damned heart out. "Shoot me, shoot me!" said Henry; "you can't kill me but once. Shoot, shoot,—and be damned! *I won't be tied!*" This he said in a tone of loud defiance; and at the same time, with a motion as quick as lightning, he with one single stroke dashed the pistols from the hand of each constable. As he did this, all hands fell upon him, and, after beating him some time, they finally overpowered him, and got him tied.

During the scuffle, I managed, I know not how, to get my pass out, and, without being discovered, put it into the fire. We were all now tied; and just as we were to leave for Easton jail, Betsy Freeland, mother of William Freeland, came to the door with her hands full of biscuits, and divided them between Henry and John. She then delivered herself of a speech, to the following effect:—addressing herself to me, she said, *"You devil! You yellow devil!* it was you that put it into the heads of Henry and John to run away. But for you, you long-legged mulatto devil! Henry nor John would never have thought of such a thing." I made no reply, and was immediately hurried off towards St. Michael's. Just a moment previous to the scuffle with Henry, Mr. Hamilton suggested the propriety of making a search for the protections which he had understood Frederick had written for himself and the rest. But, just at the moment he was about carrying his proposal into effect, his aid was needed in helping to tie Henry; and the excitement attending the scuffle caused them either to forget, or to deem it unsafe, under the circumstances, to search. So we were not yet convicted of the intention to run away.

When we got about half way to St. Michael's, while the constables having us in charge were looking ahead, Henry inquired of me what he should do with his pass. I told him to eat it with his biscuit, and own nothing; and we passed the word around, *"Own nothing;"* and *"Own nothing!"* said we all. Our confidence in each other was unshaken. We were resolved to succeed or fail together, after the calamity had befallen us as much as before. We were now prepared for any thing. We were to be dragged that morning fifteen miles behind horses, and then to be placed in the Easton jail. When we reached St. Michael's, we underwent a sort of examination. We all denied that we ever intended to run away. We did this more to bring out the evidence against us, than from any hope of getting clear of being sold; for, as I have said, we were ready for that. The fact was, we cared but little where we went, so we went together. Our greatest concern was about separation. We dreaded that more than any thing this side of death. We found the evidence against us to be the testimony of one person; our master would not tell who it was; but we came to a unanimous decision among ourselves as to who their informant was. We were sent off to the jail at Easton. When we got there, we were delivered up to the sheriff, Mr. Joseph Graham, and by him placed in jail. Henry, John, and myself, were placed in one room together—Charles, and Henry Bailey, in another. Their object in separating us was to hinder concert.

We had been in jail scarcely twenty minutes, when a swarm of slave traders, and agents for slave traders, flocked into jail to look at us, and to ascertain if we were for sale. Such a set of beings I never saw before! I felt myself surrounded by so many fiends from perdition. A band of pirates never looked more like their father, the devil. They laughed and grinned over us, saying, "Ah, my boys! we have got you, haven't we?" And after taunting us in various ways, they one by one went into an examination of us, with intent to ascertain our value. They would impudently ask us if we would not like to have them for our masters. We would make them no answer, and leave them to find out as best they could. Then they would curse and swear at us, telling us that they could take the devil out of us in a very little while, if we were only in their hands.

While in jail, we found ourselves in much more comfortable quarters than we expected when we went there. We did not get much to eat, nor that which was very good; but we had a good clean room, from the windows of which we could see what was going on in the street, which was very much better than though we had been placed in one of the dark, damp cells. Upon the whole, we got along very well, so far as the jail and its keeper were concerned. Immediately after the holidays were over, contrary to all our expectations, Mr. Hamilton and Mr. Freeland came up to Easton, and took Charles, the two Henrys, and John, out of jail, and carried them home, leaving me alone. I regarded this separation as a final one. It caused me more pain than any thing else in the whole transaction. I was ready for any thing rather than separation. I supposed that they had consulted together, and had decided that, as I was the whole cause of the intention of the others to run away, it was hard to make the innocent suffer with the guilty; and that they had, therefore, concluded to take the others home, and sell me, as a warning to the others that remained. It is due to the noble Henry to say, he seemed almost as reluctant at leaving the prison as at leaving home to come to the prison. But we knew we should, in all probability, be separated, if we were sold; and since he was in their hands, he concluded to go peaceably home.

I was now left to my fate. I was all alone, and within the walls of a stone prison. But a few days before, and I was full of hope. I expected to have been safe in a land of freedom; but now I was covered with gloom, sunk down to the utmost despair. I thought the possibility of freedom was gone. I was kept in this way about one week, at the end of which, Captain Auld, my master, to my surprise and utter astonishment, came up, and took me out, with the intention of sending me, with a gentleman of his acquaintance, into Alabama. But, from some cause or other, he did not send me to Alabama, but concluded to send me back to Baltimore, to live again with his brother Hugh, and to learn a trade.

Thus, after an absence of three years and one month, I was once more permitted to return to my old home at Baltimore. My master sent me away, because there existed against me a very great prejudice in the community, and he feared I might be killed.

WILLIAM WELLS BROWN

(c. 1816–1884)

Clotel: or, The President's Daughter, by William Wells Brown, was the first extended work of fiction by a black American writer. Brown, who was born a slave in Lexington, Kentucky, was a prolific author and his novel was not his only "first"—he was also the first black American playwright and the first to write a travel book. At age ten he was taken by his master to St. Louis, Missouri, where he worked on riverboats and in a printing office until 1834, when his master brought him to Cincinnati, Ohio, and he walked away and escaped northward. He was helped by a Quaker named Wells Brown and afterward took that name in gratitude.

Quickly acquiring an education, he turned to writing and produced a slave narrative in 1847 and a book of song-poems in 1848, *The Anti-Slavery Harp*. In 1849 Victor Hugo, president of the Paris Peace Congress, invited him to France to address that body. Brown stayed in Europe awhile and in 1853 published *Clotel* in London. The book went through three editions. He returned to the United States in 1854, when he was officially granted his freedom, and wrote a book describing his European travels, and a five-act drama, *The Escape, or a Leap for Freedom* (1858). In 1863 he published *The Black Man; His Antecedents, His Genius, and His Achievements*. The following year an American edition of his novel was published, under the title *Clotelle: A Tale of Southern States*. In the English version, Brown made his heroine the daughter of the President, drawing on an alleged account of Thomas Jefferson's fathering of a slave child. For the American edition a United States Senator was substituted for Jefferson. The following selection is from the American version. Brown wrote numerous books after the war, including *My Southern Home* (1880).

From CLOTELLE: A TALE OF SOUTHERN STATES

Chapter II

THE NEGRO SALE

As might have been expected, the day of sale brought an unusually large number together to compete for the property to be sold. Farmers, who made a business of raising slaves for the market, were there, and slave-traders, who make a business of buying human beings in the slaveraising States and taking them to the far South, were also in attendance. Men and women, too, who wished to purchase for their own use, had found their way to the slave sale.

In the midst of the throng was one who felt a deeper interest in the result of the sale than any other of the bystanders. This was young Linwood. True to his promise, he was there with a blank bank-check in his pocket, awaiting with impatience to enter the list as a bidder for the beautiful slave.

It was indeed a heart-rending scene to witness the lamentations of these slaves, all of whom had grown up together on the old homestead of Mr. Graves, and who had been treated with great kindness by that gentleman, during his life. Now they were to be separated, and form new relations and companions. Such is the precarious condition of the slave. Even when with a good master, there is no certainty of his happiness in the future.

The less valuable slaves were first placed upon the auction-block, one after another, and sold to the highest bidder. Husbands and wives were separated with a degree of indifference that is unknown in any other relation in life. Brothers and sisters were torn from each other, and mothers saw their children for the last time on earth.

It was late in the day, and when the greatest number of persons were thought to be present, when Agnes and her daughters were brought out to the place of sale. The mother was first put upon the auction-block, and sold to a noted negro trader named Jennings. Marion was next ordered to ascend the stand, which she did with a trembling step, and was sold for $1200.

All eyes were now turned on Isabella, as she was led forward by the auctioneer. The appearance of the handsome quadroon caused a deep sensation among the crowd. There she stood, with a skin as fair as most white women, her features as beautifully regular as any of her sex of pure Anglo-Saxon blood, her long black hair done up in the neatest manner, her form tall and graceful, and her whole appearance indicating one superior to her condition.

The auctioneer commenced by saying that Miss Isabella was fit to deck the drawing-room of the finest mansion in Virginia.

"How much, gentlemen, for this real Albino!—fit fancy-girl for any one! She enjoys good health, and has a sweet temper. How much do you say?"

"Five hundred dollars."

"Only five hundred for such a girl as this? Gentlemen, she is worth a deal more than that sum. You certainly do not know the value of the article you are bidding on. Here, gentlemen, I hold in my hand a paper certifying that she has a good moral character."

"Seven hundred."

"Ah, gentlemen, that is something like. This paper also states that she is very intelligent."

"Eight hundred."

"She was first sprinkled, then immersed, and is now warranted to be a devoted Christian, and perfectly trustworthy."

"Nine hundred dollars."

"Nine hundred and fifty."

"One thousand."

"Eleven hundred."

Here the bidding came to a dead stand. The auctioneer stopped, looked around, and began in a rough manner to relate some anecdote connected with the sale of slaves, which he said had come under his own observation.

At this juncture the scene was indeed a most striking one. The laughing, joking, swearing, smoking, spitting, and talking, kept up a continual hum and confusion among the crowd, while the slave-girl stood with tearful eyes, looking alternately at her mother and sister and toward the young man whom she hoped would become her purchaser.

"The chastity of this girl," now continued the auctioneer, "is pure. She has never been from under her mother's care. She is virtuous, and as gentle as a dove."

The bids here took a fresh start, and went on until $1800 was reached. The auctioneer once more resorted to his jokes, and concluded by assuring the company that Isabella was not only pious, but that she could make an excellent prayer.

"Nineteen hundred dollars."

"Two thousand."

This was the last bid, and the quadroon girl was struck off, and became the property of Henry Linwood.

This was a Virginia slave-auction, at which the bones, sinews, blood, and nerves of a young girl of eighteen was sold for $500; her moral character for $200; her superior intellect for $100; the benefits supposed to accrue from her having been sprinkled and immersed, together with a warranty of her devoted Christianity, for $300; her ability to make a good prayer for $200; and her chastity for $700 more. This, too, in a city thronged with churches, whose tall spires look like so many signals pointing to heaven, but whose ministers preach that slavery is a God-ordained institution!

The slaves were speedily separated, and taken along by their respective masters. Jennings, the slave-speculator, who had purchased Agnes and her daughter Marion, with several of the other slaves, took them to the county prison, where he usually kept his human cattle after purchasing them, previous to starting for the New Orleans market.

Linwood had already provided a place for Isabella, to which she was taken. The most trying moment for her was when she took leave of her mother and sister. The "Good-by" of the slave is unlike that of any other class in the community. It is indeed a farewell forever. With tears streaming down their cheeks, they embraced and commended each other to God, who is no respecter of persons, and before whom master and slave must one day appear.

HENRY TIMROD

(1829–1867)

Of all the poets North and South who penned lyrics having to do with the American Civil War, only three produced work that has survived its immediate occasion—Walt Whitman, Herman Melville, and Henry Timrod. The advent of the war gave Timrod, until then the author of some well-crafted but otherwise unremarkable love poems, his great theme. In the hopes and fears of his native land, Timrod found the subject that could deepen his insight and extend the range of his sensibilities. In the words of C. Hugh Holman, he attained in his work "a calmness and classic severity," and among Timrod's poems there are a half-dozen or more that stand out as the most memorable of all writings about the war by Southern authors. He has been called the "Laureate of the Confederacy," and this title is appropriate, for Timrod went beneath the surface of the war experience to get at its meanings. In poems such as "Spring," "Rain," "Charleston," and the remarkable sonnet "I know not why," he caught something of the pathos of the occasion and a sense of apprehension and despair.

Had the results of the war been other than they were, of course, Timrod's poetry would be read differently today. The modern reader can only find irony for lines such as the description of New York Harbor that closes "The Cotton Boll." But Timrod's craftsmanship, his use of language, his sensuous imagination, and his unwillingness to rely upon the poetic abstractions that characterize most of the verse of the period make his war poems moving even so.

Timrod was born in Charleston, South Carolina. His father, William Henry

Timrod, was a bookbinder and a minor poet of some talent. The younger Timrod attended school along with Paul Hamilton Hayne and later studied at the University of Georgia. A brief experience as a clerk in James L. Petigru's law office convinced him that he was not destined for the law, and he sought to find a university teaching position but instead was only able to secure employment as a private teacher. As a member of the Russell's Bookstore group he was friendly with Hayne, Simms, and others of the Charleston literati, and for *Russell's Magazine* he wrote several essays that are among the better literary criticism produced in the antebellum South.

When the war came Timrod served for a time in the army, but his poor health forced him to leave active duty. He worked as war correspondent for the Charleston *Mercury* and was present at Shiloh; he then served as a reporter in Charleston and an editor of the *South Carolinian* in Columbia. In the debacle that followed the burning of Columbia and the end of the war, Timrod could find little employment. The last several years of his life, during which he was ill with tuberculosis, were a time of suffering and destitution. To Hayne he wrote that "I would consign every line I wrote to eternal oblivion for one hundred dollars in hand."

SONNET: I KNOW NOT WHY

I know not why, but all this weary day,
Suggested by no definite grief or pain,
Sad fancies have been flitting through my brain;
Now it has been a vessel losing way,
Rounding a stormy headland; now a gray
Dull waste of clouds above a wintry main;
And then, a banner, drooping in the rain,
And meadows beaten into bloody clay.
Strolling at random with this shadowy woe
At heart, I chanced to wander hither! Lo!
A league of desolate marsh-land, with its lush,
Hot grasses in a noisome, tide-left bed,
And faint, warm airs, that rustle in the hush,
Like whispers round the body of the dead!

1861

ETHNOGENESIS

I

Hath not the morning dawned with added light?
And shall not evening call another star

ETHNOGENESIS

Out of the infinite regions of the night,
To mark this day in Heaven? At last, we are
A nation among nations; and the world
Shall soon behold in many a distant port
    Another flag unfurled!
Now, come what may, whose favor need we court?
And, under God, whose thunder need we fear?
    Thank Him who placed us here
Beneath so kind a sky—the very sun
Takes part with us; and on our errands run
All breezes of the ocean; dew and rain
Do noiseless battle for us; and the Year,
And all the gentle daughters in her train,
March in our ranks, and in our service wield
    Long spears of golden grain!
A yellow blossom as her fairy shield,
June flings her azure banner to the wind,
    While in the order of their birth
Her sisters pass, and many an ample field
Grows white beneath their steps, till now, behold,
    Its endless sheets unfold
THE SNOW OF SOUTHERN SUMMERS! Let the earth
Rejoice! beneath those fleeces soft and warm
    Our happy land shall sleep
    In a repose as deep
    As if we lay intrenched behind
Whole leagues of Russian ice and Arctic storm!

II

And what if, mad with wrongs themselves have wrought,
    In their own treachery caught,
    By their own fears made bold,
    And leagued with him of old,
Who long since in the limits of the North
Set up his evil throne, and warred with God—
What if, both mad and blinded in their rage,
Our foes should fling us down their mortal gage,
And with a hostile step profane our sod!
We shall not shrink, my brothers, but go forth
To meet them, marshaled by the Lord of Hosts,
And overshadowed by the mighty ghosts
Of Moultrie and of Eutaw—who shall foil
Auxiliars such as these? Nor these alone,

But every stock and stone
   Shall help us; but the very soil,
And all the generous wealth it gives to toil,
And all for which we love our noble land,
Shall fight beside, and through us; sea and strand,
   The heart of woman, and her hand,
Tree, fruit, and flower, and every influence,
     Gentle, or grave, or grand;
   The winds in our defence
Shall seem to blow; to us the hills shall lend
   Their firmness and their calm;
And in our stiffened sinews we shall blend
   The strength of pine and palm!

III

Nor would we shun the battle-ground,
   Though weak as we are strong;
Call up the clashing elements around,
   And test the right and wrong!
On one side, creeds that dare to teach
What Christ and Paul refrained to preach;
Codes built upon a broken pledge,
And Charity that whets a poniard's edge;
Fair schemes that leave the neighboring poor
To starve and shiver at the schemer's door,
While in the world's most liberal ranks enrolled,
He turns some vast philanthropy to gold;
Religion, taking every mortal form
But that a pure and Christian faith makes warm,
Where not to vile fanatic passion urged,
Or not in vague philosophies submerged,
Repulsive with all Pharisaic leaven,
And making laws to stay the laws of Heaven!
And on the other, scorn of sordid gain,
Unblemished honor, truth without a stain,
Faith, justice, reverence, charitable wealth,
And, for the poor and humble, laws which give,
Not the mean right to buy the right to live,
   But life, and home, and health!
To doubt the end were want of trust in God,
   Who, if he has decreed
  That we must pass a redder sea
Than that which rang to Miriam's holy glee,

Will surely raise at need
A Moses with his rod!

IV

But let our fears—if fears we have—be still,
And turn us to the future! Could we climb
Some mighty Alp, and view the coming time,
The rapturous sight would fill
      Our eyes with happy tears!
Not only for the glories which the years
Shall bring us; not for lands from sea to sea,
And wealth, and power, and peace, though these shall be;
But for the distant peoples we shall bless,
And the hushed murmurs of a world's distress:
For, to give labor to the poor,
      The whole sad planet o'er,
And save from want and crime the humblest door,
Is one among the many ends for which
      God makes us great and rich!
The hour perchance is not yet wholly ripe
When all shall own it, but the type
Whereby we shall be known in every land
Is that vast gulf which lips our Southern strand,
And through the cold, untempered ocean pours
Its genial streams, that far off Arctic shores
May sometimes catch upon the softened breeze
Strange tropic warmth and hints of summer seas.

1861

THE COTTON BOLL

While I recline
At ease beneath
This immemorial pine,
Small sphere!
(By dusky fingers brought this morning here
And shown with boastful smiles),
I turn thy cloven sheath,
Through which the soft white fibres peer,
That, with their gossamer bands,
Unite, like love, the sea-divided lands,
And slowly, thread by thread,

Draw forth the folded strands,
Than which the trembling line,
By whose frail help yon startled spider fled
Down the tall spear-grass from his swing bed,
Is scarce more fine;
And as the tangled skein
Unravels in my hands,
Betwixt me and the noonday light,
A veil seems lifted, and for miles and miles
The landscape broadens on my sight,
As, in the little boll, there lurked a spell
Like that which, in the ocean shell,
With mystic sound,
Breaks down the narrow walls that hem us round,
And turns some city lane
Into the restless main,
With all his capes and isles!

Yonder bird,
Which floats, as if at rest,
In those blue tracts above the thunder, where
No vapors cloud the stainless air,
And never sound is heard,
Unless at such rare time
When, from the City of the Blest,
Rings down some golden chime,
Sees not from his high place
So vast a cirque of summer space
As widens round me in one mighty field,
Which, rimmed by seas and sands,
Doth hail its earliest daylight in the beams
Of gray Atlantic dawns;
And, broad as realms made up of many lands,
Is lost afar
Behind the crimson hills and purple lawns
Of sunset, among plains which roll their streams
Against the Evening Star!
And lo!
To the remotest point of sight,
Although I gaze upon no waste of snow,
The endless field is white;
And the whole landscape glows,
For many a shining league away,
With such accumulated light

THE COTTON BOLL

As Polar lands would flash beneath a tropic day!
Nor lack there (for the vision grows,
And the small charm within my hands—
More potent even than the fabled one,
Which oped whatever golden mystery
Lay hid in fairy wood or magic vale,
The curious ointment of the Arabian tale—
Beyond all mortal sense
Doth stretch my sight's horizon, and I see,
Beneath its simple influence,
As if with Uriel's crown,
I stood in some great temple of the Sun,
And looked, as Uriel, down!)
Nor lack there pastures rich and fields all green
With all the common gifts of God,
For temperate airs and torrid sheen
Weave Edens of the sod;
Through lands which look one sea of billowy gold
Broad rivers wind their devious ways;
A hundred isles in their embraces fold
A hundred luminous bays;
And through yon purple haze
Vast mountains lift their plumed peaks cloud-crowned;
And, save where up their sides the ploughman creeps,
An unhewn forest girds them grandly round,
In whose dark shades a future navy sleeps!
Ye Stars, which, though unseen, yet with me gaze
Upon this loveliest fragment of the earth!
Thou Sun, that kindlest all thy gentlest rays
Above it, as to light a favorite hearth!
Ye Clouds, that in your temples in the West
See nothing brighter than its humblest flowers!
And you, ye Winds, that on the ocean's breast
Are kissed to coolness ere ye reach its bowers!
Bear witness with me in my song of praise,
And tell the world that, since the world began,
No fairer land hath fired a poet's lays,
Or given a home to man!

But these are charms already widely blown!
His be the meed whose pencil's trace
Hath touched our very swamps with grace,
And round whose tuneful way
All Southern laurels bloom;

HENRY TIMROD

The Poet of "The Woodlands," unto whom
Alike are known
The flute's low breathing and the trumpet's tone,
And the soft west wind's sighs;
But who shall utter all the debt,
O Land wherein all powers are met
That bind a people's heart,
The world doth owe thee at this day,
And which it never can repay,
Yet scarcely deigns to own!
Where sleeps the poet who shall fitly sing
The source wherefrom doth spring
That mighty commerce which, confined
To the mean channels of no selfish mart,
Goes out to every shore
Of this broad earth, and throngs the sea with ships
That bear no thunders; hushes hungry lips
In alien lands;
Joins with a delicate web remotest strands;
And gladdening rich and poor,
Doth gild Parisian domes,
Or feed the cottage-smoke of English homes,
And only bounds its blessings by mankind!
In offices like these, thy mission lies,
My Country! and it shall not end
As long as rain shall fall and Heaven bend
In blue above thee; though thy foes be hard
And cruel as their weapons, it shall guard
Thy hearth-stones as a bulwark; make thee great
In white and bloodless state;
And haply, as the years increase—
Still working through its humbler reach
With that large wisdom which the ages teach—
Revive the half-dead dream of universal peace!
As men who labor in that mine
Of Cornwall, hollowed out beneath the bed
Of ocean, when a storm rolls overhead,
Hear the dull booming of the world of brine
Above them, and a mighty muffled roar
Of winds and waters, yet toil calmly on,
And split the rock, and pile the massive ore,
Or carve a niche, or shape the archèd roof;
So I, as calmly, weave my woof
Of song, chanting the days to come,

CHARLESTON

Unsilenced, though the quiet summer air
Stirs with the bruit of battles, and each dawn
Wakes from its starry silence to the hum
Of many gathering armies. Still,
In that we sometimes hear,
Upon the Northern winds, the voice of woe
Not wholly drowned in triumph, though I know
The end must crown us, and a few brief years
Dry all our tears,
I may not sing too gladly. To Thy will
Resigned, O Lord! we cannot all forget
That there is much even Victory must regret.
And, therefore, not too long
From the great burthen of our country's wrong
Delay our just release!
And, if it may be, save
These sacred fields of peace
From stain of patriot or of hostile blood!
Oh, help us, Lord! to roll the crimson flood
Back on its course, and, while our banners wing
Northward, strike with us! till the Goth shall cling
To his own blasted altar-stones, and crave
Mercy; and we shall grant it, and dictate
The lenient future of his fate
There, where some rotting ships and crumbling quays
Shall one day mark the Port which ruled the Western seas.

1861

CHARLESTON

Calm as that second summer which precedes
 The first fall of the snow,
In the broad sunlight of heroic deeds,
 The City bides the foe.

As yet, behind their ramparts stern and proud,
 Her bolted thunders sleep—
Dark Sumter, like a battlemented cloud,
 Looms o'er the solemn deep.

No Calpe frowns from lofty cliff or scar
 To guard the holy strand;
But Moultrie holds in leash her dogs of war
 Above the level sand.

And down the dunes a thousand guns lie couched,
  Unseen, beside the flood—
Like tigers in some Orient jungle crouched
  That wait and watch for blood.

Meanwhile, through streets still echoing with trade,
  Walk grave and thoughtful men,
Whose hands may one day wield the patriot's blade
  As lightly as the pen.

And maidens, with such eyes as would grow dim
  Over a bleeding hound,
Seem each one to have caught the strength of him
  Whose sword she sadly bound.

Thus girt without and garrisoned at home,
  Day patient following day,
Old Charleston looks from roof, and spire, and dome,
  Across her tranquil bay.

Ships, through a hundred foes, from Saxon lands
  And spicy Indian ports,
Bring Saxon steel and iron to her hands,
  And Summer to her courts.

But still, along yon dim Atlantic line,
  The only hostile smoke
Creeps like a harmless mist above the brine,
  From some frail, floating oak.

Shall the Spring dawn, and she still clad in smiles,
  And with an unscathed brow,
Rest in the strong arms of her palm-crowned isles,
  As fair and free as now?

We know not; in the temple of the Fates
  God has inscribed her doom;
And, all untroubled in her faith, she waits
  The triumph or the tomb.

1862

SPRING

Spring, with that nameless pathos in the air
Which dwells with all things fair,
Spring, with her golden suns and silver rain,
Is with us once again.

SPRING

Out in the lonely woods the jasmine burns
Its fragrant lamps, and turns
Into a royal court with green festoons
The banks of dark lagoons.

In the deep heart of every forest tree
The blood is all aglee,
And there's a look about the leafless bowers
As if they dreamed of flowers.

Yet still on every side we trace the hand
Of Winter in the land,
Save where the maple reddens on the lawn,
Flushed by the season's dawn;

Or where, like those strange semblances we find
That age to childhood bind,
The elm puts on, as if in Nature's scorn,
The brown of Autumn corn.

As yet the turf is dark, although you know
That, not a span below,
A thousand germs are groping through the gloom,
And soon will burst their tomb.

Already, here and there, on frailest stems
Appear some azure gems,
Small as might deck, upon a gala day,
The forehead of a fay.

In gardens you may note amid the dearth
The crocus breaking earth;
And near the snowdrop's tender white and green,
The violet in its screen.

But many gleams and shadows need must pass
Along the budding grass,
And weeks go by, before the enamored South
Shall kiss the rose's mouth.

Still there's a sense of blossoms yet unborn
In the sweet airs of morn;
One almost looks to see the very street
Grow purple at his feet.

At times a fragrant breeze comes floating by,
And brings, you know not why,

A feeling as when eager crowds await
Before a palace gate

Some wondrous pageant; and you scarce would start,
If from a beech's heart,
A blue-eyed Dryad, stepping forth, should say,
"Behold me! I am May!"

Ah! who would couple thoughts of war and crime
With such a blessed time!
Who in the west wind's aromatic breath
Could hear the call of Death!

Yet not more surely shall the Spring awake
The voice of wood and brake,
Than she shall rouse, for all her tranquil charms,
A million men to arms.

There shall be deeper hues upon her plains
Than all her sunlit rains,
And every gladdening influence around,
Can summon from the ground.

Oh! standing on this desecrated mould,
Methinks that I behold,
Lifting her bloody daisies up to God,
Spring kneeling on the sod,

And calling, with the voice of all her rills,
Upon the ancient hills
To fall and crush the tyrants and the slaves
Who turn her meads to graves.

1863

THE UNKNOWN DEAD

The rain is plashing on my sill,
But all the winds of Heaven are still;
And so it falls with that dull sound
Which thrills us in the church-yard ground,
When the first spadeful drops like lead
Upon the coffin of the dead.
Beyond my streaming window-pane,
I cannot see the neighboring vane,
Yet from its old familiar tower
The bell comes, muffled, through the shower.

THE UNKNOWN DEAD

What strange and unsuspected link
Of feeling touched, has made me think—
While with a vacant soul and eye
I watch the gray and stony sky—
Of nameless graves on battle-plains
Washed by a single winter's rains,
Where, some beneath Virginian hills,
And some by green Atlantic rills,
Some by the waters of the West,
A myriad unknown heroes rest.
Ah! not the chiefs, who, dying, see
Their flags in front of victory,
Or, at their life-blood's noble cost
Pay for a battle nobly lost,
Claim from their monumental beds
The bitterest tears a nation sheds.
Beneath yon lonely mound—the spot
By all save some fond few forgot—
Lie the true martyrs of the fight
Which strikes for freedom and for right.
Of them, their patriot zeal and pride,
The lofty faith that with them died,
No grateful page shall farther tell
Than that so many bravely fell;
And we can only dimly guess
What worlds of all this world's distress,
What utter woe, despair, and dearth,
Their fate has brought to many a hearth.
Just such a sky as this should weep
Above them, always, where they sleep;
Yet, haply, at this very hour,
Their graves are like a lover's bower;
And Nature's self, with eyes unwet,
Oblivious of the crimson debt
To which she owes her April grace,
Laughs gayly o'er their burial-place.

1863

HENRY TIMROD

ODE

Sung on the Occasion of Decorating the
Graves of the Confederate Dead, at
Magnolia Cemetery, Charleston, S.C., 1866

I

Sleep sweetly in your humble graves,
  Sleep, martyrs of a fallen cause;
Though yet no marble column craves
  The pilgrim here to pause.

II

In seeds of laurel in the earth
  The blossom of your fame is blown,
And somewhere, waiting for its birth,
  The shaft is in the stone!

III

Meanwhile, behalf the tardy years
  Which keep in trust your storied tombs,
Behold! your sisters bring their tears,
  And these memorial blooms.

IV

Small tributes! but your shades will smile
  More proudly on these wreaths today,
Than when some cannon-moulded pile
  Shall overlook this bay.

V

Stoop, angels, hither from the skies!
  There is no holier spot of ground
Than where defeated valor lies,
  By mourning beauty crowned!

1866

LITERATURE IN THE SOUTH

We think that at no time, and in no country, has the position of an author been beset with such peculiar difficulties as the Southern writer is compelled to struggle with from the beginning to the end of his career. In no country in which literature has ever flourished has an author obtained so limited an audience. In no country, and at no period that we can recall, has an author been constrained by the indifference of the public amid which he lived, to publish with a people who were prejudiced against him. It would scarcely be too extravagant to entitle the Southern author the Pariah of modern literature. It would scarcely be too absurd if we should compare his position to that of the drawer of Shakspeare, who stands in a state of ludicrous confusion between the calls of Prince Hal upon the one side and of Poins upon the other. He is placed, in fact, much in the same relation to the public of the North and the public of the South, as we might suppose a statesman to occupy who should propose to embody in one code a system of laws for two neighbouring people, of one of which he was a constituent, and who yet altogether differed in character, institutions and pursuits. The people among whom the statesman lived would be very indignant upon finding, as they would be sure to find, that some of their interests had been neglected. The people for whom he legislated at a distance would be equally indignant upon discovering, as they would [be] sure to fancy they discovered, that not one of their interests had received proper attention. Both parties would probably unite, with great cordiality and patriotism, in consigning the unlucky statesman to oblivion or the executioner. In precisely the same manner fares the poor scribbler who has been so unfortunate as to be born South of the Potomac. He publishes a book. It is the settled conviction of the North that genius is indigenous there, and flourishes only in a Northern atmosphere. It is the equally firm conviction of the South that genius —literary genius, at least—is an exotic that will not flower on a Southern soil. Probably the book is published by a Northern house. Straightway all the newspapers of the South are indignant that the author did not choose a Southern printer, and address himself more particularly to a Southern community. He heeds their criticism, and of his next book,— published by a Southern printer—such is the secret though unacknowledged prejudice against Southern authors—he finds that more than one half of a small edition remains upon his hands. Perhaps the book contains a correct and beautiful picture of our peculiar state of society. The North is inattentive or abusive, and the South unthankful, or, at most, indifferent. Or it may happen to be only a volume of noble poetry, full of those universal thoughts and feelings which speak, not to a particular people, but to all mankind. It is censured at the South as not sufficiently Southern in spirit, while at the North it is pronounced a very fair specimen of Southern commonplace.

Both North and South agree with one mind to condemn the author and forget his book.

We do not think that we are exaggerating the embarrassments which surround the Southern writer. It cannot be denied that on the surface of newspaper and magazine literature there have lately appeared signs that his claims to respect are beginning to be acknowledged. But, in spite of this, we must continue to believe, that among a large majority of Southern readers who devour English books with avidity, there still exists a prejudice —conscious or unconscious—against the works of those authors who have grown up among themselves. This prejudice is strongest, indeed, with a class of persons whose opinions do not find expression in the public prints; but it is on that account more harmful in its evil and insidious influence. As an instance, we may mention that it is not once, but a hundred times, that we have heard the works of the first of Southern authors alluded to with contempt by individuals who had never read anything beyond the title-pages of his books. Of this prejudice there is an easy, though not a very flattering, explanation.

The truth is, it must be confessed, that though an educated, we are a provincial, and not a highly cultivated people. At least, there is among us a very general want of a high critical culture. The principles of that criticism, the basis of which is a profound psychology, are almost utterly ignored. There are scholars of pretension among us, with whom Blair's Rhetoric is still an unquestionable authority. There are schools and colleges in which it is used as a textbook. With the vast advance that has been made in critical science since the time of Blair few seem to be intimately acquainted. The opinions and theories of the last century are still held in reverence. Here Pope is still regarded by many as the most *correct* of English poets, and here, Kaimes, after having been everywhere else removed to the top shelves of libraries, is still thumbed by learned professors and declamatory sophomores. Here literature is still regarded as an epicurean amusement; not as a study, at least equal in importance, and certainly not inferior in difficulty, to law and medicine. Here no one is surprised when some fossil theory of criticism, long buried under the ruins of an exploded school, is dug up, and discussed with infinite gravity by gentlemen who know Pope and Horace by heart, but who have never read a word of Wordsworth or Tennyson, or who have read them with suspicion, and rejected them with superciliousness.

In such a state of critical science, it is no wonder that we are prudently cautious in passing a favourable judgment upon any new candidates for our admiration. It is no wonder that while we accept without a cavil books of English and Northern reputation, we yet hesitate to acknowledge our own writers, until, perhaps, having been commended by English or Northern critics, they present themselves to us with a "certain alienated majesty." There is another class of critics among us—if critics they can be called —which we must not pass over. This class seem disposed to look upon literature as they look upon a Bavarian sour-krout, a Strasbourg paté, or a New Zealand cutlet of "cold clergyman." It is a mere matter of taste. Each one feels himself at liberty to exalt the author—without reference to his real position in the world of letters, as settled by a competent tribunal—whose works afford *him* the most amusement. From such a principle, of course, the most fantastic and discordant opinions result. One regards that fanciful story, the Culprit Fay of Drake, as the greatest of American poems; and another is indignant if Tennyson be mentioned in the same breath with Longfellow. Now, it is good to be independent; but it is not good to be too independent. Some respect is certainly due to the authority of those who, by a careful and loving study of literature, have won the right to speak *ex cathedra.* Nor is that independence, but license, which is not founded upon a wide and deep knowledge of critical science, and upon a careful and respectful collation of our own conclusions, with the impartial philosophical conclusions of others.

In the course of these remarks, we have alluded to three classes of critics, the bigot, the slave, and we cannot better characterize the third, than as the autocratic. There is yet a fourth, which feels, or professes to feel, a warm interest in Southern literature, and which so far is entitled to our respect. But, unfortunately, the critical principles of this class are quite as shallow as those of any of the others; and we notice it chiefly to expose the absurdity of one of its favourite opinions, adopted from a theory which some years ago arose at the North, and which bore the name of Americanism in literature. After the lapse of a period commensurate with the distance it had to travel, it reached the remote South, where it became, with an intensity of absurdity which is admirable indeed, Southernism in literature. Now, if the theory had gone to the depth of that which constitutes true nationality, we should have no objections to urge against it. But to the understandings of these superficial critics, it meant nothing more than that an author should confine himself in the choice of his subjects to the scenery, the history, and the traditions of his own country. To be an American novelist, it was sufficient that a writer should select a story, in which one half the characters should be backwoodsmen, who talked bad Saxon, and the other half should be savages, who talked Choctaw translated into very bombastic English. To be an American poet, it was sufficient either in a style and measure imitated from Pope and Goldsmith, or in the more modern style and measure of Scott and Wordsworth, to describe the vast prairies of the West, the swamps and pine forests of the South, or the great lakes and broad rivers of the North. It signified nothing to these critics whether the tone, the spirit, or the style were caught from European writers or not. If a poet, in genuine Scott, or genuine Byron, compared his hero to a cougar or grisly bear —patriotically ignoring the Asiatic tiger or the African lion—the exclamation of the critic was, "How intensely American!"

We submit that this is a false and narrow criterion, by which to judge of the true nationality of the author. Not in the subject, except to a partial extent, but in the management of the subject, in the tone and bearings of the thought, in the drapery, the colouring, and those thousand nameless touches, which are to be felt rather than expressed, are the characteristics of a writer to be sought. It is in these particulars that an author of original genius—no matter what his subject—will manifest his nationality. In fact, true originality will be always found identical with true nationality. A painter who should paint an American landscape exactly in the style of Salvator or of Claude, ought scarcely to be entitled an American painter. A poet who should write a hymn to Niagara in the blank verse of the Ulysses or the Princess, ought not to be entitled an American poet. In a word, he alone, who, in a style evolved from his own individual nature, speaks the thoughts and feelings of his own deep heart, can be a truly national genius. In the works of such a man, the character which speaks behind and through him—as character does not always speak in the case of men of mere talent, who in some respects are usually more or less under the sway of more commanding minds—will furnish the best and highest types of the intellectual character of his countrymen, and will illustrate most correctly, as well as most subtly—perhaps most correctly because most subtly—the nature of the influences around him. In the poetry of such a man, if he be a poet, whether its scenes be laid in his native country or the land of faery, the pines of his own forests shall be heard to murmur, the music of his own rivers shall swell the diapason, the flowers of his own soil shall bud and burst, though touched perhaps with a more ethereal and lasting grace; and with a brighter and more spiritual lustre, or with a darker and holier beauty, it will be his own skies that look down upon the loveliest landscapes of his creation.

We regard the theory of Southernism in literature as a circumscription, both unnecessary and unreasonable, of the privileges of genius. Shakspeare was not less an Englishman when he wrote Antony and Cleopatra, than when he dramatized the history of the kings of England. Sir Walter was not less a Scotchman when he drew the characters of Louis XI and Charles the Bold, than when he conceived the characters of Edie Ochiltree and Balfour of Burley. We do not suppose that until this theory germinated in the brain of its foolish originator, it ever occurred to an author that in his selection of subjects, he was to be bounded by certain geographical limits. And if in addition to the many difficulties which he has to overcome, the Southern author be expected, under the penalty of being pronounced un-Southern in tone, and unpatriotic in spirit, never to pass the Potomac on one side, or the Gulf on the other, we shall despair of ever seeing within our borders a literature of such depth and comprehensiveness as will ensure it the respect of other countries, or permanence in the remembrance of posterity. No! the domain of genius is as wide as the world, and as ancient as creation. Wherever the angel of its inspiration may lead, it has the right to follow—and whether exhibited by the light of tropic suns, or of the Arctic morning, whether embodied in the persons of ancient heroes, or of modern thinkers, the eternal verities which it aims to inculcate shall find in every situation, and under every guise, their suitable place, and their proper incarnation.

We should not like to convey the impression that we undervalue the materials for prose and poetry, which may be found in Southern scenery, Southern society, or Southern history. We are simply protesting against a narrow creed, by means of which much injustice may be done to a writer, who, though not less Southern in feeling than another who displays his Southernism on the surface of his books, yet insists upon the right to clothe according to the dictates of his own taste, and locate according to the dictates of his own thoughtful judgment, the creatures of his imagination. At the same time we are not blind to the spacious field which is opened to the Southern author within his own immediate country. The vast aboriginal forests which so weightily oppress us with a sense of antiquity, the mountains, tree-clad to the summit, enclosing unexplored Elysiums, the broad belt of lowland along the ocean, with its peculiar vegetation, the live-oak, stateliest of that stately family, hung with graceful tillandsia, the historical palmetto, and the rank magnificence of swamp and thicket, the blue aureole of the passion flower, the jessamine, with its yellow and fragrant flame, and all the wild luxuriance of a bountiful Flora, the golden carpet which the rice plant spreads for the feet of autumn, and the cotton field white as with a soft, warm snow of summer—these are materials—and these are but a small part of them—from which a poet may draw an inspiration as genuine as that which touched with song the lips of English Thomson, or woke to subtler and profounder utterance the soul of English Wordsworth. Nor is the structure of our social life—so different from that of every other people, whether ancient or modern—incapable of being exhibited in a practical light. There are truths underlying the relations of master and slave; there are meanings beneath that union of the utmost freedom with a healthy conservatism, which, growing out of those relations, is characteristic of Southern thought, of which poetry may avail herself not only to vindicate our system to the eyes of the world, but to convey lessons which shall take root in the hearts of all mankind. We need not commend the poetical themes which are to be found in the history of the South; in the romance of her colonial period; in the sufferings and struggles of her revolution; in the pure patriotism of her warriors and statesmen, the sterling worth of her people, and the grace, the wit, the purity, the dignity, delicacy and self-devotion of her women. He who either in the character of poet or novelist shall associate his name with the South in one or all of the above-mentioned aspects, will have achieved a more enviable fame than any which has yet illustrated the literature of America.

We pass to a brief discussion of an error still more prevalent than the theory just dismissed. We know nothing more discouraging to an author, nothing which more clearly evinces the absence of any profound principles of criticism, than the light in which the labours of the poet and the novelist are very generally viewed at the South. The novel and the poem are almost universally characterized as light reading, and we may say are almost universally estimated as a very light and superficial sort of writing. We read novels and poems indeed, with some pleasure, but at the same time with the tacit conviction that we are engaged in a very trivial occupation; and we promise ourselves that, in order to make up for the precious moments thus thrown away, we shall hereafter redouble our diligence in the study of history or of mathematics. It is the common impression that while there is much practical utility in a knowledge of Euclid and the Calculus, no profit whatever is to be derived from works of poetry and fiction. Of two writers, one of whom should edit a treatise on the conic sections, and the other should give to the world a novel equal in tragic power and interest to the Bride of Lammermoor, the former would be considered the greater man by nine persons out of ten.

It would be from the purpose of this article to go into a minute examination of the prejudices upon which these opinions are founded. But we may be permitted a few words on the subject. What are the advantages which are supposed to result from the study of the mathematics—not, we mean, to those who are to devote their lives to science, but to that more numerous class who, immediately upon graduation, fling aside Playfair, and separate into doctors, lawyers, and politicians? The answer is, we believe, that the study of mathematics is calculated to accustom the student to habits of close reasoning, and to increase his powers of concentration. Some vague generality is usually added about its influence in strengthening the mind.

Now, it is a notorious fact that mathematicians are for the most part bad reasoners out of their particular province. As soon as they get upon topics which do not admit of precise definitions and exact demonstrations, they fall naturally enough into all sorts of blunders and contradictions. They usually beg the question at the outset, and then by means of a most unexceptionable syllogism, they come to a conclusion which, though probably false in fact, is yet, it must be confessed, always logically consistent with their premises.

Now, it will not be denied that such a method of reasoning is the very worst possible which could be employed by a lawyer or a politician. The laws, and their various interpretations, the motives, the objects, the interest in their thousand contradictory aspects, which must form the staple of the arguments of professional and public men, are not to be treated like the squares and circles of geometry. Yet that a familiarity with mathematical modes of proof does not lead to the error of using those modes of proof upon subjects to which they are wholly inapplicable, is evident to anybody who has noticed the style of argument prevalent among the very young orators who have not long cut the apron strings which tied them to a too strictly mathematical Alma Mater. They bristle all over with syllogisms, write notes in the form of captions, invariably open a speech (that is if it be not a fourth of July oration, and if they have anything to prove) with a statement, and end with Q. E. D. corollary and scholium. Not until the last theories have been erased from their memory, or until they shall have learned by repeated reverses the absurdity of which they are guilty, do they begin to reason like men of practical sense.

It must not be inferred that we are arguing against the study of the mathematics. It has its uses—though we think not the uses commonly assigned to it. These we cannot stop to particularize, but we may mention that if it could do nothing but furnish us with the clearest idea we have of the nature of absolute truths, it would still be an important study.

We shall probably be thought paradoxical when we say that we believe that the study of poetry as an art in conjunction with the science of criticism —and this not with the design of writing poetry, but merely to enable the student to appreciate and to judge of it—will afford a better preparative training than all the mathematics in the world, to the legal or political debater. Poetry, as Coleridge well remarks, has a logic of its own; and this logic being more complex, more subtle, and more uncertain than the logic of the demonstrative sciences, is far more akin than the latter can be to the dialectics of common life. And when we consider that while we are mastering this logic, we are at the same time familiarising ourselves with the deepest secrets of the human heart, imbuing our natures with the most refining influences, and storing our minds with the purest thoughts and the loveliest pictures of humanity, the utility of poetry as a study seems to be established beyond a question.

It seems strange, that in this nineteenth century, one should be called upon to vindicate poetry from aspersions which have been repeatedly and triumphantly disproved. Nevertheless, so generally accepted at the South is the prejudice which degrades poetry into a mere servant of our pleasures, that upon most ears, truths, (elsewhere so familiar as to be trite) upon which it bases a loftier pretension, fall with the startling novelty of paradox. How many look upon the imaginative faculty simply as the manufacturer of pretty conceits; how few know it as the power which, by selecting and combining materials never before brought together, in fact, produces pictures and characters in which there shall be nothing untruthful or unnatural, and which shall yet be as new to us as a lately found island in the Pacific. How many of us regard poetry as a mere creature of the fancy; how few appreciate its philosophy, or understand that beneath all the splendour of its diction and imagery, there is in its highest manifestations at least a substratum of profound and valuable thought; how very few perceive the justice of the eloquent definition of Coleridge: "That poetry is the blossom and fragrance of all human wisdom, human passions, learning, and language"; or are prepared to see, as it is expressed in the noble verse of Taylor, that

Poetry is Reason's self-sublimed;
Tis Reason's sovereignty, whereunto
All properties of sense, all dues of wit,
All fancies, images, perceptions, passions,
All intellectual ordinance grown up
From accident, necessity, or custom,
Seen to be good, and after made authentic;
All ordinance aforethought, that from science
Doth prescience take, and from experience law;
All lights and institutes of digested knowledge,
Gifts and endowments of intelligence
From sources living, from the dead bequests,—
Subserve and minister.

We hurry on to the comparative merits of history and fiction.

It is not generally understood that a novel may be more truthful than a history, in several particulars—but, perhaps, most of all in the delineation of character. The historian, hampered by facts which are not seldom contradictory, is sometimes compelled to touch and retouch his portrait of a character in order to suit those facts. Consequently, he will often give us a character not as it existed, but his idea of that character—a something, the like of which was never in heaven above, nor on the earth beneath. On the other hand, the novelist, whose only obligation is to be true to nature, at least paints us possible men and women, about whose actions we can reason almost with as much accuracy as if they had really lived, loved, acted and died. In doing this, he at once reaches a higher truth than is often attainable by the historians, and imparts to us lessons far more profitable. More of human nature can be learned from the novel of Tom Jones than from a History of the whole Roman Empire—written, at least, as histories are commonly written. Again, while it is to history we look for an account of the dynasties, the battles, sieges, revolutions, the triumphs and defeats of a nation, it is from the historical novel that we glean the best idea of that which it is infinitely more important for us to know—of the social state, the manners, morals, opinions, passions, prejudices, and habits of the people. We do not hesitate to say, that of two persons, one of whom has only read Hume's chapter on Richard I, and the other only the Ivanhoe of Scott, the latter will be by far the better acquainted with the real history of the period.

We need not say that we are not quite so silly as to believe that it is possible, by any force of argument, to bring about a reformation in the tastes of the reading community. It is, unfortunately, not in the power of a people to confer together and say, "Come, now, let us arise, and build up a literature." We cannot call meetings, and pass resolutions to this purpose, as we do with respect to turnpikes, railways, and bridges. That genuine appreciation, by which alone literature is encouraged and fostered, is a plant of slow growth. Still, we think something may be done; but in the meanwhile let it not be forgotten that, in spite of every disadvantage, the South already possesses a literature which calls for its patronage and applause. The fate of that literature is a reproach to us. Of all our Southern writers, not one but Poe has received his due measure of fame. The immense resources and versatile powers of Simms are to this day grudgingly acknowledged, or contemptuously denied. There have been writers among us who, in another country, would have been complimented with repeated editions, whose names are now almost forgotten, and whose works it is now utterly impossible to obtain. While our centre-tables are littered with the feeble moralizings of Tupper, done up in very bright morocco; and while the corners of our newspapers are graced with the glibly versified common-places of Mackey, and of writers even more worthless than Mackey, there is, perhaps, scarcely a single bookseller in the United States, on whose face we should not encounter the grin of ignorance, if we chanced to inquire for the Froissart ballads of Philip Pendleton Cooke.

It is not without mortification that we compare the reception which the North gives to its literature to the stolid indifference of the South. There, at least, Genius wears the crown, and receives the tributes which are due to it. It is true, indeed, that not a few Northern authors have owed in part their successes to the art of puffing—an art nowhere carried to such a height of excellence as in the cities of New York and Boston. It is true that through the magic of this art, many a Bottom in literature has been decked with the flowers and fed with the apricots and dewberries of a short-lived reputation. But it is also true, that there is in the reading public of the North a well-founded faith in its capacity to judge for itself, a not inconsiderable knowledge of the present state of Poetry and Art, and a cordial disposition to recognize and reward the native authors who address it.

We are not going to recommend the introduction at the South of a system of puffing. "No quarter to the dunce," whether Southern or Northern, is the motto which should be adopted by every man who has at heart the interests of his country's literature. Not by exalting mediocrity, not by setting dullness on a throne, and putting a garland on the head of vanity, shall we help in the smallest degree the cause of Southern letters. A partiality so mistaken can only serve to depreciate excellence, discourage effort, and disgust the man of real ability. We have regretted to see the tenderness with which a volume of indifferent poetry is sometimes treated—for no other reason that we could discover than that it was the work of a Southerner—by those few clever and well-meaning critics, of whom the South is not altogether destitute. The effect of this ill-judged clemency is to induce those who are indisposed to admit the claims of Southern literature upon their admiration, to look with suspicion upon every verdict of Southern criticism.

We have but one course to suggest to those who are willing, from a painful conviction of the blended servility, superficiality, and antiquated bigotry of criticism among us, to assist in bringing about a reformation. It is to speak the rude truth always. It is to declare war equally against the slaves of English and Northern opinions, and against the slaves of the conventional schools of the eighteenth century. If argument fail, perhaps satire may prove a more effective weapon. Everything like old fogyism in literature should be remorselessly ridiculed. That pert license which consults only its own uneducated taste, and that docility which truckles to the *prestige* of a foreign reputation should be alike held up to contempt. It should be shown in plain, unflattering language that the unwillingness with which native genius is acknowledged, is a bitterer slander on the country and its intellect than any of the falsehoods which defile the pages of Trollope, Dickens, Marryatt, or Basil Hall. It would be no injustice to tell those who refuse to credit that the South has done anything in prose or poetry, that in their own shallowness and stupidity they have found the best reasons for their incredulity; and they should be sternly reminded, that because a country annually gives birth to a thousand noodles, it does not follow that it may not now and then produce a man of genius. Nor should any hesitation be felt to inquire boldly into the manner in which the tastes of our youth are educated. Let it be asked on what principle we fill our chairs of belles-lettres; whether to discharge properly the duties of a critical teacher, a thorough acquaintance with English literature be not a rather indispensable requisite, and how it is that in one institution a learned professor shall maintain the Course of Time to be the greatest of English epics, and in another an equally learned professor shall deny, on the ground that he could never read it, save as a very disagreeable task, the transcendent merits of Paradise Lost. Is it not a fact, of which we may feel not unreasonably ashamed, that a student may pass four years under these misleaders of youth, and yet remain ignorant of that most important revolution in imaginative literature —to us of the present day the most important of all literary revolutions —which took place a little more than half a century ago. The influence of the new spiritual philosophy in producing a change from a sensuous to a super-sensuous poetry, the vast difference between the school represented by Wordsworth, and the school represented by Pope, the introduction of that mystical element into our verse which distinguishes it from the verse of the age of Shakspeare, the theory of that analytical criticism which examines a work of art "from the heart outwards, not from surface inwards!" and which deduces its laws from nature and truth, not from the practice of particular writers; these surely are subjects which, in an institution devoted to the purpose of education, may not be overlooked without censure. At the risk of exciting the derisive smiles of those who attach more value to the settlement of a doubtful accent, or a disputed quantity, than to a just definition of the imaginative faculty, or a correct estimation of the scope and objects of poetry, we avow our belief that a systematic study of English literature, under the guidance of proper expounders—even at the expense of the curriculum in other respects—would be attended with the highest benefits to the student and the community. Such a course of study would assist more than anything else in bringing about that improvement in taste which we need so much, and for which we must look especially to the generation now growing up about us. We do not expect much from those whose opinions are already formed. It is next to impossible thoroughly to convert a confirmed papist; and there are no prejudices so difficult to overcome as the prejudices of pedantry and age.

After all, the chief impediment to a broad, deep, and liberal culture is her own self-complacency. With a strange inconsistency, the very persons who decry Southern literature are forever extolling Southern taste, Southern learning, and Southern civilization. There is scarcely a city of any size in the South which has not its clique of amateur critics, poets and philosophers, the regular business of whom is to demonstrate truisms, settle questions which nobody else would think of discussing, to confirm themselves in opinions which have been picked up from the rubbish of seventy years agone, and above all to persuade each other that together they constitute a society not much inferior to that in which figured Burke and Johnson, Goldsmith and Sir Joshua. All of these being oracles, they are unwilling to acknowledge the claims of a professional writer, lest in doing so they should disparage their own authority. It is time that their self-complacency should be disturbed. And we propose satire as the best weapon, because against vanity it is the only effective one. He who shall convince this, and every other class of critics to which we have alluded, that they are not in advance of their age, that they are even a little behind it, will have conferred an incalculable benefit upon them, and upon the South.

We shall not admit that in exposing the deficiencies of the Southern public, we have disparaged in the slightest degree the intellect of the South. Of that intellect in its natural capacity none can conceive more highly than ourself. It is impossible not to respect a people from whom have sprung so many noble warriors, orators and statesmen. And there is that in the constitution of the Southern mind, in the Saxon, Celtic and Teutonic elements of which it is composed, and in the peculiar influences amidst which these elements have been moulded together, a promise of that blending of the philosophic in thought with the enthusiastic in feeling, which makes a literary nation. Even now, while it is in one place trammeled by musty rules and canons, and in another left to its own unguided or misguided impulses, it would be unjust to deny it a quickness of perception, which, if rightly trained, would soon convert this essay into a slander and a falsehood. We will not believe that a people with such a mental character can remain much longer under the dominion of a contracted and illiberal culture. Indeed, we think the signs of a better taste may already be noticed. The circle of careless or prejudiced readers, though large, is a narrowing circle. The circle of thoughtful and earnest students, though a small one, is a widening circle. Young authors are rising up who have won for themselves at least a partial acknowledgment of merit. The time must come at last when the public shall feel that there are ideas characterizing Southern society, as distinguished from Northern and English society, which need the exposition of a new literature. There will be a stirring of the public mind, an expectation aroused which will ensure its own gratification, a demand for Southern prose and poetry, which shall call forth the poet and prose writer from the crowds that now conceal them, and a sympathy established between author and public, which shall infuse inspiration into the one, and heighten the pleasure and profit of the other. Then, indeed, we may look for a literature of which we shall all wear the honours. We shall walk over ground made classic by the imaginations of our poets, the thoughts we speak shall find illustration in verse which has been woven by Southern hearths; and the winds that blow from the land, and the waves that wash our level coast, shall bear to other nations the names of bards who know how to embody the spirit of their country without sinking that universality which shall commend their lessons to all mankind.

PAUL HAMILTON HAYNE

(1830–1886)

Paul Hamilton Hayne was one of the very few Southern authors whose careers spanned the antebellum years and the post-Civil War era of the New South. He was born in Charleston, South Carolina, of a distinguished family. It was Hayne's uncle, Robert Y. Hayne, who argued the case for nullification in the famous Webster-Hayne debates of an earlier day. Hayne's lifelong friendship with Henry Timrod began when they attended school together in Charleston. He was graduated from the College of Charleston, studied law for a time, and began contributing poetry to literary journals. When in 1857 *Russell's Magazine* was launched, Hayne became its editor. He had also formed friendships with a number of writers in the North, including James Russell Lowell, Richard Henry Stoddard, and Richard Henry Dana, Jr., and by 1861 had published three collections of verse. Hayne served in the Confederate army for a time and wrote numerous war poems. The loss of the war also brought the loss of Hayne's wealth and possessions, including his home and most of his fine library. Almost penniless, he managed to purchase eighteen acres of uncultivated land near Augusta, Georgia, and there, with his wife and his son William, lived out his life. Except for a brief stint as a newspaper editor in Augusta, he supported himself, however meagerly, on what he earned from his poetry. He cultivated his relations with Northern authors and editors and succeeded in publishing a considerable amount of verse in the magazines. In 1873 he was able to find a publisher for the poems of his friend Timrod, and in 1882 he brought out his own *Collected Poems* with a Boston publisher.

Hayne was not a major poet; in language and idea he worked for the most part on the surface of the poem, using the poetic conventions of his day. The unsuitability of some of his language, which enabled him to image the experience of his own time and place, can be seen in a comparison of two works on the same subject, one a colloquial sonnet he wrote to invite his friend Simms to visit him and the second a nonfiction account of that visit, cited in the introduction to the Old South section of this book.

SONNET

Of all the woodland flowers of earlier spring,
These golden jasmines, each an air-hung bower,
Meet for the Queen of Fairies' tiring hour,
Seem loveliest and most fair in blossoming;
How younder mock-bird thrills his fervid wing
And long, lithe throat, where twinkling flower on flower
Rains the globed dewdrops down, a diamond shower,
O'er his brown head poised as in act to sing;
Lo! the swift sunshine floods the flowery urns,
Girding their delicate gold with matchless light,
Till the blent life of bough, leaf, blossom, burns;
Then, then outbursts the mock-bird clear and loud,
Half-drunk with perfume, veiled by radiance bright,
A star of music in a fiery cloud!

1871

ASPECTS OF THE PINES

Tall, sombre, grim, against the morning sky
    They rise, scarce touched by melancholy airs,
Which stir the fadeless foliage dreamfully,
    As if from realms of mystical despairs.

Tall, sombre, grim, they stand with dusky gleams
    Brightening to gold within the woodland's core,
Beneath the gracious noontide's tranquil beams—

PAUL HAMILTON HAYNE

But the weird winds of morning sigh no more.

A stillness, strange, divine, ineffable,
　　Broods round and o'er them in the wind's surcease,
And on each tinted copse and shimmering dell
　　Rests the mute rapture of deep hearted peace.

Last, sunset comes—the solemn joy and might
　　Borne from the West when cloudless day declines—
Low, flutelike breezes sweep the waves of light,
　　And lifting dark green tresses of the pines,

Till every lock is luminous—gently float,
　　Fraught with hale odors up the heavens afar
To faint when twilight on her virginal throat
　　Wears for a gem the tremulous vesper star.

1875

THE MOCKING-BIRD

[AT NIGHT]

A golden pallor of voluptuous light
Filled the warm southern night:
The moon, clear orbed, above the sylvan scene
Moved like a stately queen,
So rife with conscious beauty all the while,
What could she do but smile
At her own perfect loveliness below,
Glassed in the tranquil flow
Of crystal fountains and unruffled streams?
Half lost in waking dreams,
As down the loneliest forest dell I strayed,
Lo! from a neighboring glade,
Flashed through the drifts of moonshine, swiftly came
A fairy shape of flame.
It rose in dazzling spirals overhead,
Whence to wild sweetness wed,
Poured marvellous melodies, silvery trill on trill;
The very leaves grew still
On the charmed trees to hearken; while for me,
Heart-trilled to ecstasy,
I followed—followed the bright shape that flew,
Still circling up the blue,
Till as a fountain that has reached its height,

THE MOCKING BIRD

Falls back in sprays of light
Slowly dissolved, so that enrapturing lay,
Divinely melts away
Through tremulous spaces to a music-mist,
Soon by the fitful breeze
   How gently kissed
Into remote and tender silences.

1882

THE HUMORISTS

AUGUSTUS BALDWIN LONGSTREET

(1790–1870)

A native of Augusta, Georgia, A. B. Longstreet attended Moses Waddel's remarkable academy for youths in the Barnwell District of South Carolina, where Hugh Swinton Legaré, John C. Calhoun, William H. Crawford, James L. Petigru, and George McDuffie were also educated. From there he went to Yale University and the famed law school of Tapping Reeve in Litchfield, Connecticut. Properly schooled, he returned home to practice law in Augusta and throughout the rural circuit of Georgia; he got married, served in the state legislature, and became a judge in the superior court of Georgia. He also turned to newspaper editing and began contributing humorous sketches of rural Georgia life to his own and other papers. *Georgia Scenes, Characters, Incidents, etc., in the First Half Century of the Republic, By a Native Georgian* was first published in 1835 by the press of Longstreet's own newspaper, the *States Rights Sentinel* of Augusta. Republished by Harper and Bros. in New York in 1840, it achieved great popularity and has seldom been out of print since. In 1837 Longstreet joined the Methodist Church and the next year he became a minister. In Jay B. Hubbell's words, "from this time on, although really proud of the great popularity of the hastily written *Georgia Scenes*, he sometimes felt that it was not the kind of book by which a minister should be known." Subsequently, Longstreet served as president of Emory College, Centenary College, the University of Mississippi, and the University of South Carolina. He also wrote a temperance novel, *Master William Mitten* (1859). Although distinguished in his own day as an educator, his lasting fame was secured by the early humorous sketches in which, for almost the first time, he opened up the everyday folkways of the backcountry South to literary use.

THE FIGHT

In the younger days of the Republic there lived in the county of————two men, who were admitted on all hands to be the very *best men* in the county; which, in the Georgia vocabulary, means they could flog any other two men in the county. Each, through many a hard-fought battle, had acquired the mastery of his own battalion; but they lived on opposite sides of the Court-house, and in different battalions: consequently, they were but seldom thrown together. When they met, however, they were always very friendly; indeed, at their first interview, they seemed to conceive a wonderful attachment to each other, which rather increased than diminished as they became better acquainted; so that, but for the circumstance which I am about to mention, the question, which had been a thousand times asked, "Which is the best man, Billy Stallions (Stallings) or Bob Durham?" would probably never have been answered.

Billy ruled the upper battalion, and Bob the lower. The former measured six feet and an inch in his stockings, and, without a single pound of cum-brous flesh about him, weighed a hundred and eighty. The latter was an inch shorter than his rival, and ten pounds lighter; but he was much the most active of the two. In running and jumping he had but few equals in the county; and in wrestling, not one. In other respects they were nearly equal. Both were admirable specimens of human nature in its finest form. Billy's victories had generally been achieved by the tremendous power of his blows, one of which had often proved decisive of his battles; Bob's, by his adroitness in bringing his adversary to the ground. This advantage he had never failed to gain at the onset, and, when gained he never failed to improve it to the defeat of his adversary. These points of difference have involved the reader in a doubt as to the probable issue of a contest between them. It was not so, however, with the two battalions. Neither had the least difficulty in determining the point by the most natural and irresistible deductions *à priori*; and though, by the same course of reasoning, they arrived at directly opposite conclusions, neither felt its confidence in the least shaken by this circumstance. The upper battalion swore "that Billy only wanted one lick at him to knock his heart, liver, and lights out of him, and if he got two at him, he'd knock him into a cocked hat." The lower bat-talion retorted, "that he wouldn't have time to double his fist before Bob would put his head where his feet ought to be; and that, by the time he hit the ground, the meat would fly off his face so quick, that people would think it was shook off by the fall." These disputes often led to the *argumentum ad hominem*, but with such equality of success on both sides as to leave the main question just where they found it. They usually ended, however, in the common way, with a bet; and many a quart of old Jamaica (whiskey had not then supplanted rum) were staked upon the issue. Still, greatly to the annoyance of the curious, Billy and Bob continued to be good friends.

Now there happened to reside in the county just alluded to a little fellow by the name of Ransy Sniffle: a sprout of Richmond, who, in his earlier days, had fed copiously upon red clay and blackberries. This diet had given to Ransy a complexion that a corpse would have disdained to own, and an abdominal rotundity that was quite unprepossessing. Long spells of the fever and ague, too, in Ransy's youth, had conspired with clay and black-berries to throw him quite out of the order of nature. His shoulders were fleshless and elevated; his head large and flat; his neck slim and translucent; and his arms, hands, fingers, and feet were lengthened out of all proportion to the rest of his frame. His joints were large and his limbs small; and as for flesh, he could not, with propriety, be said to have any. Those parts which nature usually supplies with the most of this article—the calves of the legs, for example—presented in him the appearance of so many well-drawn blisters. His height was just five feet nothing; and his average weight in blackberry season, ninety-five. I have been thus particular in describing him, for the purpose of showing what a great matter a little fire sometimes kindleth. There was nothing on this earth which delighted Ransy so much as a fight. He never seemed fairly alive except when he was witnessing, fomenting, or talking about a fight. Then, indeed, his deep-sunken gray eye assumed something of a living fire, and his tongue acquired a volubility that bordered upon eloquence. Ransy had been kept for more than a year in the most torturing suspense as to the comparative manhood of Billy Stallings and Bob Durham. He had resorted to all his usual expedients to bring them in collision, and had entirely failed. He had faithfully reported to Bob all that had been said by the people in the upper battalion "agin him," and "he was sure Billy Stallings started it. He heard Billy say himself to Jim Brown, that he could whip him, *or any other man in his battalion";* and this he told to Bob; adding, "Dod darn his soul, if he was a little bigger, if he'd let any man *put upon* his battalion in such a way." Bob replied, "If he (Stallings) thought so, he'd better come and try it." This Ransy carried to Billy, and delivered it with a spirit becoming his own dignity and the character of his battalion, and with a colouring well calculated to give it effect. These, and many other schemes which Ransy laid for the gratification of his curiosity, entirely failed of their object. Billy and Bob continued friends, and Ransy had begun to lapse into the most tantalizing and hopeless despair, when a circumstance occurred which led to a settlement of the long-disputed question.

It is said that a hundred gamecocks will live in perfect harmony together if you do not put a hen with them; and so it would have been with Billy and Bob had there been no women in the world. But there were women in the world, and from them each of our heroes had taken to himself a wife. The good ladies were no strangers to the prowess of their husbands, and, strange as it may seem, they presumed a little upon it.

The two battalions had met at the Courthouse upon a regimental parade.

THE FIGHT

The two champions were there, and their wives had accompanied them. Neither knew the other's lady, nor were the ladies known to each other. The exercises of the day were just over, when Mrs. Stallings and Mrs. Durham stepped simultaneously into the store of Zephaniah Atwater, from "down east."

"Have you any Turkey-red?" said Mrs. S.

"Have you any curtain calico?" said Mrs. D. at the same moment.

"Yes, ladies," said Mr. Atwater, "I have both."

"Then help me first," said Mrs. D., "for I'm in a hurry."

"I'm in as great a hurry as she is, " said Mrs. S., "and I'll thank you to help me first."

"And, pray, who are you, madam?" continued the other.

"Your betters, madam," was the reply.

At this moment Billy Stallings stepped in. "Come," said he, "Nancy, let's be going; it's getting late."

"I'd a been gone half an hour ago,' she replied, "if it hadn't a' been for that impudent huzzy."

"Who do you call an impudent huzzy, you nasty, good-for-nothing, snaggle-toothed gaub of fat, you?" returned Mrs. D.

"Look here, woman," said Billy, "have you got a husband here? If you have, I'll *lick* him till he learns to teach you better manners, you *sassy* heifer you." At this moment something was seen to rush out of the store as if ten thousand hornets were stinging it; crying, "Take care—let me go—don't hold me—where's Bob Durham?" It was Ransy Sniffle, who had been listening in breathless delight to all that had passed.

"Yonder's Bob, setting on the Courthouse steps," cried one. "What's the matter?"

"Don't talk to me!" said Ransy. "Bob Durham, you'd better go long yonder, and take care of your wife. They're playing h—l with her there, in Zeph Atwater's store. Dod etarnally darn my soul, if any man was to talk to my wife as Bill Stallions is talking to yours, if I wouldn't drive blue blazes through him in less than no time."

Bob sprang to the store in a minute, followed by a hundred friends; for the bully of a county never wants friends.

"Bill Stallions," said Bob, as he entered, "what have you been saying to my wife?"

"Is that your wife?" inquired Billy, obviously much surprised and a little disconcerted.

"Yes, she is, and no man shall abuse her, I don't care who he is."

"Well," rejoined Billy, "it an't worth while to go over it; I've said enough for a fight: and, if you'll step out, we'll settle it!"

"Billy," said Bob, "are you for a fair fight?"

"I am," said Billy. "I've heard much of your manhood, and I believe I'm a better man than you are. If you will go into a ring with me, we can soon settle the dispute."

"Choose your friends," said Bob; "make your ring, and I'll be in with mine as soon as you will."

They both stepped out, and began to strip very deliberately, each battalion gathering round its champion, except Ransy, who kept himself busy in a most honest endeavour to hear and see all that transpired in both groups at the same time. He ran from one to the other in quick succession; peeped here and listened there; talked to this one, then to that one, and then to himself; squatted under one's legs and another's arms, and, in the short interval between stripping and stepping into the ring, managed to get himself trod on by half of both battalions. But Ransy was not the only one interested upon this occasion; the most intense interest prevailed everywhere. Many were the conjectures, doubts, oaths, and imprecations uttered while the parties were preparing for the combat. All the knowing ones were consulted as to the issue, and they all agreed, to a man, in one of two opinions: either that Bob would flog Billy, or Billy would flog Bob. We must be permitted, however, to dwell for a moment upon the opinion of Squire Thomas Loggins; a man who, it was said, had never failed to predict the issue of a fight in all his life. Indeed, so unerring had he always proved in this regard, that it would have been counted the most obstinate infidelity to doubt for a moment after he had delivered himself. Squire Loggins was a man who said but little, but that little was always delivered with the most imposing solemnity of look and cadence. He always wore the aspect of profound thought, and you could not look at him without coming to the conclusion that he was elaborating truth from its most intricate combinations.

"Uncle Tommy," said Sam Reynolds, "you can tell us all about it if you will; how will the fight go?"

The question immediately drew an anxious group around the squire. He raised his teeth slowly from the head of his walking cane, on which they had been resting; pressed his lips closely and thoughtfully together; threw down his eyebrows, dropped his chin, raised his eyes to an angle of twenty-three degrees, paused about half a minute, and replied, "Sammy, watch Robert Durham close in the beginning of the fight; take care of William Stallions in the middle of it; and see who has the wind at the end." As he uttered the last member of the sentence, he looked slyly at Bob's friends, and winked very significantly; whereupon they rushed, with one accord, to tell Bob what Uncle Tommy had said. As they retired, the squire turned to Billy's friends, and said, with a smile, "Them boys think I mean that Bob will whip."

Here the other party kindled into joy, and hastened to inform Billy how Bob's friends had deceived themselves as to Uncle Tommy's opinion. In the mean time, the principals and seconds were busily employed in preparing themselves for the combat. The plan of attack and defence, the manner of improving the various turns of the conflict, "the best mode of saving wind," &c., &c., were all discussed and settled. At length Billy announced himself ready, and his crowd were seen moving to the centre of the Courthouse Square; he and his five seconds in the rear. At the same time, Bob's party moved to the same point, and in the same order. The ring was now formed, and for a moment the silence of death reigned through both battalions. It was soon interrupted, however, by the cry of "Clear the way!" from Billy's seconds; when the ring opened in the centre of the upper battalion (for the order of march had arranged the centre of the two battalions on opposite sides of the circle), and Billy stepped into the ring from the east, followed by his friends. He was stripped to the trousers, and exhibited an arm, breast, and shoulders of the most tremendous portent. His step was firm, daring, and martial; and as he bore his fine form a little in advance of his friends, an involuntary burst of triumph broke from his side of the ring; and, at the same moment, an uncontrollable thrill of awe ran along the whole curve of the lower battalion.

"Look at him!" was heard from his friends; "just look at him."

"Ben, how much you ask to stand before that man two seconds?"

"Pshaw, don't talk about it! Just thinkin' about it 's broke three o' my ribs a'ready!"

"What's Bob Durham going to do when Billy let's that arm loose upon him?"

"God bless your soul, he'll think thunder and lightning a mint julip to it."

"Oh, look here, men, go take Bill Stallions out o' that ring, and bring in Phil Johnson's stud horse, so that Durham may have some chance! I don't want to see the man killed right away."

These and many other like expressions, interspersed thickly with oaths of the most modern coinage, were coming from all points of the upper battalion, while Bob was adjusting the girth of his pantaloons, which walking had discovered not to be exactly right. It was just fixed to his mind, his foes becoming a little noisy, and his friends a little uneasy at his delay, when Billy called out, with a smile of some meaning, "Where's the bully of the lower battalion? I'm getting tired of waiting."

"Here he is," said Bob, lighting, as it seemed, from the clouds into the ring, for he had actually bounded clear of the head of Ransy Sniffle into the circle. His descent was quite as imposing as Billy's entry, and excited the same feelings, but in opposite bosoms.

Voices of exultation now rose on his side.

"Where did he come from?"

"Why," said one of his seconds (all having just entered), "we were girting him up, about a hundred yards out yonder, when he heard Billy ask for the bully; and he fetched a leap over the Courthouse, and went out of sight; but I told them to come on, they'd find him here."

Here the lower battalion burst into a peal of laughter, mingled with a look of admiration, which seemed to denote their entire belief of what they had heard.

"Boys, widen the ring, so as to give him room to jump."

"Oh, my little flying wild-cat, hold him if you can! and, when you get him fast, hold lightning next."

"Ned, what do you think he's made of?"

"Steel springs and chicken-hawk, God bless you!"

"Gentlemen," said one of Bob's seconds, "I understand it is to be a fair fight; catch as catch can, rough and tumble: no man touch till one or the other halloos."

"That's the rule," was the reply from the other side.

"Are you ready?"

"We are ready."

"Then blaze away, my game cocks!"

At the word, Bob dashed at his antagonist at fullspeed; and Bill squared himself to receive him with one of his most fatal blows. Making his calculation from Bob's velocity, of the time when he would come within striking distance, he let drive with tremendous force. But Bob's onset was obviously planned to avoid this blow; for, contrary to all expectations, he stopped short just out of arm's reach, and, before Billy could recover his balance, Bob had him "all under-hold." The next second, sure enough, "found Billy's head where his feet ought to be." How it was done no one could tell; but, as if by supernatural power, both Billy's feet were thrown full half his own height in the air, and he came down with a force that seemed to shake the earth. As he struck the ground, commingled shouts, screams, and yells burst from the lower battalion, loud enough to be heard for miles. "Hurra, my little hornet!" "Save him!" "Feed him!" "Give him the Durham physic till his stomach turns!" Billy was no sooner down than Bob was on him, and lending him awful blows about the face and breast. Billy made two efforts to rise by main strength, but failed. "Lord bless you, man, don't try to get up! *Lay* still and take it! you *bleege* to have it!"

Billy now turned his face suddenly to the ground, and rose upon his hands and knees. Bob jerked up both his hands and threw him on his face. He again recovered his late position, of which Bob endeavoured to deprive him as before; but, missing one arm, he failed, and Billy rose. But he had scarcely resumed his feet before they flew up as before, and he came again to the ground. "No fight, gentlemen!" cried Bob's friends; ' the man can't stand up! Bouncing feet are bad things to fight in." His fall, however, was this time comparatively light; for, having thrown his right arm round Bob's neck, he carried his head down with him. This grasp, which was obstinately maintained, prevented Bob from getting on him, and they lay head to head, seeming, for a time, to do nothing. Presently they rose, as if by mutual consent; and, as they rose, a shout burst from both battalions. "Oh, my lark!"

cried the east, "has he foxed you? Do you begin to feel him! He's only beginning to fight; he ain't got warm yet."

"Look yonder!" cried the west; "didn't I tell you so! He hit the ground so hard it jarred his nose off. Now ain't he a pretty man as he stands? He shall have my sister Sal just for his pretty looks. I want to get in the breed of them sort o' men, to drive ugly out of my kinfolks."

I looked, and saw that Bob had entirely lost his left ear, and a large piece from his left cheek. His right eye was a little discoloured, and the blood flowed profusely from his wounds.

Bill presented a hideous spectacle. About a third of his nose, at the lower extremity, was bit off, and his face so swelled and bruised that it was difficult to discover in it anything of the human visage, much more the fine features which he carried into the ring.

They were up only long enough for me to make the foregoing discoveries, when down they went again, precisely as before. They no sooner touched the ground than Bill relinquished his hold upon Bob's neck. In this he seemed to all to have forfeited the only advantage which put him upon an equality with his adversary. But the movement was soon explained. Bill wanted this arm for other purposes than defence; and he had made arrangements whereby he knew that he could make it answer these purposes; for, when they rose again, he had the middle finger of Bob's left hand in his mouth. He was now secure from Bob's annoying trips; and he began to lend his adversary tremendous blows, every one of which was hailed by a shout from his friends. "Bullets!" "*Hoss*-kicking!" "Thunder!" "That'll do for his face; now feel his short ribs, Billy!"

I now considered the contest settled. I deemed it impossible for any human being to withstand for five seconds the loss of blood which issued from Bob's ear, cheek, nose, and finger, accompanied with such blows as he was receiving. Still he maintained the conflict, and gave blow for blow with considerable effect. But the blows of each became slower and weaker after the first three or four; and it became obvious that Bill wanted the room which Bob's finger occupied for breathing. He would therefore, probably, in a short time, have let it go, had not Bob anticipated his politeness by jerking away his hand, and making him a present of the finger. He now seized Bill again, and brought him to his knees, but he recovered. He again brought him to his knees, and he again recovered. A third effort, however, brought him down, and Bob on top of him. These efforts seemed to exhaust the little remaining strength of both; and they lay, Bill undermost and Bob across his breast, motionless, and panting for breath. After a short pause, Bob gathered his hand full of dirt and sand, and was in the act of grinding it in his adversary's eyes, when Bill cried "ENOUGH!" Language cannot describe the scene that followed; the shouts, oaths, frantic gestures, taunts, replies, and little fights, and therefore I shall not attempt it. The champions were borne off by their seconds and washed; when many a bleeding wound and ugly bruise was discovered on each which no eye had seen before.

Many had gathered round Bob, and were in various ways congratulating and applauding him, when a voice from the centre of the circle cried out, "Boys, hush and listen to me!" It proceeded from Squire Loggins, who had made his way to Bob's side, and had gathered his face up into one of its most flattering and intelligible expressions. All were obedient to the squire's command. "Gentlemen," continued he, with a most knowing smile, "is —Sammy—Reynold— in—this—company—of—gentlemen?"

"Yes," said Sam, "here I am."

"Sammy," said the squire, winking to the company and drawing the head of his cane to his mouth with an arch smile as he closed, "I —wish—you —to tell—cousin—Bobby—and—these—gentlemen here present—what —your—Uncle—Tommy—said— before—the—fight—began?"

"Oh! get away, Uncle Tom," said Sam, smiling (the squire winked), "you don't know nothing about *fighting*." (The squire winked again.) "All you know about it is how it'll begin, how it'll go on, how it'll end; that's all. Cousin Bob, when you going to fight again, just go to the old man, and let him tell you all about it. If he can't, don't ask nobody else nothing about it, I tell you."

The squire's foresight was complimented in many ways by the by-standers; and he retired, advising "the boys to be at peace, as fighting was a bad business."

Durham and Stallings kept their beds for several weeks, and did not meet again for two months. When they met, Billy stepped up to Bob and offered his hand, saying, "Bobby, you've *licked* me a fair fight; but you wouldn't have done it if I hadn't been in the wrong. I oughn't to have treated your wife as I did; and I felt so through the whole fight; and it sort o' cowed me."

"Well, Billy," said Bob, "let's be friends. Once in the fight, when you had my finger in your mouth, and was pealing me in the face and breast, I was going to halloo; but I thought of Petsy, and knew the house would be too hot for me if I got whipped when fighting for her, after always whipping when I fought for myself."

"Now that's what I always love to see," said a by-stander. "It's true I brought about the fight, but I wouldn't have done it if it hadn't o' been on account of *Miss* (Mrs.) Durham. But dod etarnally darn my soul, if I ever could stand by and see any woman put upon, much less *Miss* Durham. If Bobby hadn't been there, I'd o' took it up myself, be darned if I wouldn't, even if I'd o' got whipped for it. But we're all friends now." The reader need hardly be told that this was Ransy Sniffle.

Thanks to the Christian religion, to schools, colleges, and benevolent associations, such scenes of barbarism and cruelty as that which I have been just describing are now of rare occurrence, though they may still be occasionally met with in some of the new counties. Wherever they prevail, they are a disgrace to that community. The peace-officers who countenance them deserve a place in the Penitentiary.

THE HORSE-SWAP

During the session of the Supreme Court, in the Village of ———, about three weeks ago, when a number of people were collected in the principal street of the village, I observed a young man riding up and down the street, as I supposed, in a violent passion. He galloped this way, then that, and then the other; spurred his horse to one group of citizens, then to another, then dashed off at half speed, as if fleeing from danger; and, suddenly checking his horse, returned first in a pace, then in a trot, and then in a canter. While he was performing these various evolutions, he cursed, swore, whooped, screamed, and tossed himself in every attitude which man could assume on horseback. In short, he *cavorted* most magnanimously (a term which, in our tongue, expresses all that I have described, and a little more), and seemed to be setting all creation at defiance. As I like to see all that is passing, I determined to take a position a little nearer to him, and to ascertain, if possible, what it was that affected him so sensibly. Accordingly, I approached a crowd before which he had stopped for a moment, and examined it with the strictest scrutiny. But I could see nothing in it that seemed to have anything to do with the cavorter. Every man appeared to be in good humour, and all minding their own business. Not one so much as noticed the principal figure. Still he went on. After a semicolon pause, which my appearance seemed to produce (for he eyed me closely as I approached), he fetched a whoop, and swore that "he could out-swap any live man, woman, or child that ever walked these hills, or that ever straddled horseflesh since the days of old daddy Adam. Stranger," said he to me, "did you ever see the *Yellow* Blossom from Jasper?"

"No," said I, "but I have often heard of him."

"I'm the boy," continued he; "perhaps a *leetle,* jist a *leetle,* of the best man at a horse-swap that ever trod shoe-leather."

I began to feel my situation a little awkward, when I was relieved by a man somewhat advanced in years, who stepped up and began to survey the "*Yellow Blossom's*" horse with much apparent interest. This drew the rider's attention, and he turned the conversation from me to the stranger.

"Well, my old coon," said he, "do you want to swap *hosses?*"

"Why, I don't know,' replied the stranger; "I believe I've got a beast I'd trade with you for that one, if you like him."

"Well, fetch up your nag, my old cock; you're jist the lark I wanted to get hold of. I am perhaps a *leetle,* jist a *leetle,* of the best man at a horse-swap that ever stole *cracklins* out of his mammy's fat gourd. Where's your *hoss?*"

"I'll bring him presently; but I want to examine your horse a little."

"Oh! look at him," said the Blossom, alighting and hitting him a cut; "look at him. He's the best piece of *hoss*flesh in the thirteen united univarsal worlds. There's no sort o' mistake in little Bullet. He can pick up miles on his feet, and fling 'em behind him as fast as the next man's *hoss,* I don't care where he comes from. And he can keep at it as long as the sun can shine without resting."

During this harangue, little Bullet looked as if he understood it all, believed it, and was ready at any moment to verify it. He was a horse of goodly countenance, rather expressive of vigilance than fire; though an unnatural appearance of fierceness was thrown into it by the loss of his ears, which had been cropped pretty close to his head. Nature had done but little for Bullet's head and neck; but he managed, in a great measure, to hide their defects by bowing perpetually. He had obviously suffered severely for corn; but if his ribs and hip bones had not disclosed the fact, *he* never would have done it; for he was in all respects as cheerful and happy as if he commanded all the corn-cribs and fodder-stacks in Georgia. His height was about twelve hands; but as his shape partook somewhat of that of the giraffe, his haunches stood much lower. They were short, strait, peaked, and concave. Bullet's tail, however, made amends for all his defects. All that the artist could do to beautify it had been done; and all that horse could do to compliment the artist, Bullet did. His tail was nicked in superior style, and exhibited the line of beauty in so many directions, that it could not fail to hit the most fastidious taste in some of them. From the root it dropped into a graceful festoon; then rose in a handsome curve; then resumed its first direction; and then mounted suddenly upward like a cypress knee to a perpendicular of about two and half inches. The whole had a careless and bewitching inclination to the right. Bullet obviously knew where his beauty lay, and took all occasions to display it to the best advantage. If a stick cracked, or if any one moved suddenly about him, or coughed, or hawked, or spoke a little louder than common, up went Bullet's tail like lightning; and if the *going up* did not please, the *coming down* must of necessity, for it was as different from the other movement as was its direction. The first was a bold and rapid flight upward, usually to an angle of forty-five degrees. In this position he kept his interesting appendage until he satisfied himself that nothing in particular was to be done; when he commenced dropping it by half inches, in second beats, then in triple time, then faster and shorter, and faster and shorter still, until it finally died away imperceptibly into its natural position. If I might compare sights to sounds, I should say its *settling* was more like the note of a locust than anything else in nature.

Either from native sprightliness of disposition, from uncontrollable activity, or from an unconquerable habit of removing flies by the stamping of the feet, Bullet never stood still; but always kept up a gentle fly-scaring movement of his limbs, which was peculiarly interesting.

"I tell you, man," proceeded the Yellow Blossom "he's the best live hoss that ever trod the grit of Georgia. Bob Smart knows the hoss. Come here, Bob, and mount this hoss, and show Bullet's motions." Here Bullet bristled up, and looked as if he had been hunting for Bob all day long, and had just found him. Bob sprang on his back. "Boo-oo-oo!" said Bob, with a fluttering noise of the lips; and away went Bullet, as if in a quarter race, with all his beauties spread in handsome style.

"Now fetch him back," said Blossom. Bullet turned and came in pretty much as he went out.

"Now trot him by." Bullet reduced his tail to *"customary;"* sidled to the right and left airily, and exhibited at least three varieties of trot in the short space of fifty yards.

"Make him pace!" Bob commenced twitching the bridle and kicking at the same time. These inconsistent movements obviously (and most naturally) disconcerted Bullet; for it was impossible for him to learn, from them, whether he was to proceed or stand still. He started to trot, and was told that wouldn't do. He attempted a canter, and was checked again. He stopped, and was urged to go on. Bullet now rushed into the wide field of experiment, and struck out a gait of his own, that completely turned the tables upon his rider, and certainly deserved a patent. It seemed to have derived its elements from the jig, the minuet, and the cotillon. If it was not a pace, it certainly had *pace* in it, and no man would venture to call it anything else; so it passed off to the satisfaction of the owner.

"Walk him!" Bullet was now at home again, and he walked as if money was staked on him.

The stranger, whose name, I afterward learned, was Peter Ketch, having examined Bullet to his heart's content, ordered his son Neddy to go and bring up Kit. Neddy soon appeared upon Kit; a well-formed sorrel of the middle size, and in good order. His *tout ensemble* threw Bullet entirely in the shade, though a glance was sufficient to satisfy any one that Bullet had the decided advantage of him in point of intellect.

"Why, man," said Blossom, "do you bring such a hoss as that to trade for Bullet? Oh, I see you're no notion of trading."

"Ride him off, Neddy!" said Peter. Kit put off at a handsome lope.

"Trot him back!" Kit came in at a long, sweeping trot, and stopped suddenly at the crowd.

"Well," said Blossom, "let me look at him; maybe he'll do to plough."

"Examine him!" said Peter, taking hold of the bridle close to the mouth; "he's nothing but a tacky. He an't as *pretty* a horse as Bullet, I know; but he'll do. Start 'em together for a hundred and fifty *mile;* and if Kit an't twenty mile ahead of him at the coming out, any man may take Kit for nothing. But he's a monstrous mean horse, gentleman; any man may see that. He's the scariest horse, too, you ever saw. He won't do to hunt on, no how. Stranger, will you let Neddy have your rifle to shoot off him? Lay the rifle between his ears, Neddy, and shoot at the blaze in that stump. Tell me when his head is high enough."

Ned fired, and hit the blaze; and Kit did not move a hair's breadth.

"Neddy, take a couple of sticks, and beat on that hogshead at Kit's tail."

Ned made a tremendous rattling, at which Bullet took fright, broke his bridle, and dashed off in grand style; and would have stopped all farther negotiations by going home in disgust, had not a traveller arrested him and brought him back; but Kit did not move.

"I tell you, gentlemen," continued Peter, "he's the scariest horse you ever saw. He an't as gentle as Bullet, but he won't do any harm if you watch him. Shall I put him in a cart, gig, or wagon for you, stranger? He'll cut the same capers there he does here. He's a monstrous mean horse."

During all this time Blossom was examining him with the nicest scrutiny. Having examined his frame and limbs, he now looked at his eyes.

"He's got a curious look out of his eyes," said Blossom.

"Oh yes, sir," said Peter, "just as blind as a bat. Blind horses always have clear eyes. Make a motion at his eyes, if you please, sir."

Blossom did so, and Kit threw up his head rather as if something pricked him under the chin than as if fearing a blow. Blossom repeated the experiment, and Kit jerked back in considerable astonishment.

"Stone blind, you see, gentlemen," proceeded Peter; "but he's just as good to travel of a dark night as if he had eyes."

"Blame my buttons," said Blossom, "if I like them eyes."

"No," said Peter, "nor I neither. I'd rather have 'em made of diamonds; but they'll do, if they don't show as much white as Bullet's."

"Well," said Blossom, "make a pass at me."

"No," said Peter; "you made the banter, now make your pass."

"Well, I'm never afraid to price my hosses. You must give me twenty-five dollars boot."

"Oh, certainly; say fifty, and my saddle and bridle in. Here, Neddy, my son, take away daddy's horse."

"Well," said Blossom, "I've made my pass, now you make yours."

"I'm for short talk in a horse-swap, and therefore always tell a gentleman at once what I mean to do. You must give me ten dollars."

Blossom swore absolutely, roundly, and profanely, that he never would give boot.

"Well," said Peter, "I didn't care about trading; but you cut such high shines, that I thought I'd like to back you out, and I've done it. Gentlemen, you see I've brought him to a hack."

"Come, old man," said Blossom, "I've been joking with you. I begin to think you do want to trade; therefore, give me five dollars and take Bullet.

I'd rather lose ten dollars any time than not make a trade, though I hate to fling away a good hoss."

"Well," said Peter, "I'll be as clever as you are. Just put the five dollars on Bullet's back, and hand him over; it's a trade."

Blossom swore again, as roundly as before, that he would not give boot; and, said he, "Bullet wouldn't hold five dollars on his back, no how. But, as I bantered you, if you say an even swap, here's at you."

"I told you," said Peter, "I'd be as clever as you, therefore, here goes two dollars more, just for trade sake. Give me three dollars, and it's a bargain."

Blossom repeated his former assertion; and here the parties stood for a long time, and the by-standers (for many were now collected) began to taunt both parties. After some time, however, it was pretty unanimously decided that the old man had backed Blossom out.

At length Blossom swore he "never would be backed out for three dollars after bantering a man;" and, accordingly, they closed the trade.

"Now," said Blossom, as he handed Peter the three dollars, "I'm a man that, when he makes a bad trade, makes the most of it until he can make a better. I'm for no rues and after-claps."

"That's just my way," said Peter; "I never goes to law to mend my bargains."

"Ah, you're the kind of boy I love to trade with. Here's your hoss, old man. Take the saddle and bridle off him, and I'll strip yours; but lift up the blanket easy from Bullet's back, for he's a mighty tender-backed hoss."

The old man removed the saddle, but the blanket stuck fast. He attempted to raise it, and Bullet bowed himself, switched his tail, danced a little, and gave signs of biting.

"Don't hurt him, old man," said Blossom, archly; "take it off easy. I am, perhaps, a leetle of the best man at a horse-swap that ever catched a coon."

Peter continued to pull at the blanket more and more roughly, and Bullet became more and more *cavortish*: insomuch that, when the blanket came off, he had reached the *kicking* point in good earnest.

The removal of the blanket disclosed a sore on Bullet's back-bone that seemed to have defied all medical skill. It measured six full inches in length and four in breadth, and had as many features as Bullet had motions. My heart sickened at the sight; and I felt that the brute who had been riding him in that situation deserved the halter.

The prevailing feeling, however, was that of mirth. The laugh became loud and general at the old man's expense, and rustic witticisms were liberally bestowed upon him and his late purchase. These Blossom continued to provoke by various remarks. He asked the old man "if he thought Bullet would let five dollars lie on his back." He declared most seriously that he had owned that horse three months, and had never discovered before that he had a sore back, "or he never should have thought of trading him," &c., &c.

The old man bore it all with the most philosophic composure. He evinced no astonishment at his late discovery, and made no replies. But his son Neddy had not disciplined his feelings quite so well. His eyes opened wider and wider from the first to the last pull of the blanket; and, when the whole sore burst upon his view, astonishment and fright seemed to contend for the mastery of his countenance. As the blanket disappeared, he stuck his hands in his breeches pockets, heaved a deep sigh, and lapsed into a profound revery, from which he was only roused by the cuts at his father. He bore them as long as he could; and, when he could contain himself no longer, he began, with a certain wildness of expression which gave a peculiar interest to what he uttered: "His back's mighty bad off; but dod drot my soul if he's put it to daddy as bad as he thinks he has, for old Kit's both blind and *deef,* I'll be dod drot if he eint."

"The devil he is," said Blossom.

"Yes, dod drot my soul if he *eint.* You walk him, and see if he *eint.* His eyes don't look like it; but he'd *jist as leve go agin* the house with you, or in a ditch, as any how. Now you go try him." The laugh was now turned on Blossom; and many rushed to test the fidelity of the little boy's report. A few experiments established its truth beyond controversy.

"Neddy," said the old man, "you oughtn't to try and make people discontented with their things. Stranger, don't mind what the little boy says. If you can only get Kit rid of them little failings, you'll find him all sorts of a horse. You are a *leetle* the best man at a horse-swap that ever I got hold of; but don't fool away Kit. Come, Neddy, my son, let's be moving; the stranger seems to be getting snappish."

JOHNSON JONES
HOOPER

(1815–1862)

Johnson Jones Hooper was born in Wilmington, North Carolina, of a well-known family that had come upon impecunious days. His father, a Harvard graduate, was unable to send him to college. In 1835 he went to La Fayette, Alabama, to study law in his brother's office. He practiced law, then edited a newspaper, did reasonably well, and became involved in Alabama politics as a Whig. As the war drew near he became an ardent secessionist, and in 1861 was elected Secretary and Librarian of the Confederate Congress.

Hooper began publishing humorous sketches in Alabama that drew the attention of William T. Porter, publisher of the New York *Spirit of the Times.* Porter reprinted Hooper's humorous works and encouraged him to write for a national audience. Upon publication of *Some Adventures of Simon Suggs, Late Captain of the Tallapoosa Volunteers* in 1845, by Carey and Hart of Philadelphia, Hooper achieved a wide readership. As he grew more involved in Alabama politics he began to feel that his reputation as a literary humorist worked in his disfavor. However, Porter continued to urge him not to let his political activities stand in the way of his career as a humorist. Hooper published one more book of humor and a book on hunting.

As C. Hugh Holman has noted, *Simon Suggs* is essentially a picaresque novel. Mark Twain knew it very well, and the incident of the Dauphin at the Pokeville camp meeting in *Huckleberry Finn* is obviously modeled upon Simon Suggs' adventures along that line.

From SOME ADVENTURES OF CAPTAIN SIMON SUGGS, LATE OF THE TALLAPOOSA VOLUNTEERS

THE CAPTAIN ATTENDS A CAMP-MEETING

Captain Suggs found himself as poor at the conclusion of the Creek war, as he had been at its commencement. Although no "arbitrary," "despotic," "corrupt," and "unprincipled" judge had fined him a thousand dollars for his proclamation of martial law at Fort Suggs, or the enforcement of its rules in the case of Mrs. Haycock; yet somehow—the thing is alike inexplicable to him and to us—the money which he had contrived, by various shifts to obtain, melted away and was gone forever. To a man like the Captain, of intense domestic affections, this state of destitution was most distressing. "He could stand it himself—didn't care a d———n for it, no way," he observed, "but the old woman and the children; *that* bothered him!"

As he sat one day, ruminating upon the unpleasant condition of his "financial concerns," Mrs. Suggs informed him that "the sugar and coffee was nigh about out," and that there was not "a dozen j'ints and middlins, *all put together,* in the smoke-house." Suggs bounced up on the instant, exclaiming, "D———n it! *somebody* must suffer!" But whether this remark was intended to convey the idea that he and his family were about to experience the want of the necessaries of life; or that some other, and as yet unknown individual should "suffer" to prevent that prospective exigency, must be left to the commentators, if perchance any of that ingenious class of persons should hereafter see proper to write notes for this history. It is enough for us that we give all the facts in this connection, so that ignorance of the subsequent conduct of Captain Suggs may not lead to an erroneous judgment in respect to his words.

Having uttered the exclamation we have repeated—and perhaps, hurriedly walked once or twice across the room—Captain Suggs drew on his famous old green-blanket overcoat, and ordered his horse, and within five minutes was on his way to a camp-meeting, then in full blast on Sandy creek, twenty miles distant, where he hoped to find amusement, at least. When he arrived there, he found the hollow square of the encampment filled with people, listening to the mid-day sermon and its dozen accompanying "exhortations." A half-dozen preachers were dispensing the word; the one in the pulpit, a meek-faced old man, of great simplicity and benevolence. His voice was weak and cracked, notwithstanding which, however, he contrived to make himself heard occasionally, above the din of the exhorting, the singing, and the shouting which were going on around him. The rest were walking to and fro, (engaged in the other exercises we have indicated), among the "mourners"—a host of whom occupied the seat set apart for their especial use—or made personal appeals to the mere spectators. The excitement was intense. Men and women rolled about on the ground, or lay sobbing or shouting in promiscuous heaps. More than all, the negroes sang and screamed and prayed. Several, under the influence of what is technically called "the jerks," were plunging and pitching about with convulsive energy. The great object of all seemed to be, to see who could make the greatest noise—

> "And each—for madness ruled the hour—
> Would try his own expressive power."

"Bless my poor old soul!" screamed the preacher in the pulpit; "ef yonder aint a squad in that corner that we aint got one outen yet! It'll never do"—raising his voice—"you must come outen that! Brother Fant, fetch up that youngster in the blue coat! I see the Lord's a-workin' upon him! Fetch him along—glory—yes!—hold to him!"

"Keep the thing warm!" roared a sensual seeming man, of stout mould and florid countenance, who was exhorting among a bevy of young women, upon whom he was lavishing caresses. "Keep the thing warm, breethring! —come to the Lord, honey!" he added, as he vigorously hugged one of the damsels he sought to save.

"Oh, I've got him!" said another in exulting tones, as he led up a gawky youth among the mourners—"I've got him—he tried to git off, but—ha! Lord!"—shaking his head as much as to say, it took a smart fellow to escape him—"ha! Lord!"— and he wiped the perspiration from his face with one hand, and with the other, patted his neophyte on the shoulder —"he couldn't do it! No! Then he tried to argy wi' me—but bless the Lord! —he couldn't do that nother! Ha! Lord! I tuk him, fust in the Old

Testament—bless the Lord!—and I argyed him all thro' Kings—then I throwed him into Proverbs!— and from that, here we had it up and down, kleer down to the New Testament, and then I begun to see it work him! —then we got into Matthy, and from Matthy right straight along to Acts; and *thar* I throwed him! Y-e-s L-o-r-d!"—assuming the nasal twang and high pitch which are, in some parts, considered the perfection of rhetorical art—"Y-e-s L-o-r-d! and h-e-r-e he is! Now g-i-t down thar," addressing the subject, "and s-e-e ef the L-o-r-d won't do somethin' f-o-r you!" Having thus deposited his charge among the mourners, he started out, summarily to convert another soul!

"Gl-o-*ree*!" yelled a huge, greasy negro woman, as in a fit of the jerks, she threw herself convulsively from her feet, and fell "like a thousand of brick," across a diminutive old man in a little round hat, who was squeaking consolation to one of the mourners.

"Good Lord, have mercy!" ejaculated the little man earnestly and unaffectedly, as he strove to crawl from under the sable mass which was crushing him.

In another part of the square a dozen old women were singing. They were in a state of absolute ecstasy, as their shrill pipes gave forth,

> "I rode on the sky,
> Quite ondestified I,
> And the moon it was under my feet!"

Near these last, stood a delicate woman in that hysterical condition in which the nerves are incontrollable, and which is vulgarly—and almost blasphemously—termed the "holy laugh." A hideous grin distorted her mouth, and was accompanied with a maniac's chuckle; while every muscle and nerve of her face twitched and jerked in horrible spasms.*

Amid all this confusion and excitement Suggs stood unmoved. He viewed the whole affair as a grand deception—a sort of "opposition line" running against his own, and looked on with a sort of professional jealousy. Sometimes he would mutter running comments upon what passed before him.

"Well now," said he, as he observed the full-faced brother who was "officiating" among the women, "that ere feller takes *my* eye!—thar he's

---

* The reader is requested to bear in mind, that the scenes described in this chapter are not *now* to be witnessed. Eight or ten years ago, all classes of population of the Creek country were very different from what they now are. Of course, no disrespect is intended to any denomination of Christians. We believe that camp-meetings are not peculiar to any church, though most usual in the Methodist—a denomination whose respectability in Alabama is attested by the fact, that *very many* of its worthy clergymen and lay members, hold honourable and profitable offices in the gift of the state legislature; of which, indeed, almost a controlling portion are themselves Methodists. [Author's note]

been this half-hour, a-figurin amongst them galls, and's never said the fust word to nobody else. Wonder what's the reason these here preachers never hugs up the old, ugly women? Never seed one do it in my life—the sperrit never moves 'em that way! It's nater tho'; and the women, *they* never flocks round one o' the old dried-up breethring—bet two to one old splinter-legs thar,"—nodding at one of the ministers—"won't git a chance to say turkey to a good-looking gall to-day! Well! who blames 'em? Nater will be nater, all the world over; and I judge ef I was a preacher, I should save the purtiest souls fust, myself!"

While the Captain was in the middle of this conversation with himself, he caught the attention of the preacher in the pulpit, who inferring from an indescribable something about his appearance that he was a person of some consequence, immediately determined to add him at once to the church if it could be done; and to that end began a vigorous, direct personal attack.

"Breethring," he exclaimed, "I see yonder a man that's a sinner; I *know* he's a sinner! Thar he stands," pointing to Simon, "a missubble old crittur, with his head a-blossomin for the grave! A few more short years, and d-o-w-n he'll go to perdition, lessen the Lord have mer-cy on him! Come up here, you old hoary-headed sinner, a-n-d git down upon your knees, a-n-d put up your cry for the Lord to snatch you from the bottomless pit! You're ripe for the devil—you're b-o-u-n-d for hell, and the Lord only knows what'll become of you!"

"D———n it," thought Suggs, "*ef* I only had you down in the krick swamp for a minit or so, *I'd* show you who's *old!* *I'd* alter your tune *mighty* sudden, you sassy, 'saitful old rascal!" But he judiciously held his tongue and gave no utterance to the thought.

The attention of many having been directed to the Captain by the preacher's remarks, he was soon surrounded by numerous well-meaning, and doubtless very pious persons, each one of whom seemed bent on the application of his own particular recipe for the salvation of souls. For a long time the Captain stood silent, or answered the incessant stream of exhortation only with a sneer; but at length, his countenance began to give token of inward emotion. First his eye-lids twitched—then his upper lip quivered —next a transparent drop formed on one of his eye-lashes, and a similar one on the tip of his nose—and, at last, a sudden bursting of air from nose and mouth, told that Captain Suggs was overpowered by his emotions. At the moment of the explosion, he made a feint as if to rush from the crowd, but he was in experienced hands, who well knew that the battle was more than half won.

"Hold to him!" said one—"it's a-workin in him as strong as a Dick horse!"

"Pour it into him," said another, "it'll all come right directly!"

"That's the way I love to see 'em do," observed a third; "when you begin to draw the water from their eyes, taint gwine to be long afore you'll have 'em on their knees!"

And so they clung to the Captain manfully, and half dragged, half led him to the mourner's bench; by which he threw himself down, altogether unmanned, and bathed in tears. Great was the rejoicing of the brethren, as they sang, shouted, and prayed around him—for by this time it had come to be generally known that the "convicted" old man was Captain Simon Suggs, the very "chief of sinners" in all that region.

The Captain remained grovelling in the dust during the usual time, and gave vent to even more than the requisite number of sobs, and groans, and heart-piercing cries. At length, when the proper time had arrived, he bounced up, and with a face radiant with joy, commenced a series of vaultings and tumblings, which "laid in the shade" all previous performances of the sort at that camp-meeting. The brethren were in ecstasies at this demonstrative evidence of completion of the work; and whenever Suggs shouted "Gloree!" at the top of his lungs, every one of them shouted it back, until the woods rang with echoes.

The effervescence having partially subsided, Suggs was put upon his pins to relate his experience, which he did somewhat in this style—first brushing the tear-drops from his eyes, and giving the end of his nose a preparatory wring with his fingers, to free it of the superabundant moisture:

"Friends," he said, "it don't take long to curry a short horse, accordin' to the old sayin', and I'll give you the perticklers of the way I was 'brought to a knowledge' "—here the Captain wiped his eyes, brushed the tip of his nose and snuffled a little—"in les'n no time."

"Praise the Lord!" ejaculated a bystander.

"You see I come here full o' romancin' and devilment, and jist to make game of all the purceedins. Well, sure enough, I done so for some time, and was a-thinkin how I should play some trick—"

"Dear soul alive! *don't* he talk sweet!" cried an old lady in black silk —"Whar's John Dobbs? You Sukey!" screaming at a negro woman on the other side of the square—"ef you don't hunt up your mass John in a minute, and have him here to listen to this 'sperience, I'll tuck you up when I git home and give yau a hundred and fifty lashes, madam!—see ef I don't! Blessed Lord!"—referring again to the Captain's relation—"ain't it a *precious* 'scource!"

"I was jist a-thinkin' how I should play some trick to turn it all into redecule, when they began to come round me and talk. Long at fust I didn't mind it, but arter a little that brother"— pointing to the reverend gentleman who had so successfully carried the unbeliever through the Old and New Testaments, and who Simon was convinced was the "big dog of the tanyard"—"that brother spoke a word that struck me kleen to the heart, and run all over me, like fire in dry grass—"

"*I-I-I* can bring 'em!" cried the preacher alluded to, in a tone of exultation—"Lord thou knows ef thy servant can't stir 'em up, nobody else needn't try—but the glory aint mine! I'm a poor worrum of the dust," he added, with ill-managed affectation.

"And so from that I felt somethin' a-pullin' me inside—"

"Grace! grace! nothin' but grace!" exclaimed one; meaning that "grace" had been operating in the Captain's gastric region.

"And then," continued Suggs, "I wanted to git off, but they hilt me, and bimeby I felt so missuble, I had to go yonder"—pointing to the mourners' seat—"and when I lay down thar it got wuss and wuss, and 'peared like somethin' was a-mashin' down on my back—"

"That was his load o' sin," said one of the brethren— "never mind, it'll tumble off presently; see ef it don't!" and he shook his head professionally and knowingly.

"And it kept a-gittin heavier and heavier, ontwell it looked like it might be a four year old steer, or a big pine log, or somethin' of that sort—"

"Glory to my soul," shouted Mrs. Dobbs, "it's the sweetest talk I *ever* hearn! You Sukey! aint you got John yit? never mind, my lady, *I*'ll settle wi' you!" Sukey quailed before the finger which her mistress shook at her.

"And arter awhile," Suggs went on, " 'peared like I fell into a trance, like, and I seed—"

"Now we'll git the good on it!" cried one of the sanctified.

"And I seed the biggest, longest, rip-roarenest, blackest, scaliest—" Captain Suggs paused, wiped his brow, and ejaculated "Ah, L-o-r-d!" so as to give full time for curiosity to become impatience to know what he saw.

"*Sarpent!* warn't it?" asked one of the preachers.

"No, not a sarpent," replied Suggs, blowing his nose.

"Do tell us *what* it war, soul alive!—whar *is* John?" said Mrs. Dobbs.

"Allegator!" said the Captain.

"Alligator!" replied every woman present, and screamed for very life.

Mrs. Dobbs' nerves were so shaken by the announcement, that after repeating the horrible word, she screamed to Sukey, "you Sukey, I say, you Su-u-ke-e-y! ef you let John come a-nigh this way, whar the dreadful alliga —shaw! what am I thinkin' bout? 'Twarn't nothin' but a vishin'!"

"Well," said the Captain in continuation, "the allegator kept a-comin' and a-comin' to'ards me, and his great long jaws a-gapin' open like a ten-foot pair o' tailors' shears—"

"Oh! oh! oh! Lord! gracious above!" cried the women.

"SATAN!" was the laconic ejaculation of the oldest preacher present, who thus informed the congregation that it was the devil which had attacked Suggs in the shape of an alligator.

"And then I concluded the jig was up, 'thout I could block his game some way; for I seed his idee was to snap off my head—"

The women screamed again.

"So I fixed myself jist like I was purfectly willin' for him to take my head, and rather he'd do it as not"—here the women shuddered perceptibly —"and so I hilt my head straight out"—the Captain illustrated by elongating his neck—"and when he come up and was a gwine to *shet down* on it, I jist pitched in a big rock which choked him to death, and that minit I felt the weight slide off, and I had the best feelins—sorter like you'll have from *good* sperrits—any body ever had!"

"Didn't I *tell* you so? Didn't I *tell* you so?" asked the brother who had predicted the off-tumbling of the load of sin. "Ha, Lord! fool *who!* I've been *all* along thar!—yes, *all along thar!* and I know every inch of the way jist as good as I do the road home!"—and then he turned round and round, and looked at all, to receive a silent tribute to his superior penetration.

Captain Suggs was now the "lion of the day." Nobody could pray so well, or exhort so movingly, as "brother Suggs." Nor did his natural modesty prevent the proper performance of appropriate exercises. With the reverend Bela Bugg (him to whom, under providence, he ascribed his conversion), he was a most especial favourite. They walked, sang, and prayed together for hours.

"Come, come up; thar's room for all!" cried brother Bugg, in his evening exhortation. "Come to the 'seat,' and ef you won't pray yourselves, let *me* pray for you!"

"Yes!" said Simon, by way of assisting his friend; "it's a game that all can win at! Ante up! ante up, boys—friends I mean—don't back out!"

"Thar aint a sinner here," said Bugg, "no matter ef his soul's black as a nigger, but what thar's room for him!"

"No matter what sort of a hand you've got," added Simon in the fulness of his benevolence; "take stock! Here am *I*, the wickedest and blindest of sinners—has spent my whole life in the sarvice of the devil—has now come in on *narry pair* and won a *pile!*" and the Captain's face beamed with holy pleasure.

"D-o-n-'t be afeard!" cried the preacher; "come along! the meanest won't be turned away! humble yourselves and come!"

"No!" said Simon, still indulging in his favourite style of metaphor; "the bluff game aint played here! No runnin' of a body off! Every body holds four aces, and when you bet, you win!"

And thus the Captain continued, until the services were concluded, to assist in adding to the number at the mourners' seat; and up to the hour of retiring, he exhibited such enthusiasm in the cause, that he was unanimously voted to be the most efficient addition the church had made during that meeting.

The next morning, when the preacher of the day first entered the pulpit, he announced that "brother Simon Suggs," mourning over his past iniquities, and desirous of going to work in the cause as speedily as possible, would take up a collection to found a church in his own neighborhood, at which he hoped to make himself useful as soon as he could prepare himself for the ministry, which the preacher didn't doubt, would be in a very few weeks, as brother Suggs was "a man of mighty good judge*ment*, and of *a great discorse.*" The funds were to be collected by "brother Suggs," and held in trust by brother Bela Bugg, who was the financial officer of the circuit, until some arrangement could be made to build a suitable house.

"Yes, breethring," said the Captain, rising to his feet; "I want to start a little 'sociation close to me, and I want you all to help. I'm mighty poor myself, as poor as any of you—don't leave breethring"—observing that several of the well-to-do were about to go off—"don't leave; ef you aint able to afford any thing, jist give us your blessin' and it'll be all the same!"

This insinuation did the business, and the sensitive individuals reseated themselves.

"It's mighty little of this world's goods I've got," resumed Suggs, pulling off his hat and holding it before him; "but I'll bury *that* in the cause any how," and he deposited his last five-dollar bill in the hat.

There was a murmur of approbation at the Captain's liberality throughout the assembly.

Suggs now commenced collecting, and very prudently attacked first the gentlemen who had shown a disposition to escape. These, to exculpate themselves from anything like poverty, contributed handsomely.

"Look here, breethring," said the Captain, displaying the banknotes thus received, "brother Snooks has drapt a five wi' me, and Brother Snodgrass a ten! In course 'taint expected that you *that aint as well off as them,* will give *as much;* let every one give *accordin'* to ther means."

This was another chain-shot that raked as it went!

"Who so low" as not to be able to contribute as much as Snooks and Snodgrass?

"Here's all the *small* money I've got about me," said a burly old fellow, ostentatiously handing to Suggs, over the heads of a half dozen, a ten dollar bill.

"That's what I call maganimus!" exclaimed the Captain; "that's the way *every* rich man ought to do!"

These examples were followed, more or less closely, by almost all present, for Simon had excited the pride of purse of the congregation, and a very handsome sum was collected in a very short time.

The reverend Mr. Bugg, as soon as he observed that our hero had obtained all that was to be had at that time, went to him and inquired what amount had been collected. The Captain replied that it was still uncounted, but that it couldn't be much under a hundred.

"Well, brother Suggs, you'd better count it and turn it over to me now. I'm goin' to leave presently."

"No!" said Suggs—"can't do it!"

"Why?—what's the matter?" inquired Bugg.

"It's got to be *prayed over,* fust!" said Simon, a heavenly smile illuminating his whole face.

"Well," replied Bugg, "less go one side and do it!"

"No!" said Simon, solemnly.

Mr. Bugg gave a look of inquiry.

"You see that krick swamp?" asked Suggs—"I'm gwine down in *thar,* and I'm gwine to lay this money down *so*" —showing how he would place it on the ground—"and I'm gwine to git on these here knees"—slapping the right one—"and I'm *n-e-v-e-r* gwine to quit the grit ontwell I feel it's got the blessin'! And nobody aint got to be thar but me!"

Mr. Bugg greatly admired the Captain's fervent piety, and bidding him Godspeed, turned off.

Captain Suggs "struck for" the swamp sure enough, where his horse was already hitched. "Ef them fellers aint done to a cracklin," he muttered to himself as he mounted, "*I*'ll never bet on two pair agin! They're peart at the snap game, theyselves; but they're badly lewed this hitch! Well! Live and let live is a good old motter, and it's my sentiments adzactly!" And giving the spur to his horse, off he cantered.

GEORGE WASHINGTON HARRIS

(1814–1869)

In Harris's chronicle of *Sut Lovingood: Yarns Spun by a 'Nat'ral Born Durn'd Fool* (1867), rural Southern humor moves far away from its origins in the "frame" story, which is told by a cultivated, genteel narrator, and into the unmediated idiom, concerns, and attitudes of vernacular lowlife. Harris was born in Pennsylvania and grew up in Knoxville, Tennessee. His education was scanty. He worked as a railroad conductor, steamboat captain, postmaster, sawmill manager, skilled metalworker and jeweler, and at other trades. He became involved in politics as a Democrat and, even though East Tennessee was Unionist, he was an outspoken secessionist. None of his business ventures ever really prospered. He died in 1869 on the way back from Virginia, on a railroad trip to promote business interests, and his last words were to the effect that he had been poisoned.

Harris began writing humorous sketches in the 1840s, publishing some of them in the *Spirit of the Times.* The Sut Lovingood stories began to appear in

1854, some of them written to support Democratic Party objectives and, after the war broke out, to attack Lincoln and the Unionists. Not until after the war were the Lovingood stories collected into book form. Mark Twain reviewed them for a San Francisco newspaper, predicting that the volume would sell in the West but that "the Eastern people will call it coarse and possibly taboo it." The view of human nature exhibited in them is hardly ethereal or idealistic; Sut Lovingood is unregenerate and physical, encumbered by an ungainly body, and given to crudeness, pain, and misery—but his humor is directed against pretense and humbuggery, which he despises. In Milton Rickels's summation, "the stories recount crude practical jokes; the imagery provides the counterpoint, sounding a world only occasionally satisfying, but more often harsh, hypocritical, wicked, transitory, and meaningless."

From SUT LOVINGOOD: YARNS SPUN BY A 'NAT'RAL BORN DURN'D FOOL

RARE RIPE GARDEN SEED

"I tell yu now, I minds my fust big skeer jis' es well as rich boys minds thar fust boots, ur seein the fust spotted hoss sirkis. The red top ove them boots am still a rich red stripe in thar minds, an' the burnin red ove my fust skeer hes lef es deep a scar ontu my thinkin works. Mam hed me a standin atwixt her knees. I kin feel the knobs ove her jints a-rattlin a-pas' my ribs yet. She didn't hev much petticoats tu speak ove, an' I hed but one, an' hit wer calliker slit frum the nap ove my naik tu the tail, hilt tugether at the top wif a draw-string, an' at the bottom by the hem; hit wer the handiest close I ever seed, an' wud be pow'ful cumfurtin in summer if hit warn't fur the flies. Ef they was good to run in, I'd war one yet. They beats pasted shuts, an' britches, es bad es a feather bed beats a bag ove warnut shells fur sleepin on.

"Say, George, wudn't yu like tu see me intu one 'bout haf fadid, slit, an' a-walkin jis' so, up the middil street ove yure city chuch, a-aimin fur yure pew pen, an' hit chock full ove yure fine city gal friends, jis' arter the peopil hed sot down frum the fust prayer, an' the orgin beginin tu groan; what wud yu du in sich a margincy? say hoss?"

"Why, I'd shoot you dead, Monday morning before eight o'clock," was my reply.

"Well, I speck yu wud; but yu'd take a rale ole maid faint fus, rite amung them ar gals. Lordy! wudn't yu be shamed ove me! Yit why not ten chuch in sich a suit, when yu hesn't got no store clothes?

"Well, es I wer sayin mam wer feedin us brats ontu mush an' milk, wifout the milk, an' es I were the baby then, she hilt me so es tu see that I got my sheer. Whar thar ain't enuf feed, big childer roots littil childer outen the troff, an' gobbils up thar part. Jis' so the yeath over: bishops eats el'ders, elders eats common peopil; they eats sich cattil es me, I eats possums, possums eats chickins, chickins swallers wums, an' wums am content tu eat dus, an' the dus am the aind ove hit all. Hit am all es regilur es the souns frum the tribil down tu the bull base ove a fiddil in good tchune, an' I speck hit am right, ur hit wudn't be 'lowed.

" *'The sheriff!'* his'd mam in a keen trimblin whisper; hit sounded tu me like the skreech ove a hen when she sez 'hawk,' tu her little rounsturn'd, fuzzy, bead-eyed, stripid-backs.

"I actid jis adzacly as they dus; I darted on all fours onder mam's petticoatails, an' thar I met, face tu face, the wooden bowl, an' the mush, an' the spoon what she slid onder frum tuther side. I'se mad at mysef yet, fur rite thar I show'd the fust flash ove the nat'ral born durn fool what I now is. I orter et hit all up, in jestis tu my stumick an' my growin, while the sheriff wer levying ontu the bed an' the cheers. Tu this day, ef enybody sez 'sheriff,' I feels skeer, an' ef I hears constabil menshun'd, my laigs goes thru runnin moshuns, even ef I is asleep. Did yu ever watch a dorg dreamin ove rabbit huntin? Thems the moshuns, an' the feelin am the rabbit's.

"Sherifs am orful 'spectabil peopil; everybody looks up tu em. I never adzacly seed the 'spectabil part mysef. I'se too fear'd ove em, I reckon, tu 'zamin fur hit much. One thing I knows, no country atwix yere an' Tophit kin ever 'lect me tu sell out widders' plunder, ur poor men's co'n, an' the tho'ts ove hit gins me a good feelin; hit sorter flashes thru my heart when I thinks ove hit. I axed a passun onst, whan hit cud be, an' he pernounced hit to be *onregenerit pride,* what I orter squelch in prayer, an' in tendin chuch on colleckshun days. I wer in hopes hit mout be 'ligion, ur sense, a-soakin intu me; hit feels good, enyhow, an' I don't keer ef every suckit rider outen jail knows hit. Sheriffs' shuts allers hes nettil dus ur fleas inside ove em when they lies down tu sleep, an' I'se glad ove hit, fur they'se allers discumfortin me, durn em. I scarcely ever git tu drink a ho'n, ur eat a mess in peace. I'll hurt one sum day, see ef I don't. Show me a sheriff a-steppin softly roun, an' a-sorter sightin at me, an' I'll show yu a far sampil ove the speed ove a express ingine, fired up wif rich, dry, rosiny skeers. They don't ketch me *much,* usin only human laigs es wepuns.

"Ole John Doltin wer a 'spectabil sheriff, monsusly so, an' hed the bes' scent fur poor fugatif devils, an' wimen, I ever seed; he wer sure fire. Well, he toted a warrun fur this yere skinful ove durn'd fool, 'bout that ar misfortnit nigger meetin bisness, ontil he wore hit intu six seperit squar bits, an' hed wore out much shoe leather a-chasin ove me. I'd foun a doggery in full milk, an' hated pow'ful bad tu leave that settilment while hit suck'd free; so I sot intu sorter try an' wean him off frum botherin me so much. I suckseedid so well that he not only quit racin ove me, an' wimen, but he wer tetotaly spiled es as a sheriff, an' los' the 'spectabil seckshun ove his karac-

ter. Tu make yu fool fellers onderstan how hit wer done, I mus' interjuice
yure minds tu one Wat Mastin, a bullit-headed yung blacksmith.

"Well, las' year—no hit wer the year afore las'—in struttin an' gobblin
time, Wat felt his keepin right warm, so he sot intu bellerin an' pawin up
dus in the neighborhood roun the ole widder McKildrin's. The more dus he
flung up, the wus he got, until at las' he jis cudn't stan the ticklin sensashuns
anuther minnit; so he put fur the county clark's offis, wif his hans sock'd
down deep intu his britchis pockets, like he wer fear'd ove pick-pockets, his
back roach'd roun, an' a-chompin his teef ontil he splotch'd his whiskers wif
foam. Oh! he wer yearnis' hot, an' es restless es a cockroach in a hot skillit."

"What was the matter with this Mr. Mastin? I cannot understand you,
Mr. Lovingood; had he hydrophobia?" remarked a man in a square-tail
coat, and cloth gaiters, who was obtaining subscribers for some forthcom-
ing Encyclopedia of Useful Knowledge, who had quartered at our camp,
uninvited, and really unwanted.

"What du yu mean by high-dry-foby?" and Sut looked puzzled.

"A madness produced by being bit by some rabid animal," explained
Square-tail, in a pompous manner.

"Yas, hoss, he hed high-dry-foby *orful*, an' Mary McKildrin, the widder
McKildrin's only darter, hed gin him the complaint; I don't know whether
she bit 'im ur not; he mout a-cotch hit frum her bref, an' he wer now in the
roach back, chompin stage ove the sickness, so he wer arter the clark fur a
tickit tu the hospital. Well, the clark sole 'im a piece ove paper, part printin
an' part ritin, wif a picter ove two pigs' hearts, what sum boy had shot a
arrer thru, an' lef hit stickin, printed at the top. That paper wer a splicin
pass—sum calls hit a par ove licins—an' that very nite he tuck Mary, fur
better, fur wus, tu hev an' tu hole tu him his heirs, an'—"

"Allow me to interrupt you," said our guest; "you do not quote the marriage ceremony correctly."

"Yu go tu *hell,* mistofer; yu bothers me."

This outrageous rebuff took the stranger all aback, and he sat down.

"Whar were I? Oh yas, he married Mary tight an' fas', an' nex day he
were abil tu be about. His coat tho', an' his trousis look'd jis' a skrimshun
too big, loose like, an' heavy tu tote. I axed him ef he felt soun. He sed yas,
but he'd welded a steamboat shaftez the day afore, an' wer sorter tired like.
Thar he tole a durn lie, fur he'd been a-ho'nin up dirt mos' ove the day,
roun the widder's garden, an' bellerin in the orchard. Mary an' him sot
squar intu hous'-keepin, an' 'mung uther things he bot a lot ove *rar ripe
garden-seed,* from a Yankee peddler. Rar ripe co'n, rar ripe peas, rar ripe
taters, rar ripe everything, an' the two yung durn'd fools wer dreadfully
exercis'd 'bout hit. Wat sed he ment tu git him a rar ripe hammer an' anvil,
an' Mary vow'd tu grashus, that she'd hev a rar ripe wheel an' loom, ef
money wud git em. Purty soon arter he hed made the garden, he tuck a
noshun tu work a spell down tu Ataylanty, in the railroad shop, es he sed he

hed a sorter ailin in his back, an' he tho't weldin rail car-tire an' ingine axil-trees, were lighter work nur sharpinin plows, an' puttin lap-links in trace-chains. So down he went, an' foun hit agreed wif him, fur he didn't cum back ontil the middil ove August. The fust thing he seed when he landid intu his cabin-door, wer a shoebox wif rockers onder it, an' the nex thing he seed, wer Mary hersef, propped up in bed, an' the nex thing he seed arter that, wer a par ove littil rat-eyes a-shinin abuv the aind ove the quilt, ontu Mary's arm, an' the next an' last thing he seed wer the two littil rat-eyes aforesed, a-turnin into two hundred thousand big green stars, an' a-swingin roun an' roun the room, faster an' faster, ontil they mix'd intu one orful green flash. He drap't intu a limber pile on the floor. The durn'd fool what hed weldid the steamboat shaftez hed fainted safe an' soun es a gal skeered at a mad bull. Mary fotch a weak cat-scream, an' kivered her hed, an' sot intu work ontu a whifflin dry cry, while littil Rat-eyes gin hitssef up tu suckin. Cryin an' suckin bof at onst ain't far; mus' cum pow'ful strainin on the wet seckshun ove an' 'oman's constitushun; yet hit am ofen dun, an' more too. Ole Missis McKildrin, what wer a-nussin Mary, jis' got up frum knittin, an' flung a big gourd ove warter squar intu Wat's face, then she fotch a glass bottil ove swell-skull whisky outen the three-cornered cupboard, an' stood furnint Wat, a-holdin hit in wun han, an' the tin-cup in tuther, waitin fur Wat tu cum to. She were the piusses lookin ole 'oman jis' then, yu ever seed outside ove a prayer-meetin. Arter a spell, Wat begun to move, twitchin his fingers, an' battin his eyes, sorter 'stonished like. That pius lookin statue sed tu him:

" 'My son, jis' take a drap ove sperrits, honey. Yu'se very sick, dumplin, don't take on darlin, ef yu kin help hit, ducky, fur poor Margarit Jane am mons'ous ailin, an' the leas' nise ur takin on will kill the poor sufferin dear, an' yu'll loose yure tuckil ducky duv ove a sweet wifey, arter all she's dun gone thru for yu. My dear son Watty, yu mus' consider her feelins a littil.'
Sez Wat, a-turnin up his eyes at that vartus ole relick, sorter sick like—

" 'I is a-consuderin em a heap, rite now.'

" 'Oh that's right, my good kine child.'

"Oh dam ef ole muther-in-lors can't plaster humbug over a feller, jis' es saft an' easy es they spreads a camrick hanketcher over a three hour ole baby's face; yu don't feel hit at all, but hit am thar, a plum inch thick, an' stickin fas es court-plaster. She raised Wat's head, an' sot the aidge ove the tin cup agin his lower teef, an' turned up the bottim slow an' keerful, a-winkin at Mary, hu wer a-peepin over the aidge ove the coverlid, tu see ef Wat *tuck the perskripshun,* for a heap ove famerly cumfort 'pended on that ar ho'n ove sperrits. *Wun* ho'n allers saftens a man, the yeath over. Wat keep a-battin his eyes, wus nur a owl in daylight; at las' he raised hissef ontu wun elbow, an' rested his head in that han, sorter weak like. Sez he, mons'ous trimblin an' slow: 'Aprile—May—June—July—an' mos'—haf—ove —August,' a-countin the munths ontu the fingers ove tuther han, wif the thumb, a-shakin ove his head, an' lookin at his spread fingers like they warn't his'n, ur they were nastied wif sumfin. Then he counted em agin, slower, Aprile—May—June—July—an', mos' haf ove August, an' he run his thumb atwixt his fingers, es meanin mos' haf ove August, an' look'd at the pint ove hit, like hit mout be a snake's head. He raised his eyes tu the widder's face, who were standin jis' es steady es a hitchin pos', an' still a-warin that pius 'spression ontu her pussonal feturs, an' a flood ove saft luv fur Wat, a-shining straight frum her eyes intu his'n. Sez he, 'That jis' makes four munths, an' mos' a half, don't hit, Missis McKildrin?' She never sed one word. Wat reached fur the hath, an' got a dead fire-coal; then he made a mark clean acrost a floor-plank. Sez he, 'Aprile,' a-holdin down the coal ontu the aind ove the mark, like he wer fear'd hit mout blow away afore he got hit christened Aprile. Sez he, 'May'—an' he marked across the board agin; then he counted the marks, one, two, a-dottin at em wif the coal. 'June,' an' he marked agin, one, two, three; counted wif the pint ove the coal. He scratched his head wif the littil finger ove the han holdin the char-coal, an' he drawed hit slowly acrost the board agin, peepin onder his wrist tu see when hit reached the crack, an' sez he 'July,' es he lifted the coal; 'one, two three, four,' countin frum lef tu right, an' then frum right tu lef. 'That haint but four, no way I kin fix hit. Ole Pike hissef cudn't make hit five, ef he were tu sifer ontu hit ontil his laigs turned into figger eights.' Then he made a mark, haf acrost a plank, spit on his finger, an' rubbed off a haf inch ove the aind, an' sez he, 'Mos' haf ove August.' He looked up at the widder, an' thar she were, same as ever, still a-holdin the flask agin her bussum, an' sez he 'Four months, an' mos' a haf. *Haint enuf, is hit mammy?* hits jus' 'bout (lackin a littil) *haf enuf,* haint hit, mammy?"

"Missis McKildrin shuck her head sorter onsartin like, an' sez she, 'Take a drap more sperrits, Watty, my dear pet; dus yu mine buyin that ar rar ripe seed, frum the peddler?' Wat nodded his head, an' looked 'what ove hit,' but didn't say hit.

" 'This is what cums ove hit, an' four months an' a half am rar ripe time fur babys, adzactly. Tu be sure, hit lacks a day ur two, but Margarit Jane wer allers a pow'ful interprizin gal, an' a yearly rizer.' Sez Wat.

" 'How about the 'taters?'

" 'Oh, *we* et 'taters es big es goose aigs, afore old Missis Collinze's blossomed.'

" 'How 'bout co'n?'

" 'Oh, we shaved down roasin years afore hern tassel'd———'

" 'An' peas?'

" 'Yes son, we hed gobs an' lots in three weeks. Everything cums in adzackly half the time that it takes the ole sort, an' yu *knows,* my darlin son, yu planted hit waseful. I tho't then yu'd rar ripe everything on the place. Yu planted *often,* too, didn't yu luv? fur fear hit wudn't cum up.'

" 'Ye-ye-s-s he—he did,' sed Mary a-cryin. Wat studied pow'ful deep a spell, an' the widder jis' waited. Widders allers wait, an' allers win. At las, sez he, 'Mammy.' She looked at Mary, an' winked these yere words at her, es plain es she cud a-talked em. 'Yu hearn him call me *mammy twiste.* I'se *got him* now. His back-bone's a-limberin fas', he'll own the baby yet, see ef he don't. Jis' hole still my darter, an' let yer mammy knead this dough, then yu may bake hit es brown es yu please.'

" 'Mammy, when I married on the fust day of Aprile'——— The widder look'd oneasy; she tho't he mout be a-cupplin that day, his weddin, an' the idear, dam fool, tugether. But he warn't, fur he sed 'That day I gin ole man Collins my note ove han fur a hundred dullars, jew in one year arter date, the balluns on this lan. Dus yu think that ar seed will change the *time* eny, ur will hit alter the *amount*?' An' Wat looked at her powerful ankshus. She raised the whisky bottil way abuv her head, wif her thumb on the mouf, an' fotch the bottim down ontu her han, spat. Sez she, 'Watty, my dear b'lovid son, pripar tu pay *two* hundred dullars 'bout the fust ove October, fur hit'll be jew jis' then, *es* sure es that littil black-eyed angel in the bed thar, am yer darter.'

"Wat drap't his head, an' sed, *'Then hits a dam sure thing.'* Rite yere, the baby fotch a rattlin loud squall, (I speck Mary wer sorter figetty jis' then, an' hurt hit). 'Yas,' sez Wat, a-wallin a red eye to'ards the bed; 'my littil she —what were hit yu called her name, mammy?' 'I called her a sweet littil angel, an' she is wun, es sure es yu're her daddy, my b'loved son.' 'Well,' sez Wat, 'my littil sweet, patent rar ripe she angel, ef yu lives tu marryin time, yu'll 'stonish sum man body outen his shut, ef you don't rar ripe lose hits vartu arter the fust plantin, that's all.' He rared up on aind, wif his mouf pouch'd out. He had a pow'ful forrid, fur-reachin, bread funnel, enyhow —cud a-bit the aigs outen a catfish, in two-foot warter, wifout wettin his eyebrows. 'Dod durn rar ripe seed, an' rar ripe pedlers, an' rar ripe notes tu the hottes' corner ove———'

" 'Stop Watty, *darlin,* don't swar; 'member yu belongs tu meetin.'

" 'My blacksmith's fire,' ainded Wat, an he studied a long spell; sez he,

" 'Did you save eny ove that infunnel doubil-trigger seed?' 'Yas,' sez the widder, 'thar in that bag by the cupboard.' Wat got up ofen the floor, tuck a countin sorter look at the charcoal marks, an' reached down the bag; he went tu the door an' called 'Suke, muley! Suke, Suke, cow, chick, chick, chicky chick.' 'What's yu gwine tu du now, my dear son?' sed Missis McKildrin. 'I'se jis' gwine tu feed this actif *smart* truck tu the cow, an' the hens, that's what I'se gwine tu du. Ole muley haint hed a calf in two years, an' I'll eat sum rar ripe aigs.' Mary now venter'd tu speak: 'Husban, I ain't sure hit'll work on hens; cum an' kiss me my luv.' 'I haint sure hit'll work on hens, either,' sed Wat. 'They's powerful onsartin in thar ways, well es wimen,' an' he flung out a hanful spiteful like. 'Takin the rar ripe invenshun all tugether, frum 'taters an' peas tu notes ove han, an' childer, I can't say I likes hit much,' an' he flung out anuther hanful. 'Yer mam hed thuteen the ole way, an' ef this truck stays 'bout the hous', yu'se good fur twenty-six, maybe thuty, fur yu'se a pow'ful interprizin gal, yer mam sez,' an' he flung out anuther hanful, overhandid, es hard es ef he wer flingin rocks at a stealin sow. 'Make yere mine easy,' sed the widder; 'hit never works on married folks only the fust time.' 'Say them words agin,' sed Wat, 'I's glad tu hear em. Is hit the same way wif notes ove han?' 'I speck hit am,' answer'd the widder, wif jis' a taste ove strong vinegar in the words, es she sot the flask in the cupboard wif a push.

"Jis' then ole Doltin, the sheriff, rid up, an' started 'stonished when he seed Wat, but he, quick es an 'oman kin hide a strange hat, drawed the puckerin-string ove that legil face ove his'n, an' fotch hit up tu the 'know'd yu wer at home' sorter look, an' wishin Wat much joy, sed he'd fotch the baby a present, a par ove red shoes, an' a calliker dress, fur the luv he bore hits granmam. Missis McKildrin tole him what the rar ripe hed dun, an' he swore hit allers worked jis' that way, an' wer 'stonished at Wat's not knowin hit; an' they talked so fas', an' so much, that the more Wat listened the less he know'd.

"Arter the sheriff lef, they onrolled the bundil, an' Wat straitched out the calliker in the yard. He step't hit off keerfully, ten yards, an a littil the rise. He puss'd up his mouf, an' blow'd out a whistil seven foot long, lookin up an' down the middil stripe ove the drygoods, frum aind tu aind. Sez he, 'Missis McKildrin, that'll make Rar Ripe a good *full* frock, won't hit?' 'Y-a-s,' sed she, wif her hans laid up along her jaw, like she wer studyin the thing keerfully. 'My son, I thinks hit will, an' I wer jis' a-thinkin ef hit were cut tu 'vantage, thar *mout* be nuff lef, squeezed out tu make yu a Sunday shutin shut, makin the ruffils an' ban outen sumthin else.' 'Put hit in the bag what the rar ripe wer in, an' by mornin thar.'ll be nuff fur the ruffils an' bans, an' yu mout make the tail tu drag the yeath, wifout squeezin ur pecin', sez Wat, an' he put a few small wrinkils in the pint ove his nose, what seemed tu bother the widder tu make out the meanin ove; they look'd mons'ous like the outward signs ove an onb'lever. Jis' then his eyes sot fas' ontu sumthin a-lyin on the groun whar he'd onrolled the bundil; he walk'd up tu hit slow, sorter like a feller goes up tu a log, arter he thinks he seed a snake run onder. He walk'd clean roun hit twiste, never takin his eyes ofen hit. At las' he lifted hit on his instep, an' hilt out his laig strait at that widdered muther-in-lor ove his'n. Sez he, "What mout yu call that? Red baby's shoes don't giner'lly hev teeth, dus they?' 'Don't yu *know* hits a tuckin comb, Watty? The store-keeper's made a sorter blunder, I speck,' sed that vartus petticoatful ove widderhood. 'Maybe he hes; I'se durn sure I *hes*,' sed Wat, an' he wrinkil'd his nose again, mons'ous botherinly tu that watchful widder. He scratched his head a spell; sez he, 'Ten yards an' the rise fur a baby's frock, *an' hit rar ripe at that, gits me;* an' that ar tuckin comb gits me wus.' 'Oh, fiddlesticks an' flusterashun,' sez she. 'Save the comb; baby'll soon want hit.' 'That's so, mammy, I'm dam ef hit don't,' an' he slip't his foot frum

onder hit, an' hit scarcely totch the yeath afore he stomp't hit, an' the teeth
flew all over the widder. He look'd like he'd been stompin a blowin adder,
an' went apas' the 'oman intu the cabin, in a rale Aprile tucky gobbler strut.
When he tore the rapper off the sheriff's present, I seed a littil bit ove white
paper fall out. Onbenowenst tu enybody, I sot my foot ontu hit, an' when
they went in I socked hit deep intu my pocket, an' went over tu the still-
'ous. I tuck Jim Dunkin out, an' arter swarin 'im wif a uplifted han', tu keep
dark, got him tu read hit tu me, ontil hit wer printed on the mindin seckshun ove my brain. Hit run jis' so:

> "My Sweet Mary:
> I mayn't git the chance tu talk eny tu yu, so when Wat gits home,
> an' axes enything 'bout the *comb* an' *calliker,* yu tell him yer mam
> foun the bundil in the road. She'll back yu up in that ar statemint,
> ontil thar's enuf white fros' in hell tu kill snap-beans.
> *Notey Beney.*—I hope Wat'll stay in Atlanty ontil the merlenium,
> don't yu, my dear duv?
> > Yures till deth,
> > > Doltin.

An' tu that ar las' remark he'd sot a big D. I reckon he ment that fur dam
Wat.

"Now, I jis' know'd es long es I hed that paper, I hilt four aces ontu the
sheriff, an' I ment tu bet on the han', an' *go halves wif Wat,* fur I wer sorry
fur him, he wer so infunely 'posed upon. I went tu school tu Sicily Burns, tu
larn 'oman tricks, an' I tuck a dirplomer, I did, an' now I'd jes' like tu see
the pussonal feeters ove the she 'oman what cud stock rar ripe kerds on me,
durn'd fool es I is. I hed a talk wif Wat, an' soon foun out that his mine hed
simmer'd down intu a strong belief that the sheriff an' Mary wer doin thar
weavin in the same loom.

"Then I show'd him my four aces, an' that chip made the pot bile over,
an' he jis' 'greed tu be led by me, spontanashusly.

"Jis' think on that fac' a minnit boys; a man what hed sense enuf tu turn
a hoss shoe, an' then nail hit on toe aind foremos bein led by me, looks
sorter like a plum tree barin tumil bug-balls, but hit wer jis' so, an' durn my
pictur, ef I didn't lead him tu victory, strait along.

"Wat narrated hit, that he b'leved strong in rar ripe, frum beans, thru
notes ove han, plum tu babys, an' that his cabin shud never be wifout hit.
The widder wer cheerful, Mary wer luvin, an' the sheriff wer told on the sly,
by ole Mister McKildrin's remainin, an' mos' pius she half, that Wat wer es
plum blind es ef his eyes wer two tuckil aigs. So the wool grow'd over *his*
eyes, ontil hit wer fit tu shear, an' *dam ef I warn't at the shearin.*

"Things, tharfore, went smoof, an' es quiet es a greased waggin, runnin
in san. Hits allers so, jis' afore a tarin big storm.

"By the time littil Rar Ripe wer ten weeks ole, Doltin begun tu be pow'ful plenty in the neighborhood. Even the brats know'd his hoss's tracks, an' go whar he wud, the road led ni ontu Wat's, ur the widder's, tu git thar. My time tu play my four aces hed 'bout cum."

"And so has orderly bed time. I wish to repose," remarked the man of Useful Knowledge, in the square-tail coat, and cloth gaiters.

Sut opened his eyes in wonder.

"Yu wish to du what?"

"I wish to go to sleep."

"Then why the h—l didn't yu say so? Yu mus' talk Inglish tu me, ur not git yersef onderstood. I warn't edikated at no Injun ur nigger school. Say, bunty, warn't yu standid deep in sum creek, when the taylure man put the string to yu, fur that ar cross atwix a rounabout an' a flour barril, what yu'se got on in place of a coat?"

My self-made guest looked appealingly at me, as he untied his gaiters, evidently deeply insulted. I shook my head at Sut, who was lying on his breast, with his arms crossed for a pillow, but with head elevated like a lizard's, watching the traveler's motions with great interest.

"Say, George, what dus repose mean? That wurd wer used at me jis' now."

"Repose means rest."

"Oh, the devil hit dus! I'se glad tu hear hit, I tho't hit wer pussonal. I kin repose now, mysef. Say, ole Onsightly Peter, repose sum tu, ef yu kin in that flour barril. I ain't gwine tu hunt fur yure har ontil mor————" and Sut slept. When morning broke, the Encyclopedia, or Onsightly Peter as Sut pronounced it, had

> "Folded his tent like the Arab,
> And as silently stole away."

JOSEPH GLOVER BALDWIN

(1815–1864)

Joseph Glover Baldwin was born of fairly well-to-do parents near Winchester, Virginia, and was privately educated. He read law and was admitted to the bar, but in 1836 at the age of 21 he decided to seek greener legal pastures than those in the Valley of Virginia, and so emigrated to the recently opened Mississippi-Alabama territory. There he prospered, first at DeKalb, Mississippi, then at Greenville and Mobile in Alabama. He enjoyed and was well adapted to thrive in the catch-as-catch-can legal life of the Old Southwest, with its wide-open land dealings and boom-or-bust economy. In the early 1850s he began writing humorous sketches and accounts of the legal and social doings in the new country. These were published not in local newspapers, as was the case with most of the other writings of the Southwest humor school, but in John Reuben Thompson's *Southern Literary Messenger* in Richmond. They were thus designed to amuse a more cultivated audience, in particular that of lawyers, and when they appeared in book form as the *Flush Times of Alabama and Mississippi,* published by D. Appleton and Co. in New York in 1853, they were dedicated "to 'THE OLD FOLKS AT HOME,' my friends in the valley of the Shenandoah." Baldwin, like most of the Southwest humorists, was a Whig and a political conservative, and his anti-Jackson, anti-Jefferson bias figures prominently in his second book, *Party Leaders* (1855), which includes comparative sketches of a number of leading American political figures.

By 1854 Baldwin had apparently found life in Alabama too settled and politically too Democratic for his tastes and he moved out to California where he established a lucrative law practice, helped to put down vigilante rule, and became associate justice of the state supreme court.

From FLUSH TIMES OF ALABAMA AND MISSISSIPPI

HOW THE TIMES SERVED THE VIRGINIANS. VIRGINIANS IN A NEW COUNTRY. THE RISE, DECLINE, AND FALL OF THE RAG EMPIRE

The disposition to be proud and vain of one's country, and to boast of it, is a natural feeling, indulged or not in respect to the pride, vanity, and boasting, according to the character of the native: but, with a Virginian, it is a passion. It inheres in him even as the flavor of a York river oyster in that bivalve, and no distance of deportation, and no trimmings of a gracious prosperity, and no pickling in the sharp acids of adversity, can destroy it. It is a part of the Virginia character—just as the flavor is a distinctive part of the oyster—"which cannot, save by annihilating, die." It is no use talking about it—the thing may be right, or wrong:—like Falstaff's victims at Gadshill, it is past praying for: it is a sort of cocoa grass that has got into the soil, and has so matted over it, and so *fibred* through it, as to have become a part of it; at least, there is no telling which is the grass and which is the soil; and certainly it is useless labor to try to root it out. You may destroy the soil, but you can't root out the grass.

Patriotism with a Virginian is a noun personal. It is the Virginian himself and something over. He loves Virginia *per se* and *propter se:* he loves her for herself and for himself—because *she is* Virginia and—everything else beside. He loves to talk about her: out of the abundance of the heart the mouth speaketh. It makes no odds where he goes, he carries Virginia with him; not in the entirety always—but the little spot he came from is Virginia —as Swedenborg says the smallest part of the brain is an abridgment of all of it. "*Cœlum non animum mutant qui trans mare currunt,*" was made for a Virginian. He never gets acclimated elsewhere; he never loses citizenship to the old Home. The right of expatriation is a pure abstraction to him. He may breathe in Alabama, but he lives in Virginia. His treasure is there, and his heart also. If he looks at the Delta of the Mississippi, it reminds him of James River "low grounds;" if he sees the vast prairies of Texas, it is a memorial of the meadows of the Valley. Richmond is the centre of attraction, the *depot* of all that is grand, great, good and glorious. "It is the Kentucky of a place," which the preacher described Heaven to be to the Kentucky congregation.

Those who came many years ago from the borough towns, especially from the vicinity of Williamsburg, exceed, in attachment to their birthplace, if possible, the *emigrés* from the metropolis. It is refreshing in these costermonger times, to hear them speak of it:—they remember it when the old burg was the seat of fashion, taste, refinement, hospitality, wealth, wit, and all social graces; when genius threw its spell over the public assemblages and illumined the halls of justice, and when beauty brightened the social hour with her unmatched and matchless brilliancy.

Then the spirited and gifted youths of the College of old William and Mary, some of them just giving out the first scintillations of the genius that afterwards shone refulgent in the forum and the senate, added to the attractions of a society gay, cultivated and refined beyond example—*even* in the Old Dominion. A hallowed charm seems to rest upon the venerable city, clothing its very dilapidation in a drapery of romance and of serene and classic interest: as if all the sweet and softened splendor which invests the "Midsummer Night's Dream" were poured in a flood of mellow and poetic radiance over the now quiet and half "deserted village." There is something in the shadow from the old college walls, cast by the moon upon the grass and sleeping on the sward, that throws a like shadow soft, sad and melancholy upon the heart of the returning pilgrim who saunters out to view again, by moonlight, his old *Alma Mater*—the nursing mother of such a list and such a line of statesmen and heroes.

There is nothing presumptuously forward in this Virginianism. The Virginian does not make broad his phylacteries and crow over the poor Carolinian and Tennesseeian. He does not reproach him with his misfortune of birthplace. No, he thinks the affliction is enough without the triumph. The franchise of having been born in Virginia, and the prerogative founded thereon, are too patent of honor and distinction to be arrogantly pretended.

The bare mention is enough. He finds occasion to let the fact be known, and then the fact is fully able to protect and take care of itself. Like a ducal title, there is no need of saying more than to name it: modesty then is a becoming and expected virtue; forbearance to boast is true dignity.

The Virginian is a magnanimous man. He never throws up to a Yankee the fact of his birthplace. He feels on the subject as a man of delicacy feels in alluding to a rope in the presence of a person, one of whose brothers "stood upon nothing and kicked at the U. S.," or to a female indiscretion, where there had been scandal concerning the family. So far do they carry this refinement, that I have known one of my countrymen, on occasion of a Bostonian owning where he was born, generously protest that he had never heard of it before. As if honest confession half obliterated the shame of the fact. Yet he does not lack the grace to acknowledge worth or merit in another, wherever the native place of that other: for it is a common thing to hear them say of a neighbor, "he is a clever fellow, *though* he *did* come from New Jersey or even Connecticut."

In politics the Virginian is learned much beyond what is written—for they have heard a great deal of speaking on that prolific subject, especially by one or two Randolphs and any number of Barbours. They read the same papers here they read in Virginia—the *Richmond Enquirer* and the *Richmond Whig*. The Democrat stoutly asseverates a fact, and gives *the Enquirer* as his authority with an air that means to say, *that* settles it: while the Whig quoted Hampden Pleasants with the same confidence. But the faculty of personalizing everything which the exceeding social turn of a Virginian gives him, rarely allowed a reference to the paper, *eo nomine;* but made him refer to the editor: as "Ritchie said" so and so, or "Hampden Pleasants said" this or that. When two of opposite politics got together, it was amusing, if you had nothing else to do that day, to hear the discussion. I never knew a debate that did not start *ab urbe condita.* They not only went back to first principles, but also to first times; nor did I ever hear a discussion in which old John Adams and Thomas Jefferson did not figure—as if an interminable dispute had been going on for so many generations between those disputatious personages; as if the quarrel had begun before time, but was not to end with it. But the strangest part of it to me was, that the dispute seemed to be going on without poor Adams having any defence or champion; and never waxed hotter than when both parties agreed in denouncing the man of Braintree as the worst of public sinners and the vilest of political heretics. They both agreed on one thing, and that was to refer the matter to the Resolutions of 1798-99; which said Resolutions, like Goldsmith's "Good Natured Man," arbitrating between Mr. and Mrs. Croaker, seemed so impartial that they agreed with both parties on every occasion.

Nor do I recollect of hearing any question debated that did not resolve itself into a question of constitution—strict construction, &c.,—the constitution being a thing of that curious virtue that its chief excellency consisted in not allowing the government to do any thing; or in being a regular prize fighter that knocked all laws and legislators into a cocked hat, except those of the objector's party.

Frequent reference was reciprocally made to "gorgons, hydras, and chimeras dire," to black cockades, blue lights, Essex juntos, the Reign of Terror, and some other mystic entities—but who or what these monsters were, I never could distinctly learn; and was surprised, on looking into the history of the country, to find that, by some strange oversight, no allusion was made to them.

Great is the Virginian's reverence of great men, that is to say, of great Virginians. This reverence is not Unitarian. He is a Polytheist. He believes in a multitude of Virginia Gods. As the Romans of every province and village had their tutelary or other divinities, besides having divers national gods, so the Virginian of every county has his great man, the like of whom cannot be found in the new country he has exiled himself to. This sentiment of veneration for talent, especially for speaking talent,—this amiable propensity to lionize men, is not peculiar to any class of Virginians among us: it abides in all. I was amused to hear "old Culpepper," as we call him (by nickname derived from the county he came from), declaiming in favor of the Union. "What, gentlemen," said the old man, with a sonorous swell —"what, burst up this glorious Union! and who, if *this* Union is torn up, could write another? Nobody except Henry Clay and J— S. B—, of Culpepper—and may be *they* wouldn't—and what then would you do for another?"

The greatest compliment a Virginian can ever pay to a speaker, is to say that he reminds him of a Col. Broadhorn or a Captain Smith, who represented some royal-named county some forty years or less in the Virginia House of Delegates; and of whom, the auditor, of course, has heard, as he made several speeches in the capitol at Richmond. But the force of the compliment is somewhat broken, by a long narrative, in which the personal reminiscences of the speaker go back to sundry sketches of the Virginia statesman's efforts, and recapitulations of his sayings, interspersed *par parenthèse*, with many valuable notes illustrative of his pedigree and performances; the whole of which, given with great historical fidelity of detail, leaves nothing to be wished for except the point, or rather, two points, the gist and the period.

It is not to be denied that Virginia is the land of orators, heroes and statesmen; and that, directly or indirectly, she has exerted an influence upon the national councils nearly as great as all the rest of the States combined. It is wonderful that a State of its size and population should have turned out such an unprecedented quantum of talent, and of talent as various in kind as prodigious in amount. She has reason to be proud; and the other States so largely in her debt (for, from Cape May to Puget's Sound she has colonized the other States and the territories with her surplus talent,) ought to allow her the harmless privilege of a little bragging. In the showy talent of oratory has she especially shone. To accomplish her in this art the State has been turned into a debating society, and while she has been *talking* for the benefit of the nation, as she thought, the other, and, by nature, less favored States, have been *doing* for their own. Consequently, what she has gained in reputation, she has lost in wealth and *material aids.* Certainly the Virginia character has been less distinguished for its practical than its ornamental traits, and for its business qualities than for its speculative temper. *Cui bono* and utilitarianism, at least until latterly, were not favorite or congenial inquiries and subjects of attention to the Virginia politician. What the Virginian was upon his native soil, that he was abroad; indeed, it may be said that the *amor patriæ*, strengthened by absence, made him more of a conservative abroad than he would have been if he had staid at home; for most of them here would not, had they been consulted, have changed either of the old constitutions.

. . .

In the fulness of time the new era had set in—the era of the second great experiment of independence: the experiment, namely, of credit without capital, and enterprise without honesty. The Age of Brass had succeeded the Arcadian period when men got rich by saving a part of their earnings, and lived at their own cost and in ignorance of the new plan of making fortunes on the profits of what they owed. A new theory, not found in the works on political economy, was broached. It was found out that the prejudice in favor of the metals (brass excluded) was an absurd superstition; and that, in reality, any thing else, which the parties interested in giving it currency chose, might serve as a representative of value and medium for exchange of property; and as gold and silver had served for a great number of years as representatives, the republican doctrine of rotation in office required they should give way. Accordingly it was decided that Rags, a very familiar character, and very popular and easy of access, should take their place. Rags belonged to the school of progress. He was representative of the then Young America. His administration was not tame. It was *very* spirited. It was based on the Bonapartist idea of keeping the imagination of the people excited. The leading fiscal idea of his system was to *democratize* capital, and to make, for all purposes of trade, credit and enjoyment of wealth, the man that had *no* money a little richer, if anything, than the man that had a million. The principle of success and basis of operation, though inexplicable in the hurry of the time, is plain enough now: it was faith. Let the public believe that a smutted rag is money, it is money: in other words, it was a sort of financial biology, which made, at night, the thing conjured for, the thing that was seen, so far as the patient was concerned, while the fit was on him—except that now a man does not do his trading when under the mesmeric influence: in the flush times he did.

This country was just settling up. Marvellous accounts had gone forth of the fertility of its virgin lands; and the productions of the soil were commanding a price remunerating to slave labor as it had never been remunerated before. Emigrants came flocking in from all quarters of the Union, especially from the slaveholding States. The new country seemed to be a reservoir, and every road leading to it a vagrant stream of enterprise and adventure. Money, or what passed for money, was the only cheap thing to be had. Every crossroad and every avocation presented an opening, —through which a fortune was seen by the adventurer in near perspective. Credit was a thing of course. To refuse it—if the thing was ever done—were an insult for which a bowie-knife were not a too summary or exemplary a means of redress. The State banks were issuing their bills by the sheet, like a patent steam printing-press *its* issues; and no other showing was asked of the applicant for the loan than an authentication of his great distress for money. Finance, even in its most exclusive quarter, had thus already got, in this wonderful revolution, to work upon the principles of the charity hospital. If an overseer grew tired of supervising a plantation and felt a call to the mercantile life, even if he omitted the compendious method of buying out a merchant wholesale, stock, house and good will, and laying down, at once, his bullwhip for the yard-stick—all he had to do was to go on to New-York, and present himself in Pearl-street with a letter avouching his citizenship, and a clean shirt, and he was regularly given a through ticket to speedy bankruptcy.

Under this stimulating process prices rose like smoke. Lots in obscure villages were held at city prices; lands, bought at the minimum cost of government, were sold at from thirty to forty dollars per acre, and considered dirt cheap at that. In short, the country had got to be a full ante-type of California, in all except the gold. Society was wholly unorganized: there was no restraining public opinion: the law was well-nigh powerless—and religion scarcely was heard of except as furnishing the oaths and *technics* of profanity. The world saw a fair experiment of what it would have been, if the fiat had never been pronounced which decreed subsistence as the price of labor.

Money, got without work, by those unaccustomed to it, turned the heads of its possessors, and they spent it with a recklessness like that with which they gained it. The pursuits of industry neglected, riot and coarse debauchery filled up the vacant hours. "Where the carcass is, there will the eagles be gathered together"; and the eagles that flocked to the Southwest, were of the same sort as the *black eagles* the Duke of Saxe-Weimar saw on his celebrated journey to the Natural Bridge. "The cankers of a long peace and a calm world"—there were no Mexican wars and filibuster expeditions in those days—gathered in the villages and cities by scores.

Even the little boys caught the taint of the general infection of morals;

and I knew one of them—Jim Ellett by name—to give a man ten dollars to hold him up to bet at the table of a faro-bank. James was a fast youth; and I sincerely hope he may not fulfil his early promise, and some day be *assisted up still higher.*

The groceries—*vulgice* doggeries—were in full blast in those days, no village having less than a half-dozen all busy all the time: gaming and horse-racing were polite and well patronized amusements. I knew a Judge to adjourn two courts (or court twice) to attend a horse-race, at which he officiated judicially and ministerially, and with more appropriateness than in the judicial chair. Occasionally the scene was diversified by a murder or two, which though perpetrated from behind a corner, or behind the back of the deceased, whenever the accused *chose* to stand his trial, was always found to have been committed in self-defence, securing the homicide an honorable acquittal *at the hands of his peers.*

The old rules of business and the calculations of prudence were alike disregarded, and profligacy, in all the departments of the *crimen falsi,* held riotous carnival. Larceny grew not only respectable, but genteel, and ruffled it in all the pomp of purple and fine linen. Swindling was raised to the dignity of the fine arts. Felony came forth from its covert, put on more seemly habiliments, and took its seat with unabashed front in the upper places of the synagogue. Before the first circles of the patrons of this brilliant and dashing villainy, Blunt Honesty felt as abashed as poor Halbert Glendinning by the courtly refinement and supercilious airs of Sir Piercie Shafton.

Public office represented, by its incumbents, the state of public morals with some approach to accuracy. Out of sixty-six receivers of public money in the new States, sixty-two were discovered to be defaulters; and the agent, sent to look into the affairs of a peccant office-holder in the South-West, reported him *minus* some tens of thousands, but advised the government to retain him, for a reason one of Æsop's fables illustrates: the agent ingeniously surmising that the appointee succeeding would do his stealing without any regard to the proficiency already made by his predecessor; while the present incumbent would probably consider, in mercy to the treasury, that he *had* done *something* of the pious duty of providing for his household.

.   .   .

With the change of times and the imagination of wealth easily acquired came a change in the thoughts and habits of the people. "Old times were changed—old manners gone." Visions of affluence, such as crowded Dr. Samuel Johnson's mind, when advertising a sale of Thrale's Brewery, and casting a soft sheep's eye towards Thrale's widow, thronged upon the popular fancy. Avarice and hope joined partnership. It was strange how the reptile arts of humanity, as at a faro table, warmed into life beneath their heat. The *cacoethes accrescendi* became epidemic. It seized upon the universal community. The pulpits even were not safe from its insidious invasion. What men anxiously desire they willingly believe; and all believed a good time was coming—nay, had come.

"Commerce was king"—and Rags, Tag and Bobtail his cabinet council. Rags was treasurer. Banks, chartered on a specie basis, did a very flourishing business on the promissory notes of the individual stockholders ingeniously substituted in lieu of cash. They issued ten for one, the *one* being fictitious. They generously loaned all the directors could not use themselves, and were not choice whether Bardolph was the endorser for Falstaff, or Falstaff borrowed on his own proper credit, or the funds advanced him by Shallow. The stampede towards the golden temple became general: the delusion prevailed far and wide that this thing was not a burlesque on commerce and finance. Even the directors of the banks began to have their doubts whether the intended swindle was not a failure. Like Lord Clive, when reproached for extortion to the extent of some millions in Bengal, they exclaimed, after the bubble burst, "When they thought of what they had got, and what they might have got, they were astounded at their own moderation."

The old capitalists for a while stood out. With the Tory conservatism of cash in hand, worked for, they couldn't reconcile their old notions to the new regime. They looked for the thing's ending, and *then* their time. But the stampede still kept on. Paper fortunes still multiplied—houses and lands changed hands—real estate see-sawed up as morals went down on the other end of the plank—men of straw, corpulent with bank bills, strutted past them on 'Change. They began, too, to think there might be something in this new thing. Peeping cautiously, like hedge-hogs out of their holes, they saw the stream of wealth and adventurers passing by—then, looking carefully around, they inched themselves half way out—then, sallying forth and snatching up a morsel, ran back, until, at last, grown more bold, *they* ran out too with their hoarded store, in full chase with the other unclean beasts of adventure. They never got back again. Jonah's gourd withered one night, and next morning the vermin that had nestled under its broad shade were left unprotected, a prey to the swift retribution that came upon them. They were left naked, or only clothed themselves with cursing (the Specie Circular on the United States Bank) as with a garment. To drop the figure: Shylock himself couldn't live in those times, so reversed was every thing. Shaving paper and loaning money at a usury of fifty per cent, was for the first time since the Jews left Jerusalem, a breaking business to the operator.

The condition of society may be imagined:—vulgarity—ignorance —fussy and arrogant pretension—unmitigated rowdyism—bullying insolence, if they did not rule the hour, *seemed* to wield unchecked dominion. The workings of these choice spirits were patent upon the face of society; and the modest, unobtrusive, retiring men of worth and character (for there were many, perhaps a large majority of such) were almost lost sight of in the hurly-burly of those strange and shifting scenes.

Even in the professions were the same characteristics visible. Men dropped down into their places as from the clouds. Nobody knew who or what they were, except as they claimed, or as a surface view of their characters indicated. Instead of taking to the highway and magnanimously calling upon the wayfarer to stand and deliver, or to the fashionable larceny of credit without prospect or design of paying, some unscrupulous horse-doctor would set up his sign as "Physician and Surgeon," and draw his lancet on you, or fire at random a box of his pills into your bowels, with a vague chance of hitting some disease unknown to him, but with a better prospect of killing the patient, whom or whose administrator he charged some ten dollars a trial for his markmanship.

A superannuated justice or constable in one of the old States was metamorphosed into a lawyer; and though he knew not the distinction between a *fee tail* and a *female,* would undertake to construe, off-hand, a will involving all the subtleties of *uses and trusts.*

But this state of things could not last for ever: society cannot always stand on its head with its heels in the air.

The Jupiter Tonans of the White House saw the monster of a free credit prowling about like a beast of apocalyptic vision, and marked him for his prey. Gathering all his bolts in his sinewy grasp, and standing back on his heels, and waving his wiry arm, he let them all fly, hard and swift upon all the hydra's heads. Then came a crash, as "if the ribs of nature broke," and a scattering, like the bursting of a thousand magazines, and a smell of brimstone, as if Pandemonium had opened a window next to earth for ventilation,—and all was silent. The beast never stirred in his tracks. To get down from the clouds to level ground, the Specie Circular was issued without warning, and the splendid lie of a false credit burst into fragments. It came in the midst of the dance and the frolic—as Tam O'Shanter came to disturb the infernal glee of the warlocks, and to disperse the rioters. Its effect was like that of a general creditor's bill in the chancery court, and a marshalling of all the assets of the trades-people. Gen. Jackson was no fairy; but he did some very pretty fairy work, in converting the bank bills back again into rags and oak-leaves. Men worth a million were insolvent for two millions: promising young cities marched back again into the wilderness. The ambitious town plat was re-annexed to the plantation, like a country girl taken home from the city. The frolic was ended, and what headaches, and feverish limbs the next morning! The retreat from Moscow was performed over again, and "Devil take the hindmost" was the tune to which the soldiers of fortune marched. The only question was as to the means of escape, and the nearest and best route to Texas. The sheriff was as busy as a militia adjutant on review day; and the lawyers were mere wreckers, earning salvage. Where are ye now my ruffling gallants? Where now the braw cloths and watch chains and rings and fine horses? Alas! for ye—they are glimmering among the things that were—the wonder of an hour! They live only in memory, as unsubstantial as the promissory notes ye gave for them. When it came to be tested, the whole matter was found to be hollow and fallacious. Like a sum ciphered out through a long column, the first figure an error, the whole, and all the parts were wrong, throughout the entire calculation.

Such is a charcoal sketch of the interesting region—now inferior to none in resources, and the character of its population—during the FLUSH TIMES; a period constituting an episode in the commercial history of the world —the reign of humbug, and wholesale insanity, just overthrown in time to save the whole country from ruin. But while it lasted, many of our country-men came into the South-West in time to get "a benefit." The *auri sacra fames* is a catching disease. Many Virginians had lived too fast for their for-tunes, and naturally desired to recuperate: many others, with a competency, longed for wealth; and others again, with wealth, yearned—the common frailty—for still more. Perhaps some friend or relative, who had come out, wrote back flattering accounts of the El Dorado, and fired with dissatisfac-tion those who were doing well enough at home, by the report of his real or imagined success; for who that ever moved off, was not "doing well" in the new country, himself or friends being chroniclers?

Superior to many of the settlers in elegance of manners and general intel-ligence, it was the weakness of the Virginian to imagine he was superior too in the essential art of being able to hold his hand and make his way in a new country, and especially *such* a country, and at *such* a time. What a mistake that was! The times were out of joint. It was hard to say whether it were more dangerous to stand still or to move. If the emigrant stood still, he was consumed, by no slow degrees, by expenses: if he moved, ten to one he went off in a galloping consumption, by a ruinous investment. Expenses then—necessary articles about three times as high, and extra articles still more extra-priced—were a different thing in the new country from what they were in the old. In the old country, a jolly Virginian, starting the busi-ness of free living on a capital of a plantation, and fifty or sixty negroes, might reasonably calculate, if no ill luck befell him, by the aid of a usurer, and the occasional sale of a negro or two, to hold out without declared insolvency, until a green old age. His estate melted like an estate in chan-cery, under the gradual thaw of expenses; but in this fast country, it went by the sheer cost of living—some *poker* losses included—like the fortune of the confectioner in California, who failed for one hundred thousand dollars in the six months keeping of a candy-shop. But all the habits of his life, his taste, his associations, his education—every thing—the trustingness of his disposition—his want of business qualifications —his sanguine temper—all that was Virginian in him, made him the prey, if not of imposture, at least of unfortunate speculations. Where the keenest jockey often was bit, what

chance had *he?* About the same that the verdant Moses had with the venerable old gentleman, his father's friend, at the fair, when he traded the
Vicar's pony for the green spectacles. But how could he believe it? how
could he believe that that stuttering, grammarless Georgian, who had never
heard of the resolutions of '98, could beat him in a land trade? "Have no
money dealings with my father," said the friendly Martha to Lord Nigel,
"for, idiot though he seems, he will make an ass of thee." What a pity some
monitor, equally wise and equally successful with old Trapbois' daughter,
had not been at the elbow of every Virginian! "Twad frae monie a blunder
free'd him—an' foolish notion."

If he made a bad bargain, how could he expect to get rid of it? *He* knew
nothing of the elaborate machinery of ingenious chicane,—such as feigning
bankruptcy—fraudulent conveyances—making over to his wife—running
property—and had never heard of such tricks of trade as sending out coffins
to the graveyard, with negroes inside, carried off by sudden spells of imaginary disease, to be "resurrected," in due time, grinning, on the banks of the
Brazos.

The new philosophy, too, had commended itself to his speculative temper. He readily caught at the idea of a new spirit of the age having set in,
which rejected the saws of Poor Richard as being as much out of date as his
almanacs. He was already, by the great rise of property, compared to his
condition under the old-time prices, rich; and what were a few thousands of
debt, which two or three crops would pay off, compared to the value of his
estate? (He never thought that the value of property might come down,
while the debt was a fixed fact.) He lived freely, for it was a liberal time, and
liberal fashions were in vogue, and it was not for a Virginian to be behind
others in hospitality and liberality. He required credit and security, and, of
course, had to stand security in return. When the crash came, and no
"accommodations" could be had, except in a few instances, and in those on
the most ruinous terms, he fell an easy victim. They broke by neighbor-
hoods. They usually endorsed for each other, and when one fell—like the
child's play of putting bricks on end at equal distances, and dropping the
first in the line against the second, which fell against the third, and so on to
the last—all fell; each got broke as security, and yet few or none were able
to pay their own debts! So powerless of protection were they in those times,
that the witty H. G. used to say they reminded him of an oyster, both shells
torn off, lying on the beach, with the sea-gulls screaming over them; the
only question being, *which* should "gobble them up."

There was one consolation—if the Virginian involved himself like a fool,
he suffered himself to be sold out like a gentleman. When his card house of
visionary projects came tumbling about his ears, the next question was, the
one Webster plagiarised—"Where am I to go?" Those who had fathers,
uncles, aunts, or other like dernier resorts, in Virginia, limped back with
feathers moulted and crestfallen, to the old stamping ground, carrying the

returned Californian's fortune of ten thousand dollars—six bits in money, and the balance in experience. Those who were in the condition of the prodigal, (barring the father, the calf—the fatted one I mean—and the fiddle,) had to turn their accomplishments to account; and many of them, having lost all by eating and drinking, sought the retributive justice from meat and drink, which might, at least, support them in poverty. Accordingly, they kept tavern, and made a barter of hospitality, a business, the only disagreeable part of which was receiving the money, and the only one I know of for which a man can eat and drink himself into qualification. And while I confess I never knew a Virginian, out of the State, to keep a bad tavern, I never knew one to draw a solvent breath from the time he opened house, until death or the sheriff closed it.

Others again got to be, not exactly overseers, but some nameless thing, the duties of which were nearly analogous, for some more fortunate Virginian, who had escaped the wreck, and who had got his former boon companion to live with him on board, or other wages, in some such relation that the friend was not often found at table at the dinings given to the neighbors, and had got to be called Mr. Flournoy instead of Bob, and slept in an outhouse in the yard, and only read the *Enquirer* of nights and Sundays.

. . .

One thing I will say for the Virginians—I never knew one of them, under any pressure, extemporize a profession. The sentiment of reverence for the mysteries of medicine and law was too large for a deliberate quackery; as to the pulpit, a man might as well do his starving without the hypocrisy.

But others were not so nice. I have known them to rush, when the wolf was after them, from the counting-house or the plantation, into a doctor's shop or a law office, as if those places were the sanctuaries from the avenger; some pretending to be doctors that did not know a liver from a gizzard, administering medicine by the guess, without knowing enough of pharmacy to tell whether the stuff exhibited in the big-bellied blue, red and green bottles at the show-windows of the apothecaries' shops, was given by the drop or the half-pint.

Divers others left, but what became of them, I never knew any more than they know what becomes of the sora after frost.

Many were the instances of suffering; of pitiable misfortune, involving and crushing whole families; of pride abased; of honorable sensibilities wounded; of the provision for old age destroyed; of the hopes of manhood overcast: of independence dissipated, and the poor victim without help, or hope, or sympathy, forced to petty shifts for a bare subsistence, and a ground-scuffle, for what in happier days, he threw away. But there were too many examples of this sort for the expenditure of a useless compassion; just as the surgeon after a battle, grows case-hardened, from an excess of objects of pity.

My memory, however, fixes itself on one honored exception, the noblest of the noble, the best of the good. Old Major Willis Wormley had come in long before the *new era.* He belonged to the old school of Virginians. Nothing could have torn him from the Virginia he loved, as Jacopi Foscari, Venice, but the marrying of his eldest daughter, Mary, to a gentleman of Alabama. The Major was something between, or made of about equal parts, of Uncle Toby and Mr. Pickwick, with a slight flavor of Mr. Micawber. He was the soul of kindness, disinterestedness and hospitality. Love to every thing that had life in it, burned like a flame in his large and benignant soul; it flowed over in his countenance, and glowed through every feature, and moved every muscle in the frame it animated. The Major lived freely, was rather corpulent, and had not a lean thing on his plantations; the negroes; the dogs; the horses; the cattle; the very chickens, wore an air of corpulent complacency, and bustled about with a good-humored rotundity. There was more laughing, singing and whistling at "Hollywood," than would have set up a dozen Irish fairs. The Major's wife had, from a long life of affection, and the practice of the same pursuits, and the indulgence of the same feelings and tastes, got so much like him, that she seemed a feminine and modest edition of himself. Four daughters were all that remained in the family—two had been married off—and they had no son. The girls ranged from sixteen to twenty-two, fine, hearty, whole-souled, wholesome, cheerful lasses, with constitutions to last, and a flow of spirits like mountain springs —not beauties, but good housewife girls, whose open countenances, and neat figures, and rosy cheeks, and laughing eyes, and frank and cordial manners, made them, at home, abroad, on horseback or on foot, at the piano or discoursing on the old English books, or Washington Irving's Sketch Book, a favorite in the family ever since it was written, as entertaining and as well calculated to fix solid impressions on the heart, as any four girls in the country. The only difficulty was, they were so much alike, that you were put to fault which to fall in love with. They were all good housewives, or women, rather. But Mrs. Wormley, or Aunt Wormley, as we called her, was as far ahead of any other woman in that way, as could be found this side of the Virginia border. If there was any thing good in the culinary line that she couldn't make, I should like to know it. The Major lived on the main stage road, and if any decently dressed man ever passed the house after sundown, he escaped by sheer accident. The house was greatly visited. The Major knew everybody, and everybody near him knew the Major. The stage coach couldn't stop long, but in the hot summer days, about noon, as the driver tooted his horn at the top of the red hill, two negro boys stood opposite the door, with trays of the finest fruit, and a pitcher of cider for the refreshment of the wayfarers. The Major himself being on the look-out, with his hands over his eyes, bowing—as he only could bow—vaguely into the coach, and looking wistfully, to find among the passengers an acquaintance whom he could prevail upon to get out and stay a week with him. There wasn't a poor neighbor to whom the Major had not been as good as an insurer, without premium, for his stock, or for his crop; and from the way he rendered the service, you would think he was the party obliged—as he was.

This is not, in any country I have ever been in, a money-making business; and the Major, though he always made good crops, must have broke at it long ago, but for the fortunate death of a few Aunts, after whom the girls were named, who, paying their several debts of nature, left the Major the means to pay his less serious, but still weighty obligations.

The Major—for a wonder, being a Virginian—had no partisan politics. He could not have. His heart could not hold anything that implied a warfare upon the thoughts or feelings of others. He voted all the time for his friend, that is, the candidate living nearest to him, regretting, generally, that he did not have another vote for the other man.

It would have done a Comanche Indian's heart good to see all the family together—grand-children and all—of a winter evening, with a guest or two, to excite sociability a little—not company enough to embarrass the manifestations of affection. Such a concordance—as if all hearts were attuned to the same feeling—the old lady knitting in the corner—the old man smoking his pipe opposite—both of their fine faces radiating in the pauses of the laugh, the jest, or the caress, the infinite satisfaction within.

It was enough to convert an abolitionist, to see the old Major when he came home from a long journey of two days to the county town; the negroes running in a string to the buggy; this one to hold the horse, that one to help the old man out, and the others to inquire how he was; and to observe the benignity with which—the kissing of the girls and the old lady hardly over—he distributed a piece of calico here, a plug of tobacco there, or a card of *town* ginger-bread to the little snow-balls that grinned around him; what was given being but a small part of the gift, divested of the kind, cheerful, rollicking way the old fellow had of giving it.

The Major had given out his autograph (as had almost everybody else) as endorser on three several bills of exchange, of even tenor and date, and all maturing at or about the same time. His friend's friend failed to pay as he or his firm agreed, the friend himself did no better, and the Major, before he knew anything at all of his danger, found a writ served upon him, and was told by his friend that he was dead broke, and all he could give him was his sympathy; the which, the Major as gratefully received as if it was a legal tender and would pay the debt. The Major's friends advised him he could get clear of it; that notice of protest not having been sent to the Major's post-office, released him; but the Major wouldn't hear of such a defence, he said *his* understanding was, that he was to pay the debt if his friend didn't; and to slip out of it by a quibble, was little better than pleading the gambling act. Besides, what would the lawyers say? And what would be said by his old friends in Virginia, when it reached their ears, that he had plead want of notice, to get clear of a debt, when everybody knew it was the same thing as if he had got notice. And if this defence were good at law, it would not be in equity; and if they took it into chancery, it mattered not what became of the case, the property would all go, and he never could expect to see the last of it. No, no; he would pay it, and had as well set about it at once.

The rumor of the Major's condition spread far and wide. It reached old N. D., "an angel," whom the Major had "entertained," and one of the few that ever travelled that road. He came, post haste, to see into the affair; saw the creditor; made him, upon treat of defence, agree to take half the amount, and discharge the Major; advanced the money, and took the Major's negroes—except the houseservants—and put them on his Mississippi plantation to work out the debt.

The Major's heart pained him at the thought of the negroes going off; he couldn't witness it; though he consoled himself with the idea of the discipline and exercise being good for the health of sundry of them who had contracted sedentary diseases.

The Major turned his house into a tavern—that is, changed its name —put up a sign, and three weeks afterwards, you couldn't have told that anything had happened. The family were as happy as ever—theMajor never having put on airs of arrogance in prosperity, felt no humiliation in adversity; the girls were as cheerful, as bustling, and as light-hearted as ever, and seemed to think of the duties of hostesses as mere bagatelles, to enliven the time. The old Major was as profluent of anecdotes as ever, and never grew tired of telling the same ones to every new guest; and yet, the Major's anecdotes were all of Virginia growth, and not one of them under the legal age of twenty-one. If the Major had worked his negroes as he had those anecdotes, he would have been able to pay off the bills of exchange without any difficulty.

The old lady and the girls laughed at the anecdotes, though they must have heard them at least a thousand times, and knew them by heart; for the Major told them without the variations; and the other friends of the Major laughed too; indeed, with such an air of thorough benevolence, and in such a truly social spirit did the old fellow proceed "the tale to unfold," that a Cassius-like rascal that wouldn't laugh, whether he saw anything to laugh at or not, ought to have been sent to the Penitentiary for life—half of the time to be spent in solitary confinement.

THOMAS BANGS THORPE

(1815–1875)

The importance of Thomas Bangs Thorpe as a writer in the Southern literary tradition was established with his writing of "The Big Bear of Arkansas," in which he draws on the tall-tale tradition and rural myth to present a story that comically symbolizes the white man's conquest of the American wilderness.

Thorpe was a native of Massachusetts and studied at Wesleyan University in Connecticut, where he also worked at painting. Because of his poor health, several of his Southern classmates urged him to move south, and he settled in at Baton Rouge, Louisiana, where for the next twenty years he wrote and painted. He also saw duty as a Whig politician, a newspaper editor, a Mexican War correspondent, and a contributor of both art and literary sketches to sporting magazines, such as the *Spirit of the Times*.

In 1853 Thorpe returned to New York where he made his living as a writer. He collected and revised his backwoods sketches, publishing them as *The Hive of "The Bee-Hunter"* (1854), wrote an antislavery novel, and exhibited his paintings regularly. When the war came he was appointed colonel in the United States Army and for two years served in occupied New Orleans as an army administrator. Afterwards he continued with his writing and painting and held a post at the New York Customs House.

"The Big Bear of Arkansas," which had great popularity in its day, gives definitive treatment to a tall tale that long fascinated American readers, and that in the twentieth century would provide the occasion for William Faulkner's great mythic, nature story, "The Bear." Thorpe's approach is considerably more comic, even risque; he ends with a carefully disguised scatalogical joke.

THE BIG BEAR OF ARKANSAS

A steamboat on the Mississippi frequently, in making her regular trips, carries between places varying from one to two thousand miles apart; and as these boats advertise to land passengers and freight at "all intermediate landings," the heterogeneous character of the passengers of one of these up-country boats can scarcely be imagined by one who has never seen it with his own eyes. Starting from New Orleans in one of these boats, you will find yourself associated with men from every state in the Union, and from every portion of the globe; and a man of observation need not lack for amusement or instruction in such a crowd, if he will take the trouble to read the great book of character so favourably opened before him. Here may be seen jostling together the wealthy Southern planter, and the pedlar of tin-ware from New England—the Northern merchant, and the Southern jockey—a venerable bishop, and a desperate gambler—the land speculator, and the honest farmer—professional men of all creeds and characters—Wolvereens, Suckers, Hoosiers, Buckeyes, and Corn-crackers, beside a "plentiful sprinkling" of the half-horse and half-alligator species of men, who are peculiar to "old Mississippi," and who appear to gain a livelihood simply by going up and down the river. In the pursuit of pleasure or business, I have frequently found myself in such a crowd.

On one occasion, when in New Orleans, I had occasion to take a trip of a few miles up the Mississippi, and I hurried on board the well-known "high-pressure-and-beat-every-thing" steamboat *Invincible*, just as the last note of the last bell was sounding; and when the confusion and bustle that is natural to a boat's getting under way had subsided, I discovered that I was associated in as heterogeneous a crowd as was ever got together. As my trip was to be of a few hours' duration only, I made no endeavours to become acquainted with my fellow passengers, most of whom would be together many days. Instead of this, I took out of my pocket the "latest paper," and more critically than usual examined its contents; my fellow passengers at the same time disposed themselves in little groups. While I was thus busily employed in reading, and my companions were more busily employed in discussing such subjects as suited their humours best, we were startled most unexpectedly by a loud Indian whoop, uttered in the "social hall," that part of the cabin fitted off for a bar; then was to be heard a loud crowing, which would not have continued to have interested us—such sounds being quite common in that place of spirits—had not the hero of these windy accomplishments stuck his head into the cabin and hallooed out, "Hurra for the Big Bar of Arkansaw!" and then might be heard a confused hum of voices, unintelligible, save in such broken sentences as "horse," "screamer," "lightning is slow," etc. As might have been expected, this continued interruption attracted the attention of every one in the cabin; all conversation dropped, and in the midst of this surprise the "Big Bar" walked into the cabin, took a chair, put his feet on the stove, and looking back over his shoulder, passed the general and familiar salute of "Strangers, how are you?" He then expressed himself as much at home as if he had been at "the Forks of Cypress," and "perhaps a little more so." Some of the company at this familiarity looked a little angry, and some astonished; but in a moment every face was wreathed in a smile. There was something about the intruder that won the heart on sight. He appeared to be a man enjoying perfect health and contentment: his eyes were as sparkling as diamonds, and good-natured to simplicity. Then his perfect confidence in himself was irresistibly droll. "Perhaps," said he, "gentlemen," running on without a person speaking, "perhaps you have been to New Orleans often; I never made *the first visit before*, and I don't intend to make another in a crow's life. I am thrown away in that ar place, and useless, that ar a fact. Some of the gentlemen thar called me *green*—well, perhaps I am, said I, *but I arn't so at home*; and if I ain't off my trail much, the heads of them perlite chaps themselves weren't much the hardest; for according to my notion, they were real *know-nothings*, green as a pumpkin-vine—couldn't, in farming, I'll bet, raise a crop of turnips; and as for shooting, they'd miss a barn if the door was swinging, and that, too, with the best rifle in the country. And then they talked to me 'bout hunting, and laughed at my calling the principal game in Arkansaw poker, and high-low-jack. 'Perhaps,' said I, 'your prefer chickens and rolette'; at this they laughed harder than ever, and asked me if I lived in the woods, and didn't know what *game* was? At this I rather think I laughed. 'Yes,' I roared, and says, 'Strangers, if you'd asked me *how we got our meat* in Arkansaw, I'd a told you at once, and given you a list of varmints that would make a caravan, beginning with the bar, and ending off with the cat; that's *meat* though, not game.' Game, indeed, that's what city folks call it; and with them it means chippen-birds and shitepokes; maybe such trash live in my diggens, but I arn't noticed them yet; a bird any way is too trifling. I never did shoot at but one, and I'd never forgiven myself for that, had it weighed less than forty pounds. I wouldn't draw a rifle on anything less than that, and when I meet with another wild turkey of the same weight I will drap him."

"A wild turkey weighing forty pounds!" exclaimed twenty voices in the cabin at once.

"Yes, strangers, and wasn't it a whopper? You see, the thing was so fat that it couldn't fly far; and when he fell out of the tree, after I shot him, on striking the ground he bust open behind, and the way the pound gobs of tallow rolled out of the opening was perfectly beautiful."

"Where did all that happen?" asked a cynical-looking Hoosier.

"Happen! happened in Arkansaw: where else could it have happened, but in the creation state, the finishing-up country—a state where the *sile* runs down to the centre of the 'arth, and government gives you a title to every inch of it? Then its airs—just breathe them, and they will make you snort like a horse. It's a state without a fault, it is."

"Excepting mosquitoes," cried the Hoosier.

"Well, stranger, except them; for it ar a fact that they are rather *enormous*, and do push themselves in somewhat troublesome. But, stranger, they never stick twice in the same place; and give them a fair chance for a few months, and you will get as much above noticing them as an alligator. They can't hurt my feelings, for they lay under the skin; and I never knew but one case of injury resulting from them, and that was to a Yankee; and they take worse to foreigners, any how, than they do to natives. But the way they used that fellow up! first they punched him until he swelled up and busted; then he su-per-a-ted, as the doctor called it, until he was as raw as beef; then he took the ager owing to the warm weather, and finally he took a steamboat and left the country. He was the only man that ever took mosquitoes to heart that I know of. But mosquitoes is natur, and I never find fault with her. If they ar large, Arkansaw is large, her varmints ar large, her trees ar large, her rivers ar large, and a small mosquito would be of no more use in Arkansaw than preaching in a cane-break."

This knock-down argument in favour of big mosquitoes used the Hoosier up, and the logician started on a new track, to explain how numerous bear were in his "diggins," where he represented them to be "about as plenty as blackberries, and a little plentifuler."

Upon the utterance of this assertion, a timid little man near me inquired if the bear in Arkansaw ever attacked the settlers in numbers.

"No," said our hero, warming with the subject, "no, stranger, for you see it ain't the natur of bar to go in droves; but the way they squander about in pairs and single ones is edifying. And then the way I hunt them the old black rascals know the crack of my gun as well as they know a pig's squealing. They grow thin in our parts, it frightens them so, and they do take the noise dreadfully, poor things. That gun of mine is perfect *epidemic among bar*; if not watched closely, it will go off as quick on a warm scent as my dog Bowie-knife will: and then that dog—whew! why the fellow thinks that the world is full of bar, he finds them so easy. It's lucky he don't talk as well as think; for with his natural modesty, if he should suddenly learn how much he is acknowledged to be ahead of all other dogs in the universe, he would be astonished to death in two minutes. Strangers, the dog knows a bar's way as well as a horse-jockey knows a woman's; he always barks at the right time, bites at the exact place, and whips without getting a scratch. I never could tell whether he was made expressly to hunt bar, or whether bar was made expressly for him to hunt; any way, I believe they were ordained to go together as naturally as Squire Jones says a man and woman is, when he moralizes in marrying a couple. In fact, Jones once said, said he, 'Marriage according to law is a civil contract of divine origin; it's common to all countries as well as Arkansaw, and people take to it as naturally as Jim Doggett's Bowie-knife takes to bar.' "

"What season of the year do your hunts take place?" inquired a gentlemanly foreigner, who, from some peculiarities of his baggage, I suspected to be an Englishman, on some hunting expedition, probably at the foot of the Rocky Mountains.

"The season for bar hunting, stranger," said the man of Arkansaw, "is generally all the year round, and the hunts take place about as regular. I read in history that varmints have their fat season, and their lean season. That is not the case in Arkansaw, feeding as they do upon the *spontenacious* productions of the sile, they have one continued fat season the year round; though in winter things in this way is rather more greasy than in summer,

I must admit. For that reason bar with us run in warm weather, but in winter, they only waddle. Fat, fat! it's an enemy to speed; it tames everything that has plenty of it. I have seen wild turkeys, from its influence, as gentle as chickens. Run a bar in this fat condition, and the way it improves the critter for eating is amazing; it sort of mixes the ile up with the meat, until you can't tell t'other from which. I've done this often. I recollect one perty morning in particular, of putting an old fellow on the stretch, and considering the weight he carried, he run well. But the dogs soon tired him down, and when I came up with him wasn't he in a beautiful sweat—I might say fever; and then to see his tongue sticking out of his mouth a foot, and his sides sinking and opening like a bellows, and his cheeks so fat he couldn't look cross. In this fix I blazed at him, and pitch me naked into a briar patch if the steam didn't come out of the bullet-hole ten foot in a straight line. The fellow, I reckon, was made on the high-pressure system, and the lead sort of bust his biler."

"That column of steam was rather curious, or else the bear must have been *warm*," observed the foreigner, with a laugh.

"Stranger, as you observe, that bar was WARM, and the blowing off of the steam show'd it, and also how hard the varmint had been run. I have no doubt if he had kept on two miles farther his insides would have been stewed; and I expect to meet with a varmint yet of extra bottom, who will run himself into a skinfull of bar's grease: it is possible, much onlikelier things have happened."

"Whereabouts are these bears so abundant?" inquired the foreigner, with increasing interest.

"Why, stranger, they inhabit the neighbourhood of my settlement, one of the prettiest places on old Mississippi—a perfect location, and no mistake; a place that had some defects until the river made the 'cut-off' at 'Shirt-tail bend,' and that remedied the evil, as it brought my cabin on the edge of the river—a great advantage in wet weather, I assure you, as you can now roll a barrel of whiskey into my yard in high water from a boat, as easy as falling off a log. It's a great improvement, as toting it by land in a jug, as I used to do, *evaporated* it too fast, and it became expensive. Just stop with me, stranger, a month or two, or a year if you like, and you will appreciate my place. I can give you plenty to eat; for beside hog and hominy, you can have bar-ham, and bar-sausages, and a mattrass of bar-skins to sleep on, and a wildcat-skin, pulled off hull, stuffed with corn-shucks, for a pillow. That bed would put you to sleep if you had the rheumatics in every joint in your body. I call that ar bed a *quietus*. Then look at my land—the government ain' got another such a piece to dispose of. Such timber, and such bottom land, why you can't preserve any thing natural you plant in it unless you pick it young, things thar will grow out of shape so quick. I once planted in those diggins a few potatoes and beets; they took a fine start, and after that an ox team couldn't have kept them from growing. About that time I went off to old Kentuck on bisiness, and did not hear from them things in three months, when I accidentally stumbled on a fellow who had stopped at my place, with an idea of buying me out. 'How did you like things?' said I. 'Pretty well,' said he; 'the cabin is convenient, and the timber land is good; but that bottom land ain't worth the first red cent.' 'Why?' said I. ' 'Cause,' said he. ' 'Cause what?' said I. ' 'Cause it's full of cedar stumps and Indian mounds,' said he *and it can't be cleared.'* 'Lord,' said I, 'them ar "cedar stumps" is beets, and them ar "Indian mounds" ar tater hills.' As I expected, the crop was overgrown and useless; the sile is too rich, *and planting in Arkansaw is dangerous.* I had a good-sized sow killed in that same bottom land. The old thief stole an ear of corn, and took it down where she slept at night to eat. Well, she left a grain or two on the ground, and lay down on them; before morning the corn shot up, and the percussion killed her dead. I don't plant any more; natur intended Arkansaw for a hunting ground, and I go according to natur."

The questioner who thus elicited the description of our hero's settlement, seemed to be perfectly satisfied and said no more; but the "Big Bar of Arkansaw" rambled on from one thing to another with a volubility perfectly astonishing, occasionally disputing with those around him, particularly with a "live Sucker" from Illinois, who had the daring to say that our Arkansaw friend's stories "smelt rather tall."

In this manner the evening was spent; but conscious that my own association with so singular a personage would probably end before morning, I asked him if he would not give me a description of some particular bear hunt; adding that I took great interest in such things, though I was no sportsman. The desire seemed to please him, and he squared himself round towards me, saying, that he could give me an idea of a bar hunt that was never beat in this world, or in any other. His manner was so singular, that half of his story consisted in his excellent way of telling it, the great peculiarity of which was the happy manner he had of emphasizing the prominent parts of his conversation. As near as I can recollect, I have italicized them, and given the story in his own words.

"Stranger," said he, "in bar hunts *I am numerous*, and which particular one, as you say, I shall tell, puzzles me. There was the old she devil I shot at the Hurricane last fall—then there was the old hog thief I popped over at the Bloody Crossing, and then—Yes, I have it! I will give you an idea of a hunt, in which the greatest bar was killed that ever lived, *none excepted*; about an old fellow that I hunted, more or less, for two or three years; and if that ain't a particular bar hunt, I ain't got one to tell. But in the first place, stranger let me say, I am pleased with you, because you ain't ashamed to gain information by asking, and listening, and that's what I say to Countess's pups every day when I'm home; and I have got great hopes of them ar pups, because they are continually *nosing* about; and though they stick it sometimes in the wrong place, they gain experience any how, and may learn something useful to boot. Well, as I was saying about this big bar, you see when I and some more first settled in our region, we were driven to hunting naturally; we soon liked it, and after that we found it an easy matter to make the thing our business. One old chap who had pioneered 'afore us, gave us to understand that we had settled in the right place. He dwelt upon its merits until it was affecting, and showed us, to prove his assertions, more marks on the sassafras trees than I ever saw on a tavern door 'lection time. 'Who keeps that ar reckoning?' said I. 'The bar,' said he. 'What for?' said I. 'Can't tell,' said he; 'but so it is; the bar bite the bark and wood too, at the highest point from the ground they can reach, and you can tell, by the marks,' said he, 'the length of the bar to an inch.' 'Enough,' said I; 'I've learned something here a'ready, and I'll put it in practice.'

"Well, stranger, just one month from that time I killed a bar, and told its exact length before I measured it, by those very marks; and when I did that, I swelled up considerable—I've been a prouder man ever since. So I went on, larning something every day, until I was reckoned a buster, and allowed to be decidedly the best bar hunter in my district; and that is a reputation as much harder to earn than to be reckoned first man in Congress, as an iron ramrod is harder than a toadstool. Did the varmints grow over-cunning by being fooled with by green-horn hunters, and by this means get troublesome, they send for me as a matter of course; and thus I do my own hunting, and most of my neighbours'. I walk into the varmints though, and it has become about as much the same to me as drinking. It is told in two sentences—a bar is started, and he is killed. The thing is somewhat monotonous now—I know just how much they will run, where they will tire, how much they will growl, and what a thundering time I will have in getting them home. I could give you this history of the chase with all particulars at the commencement, I know the signs so well—*Stranger, I'm certain.* Once I met with a match though, and I will tell you about it; for a common hunt would not be worth relating.

"On a fine fall day, long time ago, I was trailing about for bar, and what should I see but fresh marks on the sassafras trees, about eight inches above any in the forests that I knew of. Says I, 'them marks is a hoax, or it indicates the d———t bar that was ever grown.' In fact, stranger, I couldn't believe it was real, and I went on. Again I saw the same marks, at the same height, and *I knew the thing lived.* That conviction came home to my soul like an earthquake. Says I, 'here is something a-purpose for me: that bar is mine, or I give up the hunting business.' The very next morning what should I see but a number of buzzards hovering over my cornfield. 'The rascal has been there,' said I, 'for that sign is certain'; and, sure enough, on examining, I found the bones of what had been as beautiful a hog the day before as was ever raised by a Buckeye. Then I tracked the critter out of the field to the woods, and all the marks he left behind, showed me that he was *the bar*.

"Well, stranger, the first fair chase I ever had with that big critter, I saw him no less than three distinct times at a distance: the dogs run him over eighteen miles and broke down, my horse gave out, and I was as nearly used up as a man can be, made on *my* principle, *which is patent*. Before this adventure, such things were unknown to me as possible; but, strange as it was, that bar got me used to it before I was done with him; for he got so at last, that he would leave me on a long chase *quite* easy. How he did it, I never could understand. That a bar runs at all, is puzzling; but how this one could tire down and bust up a pack of hounds and a horse, that were used to overhauling everything they started after in no time, was past my understanding. Well, stranger, that bar finally got so sassy, that he used to help himself to a hog off my premises whenever he wanted one; the buzzards followed after what he left, and so between *bar and buzzard*, I rather think I was *out of pork*.

"Well, missing that bar so often took hold of my vitals, and I wasted away. The thing had been carried too far, and it reduced me in flesh faster than an ager. I would see that bar in every thing I did; *he hunted me*, and that, too, like a devil, which I began to think he was. While in this fix, I made preparations to give him a last brush, and be done with it. Having completed every thing to my satisfaction, I started at sunrise, and to my great joy, I discovered from the way the dogs run, that they were near him; finding his trial was nothing, for that had become as plain to the pack as a turnpike road. On we went, and coming to an open country, what should I see but the bar very leisurely ascending a hill, and the dogs close at his heels, either a match for him in speed, or else he did not care to get out of their way—I don't know which. But wasn't he a beauty, though? I loved him like a brother.

"On he went, until he came to a tree, the limbs of which formed a crotch about six feet from the ground. Into this crotch he got and seated himself, the dogs yelling all around it; and there he sat eyeing them as quiet as a pond in low water. A green-horn friend of mine, in company, reached shooting distance before me, and blazed away, hitting the critter in the centre of his forehead. The bar shook his head as the ball struck it, and then walked down from that tree as gently as a lady would from a carriage. 'Twas a beautiful sight to see him do that—he was in such a rage that he seemed to be as little afraid of the dogs as if they had been sucking pigs; and the dogs warn't slow in making a ring around him at a respectful distance, I tell you; even Bowie-knife, himself, stood off. Then the way his eyes flashed—why the fire of them would have singed a cat's hair; in fact that bar was in a *wrath all over*. Only one pup came near him, and he was brushed out so totally with the bar's left paw, that he entirely disappeared, and that made the old dogs more cautious still. In the meantime, I came up, and taking deliberate aim as a man should do, at his side, just back of his foreleg, *if my gun did not snap*, call me a coward, and I won't take it personal. Yes, stranger, *it snapped*, and I could not find a cap about my person. While in this predicament, I turned round to my fool friend—says I, 'Bill,' says I, 'you're an ass—you're a fool—you might as well have tried to kill that bar by barking the tree under his belly, as to have done it by hitting him in the head. Your shot has made a tiger of him, and blast me, if a dog gets killed or wounded when they come to blows, I will stick my knife into your liver, I will—' my wrath was up. I had lost my caps, my gun had snapped, the fellow with me had fired at the bar's head, and I expected every moment to see him close in with the dogs, and kill a dozen of them at least. In this thing I was mistaken, for the bar leaped over the ring formed by the dogs, and giving a fierce growl, was off—the pack, of course, in full cry after him. The run this time was short, for coming to the edge of a lake the varmint jumped in, and swam to a little island in the lake, which it reached just a moment before the dogs. 'I'll have him now,' said I, for I had found my caps in the *lining of my coat*—so, rolling a log into the lake, I paddled myself across to the island, just as the dogs had cornered the bar in a thicket. I rushed up and fired—at the same time the critter leaped over the dogs and came within three feet of me, running like mad; he jumped into the lake, and tried to mount the log I had just deserted, but every time he got half his body on it, it would roll over and send him under; the dogs, too, got around him, and pulled him about, and finally Bowie-knife clenched with him, and they sunk into the lake together. Stranger, about this time, I was excited, and I stripped off my coat, drew my knife, and intended to have taken a part with Bowie-knife myself, when the bar rose to the surface. But the varmint staid under—Bowie-knife came up alone, more dead than alive, and with the pack came ashore. 'Thank God,' said I, 'the old villain has got his deserts at last.' Determined to have the body, I cut a grape-vine for a rope, and dove down where I could see the bar in the water, fastened my queer rope to his leg, and fished him, with great difficulty, ashore. Stranger, may I be chawed to death by young alligators, if the thing I looked at wasn't a *she bar, and not the old critter after all*. The way matters got mixed on that island was onaccountably curious, and thinking of it made me more than ever convinced that I was hunting the devil himself. I went home that night and took to my bed—the thing was killing me. The entire team of Arkansaw in bar-hunting, acknowledged himself used up, and the fact sunk into my feelings like a snagged boat will in the Mississippi. I grew as cross as a bar with two cubs and a sore tail. The thing got out 'mong my neighbours, and I was asked how come on that individu-al that never lost a bar when once started? and if that same individ-u-al didn't wear telescopes when he turned a she bar, of ordinary size, into an old he one, a little larger than a horse? 'Perhaps,' said I, 'friends'—getting wrathy—'perhaps you want to call somebody a liar.' 'Oh, no,' said they, 'we only heard such things

as being *rather common* of late, but we don't believe one word of it; oh, no,'
—and then they would ride off and laugh like so many hyenas over a dead
nigger. It was too much, and I determined to catch that bar, go to Texas, or
die,—and I made my preparations accordin'. I had the pack shut up and
rested. I took my rifle to pieces and iled it. I put caps in every pocket about
my person, *for fear of the lining.* I then told my neighbours, that on Monday
morning—naming the day—I would start THAT BAR, and bring him home
with me, or they might divide my settlement among them, the owner having
disappeared. Well, stranger, on the morning previous to the great day of my
hunting expedition, I went into the woods near my house, taking my gun
and Bowie-knife along, just *from habit,* and there sitting down also from
habit, what should I see, getting over my fence, but *the bar!* Yes, the old
varmint was within a hundred yards of me, and the way he walked *over that
fence*—stranger, he loomed up like a *black mist,* he seemed so large, and he
walked right towards me. I raised myself, took deliberate aim, and fired.
Instantly the varmint wheeled, gave a yell, and *walked through the fence* like
a falling tree would through a cobweb. I started after, but was tripped up by
my inexpressibles, which either from habit, or the excitement of the
moment, were about my heels, and before I had really gathered myself up, I
heard the old varmint groaning in a thicket near by, like a thousand sinners,
and by the time I reached him he was a corpse. Stranger, it took five niggers
and myself to put that carcase on a mule's back, and old long-ears waddled
under the load, as if he was foundered in every leg of his body, and with a
common whopper of a bar, he would have trotted off, and enjoyed himself.
'Twould astonish you to know how big he was: I made a *bedspread of his
skin,* and the way it used to cover my bar mattress, and leave several feet on
each side to tuck up, would have delighted you. It was in fact a creation bar,
and if it had lived in Samson's time, and had met him, in a fair fight, it
would have licked him in the twinkling of a dice-box. But, strangers, I never
like the way I hunted, and *missed him.* There is something curious about it, I
could never understand,—and I never was satisfied at his giving in so easy
at last. Perhaps, he had heard of my preparations to hunt him the next day,
so he just come in, like Capt. Scott's coon, to save his wind to grunt with in
dying; but that ain't likely. My private opinion is, that that bar was an
unhuntable bar, and died when his time come."

When the story was ended, our hero sat some minutes with his auditors
in a grave silence; I saw there was a mystery to him connected with the bear
whose death he had just related, that had evidently made a strong impression on his mind. It was also evident that there was some superstitious awe
connected with the affair,—a feeling common with all "children of the
wood," when they meet with any thing out of their everyday experience. He
was the first one, however, to break the silence, and jumping up, he asked
all present to "liquor" before going to bed,—a thing which he did, with a
number of companions, evidently to his heart's content.

THOMAS BANGS THORPE

Long before day, I was put ashore at my place of destination, and I can only follow with the reader, in imagination, our Arkansas friend, in his adventures at the "Forks of Cypress" on the Mississippi.

PART THREE

AFTER THE WAR

There was an almost complete changing of the guard in Southern literature in the years immediately following the end of the Civil War. Only Paul Hayne and John Esten Cooke continued their literary careers into the 1870s, and neither attained important literary achievement. William Gilmore Simms spent the last five years of his life grinding out prose for second-rate magazines to support his family before his death in 1870. Henry Timrod died of tuberculosis within two years of the close of the fighting. The heyday of the Southwestern Humorists was almost at an end, though George Washington Harris wrote for a few years longer. A new form of literature was in the offing. In the middle 1870s the Southern literature of "local color" began to gain widespread popularity in the national magazines, and almost every one of the prominent practitioners was new to the literary scene.

There was little opportunity for a writer to earn a living by the pen within the postwar South, for there was no money to pay for books or magazines. Financially and commercially the region was devastated. In antebellum times capital had been invested in land and in slaves. Without people to work it, the land was worthless. A system of sharecropping and tenant farming was developed that, except in years of good farm prices (which became ever more rare during the 1870s and 1880s), meant poverty, debt, and bare subsistence. "Ten cent cotton and forty cent meat," the saying went, "how in the hell can a poor man eat?" As for the towns and cities, there was little prosperity there too. The entire South was in a state of destitution, and the scars of the war and the Reconstruction were years in the healing.

The politics of the 1880s and 1890s were tumultuous and dirty. The white farmers of the Upcountry, in desperate economic shape because of failing farm prices, sought to overthrow the hegemony of the old financial and planter leadership, and class conflict shook the foundations of the Democratic Party. Black Southerners, now freed from slavery—but without land, education, opportunity, or the ability to protect themselves politically —became the focal point of some extraordinarily nasty political campaigning. Laws were passed fixing a permanent status of segregated inferiority for blacks, and the annual occurrence of lynchings and violence grew alarmingly for a time. Meanwhile, the rural South remained poor, isolated, and backward, while—except in a few areas such as the North Alabama iron region, piedmont North Carolina, Atlanta, and Richmond—the towns and cities of the South experienced little of the growth and prosperity that characterized the American nation as a whole during the Age of Enterprise.

Paradoxically, beginning in the 1870s the literature of the South began prospering as never before. For now that the results of the Civil War had resolved the question of national identity for good, at least insofar as the threat of political separation was concerned, there arose throughout the nation a growing fascination with the varieties and divergences of American life and ways. The new mass-circulation magazines, which dominated American culture during the popularity of the Genteel Tradition in the later nineteenth century, were ready markets for stories that could describe the oddities, the quaintness, and the picturesque ways of language and events in the regions remote from the cities of the Northeast. Perhaps as a reaction to the swift-growing urbanization of the great cities, local color in American literature flourished and, though there were a great many practitioners of it in other regions, no other part of the country proved so well equipped to offer stories exhibiting quaint customs and divergent patterns of life as the South. Not only were there such distinct subcultures as the Creoles and Cajuns of once-French Louisiana, or the remote mountain folk of the Appalachians, but now that slavery was no longer an issue, the black folk who lived on the land could provide the models for a faithful literary peasantry. Harriet Beecher Stowe's Uncle Tom now became Joel Chandler Harris's Uncle Remus. Moreover, reunion was very much in vogue, and since the issues that had led to secession and war had in an important sense been artificial forces of division among a people that north and south were much more similar than different in their ways and their values, now that the war was done there was a premium upon popular literature that could help bring about national unity. Thus the Confederate heritage, once a badge of treason in the immediate postwar period, soon took on the glamour and excitement of a lost cause. Defeated valor made for excellent literary romance. The plantation novel, first developed by John Pendleton Kennedy in the 1830s, attained full development now that the old plantation was a thing of the past; the image of ordered, serene elegance and grace, a life properly settled and aristocratic, free of money-grubbing and hard toil (even the slaves scarcely worked), proved even more attractive to the urban American imagination now that it could offer the chivalry and the pathos of a lost Arcadia. As the onetime Abolitionist and Reconstruction Judge Albion Tourgee wrote in vexation in 1888, "not only is the epoch of the war the favorite field of American fiction today, but the Confederate soldier is the popular hero. Our literature has become not only Southern in type but distinctly Confederate in sympathy."

The lone Southern local colorist who dissented from the growing national consensus that blacks were second-class citizens was George W. Cable. This former Confederate soldier, whose tales of Creole life in New Orleans were widely popular in the late 1870s and 1880s, soon came to feel that the South was making à grievous mistake in relegating its black citizens to permanent political and social inferiority. His warnings fell on deaf ears, however, and his Northern editors became more and more reluctant to publish his polemics against racial injustice. In the decade of the 1890s he abandoned the Creole scenes which he depicted in his fiction to write a realistic novel about Southern problems, entitled *John March, Southerner* (1895). It was all but ignored, and thereafter he gave up his futile struggle.

Another Southerner, Joel Chandler Harris of Georgia, won international fame for his dialect stories of Brer Rabbit and other animal inhabitants of the

Southern countryside who lived back in the days when creatures could talk. The kindly old black man who recounted the tales has been seen as the embodiment of the local-color stereotype—the childlike, docile "uncle," happy in his inferior status. Yet it may be that the objections to the Uncle Remus stories as examples of racial stereotyping are too facile. It is the rabbit, not Remus, who is the hero of these stories, and the manner in which this rabbit—living in a world populated by foxes, wolves, bears, and other powerful creatures—slyly and zestfully outwits his foes is more than a little suggestive of the black man's situation in a society controlled and dominated by whites. It was not that Harris, an associate of Henry W. Grady and editorial writer for the Atlanta *Constitution*, openly dissented from the racial views of his time, but rather that in (and only in) the animal stories he was able to write, however humorously, with a realism about things as they actually were in a way that could transcend the assumptions of his society.

It was Thomas Nelson Page of Virginia, however, who in his stories epitomized the local-color tableau of the happy days back on the old plantation. His faithful black retainers who narrate his stories exist to extol the days before the war, when

> Niggers didn' hed nothin t' all to do—jes' hed to 'ten' to de feedin' an' cleanin' de hosses, and doin' what de marster tell 'em to do; an' when dey wuz sick, dey had things sont 'em out de house, an' de same doctor xome to see 'em what 'ten' to de white folks when dey wuz po'ly. Dyar warn' no trouble nor nothin'.

In some of Page's stories gallant Southern ladies fall in love despite themselves with high-minded, young Union officers of aristocratic families, whom they ultimately marry and with whom they restore the plantation to the peace of the good old days. In these stories we can see the impulse toward sectional reconciliation. Other stories, such as his masterpiece "Marse Chan," rang the changes on the purity and heroism of the splendid young Southern chivalry who mistakenly perhaps, but with the highest of moral intentions, rode off to war in 1861 to defend their community against the invaders.

Because the form for depicting black folk in fiction was the local color dialect story, a young Ohio-born, North Carolina black writer, Charles Waddell Chesnutt, turned automatically to it for his tales of life in the rural South before and after the war. But Chesnutt had a very different goal in mind than a writer such as Page, and what he did was to use the local color "frame" story, in which an old black man tells his white superiors a tale in dialect in order to show how slavery and racial injustice looked to the blacks involved in it. The narrator, Julius, would tell tales of conjuring among the blacks—but never for the sake of tale-telling alone; the storyteller always had a purpose in mind, and his objective was always to secure some advantage—usually economic —from the Northern-born white owners of the postwar plantation. When Chesnutt sought to write other stories that did not use the dialect convention, but dealt openly and directly with racial matters, he found little interest among the magazine editors of the 1890s. His three novels, which also made strong racial commentaries, were also largely unsuccessful commercially.

The leading Southern author of the day, however, and by all odds the single major American literary figure among all his Southern contemporaries, was Mark Twain—a Missourian of Virginia and Kentucky descent who grew up in a slave-holding community, worked for several years as a river pilot on the Mississippi between St. Louis and New Orleans, enlisted briefly in a Confederate militia outfit when war came, and then went West to the Nevada territory. It was while he was working in the Far West that Samuel L. Clemens invented the penname Mark Twain, and when he made his entry on the national literary scene immediately after the war it was in the guise of a Westerner, not a Southerner. Yet his greatest art was not drawn from his western experience, but from his childhood and young manhood in Hannibal and on the Mississippi.

Clemens began as a writer with newspaper humor, written directly in the manner and style of the Southwestern humorists whose work he knew and admired. As he began writing professionally, however, his range deepened, and he developed the humorous contrast between the realistic vernacular attitudes and values of that kind of writing and the more traditional ideals and standards of the formal literature of his day into a searching scrutiny of American life. In his masterpiece, *The Adventures of Huckleberry Finn* (1884), he used the language and insights of a largely uneducated youth of disadvantaged status to tell the story of a raft trip down the Mississippi in the company of a fugitive slave. Through Huck Finn, Twain exposed the falseness, hypocrisy, and artificiality of the society along the shore. In its telling the story develops a stunning contrast between the ideal of innocence and freedom on the river, and the necessity of living and dealing with the world on the shore—the world in which the protagonist must dissemble and disguise himself in order to preserve his own integrity. In *Huckleberry Finn* Mark Twain was able to bring together within a single work of high literary art the vernacular idiom with the perspective of everyday American language, and the concern for values with the ultimate meaning of formal literature. Thus, in effect, as Ernest Hemingway was later to remark, Mark Twain created the language of American literature.

He was, as his friend William Dean Howells wrote of him, "the most desouthernized Southerner I ever knew"—referring to his notorious denunciations of slavery and racial injustice and his oft-expressed distaste for the Southern pseudo-Gothic cultural style. But while as a businessman in Connecticut he threw himself energetically into the money-making frenzy of the

Gilded Age, the forces of his creative imagination held ferociously on, in hatred and in pride, to the faraway country of his youth. In comedy he strove to articulate and resolve the tensions, incongruities, and contradictions that his relentless self-scrutiny and memory kept discovering. His great weapon was laughter. When finally it failed, he was left high and dry, dictating rambling memories to a secretary, along with furious but ineffective tirades against a hostile universe. By accident of time and place, Sam Clemens was jarred loose from the Southern community in a way that none of his literary contemporaries were. Not for generations after his time would there be other Southern authors who would find themselves both tied to and dissociated imaginatively from the place of their origins in something like the way he had been. When that day came in the years after the First World War, the twentieth-century Southern Literary Renascence would get under way.

SAMUEL LANGHORNE CLEMENS
("Mark Twain")
(1835–1910)

The enduring works of Samuel L. Clemens are set in the small Missouri town where he grew up—more Southern than Western in its customs, beliefs, and institutions—and on the great river that flowed from St. Louis and Cairo to New Orleans, along which he worked as a pilot. It is Mark Twain's fictional representation of this early experience, rather than that of the Far West, where he went to live briefly in his late twenties before emerging on the national literary scene, that earned him the lasting literary reputation that, at first, because he was considered merely a "funnyman," was withheld from him.

Clemens' father, John Marshall Clemens, was a Virginian. However, like many other Virginians of respectable families but uncertain prospects, he went West to seek his fortune with less than satisfactory results. Indeed, in certain important ways the career of the elder Clemens in the new country very much resembled that life as chronicled by Joseph G. Baldwin in *Flush Times of Alabama and Mississippi*. He married a Kentuckian, Jane Lampson, and after a venture in Tennessee moved out to Missouri, where in 1835 Sam Clemens was born in the town of Florida; they then settled in Hannibal a few years later. When the elder Clemens died, Mark Twain was twelve years old.

SAMUEL LANGHORNE CLEMENS

He was apprenticed to a printer, and beginning in 1853 he travelled about as a journeyman compositor, working in New York, Philadelphia, Cincinnati, St. Louis, and Keokuk. He then took up river piloting, serving his apprenticeship under Horace Bixby and becoming a full-fledged steamboat pilot. His days on the river ended with the outbreak of the Civil War. Sam Clemens enlisted in the Marion Rangers, a Confederate cavalry unit, but served only a few weeks. When his brother Orion, an ardent Unionist, was appointed Secretary of the Territory of Nevada, he went West with him, later working as a miner and a newspaperman. Meanwhile, he had begun writing, and his fame began reaching the East Coast. The *Alta Californian* financed his passage aboard a shipload of tourists bound for the Mediterranean and the Holy Land, and his account of this voyage, *The Innocents Abroad* (1869), was widely successful. He had also become a popular humorous lecturer.

In 1870 he married Olivia Langdon, daughter of a prosperous coal dealer, in Elmira, New York, and settled into a brief career as a newspaper editor. In 1871 he published *Roughing It*, an account of his years in the Far West. He then moved to Hartford, Connecticut, and thereafter devoted his energies to writing, reading, and lecturing, and also to getting involved in all types of business enterprises and investments, including his own publishing company, the Charles L. Webster Company, which sold large printings of his own and other books. Among those published was the *Memoirs* of General U. S. Grant, which was sold by door-to-door subscription. Among the books he wrote in this period are *The Adventures of Tom Sawyer* (1876), *The Prince and the Pauper* (1882), *Life on the Mississippi* (1883), *Adventures of Huckleberry Finn* (1884), *A Connecticut Yankee in King Arthur's Court* (1889), and *Pudd'nhead Wilson* (1894).

Clemens' financial investments, particularly that in a typesetting machine, eventually became too severe a drain on his resources, and in 1894 his publishing firm went into bankruptcy. With the advice of the financier Henry H. Rogers of the Standard Oil Company, he settled his debts and for the remainder of his life enjoyed financial security. His last years were saddened, however, by the death of two of his daughters and of his wife. He died in 1910. Little of the writing done in his last two decades is among his most memorable, though there are individual pieces of considerable power, including some scathing attacks on American materialism, imperialism, and racial injustice.

It was in 1874 that Clemens "discovered" the possibilities of using Hannibal and the Mississippi as subjects for literature. He wrote a series of sketches for the *Atlantic Monthly*, edited by his friend William Dean Howells, describing the transformation of a cub into a fully accredited river pilot. Significantly, he made the cub some years younger than he had been when he first took up the study of river piloting, thus enabling him to distance the protagonist from himself and achieve fictional depth. In a famous passage he describes a sunrise on the river as a tourist might see it, producing a paragraph of conventional literary rhapsodizing, but Twain then shows what these apparently innocent details mean to the trained eye of the pilot and concludes with a lament for the loss of the capacity for detached contemplation of the beautiful. Yet the passage describing the river as seen by the pilot is far more convincing imaginatively because of its strong evocation of the reality of the river itself.

From the writing of "Old Times on the Mississippi" (as it was entitled in its serial publication in *The Atlantic Monthly*) to *Tom Sawyer* and *Huckleberry Finn* there ensued a deeper, more fictionalized, and, therefore, more critically imaginative portrayal of the life and times of his youth and young manhood; this new depth culminated in the powerful contrast between the freedom of life aboard the raft, away from society in nature, and the corruption, materialism, sentimentality, and emotional frustration of the society along the shore as depicted in *Huckleberry Finn*, making it one of the great works of fiction. In language, in moral insight, in detailed description, and in rich observation Mark Twain made of the interplay between his childhood memories and his adult insights a dialectical exploration within the consciousness of Huckleberry Finn, whereby his own youthful Southern experience was given lasting artistic definition.

From OLD TIMES ON THE MISSISSIPPI

THE BOYS' AMBITION

When I was a boy, there was but one permanent ambition among my comrades in our village on the west bank of the Mississippi River. That was, to be a steamboatman. We had transient ambitions of other sorts, but they were only transient. When a circus came and went, it left us all burning to become clowns; the first negro minstrel show that ever came to our section left us all suffering to try that kind of life; now and then we had a hope that, if we lived and were good, God would permit us to be pirates. These ambitions faded out, each in its turn; but the ambition to be a steamboatman always remained.

Once a day a cheap, gaudy packet arrived upward from St. Louis, and another downward from Keokuk. Before these events, the day was glorious with expectancy; after them, the day was a dead and empty thing. Not only the boys, but the whole village, felt this. After all these years I can picture that old time to myself now, just as it was then: the white town drowsing in the sunshine of a summer's morning; the streets empty, or pretty nearly so; one or two clerks sitting in front of the Water Street stores, with their splint-bottomed chairs tilted back against the wall, chins on breasts, hats slouched over their faces, asleep—with shingle-shavings enough around to show what broke them down; a sow and a litter of pigs loafing along the sidewalk, doing a good business in watermelon rinds and seeds; two or three lonely little freight piles scattered about the "levee;" a pile of "skids" on the slope of the stone-paved wharf, and the fragrant town drunkard asleep in the shadow of them; two or three wood flats at the head of the wharf, but nobody to listen to the peaceful lapping of the wavelets against them; the great Mississippi, the majestic, the magnificent Mississippi, rolling its mile-wide tide along, shining in the sun; the dense forest away on the other side; the "point" above the town, and the "point" below, bounding the river-glimpse and turning it into a sort of sea, and withal a very still and brilliant and lonely one. Presently a film of dark smoke appears above one of those remote "points;" instantly a negro drayman, famous for his quick eye and prodigious voice, lifts up the cry "S-t-e-a-m-boat a-comin'!" and the scene changes! The town drunkard stirs, the clerks wake up, a furious clatter of drays follows, every house and store pours out a human contribution, and all in a twinkling the dead town is alive and moving. Drays, carts, men, boys, all go hurrying from many quarters to a common centre, the wharf. Assembled there, the people fasten their eyes upon the coming boat as upon a wonder they are seeing for the first time. And the boat *is* rather a handsome sight, too. She is long and sharp and trim and pretty; she has two tall fancy-topped chimneys, with a gilded device of some kind swung between them; a fanciful pilot-house, all glass and "gingerbread," perched on top of the "texas" deck behind them; the paddle-boxes are gorgeous with a picture or with gilded rays above the boat's name; the boiler deck, the hurricane deck, and the texas deck are fenced and ornamented with clean white railings; there is a flag gallantly flying from the jack-staff; the furnace doors are open and the fires glaring bravely; the upper decks are black with passengers; the captain stands by the big bell, calm, imposing, the envy of all; great volumes of the blackest smoke are rolling and tumbling out of the chimneys—a husbanded grandeur created with a bit of pitch pine just before arriving at a town; the crew are grouped on the forecastle; the broad stage is run far out over the port bow, and an envied deck-hand stands picturesquely on the end of it with a coil of rope in his hand; the pent steam is screaming through the gauge-cocks; the captain lifts his hand, a bell rings, the wheels stop; then they turn back, churning the water to foam, and the steamer is at rest. Then such a scramble as there is to get aboard, and to get ashore, and to take in freight and to discharge freight, all at one and the same time; and such a yelling and cursing as the mates facilitate it all with! Ten minutes later the steamer is under way again, with no flag on the jack-staff and no black smoke issuing from the chimneys. After ten more minutes the town is dead again, and the town drunkard asleep by the skids once more.

My father was a justice of the peace, and I supposed he possessed the power of life and death over all men and could hang anybody that offended him. This was distinction enough for me as a general thing; but the desire to be a steamboatman kept intruding, nevertheless. I first wanted to be a cabin-boy, so that I could come out with a white apron on and shake a table-cloth over the side, where all my old comrades could see me; later I thought I would rather be the deck-hand who stood on the end of the stage-plank with the coil of rope in his hand, because he was particularly conspicuous. But these were only day-dreams,—they were too heavenly to be contemplated as real possibilities. By and by one of our boys went away. He was not heard of for a long time. At last he turned up as apprentice engineer or "striker" on a steamboat. This thing shook the bottom out of all my Sunday-school teachings. That boy had been notoriously worldly, and I just the reverse; yet he was exalted to this eminence, and I left in obscurity and misery. There was nothing generous about this fellow in his greatness. He would always manage to have a rusty bolt to scrub while his boat tarried at our town, and he would sit on the inside guard and scrub it, where we all could see him and envy him and loathe him. And whenever his boat was laid up he would come home and swell around the town in his blackest and greasiest clothes, so that nobody could help remembering that he was a steamboatman; and he used all sorts of steamboat technicalities in his talk, as if he were so used to them that he forgot common people could not understand them. He would speak of the "labboard" side of a horse in an easy, natural way that would make one wish he was dead. And he was always talking about "St. Looey" like an old citizen; he would refer casually to occasions when he was "coming down Fourth Street," or when he was "passing by the Planter's House," or when there was a fire and he took a turn on the brakes of "the old Big Missouri;" and then he would go on and lie about how many towns the size of ours were burned down there that day. Two or three of the boys had long been persons of consideration among us because they had been to St. Louis once and had a vague general knowledge of its wonders, but the day of their glory was over now. They lapsed into a humble silence, and learned to disappear when the ruthless "cub"-engineer approached. This fellow had money, too, and hair oil. Also an ignorant silver watch and a showy brass watch-chain. He wore a leather belt and used no suspenders. If ever a youth was cordially admired and hated by his comrades, this one was. No girl could withstand his charms. He "cut out" every boy in the village. When his boat blew up at last, it diffused a tranquil contentment among us such as we had not known for months. But when he came home the next week, alive, renowned, and appeared in church all battered up and bandaged, a shining hero, stared at and wondered over by everybody, it seemed to us that the partiality of Providence for an undeserving reptile had reached a point where it was open to criticism.

This creature's career could produce but one result, and it speedily followed. Boy after boy managed to get on the river. The minister's son became an engineer. The doctor's and the postmaster's sons became "mud clerks;" the wholesale liquor dealer's son became a barkeeper on a boat;

four sons of the chief merchant, and two sons of the county judge, became pilots. Pilot was the grandest position of all. The pilot, even in those days of trivial wages, had a princely salary—from a hundred and fifty to two hundred and fifty dollars a month, and no board to pay. Two months of his wages would pay a preacher's salary for a year. Now some of us were left disconsolate. We could not get on the river—at least our parents would not let us.

So by and by I ran away. I said I would never come home again till I was a pilot and could come in glory. But somehow I could not manage it. I went meekly aboard a few of the boats that lay packed together like sardines at the long St. Louis wharf, and very humbly inquired for the pilots, but got only a cold shoulder and short words from mates and clerks. I had to make the best of this sort of treatment for the time being, but I had comforting day-dreams of a future when I should be a great and honored pilot, with plenty of money, and could kill some of these mates and clerks and pay for them.

I WANT TO BE A CUB-PILOT

Months afterward the hope within me struggled to a reluctant death, and I found myself without an ambition. But I was ashamed to go home. I was in Cincinnati, and I set to work to map out a new career. I had been reading about the recent exploration of the river Amazon by an expedition sent out by our government. It was said that the expedition, owing to difficulties, had not thoroughly explored a part of the country lying about the headwaters, some four thousand miles from the mouth of the river. It was only about fifteen hundred miles from Cincinnati to New Orleans, where I could doubtless get a ship. I had thirty dollars left; I would go and complete the exploration of the Amazon. This was all the thought I gave to the subject. I never was great in matters of detail. I packed my valise, and took passage on an ancient tub called the "Paul Jones," for New Orleans. For the sum of sixteen dollars I had the scarred and tarnished splendor of "her" main saloon principally to myself, for she was not a creature to attract the eye of wiser travelers.

When we presently got under way and went poking down the broad Ohio, I became a new being, and the subject of my own admiration. I was a traveller! A word never had tasted so good in my mouth before. I had an exultant sense of being bound for mysterious lands and distant climes which I never have felt in so uplifting a degree since. I was in such a glorified condition that all ignoble feelings departed out of me, and I was able to look down and pity the untravelled with a compassion that had hardly a trace of contempt in it. Still, when we stopped at villages and wood-yards, I could not help lolling carelessly upon the railings of the boiler deck to enjoy the envy of the country boys on the bank. If they did not seem to discover me, I presently sneezed to attract their attention, or moved to a position where they could not help seeing me. And as soon as I knew they saw me I gaped and stretched, and gave other signs of being mightily bored with travelling.

I kept my hat off all the time, and stayed where the wind and the sun could strike me, because I wanted to get the bronzed and weather-beaten look of an old traveller. Before the second day was half gone, I experienced a joy which filled me with the purest gratitude; for I saw that the skin had begun to blister and peel off my face and neck. I wished that the boys and girls at home could see me now.

We reached Louisville in time—at least the neighborhood of it. We stuck hard and fast on the rocks in the middle of the river, and lay there four days. I was now beginning to feel a strong sense of being a part of the boat's family, a sort of infant son to the captain and younger brother to the officers. There is no estimating the pride I took in this grandeur, or the affection that began to swell and grow in me for those people. I could not know how the lordly steamboatman scorns that sort of presumption in a mere landsman. I particularly longed to acquire the least trifle of notice from the big stormy mate, and I was on the alert for an opportunity to do him a service to that end. It came at last. The riotous powwow of setting a spar was going on down on the forecastle, and I went down there and stood around in the way—or mostly skipping out of it—till the mate suddenly roared a general order for somebody to bring him a capstan bar. I sprang to his side and said: "Tell me where it is—I 'll fetch it!"

If a rag-picker had offered to do a diplomatic service for the Emperor of Russia, the monarch could not have been more astounded than the mate was. He even stopped swearing. He stood and stared down at me. It took him ten seconds to scrape his disjointed remains together again. Then he said impressively: "Well, if this don't beat hell!" and turned to his work with the air of a man who had been confronted with a problem too abstruse for solution.

I crept away, and courted solitude for the rest of the day. I did not go to dinner; I stayed away from supper until everybody else had finished. I did not feel so much like a member of the boat's family now as before. However, my spirits returned, in instalments, as we pursued our way down the river. I was sorry I hated the mate so, because it was not in (young) human nature not to admire him. He was huge and muscular, his face was bearded and whiskered all over; he had a red woman and a blue woman tattooed on his right arm,—one on each side of a blue anchor with a red rope to it; and in the matter of profanity he was sublime. When he was getting out cargo at a landing, I was always where I could see and hear. He felt all the majesty of his great position, and made the world feel it, too. When he gave even the simplest order, he discharged it like a blast of lightning, and sent a long, reverberating peal of profanity thundering after it. I could not help contrasting the way in which the average landsman would give an order, with the mate's way of doing it. If the landsman should wish the gang-plank moved a foot farther forward, he would probably say: "James, or William, one of you push the plank forward, please;" but put the mate in his place, and he would roar out: "Here, now, start that gang-plank for'ard! Lively, now! *What* 're you about! Snatch it! *snatch* it! There! there! Aft again! aft again! Don't you hear me? Dash it to dash! are you going to *sleep* over it! *'Vast* heaving. 'Vast heaving, I tell you! Going to heave it clear astern? WHERE 're you going with that barrel! *for'ard* with it 'fore I make you swallow it, you dash-dash-dash-*dashed* split between a tired mud-turtle and a crippled hearse-horse!"

I wished I could talk like that.

When the soreness of my adventure with the mate had somewhat worn off, I began timidly to make up to the humblest official connected with the boat—the night watchman. He snubbed my advances at first, but I presently ventured to offer him a new chalk pipe, and that softened him. So he allowed me to sit with him by the big bell on the hurricane deck, and in time he melted into conversation. He could not well have helped it, I hung with such homage on his words and so plainly showed that I felt honored by his notice. He told me the names of dim capes and shadowy islands as we glided by them in the solemnity of the night, under the winking stars, and by and by got to talking about himself. He seemed over-sentimental for a man whose salary was six dollars a week—or rather he might have seemed so to an older person than I. But I drank in his words hungrily, and with a faith that might have moved mountains if it had been applied judiciously. What was it to me that he was soiled and seedy and fragrant with gin? What was it to me that his grammar was bad, his construction worse, and his profanity so void of art that it was an element of weakness rather than strength in his conversation? He was a wronged man, a man who had seen trouble, and that was enough for me. As he mellowed into his plaintive history his tears dripped upon the lantern in his lap, and I cried, too, from sympathy. He said he was the son of an English nobleman—either an earl or an alderman, he could not remember which, but believed he was both; his father, the nobleman, loved him, but his mother hated him from the cradle; and so while he was still a little boy he was sent to "one of them old, ancient colleges"—he couldn't remember which; and by and by his father died and his mother seized the property and "shook" him, as he phrased it. After his mother shook him, members of the nobility with whom he was acquainted used their influence to get him the position of "loblolly-boy in a ship;" and from that point my watchman threw off all trammels of date and locality and branched out into a narrative that bristled all along with incredible adventures; a narrative that was so reeking with bloodshed, and so crammed with hair-breadth escapes and the most engaging and unconscious personal villanies, that I sat speechless, enjoying, shuddering, wondering, worshipping.

It was a sore blight to find out afterwards that he was a low, vulgar, ignorant, sentimental, half-witted humbug, an untravelled native of the wilds of Illinois, who had absorbed wildcat literature and appropriated its marvels, until in time he had woven odds and ends of the mess into this yarn, and then gone on telling it to fledglings like me, until he had come to believe it himself.

A CUB-PILOT'S EXPERIENCE

What with lying on the rocks four days at Louisville, and some other delays, the poor old "Paul Jones" fooled away about two weeks in making the voyage from Cincinnati to New Orleans. This gave me a chance to get acquainted with one of the pilots, and he taught me how to steer the boat, and thus made the fascination of river life more potent than ever for me.

It also gave me a chance to get acquainted with a youth who had taken deck passage—more's the pity; for he easily borrowed six dollars of me on a promise to return to the boat and pay it back to me the day after we should arrive. But he probably died or forgot, for he never came. It was doubtless the former, since he had said his parents were wealthy, and he only travelled deck passage because it was cooler.

I soon discovered two things. One was that a vessel would not be likely to sail for the mouth of the Amazon under ten or twelve years; and the other was that the nine or ten dollars still left in my pocket would not suffice for so impossible an exploration as I had planned, even if I could afford to wait for a ship. Therefore it followed that I must contrive a new career. The "Paul Jones" was now bound for St. Louis. I planned a siege against my pilot, and at the end of three hard days he surrendered. He agreed to teach me the Mississippi River from New Orleans to St. Louis for five hundred dollars, payable out of the first wages I should receive after graduation. I entered upon the small enterprise of "learning" twelve or thirteen hundred miles of the great Mississippi River with the easy confidence of my time of life. If I had really known what I was about to require of my faculties, I should not have had the courage to begin. I supposed that all a pilot had to do was to keep his boat in the river, and I did not consider that that could be much of a trick, since it was so wide.

The boat backed out from New Orleans at four in the afternoon, and it was "our watch" until eight. Mr. Bixby, my chief, "straightened her up," plowed her along past the sterns of the other boats that lay at the Levee, and then said, "Here, take her; shave those steamships as close as you'd peel an apple." I took the wheel, and my heart-beat fluttered up into the hundreds; for it seemed to me that we were about to scrape the side off every ship in the line, we were so close. I held my breath and began to claw the boat away from the danger; and I had my own opinion of the pilot who had known no better than to get us into such peril, but I was too wise to express it. In half a minute I had a wide margin of safety intervening between the "'Paul Jones" and the ships; and within ten seconds more I was set aside in disgrace, and Mr. Bixby was going into danger again and flaying me alive with abuse of my cowardice. I was stung, but I was obliged to admire the easy confidence with which my chief loafed from side to side of his wheel, and trimmed the ships so closely that disaster seemed ceaselessly imminent. When he had cooled a little he told me that the easy water was close ashore and the current outside, and therefore we must hug the bank, up-stream, to get the benefit of the former, and stay well out, down-stream, to take advantage of the latter. In my own mind I resolved to be a down-stream pilot and leave the up-streaming to people dead to prudence.

Now and then Mr. Bixby called my attention to certain things. Said he, "This is Six-Mile Point." I assented. It was pleasant enough information, but I could not see the bearing of it. I was not conscious that it was a matter of any interest to me. Another time he said, "This is Nine-Mile Point." Later he said, "This is Twelve-Mile Point." They were all about level with the water's edge; they all looked about alike to me; they were monotonously unpicturesque. I hoped Mr. Bixby would change the subject. But no; he would crowd up around a point, hugging the shore with affection, and then say: "The slack water ends here, abreast this bunch of China trees; now we cross over." So he crossed over. He gave me the wheel one or twice, but I had no luck. I either came near chipping off the edge of a sugar-plantation, or I yawed too far from shore, and so dropped back into disgrace again and got abused.

The watch was ended at last, and we took supper and went to bed. At midnight the glare of a lantern shone in my eyes, and the night watchman said: —

"Come! turn out!"

And then he left. I could not understand this extraordinary procedure; so I presently gave up trying to, and dozed off to sleep. Pretty soon the watchman was back again, and this time he was gruff. I was annoyed. I said: —

"What do you want to come bothering around here in the middle of the night for? Now, as like as not, I'll not get to sleep again to-night."

The watchman said: —

"Well, if this an't good, I'm blest."

The "off-watch" was just turning in, and I heard some brutal laughter from them and such remarks as "Hello, watchman! an't the new cub turned out yet? He's delicate, likely. Give him some sugar in a rag, and send for the chambermaid to sing rock-a-by-baby to him."

About this time Mr. Bixby appeared on the scene. Something like a minute later I was climbing the pilot-house steps with some of my clothes on and the rest in my arms. Mr. Bixby was close behind, commenting. Here was something fresh—this thing of getting up in the middle of the night to go to work. It was a detail in piloting that had never occurred to me at all. I knew that boats ran all night, but somehow I had never happened to reflect that somebody had to get up out of a warm bed to run them. I began to fear that piloting was not quite so romantic as I had imagined it was; there was something very real and worklike about this new phase of it.

It was a rather dingy night, although a fair number of stars were out. The big mate was at the wheel, and he had the old tub pointed at a star and was holding her straight up the middle of the river. The shores on either hand were not much more than half a mile apart, but they seemed wonderfully far away and ever so vague and indistinct. The mate said: —

"We've got to land at Jones's plantation, sir."

The vengeful spirit in me exulted. I said to myself, I wish you joy of your job, Mr. Bixby; you'll have a good time finding Mr. Jones's plantation such a night as this; and I hope you never *will* find it as long as you live.

Mr. Bixby said to the mate: —

"Upper end of the plantation, or the lower?"

"Upper."

"I can't do it. The stumps there are out of water at this stage. It's no great distance to the lower, and you'll have to get along with that."

"All right, sir. If Jones don't like it, he'll have to lump it, I reckon."

And then the mate left. My exultation began to cool and my wonder to come up. Here was a man who not only proposed to find this plantation on such a night, but to find either end of it you preferred. I dreadfully wanted to ask a question, but I was carrying about as many short answers as my cargo-room would admit of, so I held my peace. All I desired to ask Mr. Bixby was the simple question whether he was ass enough to really imagine he was going to find that plantation on a night when all plantations were exactly alike and all of the same color. But I held in. I used to have fine inspirations of prudence in those days.

Mr. Bixby made for the shore and soon was scraping it, just the same as if it had been daylight. And not only that, but singing —

"Father in heaven, the day is declining," etc.

It seemed to me that I had put my life in the keeping of a peculiarly reckless outcast. Presently he turned on me and said: —

"What's the name of the first point above New Orleans?"

I was gratified to be able to answer promptly, and I did. I said I did n't know.

"Don't *know?*"

This manner jolted me. I was down at the foot again, in a moment. But I had to say just what I had said before.

"Well, you're a smart one," said Mr. Bixby. "What's the name of the *next* point?"

Once more I did n't know.

"Well, this beats anything. Tell me the name of *any* point or place I told you."

I studied a while and decided that I could n't.

"Look here! What do you start out from, above Twelve-Mile Point, to cross over?"

"I—I—don't know."

"You—you—don't know?" mimicking my drawling manner of speech. "What *do* you know?"

"I—I—nothing, for certain."

"By the great Caesar's ghost, I believe you! You're the stupidest dunder-head I ever saw or heard of, so help me Moses! The idea of *you* being a pilot — *you!* Why, you don't know enough to pilot a cow down a lane."

Oh, but his wrath was up! He was a nervous man, and he shuffled from one side of his wheel to the other as if the floor was hot. He would boil awhile to himself, and then overflow and scald me again.

"Look here! What do you suppose I told you the names of those points for?"

I tremblingly considered a moment, and then the devil of temptation provoked me to say : —

"Well to—to—be entertaining, I thought."

This was a red rag to the bull. He raged and stormed so (he was crossing the river at the time) that I judged it made him blind, because he ran over the steering-oar of a trading-scow. Of course the traders sent up a volley of red-hot profanity. Never was a man so grateful as Mr. Bixby was: because he was brim ful, and here were subjects who would *talk back*. He threw open a window, thrust his head out, and such an irruption followed as I never had heard before. The fainter and farther away the scowmen's curses drifted, the higher Mr. Bixby lifted his voice and the weightier his adjectives grew. When he closed the window he was empty. You could have drawn a seine through his system and not caught curses enough to disturb your mother with. Presently he said to me in the gentlest way : —

"My boy, you must get a little memorandum-book; and every time I tell you a thing, put it down right away. There's only one way to be a pilot, and that is to get this entire river by heart. You have to know it just like A B C."

That was a dismal revelation to me; for my memory was never loaded with anything but blank cartridges. However, I did not feel discouraged long. I judged that it was best to make some allowances, for doubtless Mr. Bixby was "stretching." Presently he pulled a rope and struck a few strokes on the big bell. The stars were all gone now, and the night was as black as ink. I could hear the wheels churn along the bank, but I was not entirely certain that I could see the shore. The voice of the invisible watchman called up from the hurricane deck: —

"What's this, sir?"

"Jones's plantation."

I said to myself, I wish I might venture to offer a small bet that it is n't. But I did not chirp. I only waited to see. Mr. Bixby handled the engine bells, and in due time the boat's nose came to the land, a torch glowed from the forecastle, a man skipped ashore, a darky's voice on the bank said, "Gimme de k'yarpetbag, Mars' Jones," and the next moment we were standing up the river again, all serene. I reflected deeply a while, and then said,—but not aloud,—Well, the finding of that plantation was the luckiest accident that ever happened; but it could n't happen again in a hundred years. And I fully believed it *was* an accident, too.

By the time we had gone seven or eight hundred miles up the river, I had learned to be a tolerably plucky upstream steersman, in daylight, and before we reached St. Louis I had made a trifle of progress in night-work, but only a trifle. I had a note-book that fairly bristled with the names of towns, "points," bars, islands, bends, reaches, etc.; but the information was to be found only in the note-book—none of it was in my head. It made my heart ache to think I had only got half of the river set down; for as our watch was four hours off and four hours on, day and night, there was a long four-hour gap in my book for every time I had slept since the voyage began.

My chief was presently hired to go on a big New Orleans boat, and I packed my satchel and went with him. She was a grand affair. When I stood in her pilot-house I was so far above the water that I seemed perched on a mountain; and her decks stretched so far away, fore and aft, below me, that I wondered how I could ever have considered the little "Paul Jones" a large craft. There were other differences, too. The "Paul Jones's" pilothouse was a cheap, dingy, battered rattle-trap, cramped for room: but here was a sumptuous glass temple; room enough to have a dance in; showy red and gold window-curtains; an imposing sofa; leather cushions and a back to the high bench where visiting pilots sit, to spin yarns and "look at the river;" bright fanciful "cuspadores," instead of a broad wooden box filled with sawdust; nice new oilcloth on the floor; a hospitable big stove for winter; a wheel as high as my head, costly with inlaid work; a wire tiller-rope; bright brass knobs for the bells; and a tidy, white-aproned, black "texas-tender," to bring up tarts and ices and coffee during mid-watch, day and night. Now this was "something like;" and so I began to take heart once more to believe that piloting was a romantic sort of occupation after all. The moment we were under way I began to prowl about the great steamer and fill myself with joy. She was as clean and as dainty as a drawing-room; when I looked down her long, gilded saloon, it was like gazing through a splendid tunnel; she had an oil-picture, by some gifted sign-painter, on every stateroom door; she glittered with no end of prism-fringed chande-liers; the clerk's office was elegant, the bar was marvellous, and the bar-keeper had been barbered and upholstered at incredible cost. The boiler deck (*i.e.*, the second story of the boat, so to speak), was as spacious as a church, it seemed to me; so with the forecastle; and there was no pitiful handful of deck-hands, firemen, and roustabouts down there, but a whole battalion of men. The fires were fiercely glaring from a long row of fur-naces, and over them were eight huge boilers! This was unutterable pomp. The mighty engines—but enough of this. I had never felt so fine before. And when I found that the regiment of natty servants respectfully "sir'd" me, my satisfaction was complete.

.   .   .

CONTINUED PERPLEXITIES

There was no use in arguing with a person like this. I promptly put such a strain on my memory that by and by even the shoal water and the countless crossing-marks began to stay with me. But the result was just the same. I never could more than get one knotty thing learned before another pre-sented itself. Now I had often seen pilots gazing at the water and pretending to read it as if it were a book; but it was a book that told me nothing. A time came at last, however, when Mr. Bixby seemed to think me far enough advanced to bear a lesson on water-reading. So he began: —

"Do you see that long, slanting line on the face of the water? Now, that 's a reef. Moreover it 's a bluff reef. There is a solid sandbar under it that is nearly as straight up and down as the side of a house. There is plenty of water close up to it, but mighty little on top of it. If you were to hit it you would knock the boat's brains out. Do you see where the line fringes out at the upper end and begins to fade away?"

"Yes, sir."

"Well, that is a low place; that is the head of the reef. You can climb over there, and not hurt anything. Cross over, now, and follow along close under the reef—easy water there—not much current."

I followed the reef along till I approached the fringed end. Then Mr. Bixby said, —

"Now get ready. Wait till I give the word. She won't want to mount the reef; a boat hates shoal water. Stand by—wait—*wait*—keep her well in hand. *Now* cramp her down! Snatch her! snatch her!"

He seized the other side of the wheel and helped to spin it around until it was hard down, and then we held it so. The boat resisted, and refused to answer for a while, and next she came surging to starboard, mounted the reef, and sent a long, angry ridge of water foaming away from her bows.

"Now watch her; watch her like a cat, or she 'll get away from you. When she fights strong and the tiller slips a little, in a jerky, greasy sort of way, let up on her a trifle; it is the way she tells you at night that the water is too shoal; but keep edging her up, little by little, toward the point. You are well up on the bar, now; there is a bar under every point, because the water that comes down around it forms an eddy and allows the sediment to sink. Do you see those fine lines on the face of the water that branch out like the ribs of a fan? Well, those are little reefs; you want to just miss the ends of them, but run them pretty close. Now look out—look out! Don't you crowd that slick, greasy-looking place; there ain't nine feet there; she won't stand it. She begins to smell it; look sharp, I tell you! Oh, blazes, there you go! Stop the starboard wheel! Quick! Ship up to back! Set her back!"

The engine bells jingled and the engines answered promptly, shooting white columns of steam far aloft out of the 'scape pipes, but it was too late. The boat had "smelt" the bar in good earnest; the foamy ridges that radiated from her bows suddenly disappeared, a great dead swell came rolling forward, and swept ahead of her, she careened far over to larboard, and went tearing away toward the other shore as if she were about scared to death. We were a good mile from where we ought to have been, when we finally got the upper hand of her again.

During the afternoon watch the next day, Mr. Bixby asked me if I knew how to run the next few miles. I said: —

"Go inside the first snag above the point, outside the next one, start out from the lower end of Higgins's wood-yard, make a square crossing, and—

"That 's all right. I 'll be back before you close up on the next point."

But he was n't. He was still below when I rounded it and entered upon a piece of the river which I had some misgivings about. I did not know that he was hiding behind a chimney to see how I would perform. I went gayly along, getting prouder and prouder, for he had never left the boat in my sole charge such a length of time before. I even got to "setting" her and letting the wheel go, entirely, while I vaingloriously turned my back and inspected the stern marks and hummed a tune, a sort of easy indifference which I had prodigiously admired in Bixby and other great pilots. Once I inspected rather long, and when I faced to the front again my heart flew into my mouth so suddenly that if I had n't clapped my teeth together I should have lost it. One of those frightful bluff reefs was stretching its deadly length right across our bows! My head was gone in a moment; I did not know which end I stood on; I gasped and could not get my breath; I spun the wheel down with such rapidity that it wove itself together like a spider's web; the boat answered and turned square away from the reef, but the reef followed her! I fled, but still it followed still it kept—right across my bows! I never looked to see where I was going, I only fled. The awful crash was imminent. Why did n't that villain come? If I committed the crime of ringing a bell, I might get thrown overboard. But better that than kill the

boat. So in blind desperation I started such a rattling "shivaree" down below as never had astounded an engineer in this world before, I fancy. Amidst the frenzy of the bells the engines began to back and fill in a furious way, and my reason forsook its throne—we were about to crash into the woods on the other side of the river. Just then Mr. Bixby stepped calmly into view on the hurricane deck. My soul went out to him in gratitude. My distress vanished; I would have felt safe on the brink of Niagara, with Mr. Bixby on the hurricane deck. He blandly and sweetly took his tooth-pick out of his mouth between his fingers, as if it were a cigar,—we were just in the act of climbing an overhanging big tree, and the passengers were scudding astern like rats,—and lifted up these commands to me ever so gently:
—

"Stop the starboard. Stop the larboard. Set her back on both."

The boat hesitated, halted, pressed her nose among the boughs a critical instant, then reluctantly began to back away.

"Stop the larboard. Come ahead on it. Stop the starboard. Come ahead on it. Point her for the bar."

I sailed away as serenely as a summer's morning. Mr. Bixby came in and said, with mock simplicity, —

"When you have a hail, my boy, you ought to tap the big bell three times before you land, so that the engineers can get ready."

I blushed under the sarcasm, and said I had n't had any hail.

"Ah! Then it was for wood, I suppose. The officer of the watch will tell you when he wants to wood up."

I went on consuming, and said I was n't after wood.

"Indeed? Why, what could you want over here in the bend, then? Did you ever know of a boat following a bend up-stream at this stage of the river?"

"No, sir,—and I was n't trying to follow it. I was getting away from a bluff reef."

"No, it was n't a bluff reef; there is n't one within three miles of where you were."

"But I saw it. It was as bluff as that one yonder."

"Just about, Run over it!"

"Do you give it as an order?"

"Yes. Run over it!"

"If I don't, I wish I may die."

"All right; I am taking the responsibility."

I was just as anxious to kill the boat, now, as I had been to save it before. I impressed my orders upon my memory, to be used at the inquest, and made a straight break for the reef. As it disappeared under our bows I held my breath; but we slid over it like oil.

"Now, don't you see the difference? It was n't anything but a *wind* reef. The wind does that."

"So I see. But it is exactly like a bluff reef. How am I ever going to tell them apart?"

"I can't tell you. It is an instinct. By and by you will just naturally *know* one from the other, but you never will be able to explain why or how you know them apart."

It turned out to be true. The face of the water, in time, became a wonderful book—a book that was a dead language to the uneducated passenger, but which told its mind to me without reserve, delivering its most cherished secrets as clearly as if it uttered them with a voice. And it was not a book to be read once and thrown aside, for it had a new story to tell every day. Throughout the long twelve hundred miles there was never a page that was void of interest, never one that you could leave unread without loss, never one that you would want to skip, thinking you could find higher enjoyment in some other thing. There never was so wonderful a book written by man; never one whose interest was so absorbing, so unflagging, so sparklingly renewed with every re-perusal. The passenger who could not read it was charmed with a peculiar sort of faint dimple on its surface (on the rare occasions when he did not overlook it altogether); but to the pilot that was an *italicized* passage; indeed, it was more than that, it was a legend of the largest capitals, with a string of shouting exclamation points at the end of it; for it meant that a wreck or a rock was buried there that could tear the life out of the strongest vessel that ever floated. It is the faintest and simplest expression the water ever makes, and the most hideous to a pilot's eye. In truth, the passenger who could not read this book saw nothing but all manner of pretty pictures in it, painted by the sun and shaded by the clouds, whereas to the trained eye these were not pictures at all, but the grimmest and most dead-earnest of reading-matter.

Now when I had mastered the language of this water and had come to know every trifling feature that bordered the great river as familiarly as I knew the letters of the alphabet, I had made a valuable acquisition. But I had lost something, too. I had lost something which could never be restored to me while I lived. All the grace, the beauty, the poetry, had gone out of the majestic river! I still keep in mind a certain wonderful sunset which I witnessed when steamboating was new to me. A broad expanse of the river was turned to blood; in the middle distance the red hue brightened into gold, through which a solitary log came floating, black and conspicuous; in one place a long, slanting mark lay sparkling upon the water; in another the surface was broken by boiling, tumbling rings, that were as many-tinted as an opal; where the ruddy flush was faintest, was a smooth spot that was covered with graceful circles and radiating lines, ever so delicately traced; the shore on our left was densely wooded, and the sombre shadow that fell from this forest was broken in one place by a long ruffled trail that shone like silver; and high above the forest wall a clean-stemmed dead tree waved a single leafy bough that glowed like a flame in the unobstructed splendor that was flowing from the sun. There were graceful curves, reflected images, woody heights, soft distances; and over the whole scene, far and near, the dissolving lights drifted steadily, enriching it, every passing moment, with new marvels of coloring.

I stood like one bewitched. I drank it in, in a speechless rapture. The world was new to me, and I had never seen anything like this at home. But as I have said, a day came when I began to cease from noting the glories and the charms which the moon and the sun and the twilight wrought upon the river's face; another day came when I ceased altogether to note them. Then, if that sunset scene had been repeated, I should have looked upon it without rapture, and should have commented upon it, inwardly, after this fashion: This sun means that we are going to have wind to-morrow; that floating log means that the river is rising, small thanks to it; that slanting mark on the water refers to a bluff reef which is going to kill somebody's steamboat one of these nights, if it keeps on stretching out like that; those tumbling "boils" show a dissolving bar and a changing channel there; the lines and circles in the slick water over yonder are a warning that that troublesome place is shoaling up dangerously; that silver streak in the shadow of the forest is the "break" from a new snag, and he has located himself in the very best place he could have found to fish for steamboats; that tall dead tree, with a single living branch, is not going to last long, and then how is a body ever going to get through this blind place at night without the friendly old landmark?

No, the romance and beauty were all gone from the river. All the value any feature of it had for me now was the amount of usefulness it could furnish toward compassing the safe piloting of a steamboat. Since those days, I have pitied doctors from my heart. What does the lovely flush in a beauty's cheek mean to a doctor but a "break" that ripples above some deadly disease? Are not all her visible charms sown thick with what are to him the signs and symbols of hidden decay? Does he ever see her beauty at all, or does n't he simply view her professionally, and comment upon her unwholesome condition all to himself? And does n't he sometimes wonder whether he has gained most or lost most by learning his trade?

. . .

RANK AND DIGNITY OF PILOTING

In my preceding chapters I have tried, by going into the minutiæ of the science of piloting, to carry the reader step by step to a comprehension of what the science consists of; and at the same time I have tried to show him that it is a very curious and wonderful science, too, and very worthy of his attention. If I have seemed to love my subject, it is no surprising thing, for I loved the profession far better than any I have followed since, and I took a measureless pride in it. The reason is plain: a pilot, in those days, was the only unfettered and entirely independent human being that lived in the earth. Kings are but the hampered servants of parliament and the people; parliaments sit in chains forged by their constituency; the editor of a newspaper cannot be independent, but must work with one hand tied behind him by party and patrons, and be content to utter only half or two thirds of his mind; no clergyman is a free man and may speak the whole truth, regardless of his parish's opinions; writers of all kinds are manacled servants of the public. We write frankly and fearlessly, but then we "modify" before we print. In truth, every man and woman and child has a master, and worries and frets in servitude; but in the day I write of, the Mississippi pilot had *none*. The captain could stand upon the hurricane deck, in the pomp of a very brief authority, and give him five or six orders while the vessel backed into the stream, and then that skipper's reign was over. The moment that the boat was under way in the river, she was under the sole and unquestioned control of the pilot. He could do with her exactly as he pleased, run her when and whither he chose, and tie her up to the bank whenever his judgment said that that course was best. His movements were entirely free; he consulted no one, he received commands from nobody, he promptly resented even the merest suggestions. Indeed, the law of the United States forbade him to listen to commands or suggestions, rightly considering that the pilot necessarily knew better how to handle the boat than anybody could tell him. So here was the novelty of a king without a keeper, an absolute monarch who was absolute in sober truth and not by a fiction of words. I have seen a boy of eighteen taking a great steamer serenely into what seemed almost certain destruction, and the aged captain standing mutely by, filled with apprehension but powerless to interfere. His interference, in that particular instance, might have been an excellent thing, but to permit it would have been to establish a most pernicious precedent. It will easily be guessed, considering the pilot's boundless authority, that he was a great personage in the old steamboating days. He was treated with marked courtesy by the captain and with marked deference by all the officers and servants; and this deferential spirit was quickly communicated to the passengers, too. I think pilots were about the only people I ever knew who failed to show, in some degree, embarrassment in the presence of travelling foreign princes. But then, people in one's own grade of life are not usually embarrassing objects.

By long habits, pilots came to put all their wishes in the form of commands. It "gravels" me, to this day, to put my will in the weak shape of a request, instead of launching it in the crisp language of an order.

In those old days, to load a steamboat at St. Louis, take her to New Orleans and back, and discharge cargo, consumed about twenty-five days, on an average. Seven or eight of these days the boat spent at the wharves of St.

Louis and New Orleans, and every soul on board was hard at work, except the two pilots; *they* did nothing but play gentleman up town, and receive the same wages for it as if they had been on duty. The moment the boat touched the wharf at either city, they were ashore; and they were not likely to be seen again till the last bell was ringing and everything in readiness for another voyage.

When a captain got hold of a pilot of particularly high reputation, he took pains to keep him. When wages were four hundred dollars a month on the Upper Mississippi, I have known a captain to keep such a pilot in idleness, under full pay, three months at a time, while the river was frozen up. And one must remember that in those cheap times four hundred dollars was a salary of almost inconceivable splendor. Few men on shore got such pay as that, and when they did they were mightily looked up to. When pilots from either end of the river wandered into our small Missouri village, they were sought by the best and the fairest, and treated with exalted respect. Lying in port under wages was a thing which many pilots greatly enjoyed and appreciated; especially if they belonged in the Missouri River in the heyday of that trade (Kansas times), and got nine hundred dollars a trip, which was equivalent to about eighteen hundred dollars a month. Here is a conversation of that day. A chap out of the Illinois River, with a little stern-wheel tub, accosts a couple of ornate and gilded Missouri River pilots: —

"Gentlemen, I've got a pretty good trip for the up-country, and shall want you about a month. How much will it be?"

"Eighteen hundred dollars apiece."

"Heavens and earth! You take my boat, let me have your wages, and I'll divide!"

I will remark, in passing, that Mississippi steamboatmen were important in landsmen's eyes (and in their own, too, in a degree) according to the dignity of the boat they were on. For instance, it was a proud thing to be of the crew of such stately craft as the "Aleck Scott" or the "Grand Turk." Negro firemen, deck hands, and barbers belonging to those boats were distinguished personages in their grade of life, and they were well aware of that fact, too. A stalwart darkey once gave offense at a negro ball in New Orleans by putting on a good many airs. Finally one of the managers bustled up to him and said, —

"Who *is* you, any way? Who *is* you? dat's what *I* wants to know!"

The offender was not disconcerted in the least, but swelled himself up and threw that into his voice which showed that he knew he was not putting on all those airs on a stinted capital.

"Who *is* I? Who *is* I? I let you know mighty quick who I is! I want you niggers to understan' dat I fires de middle do' on de 'Aleck Scott!'"

That was sufficient.

The barber of the "Grand Turk" was a spruce young negro, who aired his importance with balmy complacency, and was greatly courted by the circle in which he moved. The young colored population of New Orleans were much given to flirting, at twilight, on the banquettes of the back streets. Somebody saw and heard something like the following, one evening, in one of those localities. A middle-aged negro woman projected her head through a broken pane and shouted (very willing that the neighbors should hear and envy), "You Mary Ann, come in de house dis minute! Stannin' out dah foolin' 'long wid dat low trash, an' heah's de barber off'n de 'Gran' Turk' wants to conwerse wid you!"

My reference, a moment ago, to the fact that a pilot's peculiar official position placed him out of the reach of criticism or command, brings Stephen W——naturally to my mind. He was a gifted pilot, a good fellow, a tireless talker, and had both wit and humor in him. He had a most irreverent independence, too, and was deliciously easy-going and comfortable in the presence of age, official dignity, and even the most august wealth. He always had work, he never saved a penny, he was a most persuasive borrower, he was in debt to every pilot on the river, and to the majority of captains. He could throw a sort of splendor around a bit of harum-scarum, devil-may-care piloting, that made it almost fascinating—but not to everybody. He made a trip with good old Captain Y—— once, and was "relieved" from duty when the boat got to New Orleans. Somebody expressed surprise at the discharge. Captain Y—— shuddered at the mere mention of Stephen. Then his poor, thin old voice piped out something like this:

"Why, bless me! I would n't have such a wild creature on my boat for the world—not for the whole world! He swears, he sings, he whistles, he yells —I never saw such an Injun to yell. All times of the night—it never made any difference to him. He would just yell that way, not for anything in particular, but merely on account of a kind of devilish comfort he got out of it. I never could get into a sound sleep but he would fetch me out of bed, all in a cold sweat, with one of those dreadful war-whoops. A queer being,—very queer being; no respect for anything or anybody. Sometimes he called me 'Johnny.' And he kept a fiddle, and a cat. He played execrably. This seemed to distress the cat, and so the cat would howl. Nobody could sleep where that man—and his family—was. And reckless ? There never was anything like it. Now you may believe it or not, but as sure as I am sitting here, he brought my boat a-tilting down through those awful snags at Chicot under a rattling head of steam, and the wind a-blowing like the very nation, at that! My officers will tell you so. They saw it. And, sir, while he was a-tearing right down through those snags, and I a-shaking in my shoes and praying, I wish I may never speak again if he didn't pucker up his mouth and go to *whistling*! Yes, sir; whistling 'Buffalo gals, can't you come out to-night, can't you come out to-night, can't you come out to-night;' and doing it as calmly as if we were attending a funeral and were n't related to the corpse. And when I remonstrated with him about it, he smiled down on me as if I was his child, and told me to run in the house and try to be good, and not be meddling with my superiors!"

Once a pretty mean captain caught Stephen in New Orleans out of work and as usual out of money. He laid steady siege to Stephen, who was in a very "close place," and finally persuaded him to hire with him at one hundred and twenty-five dollars per month, just half wages, the captain agreeing not to divulge the secret and so bring down the contempt of all the guild upon the poor fellow. But the boat was not more than a day out of New Orleans before Stephen discovered that the captain was boasting of his exploit, and that all the officers had been told. Stephen winced, but said nothing. About the middle of the afternoon the captain stepped out on the hurricane deck, cast his eye around, and looked a good deal surprised. He glanced inquiringly aloft at Stephen, but Stephen was whistling placidly, and attending to business. The captain stood around a while in evident discomfort, and once or twice seemed about to make a suggestion; but the etiquette of the river taught him to avoid that sort of rashness, and so he managed to hold his peace. He chafed and puzzled a few minutes longer, then retired to his apartments. But soon he was out again, and apparently more perplexed than ever. Presently he ventured to remark, with deference,

—

"Pretty good stage of the river now, ain't it, sir?"

"Well, I should say so! Bank-full *is* a pretty liberal stage."

"Seems to be a good deal of current here."

"Good deal don't describe it! It's worse than a mill-race."

"Is n't it easier in toward shore than it is out here in the middle?"

"Yes, I reckon it is; but a body can't be too careful with a steamboat. It's pretty safe out here; can't strike any bottom here, you can depend on that."

The captain departed, looking rueful enough. At this rate, he would probably die of old age before his boat got to St. Louis. Next day he appeared on deck and again found Stephen faithfully standing up the middle of the river, fighting the whole vast force of the Mississippi, and whistling the same placid tune. This thing was becoming serious. In by the shore was a slower boat clipping along in the easy water and gaining steadily; she began to make for an island chute; Stephen stuck to the middle of the river. Speech was *wrung* from the captain. He said, —

"Mr. W————., don't that chute cut off a good deal of distance?"

"I think it does, but I don't know."

"Don't know! Well, is n't there water enough in it now to go through?"

"I expect there is, but I am not certain."

"Upon my word this is odd! Why, those pilots on that boat yonder are going to try it. Do you mean to say that you don't know as much as they do?"

"*They!* Why, *they* are two-hundred-and-fifty-dollar pilots! But don't you be uneasy; I know as much as any man can afford to know for a hundred and twenty-five!"

The captain surrendered.

Five minutes later Stephen was bowling through the chute and showing the rival boat a two-hundred-and-fifty-dollar pair of heels.

GEORGE WASHINGTON CABLE

(1844–1925)

Born in New Orleans to a family of mixed Virginian and New England ancestry and strong Calvinist belief, Cable grew up during the years when the city was still the chief export center for the burgeoning steamboat traffic of the Mississippi River system, transshipping cotton and other products of the Mississippi, Red, Missouri, and Ohio River areas to Europe and to the American Northeast. During the Civil War Cable served as a Confederate cavalryman and was twice wounded. He returned home after the war, secured work as a clerk, and soon began contributing a column of sketches and miscellaneous writings to the New Orleans *Picayune*. In 1873 *Scribner's Monthly* accepted his story " 'Sieur George," which together with additional stories of Creole New Orleans and Louisiana life became a book, *Old Creole Days*, in 1879. The volume was the first important work of Southern local-color literature. Heartened by his success with short fiction Cable began a novel, *The Grandissimes*, the reception of which, upon publication in 1880, impelled him to resign his post at the New Orleans Cotton Exchange and become a full-time writer. In 1884 he published a history, *The Creoles of Louisiana*, and a second novel, *Dr. Sevier*. Cable's presentation of antebellum Creole society drew the ire of leading Creoles, including Charles Etienne Gayarré, while his growing public dissent on the race issue developed into a definite break with Southern opinion. He had meanwhile begun extensive public lecturing and readings in the Northeast and Midwest, and in 1884, both in order to be nearer his literary and speaking assignments and because of growing hostility toward him in New Orleans, he moved his family to Simsbury, Connecticut, and a year later to Northampton, Massachusetts, where he resided for the remainder of his life. In 1884 and 1885 he took part in a celebrated joint-reading tour with Mark Twain.

Cable's work in fiction waned during the 1880s as he undertook a vigorous campaign on the lecture platform and in print to awaken the conscience of what he called the "silent South" to the wrong done to its black citizens. However, his outspoken views brought only hostility in the South and growing apathy in the North. In 1895 he published a new novel, *John March, Southerner*, set in northern Georgia. Though marred by a sentimental love plot, it recreates some of the problems and possibilities of the post-Reconstruction South such as were offered in no other fiction of the day. The novel was virtually ignored, however, and for a decade and more, except for some short stories and one psychological study of jealousy, *Bylow Hill* (1901), Cable turned to the writing of historical costume romance, including *The Cavalier* (1901), which was a best-seller, *Kincaid's Battery* (1908), and *Gideon's Band* (1914). Late in his life, however, Cable returned to Southern problems with two works of fiction, *Lovers of Louisiana* and *The Flower of the Chapdelaines*, both published in 1918. He died in Florida and was buried in Northampton.

BELLES DEMOISELLES PLANTATION

The original grantee was Count——, assume the name to be De Charleu; the old Creoles never forgive a public mention. He was the French king's commissary. One day, called to France to explain the lucky accident of the commissariat having burned down with his account-books inside, he left his wife, a Choctaw Comptesse, behind.

Arrived at court, his excuses were accepted, and that tract granted him where afterwards stood Belles Demoiselles Plantation. A man cannot remember every thing! In a fit of forgetfulness he married a French gentlewoman, rich and beautiful, and "brought her out." However, "All's well that ends well;" a famine had been in the colony, and the Choctaw Comptesse had starved, leaving nought but a half-caste orphan family lurking on the edge of the settlement, bearing our French gentlewoman's own new name, and being mentioned in Monsieur's will.

And the new Comptesse—she tarried but a twelve-month, left Monsieur a lovely son, and departed, led out of this vain world by the swamp-fever.

From this son sprang the proud Creole family of De Charleu. It rose straight up, up, up, generation after generation, tall, branchless, slender, palm-like; and finally, in the time of which I am to tell, flowered with all the rare beauty of a century-plant, in Artemise, Innocente, Felicité, the twins Marie and Martha, Leontine and little Septima; the seven beautiful daughters for whom their home had been fitly named Belles Demoiselles.

The Count's grant had once been a long Pointe, round which the Mississippi used to whirl, and seethe, and foam, that it was horrid to behold. Big whirlpools would open and wheel about in the savage eddies under the low bank, and close up again, and others open, and spin, and disappear. Great circles of muddy surface would boil up from hundreds of feet below, and gloss over, and seem to float away,—sink, come back again under water, and with only a soft hiss surge up again, and again drift off, and vanish. Every few minutes the loamy bank would tip down a great load of earth upon its besieger, and fall back a foot,—sometimes a yard,—and the writhing river would press after, until at last the Pointe was quite swallowed up, and the great river glided by in a majestic curve, and asked no more; the bank stood fast, the "caving" became a forgotten misfortune, and the diminished grant was a long, sweeping, willowy bend, rustling with miles of sugar-cane.

Coming up the Mississippi in the sailing craft of those early days, about the time one first could descry the white spires of the old St. Louis Cathedral, you would be pretty sure to spy, just over to your right under the levee, Belles Demoiselles Mansion, with its broad veranda and red painted cypress roof, peering over the embankment, like a bird in the nest, half hid by the avenue of willows which one of the departed De Charleus,—he that married a Marot,—had planted on the levee's crown.

The house stood unusually near the river, facing eastward, and standing four-square, with an immense veranda about its sides, and a flight of steps in front spreading broadly downward, as we open arms to a child. From the veranda nine miles of river were seen; and in their compass, near at hand, the shady garden full of rare and beautiful flowers; farther away broad fields of cane and rice, and the distant quarters of the slaves, and on the horizon everywhere a dark belt of cypress forest.

The master was old Colonel De Charleu,—Jean Albert Henri Joseph De Charleu-Marot, and "Colonel" by the grace of the first American governor. Monsieur,—he would not speak to any one who called him "Colonel," —was a hoary-headed patriarch. His step was firm, his form erect, his intellect strong and clear, his countenance classic, serene, dignified, commanding, his manners courtly, his voice musical,—fascinating. He had had his vices,—all his life; but had borne them, as his race do, with a serenity of conscience and a cleanness of mouth that left no outward blemish on the surface of the gentleman. He had gambled in Royal Street, drunk hard in Orleans Street, run his adversary through in the duelling-ground at Slaughter-house Point, and danced and quarrelled at the St. Philippe-street-theatre quadroon balls. Even now, with all his courtesy and bounty, and a hospitality which seemed to be entertaining angels, he was bitter-proud and penurious, and deep down in his hard-finished heart loved nothing but himself, his name, and his motherless children. But these!—their ravishing beauty was all but excuse enough for the unbounded idolatry of their father. Against these seven goddesses he never rebelled. Had they even required him to defraud old De Carlos —

I can hardly say.

Old De Carlos was his extremely distant relative on the Choctaw side. With this single exception, the narrow thread-like line of descent from the Indian wife, diminished to a mere strand by injudicious alliances, and deaths in the gutters of old New Orleans, was extinct. The name, by Spanish contact, had become De Carlos; but this one surviving bearer of it was known to all, and known only, as Injin Charlie.

One thing I never knew a Creole to do. He will not utterly go back on the ties of blood, no matter what sort of knots those ties may be. For one reason, he is never ashamed of his or his father's sins; and for another,—he will tell you—he is "all heart!"

So the different heirs of the De Charleu estate had always strictly regarded the rights and interests of the De Carloses, especially their ownership of a block of dilapidated buildings in a part of the city, which had once been very poor property, but was beginning to be valuable. This block had much more than maintained the last De Carlos through a long and lazy lifetime, and, as his household consisted only of himself, and an aged and crippled negress, the inference was irresistible that he "had money." Old Charlie, though by *alias* an "Injin," was plainly a dark white man, about as old as Colonel De Charleu, sunk in the bliss of deep ignorance, shrewd, deaf, and, by repute at least, unmerciful.

The Colonel and he always conversed in English. This rare accomplishment, which the former had learned from his Scotch wife,—the latter from up-river traders,—they found an admirable medium of communication, answering, better than French could, a similar purpose to that of the stick which we fasten to the bit of one horse and breast-gear of another, whereby each keeps his distance. Once in a while, too, by way of jest, English found its way among the ladies of Belles Demoiselles, always signifying that their sire was about to have business with old Charlie.

Now a long-standing wish to buy out Charlie troubled the Colonel. He had no desire to oust him unfairly; he was proud of being always fair; yet he did long to engross the whole estate under one title. Out of his luxurious idleness he had conceived this desire, and thought little of so slight an obstacle as being already somewhat in debt to old Charlie for money borrowed, and for which Belles Demoiselles was, of course, good, ten times over. Lots, buildings, rents, all, might as well be his, he thought, to give, keep, or destroy. "Had he but the old man's heritage. Ah! he might bring that into existence which his *belles demoiselles* had been begging for, 'since many years;' a home—and such a home,—in the gay city. Here he should tear down this row of cottages, and make his garden wall; there that long rope-walk should give place to vine-covered arbors; the bakery yonder should make way for a costly conservatory; that wine warehouse should come down, and the mansion go up. It should be the finest in the State. Men should never pass it, but they should say—'the palace of the De Charleus; a family of grand descent, a people of elegance and bounty, a line as old as France, a fine old man, and seven daughters as beautiful as happy; whoever dare attempt to marry there must leave his own name behind him!'

"The house should be of stones fitly set, brought down in ships from the land of 'les Yankees,' and it should have an airy belvedere, with a gilded image tip-toeing and shining on its peak, and from it you should see, far across the gleaming folds of the river, the red roof of Belles Demoiselles, the country-seat. At the big stone gate there should be a porter's lodge, and it should be a privilege even to see the ground."

Truly they were a family fine enough, and fancy-free enough to have fine wishes, yet happy enough where they were, to have had no wish but to live there always.

To those, who, by whatever fortune, wandered into the garden of Belles Demoiselles some summer afternoon as the sky was reddening towards evening, it was lovely to see the family gathered out upon the tiled pavement at the foot of the broad front steps, gayly chatting and jesting, with that ripple of laughter that comes so pleasingly from a bevy of girls. The father would be found seated in their midst, the centre of attention and compliment, witness, arbiter, umpire, critic, by his beautiful children's unanimous appointment, but the single vassal, too, of seven absolute sovereigns.

Now they would draw their chairs near together in eager discussion of some new step in the dance, or the adjustment of some rich adornment. Now they would start about him with excited comments to see the eldest fix a bunch of violets in his button-hole. Now the twins would move down a walk after some unusual flower, and be greeted on their return with the high pitched notes of delighted feminine surprise.

As evening came on they would draw more quietly about their paternal centre. Often their chairs were forsaken, and they grouped themselves on the lower steps, one above another, and surrendered themselves to the tender influences of the approaching night. At such an hour the passer on the river, already attracted by the dark figures of the broad-roofed mansion, and its woody garden standing against the glowing sunset, would hear the voices of the hidden group rise from the spot in the soft harmonies of an evening song; swelling clearer and clearer as the thrill of music warmed them into feeling, and presently joined by the deeper tones of the father's voice; then, as the daylight passed quite away, all would be still, and he would know that the beautiful home had gathered its nestlings under its wings.

And yet, for mere vagary, it pleased them not to be pleased.

"Arti!" called one sister to another in the broad hall, one morning, —mock amazement in her distended eyes,—"something is goin' to took place!"

"*Comm-e-n-t?*"—long-drawn perplexity.

"Papa is goin' to town!"

The news passed up stairs.

"Inno!"—one to another meeting in a doorway,—"something is goin' to took place!"

"*Qu'est-ce-que c'est!*"—vain attempt at gruffness.

"Papa is goin' to town!"

The unusual tidings were true. It was afternoon of the same day that the Colonel tossed his horse's bridle to his groom, and stepped up to old Charlie, who was sitting on his bench under a China-tree, his head as was his fashion, bound in a Madras handkerchief. The "old man" was plainly under the effect of spirits and smiled a deferential salutation without trusting himself to his feet.

"Eh, well Charlie!"—the Colonel raised his voice to suit his kinsman's deafness,—"how is those times with my friend Charlie?"

"Eh?" said Charlie, distractedly.

"Is that goin' well with my friend Charlie?"

"In de house,—call her," —making a pretence of rising.

"*Non, non!* I don't want,"—the speaker paused to breathe—"ow is collection?"

"Oh!" said Charlie, "every day he make me more poorer!"

"What do you hask for it?" asked the planter indifferently, designating the house by a wave of his whip.

"Ask for w'at?" said Injin Charlie.

"De *house!* What you ask for it?"

"I don't believe," said Charlie.

"What you would *take* for it!" cried the planter.

"Wait for w'at?"

"What you would *take* for the whole block?"

"I don't want to sell him!"

"I'll give you *ten thousand dollah* for it."

"Ten t'ousand dollah for dis house? Oh, no, dat is no price. He is blame good old house,—dat old house." (Old Charlie and the Colonel never swore in presence of each other.) "Forty years dat old house didn't had to be paint! I easy can get fifty t'ousand dollah for dat old house."

"Fifty thousand picayunes; yes," said the Colonel.

"She's a good house. Can make plenty money," pursued the deaf man.

"That's what make you so rich, eh, Charlie?"

"*Non*, I don't make nothing. Too blame clever, me, dat's de troub'. She's a good house,—make money fast like a steamboat,—make a barrel full in a week! Me, I lose money all de days. Too blame clever."

"Charlie!"

"Eh?"

"Tell me what you'll take."

"Make? I don't make *nothing*. Too blame clever."

"What will you *take?*"

"Oh! I got enough already,—half drunk now."

"What will you take for the 'ouse?"

"You want to buy her?"

"I don't know,"—(shrug),—"may*be*,—if you sell it cheap."

"She's a bully old house."

There was a long silence. By and by old Charlie commenced —

"Old Injin Charlie is a low-down dog."

"*C'est vrai, oui!*" retorted the Colonel in an undertone.

"He's got Injin blood in him."

The Colonel nodded assent.

"But he's got some blame good blood, too, ain't it?"

The Colonel nodded impatiently.

"*Bien!* Old Charlie's Injin blood says, 'sell de house, Charlie, you blame old fool!' *Mais*, old Charlie's good blood says, 'Charlie! if you sell dat old house, Charlie, you low-down old dog, Charlie, what de Compte De Charleu make for you grace-gran'-muzzer, de dev' can eat you, Charlie, I don't care.'"

"But you'll sell it anyhow, won't you, old man?"

"No!" And the *no* rumbled off in muttered oaths like thunder out on the Gulf. The incensed old Colonel wheeled and started off.

"Curl!" (Colonel) said Charlie, standing up unsteadily.

The planter turned with an inquiring frown.

"I'll trade with you!" said Charlie.

The Colonel was tempted. " 'Ow'l you trade?" he asked.

"My house for yours!"

The old Colonel turned pale with anger. He walked very quickly back, and came close up to his kinsman.

"Charlie!" he said.

"Injin Charlie,"—with a tipsy nod.

But by this time self-control was returning. "Sell Belles Demoiselles to you?" he said in a high key, and then laughed "Ho, ho, ho!" and rode away.

A cloud, but not a dark one, overshadowed the spirits of Belles Demoiselles' plantation. The old master, whose beaming presence had always made him a shining Saturn, spinning and sparkling within the bright circle of his daughters, fell into musing fits, started out of frowning reveries, walked often by himself, and heard business from his overseer fretfully.

No wonder. The daughters knew his closeness in trade, and attributed to it his failure to negotiate for the Old Charlie buildings,—so to call them. They began to depreciate Belles Demoiselles. If a north wind blew, it was too cold to ride. If a shower had fallen, it was too muddy to drive. In the morning the garden was wet. In the evening the grasshopper was a burden. *Ennui* was turned into capital; every headache was interpreted a premonition of ague; and when the native exuberance of a flock of ladies without a want or a care burst out in laughter in the father's face, they spread their French eyes, rolled up their little hands, and with rigid wrists and mock vehemence vowed and vowed again that they only laughed at their misery, and should pine to death unless they could move to the sweet city. "Oh! the theatre! Oh! Orleans Street! Oh! the masquerade! the Place d'Armes! the ball!" and they would call upon Heaven with French irreverence, and fall into each other's arms, and whirl down the hall singing a waltz, end with a grand collision and fall, and, their eyes streaming merriment, lay the blame on the slippery floor, that would some day be the death of the whole seven.

Three times more the fond father, thus goaded, managed, by accident, —business accident,—to see old Charlie and increase his offer; but in vain. He finally went to him formally.

"Eh?" said the deaf and distant relative. "For what you want him, eh? Why you don't stay where you halways be 'appy? Dis is a blame old rat-hole,—good for old Injin Charlie,—da's all. Why you don't stay where you be halways 'appy? Why you don't buy somewheres else?"

"That's none of your business," snapped the planter. Truth was, his reasons were unsatisfactory even to himself.

A sullen silence followed. Then Charlie spoke:

"Well, now, look here; I sell you old Charlie's house."

"*Bien!* and the whole block," said the Colonel.

"Hold on," said Charlie. "I sell you de 'ouse and de block. Den I go and git drunk, and go to sleep, de dev' comes along and says, 'Charlie! old Charlie, you blame low-down old dog, wake up! What you doin' here? Where's de 'ouse what Monsieur le Compte give your grace-gran-muzzer? Don't you see dat fine gentyman, De Charleu, done gone and tore him down and make him over new, you blame old fool, Charlie, you low-down old Injin dog!' "

"I'll give you forty thousand dollars," said the Colonel.

"For de 'ouse?"

"For all."

The deaf man shook his head.

"Forty-five!" said the Colonel.

"What a lie? For what you tell me 'What a lie?' I don't tell you no lie."

"*Non, non!* I give you *forty-five!*" shouted the Colonel.

Charlie shook his head again.

"Fifty!"

He shook it again.

The figures rose and rose to —

"Seventy-five!"

The answer was an invitation to go away and let the owner alone, as he was, in certain specified respects, the vilest of living creatures, and no company for a fine gentyman.

The "fine gentyman" longed to blaspheme,—but before old Charlie!—in the name of pride, how could he? He mounted and started away.

"Tell you what I'll make wid you," said Charlie.

The other, guessing aright, turned back without dismounting, smiling.

"How much Belles Demoiselles hoes me now?" asked the deaf one.

"One hundred and eighty thousand dollars," said the Colonel, firmly.

"Yass," said Charlie. "I don't want Belles Demoiselles."

The old Colonel's quiet laugh intimated it made no difference either way.

"But me," continued Charlie, "me,—I'm got le Compte De Charleu's blood in me, any'ow,—a litt' bit, any'ow, ain't it?"

The Colonel nodded that it was.

"*Bien!* If I go out of dis place and don't go to Belles Demoiselles, de peoples will say,—dey will say, 'Old Charlie he been all doze time tell a blame *lie!* He ain't no kin to his old grace-gran-muzzer, not a blame bit! He don't got nary drop of De Charleu blood to save his blame low-down old Injin soul!' No, sare! What I want wid money, den? No, sare! My place for yours!"

He turned to go into the house, just too soon to see the Colonel make an ugly whisk at him with his riding-whip. Then the Colonel, too, moved off.

Two or three times over, as he ambled homeward, laughter broke through his annoyance, as he recalled old Charlie's family pride and the presumption of his offer. Yet each time he could but think better of—not the offer to swap, but the preposterous ancestral loyalty. It was so much better than he could have expected from his "low-down" relative, and not unlike his own whim withal—the proposition which went with it was forgiven.

This last defeat bore so harshly on the master of Belles Demoiselles, that the daughters, reading chagrin in his face, began to repent. They loved their father as daughters can, and when they saw their pretended dejection harassing him seriously they restrained their complaints, displayed more than ordinary tenderness, and heroically and ostentatiously concluded there was no place like Belles Demoiselles. But the new mood touched him more than the old, and only refined his discontent. Here was a man, rich without the care of riches, free from any real trouble, happiness as native to his house as perfume to his garden, deliberately, as it were with premeditated malice, taking joy by the shoulder and bidding her be gone to town, whither he might easily have followed, only that the very same ancestral nonsense that kept Injin Charlie from selling the old place for twice its value prevented him from choosing any other spot for a city home.

But by and by the charm of nature and the merry hearts around him prevailed; the fit of exalted sulks passed off, and after a while the year flared up at Christmas, flickered, and went out.

New Year came and passed; the beautiful garden of Belles Demoiselles put on its spring attire; the seven fair sisters moved from rose to rose; the cloud of discontent had warmed into invisible vapor in the rich sunlight of family affection, and on the common memory the only scar of last year's wound was old Charlie's sheer impertinence in crossing the caprice of the De Charleus. The cup of gladness seemed to fill with the filling of the river.

How high that river was! Its tremendous current rolled and tumbled and spun along, hustling the long funeral flotillas of drift,—and how near shore it came! Men were out day and night, watching the levee. On windy nights even the old Colonel took part, and grew light-hearted with occupation and excitement, as every minute the river threw a white arm over the levee's top, as though it would vault over. But all held fast, and, as the summer drifted in, the water sunk down into its banks and looked quite incapable of harm.

On a summer afternoon of uncommon mildness, old Colonel Jean Albert Henri Joseph De Charleu-Marot, being in a mood for revery, slipped the custody of his feminine rulers and sought the crown of the levee, where it was his wont to promenade. Presently he sat upon a stone bench,—a favorite seat. Before him lay his broad-spread fields; near by, his lordly mansion; and being still,—perhaps by female contact,—somewhat sentimental, he fell to musing on his past. It was hardly worthy to be proud of. All its morning was reddened with mad frolic, and far toward the meridian it was marred with elegant rioting. Pride had kept him well-nigh useless, and despised the honors won by valor; gaming had dimmed prosperity; death had taken his heavenly wife; voluptuous ease had mortgaged his lands; and yet his house still stood, his sweet-smelling fields were still fruitful, his name was fame enough; and yonder and yonder, among the trees and flowers, like angels walking in Eden, were the seven goddesses of his only worship.

Just then a slight sound behind him brought him to his feet. He cast his eyes anxiously to the outer edge of the little strip of bank between the levee's base and the river. There was nothing visible. He paused, with his ear toward the water, his face full of frightened expectation. Ha! There came a single plashing sound, like some great beast slipping into the river, and little waves in a wide semi-circle came out from under the bank and spread over the water!

"My God!"

He plunged down the levee and bounded through the low weeds to the edge of the bank. It was sheer, and the water about four feet below. He did not stand quite on the edge, but fell upon his knees a couple of yards away, wringing his hands, moaning and weeping, and staring through his watery eyes at a fine, long crevice just discernible under the matted grass, and curving outward on either hand toward the river.

"My God!" he sobbed aloud; "my God!" and even while he called, his God answered: the tough Bermuda grass stretched and snapped, the crevice slowly became a gape, and softly, gradually, with no sound but the closing of the water at last, a ton or more of earth settled into the boiling eddy and disappeared.

At the same instant a pulse of the breeze brought from the garden behind, the joyous, thoughtless laughter of the fair mistresses of Belles Demoiselles.

The old Colonel sprang up and clambered over the levee. Then forcing himself to a more composed movement, he hastened into the house and ordered his horse.

"Tell my children to make merry while I am gone," he left word. "I shall be back to-night," and the horse's hoofs clattered down a by-road leading to the city.

"Charlie," said the planter, riding up to a window, from which the old man's nightcap was thrust out, "what you say, Charlie,—my house for yours, eh, Charlie—what you say?"

"Ello!" said Charlie; "from where you come from dis time of to-night?"

"I come from the Exchange in St. Louis Street." (A small fraction of the truth.)

"What you want?" said matter-of-fact Charlie.

"I come to trade."

The low-down relative drew the worsted off his ears. "Oh! yass," he said with an uncertain air.

"Well, old man Charlie, what you say: my house for yours,—like you said,—eh, Charlie?"

"I dunno," said Charlie; "it's nearly mine now. Why you don't stay dare youse'f?"

"*Because I don't want!*" said the Colonel savagely.

"Is dat reason enough for you? You better take me in de notion, old man, I tell you,—yes!"

Charlie never winced; but how his answer delighted the Colonel! Quoth Charlie:

"I don't care—I take him!—*mais*, possession give right off."

"Not the whole plantation, Charlie; only"—

"I don't care," said Charlie; "we easy can fix dat. *Mais*, what for you don't want to keep him? I don't want him. You better keep him."

"Don't you try to make no fool of me, old man," cried the planter.

"Oh, no!" said the other. "Oh, no! but you make a fool of yourself, ain't it?"

The dumbfounded Colonel stared; Charlie went on:

"Yass! Belles Demoiselles is more wort' dan tree block like dis one. I pass by dare since two weeks. Oh, pritty Belles Demoiselles! De cane was wave in de wind, de garden smell like a bouquet, de white-cap was jump up and down on de river; seven *belles demoiselles* was ridin' on horses. 'Pritty, pritty, pritty!' says old Charlie. Ah! *Monsieur le père*, 'ow 'appy, 'appy, 'appy!"

"Yass!" he continued—the Colonel still staring—"le Compte De Charleu have two familie. One was low-down Choctaw, one was high up *noblesse*. He gave the low-down Choctaw dis old rat-hole; he give Belles Demoiselles to you gran-fozzer; and now you don't be *satisfait*. What I'll do wid Belles Demoiselles? She'll break me in two years, yass. And what you'll do wid old Charlie's house, eh? You'll tear her down and make you'se'f a blame old fool. I rather wouldn't trade!"

The planter caught a big breathful of anger, but Charlie went straight on:

"I rather wouldn't, *mais* I will do it for you;—just the same, like Monsieur le Compte would say, 'Charlie, you old fool, I want to shange houses wid you.' "

So long as the Colonel suspected irony he was angry, but as Charlie seemed, after all, to be certainly in earnest, he began to feel conscience-stricken. He was by no means a tender man, but his lately-discovered misfortune had unhinged him, and this strange, undeserved, disinterested family fealty on the part of Charlie touched his heart. And should he still try to lead him into the pitfall he had dug? He hesitated;—no, he would show him the place by broad daylight, and if he chose to overlook the "caving bank," it would be his own fault;—a trade's a trade.

"Come," said the planter, "come at my house tonight; to-morrow we look at the place before breakfast, and finish the trade."

"For what?" said Charlie.

"Oh, because I got to come in town in the morning."

"I don't want," said Charlie. "How I'm goin' to come dere?"

"I git you a horse at the liberty stable."

"Well—anyhow—I don't care—I'll go." And they went.

When they had ridden a long time, and were on the road darkened by hedges of Cherokee rose, the Colonel called behind him to the "low-down" scion:

"Keep the road, old man."

"Eh?"

"Keep the road."

"Oh, yes; all right; I keep my word; we don't goin' to play no tricks, eh?"

But the Colonel seemed not to hear. His ungenerous design was beginning to be hateful to him. Not only old Charlie's unprovoked goodness was prevailing; the eulogy on Belles Demoiselles had stirred the depths of an intense love for his beautiful home. True, if he held to it, the caving of the bank, at its present fearful speed, would let the house into the river within three months; but were it not better to lose it so, than sell his birthright? Again,—coming back to the first thought,—to betray his own blood! It was only Injin Charlie; but had not the De Charleu blood just spoken out in him? Unconsciously he groaned.

After a time they struck a path approaching the plantation in the rear, and a little after, passing from behind a clump of live-oaks, they came in sight of the villa. It looked so like a gem, shining through its dark grove, so like a great glow-worm in the dense foliage, so significant of luxury and gayety, that the poor master, from an overflowing heart, groaned again.

"What?" asked Charlie.

The Colonel only drew his rein, and, dismounting mechanically, contemplated the sight before him. The high, arched doors and windows were thrown wide to the summer air; from every opening the bright light of numerous candelabra darted out upon the sparkling foliage of magnolia and bay, and here and there in the spacious verandas a colored lantern swayed in the gentle breeze. A sound of revel fell on the ear, the music of harps; and across one window, brighter than the rest, flitted, once or twice, the shadows of dancers. But oh! the shadows flitting across the heart of the fair mansion's master!

"Old Charlie," said he, gazing fondly at his house, "You and me is both old, eh?"

"Yaas," said the stolid Charlie.

"And we has both been bad enough in our time, eh, Charlie?"

Charlie, surprised at the tender tone, repeated, "Yaas."

"And you and me is mighty close?"

"Blame close, yaas."

"But you never know me to cheat, old man!"

"No,"—impassively.

"And do you think I would cheat you now?"

"I dunno," said Charlie. "I don't believe."

"Well, old man, old man,"—his voice began to quiver,—"I sha'n't cheat you now. My God!—old man, I tell you—you better not make the trade!"

"Because for what?" asked Charlie in plain anger; but both looked quickly toward the house! The Colonel tossed his hands wildly in the air, rushed forward a step or two, and giving one fearful scream of agony and fright, fell forward on his face in the path. Old Charlie stood transfixed with horror. Belles Demoiselles, the realm of maiden beauty, the home of merriment, the house of dancing, all in the tremor and glow of pleasure, suddenly sunk, with one short, wild wail of terror—sunk, sunk, down, down, down, into the merciless, unfathomable flood of the Mississippi.

Twelve long months were midnight to the mind of the childless father; when they were only half gone, he took his bed; and every day, and every night, old Charlie, the "low-down," the "fool," watched him tenderly, tended him lovingly, for the sake of his name, his misfortunes, and his broken heart. No woman's step crossed the floor of the sick-chamber, whose western dormer-windows overpeered the dingy architecture of old Charlie's block; Charlie and a skilled physician, the one all interest, the other all gentleness, hope, and patience—these only entered by the door; but by the window came in a sweet-scented evergreen vine, transplanted from the caving bank of Belles Demoiselles. It caught the rays of sunset in its flowery net and let then softly in upon the sick man's bed; gathered the glancing beams of the moon at midnight, and often wakened the sleeper to look, with his mindless eyes, upon their pretty silver fragments strewn upon the floor.

By and by there seemed—there was—a twinkling dawn of returning reason. Slowly, peacefully, with an increase unseen from day to day, the light of reason came into the eyes, and speech became coherent; but withal there came a failing of the wrecked body, and the doctor said that monsieur was both better and worse.

One evening, as Charlie sat by the vine-clad window with his fireless pipe in his hand, the old Colonel's eyes fell full upon his own, and rested there.

"Charl—," he said with an effort, and his delighted nurse hastened to the bedside and bowed his best ear. There was an unsuccessful effort or two, and then he whispered, smiling with sweet sadness,—

"We didn't trade."

The truth, in this case, was a secondary matter to Charlie; the main point was to give a pleasing answer. So he nodded his head decidedly, as who should say—"Oh yes, we did, it was a bona-fide swap!" but when he saw the smile vanish, he tried the other expedient and shook his head with still more vigor, to signify that they had not so much as approached a bargain; and the smile returned.

Charlie wanted to see the vine recognized. He stepped backward to the window with a broad smile, shook the foliage, nodded and looked smart.

"I know," said the Colonel, with beaming eyes, "—many weeks."

The next day—

"Charl—"

The best ear went down.

"Send for a priest."

The priest came, and was alone with him a whole afternoon. When he left, the patient was very haggard and exhausted, but smiled and would not suffer the crucifix to be removed from his breast.

One more morning came. Just before dawn Charlie, lying on a pallet in the room, thought he was called, and came to the bedside.

"Old man," whispered the failing invalid, "is it caving yet?"

Charlie nodded.

"It won't pay you out."

"Oh, dat makes not'ing," said Charlie. Two big tears rolled down his brown face. "Dat makes not'in."

The Colonel whispered once more:

"*Mes belles demoiselles!* in paradise;—in the garden—I shall be with them at sunrise;" and so it was.

MARY NOAILLES MURFREE

(1850–1922)

Although Mary Noailles Murfree knew the mountains of Tennessee only as a summer visitor, it was she who made popular the life of the Southern mountain people as a subject for literature. Her tales of laconic, hard-toiling primitive mountaineers were immensely successful during the 1880s and early 1890s, at the height of the local-color vogue when an American reading public was hungry for accounts of the outlying and remote provinces of the nation.

Miss Murfree was born in Murfreesboro, Tennessee, into a family long prominent in Tennessee life. Her father was a noted lawyer and property owner. She was educated in Nashville, where the family moved in 1856, and in Philadelphia. The defeat of the Civil War wiped out most of her father's fortune, and she then began writing, publishing under the penname of "Charles Egbert Craddock." Her stories met with considerable acclaim, and her first collection, *In the Tennessee Mountains* (1884), was followed by numerous other novels and collections of stories about the mountain folk, including *The Prophet of the Great Smoky Mountains* (1885) and *In the Stranger People's Country* (1891). The account of her arrival—a spinster, crippled and of slight stature—at the office of the *Atlantic Monthly* in Boston in 1885 and the astonishment of the editor, Thomas Bailey Aldrich, at her shy announcement that she was none other than "Charles Egbert Craddock," was well known in the literary circles of the day.

When the vogue for local-color fiction waned in the late 1890s, Miss Murfree turned to historical romance, and also produced a number of works for children. She was unable, however, to retain her popularity, and in her closing years found it difficult to get her stories published. In 1912 she sold the full rights to her fifteen books to the Houghton Mifflin Company for $1,159.81. She died in destitute circumstances.

THE "HARNT" THAT WALKS CHILHOWEE

June had crossed the borders of Tennessee. Even on the summit of Chilhowee Mountain, the apples in Peter Giles's orchard were beginning to redden, and his Indian corn, planted on so steep a declivity that the stalks seemed to have much ado to keep their footing, was crested with tassels and plumed with silk. Among the dense forests, seen by no man's eye, the elder was flying its creamy banners in honor of June's coming, and, heard by no man's ear, the pink and white bells of the azalea rang out melodies of welcome.

"An' it air a toler'ble for'ard season. Your wheat looks likely; an' yer gyarden truck air thrivin' powerful. Even that cold spell we-uns hed about the full o' the moon in May ain't done sot it back none, it 'pears like ter me. But, 'cording ter my way o' thinkin', ye hev got chickens enough hyar ter eat off every pea-bloom ez soon ez it opens." And Simon Burney glanced with a gardener's disapproval at the numerous fowls, lifting their red combs and tufted top-knots here and there among the thick clover under the apple-trees.

"Them's Clarsie's chickens,—my darter, ye know," drawled Peter Giles, a pale, listless, and lank mountaineer. "An' she hev been gin ter onderstand ez they hev got ter be kep' out 'n the gyarden; 'thout," he added indulgently,—"'thout I 'm a-plowin', when I lets 'em foller in the furrow ter pick up worms. But law! Clarsie is so spry that she don't ax no better 'n ter be let ter run them chickens off 'n the peas."

Then the two men tilted their chairs against the posts of the little porch in front of Peter Giles's log cabin, and puffed their pipes in silence. The panorama spread out before them showed misty and dreamy among the delicate spiral wreaths of smoke. But was that gossamer-like illusion, lying upon the far horizon, the magic of nicotian, or the vague presence of distant heights? As ridge after ridge came down from the sky in ever-graduating shades of intense blue, Peter Giles might have told you that this parallel system of enchantment was only "the mountings": that here was Foxy, and there was Big Injun, and still beyond was another, which he had "hearn tell ran spang up into Virginny." The sky that bent to clasp this kindred blue was of varying moods. Floods of sunshine submerged Chilhowee in liquid gold, and revealed that dainty outline limned upon the northern horizon; but over the Great Smoky mountains clouds had gathered, and a gigantic rainbow bridged the valley.

Peter Giles's listless eyes were fixed upon a bit of red clay road, which was visible through a gap in the foliage far below. Even a tiny object, that ant-like crawled upon it, could be seen from the summit of Chilhowee. "I reckon that 's my brother's wagon an' team," he said, as he watched the moving atom pass under the gorgeous triumphal arch. "He 'lowed he war goin' ter the Cross-Roads ter-day."

Simon Burney did not speak for a moment. When he did, his words seemed widely irrelevant. "That 's a likely gal o' yourn," he drawled, with an odd constraint in his voice,—"a likely gal, that Clarsie."

There was a quick flash of surprise in Peter Giles's dull eyes. He covertly surveyed his guest, with an astounded curiosity rampant in his slow brains. Simony Burney had changed color; an expression of embarrassment lurked in every line of his honest, florid, hard-featured face. An alert imagination might have detected a deprecatory self-consciousness in every gray hair that striped the black beard raggedly fringing his chin.

"Yes," Peter Giles at length replied, "Clarsie air a likely enough gal. But she air mightily sot ter hevin' her own way. An' ef 't ain't give ter her peace-able-like, she jes' takes it, whether or no."

This statement, made by one presumably fully informed on the subject, might have damped the ardor of many a suitor,—for the monstrous truth was dawning on Peter Giles's mind that suitor was the position to which this slow, elderly widower aspired. But Simon Burney, with that odd, all-pervading constraint still prominently apparent, mildly observed, "Waal, ez much ez I hev seen of her goin's-on, it 'pears ter me ez her way air a mighty good way. An' it ain't comical that she likes it."

Urgent justice compelled Peter Giles to make some amends to the absent Clarissa. "That 's a fac'," he admitted. "An' Clarsie ain't no hand ter jaw. She don't hev no words. But then," he qualified, truth and consistency alike constraining him, "she air a toler'ble hard-headed gal. That air a true word. Ye mought ez well try ter hender the sun from shining ez ter make that thar Clarsie Giles do what she don't want ter do."

To be sure, Peter Giles had a right to his opinion as to the hardness of his own daughter's head. The expression of his views, however, provoked Simon Burney to wrath; there was something astir within him that in a wor-thier subject might have been called a chivalric thrill, and it forbade him to hold his peace. He retorted: "Of course ye kin say that, ef so minded; but ennybody ez hev got eyes kin see the change ez hev been made in this hyar place sence that thar gal hev been growed. I ain't a-purtendin' ter know that thar Clarsie ez well ez you-uns knows her hyar at home, but I hev seen enough, an' a deal more 'n enough, of her goin's-on, ter know that what she does ain't done fur *herself*. An' ef she will hev her way, it air fur the good of the whole tribe of ye. It 'pears ter me ez thar ain't many gals like that thar Clarsie. An' she air a merciful critter. She air mighty savin' of the feelin's of everything, from the cow an' the mare down ter the dogs, an' pigs, an' chickens; always a-feedin' of 'em jes' ter the time, an' never draggin', an' clawin', an' beatin' of 'em. Why, that thar Clarsie can't put her foot out 'n the door, that every dumb beastis on this hyar place ain't a-runnin' ter git nigh her. I hev seen them pigs mos' clib the fence when she shows her face at the door. 'Pears ter me ez that thar Clarsie could tame a b'ar, ef she looked at him a time or two, she 's so savin' o' the critter's feelin's! An' thar 's that old yaller dog o' yourn," pointing to an ancient cur that was blinking in the sun, "he 's older 'n Clarsie, an' no 'count in the worl'. I hev hearn ye say forty times that ye would kill him, 'ceptin' that Clarsie pur-tected him, an' hed sot her heart on his a-livin' along. An' all the home-folks, an' everybody that kems hyar to sot an' talk awhile, never misses a chance ter kick that thar old dog, or poke him with a stick, or cuss him. But Clarsie!—I hev seen that gal take the bread an' meat off'n her plate, an' give it ter that old dog, ez 'pears ter me ter be the worst dispositionest dog I ever see, an' no thanks lef' in him. He hain't hed the grace ter wag his tail fur twenty year. That thar Clarsie air surely a merciful critter, an' a mighty spry, likely young gal, besides."

Peter Giles sat in stunned astonishment during this speech, which was delivered in a slow, drawling monotone, with frequent meditative pauses, but nevertheless emphatically. He made no reply, and as they were once more silent there rose suddenly the sound of melody upon the air. It came from beyond that tumultuous stream that raced with the wind down the mountain's side; a great log thrown from bank to bank served as bridge. The song grew momentarily more distinct; among the leaves there were fugitive glimpses of blue and white, and at last Clarsie appeared, walking lightly along the log, clad in her checked homespun dress, and with a pail upon her head.

She was a tall, lithe girl, with that delicately transparent complexion often seen among the women of these mountains. Her lustreless black hair lay along her forehead without a ripple or wave; there was something in the expression of her large eyes that suggested those of a deer,—something free, untamable, and yet gentle. " 'T ain't no wonder ter me ez Clarsie is all tuk up with the wild things, an' critters ginerally," her mother was wont to say. "She sorter looks like 'em, I 'm a-thinkin'."

As she came in sight there was a renewal of that odd constraint in Simon Burney's face and manner, and he rose abruptly. "Waal," he said, hastily, going to his horse, a raw-boned sorrel, hitched to the fence, "it 's about time I war a-startin' home, I reckons."

He nodded to his host, who silently nodded in return, and the old horse jogged off with him down the road, as Clarsie entered the house and placed the pail upon a shelf.

"Who d' ye think hev been hyar a-speakin' of compli*mints* on ye, Clarsie?" exclaimed Mrs. Giles, who had overheard through the open door every word of the loud, drawling voice on the porch.

Clarsie's liquid eyes widened with surprise, and a faint tinge of rose sprang into her pale face, as she looked an expectant inquiry at her mother.

Mrs. Giles was a slovenly, indolent woman, anxious, at the age of forty-five, to assume the prerogatives of advanced years. She had placed all her domestic cares upon the shapely shoulders of her willing daughter, and had betaken herself to the chimney-corner and a pipe.

"Yes, thar hev been somebody hyar a-speakin' of compli*mints* on ye, Clarsie," she reiterated, with chuckling amusement. "He war a mighty peart, likely boy,—that he war!"

Clarsie's color deepened.

"Old Simon Burney!" exclaimed her mother, in great glee at the incongruity of the idea, "*Old Simon Burney!*—jes' a-sittin' out thar, a-wastin' the time, an' a-burnin' of daylight—jes' ez perlite an' smilin' ez a basket of chips—a-speakin' of compli*mints* on ye!'"

There was a flash of laughter among the sylvan suggestions of Clarsie's eyes,—a flash as of sudden sunlight upon water. But despite her mirth she seemed to be unaccountably disappointed. The change in her manner was not noticed by her mother, who continued banteringly, —

"Simon Burney air a mighty pore old man. Ye oughter be sorry fur him, Clarsie. Ye must n't think less of folks than ye does of the dumb beastis, —that ain't religion. Ye knows ye air sorry fur mos' everything; why not fur this comical old consarn? Ye oughter marry him ter take keer of him. He said ye war a merciful critter; now is yer chance ter show it! Why, air ye a-goin' ter weavin', Clarsie, jes' when I wants ter talk ter ye 'bout 'n old Simon Burney? But law! I knows ye kerry him with ye in yer heart."

The girl summarily closed the conversation by seating herself before a great hand-loom; presently the persistent thump, thump, of the batten and the noisy creak of the treadle filled the room, and through all the long, hot afternoon her deft, practiced hands lightly tossed the shuttle to and fro.

The breeze freshened, after the sun went down, and the hop and gourd vines were all astir as they clung about the little porch where Clarsie was sitting now, idle at last. The rain clouds had disappeared, and there bent over the dark, heavily wooded ridges a pale blue sky, with here and there the crystalline sparkle of a star. A halo was shimmering in the east, where the mists had gathered about the great white moon, hanging high above the mountains. Noiseless wings flitted through the dusk; now and then the bats swept by so close as to wave Clarsie's hair with the wind of their flight. What an airy, glittering, magical thing was that gigantic spider-web suspended between the silver moon and her shining eyes! Ever and anon there came from the woods a strange, weird, long-drawn sigh, unlike the stir of the wind in the trees, unlike the fret of the water on the rocks. Was it the voiceless sorrow of the sad earth? There were stars in the night besides those known to astronomers: the stellular fireflies gemmed the black shadows with a fluctuating brilliancy; they circled in and out of the porch, and touched the leaves above Clarsie's head with quivering points of light. A steadier and an intenser gleam was advancing along the road, and the sound of languid footsteps came with it; the aroma of tobacco graced the atmosphere, and a tall figure walked up to the gate.

"Come in, come in," said Peter Giles, rising, and tendering the guest a chair. "Ye air Tom Pratt, ez well ez I kin make out by this light. Waal, Tom, we hain't furgot ye sence ye done been hyar."

As Tom had been there on the previous evening, this might be considered a joke, or an equivocal compliment. The young fellow was restless and awkward under it, but Mrs. Giles chuckled with great merriment.

"An' how air ye a-comin' on, Mrs. Giles?" he asked propitiatorily.

"Jes' toler'ble, Tom. Air they all well ter yer house?"

"Yes, they 're toler'ble well, too." He glanced at Clarsie, intending to address to her some polite greeting, but the expression of her shy, half-startled eyes, turned upon the far-away moon, warned him. "Thar never war a gal so skittish," he thought. "She 'd run a mile, skeered ter death, ef I said a word ter her."

And he was prudently silent.

"Waal," said Peter Giles, "what 's the news out yer way, Tom? Ennything a-goin' on?"

"Thar war a shower yander on the Backbone; it rained toler'ble hard fur a while, an' sot up the corn wonderful. Did ye git enny hyar?"

"Not a drap."

" 'Pears ter me ez I kin see the clouds a-circlin' round Chilhowee, an' a-rainin' on everybody's cornfield 'ceptin' ourn," said Mrs. Giles. "Some folks is the favored of the Lord, an' t' others hev ter work fur everything an' git nuthin'. Waal, waal; we-uns will see our reward in the nex' worl'. Thar 's a better worl' than this, Tom."

"That's a fac'," said Tom, in orthodox assent.

"An' when we leaves hyar once, we leaves all trouble an' care behind us, Tom; fur we don't come back no more." Mrs. Giles was drifting into one of her pious moods.

"I dunno," said Tom. "Thar hev been them ez hev."

"Hev what?" demanded Peter Giles, startled.

"Hev come back ter this hyar yearth. Thar's a harnt that walks Chilhowee every night o' the worl'. I know them ez hev seen him."

Clarsie's great dilated eyes were fastened on the speaker's face. There was a dead silence for a moment, more eloquent with these looks of amazement than any words could have been.

"I reckons ye remember a puny, shriveled little man, named Reuben Crabb, ez used ter live yander, eight mile along the ridge ter that thar big sulphur spring," Tom resumed, appealing to Peter Giles. "He war born with only one arm."

"I 'members him," interpolated Mrs. Giles, vivaciously. "He war a might porely, sickly little critter, all the days of his life. 'Twar a wonder he war ever raised ter be a man,—an' a pity, too. An' 't war powerful comical, the way of his takin' off; a stunted, one-armed little critter a-ondertakin' ter fight folks an' shoot pistols. He hed the use o' his one arm, sure."

"Waal," said Tom, "his house ain't thar now, 'kase Sam Grim's brothers burned it ter the ground fur his a-killin' of Sam. That warn't all that war done ter Reuben fur killin' of Sam. The sheriff run Reuben Crabb down this hyar road 'bout a mile from hyar,—mebbe less,—an' shot him dead in the road, jes' whar it forks. Waal, Reuben war in company with another evil-doer,—*he* war from the Cross-Roads, an' I furgits what he hed done, but he war a-tryin' ter hide in the mountings, too; an' the sheriff lef' Reuben a-lying thar in the road, while he tries ter ketch up with the t'other; but his horse got a stone in his hoof, an' he los' time, an' hed ter gin it up. An' when he got back ter the forks o' the road whar he had lef' Reuben a-lyin' dead, thar war nuthin' thar 'ceptin' a pool o' blood. Waal, he went right on ter Reuben's house, an' them Grim boys hed burnt it ter the ground; but he seen Reuben's brother Joel. An' Joel, he tole the sheriff that late that evenin' he hed tuk Reuben's body out 'n the road an' buried it, 'kase it hed been lyin' thar in the road ever sence early in the mornin', an' he could n't leave it thar all night, an' he hed n't no shelter fur it, sence the Grim boys hed burnt down the house. So he war obleeged ter bury it. An' Joel showed the sheriff a new-made grave, an' Reuben's coat whar the sheriff's bullet hed gone in at the back an' kem out'n the breast. The sheriff 'lowed ez they 'd fine Joel fifty dollars fur a-buryin' of Reuben afore the cor'ner kem; but they never done it, ez I knows on. The sheriff said that when the cor'ner kem the body would be tuk up fur a 'quest. But thar hed been a powerful big frishet, an' the river 'twixt the cor'ner's house an' Chilhowee could n't be forded fur three weeks. The cor'ner never kem, an' so thar it all stayed. That war four year ago."

"Waal," said Peter Giles, dryly, "I ain't seen no harnt yit. I knowed all that afore."

Clarsie's wondering eyes upon the young man's moonlit face had elicited these facts, familiar to the elders, but strange, he knew, to her.

"I war jes' a-goin' on ter tell," said Tom, abashed. "Waal, ever sence his brother Joel died, this spring, Reuben's harnt walks Chilhowee. He war seen week afore las', 'bout daybreak, by Ephraim Blenkins, who hed been a-fishin', an' war a-goin' home. Eph happened ter stop in the laurel ter wind up his line, when all in a minit he seen the harnt go by, his face white, an' his eye-balls like fire, an' puny an' one-armed, jes' like he lived. Eph, he owed me a haffen day's work; I holped him ter plow las' month, an' so he kem ter-day an' hoed along cornsider'ble ter pay fur it. He say he believes the harnt never seen him, 'kase it went right by. He 'lowed ef the harnt hed so much ez cut one o' them blazin' eyes round at him he could n't but hev drapped dead. Waal, this mornin', 'bout sunrise, my brother Bob's little gal, three year old, strayed off from home while her mother war out milkin' the cow. An' we went a-huntin' of her, mightily worked up, 'kase thar hev been a b'ar prowlin' round our cornfield twict this summer. An' I went to the right, an' Bob went to the lef'. An' he say ez he war a-pushin' 'long through the laurel, he seen the bushes ahead of him a-rustlin'. An' he jes' stood still an' watched 'em. An' fur a while the bushes war still too; an' then they moved jes' a little, fust this way an' then that, till all of a suddint the leaves opened, like the mouth of hell mought hev done, an' thar he seen Reuben Crabb's face! He say he never seen sech a face! Its mouth war open, an' its eyes war a-startin' out 'n its head, an' its skin war white till it war blue; an' ef the devil hed hed it a-hangin' over the coals that minit it could n't hev looked no more skeered. But that war all that Bob seen, 'kase he jes' shet his eyes an' screeched an' screeched like he war *de*stracted. An' when he stopped a second ter ketch his breath he hearn su'thin' a-answerin' him back, sorter weak-like, an' thar war little Peggy a-pullin' through the laurel. Ye know she 's too little ter talk good, but the folks down ter our house believes she seen the harnt, too."

"My Lord!" exclaimed Peter Giles. "I 'low I could n't live a minit ef I war ter see that thar harnt that walks Chilhowee!"

"I know *I* could n't," said his wife.

"Nor me, nuther," murmured Clarsie.

"Waal," said Tom resuming the thread of his narrative, "we hev all been a-talkin' down yander ter our house ter make out the reason why Reuben Crabb's harnt hev sot out ter walk *jes' sence his brother Joel died*,—'kase it war never seen afore then. An' ez nigh ez we kin make it out, the reason is 'kase thar's nobody lef' in this hyar worl' what believes he warn't ter blame in that thar killin' o' Sam Grim. Joel always swore ez Reuben never killed him no more 'n nuthin'; that Sam's own pistol went off in his own hand, an' shot him through the heart jes' ez he war a-drawin' of it ter shoot Reuben Crabb. An' I hev hearn other men ez war a-standin' by say the same thing, though them Grims tells another tale; but ez Reuben never owned no pistol in his life, nor kerried one, it don't 'pear ter me ez what them Grims say air reasonable. Joel always swore ez Sam Grim war a mighty mean man,—a great big feller like him a-rockin' of a deformed little critter, an' a-mockin' of him, an' a-hittin' of him. An' the day of the fight Sam jes' knocked him down fur nuthin' at all; an' afore ye could wink Reuben jumped up suddint, an' flew at him like an eagle, an' struck him in the face. An' then Sam drawed his pistol, an' it went off in his own hand, an' shot him through the heart, an' killed him dead. Joel said that ef he could hev kep' that pore little critter Reuben still, an' let the sheriff arrest him peaceable-like, he war sure the jury would hev let him off; 'kase how war Reuben a-goin' ter shoot ennybody when Sam Grim never left a-holt of the only pistol between 'em, in life, or in death? They tells me they hed ter bury Sam Grim with that thar pistol in his hand; his grip war too tight fur death to unloose it. But Joel said that Reuben war sartain they'd hang him. He hedn't never seen no jestice from enny one man, an' he could n't look fur it from twelve men. So he jes' sot out ter run through the woods, like a painter or a wolf, ter be hunted by the sheriff, an' he war run down an' kilt in the road. Joel said *he* kep' up arter the sheriff ez well ez he could on foot,—fur the Crabbs never hed no horse,—ter try ter beg fur Reuben, ef he war cotched, an' tell how little an' how weakly he war. I never seen a young man's head turn white like Joel's done; he said he reckoned it war his troubles. But ter the las' he stuck ter his rifle faithful. He war a powerful hunter; he war out rain or shine, hot or cold, in sech weather ez other folks would think thar war n't no use in tryin' ter do nuthin' in. I'm mightily afeard o' seein' Reuben, now, that's a fac'," concluded Tom, frankly; " 'kase I hev hearn tell, an' I believes it, that ef a harnt speaks ter ye, it air sartain ye 're bound ter die right then."

" 'Pears ter me," said Mrs. Giles, "ez many mountings ez thar air round hyar, he mought hev tuk ter walkin' some o' them, stiddier Chilhowee."

There was a sudden noise close at hand: a great inverted splintbasket, from which came a sound of flapping wings, began to move slightly back and forth. Mrs. Giles gasped out an ejaculation of terror, the two men sprang to their feet, and the coy Clarsie laughed aloud in an exuberance of delighted mirth, forgetful of her shyness. "I declar' ter goodness, you-uns air all skeered fur true! Did ye think it war the harnt that walks Chilhowee?"

"What's under that thar basket?" demanded Peter Giles, rather sheepishly, as he sat down again.

"Nuthin' but the duck-legged Dominicky," said Clarsie, "what air bein' broke up from settin'." The moonlight was full upon the dimpling merriment in her face, upon her shining eyes and parted red lips, and her gurgling laughter was pleasant to hear. Tom Pratt edged his chair a trifle nearer, as he, too, sat down.

"Ye ought n't never ter break up a duck-legged hen, nor a Dominicky, nuther," he volunteered, " 'kase they air sech a good kind 'o hen ter kerry chickens; but a hen that is duck-legged an' Dominicky too oughter be let ter set, whether or no."

Had he been warned in a dream, he could have found no more secure road to Clarsie's favor and interest than a discussion of the poultry. "I'm a-thinkin'," she said, "that it air too hot fur hens ter set now, an' 't will be till the las' of August."

"It don't 'pear ter me ez it air hot much in June up hyar on Chilhowee, —thar 's a differ, I know, down in the valley; but till July, on Chilhowee, it don't 'pear ter me ez it air too hot ter set a hen. An' a duck-legged Dominicky air mighty hard ter break up."

"That's a fac'," Clarsie admitted; "but I 'll hev ter do it, somehow, 'kase I ain't got no eggs fur her. All my hens air kerryin' of chickens."

"Waal!" exclaimed Tom, seizing his opportunity, "I 'll bring ye some ter-morrer night, when I come agin. We-uns hev got eggs ter our house."

"Thanky," said Clarsie, shyly smiling.

This unique method of courtship would have progressed very prosperously but for the interference of the elders, who are an element always more or less adverse to love-making. "Ye oughter turn out yer hen now, Clarsie," said Mrs. Giles, "ez Tom air a-goin' ter bring ye some eggs ter-morrer. I wonder ye don't think it 's mean ter keep her up longer 'n ye air obleeged ter. Ye oughter remember ye war called a merciful critter jes' ter-day."

Clarsie rose precipitately, raised the basket, and out flew the "duck-legged Dominicky," with a frantic flutter and hysterical cackling. But Mrs. Giles was not to be diverted from her purpose; her thoughts had recurred to the absurd episode of the afternoon, and with her relish of the incongruity of the joke she opened upon the subject at once.

"Waal, Tom," she said, "we'll be hevin' Clarsie married, afore long, I'm a-thinkin'." The young man sat bewildered. He, too, had entertained views concerning Clarsie's speedy marriage, but with a distinctly personal application; and this frank mention of the matter by Mrs. Giles had a sinister suggestion that perhaps her ideas might be antagonistic. "An' who d 'ye think hev been hyar ter-day, a-speakin' of compli*mints* on Clarsie?" He could not answer, but he turned his head with a look of inquiry, and Mrs. Giles continued. "He is a mighty peart, likely boy,—*he* is."

There was a growing anger in the dismay on Tom Pratt's face; he leaned forward to hear the name with a fiery eagerness, altogether incongruous with his usual lack-lustre manner.

"Old Simon Burney!" cried Mrs. Giles, with a burst of laughter. "*Old Simon Burney!* Jes' a-speakin' of compli*mints* on Clarsie!"

The young fellow drew back with a look of disgust. "Why, he 's a old man; he ain't no fit husband fur Clarsie."

"Don't ye be too sure ter count on that. I war jes' a-layin' off ter tell Clarsie that a gal oughter keep mighty clar o' widowers, 'thout she wants ter marry one. Fur I believes," said Mrs. Giles, with a wild flight of imagination, "ez them men hev got some sort 'n trade with the Evil One, an' he gives 'em the power ter witch the gals, somehow, so 's ter git 'em ter marry; 'kase I don't think that any gal that 's got good sense air a-goin' ter be a man's second ch'ice, an' the mother of a whole pack of step-chil'ren, 'thout she air under some sort 'n spell. But them men carries the day with the gals, ginerally, an' I 'm a-thinkin' they 're banded with the devil. Ef I war a gal, an' a smart, peart boy like Simon Burney kem around a-speakin' of compli*mints*, an' sayin' I war a merciful critter, I 'd jes' give it up, an' marry him fur second ch'ice. Thar 's one blessin'," she continued, contemplating the possibility in a cold-blooded fashion positively revolting to Tom Pratt: "he ain't got no tribe of chil'ren fur Clarsie ter look arter; nary chick nor child hev old Simon Burney got. He hed two, but they died."

The young man took leave presently, in great depression of spirit,—the idea that the widower was banded with the powers of evil was rather overwhelming to a man whose dependence was in merely mortal attractions; and after he had been gone a little while Clarsie ascended the ladder to a nook in the roof, which she called her room.

For the first time in her life her slumber was fitful and restless, long intervals of wakefulness alternating with snatches of fantastic dreams. At last she rose and sat by the rude window, looking out through the chestnut leaves at the great moon, which had begun to dip toward the dark uncertainty of the western ridges, and at the shimmering, translucent, pearly mists that filled the intermediate valley. All the air was dew and incense; so subtle and penetrating an odor came from that fir-tree beyond the fence that it seemed as if some invigorating infusion were thrilling along her veins; there floated upward, too, the warm fragrance of the clover, and every breath of the gentle wind brought from over the stream a thousand blended, undistinguishable perfumes of the deep forests beyond. The moon's idealizing glamour had left no trace of the uncouthness of the place which the daylight revealed; the little log house, the great overhanging chestnut-oaks, the jagged precipice before the door, the vague outlines of the distant ranges, all suffused with a magic sheen, might have seemed a stupendous alto-rilievo in silver repoussé. Still, there came here and there the sweep of the bat's dusky wings; even they were a part of the night's witchery. A tiny owl perched for a moment or two amid the dew-tipped chestnut-leaves, and gazed with great round eyes at Clarsie as solemnly as she gazed at him.

"I 'm thankful enough that ye hed the grace not ter screech while ye war hyar," she said, after the bird had taken his flight. "I ain't ready ter die yit, an' a screech-ow*el* air the sure sign."

She felt now and then a great impatience with her wakeful mood. Once she took herself to task: "Jes' a-sittin' up hyar all night, the same ez ef I war a fox, or that thar harnt that walks Chilhowee!"

And then her mind reverted to Tom Pratt, to old Simon Burney, and to her mother's emphatic and oracular declaration that widowers are in league with Satan, and that the girls upon whom they cast the eye of supernatural fascination have no choice in the matter. "I wish I knowed ef that thar sayin' war true," she murmured, her face still turned to the western spurs, and the moon sinking so slowly toward them.

With a sudden resolution she rose to her feet. She knew a way of telling fortunes which was, according to tradition, infallible, and she determined to try it, and ease her mind as to her future. Now was the propitious moment. "I hev always hearn that it won't come true 'thout ye try it jes' before day-break, an' a-kneelin' down at the forks of the road." She hesitated a moment and listened intently. "They 'd never git done a-laffin' at me, ef they fund it out," she thought.

There was no sound in the house, and from the dark woods arose only those monotonous voices of the night, so familiar to her ears that she accounted their murmurous iteration as silence too. She leaned far out of the low window, caught the wide-spreading branches of the tree beside it, and swung herself noiselessly to the ground. The road before her was dark with the shadowy foliage and dank with the dew; but now and then, at long intervals, there lay athwart it a bright bar of light, where the moonshine fell through a gap in the trees. Once, as she went rapidly along her way, she saw speeding across the white radiance, lying just before her feet, the ill-omened shadow of a rabbit. She paused, with a superstitious sinking of the heart, and she heard the animal's quick, leaping rush through the bushes near at hand; but she mustered her courage, and kept steadily on. " 'T ain't no use a-goin' back ter git shet o' bad luck," she argued. "Ef old Simon Burney air my fortune, he 'll come whether or no,—ef all they say air true."

The serpentine road curved to the mountain's brink before it forked, and there was again that familiar picture of precipice, and far-away ridges, and shining mist, and sinking moon, which was visibly turning from silver to gold. The changing lustre gilded the feathery ferns that grew in the marshy dip. Just at the angle of the divergent paths there rose into the air a great mass of indistinct white blossoms, which she knew were the exquisite mountain azaleas, and all the dark forest was starred with the blooms of the laurel.

She fixed her eyes upon the mystic sphere dropping down the sky, knelt among the azaleas at the forks of the road, and repeated the time-honored invocation: —

"Ef I'm a-goin' ter marry a young man, whistle, Bird, whistle. Ef I'm a-goin' ter marry an old man, low, Cow, low. Ef I ain't a-goin' ter marry nobody, knock, Death, knock."

There was a prolonged silence in the matutinal freshness and perfume of the woods. She raised her head, and listened attentively. No chirp of half-a-wakened bird, no tapping of woodpecker, or the mysterious deathwatch; but from far along the dewy aisles of the forest, the ungrateful Spot, that Clarsie had fed more faithfully than herself, lifted up her voice, and set the echoes vibrating. Clarsie, however, had hardly time for a pang of disappointment. While she still knelt among the azaleas her large deer-like eyes were suddenly dilated with terror. From around the curve of the road came the quick beat of hastening footsteps, the sobbing sound of panting breath, and between her and the sinking moon there passed an attenuated, one-armed figure, with a pallid, sharpened face, outlined for a moment on its brilliant disk, and dreadful starting eyes, and quivering open mouth. It disappeared in an instant among the shadows of the laurel, and Clarsie, with a horrible fear clutching at her heart, sprang to her feet.

Her flight was arrested by other sounds. Before her reeling senses could distinguish them, a party of horsemen plunged down the road. They reined in suddenly as their eyes fell upon her, and their leader, an eager, authoritative man, was asking her a question. Why could she not understand him? With her nerveless hands feebly catching at the shrubs for support, she listened vaguely to his impatient, meaningless words, and saw with helpless deprecation the rising anger in his face. But there was no time to be lost. With a curse upon the stupidity of the mountaineer, who couldn't speak when she was spoken to, the party sped on in a sweeping gallop, and the rocks and the steeps were hilarious with the sound.

When the last faint echo was hushed, Clarsie tremblingly made her way out into the road; not reassured, however, for she had a frightful conviction that there was now and then a strange stir in the laurel, and that she was stealthily watched. Her eyes were fixed upon the dense growth with a morbid fascination, as she moved away; but she was once more rooted to the spot when the leaves parted and in the golden moonlight the ghost stood before her. She could not nerve herself to run past him, and he was directly in her way homeward. His face was white, and lined, and thin; that pitiful quiver was never still in the parted lips; he looked at her with faltering, beseeching eyes. Clarsie's merciful heart was stirred. "What ails ye, ter come back hyar, an' foller me?" she cried out, abruptly. And then a great horror fell upon her. Was not one to whom a ghost should speak doomed to death, sudden and immediate?

The ghost replied in a broken, shivering voice, like a wail of pain, "I war a-starvin',—I war a-starvin'," with despairing iteration.

It was all over, Clarsie thought. The ghost had spoken, and she was a doomed creature. She wondered that she did not fall dead in the road. But while those beseeching eyes were fastened in piteous appeal on hers, she could not leave him. "I never hearn that 'bout ye," she said, reflectively. "I knows ye hed awful troubles while ye war alive, but I never knowed ez ye war starved."

Surely that was a gleam of sharp surprise in the ghost's prominent eyes, succeeded by a sly intelligence.

"Day is nigh ter breakin'," Clarsie admonished him, as the lower rim of the moon touched the silver mists of the west. "What air ye a-wantin' of me?"

There was a short silence. Mind travels far in such intervals. Clarsie's thoughts had overtaken the scenes when she should have died that sudden terrible death: when there would be no one left to feed the chickens; when no one would care if the pigs cried with the pangs of hunger, unless indeed, it were time for them to be fattened before killing. The mare,—how often would she be taken from the plow, and shut up for the night in her shanty without a drop of water, after her hard day's work! Who would churn, or spin, or weave? Clarsie could not understand how the machinery of the universe would go on without her. And Towse, poor Towse! He was a useless cumberer of the ground, and it was hardly to be supposed that after his protector was gone he would be spared a blow or a bullet, to hasten his lagging death. But Clarsie still stood in the road, and watched the face of the ghost, as he, with his eager, starting eyes, scanned her open, ingenuous countenance.

"Ye do ez ye air bid, or it 'll be the worse for ye," said the "harnt," in the same quivering, shrill tone. "Thar 's hunger in the nex' worl' ez well ez in this, an' ye bring me some vittles hyar this time ter-morrer, an' don't ye tell nobody ye hev seen me, nuther, or it'll be the worse for ye."

There was a threat in his eyes as he disappeared in the laurel, and left the girl standing in the last rays of moonlight.

A curious doubt was stirring in Clarsie's mind when she reached home, in the early dawn, and heard her father talking about the sheriff and his posse, who had stopped at the house in the night, and roused its inmates, to know if they had seen a man pass that way.

"Clarsie never hearn none o' the noise, I'll be bound, 'kase she always sleeps like a log," said Mrs. Giles, as her daughter came in with the pail, after milking the cow. "Tell her 'bout 'n it."

"They kem a-bustin' along hyar a while afore day-break, a-runnin' arter the man," drawled Mr. Giles, dramatically. "An' they knocked me up, ter know ef ennybody hed passed. An' one o' them men—I never seen none of 'em afore; they 's all valley folks, I 'm a-thinkin'—an' one of 'em bruk his saddle-girt' a good piece down the road, an' he kem back ter borrer mine; an' ez we war a-fixin' of it, he tole me what they war all arter. He said that word war tuk ter the sheriff down yander in the valley—'pears ter me them town-folks don't think nobody in the mountings hev got good sense—word war tuk ter the sheriff 'bout this one-armed harnt that walks Chilhowee; an' he sot it down that Reuben Crabb war n't dead at all, an' Joel jes' pur-tended ter hev buried him, an' it air Reuben hisself that walks Chilhowee. An' thar air two hundred dollars blood-money reward fur ennybody ez kin ketch him. These hyar valley folks air powerful cur'ous critters,—two hun-derd dollars blood-money reward fur that thar harnt that walks Chilhowee! I jes' sot myself ter laffin' when that thar cuss tole it so solemn. I jes' 'lowed ter him ez he could n't shoot a harnt nor hang a harnt, an' Reuben Crabb hed about got done with his persecutions in this worl'. An' he said that by the time they hed scoured this mounting, like they hed laid off ter do, they would find that that thar puny little harnt war nuthin' but a mortal man, an' could be kep' in a jail ez handy ez enny other flesh an' blood. He said the sheriff 'lowed ez the reason Reuben hed jes' taken ter walk Chilhowee sence Joel died is 'kase thar air nobody ter feed him, like Joel done, mebbe, in the nights; an' Reuben always war a pore, one-armed, weakly critter, what can't even kerry a gun, an' he air driv by hunger out'n the hole whar he stays, ter prowl round the cornfields an' hen coops ter steal suthin',—an' that 's how he kem ter be seen frequent. The sheriff 'lowed that Reuben can't find enough roots an' yerbs ter keep him up; but law!—a harnt eatin'! It jes' sot me off ter laffin'. Reuben Crabb hev been too busy in torment fur the las' four year ter be a-studyin' 'bout eatin'; an' it air his harnt that walks Chilhowee."

The next morning, before the moon sank, Clarsie, with a tin pail in her hand, went to meet the ghost at the appointed place. She understood now why the terrible doom that falls upon those to whom a spirit may chance to speak had not descended upon her, and that fear was gone; but the secrecy of her errand weighed heavily. She had been scrupulously careful to put into the pail only such things as had fallen to her share at the table, and which she had saved from the meals of yesterday. "A gal that goes a-robbin' fur a hongry harnt," was her moral reflection, "oughter be throwed boda-ciously off'n the bluff."

She found no one at the forks of the road. In the marshy dip were only the myriads of mountain azaleas, only the masses of feathery ferns, only the constellated glories of the laurel blooms. A sea of shining white mist was in the valley, with glinting golden rays striking athwart it from the great cresset of the sinking moon; here and there the long, dark, horizontal line of a distant mountain's summit rose above the vaporous shimmer, like a dreary, sombre island in the midst of enchanted waters. Her large, dreamy eyes, so wild and yet so gentle, gazed out through the laurel leaves upon the floating gilded flakes of light, as in the deep coverts of the mountain, where the fulvous-tinted deer were lying, other eyes, as wild and as gentle, dreamily watched the vanishing moon. Overhead, the filmy, lace-like clouds, fretting the blue heavens, were tinged with a faint rose. Through the trees she caught a glimpse of the red sky of dawn, and the glister of a great lucent, tremulous star. From the ground, misty blue exhalations were rising, alternating with the long lines of golden light yet drifting through the woods. It was all very still, very peaceful, almost holy. One could hardly believe that these consecrated solitudes had once reverberated with the echoes of man's death-dealing ingenuity, and that Reuben Crabb had fallen, shot through and through, amid that wealth of flowers at the forks of the road. She heard suddenly the far-away baying of a hound. Her great eyes dilated, and she lifted her head to listen. Only the solemn silence of the woods, the slow sinking of the noiseless moon, the voiceless splendor of that eloquent daystar.

Morning was close at hand, and she was beginning to wonder that the ghost did not appear, when the leaves fell into abrupt commotion, and he was standing in the road, beside her. He did not speak, but watched her with an eager, questioning intentness, as she placed the contents of the pail upon the moss at the roadside. "I'm a-comin' agin ter-morrer," she said, gently. He made no reply, quickly gathered the food from the ground, and disappeared in the deep shades of the woods.

She had not expected thanks, for she was accustomed only to the gratitude of dumb beasts; but she was vaguely conscious of something wanting, as she stood motionless for a moment, and watched the burnished rim of the moon slip down behind the western mountains. Then she slowly walked along her misty way in the dim light of the coming dawn. There was a footstep in the road behind her; she thought it was the ghost once more. She turned, and met Simon Burney, face to face. His rod was on his shoulder, and a string of fish was in his hand.

"Ye air a-doin' wrongful, Clarsie," he said, sternly. "It air agin the law fur folks ter feed an' shelter them ez is a-runnin' from jestice. An' ye 'll git yerself inter trouble. Other folks will find ye out, besides me, an' then the sheriff 'll be up hyar arter ye."

The tears rose to Clarsie's eyes. This prospect was infinitely more terrifying than the awful doom which follows the horror of a ghost's speech.

"I can't holp it," she said, however, doggedly swinging the pail back and forth. "I can't gin my consent ter starvin' of folks even ef they air a-hidin' an' a-runnin' from jestice."

"They mought put ye in jail, too,—I dunno," suggested Simon Burney.

"I can't holp that, nuther," said Clarsie, the sobs rising, and the tears falling fast. "Ef they comes an' gits me, and puts me in the pen'tiary away down yander, somewhars in the valley, like they done Jane Simpkins, fur a-cuttin' of her step-mother's throat with a butcher-knife, while she war asleep,—though some said Jane war crazy,—I can't gin my consent ter starvin' of folks."

A recollection came over Simon Burney of the simile of "hendering the sun from shining."

"She hev done sot it down in her mind," he thought, as he walked on beside her and looked at her resolute face. Still he did not relinquish his effort.

"Doin' wrong, Clarsie, ter aid folks what air a-doin' wrong, an' mebbe *hev* done wrong, air powerful hurtful ter everybody, an' henders the law an' jestice."

"I can't holp it," said Clarsie.

"It 'pears toler'ble comical ter me," said Simon Burney, with a sudden perception of a curious fact which has proved a marvel to wiser men, "that no matter how good a woman is, she ain't got no respect fur the laws of the country, an' don't sot no store by jestice." After a momentary silence he appealed to her on another basis. "Somebody will ketch him arter a while, ez sure ez ye air born. The sheriff 's a-sarchin' now, an' by the time that words gits around, all the mounting boys 'll turn out, 'kase thar air two hunderd dollars blood-money fur him. An then he 'll think, when they ketches him,—an' everybody 'll say so, too,—ez ye war constant in feedin' him jes' ter 'tice him ter comin' ter one place, so ez ye could tell somebody whar ter go ter ketch him, an' make them gin ye haffen the blood-money, mebbe. That 's what the mounting will say, mos' likely."

"I can't holp it," said Clarsie, once more.

He left her walking on toward the rising sun, and retraced his way to the forks of the road. The jubilant morning was filled with the song of birds; the sunlight flashed on the dew; all the delicate enameled bells of the pink and white azaleas were swinging tremulously in the wind; the aroma of ferns and mint rose on the delicious fresh air. Presently he checked his pace, creeping steathily on the moss and grass beside the road rather than in the beaten path. He pulled aside the leaves of the laurel with no more stir than the wind might have made, and stole cautiously through its dense growth, till he came suddenly upon the puny little ghost, lying in the sun at the foot of a tree. The frightened creature sprang to his feet with a wild cry of terror, but before he could move a step he was caught and held fast in the strong grip of the stalwart mountaineer beside him. "I hev kem hyar ter tell ye a word, Reuben Crabb," said Simon Burney. "I hev kem hyar ter tell ye that the whole mounting air a-goin' ter turn out ter sarch fur ye; the sheriff air a-ridin' now, an' ef ye don't come along with me they 'll hev ye afore night, 'kase thar air two hundred dollars reward fur ye."

What a piteous wail went up to the smiling blue sky, seen through the dappling leaves above them! What a horror, and despair, and prescient agony were in the hunted creature's face! The ghost struggled no longer; he slipped from his feet down upon the roots of the tree, and turned that woful face, with its starting eyes and drawn muscles and quivering parted lips, up toward the unseeing sky.

"God A'mighty, man!" exclaimed Simon Burney, moved to pity. "Why n't ye quit this hyar way of livin' in the woods like ye war a wolf? Why n't ye come back an' stand yer trial? From all I' ve hearn tell, it 'pears ter me ez the jury air obleeged ter let ye off, an' I 'll take keer of ye agin them Grims."

"I hain't got no place ter live in," cried out the ghost, with a keen despair.

Simon Burney hesitated, Reuben Crabb was possibly a murderer,—at the best could but be a burden. The burden, however, had fallen in his way, and he lifted it.

"I tell ye now, Reuben Crabb," he said, "I ain't a-goin' ter holp no man ter break the law an' hender jestice; but ef ye will go an' stand yer trial, I'll take keer of ye agin them Grims ez long ez I kin fire a rifle. An' arter the jury hev done let ye off, ye air welcome ter live along o' me at my house till ye die. Ye air no-'count ter work, I know, but I ain't a-goin' ter grudge ye fur a livin' at my house."

And so it came to pass that the reward set upon the head of the harnt that walked Chilhowee was never claimed.

With his powerful ally, the forlorn little spectre went to stand his trial, and the jury acquitted him without leaving the box. Then he came back to the mountains to live with Simon Burney. The cruel gibes of his burly mockers that had beset his feeble life from his childhood up, the deprivation and loneliness and despair and fear that had filled those days when he walked Chilhowee, had not improved the harnt's temper. He was a helpless creature, not able to carry a gun or plow, and the years that he spent smoking his cob-pipe in Simon Burney's door were idle years and unhappy. But Mrs. Giles said she thought he was "a mighty lucky little critter: fust, he hed Joel ter take keer of him an' feed him, when he tuk ter the woods ter pertend he war a harnt; an' they do say now that Clarsie Pratt, afore she war married, used ter kerry him vittles, too; an' then old Simon Burney tuk him up an' fed him ez plenty ez ef he war a good workin' hand, an' gin him clothes an' house-room, an' put up with his jawin' jes' like he never hearn a word of it. But law! some folks dunno when they air well off."

There was only a sluggish current of peasant blood in Simon Burney's veins, but a prince could not have dispensed hospitality with a more royal hand. Ungrudgingly he gave of his best; valiantly he defended his thankless guest at the risk of his life; with a moral gallantry he struggled with his sloth, and worked early and late, that there might be enough to divide. There was no possibility of a recompense for him, not even in the encomiums of discriminating friends, nor the satisfaction of tutored feelings and a practiced spirited discernment; for he was an uncouth creature, and densely ignorant.

The grace of culture is, in its way, a fine thing, but the best that art can do—the polish of a gentleman—is hardly equal to the best that Nature can do in her higher moods.

THOMAS NELSON PAGE

(1853–1922)

The dialect stories in Thomas Nelson Page's *In Ole Virginia*, Ellen Glasgow wrote, "are firm and round and as fragrant as dried rose-leaves." More than any other writer, it was Page who glamorized Virginia plantation life "befo' de wah." For two decades he was one of the leading Southern local colorists.

Page came by his nostalgia for antebellum plantation life honestly. Born in Hanover County, Virginia, he was descended from two distinguished Virginia families, the Nelsons and the Pages. He was a student at Washington College when Robert E. Lee was its president; he studied law at the University of Virginia and then practiced it in Hanover County ,and Richmond, Virginia. Publication of a black dialect poem, "Uncle Gabe's White Folks," in 1877 launched him on a career as interpreter of the antebellum glamour and faded postwar glory of plantation society. In 1884 *The Century Magazine* published his story, "Marse Chan," perhaps the quintessential work in the plantation sub-genre. It was a great success, and Page followed it with other dialect stories such as "Unc' Edinburg's Drowndin" and "Meh Lady." These and three other stories were brought out in book form in 1887 as *In Ole Virginia*. Page's popularity continued with children's stories and other tales of plantation life, and he also wrote essays and articles extolling the happy days before the war and the nobility of those who kept the faith. He defended the South's course of action before 1861 and argued for his region's racial beliefs. In 1898 he published his first full-length novel, *Red Rock*, a chronicle of Reconstruction written according to the standard white Southern view. In 1903 *Gordon Keith*, a novel of the New South, was published. He wrote numerous other works of fiction and nonfiction, including a "problem" novel about urban life, *John Marvel, Assistant* (1909). He also published a biography of Robert E. Lee in 1911, and at his death in 1922 he left an unfinished novel, *Red Riders.*

In 1886 Page married Anne Seddon Bruce. Her death two years later was a grievous blow and for several years afterward he could not write. In 1893 he married Mrs. Florence Lathrop Field of Chicago, a sister-in-law of Marshall Field. The Pages settled in Washington and began playing a notable role in social life and in politics. In 1913 President Woodrow Wilson appointed him ambassador to Italy and he served in that post until 1919. He died at "Oakland," the Hanover County house in which he had been born.

Page's depiction of antebellum life in "Meh Lady" and other similar stories was one of glamorous young aristocrats and faithful black retainers, and the coming of the War was depicted as the end of a Golden Age. His blacks are all gentle and humble, happy in their role as slaves, and the presence of the rural white middle class, which was the largest element in the Virginia population, almost never intrudes in his idyllic representation of the good old times.

MARSE CHAN

A TALE OF OLD VIRGINIA

One afternoon, in the autumn of 1872, I was riding leisurely down the sandy road that winds along the top of the water-shed between two of the smaller rivers of eastern Virginia. The road I was travelling, following "the ridge" for miles, had just struck me as most significant of the character of the race whose only avenue of communication with the outside world it had formerly been. Their once splendid mansions, now fast falling to decay, appeared to view from time to time, set back far from the road, in proud seclusion, among groves of oak and hickory, now scarlet and gold with the early frost. Distance was nothing to this people; time was of no consequence to them. They desired but a level path in life, and that they had, though the way was longer, and the outer world strode by them as they dreamed.

I was aroused from my reflections by hearing some one ahead of me calling, "Heah!—heah—whoo-oop, heah!"

Turning the curve in the road, I saw just before me a negro standing, with a hoe and a watering-pot in his hand. He had evidently just gotten over the "worm-fence" into the road, out of the path which led zigzag across the "old field" and was lost to sight in the dense growth of sassafras. When I rode up, he was looking anxiously back down this path for his dog. So engrossed was he that he did not even hear my horse, and I reined in to wait until he should turn around and satisfy my curiosity as to the handsome old place half a mile off from the road.

The numerous out-buildings and the large barns and stables told that it had once been the seat of wealth, and the wild waste of sassafras that covered the broad fields gave it an air of desolation that greatly excited my interest. Entirely oblivious of my proximity, the negro went on calling "Whoo-oop, heah!" until along the path, walking very slowly and with great dignity, appeared a noble-looking old orange and white setter, gray with age, and corpulent with excessive feeding. As soon as he came in sight, his master began:

"Yes, dat you! You gittin' deaf as well as bline, I s'pose! Kyarnt heah me callin', I reckon? Whyn't yo' come on, dawg?"

The setter sauntered slowly up to the fence and stopped, without even deigning a look at the speaker, who immediately proceeded to take the rails down, talking meanwhile:

"Now, I got to pull down de gap, I s'pose! Yo' so sp'ilt yo' kyahn hardly walk. Jes' ez able to git over it as I is! Jes' like white folks—think 'cuz you's white and I's black, I got to wait on yo' all de time. Ne'm mine, I ain' gwi' do it!"

The fence having been pulled down sufficiently low to suit his dogship, he marched sedately through, and, with a hardly perceptible lateral movement of his tail, walked on down the road. Putting up the rails carefully, the negro turned and saw me.

"Sarvent, marster," he said, taking his hat off. Then, as if apologetically for having permitted a stranger to witness what was merely a family affair, he added: "He know I don' mean nothin' by what I sez. He's Marse Chan's dawg, an' he's so ole he kyahn git long no pearter. He know I'se jes' prodjickin' wid 'im."

"Who is Marse Chan?" I asked; "and whose place is that over there, and the one a mile or two back—the place with the big gate and the carved stone pillars?"

"Marse Chan," said the darky, "he's Marse Channin'—my young marster; an' dem places—dis one's Weall's, an' de one back dyar wid de rock gate-pos's is ole Cun'l Chahmb'lin's. Dey don' nobody live dyar now, 'cep' niggers. Arfter de war some one or nurr bought our place, but his name done kind o' slipped me. I nuver hearn on 'im befo'; I think dey's half-strainers. I don' ax none on 'em no odds. I lives down de road heah, a little piece, an' I jes' steps down of a evenin' and looks arfter de graves."

"Well, where is Marse Chan?" I asked.

"Hi! don' you know? Marse Chan, he went in de army. I was wid im. Yo' know he warn' gwine an' lef' Sam."

"Will you tell me all about it?" I said, dismounting.

Instantly, and as if by instinct, the darky stepped forward and took my bridle. I demurred a little; but with a bow that would have honored old Sir Roger, he shortened the reins, and taking my horse from me, led him along.

"Now tell me about Marse Chan," I said.

"Lawd, marster, hit's so long ago, I'd a'most forgit all about it, ef I hedn' been wid him ever sence he wuz born. Ez 'tis, I remembers it jes' like 'twuz yistiddy. Yo' know Marse Chan an' me—we wuz boys togerr. I wuz older'n he wuz, jes' de same ez he wuz whiter'n me. I wuz born plantin' corn time, de spring arfter big Jim an' de six steers got washed away at de upper ford right down dyar b'low de quarters ez he wuz a bringin' de Chris'mas things home; an' Marse Chan, he warn' born tell mos' to de harves' arfter my sister Nancy married Cun'l Chahmb'lin's Torm, 'bout eight years arfterwoods.

"Well, when Marse Chan wuz born, dey wuz de grettes' doin's at home you ever did see. De folks all hed holiday, jes' like in de Chris'mas. Ole marster (we didn' call 'im *ole* marster tell arfter Marse Chan wuz born—befo' dat he wuz jes' de marster, so)—well, ole marster, his face fyar shine wid pleasure, an' all de folks wuz mighty glad, too, 'cause dey all loved ole marster, and aldo' dey did step aroun' right peart when ole marster was lookin' at 'em, dyar warn' nyar han' on de place but what, ef he wanted anythin', would walk up to de back poach, an' say he warn' to see de marster, an' ev'ybody wuz talkin' 'bout de young marster, an' de maids an' de wimmens 'bout de kitchen wuz sayin' how 'twuz de purties' chile dey ever see; an' at dinner-time de mens (all on 'em hed holiday) come roun' de poach an' ax how de missis an' de young marster wuz, an' ole marster come out on de poach an' smile wus'n a 'possum, an' sez, 'Thankee! Bofe doin' fust rate, boys;' an' den he stepped back in de house, sort o' laughin' to hisse'f, an' in a minute he come out ag'in wid de baby in he arms, all wrapped up in flannens an' things, an' sez, 'Heah he is, boys.' All de folks den, dey went up on de poach to look at 'im, drappin' dey hats on de steps, an' scrapin' dey feets ez dey went up. An' pres'n'y ole marster, lookin' down at we all chil'en all packed togerr down dyah like a parecel o' sheep-burrs, cotch sight o' *me* (he knowed my name, 'cause I use' to hole he hoss fur 'im sometimes; but he didn' know all de chil'en by name, dey wuz so many on 'em), an' he sez, 'Come up heah.' So up I goes tippin', skeered like, an' old marster sez, 'Ain' you Mymie's son?' 'Yass, seh,' sez I. 'Well,' sez he, 'I'm gwine to give you to yo' young Marse Channin' to be his body-servant, ' an' he put de baby right in my arms (it's de truth I'm tellin' yo'!), an' yo' jes' ought to a-heard de folks sayin', 'Lawd! marster, dat boy'll drap dat chile!' 'Naw, he won't,' sez marster; 'I kin trust 'im.' And den he sez: 'Now, Sam, from dis time you belong to yo' young Marse Channin'; I wan' you to tek keer on 'im ez long ez he lives. You are to be his boy from dis time. An' now,' he sez, 'carry 'im in de house.' An' he walks arfter me an' opens de do's fur me, an' I kyars 'im in my arms, an' lays 'im down on de bed. An from dat time I was tooken in de house to be Marse Channin's body-servant.

"Well, you nuver see a chile grow so. Pres'n'y he growed up right big, an' ole marster sez he must have some edication. So he sont 'im to school to ole Miss Lawry down dyar, dis side o' Cun'l Chahmb'lin's, an' I use' to go 'long wid 'im an' tote he books an' we all's snacks; an' when he larnt to read an' spell right good, an' got 'bout so-o big, ole Miss Lawry she died, an' ole marster said he mus' have a man to teach 'im an' trounce 'im. So we all went to Mr. Hall, whar kep' de school-house beyant de creek, an' dyar we went ev'y day, 'cep Sat'd'ys of co'se, an' sich days ez Marse Chan din' warn' go, an' ole missis begged 'im off.

"Hit wuz down dyar Marse Chan fust took notice o' Miss Anne. Mr. Hall, he taught gals ez well ez boys, an' Cun'l Chahmb'lin he sont his daughter (dat's Miss Anne I'm talkin' about). She wuz a leetle bit o' gal when she fust come. Yo' see, her ma wuz dead, an' ole Miss Lucy Chahmb'lin, she lived wid her brurr an' kep' house for 'im; an' he wuz so busy wid politics, he didn' have much time to spyar, so he sont Miss Anne to Mr. Hall's by a 'ooman wid a note. When she come dat day in de school-house, an' all de chil'en looked at her so hard, she tu'n right red, an' 'tried to pull her long curls over her eyes, an' den put bofe de backs of her little han's in her two eyes, an' begin to cry to herse'f. Marse Chan he was settin' on de een' o' de bench nigh de do', an' he jes' reached out an' put he arm roun' her an' drawed her up to 'im. An' he kep' whisperin' to her, an' callin' her name, an' coddlin' her; an' pres'n'y she took her han's down an' begin to laugh.

"Well, dey 'peared to tek' a gre't fancy to each urr from dat time. Miss Anne she warn' nuthin' but a baby hardly, an' Marse Chan he wuz a good big boy 'bout mos' thirteen years ole, I reckon. Hows'ever, dey sut'n'y wuz sot on each urr an' (yo' heah me!) ole marster an' Cun'l Chahmb'lin dey 'peared to like it 'bout well ez de chil'en. Yo' see, Cun'l Chahmb'lin's place j'ined ourn, an' it looked jes' ez natural fur dem two chil'en to marry an' mek it one plantation, ez it did fur de creek to run down de bottom from our place into Cun'l Chahmb'lin's. I don' rightly think de chil'en thought 'bout gittin' *married*, not den, no mo'n I thought 'bout marryin' Judy when she wuz a little gal at Cun'l Chahmb'lin's, runnin' 'bout de house, huntin' fur Miss Lucy's spectacles; but dey wuz good frien's from de start. Marse Chan he use' to kyar Miss Anne's books fur her ev'y day, an' ef de road wuz muddy or she wuz tired, he use' to tote her; an' 'twarn' hardly a day passed dat he didn't kyar her some'n' to school—apples or hick'y nuts, or some'n. He wouldn' let none o' de chil'en tease her, nurr. Heh! One day, one o' de boys poked he finger at Miss Anne, and arfter school Marse Chan he axed 'im 'roun' hine de school-house out o' sight, an' ef he didn' whop 'im!

"Marse Chan, he wuz de peartes' scholar ole Mr. Hall hed, an' Mr. Hall he wuz mighty proud o' 'im. I don' think he use' to beat 'im ez much ez he did de urrs, aldo' he wuz de head in all debilment dat went on, jes' ez he wuz in sayin' he lessons.

"Heh! one day in summer, jes' fo' de school broke up, dyah come up a storm right sudden, an' riz de creek (dat one yo' cross' back yonder), an' Marse Chan he toted Miss Anne home on he back. He ve'y off'n did dat when de parf wuz muddy. But dis day when dey come to de creek, it had done washed all de logs 'way. 'Twuz still mighty high, so Marse Chan he put Miss Anne down, an' he took a pole an' waded right in. Hit took 'im long up to de shoulders. Den he waded back, an' took Miss Anne up on his head an' kyared her right over. At fust she wuz skeered; but he tol' her he could swim an' wouldn' let her git hu't, an' den she let 'im kyar her 'cross, she hol'in' his han's. I warn' 'long dat day, but he sut'n'y did dat thing.

"Ole marster he wuz so pleased 'bout it, he giv' Marse Chan a pony; an' Marse Chan rode 'im to school de day arfter he come, so proud, an' sayin' how he wuz gwine to let Anne ride behine 'im; an' when he come home dat evenin' he wuz walkin'. 'Hi! where's yo' pony?' said ole marster. 'I give 'im to Anne,' says Marse Chan. 'She liked 'im, an'—I kin walk.' 'Yes,' sez ole marster, laughin', 'I s'pose you's already done giv' her yo'se'f, an' nex' thing I know you'll be givin' her this plantation and all my niggers.'

"Well, about a fortnight or sich a matter arfter dat, Cun'l Chahmb'lin sont over an' invited all o' we all over to dinner, an' Marse Chan wuz 'spressly named in de note whar Ned brought; an' arfter dinner he made ole Phil, whar wuz his ker'ige-driver, bring roun' Marse Chan's pony wid a little side-saddle on 'im, an' a beautiful little hoss wid a bran'-new saddle an' bridle on 'im; an' he gits up an' meks Marse Chan a gre't speech, an' presents 'im de little hoss; an' den he calls Miss Anne, an' she comes out on de poach in a little ridin' frock, an' dey puts her on her pony, an' Marse Chan mounts his hoss, an' dey goes to ride, while de grown folks is a-laughin' an' chattin' an' smokin' dey cigars.

"Dem wuz good ole times, marster—de bes' Sam ever see! Dey wuz, in fac'! Niggers didn' hed nothin' 't all to do—jes' hed to 'ten' to de feedin' an' cleanin' de hosses, an' doin' what de marster tell 'em to do; an' when dey wuz sick, dey had things sont 'em out de house, an' de same doctor come to see 'em whar 'ten' to de white folks when dey wuz po'ly. Dyar warn' no trouble nor nothin.

"Well, things tuk a change arfter dat. Marse Chan he went to de bo'din' school, whar he use' to write to me constant. Ole missis use' to read me de letters, an' den I'd git Miss Anne to read 'em ag'in to me when I'd see her. He use' to write to her too, an' she use' to write to him too. Den Miss Anne she wuz sont off to school too. An' in de summer time dey'd bofe come home, an' yo' hardly knowed whether Marse Chan lived at home or over at Cun'l Chahmb'lin's. He wuz over dyah constant. 'Twuz always ridin' or fishin' down dyah in de river; or sometimes he' go over dyah, an' 'im an' she'd go out an' set in de yard onder de trees; she settin' up mekin' out she wuz knittin' some sort o' bright-cullored some'n', wid de grarss growin all up 'g'inst her, an' her hat th'owed back on her neck, an' he readin' to her

out books; an' sometimes dey'd bofe read out de same book, fust one an'
den todder. I use' to see 'em! Dat wuz when dey wuz growin' up like.

"Den ole marster he run for Congress, an' ole Cun'l Chahmb'lin he wuz
put up to run 'g'inst ole marster by de Dimicrats; but ole marster he beat
'im. Yo' know he wuz gwine do dat! Co'se he wuz! Dat made ole Cun'l
Chahmb'lin mighty mad, and dey stopt visitin' each urr reg'lar, like dey had
been doin' all 'long. Den Cun'l Chahmb'lin he sort o' got in debt, an' sell
some o' he niggers, an' dat's de way de fuss begun. Dat's whar de lawsuit
cum from. Ole marster he didn' like nobody to sell niggers, an' knowin' dat
Cun'l Chahmb'lin wuz sellin' o' his, he writ an' offered to buy his M'ria an'
all her chil'en, 'cause she hed married our Zeek'yel. An' don' yo' think,
Cun'l Chahmb'lin axed ole marster mo' 'n th'ee niggers wuz wuth fur M'ria!
Befo' ole marster bought her, dough, de sheriff cum an' levelled on M'ria
an' a whole parecel o' urr niggers. Ole marster he went to de sale an' bid for
'em; but Cun'l Chahmb'lin he got some one to bid 'g'inst ole marster. Dey
wuz knocked out to ole marster dough, an' den dey hed a big lawsuit, an'
ole marster wuz agwine to co't, off an' on, fur some years, till at lars' de co't
decided dat M'ria belonged to ole marster. Ole Cun'l Chahmb'lin den wuz
so mad he sued ole marster for a little strip o' lan' down dyah on de line
fence, whar he said belonged to 'im. Evy'body knowed hit belonged to ole
marster. Ef yo' go down dyah now, I kin show it to yo', inside de line fence,
whar it hed done bin ever since long befo' Cun'l Chahmb'lin wuz born. But
Cun'l Chahmb'lin wuz a mons'us perseverin' man, an' ole marster he
wouldn' let nobody run over 'im. No, dat he wouldn'! So dey wuz agwine
down to co't about dat, fur I don' know how long, till ole marster beat 'im.

"All dis time, yo' know, Marse Chan wuz agoin' back'ads an' for'ads to
college, an' wuz growed up a ve'y fine young man. He wuz a ve'y likely
gent'man! Miss Anne she hed done mos' growed up too—wuz puttin' her
hyar up like ole missis use' to put hers up, an' 't wuz jes' ez bright ez de
sorrel's mane when de sun cotch on it, an' her eyes wuz gre't big dark eyes,
like her pa's, on'y bigger an' not so fierce, an' 'twarn' none o' de young
ladies ez purty ez she wuz. She an' Marse Chan still set a heap o' sto' by one
'nurr, but I don' think dey wuz easy wid each urr ez when he used to tote
her home from school on his back. Marse Chan he use' to love de ve'y
groun' she walked on, dough, in my 'pinion. Heh! His face 'twoud light up
whenever she come into chu'ch, or anywhere, jes' like de sun hed come
th'oo a chink on it suddenly.

"Den ole marster lost he eyes. D' yo' ever heah 'bout dat? Heish! Didn'
yo'? Well, one night de big barn cotch fire. De stables, yo' know, wuz under
de big barn, an' all de hosses wuz in dyah. Hit'peared to me like 'twarn' no
time befo' all de folks an' de neighbors dey come, an' dey wuz a-totin'
water, an' a-tryin' to save de po' critters, and dey got a heap on 'em out; but
de ker'ige-hosses dey wouldn' come out, an' dey wuz a-runnin' back'ads an'
for'ads inside de stalls a-nikerin' an a-screamin', like dey knowed dey time

hed come. Yo' could heah 'em so pitiful, an' pres'n'y old marster said to Ham Fisher (he wuz de ker'ige-driver), 'Go in dyah an' try to save 'em; don' let 'em bu'n to death.' An' Ham he went right in. An' jest arfter he got in, de shed whar it hed fus' cotch fell in, an' de sparks shot 'way up in de air; an' Ham didn' come back, an' de fire begun to lick out under de eaves over whar de ker'ige hosses' stalls wuz, an' all of a sudden ole marster tu'ned an' kissed ole missis, who wuz standin' nigh him, wid her face jes' ez white ez a sperit's, an', befo' anybody knowed what he wuz gwine do, jumped right in de do', an' de smoke come po'in' out behine 'im. Well, seh, I nuver 'spects to heah tell Judgment sich a soun' ez de folks set up! Ole missis she jes' drapt down on her knees in de mud an' prayed out loud. Hit 'peared like her pra'r wuz heard; for in a minit, right out de same do', kyarin' Ham Fisher in his arms, come ole marster, wid his clo's all blazin'. Dey flung water on 'im, an' put 'im out; an', ef you b'lieve me, yo' wouldn' a-knowed 'twuz ole marster. Yo' see, he hed find Ham Fisher done fall down in de smoke right by the ker'ige-hoss' stalls, whar he sont him, an' he hed to tote 'im back in his arms th'oo de fire what hed done cotch de front part o' de stable, and to keep de flame from gittin' down Ham Fisher's th'ote he hed tuk off his own hat and mashed it all over Ham Fisher's face, an' he hed kep' Ham Fisher from bein' so much bu'nt; but he wuz bu'nt dreadful! His beard an' hyar wuz all nyawed off, an' his face an' han's an' neck wuz scorified terrible. Well, he jes' laid Ham Fisher down, an' then he kind o' staggered for'ad, an' ole missis ketch' 'im in her arms. Ham Fisher, he warn' bu'nt so bad, an' he got out in a month or two; an' arfter a long time, ole marster he got well, too; but he wuz always stone blind arfter that. He nuver could see none from dat night.

"Marse Chan he comed home from college toreckly, an' he sut'n'y did nuss ole marster faithful—jes' like a 'ooman. Den he took charge of de plantation arfter dat; an' I use' to wait on 'im jes' like when we wuz boys togedder; an' sometimes we'd slip off an' have a fox-hunt, an' he'd be jes' like he wuz in ole times, befo' ole marster got bline, an' Miss Anne Chahmb'lin stopt comin' over to our house, an' settin' onder de trees, readin' out de same book.

"He sut'n'y wuz good to me. Nothin' nuver made no diffunce 'bout dat. He nuver hit me a lick in his life—an' nuver let nobody else do it, nurr.

"I 'members one day, when he wuz a leetle bit o' boy, ole marster hed done tole we all chil'en not to slide on de straw-stacks; an' one day me an' Marse Chan thought ole marster hed done gone 'way from home. We watched him git on he hoss an' ride up de road out o' sight, an' we wuz out in de field a-slidin' an a-slidin', when up comes ole marster. We started to run; but he hed done see us, an' he called us to come back; an' sich a whuppin' ez he did gi' us!

"Fust he took Marse Chan, an' den he teched me up. He nuver hu't me, but in co'se I wuz a-hollerin' ez hard ez I could stave it, 'cause I knowed dat wuz gwine mek him stop. Marse Chan he hed'n open he mouf long ez ole marster wuz tunin' 'im; but soon ez he commence warmin' me an' I begin to holler, Marse Chan he bu'st out cryin', an' stept right in befo' ole marster, an' ketchin' de whup, sed:

" 'Stop, seh! Yo' sha'n't whup 'im; he b'longs to me, an' ef you hit 'im another lick I'll set 'im free!'

"I wish yo' hed see ole marster. Marse Chan he warn' mo'n eight years ole, an' dyah dey wuz—old marster stan'in' wid he whup raised up, an' Marse Chan red an' cryin', hol'in' on to it, an' sayin' I b'longst to 'im.

"Ole marster, he raise' de whup, an' den he drapt it, an' broke out in a smile over he face, an' he chuck' Marse Chan onder de chin, an' tu'n right roun' an' went away, laughin' to hisse'f, an' I heah' 'im tellin' ole missis dat evenin', an' laughin' 'bout it.

" 'Twan' so mighty long arfter dat when dey fust got to talkin' 'bout de war. Dey wuz a-dictatin' back'ads an' for'ds 'bout it fur two or th'ee years 'fo' it come sho' nuff, you know. Ole marster, he was a Whig, an' of co'se Marse Chan he tuk after he pa. Cun'l Chahmb'lin, he wuz a Dimicrat. He wuz in favor of de war, an' ole marster and Marse Chan dey wuz agin' it. Dey wuz a-talkin' 'bout it all de time, an' purty soon Cun'l Chahmb'lin he went about ev'vywhar speakin' an' noratin' 'bout Ferginia ought to secede; an' Marse Chan he wuz picked up to talk agin' 'im. Dat wuz de way dey come to fight de duil. I sut'n'y wuz skeered fur Marse Chan dat mawnin', an' he was jes' ez cool! Yo' see, it happen so: Marse Chan he wuz a-speakin' down at de Deep Creek Tavern, an' he kind o' got de bes' of ole Cun'l Chahmb'lin. All de white folks laughed an' hoorawed, an' ole Cun'l Chahmb'lin—my Lawd! I t'ought he'd a' bu'st, he was so mad. Well, when it come to his time to speak, he jes' light into Marse Chan. He call 'im a traitor, an' a ab'litionis', an' I don't know what all. Marse Chan, he jes' kep' cool till de ole Cun'l light into he pa. Ez soon ez he name ole marster, I seen Marse Chan sort o' lif' up he head. D' yo' ever see a hoss rar he head up right sudden at night when he see somethin' comin' to'ds 'im from de side an' he don't know what 'tis? Ole Cun'l Chahmb'lin he went right on. He said ole marster hed taught Marse Chan; dat ole marster wuz a wuss ab'litionis' dan he son. I looked at Marse Chan, an' sez to myse'f: 'Fo' Gord! old Cun'l Chahmb'lin better min', an' I hedn' got de wuds out, when ole Cun'l Chahmb'lin 'cuse' old marster o' cheatin' 'im out o' he niggers, an' stealin' piece o' he lan'—dat's de lan' I tole you 'bout. Well, seh, nex' think I knowed, I heahed Marse Chan—hit all happen right 'long togerr, like lightnin' and thunder when they hit right at you—I heah 'im say:

" 'Cun'l Chahmb'lin, what you say is false, an' yo' know it to be so. You have wilfully slandered one of de pures' an' nobles' men Gord ever made, an' nothin' but yo' gray hyars protects you.'

"Well, ole Cun'l Chahmb'lin, he ra'ed an' he pitch'd. He said he wan' too ole, an' he'd show 'im so.

" 'Ve'y well,' says Marse Chan.

"De meetin broke up den. I wuz hol'in' de hosses out dyar in de road by de een' o' de poach, an' I see Marse Chan talkin' an' talkin' to Mr. Gordon an' anudder gent'man, and den he come out an' got on de sorrel an' galloped off. Soon ez he got out o' sight he pulled up, an' we walked along tell we come to de road whar leads off to'ds Mr. Barbour's. He wuz de big lawyer o' de country. Dar he tu'ned off. All dis time he hedn' sed a wud, 'cep' to kind o' mumble to hisse'f now and den. When we got to Mr. Barbour's, he got down an' went in. Dat wuz in de late winter; de folks wuz jes' beginnin' to plough fur corn. He stayed dyar 'bout two hours, an' when he come out Mr. Barbour come out to de gate wid 'im an' shake hans arfter he got up in de saddle. Den we all rode off. 'Twuz late den—good dark; an' we rid ez hard ez we could, tell we come to de ole school-house at ole Cun'l Chahmb'lin's gate. When we got dar, Marse Chan got down an' walked right slow 'roun' de house. Arfter lookin' roun' a little while an' tryin' de do' to see ef it wuz shet, he walked down de road tell he got to de creek. He stop' dyar a little while an' picked up two or three little rocks an' frowed 'em in, an' pres'n'y he got up an' we come on home. Ez he got down, he tu'ned to me an', rubbin' de sorrel's nose, said: 'Have 'em well fed, Sam; I'll want 'em early in de mawnin'.'

"Dat night at supper he laugh an' talk, an' he set at de table a long time. Arfter ole marster went to bed, he went in de charmber an' set on de bed by 'im talkin' to 'im an tellin' 'im 'bout de meetin' an' e'vything; but he nuver mention ole Cun'l Chahmb'lin's name. When he got up to come out to de office in de yard, whar he slept, he stooped down an' kissed 'im jes' like he wuz a baby layin' dyar in de bed, an' he'd hardly let ole missis go at all. I knowed some'n wuz up, an' nex mawnin' I called 'im early befo' light, like he tole me, an' he dressed an' come out pres'n'y jes' like he wuz goin' to church. I had de hosses ready, an' we went out de back way to'ds de river. Ez we rode along, he said:

" 'Sam, you an' I wuz boys togedder, wa'n't we?'

" 'Yes,' sez I, 'Marse Chan, dat we wuz.'

" 'You have been ve'y faithful to me,' sez he, 'an' I have seen to it that you are well provided fur. You want to marry Judy, I know, an' you'll be able to buy her ef you want to.'

"Den he tole me he wuz goin' to fight a duil, an' in case he should git shot, he had set me free an' giv' me nuff to tek keer o' me an' my wife ez long ez we lived. He said he'd like me to stay an' tek keer o' ole marster an' ole missis ez long ez dey lived, an' he said it wouldn' be very long, he reckoned. Dat wuz de only time he voice broke—when he said dat; an' I couldn' speak a wud, my th'oat choked me so.

"When we come to de river, we tu'ned right up de bank, an' arfter ridin' 'bout a mile or sich a matter, we stopped whar dey wuz a little clearin' wid elder bushes on one side an' two big gum-trees on de urr, an' de sky wuz all red, an' de water down to'ds whar the sun wuz comin' wuz jes' like de sky.

"Pres'n'y Mr. Gordon he come, wid a 'hogany box 'bout so big 'fore 'im, an' he got down, an' Marse Chan tole me to tek all de hosses an' go 'roun' behine de bushes whar I tell you 'bout—off to one side; an' 'fore I got 'roun' dar, ole Cun'l Chahmb'lin an' Mr. Hennin an' Dr. Call come ridin' from t'urr way, to'ds ole Cun'l Chahmb'lin's. When dey hed tied dey hosses, de urr gent'mens went up to whar Mr. Gordon wuz, an' arfter some chattin' Mr. Hennin step' off 'bout fur ez 'cross dis road, or mebbe it mout be a little furder; an' den I seed 'em th'oo de bushes loadin' de pistils, an' talk a little while; an' den Marse Chan an' ole Cun'l Chahmb'lin walked up wid de pistils in dey han's, an' Marse Chan he stood wid his face right to'ds de sun. I seen it shine on him jez' ez it come up over de low groun's, an' he look like he did sometimes when he come out of church. I wuz so skeered I couldn' say nothin'. Ole Cun'l Chahmb'lin could shoot fust rate, an' Marse Chan he never missed.

"Den I heared Mr. Gordon say, 'Gent'mens, is yo' ready?' and bofe of 'em sez, 'Ready,' jes' so.

"An' he sez, 'Fire, one, two'—an' ez he said 'one,' ole Cun'l Chahmb'lin raised he pistil an' shot right at Marse Chan. De ball went th'oo his hat. I seen he hat sort o' settle on he head ez de bullit hit it, an' *he* jes' tilted his pistil up in de a'r an' shot—*bang*; an' ez de pistil went bang, he sez to Cun'l Chahmb'lin, 'I mek you a present to yo' fam'ly, seh!'

"Well, dey had some talkin' arfter dat. I didn't git rightly what it wuz; but it 'peared like Cun'l Chahmb'lin he warn't satisfied, an' wanted to have anurr shot. De seconds dey wuz talkin', an' pres'n'y dey put de pistils up, an' Marse Chan an' Mr. Gordon shook han's wid Mr. Hennin an' Dr. Call, an' come an' got on dey hosses. An' Cun'l Chahmb'lin he got on his horse an' rode away wid de urr gent'mens, lookin' like he did de day befo' when all de people laughed at 'im.

"I b'lieve old Cun'l Chahmb'lin wan' to shoot Marse Chan, anyway!

"We come on home to breakfast, I totin' de box wid de pistils befo' me on de roan. Would you b'lieve me, seh, Marse Chan he nuver said a wud 'bout it to ole marster or nobody. Ole missis didn't fin' out 'bout it for mo'n a month, an' den, Lawd! how she did cry and kiss Marse Chan; an' ole marster, aldo' he never say much, he wuz jes' ez please' ez ole missis. He call' me in de room an' made me tole 'im all 'bout it, an' when I got th'oo he gi' me five dollars an' a pyar of breeches.

"But ole Cun'l Chahmb'lin he nuver did furgive Marse Chan, an' Miss Anne she got mad too. Wimmens is mons'us onreasonable nohow. Dey's jes' like a catfish: you can n' tek hole on 'em like udder folks, an' when you gits 'm yo' can n' always hole 'em.

"What meks me think so? Heaps o' things—dis: Marse Chan he done gi' Miss Anne her pa jes' ez good ez I gi' Marse Chan's dawg sweet 'taters, an' she git mad wid 'im ez if he hed kill 'im 'stid o' sen'in' 'im back to her dat mawnin' whole an' soun'. B'lieve me! she wouldn' even speak to him arfter dat!

"Don' I 'member dat mawnin'!

"We wuz gwine fox-huntin', 'bout six weeks or sich a matter arfter de duil, an' we met Miss Anne ridin' 'long wid anurr lady an' two gent'mens whar wuz stayin' at her house. Dyar wuz always some one or nurr dyar co'ting her. Well, dat mawnin' we meet 'em right in de road. 'Twuz de fust time Marse Chan had see her sence de duil, an' he raises he hat ez he pahss, an' she looks right at 'im wid her head up in de yair like she nuver see 'im befo' in her born days; an' when she comes by me, she sez, 'Good-mawnin', Sam!' Gord! I nuver see nuthin' like de look dat come on Marse Chan's face when she pahss 'im like dat. He gi' de sorrel a pull dat fotch 'im back settin' down in de san' on he haunches. He ve'y lips wuz white. I tried to keep up wid 'im, but 'twarn' no use. He sont me back home pres'n'y, an' he rid on. I sez to myself, 'Cun'l Chahmb'lin, don' yo' meet Marse Chan dis mawnin'. He ain' bin lookin' 'roun' de ole school-house, whar he an' Miss Anne use' to go to school to ole Mr. Hall together, fur nuffin'. He won' stan' no prodjickin' to-day.'

"He nuver come home dat night tell 'way late, an' ef he'd been fox-huntin' it mus' ha' been de ole red whar lives down in de greenscum mashes he'd been chasin'. De way de sorrel wuz gormed up wid sweat an' mire sut'n'y did hu't me. He walked up to de stable wid he head down all de way, an' I'se seen 'im go eighty miles of a winter day, an' prance into de stable at night ez fresh ez ef he hed jes' cantered over to ole Cun'l Chahmb'lin's to supper. I nuver seen a hoss beat so sence I knowed de fetlock from de fo'lock, an' bad ez he wuz he wan' ez bad ez Marse Chan.

"Whew! he didn't git over dat thing, seh—he nuver did git over it.

"De war come on jes' den, an Marse Chan wuz elected cap'n; but he wouldn' tek it. He said Firginia hadn' seceded, an' he wuz gwine stan' by her. Den dey 'lected Mr. Gordon cap'n.

"I sut'n'y did wan' Marse Chan to tek de place, cuz I knowed he wuz gwine tek me wid 'im. He wan' gwine widout Sam. An' beside, he look so po' an' thin, I thought he wuz gwine die.

"Of co'se, ole missis she heard 'bout it, an' she met Miss Anne in de road, an' cut her jes' like Miss Anne cut Marse Chan.

"Ole missis, she wuz proud ez anybody! So we wuz mo' strangers dan ef we hadn' live' in a hunderd miles of each urr. An' Marse Chan he wuz gittin' thinner an' thinner, an' Firginia she come out, an' den Marse Chan he went to Richmond an' listed, an' come back an' sey he wuz a private, an' he didn' know whe'r he could take me or not. He writ to Mr. Gordon, hows'ever, an' 'twuz 'cided dat when he went I wuz to go 'long an' wait on him an' de cap'n too. I didn' min' dat, yo' know, long ez I could go wid Marse Chan, an' I like' Mr. Gordon anyways.

"Well, one night Marse Chan come back from de offis wid a telegram dat say, 'Come at once,' so he wuz to start nex' mawnin'. He uniform wuz all ready, gray wid yaller trimmin's, an' mine wuz ready too, an' he had ole marster's sword, whar de State gi' 'im in de Mexikin war; an' he trunks wuz all packed wid ev'rything in 'em, an' my chist was packed too, an' Jim Rasher he druv 'em over to de depo' in de waggin, an' we wuz to start nex' mawnin' 'bout light. Dis wuz 'bout de las' o' spring, you know. Dat night ole missis made Marse Chan dress up in he uniform, an' he sut'n'y did look splendid, wid he long mustache an' he wavin' hyar an' he tall figger.

"Arfter supper he come down an' sez: 'Sam, I wan' you to tek dis note an' kyar it over to Cun'l Chahmb'lin's, an' gi' it to Miss Anne wid yo' own han's, an' bring me wud what she sez. Don' let any one know 'bout it, or know why you've gone.' 'Yes, seh,' sez I.

"Yo' see, I knowed Miss Anne's maid over at ole Cun'l Chahmbl'in's —dat wuz Judy whar is my wife now—an' I knowed I could wuk it. So I tuk de roan an' rid over, an' tied 'im down de hill in de cedars, an' I wen' 'roun' to de back yard. 'Twuz a right blowy sort o' night; de moon wuz jes' risin', but de clouds wuz so big it didn' shine 'cep' th'oo a crack now an' den. I soon foun' my gal, an' arfter tellin' her two or three lies 'bout herse'f, I got her to go in an' ax Miss Anne to come to de do'. When she come, I gi' her de note, an' arfter a little while she bro't me anurr, an' I tole her good-by, an' she gi' me a dollar, an' I come home an' gi' de letter to Marse Chan. He read it, an' tole me to have de hosses ready at twenty minits to twelve at de corner of de garden. An' jes' befo' dat he come out ez ef he wuz gwine to bed, but instid he come, an' we all struck out to'ds Cun'l Chahmb'lin's. When we got mos' to de gate, de hosses got sort o' skeered, an' I see dey wuz some'n or somebody standin' jes' inside; an' Marse Chan he jumpt off de sorrel an' flung me de bridle and he walked up.

"She spoke fust ('twuz Miss Anne had done come out dyar to meet Marse Chan), an' she sez, jes' ez cold ez a chill, 'Well, seh, I granted your favor. I wished to relieve myself of de obligations you placed me under a few months ago, when you made me a present of my father, whom you fust insulted an' then prevented from gittin' satisfaction.'

"Marse Chan he didn' speak fur a minit, an' den he said: 'Who is with you?' (Dat wuz ev'y wud.)

" 'No one,' sez she; 'I came alone.'

" 'My God!' sez he, 'you didn' come all through those woods by yourse'f at this time o' night?'

" 'Yes, I'm not afraid,' sez she. (An' heah dis nigger! I don' b'lieve she wuz.)

"De moon come out, an' I cotch sight o' her stan'in' dyar in her white dress, wid de cloak she had wrapped herse'f up in drapped off on de groun', an' she didn' look like she wuz 'feared o' nuthin'. She wuz mons'us purty ez she stood dyar wid de green bushes behine her, an' she hed jes' a few flowers in her breas'—right hyah—and some leaves in her sorrel hyar; an' de moon come out an' shined down on her hyar an' her frock, an' 'peared like de light wuz jes' stan'in' off it ez she stood dyar lookin' at Marse Chan wid her head tho'd back, jes' like dat mawnin' when she pahss Marse Chan in de road widout speakin' to 'im, an' sez to me, 'Good mawnin', Sam.'

"Marse Chan, he den tole her he hed come to say good-by to her, ez he wuz gwine 'way to de war nex' mawnin'. I wuz watchin' on her, an' I tho't, when Marse Chan tole her dat, she sort o' started an' looked up at 'im like she wuz mighty sorry, an' 'peared like she didn' stan' quite so straight arfter dat. Den Marse Chan he went on talkin' right fars to her; an' he tole her how he had loved her ever sence she wuz a little bit o' baby mos', an' how he nuver 'membered de time when he hedn' 'spected to marry her. He tole her it wuz his love for her dat hed made 'im stan' fust at school an' collige, an' hed kep' 'im good an' pure; an' now he wuz gwine 'way, wouldn' she let it be like 'twuz in ole times, an' ef he come back from de war wouldn' she try to think on him ez she use' to do when she wuz a little guirl?

"Marse Chan he had done been talkin' so serious, he hed done tuk Miss Anne's han', an' wuz lookin' down in her face like he wuz list'nin' wid his eyes.

"Arfter a minit Miss Anne she said somethin', an' Marse Chan he cotch her urr han' an' sez:

" 'But if you love me, Anne?'

"When he said dat, she tu'ned her head 'way from 'im, an' wait' a minit, an' den she said—right clear:

" 'But I don' love yo'.' (Jes' dem th'ee wuds!) De wuds fall right slow —like dirt falls out a spade on a coffin when yo's buryin' anybody, an' seys, 'Uth to uth.' Marse Chan he jes' let her hand drap, an' he stiddy hisse'f g'inst de gate-pos', an' he didn' speak torekly. When he did speak, all he sez wuz:

" 'I mus' see you home safe.'

"I 'clar, marster, I didn' know 'twuz Marse Chan's voice tell I look at 'im right good. Well, she wouldn' let 'im go wid her. She jes' wrap' her cloak 'roun' her shoulders, an' wen' 'long back by herse'f, widout doin' more'n jes' look up once at Marse Chan leanin' dyah 'g'inst de gate-pos' in he sodger clo's, wid he eyes on de groun'. She said 'Good-by' sort o' sorf, an' Marse Chan, widout lookin' up, shake han's wid her, an' she wuz done gone down de road. Soon ez she got 'mos' 'roun de curve, Marse Chan he followed her, keepin' under de trees so ez not to be seen, an' I led de hosses on down de road behine 'im. He kep' 'long behine her tell she wuz safe in de house, an' den he come an' got on he hoss, an' we all come home.

"Nex' mawnin' we all come off to j'ine de army. An' dey wuz a-drillin' an a'drillin' all 'bout for a while an' dey went 'long wid all de res' o' de army, an' I went wid Marse Chan an' clean he boots, an' look arfter de tent, an' tek keer o' him an' de hosses. An' Marse Chan, he wan' a bit like he use' to be. He wuz so solum an' moanful all de time, at leas' 'cep' when dyah wuz gwine to be a fight. Den he'd peartin' up, an' he alwuz rode at de head o' de company, 'cause he wuz tall; an' hit wan' on'y in battles whar all his company wuz dat *he* went, but he use' to volunteer whenever de cun'l wanted anybody to fine out anythin', an' 'twuz so dangersome he didn' like to mek one man go no sooner'n anurr, yo' know, an' ax'd who'd volunteer. *He* 'peared to like to go prowlin' aroun' 'mong dem Yankees, an' he use' to tek me wid 'im whenever he could. Yes, seh, he sut'n'y wuz a good sodger! He didn' mine bullets no more'n he did so many draps o' rain. But I use' to be pow'ful skeered sometimes. It jes' use' to 'pear like fun to 'im. In camp he use' to be so sorreful he'd hardly open he mouf. You'd 'a' tho't he wuz seekin', he used to look so moanful; but jes' le' 'im git into danger, an' he use' to be like ole times—jolly an' laughin' like when he wuz a boy.

"When Cap'n Gordon got he leg shot off, dey mek Marse Chan cap'n on de spot, 'cause one o' de lieutenants got kilt de same day, an' turr one (named Mr. Ronny) wan' no 'count, an' all de company said Marse Chan wuz de man.

"An' Marse Chan he wuz jes' de same. He didn' never mention Miss Anne's name, but I knowed he wuz thinkin' on her constant. One night he wuz settin' by de fire in camp, an' Mr. Ronny—he wuz de secon' lieutenant —got to talkin' 'bout ladies, an' he say all sorts o' things 'bout 'em, an' I see Marse Chan kinder lookin' mad; an' de lieutenant mention Miss Anne's name. He hed been courtin' Miss Anne 'bout de time Marse Chan fit de duil wid her pa, an' Miss Anne hed kicked 'im, dough he wuz mighty rich, 'cause he warn' nuthin' but a half-strainer, an' 'cause she like Marse Chan, I believe, dough she didn' speak to 'im; an' Mr. Ronny he got drunk, an' 'cause Cun'l Chahmb'lin tole 'im not to come dyah no more, he got mighty mad. An' dat evenin' I'se tellin' yo' 'bout, he wuz talkin', an' he mention' Miss Anne's name. I see Marse Chan tu'n he eye 'roun' on 'im an' keep it on he face, and pres'n'y Mr. Ronny said he wuz gwine hev some fun dyah yit. He didn' mention her name dat time; but he said dey wuz all on 'em a parecel of stuck-up 'risticrats, an' her pa wan' no gent'man anyway, an'—I don' know what he wuz gwine say (he nuver said it), fur ez he got dat far Marse Chan riz up an' hit 'im a crack, an' he fall like he hed been hit wid a fence-rail. He challenged Marse Chan to fight a duil, an' Marse Chan he excepted de challenge, an' dey wuz gwine fight; but some on 'em tole 'im Marse Chan wan' gwine mek a present o' him to his fam'ly, an' he got somebody to bre'k up de duil; twan' nuthin' dough, but he wuz 'fred to fight Marse Chan. An' purty soon he lef' de comp'ny.

"Well, I got one o' de gent'mens to write Judy a letter for me, an' I tole her all 'bout de fight, an' how Marse Chan knock Mr. Ronny over fur speakin' discontemptuous o' Cun'l Chahmb'lin, an' I tole her how Marse Chan wuz a-dyin' fur love o' Miss Anne. An' Judy she gits Miss Anne to read de letter fur her. Den Miss Anne she tells her pa, an'—you mind, Judy

tells me all dis arfterwards, an' she say when Cun'l Chahmb'lin hear 'bout
it, he wuz settin' on de poach, an' he set still a good while, an' den he sey to
hisse'f:

" 'Well, he carn' he'p bein' a Whig.'

"An' den he gits up an' walks up to Miss Anne an' looks at her right
hard; an' Miss Anne she hed done tu'n away her haid an' wuz makin' out
she wuz fixin' a rose-bush 'g'inst de poach; an' when her pa kep' lookin' at
her, her face got jes' de color o' de roses on de bush, and pres'n'y her pa sez:

" 'Anne!'

"An' she tu'ned roun', an' he sez:

" 'Do yo' want 'im?'

"An' she sez, 'Yes,' an' put her head on he shoulder an' begin to cry; an'
he sez:

" 'Well, I won' stan' between yo' no longer. Write to 'im an' say so.'

"We didn' know nuthin' 'bout dis den. We wuz a-fightin' an' a-fightin' all
dat time; an' come one day a letter to Marse Chan, an' I see 'im start to
read it in his tent, an' he face hit look so cu'ious, an' he han's trembled so I
couldn' mek out what wuz de matter wid 'im. An' he fol' de letter up an'
wen' out an' wen' way down 'hine de camp, an' stayed dyah 'bout nigh an
hour. Well, seh, I wuz on de lookout for 'im when he come back, an', fo'
Gord, ef he face didn' shine like a angel's! I say to myse'f, 'Um'm! ef de
glory o' Gord ain' done shine on 'im!' An' what yo' 'spose 'twuz?

"He tuk me wid 'im dat evenin', an' he tell me he hed done git a letter
from Miss Anne, an' Marse Chan he eyes look like gre't big stars, an' he
face wuz jes' like 'twuz dat mawnin' when de sun riz up over de low groun',
an' I see 'im stan'in' dyah wid de pistil in he han', lookin' at it, an' not
knowin' but what it mout be de lars' time, an' he done mek up he mine not
to shoot ole Cun'l Chahmb'lin fur Miss Anne's sake, what writ 'im de letter.

"He fol' de letter wha' was in his han' up, an' put it in he inside pocket
—right dyar on de lef' side; an' den he tole me he tho't mebbe we wuz
gwine hev some warm wuk in de nex' two or th'ee days, an' arfter dat ef
Gord speared 'im he'd git a leave o' absence fur a few days, an' we'd go
home.

"Well, dat night de orders come, an' we all hed to git over to'ds Romney;
an' we rid all night till 'bout light; an' we halted right on a little creek, an'
we stayed dyah till mos' breakfas' time, an' I see Marse Chan set down on
de groun' 'hine a bush an' read dat letter over an' over. I watch 'im, an' de
battle wuz a-goin' on, but we had orders to stay 'hine de hill, an' ev'y now
an' den de bullets would cut de limbs o' de trees right over us, an' one o'
dem big shells what goes 'Awhar—awhar—awhar'! would fall right 'mong
us; but Marse Chan he didn' mine it no mo'n nuthin'! Den it 'peared to git
closer an' thicker, and Marse Chan he calls me, an' I crep' up, an' he sez:

" 'Sam, we'se goin' to win in dis battle, an' den we'll go home an' git married; an' I'se goin' home wid a star on my collar.' An' den he sez, 'Ef I'm wounded, kyar me home, yo' hear?' An' I sez, 'Yes, Marse Chan.'

"Well, jes' den dey blowed boots an' saddles, 'an we mounted; an' de orders come to ride 'roun' de slope, an' Marse Chan's comp'ny wuz de secon', an' when we got 'roun' dyah, we wuz right in it. Hit wuz de wust place ever dis nigger got in. An' dey said, 'Charge 'em!' an' my king! ef ever you see bullets fly, dey did dat day. Hit wuz jes' like hail; an' we wen' down de slope (I long wid de res') an' up de hill right to'ds de cannons, an' de fire wuz so strong dyar (dey hed a whole rigiment o' infintrys layin' down dyar onder de cannons) our lines sort o' broke an' stop; de cun'l was kilt, an' I b'lieve dey wuz jes' 'bout to bre'k all to pieces, when Marse Chan rid up an' cotch hol' de fleg an' hollers, 'Foller me!' an' rid strainin' up de hill 'mong de cannons. I seen 'im when he went, de sorrel four good lengths ahead o' ev'y urr hoss, jes' like he use' to be in a fox-hunt, an' de whole rigiment right arfter 'im. Yo' ain' nuver hear thunder! Fust thing I knowed, de roan roll' head over heels an' flung me up 'g'inst de bank, like yo' chuck a nubbin over 'g'inst de foot o' de corn pile. An dat's what kep' me from bein' kilt, I 'spects. Judy she say she think 'twuz Providence, but I think 'twuz de bank. O' co'se, Providence put de bank dyah, but how come Providence nuver saved Marse Chan? When I look' 'roun', de roan wuz layin' dyah by me, stone dead, wid a cannon-ball gone 'mos' th'oo him, an' our men hed done swep' dem on t'urr side from de top o' de hill. 'Twan' mo'n a minit, de sorrel come gallupin' back wid his mane flyin', an' de rein hangin' down on one side to his knee. 'Dyar!' says I, 'fo' Gord! I 'specks dey done kill Marse Chan, an' I promised to tek care on him.'

"I jumped up an' run over de bank, an' dyar, wid a whole lot o' dead men, an' some not dead yit, onder one o' de guns wid de fleg still in he han', an' a bullet right th'oo he body, lay Marse Chan. I tu'n 'im over an' call 'im, 'Marse Chan!' but 'twan' no use, he wuz done gone home, sho' 'nuff. I pick' 'im up in my arms wid de fleg still in he han's, an' toted 'im back jes' like I did dat day when he wuz a baby, an' ole marster gin 'im to me in my arms, an' sez he could trus' me, an' tell me to tek keer on 'im long ez he lived. I kyar'd 'im 'way off de battlefiel' out de way o' de balls, an' I laid 'im down onder a big tree till I could git somebody to ketch de sorrel for me. He wuz cotched arfter a while, an' I hed some money, so I got some pine plank an' made a coffin dat evenin', an' wrapt Marse Chan's body up in de fleg, an' put 'im in de coffin; but I didn' nail de top on strong, 'cause I knowed ole missis wan' see 'im; an' I got a' ambulance an' set out for home dat night. We reached dyar de nex' evein', arfter travellin' all dat night an' all nex' day.

"Hit 'peared like somethin' hed tole ole missis we wuz comin' so; for when we got home she wuz waitin' for us—done drest up in her best Sunday-clo'es, an' stan'n' at de head o' de big steps, an' ole marster settin' in his big cheer—ez we druv up de hill to'ds de house, I drivin' de ambulance an' de sorrel leadin' 'long behine wid de stirrups crost over de saddle.

"She come down to de gate to meet us. We took de coffin out de ambulance an' kyar'd it right into de big parlor wid de pictures in it, whar dey use' to dance in ole times when Marse Chan wuz a school-boy, an' Miss Anne Chahmb'lin use' to come over, an' go wid ole missis into her chamber an' tek her things off. In dyar we laid de coffin on two o' de cheers, an' ole missis nuver said a wud; she jes' looked so ole an' white.

"When I had tell 'em all 'bout it, I tu'ned right 'roun' an' rid over to Cun'l Chahmb'lin's, 'cause I knowed dat wuz what Marse Chan he'd 'a' wanted me to do. I didn' tell nobody whar I wuz gwine, 'cause yo' know none on 'em hadn' nuver speak to Miss Anne, not sence de duil, an' dey didn' know 'bout de letter.

"When I rid up in de yard, dyar wuz Miss Anne a-stan'in' on de poach watchin' me ez I rid up. I tied my hoss to de fence, an' walked up de parf. She knowed by de way I walked dyar wuz somethin' de motter, an' she wuz mighty pale. I drapt my cap down on de enn' o' de steps an' went up. She nuver opened her mouf; jes' stan' right still an' keep her eyes on my face. Fust, I couldn' speak; den I cotch my voice, an' I say, 'Marse Chan, he done got he furlough.'

"Her face was mighty ashy, an' she sort o' shook, but she didn' fall. She tu'ned roun' an' said, 'Git me de ker'ige!' Dat wuz all.

"When de ker'ige come 'roun', she hed put on her bonnet, an' wuz ready. Ez she got in, she sey to me, 'Hev yo' brought him home?' an' we drove 'long, I ridin' behine.

"When we got home, she got out, an' walked up de big walk—up to de poach by herse'f. Ole missis hed done fin' de letter in Marse Chan's pocket, wid de love in it, while I wuz 'way, an' she wuz a-waitin' on de poach. Dey sey dat wuz de fust time ole missis cry when she find de letter, an' dat she sut'n'y did cry over it, pintedly.

"Well, seh, Miss Anne she walks right up de steps, mos' up to ole missis stan'in' dyar on de poach, an' jes' falls right down mos' to her, on her knees fust, an' den flat on her face right on de flo', ketchin' at ole missis' dress wid her two han's—so.

"Ole missis stood for 'bout a minit lookin' down at her, an' den she drapt down on de flo' by her, an' took her in bofe her arms.

"I couldn' see, I wuz cryin' so myse'f, an' ev'ybody wuz cryin'. But dey went in arfter a while in de parlor, an' shet de do'; an I heahd 'em say, Miss Anne she tuk de coffin in her arms an' kissed it, an' kissed Marse Chan, an' call 'im by his name, an' her darlin', an' ole missis lef' her cryin' in dyar tell some on 'em went in, an' found her done faint on de flo'.

"Judy (she's my wife) she tell me she heah Miss Anne when she axed ole missis mout she wear mo'nin' fur 'im. I don' know how dat is; but when we buried 'im nex' day, she wuz de one whar walked arfter de coffin, holdin' ole marster, an' ole missis she walked next to 'em.

"Well, we buried Marse Chan dyar in de ole grabeyard, wid de fleg wrapped roun' 'im, an' he face lookin' like it did dat mawnin' down in de low groun's, wid de new sun shinin' on it so peaceful.

"Miss Anne she nuver went home to stay arfter dat; she stay wid ole marster an' ole missis ez long ez dey lived. Dat warn' so mighty long, 'cause ole marster he died dat fall, when dey wuz fallerin' fur wheat—I had jes' married Judy den—an' ole missis she warn' long behine him. We buried her by him next summer. Miss Anne she went in de hospitals toreckly arfter ole missis died; an' jes' fo' Richmond fell she come home sick wid de fever. Yo' nuver would 'a' knowed her fur de same ole Miss Anne. She wuz light ez a piece o' peth, an' so white, 'cep her eyes an' her sorrel hyar, an' she kep' on gittin' whiter an' weaker. Judy she sut'n'y did nuss her faithful. But she nuver got no betterment! De fever an' Marse Chan's bein' kilt hed done strain her, an' she died jes' fo' de folks wuz sot free.

"So we buried Miss Anne right by Marse Chan, in a place whar ole missis hed tole us to leave, an' dey's bofe on 'em sleep side by side over in de ole grabeyard at home.

"An' will yo' please tell me, marster? Dey tells me dat de Bible sey dyar won' be marryin' nor givin' in marriage in heaven, but I don' b'lieve it signifies dat—does you?"

I gave him the comfort of my earnest belief in some other interpretation, together with several, spare "eighteen-pences," as he called them, for which he seemed humbly grateful. And as I rode away I heard him calling across the fence to his wife, who was standing in the door of a small white-washed cabin, near which we had been standing for some time:

"Judy, have Marse Chan's dawg got home?"

JOEL CHANDLER HARRIS

(1848–1908)

Joel Chandler Harris is remembered today principally for his animal stories, in which an old black man, Uncle Remus, tells a little white boy about the days when the animals could talk. Usually he relates how a saucy, impudent trickster named Brer Rabbit made his way, most often in triumph, among a world

JOEL CHANDLER HARRIS

inhabited by bears, foxes, and other creatures stronger, but less clever, than himself. Nowadays many blacks object to the use of such stories in schools and elsewhere, feeling that the stereotyped depiction of Uncle Remus as an unctuous, folksy, illiterate "Old Time Darkie" gives a false and prejudiced view of black life. This is no doubt true. But careful attention to what happens in the Remus stories will also reveal that the central figure, Brer Rabbit, is likewise a Southern rural black man, and his ability not merely to survive but to flourish in a society in which all the odds are stacked against him underlies the stories and bears considerable relevance to racial relations in the post-Reconstruction South.

Harris was born near Eatonton, Georgia, but unlike Thomas Nelson Page, the other noted white chronicler of black life in the local color era, his relationship to the plantation tradition was quite oblique. Harris was his mother's maiden name; his father was supposedly an itinerant Irish laborer who left before he was born. He grew up in Eatonton and at the age of thirteen went to work as a printer's devil at "Turnwold," the plantation of Joseph Addison Turner, who published a literary newspaper, *The Countryman*. After the Civil War Harris worked as a printer and journalist on newspapers in Forsyth, Macon, New Orleans, and Savannah, where he was the associate editor of writer William Tappan Thompson. It was in Savannah that he married.

Moving to Atlanta in 1876 with his family to escape an epidemic of yellow fever, he joined the staff of the *Constitution* under the editorship of Henry W. Grady. When a columnist who contributed dialect sketches left the newspaper's employ, Harris was pressed into service, and Uncle Remus came into being. Soon the Remus sketches were being reprinted nationally, and in 1880 he published *Uncle Remus: His Songs and His Sayings*, which became widely popular. It was followed by *Nights with Uncle Remus* (1883), *Uncle Remus and His Friends* (1892), and *Told by Uncle Remus* (1905). A fifth volume, *Uncle Remus and the Little Boy*, was published posthumously in 1910. However, the Remus stories represented only a small portion of Harris's literary output. During his lifetime he published numerous collections of short stories and sketches, among them: *Free Joe and Other Sketches* (1887), *Balaam and His Master* (1891), *Tales of the Home Folks in Peace and War* (1898), *The Chronicles of Aunt Minervy Ann* (1899), and *The Making of a Statesman* (1902), as well as two novels, *Sister Jane, Her Friends and Acquaintances* (1896), and *Gabriel Tolliver* (1902), and numerous stories for children. In 1900 Harris resigned from the *Constitution* and in 1907 was persuaded by his son Julian to edit *Uncle Remus' Magazine*.

From UNCLE REMUS: HIS SONGS AND HIS SAYINGS

THE WONDERFUL TAR-BABY STORY

"Didn't the fox *never* catch the rabbit, Uncle Remus?" asked the little boy the next evening.

"He come mighty nigh it, honey, sho's you bawn—Brer Fox did. One day atter Brer Rabbit fool 'im wid dat calamus root, Brer Fox went ter wuk en got 'im some tar, en mix it wid some turkentime, en fix up a contrapshun wat he call a Tar-Baby, en he tuck dish yer Tar-Baby en he sot 'er in de big road, en den he lay off in de bushes fer ter see wat de news wuz gwineter be. En he didn't hatter wait long, nudder, kaze bimeby here come Brer Rabbit pacin' down de road—lippity-clippity, clippity-lippity—dez ez sassy ez a jay-bird. Brer Fox, he lay low. Brer Rabbit come prancin' 'long twel he spy de Tar-Baby, en den he fotch up on his behime legs like he wuz 'stonished. De Tar-Baby, she sot dar, she did, en Brer Fox, he lay low.

" 'Mawnin'!' sez Brer Rabbit, sezee—'nice wedder dis mawnin',' sezee.

"Tar-Baby ain't sayin' nuthin', en Brer Fox, he lay low.

" 'How duz yo' smy'tums seem ter segashuate?' sez Brer Rabbit, sezee.

"Brer Fox, he wink his eye slow, en lay low, en de Tar-Baby, she ain't sayin' nuthin'.

" 'How you come on, den? Is you deaf?' sez Brer Rabbit, sezee. 'Kaze if you is, I kin holler louder,' sezee.

"Tar-Baby stay still, en Brer Fox, he lay low.

" 'Youer stuck up, dat's w'at you is,' says Brer Rabbit, sezee, 'en I'm gwineter kyore you, dat's w'at I'm a gwineter do,' sezee.

"Brer Fox, he sorter chuckle in his stummuck, he did, but Tar-Baby ain't sayin' nuthin'.

" 'I'm gwineter larn you howter talk ter 'specttubble fokes ef hit's de las' ack,' sez Brer Rabbit, sezee. 'Ef you don't take off dat hat en tell me howdy, I'm gwineter bus' you wide open,' sezee.

"Tar-Baby stay still, en Brer Fox, he lay low.

"Brer Rabbit keep on axin' 'im, en de Tar-Baby, she keep on sayin' nuthin', twel present'y Brer Rabbit draw back wid his fis', he did, en blip he tuck 'er side er de head. Right dar's whar he broke his merlasses jug. His fis' stuck, en he can't pull loose. De tar hilt 'im. But Tar-Baby, she stay still, en Brer Fox, he lay low.

" 'Ef you don't lemme loose, I'll knock you agin,' sez Brer Rabbit, sezee, en wid dat he fotch 'er a wipe wid de udder han', en dat stuck. Tar-Baby, she ain't sayin' nuthin', en Brer Fox he lay low.

" 'Tu'n me loose, fo' I kick de natal stuffin' outen you,' sez Brer Rabbit, sezee, but de Tar-Baby, she ain't sayin' nuthin'. She des hilt on, en den Brer

Rabbit lose de use er his feet in de same way. Brer Fox, he lay low. Den Brer Rabbit squall out dat ef de Tar-Baby don't tu'n 'im loose he butt 'er cranksided. En den he butted, en his head got stuck. Den Brer Fox, he sa'ntered fort', lookin' des ez innercent ez wunner yo' mammy's mockin' birds.

" 'Howdy, Brer Rabbit,' sez Brer Fox, sezee. 'You look sorter stuck up dis mawnin',' sezee, en den he rolled on de groun', en laft en laft twel he couldn't laff no mo'. 'I speck you'll take dinner wid me dis time, Brer Rabbit. I done laid in come calamus root, en I ain't gwineter take no skuse,' sez Brer Fox, sezee."

Here Uncle Remus paused, and drew a two-pound yam out of the ashes.

"Did the fox eat the rabbit?" asked the little boy to whom the story had been told.

"Dat's all de fur de tale goes," replied the old man. "He mout, en den agin he moutent. Some say Jedge B'ar come 'long en loosed 'im—some say he didn't. I hear Miss Sally callin'. You better run 'long."

HOW MR. RABBIT WAS TOO SHARP FOR MR. FOX

"Uncle Remus," said the little boy one evening, when he had found the old man with little or nothing to do, "did the fox kill and eat the rabbit when he caught him with the Tar-Baby?"

"Law, honey, ain't I tell you 'bout dat?" replied the old darkey, chuckling slyly. "I 'clar ter grashus I ought er tole you dat, but old man Nod wuz ridin' on my eyeleds 'twel a leetle mo'n I'd a dis'member'd my own name, en den on to dat here come yo' mammy a hollerin' atter you.

"W'at I tell you w'en I fus' begin? I tole you Brer Rabbit wuz a monstus soon creetur; leas'ways dat's w'at I laid out fer ter tell you. Well, den, honey, don't you go en make no udder calkalashuns, kaze in dem days Brer Rabbit en his family wuz at de head er de gang w'en enny racket wuz on han', en dar dey stayed. 'Fo' you begins fer ter wipe yo' eyes 'bout Brer Rabbit, you wait en see whar'bouts Brer Rabbit gwineter fetch up at. But dat's needer yer ner dar.

"W'en Brer Fox fine Brer Rabbit mixt up wid de Tar-Baby, he feel mighty good, en he roll on de groun' en laff. Bimeby he up'n say, sezee:

" 'Well, I speck I got you dis time, Brer Rabbit,' sezee; 'maybe I ain't, but I speck I is. You been runnin' roun' here sassin' after me a mighty long time, but I speck you done come ter de een' er de row. You bin cuttin' up yo' capers en bouncin' 'roun' in dis neighberhood ontwel you come ter b'leeve yo'sef de boss er de whole gang. En den youer allers som'ers whar you got no bizness,' sez Brer Fox, sezee. 'Who ax you fer ter come en strike up a 'quaintance wid dish yer Tar-Baby? En who stuck you up dar whar you iz? Nobody in de roun' worril. You des tuck en jam yo'se'f on dat Tar-

Baby widout waitin' fer enny invite,' sez Brer Fox, sezee, 'en dar you is, en dar you'll stay twel I fixes up a bresh-pile and fires her up, kaze I'm gwineter bobbycue you dis day, sho,' sez Brer Fox, sezee.

"Den Brer Rabbit talk mighty 'umble.

"'I don't keer w'at you do wid me, Brer Fox,' sezee, 'so you don't fling me in dat brier-patch. Roas' me, Brer Fox,' sezee, 'but don't fling me in dat brier-patch,' sezee.

"'Hit's so much trouble fer ter kindle a fier,' sez Brer Fox, sezee, "dat I speck I'll hatter hang you,' sezee.

"'Hang me des ez high as you please, Brer Fox,' sez Brer Rabbit, sezee, 'but do fer de Lord's sake don't fling me in dat brier-patch,' sezee.

"'I ain't got no string,' sez Brer Fox, sezee, 'en now I speck I'll hatter drown you,' sezee.

"'Drown me des ez deep ez you please, Brer Fox,' sez Brer Rabbit, sezee, 'but do don't fling me in dat brier-patch,' sezee.

"'Dey ain't no water nigh,' sez Brer Fox, sezee, 'en now I speck I'll hatter skin you,' sezee.

"'Skin me, Brer Fox,' sez Brer Rabbit, sezee, 'snatch out my eyeballs, t'ar out my years by de roots, en cut off my legs,' sezee, 'but do please, Brer Fox, don't fling me in dat brier-patch,' sezee.

"Co'se Brer Fox wanter hurt Brer Rabbit bad ez he kin, so he cotch 'im by de behime legs en slung 'im right in de middle er de brier-patch. Dar wuz a considerbul flutter whar Brer Rabbit struck de bushes, en Brer Fox sorter hang 'roun' fer ter see w'at wuz gwineter happen. Bimeby he hear somebody call 'im, en way up de hill he see Brer Rabbit settin' cross-legged on a chinkapin log koamin' de pitch outen his har wid a chip. Den Brer Fox know dat he bin swop off mighty bad. Brer Rabbit wuz bleedzed fer ter fling back some er his sass, en he holler out:

"'Bred en bawn in a brier-patch, Brer Fox—bred en bawn in a brier-patch!" en wid dat he skip out des ez lively ez a cricket in de embers.'"

· · ·

MR. RABBIT AND MR. BEAR

"Dar wuz one season," said Uncle Remus, pulling thoughtfully at his whiskers, "w'en Brer Fox say to hisse'f dat he speck he better whirl in en plant a goober-patch, en in dem days, mon, hit wuz tech en go. De wud wern't mo'n out'n his mouf 'fo' de groun' 'uz brok'd up en de goobers 'uz planted. Ole Brer Rabbit, he sot off en watch de motions, he did, en he sorter shet one eye en sing to his chilluns:

"'Ti-yi! Tungalee!
I eat um pea, I pick um pea.

> Hit grow in de groun', hit grow so free;
> Ti-yi! dem goober pea.'

"Sho' 'nuff w'en de goobers 'gun ter ripen up, eve'y time Brer Fox go down ter his patch, he fine whar somebody bin grabblin' 'mongst de vines, en he git mighty mad. He sorter speck who de somebody is, but ole Brer Rabbit he cover his tracks so cute dat Brer Fox dunner how ter ketch 'im. Bimeby, one day Brer Fox take a walk all roun' de groun'-pea patch, en 'twan't long fo' he fine a crack in de fence whar de rail done bin rub right smoove, en right dar he sot 'im a trap. He tuck'n ben' down a hick'ry saplin', growin' in de fence-cornder, en tie one een' un a plow-line on de top, en in de udder een' he fix a loop-knot, en dat he fasten wid a trigger right in de crack. Nex' mawnin' w'en ole Brer Rabbit come slippin' 'long en crope thoo de crack, de loop-knot kotch 'im behime de fo' legs, en de saplin' flew'd up, en dar he wuz 'twix' de heavens en de yeth. Dar he swung, en he fear'd he gwineter fall, en he fear'd he wer'n't gwineter fall.

"W'ile he wuz afixin' up a tale fer Brer Fox, he hear a lumberin' down de road, en present'y yer come ole Brer B'ar amblin' 'long fum whar he bin takin' a bee-tree. Brer Rabbit, he hail 'im:

" 'Howdy, Brer B'ar!'

"Brer B'ar, he look 'roun en bimeby he see Brer Rabbit swingin' fum de saplin', en he holler out:

" 'Heyo, Brer Rabbit! How you come on dis mawnin'?'

" 'Much oblije, I'm middlin', Brer B'ar,' sez Brer Rabbit, sezee.

"Den Brer B'ar, he ax Brer Rabbit w'at he doin' up dar in de elements, en Brer Rabbit, he up'n say he makin' dollar minnit. Brer B'ar, he say how. Brer Rabbit say he keepin' crows out'n Brer Fox's groun'-pea patch, en den he ax Brer B'ar ef he don't wanter make dollar minnit, kaze he got big fambly er chilluns fer ter take keer un, en den he make sech nice skeer-crow. Brer B'ar 'low dat he take de job, en den Brer Rabbit show 'im how ter ben' down de saplin', en 'twan't long 'fo' Brer B'ar wuz swingin' up dar in Brer Rabbit place. Den Brer Rabbit, he put out fer Brer Fox house, en w'en he got dar he sing out:

" 'Brer Fox! Oh, Brer Fox! Come out yer, Brer Fox, en I'll show you de man w'at bin stealin' yo' goobers.'

"Brer Fox, he grab up his walkin'-stick, en bofe un um went runnin' back down ter der goober-patch, en w'en dey got dar, sho 'nuff, dar wuz ole Brer B'ar.

" 'Oh, yes! youer kotch, is you?' sez Brer Fox, en 'fo' Brer B'ar could 'splain, Brer Rabbit he jump up en down, en holler out:

" 'Hit 'im in de mouf, Brer Fox; hit 'im in de mouf'; en Brer Fox, he draw back wid de walkin'-cane, en blip he tuck 'im, en eve'y time Brer B'ar'd try ter 'splain, Brer Fox'd shower down on him.

"W'iles all dis 'uz gwine on, Brer Rabbit, he slip off en git in a mudhole

en des lef' his eyes stickin' out, kaze he know'd dat Brer B'ar'd be a comin'
atter 'im. Sho 'nuff, bimeby here come Brer B'ar down de road, en w'en he
git ter de mud-hole, he say:

" 'Howdy, Brer Frog; is you seed Brer Rabbit go by yer?'

" 'He des gone by,' sez Brer Rabbit, en ole man B'ar tuck off down de
road like a skeer'd mule, en Brer Rabbit, he come out en dry hisse'f in de
sun, en go home ter his family same ez enny udder man."

"The Bear didn't catch the Rabbit, then?" inquired the little boy, sleepi-
ly.

"Jump up fum dar, honey!" exclaimed Uncle Remus, by way of reply. "I
ain't got no time fer ter be settin' yer proppin' yo' eyeleds open."

.   .   .

MR. RABBIT GROSSLY DECEIVES MR. FOX

One evening when the little boy, whose nights with Uncle Remus were as
entertaining as those Arabian ones of blessed memory, had finished supper
and hurried out to sit with his venerable patron, he found the old man in
great glee. Indeed, Uncle Remus was talking and laughing to himself at
such a rate that the little boy was afraid he had company. The truth is,
Uncle Remus had heard the child coming, and, when the rosy-cheeked
chap put his head in at the door, was engaged in a monologue, the burden
of which seemed to be—

> "Ole Molly Har',
> W'at you doin' dar,
> Settin' in de cornder
> Smokin' yo' seegyar?"

As a matter of course this vague allusion reminded the little boy of the
fact that the wicked Fox was still in pursuit of the Rabbit, and he immediately put his curiosity in the shape of a question.

"Uncle Remus, did the Rabbit have to go clean away when he got loose
from the Tar-Baby?"

"Bless gracious, honey, dat he didn't. Who? Him? You dunno nuthin'
'tall 'bout Brer Rabbit ef dat's de way you puttin' 'im down. W'at he gwine
'way fer? He moughter stayed sorter close twel de pitch rub off'n his ha'r,
but twern't menny days 'fo' he wuz lopin' up en down de neighborhood
same ez ever, en I dunno ef he wern't mo' sassier dan befo'.

"Seem like dat de tale 'bout how he got mixt up wid de Tar-Baby got
'roun' 'mongst de nabers. Leas'ways, Miss Meadows en de gals got win' un'
it, en de nex' time Brer Rabbit paid um a visit Miss Meadows tackled 'im

'bout it, en de gals sot up a monstus gigglement. Brer Rabbit, he sot up des ez cool ez a cowcumber, he did, en let 'em run on."

"Who was Miss Meadows, Uncle Remus?" inquired the little boy.

"Don't ax me, honey. She wuz in de tale, Miss Meadows en de gals wuz, en de tale I give you like hi't wer' gun ter me. Brer Rabbit, he sot dar, he did, sorter lam' like, en den bimeby he cross his legs, he did, and wink his eye slow, en up and say, sezee:

" 'Ladies, Brer Fox wuz my daddy's ridin'-hoss fer thirty year; maybe mo' but thirty year dat I knows un,' sezee; en den he paid um his 'specks, en tip his beaver, en march off, he did, des ez stiff en ez stuck up ez a fire-stick.

"Nex' day, Brer Fox cum a callin', and w'en he gun fer ter laugh 'bout Brer Rabbit, Miss Meadows en de gals, dey ups en tells 'im 'bout w'at Brer Rabbit say. Den Brer Fox grit his tushes sho' nuff, he did, en he look mighty dumpy, but w'en he riz fer ter go he up en say, sezee:

" 'Ladies, I ain't 'sputin' w'at you say, but I'll make Brer Rabbit chaw up his words en spit um out right yer whar you kin see 'im,' sezee, en wid dat off Brer Fox put.

"En w'en he got in de big road, he shuck de dew off'n his tail, en made a straight shoot fer Brer Rabbit's house. W'en he got dar, Brer Rabbit wuz spectin' un 'im, en de do' wuz shet fas'. Brer Fox knock. Nobody ain't ans'er. Brer Fox knock. Nobody ans'er. Den he knock agin—blam! blam! Den Brer Rabbit holler out mighty weak:

" 'Is dat you, Brer Fox? I want you ter run en fetch de doctor. Dat bait er pusly w'at I e't dis mawnin' is gittin' 'way wid me. Do, please, Brer Fox, run quick,' sez Brer Rabbit, sezee.

" 'I come atter you, Brer Rabbit,' sez Brer Fox, sezee. 'Dar's gwineter be a party up at Miss Meadows's,' sezee. 'All de gals 'll be dere, en I promus' dat I'd fetch you. De gals, dey 'lowed dat hit wouldn't be no party 'ceppin' I fotch you,' sez Brer Fox, sezee.

"Den Brer Rabbit say he wuz too sick, en Brer Fox say he wuzzent, en dar dey had it up and down, 'sputin' en contendin'. Brer Rabbit say he can't walk. Brer Fox say he tote 'im. Brer Rabbit say how? Brer Fox say in his arms. Brer Rabbit say he drap 'im. Brer Fox 'low he won't. Bimeby Brer Rabbit say he go ef Brer Fox tote 'im on his back. Brer Fox say he would. Brer Rabbit say he can't ride widout a saddle. Brer Fox say he git de saddle. Brer Rabbit say he can't set in saddle less he have bridle fer ter hol' by. Brer Fox say he git de bridle. Brer Rabbit say he can't ride widout bline bridle, kaze Brer Fox be shyin' at stumps 'long de road, en fling 'im off. Brer Fox say he git bline bridle. Den Brer Rabbit say he go. Den Brer Fox say he ride Brer Rabbit mos' up ter Miss Meadows's, en den he could git down en walk de balance er de way. Brer Rabbit 'greed, en den Brer Fox lipt out atter de saddle en de bridle.

"Co'se Brer Rabbit know de game dat Brer Fox wuz fixin' fer ter play, en he 'termin' fer ter outdo 'im, en by de time he koam his ha'r en twis' his mustarsh, en sorter rig up, yer come Brer Fox, saddle en bridle on, en lookin' ez peart ez a circus pony. He trot up ter de do' en stan' dar pawin' de ground en chompin' de bit same like sho 'nuff hoss, en Brer Rabbit he mount, he did, en dey amble off. Brer Fox can't see behime wid de bline bridle on, but bimeby he feel Brer Rabbit raise one er his foots.

" 'W'at you doin' now, Brer Rabbit?' sezee.

" 'Short'nin' de lef stir'p, Brer Fox,' sezee.

"Bimeby Brer Rabbit raise up de udder foot.

" 'W'at you doin' now, Brer Rabbit?' sezee.

" 'Pullin' down my pants, Brer Fox,' sezee.

"All de time, bless grashus, honey, Brer Rabbit wer puttin' on his spurrers, en w'en dey got close to Miss Meadows's, whar Brer Rabbit wuz to git off, en Brer Fox made a motion fer ter stan' still, Brer Rabbit slap de spurrers inter Brer Fox flanks, en you better b'leeve he got over groun'. W'en dey got ter de house, Miss Meadows en all de gals wuz settin' on de peazzer, en stidder stoppin' at de gat, Brer Rabbit rid on by, he did, en den come gallopin' down de road en up ter de hoss-rack, w'ich he hitch Brer Fox at, en den he santer inter de house, he did, en shake han's wid de gals, en set dar, smokin' his seegyar same ez a town man. Bimeby he draw in a long puff, en den let hit out in a cloud, en squar hisse'f back en holler out, he did:

" 'Ladies, ain't I done tell you Brer Fox wuz de ridin'-hoss fer our fambly? He sorter losin' his gait now, but I speck I kin fetch 'im all right in a mont' er so,' sezee.

"En den Brer Rabbit sorter grin, he did, en de gals giggle, en Miss Meadows, she praise up de pony, en dar wuz Brer Fox hitch fas' ter de rack, en couldn't he'p hisse'f."

"Is that all, Uncle Remus?" asked the little boy as the old man paused.

"Dat ain't all, honey, but 'twon't do fer ter give out too much cloff fer ter cut one pa'r pants," replied the old man sententiously.

FREE JOE AND THE REST OF THE WORLD

The name of Free Joe strikes humorously upon the ear of memory. It is impossible to say why, for he was the humblest, the simplest, and the most serious of all God's living creatures, sadly lacking in all those elements that suggest the humorous. It is certain, moreover, that in 1850 the soberminded citizens of the little Georgian village of Hillsborough were not inclined to take a humorous view of Free Joe, and neither his name nor his presence provoked a smile. He was a black atom, drifting hither and thither without an owner, blown about by all the winds of circumstance, and given over to shiftlessness.

The problems of one generation are the paradoxes of a succeeding one, particularly if war, or some such incident, intervenes to clarify the atmosphere and strengthen the understanding. Thus, in 1850, Free Joe represented not only a problem of large concern, but, in the watchful eyes of Hillsborough, he was the embodiment of that vague and mysterious danger that seemed to be forever lurking on the outskirts of slavery, ready to sound a shrill and ghostly signal in the impenetrable swamps, and steal forth under the midnight stars to murder, rapine, and pillage,—a danger always threatening, and yet never assuming shape; intangible, and yet real; impossible, and yet not improbable. Across the serene and smiling front of safety, the pale outlines of the awful shadow of insurrection sometimes fell. With this invisible panorama as a background, it was natural that the figure of Free Joe, simple and humble as it was, should assume undue proportions. Go where he would, do what he might, he could not escape the finger of observation and the kindling eye of suspicion. His lightest words were noted, his slightest actions marked.

Under all the circumstances it was natural that his peculiar condition should reflect itself in his habits and manners. The slaves laughed loudly day by day, but Free Joe rarely laughed. The slaves sang at their work and danced at their frolics, but no one ever heard Free Joe sing or saw him dance. There was something painfully plaintive and appealing in his attitude, something touching in his anxiety to please. He was of the friendliest nature, and seemed to be delighted when he could amuse the little children who had made a playground of the public square. At times he would please them by making his little dog Dan perform all sorts of curious tricks, or he would tell them quaint stories of the beasts of the field and birds of the air; and frequently he was coaxed into relating the story of his own freedom. That story was brief, but tragical.

In the year of our Lord 1840, when a negro-speculator of a sportive turn of mind reached the little village of Hillsborough on his way to the Mississippi region, with a caravan of likely negroes of both sexes, he found much to interest him. In that day and at that time there were a number of young men in the village who had not bound themselves over to repentance for the various misdeeds of the flesh. To these young men the negro-speculator (Major Frampton was his name) proceeded to address himself. He was a Virginian, he declared; and, to prove the statement, he referred all the festively inclined young men of Hillsborough to a barrel of peach-brandy in one of his covered wagons. In the minds of these young men there was less doubt in regard to the age and quality of the brandy than there was in regard to the negro-trader's birthplace. Major Frampton might or might not have been born in the Old Dominion,—that was a matter for consideration and inquiry,—but there could be no question as to the mellow pungency of the peach-brandy.

In his own estimation, Major Frampton was one of the most accomplished of men. He had summered at the Virginia Springs; he had been to

Philadelphia, to Washington, to Richmond, to Lynchburg, and to Charleston, and had accumulated a great deal of experience which he found useful. Hillsborough was hid in the woods of Middle Georgia, and its general aspect of innocence impressed him. He looked on the young men who had shown their readiness to test his peach-brandy, as over-grown country boys who needed to be introduced to some of the arts and sciences he had at his command. Thereupon the major pitched his tents, figuratively speaking, and became, for the time being, a part and parcel of the innocence that characterized Hillsborough. A wiser man would doubtless have made the same mistake.

The little village possessed advantages that seemed to be providentially arranged to fit the various enterprises that Major Frampton had in view. There was the auction-block in front of the stuccoed court-house, if he desired to dispose of a few of his negroes; there was a quarter-track, laid out to his hand and in excellent order, if he chose to enjoy the pleasures of horse-racing; there were secluded pine thickets within easy reach, if he desired to indulge in the exciting pastime of cock-fighting; and various lonely and unoccupied rooms in the second story of the tavern, if he cared to challenge the chances of dice or cards.

Major Frampton tried them all with varying luck, until he began his famous game of poker with Judge Alfred Wellington, a stately gentleman with a flowing white beard and mild blue eyes that gave him the appearance of a benevolent patriarch. The history of the game in which Major Frampton and Judge Alfred Wellington took part is something more than a tradition in Hillsborough, for there are still living three or four men who sat around the table and watched its progress. It is said that at various stages of the game Major Frampton would destroy the cards with which they were playing, and send for a new pack, but the result was always the same. The mild blue eyes of Judge Wellington, with few exceptions, continued to overlook "hands" that were invincible—a habit they had acquired during a long and arduous course of training from Saratoga to New Orleans. Major Frampton lost his money, his horses, his wagons, and all his negroes but one, his body-servant. When his misfortune had reached this limit, the major adjourned the game. The sun was shining brightly, and all nature was cheerful. It is said that the major also seemed to be cheerful. However this may be, he visited the courthouse, and executed the papers that gave his body-servant his freedom. This being done, Major Frampton sauntered into a convenient pine thicket, and blew out his brains.

The negro thus freed came to be known as Free Joe. Compelled, under the law, to choose a guardian, he chose Judge Wellington, chiefly because his wife Lucinda was among the negroes won from Major Frampton. For several years Free Joe had what may be called a jovial time. His wife Lucinda was well provided for, and he found it a comparatively easy matter to provide for himself; so that, taking all the circumstances into consideration, it is not matter for astonishment that he became somewhat shiftless.

When Judge Wellington died, Free Joe's troubles began. The judge's negroes, including Lucinda, went to his half-brother, a man named Calderwood, who was a hard master and a rough customer generally—a man of many eccentricities of mind and character. His neighbors had a habit of alluding to him as "Old Spite;" and the name seemed to fit him so completely, that he was known far and near as "Spite" Calderwood. He probably enjoyed the distinction the name gave him, at any rate, he never resented it, and it was not often that he missed an opportunity to show that he deserved it. Calderwood's place was two or three miles from the village of Hillsborough, and Free Joe visited his wife twice a week, Wednesday and Saturday nights.

One Sunday he was sitting in front of Lucinda's cabin, when Calderwood happened to pass that way.

"Howdy, marster?" said Free Joe, taking off his hat.

"Who are you?" exclaimed Calderwood abruptly, halting and staring at the negro.

"I'm name' Joe, marster. I'm Lucindy's ole man."

"Who do you belong to?"

"Marse John Evans is my gyardeen, marster."

"Big name—gyardeen. Show your pass."

Free Joe produced that document, and Calderwood read it aloud slowly, as if he found it difficult to get at the meaning:—

"To whom it may concern: This is to certify that the boy Joe Frampton has my permission to visit his wife Lucinda."

This was dated at Hillsborough, and signed *"John W. Evans."*

Calderwood read it twice, and then looked at Free Joe, elevating his eyebrows, and showing his discolored teeth.

"Some mighty big words in that there. Evans owns this place, I reckon. When's he comin' down to take hold?"

Free Joe fumbled with his hat. He was badly frightened.

"Lucindy say she speck you wouldn't min' my comin', long ez I behave, marster."

Calderwood tore the pass in pieces and flung it away.

"Don't want no free niggers 'round here," he exclaimed. "There's the big road. It'll carry you to town. Don't let me catch you here no more. Now, mind what I tell you."

Free Joe presented a shabby spectacle as he moved off with his little dog Dan slinking at his heels. It should be said in behalf of Dan, however, that his bristles were up, and that he looked back and growled. It may be that the dog had the advantage of insignificance, but it is difficult to conceive how a dog bold enough to raise his bristles under Calderwood's very eyes could be as insignificant as Free Joe. But both the negro and his little dog seemed to give a new and more dismal aspect to forlornness as they turned into the road and went toward Hillsborough.

After this incident Free Joe appeared to have clearer ideas concerning his peculiar condition. He realized the fact that though he was free he was more helpless than any slave. Having no owner, every man was his master. He knew that he was the object of suspicion, and therefore all his slender resources (ah! how pitifully slender they were!) were devoted to winning, not kindness and appreciation, but toleration; all his efforts were in the direction of mitigating the circumstances that tended to make his condition so much worse than that of the negroes around him,—negroes who had friends because they had masters.

So far as his own race was concerned, Free Joe was an exile. If the slaves secretly envied him his freedom (which is to be doubted, considering his miserable condition), they openly despised him, and lost no opportunity to treat him with contumely. Perhaps this was in some measure the result of the attitude which Free Joe chose to maintain toward them. No doubt his instinct taught him that to hold himself aloof from the slaves would be to invite from the whites the toleration which he coveted, and without which even his miserable condition would be rendered more miserable still.

His greatest trouble was the fact that he was not allowed to visit his wife; but he soon found a way out of this difficulty. After he had been ordered away from the Calderwood place, he was in the habit of wandering as far in that direction as prudence would permit. Near the Calderwood place, but not on Calderwood's land, lived an old man named Micajah Staley and his sister Becky Staley. These people were old and very poor. Old Micajah had a palsied arm and hand; but, in spite of this, he managed to earn a precarious living with his turning-lathe.

When he was a slave Free Joe would have scorned these representatives of a class known as poor white trash, but now he found them sympathetic and helpful in various ways. From the back door of their cabin he could hear the Calderwood negroes singing at night, and he sometimes fancied he could distinguish Lucinda's shrill treble rising above the other voices. A large poplar grew in the woods some distance from the Staley cabin, and at the foot of this tree Free Joe would sit for hours with his face turned toward Calderwood's. His little dog Dan would curl up in the leaves near by, and the two seemed to be as comfortable as possible.

One Saturday afternoon Free Joe, sitting at the foot of this friendly poplar, fell asleep. How long he slept, he could not tell; but when he awoke little Dan was licking his face, the moon was shining brightly, and Lucinda his wife stood before him laughing. The dog, seeing that Free Joe was asleep, had grown somewhat impatient, and he concluded to make an excursion to the Calderwood place on his own account. Lucinda was inclined to give the incident a twist in the direction of superstition.

"I 'uz settin' down front er de fireplace," she said, "cookin' me some meat, w'en all of a sudden I year sumpin at de do'—scratch, scratch. I tuck'n tu'n de meat over, en make out I aint year it. Bimeby it come dar 'gin —scratch, scratch. I up en open de do', I did, en, bless de Lord! dar wuz little Dan, en it look like ter me dat his ribs done grow tergeer. I gin 'im some bread, en den, w'en he start out, I tuck'n foller 'im, kaze, I say ter myse'f, maybe my nigger man mought be some'rs 'roun'. Dat ar little dog got sense, mon."

Free Joe laughed and dropped his hand lightly on Dan's head. For a long time after that he had no difficulty in seeing his wife. He had only to sit by the poplar-tree until little Dan could run and fetch her. But after a while the other negroes discovered that Lucinda was meeting Free Joe in the woods, and information of the fact soon reached Calderwood's ears. Calderwood was what is called a man of action. He said nothing; but one day he put Lucinda in his buggy, and carried her to Macon, sixty miles away. He carried her to Macon, and came back without her; and nobody in or around Hillsborough, or in that section, ever saw her again.

For many a night after that Free Joe sat in the woods and waited. Little Dan would run merrily off and be gone a long time, but he always came back without Lucinda. This happened over and over again. The "willis-whistlers" would call and call, like phantom huntsmen wandering on a far-off shore; the screech-owl would shake and shiver in the depths of the woods; the night-hawks, sweeping by on noiseless wings, would snap their beaks as though they enjoyed the huge joke of which Free Joe and little Dan were the victims; and the whip-poor-wills would cry to each other through the gloom. Each night seemed to be lonelier than the preceding, but Free Joe's patience was proof against loneliness. There came a time, however, when little Dan refused to go after Lucinda. When Free Joe motioned him in the direction of the Calderwood place, he would simply move about uneasily and whine; then he would curl up in the leaves and make himself comfortable.

One night, instead of going to the poplar-tree to wait for Lucinda, Free Joe went to the Staley cabin, and, in order to make his welcome good, as he expressed it, he carried with him an armful of fat-pine splinters. Miss Becky Staley had a great reputation in those parts as a fortune-teller, and the schoolgirls, as well as older people, often tested her powers in this direction, some in jest and some in earnest. Free Joe placed his humble offering of light-wood in the chimney-corner, and then seated himself on the steps, dropping his hat on the ground outside.

"Miss Becky," he said presently, "whar in de name er gracious you reckon Lucindy is?"

"Well, the Lord he'p the nigger!" exclaimed Miss Becky, in a tone that seemed to reproduce, by some curious agreement of sight with sound, her general aspect of peakedness. "Well, the Lord he'p the nigger! haint you been a-seein' her all this blessed time? She's over at old Spite Calderwood's, if she's anywheres, I reckon.'

"No'm, dat I aint, Miss Becky. I aint seen Lucindy in now gwine on mighty nigh a mont'."

"Well, it haint a-gwine to hurt you," said Miss Becky, somewhat sharply. "In my day an' time it wuz allers took to be a bad sign when niggers got to honeyin' 'roun' an' gwine on."

"Yessum," said Free Joe, cheerfully assenting to the proposition —"yessum, dat's so, but me an' my ole 'oman, we 'uz raise tergeer, en dey aint bin many days w'en we 'uz 'way fum one n'er like we is now."

"Maybe she's up an' took up wi' some un else," said Micajah Staley from the corner. "You know what the sayin' is, 'New master, new nigger.' "

"Dat's so, dat's de sayin', but tain't wid my ole 'oman like 'tis wid yuther niggers. Me en her wuz des natally raise up tergeer. Dey's lots likelier niggers dan w'at I is," said Free Joe, viewing his shabbiness with a critical eye, " but I knows Lucindy mos' good ez I does little Dan dar—dat I does."

There was no reply to this, and Free Joe continued,—

"Miss Becky, I wish you please, ma'am, tạke en run yo' kyards en see sump'n n'er 'bout Lucindy; kaze ef she sick, I'm gwine dar. Dey ken take en take me up en gimme a stroppin', but I'm gwine dar."

Miss Becky got her cards, but first she picked up a cup, in the bottom of which were some coffee-grounds. These she whirled slowly round and round, ending finally by turning the cup upside down on the hearth and allowing it to remain in that position.

"I'll turn the cup first," said Miss Becky, "and then I'll run the cards and see what they say."

As she shuffled the cards the fire on the hearth burned low, and in its fitful light the gray-haired, thin-featured woman seemed to deserve the weird reputation which rumor and gossip had given her. She shuffled the cards for some moments, gazing intently in the dying fire; then, throwing a piece of pine on the coals, she made three divisions of the pack, disposing them about in her lap. Then she took the first pile, ran the cards slowly through her fingers, and studied them carefully. To the first she added the second pile. The study of these was evidently not satisfactory. She said nothing, but frowned heavily; and the frown deepened as she added the rest of the cards until the entire fifty-two had passed in review before her. Though she frowned, she seemed to be deeply interested. Without changing the relative position of the cards, she ran them all over again. Then she threw a larger piece of pine on the fire, shuffled the cards afresh, divided them into three piles, and subjected them to the same careful and critical examination.

"I can't tell the day when I've seed the cards run this a-way," she said after a while. "What is an' what aint, I'll never tell you; but I know what the cards sez."

"W'at does dey say, Miss Becky?" the negro inquired, in a tone the solemnity of which was heightened by its eagerness.

"They er runnin' quare. These here that I'm a-lookin' at," said Miss Becky, "they stan' for the past. Them there, they er the present; and the t'others, they er the future. Here's a bundle,"—tapping the ace of clubs with her thumb,—"an' here's a journey as plain as the nose on a man's face. Here's Lucinda"—

"Whar she, Miss Becky?"

"Here she is—the queen of spades."

Free Joe grinned. The idea seemed to please him immensely.

"Well, well, well!" he exclaimed. "Ef dat don't beat my time! De queen er spades! W'en Lucindy year dat hit'll tickle 'er, sho'!"

Miss Becky continued to run the cards back and forth through her fingers.

"Here's a bundle an' a journey, and here's Lucinda. An' here's ole Spite Calderwood."

She held the cards toward the negro and touched the king of clubs.

"De Lord he'p my soul!" exclaimed Free Joe with a chuckle. "De faver's dar. Yesser, dat's him! W'at de matter 'long wid all un um, Miss Becky?"

The old woman added the second pile of cards to the first, and then the third, still running them through her fingers slowly and critically. By this time the piece of pine in the fireplace had wrapped itself in a mantle of flame, illuminating the cabin and throwing into strange relief the figure of Miss Becky as she sat studying the cards. She frowned ominously at the cards and mumbled a few words to herself. Then she dropped her hands in her lap and gazed once more into the fire. Her shadow danced and capered on the wall and floor behind her, as if, looking over her shoulder into the future, it could behold a rare spectacle. After a while she picked up the cup that had been turned on the hearth. The coffee-grounds, shaken around, presented what seemed to be a most intricate map.

"Here's the journey," said Miss Becky, presently; "here's the big road, here's rivers to cross, here's the bundle to tote." She paused and sighed. "They haint no names writ here, an' what it all means I'll never tell you. Cajy, I wish you'd be so good as to han' me my pipe."

"I haint no hand wi' the kyards," said Cajy, as he handed the pipe, "but I reckon I can patch out your misinformation, Becky, bekaze the other day, whiles I was a-finishin' up Mizzers Perdue's rollin-'pin, I hearn a rattlin' in the road. I looked out, an' Spite Calderwood was a-drivin' by in his buggy, an' thar sot Lucinda by him. It'd in-about drapt out er my min'.'"

Free Joe sat on the door-sill and fumbled at his hat, flinging it from one hand to the other.

"You aint see um gwine back, is you, Mars Cajy?" he asked after a while.

"Ef they went back by this road," said Mr. Staley, with the air of one who is accustomed to weigh well his words, "it must 'a' bin endurin' of the time whiles I was asleep, bekaze I haint bin no furder from my shop than to yon bed."

"Well, sir!" exclaimed Free Joe in an awed tone, which Mr. Staley seemed to regard as a tribute to his extraordinary powers of statement.

"Ef it's my beliefs you want," continued the old man, "I'll pitch 'em at you fair and free. My beliefs is that Spite Calderwood is gone an' took Lucindy outen the county. Bless your heart and soul! when Spite Calderwood meets the Old Boy in the road they'll be a turrible scuffle. You mark what I tell you."

Free Joe, still fumbling with his hat, rose and leaned against the door-facing. He seemed to be embarrassed. Presently he said,—

"I speck I better be gittin' 'long. Nex' time I see Lucindy, I'm gwine tell 'er w'at Miss Becky say 'bout de queen er spades—dat I is. Ef dat don't tickle 'er, dey ain't no nigger 'oman never bin tickle'."

He paused a moment, as though waiting for some remark or comment, some confirmation of misfortune, or, at the very least, some indorsement of his suggestion that Lucinda would be greatly pleased to know that she had figured as the queen of spades; but neither Miss Becky nor her brother said any thing.

"One minnit ridin' in the buggy 'longside er Mars Spite, en de nex' highfalutin' 'roun' playin' de queen er spades. Mon, deze yer nigger gals gittin' up in de pictur's; dey sholy is."

With a brief "Good-night, Miss Becky, Mars Cajy," Free Joe went out into the darkness, followed by little Dan. He made his way to the poplar, where Lucinda had been in the habit of meeting him, and sat down. He sat there a long time; he sat there until little Dan, growing restless, trotted off in the direction of the Calderwood place. Dozing against the poplar, in the gray dawn of the morning, Free Joe heard Spite Calderwood's fox-hounds in full cry a mile away.

"Shoo!" he exclaimed, scratching his head, and laughing to himself, "dem ar dogs is des a-warmin' dat old fox up."

But it was Dan the hounds were after, and the little dog came back no more. Free Joe waited and waited, until he grew tired of waiting. He went back the next night and waited, and for many nights thereafter. His waiting was in vain, and yet he never regarded it as in vain. Careless and shabby as he was, Free Joe was thoughtful enough to have his theory. He was convinced that little Dan had found Lucinda, and that some night when the moon was shining brightly through the trees, the dog would rouse him from his dreams as he sat sleeping at the foot of the poplar-tree, and he would open his eyes and behold Lucinda standing over him, laughing merrily as of old; and then he thought what fun they would have about the queen of spades.

How many long nights Free Joe waited at the foot of the poplar-tree for Lucinda and little Dan, no one can ever know. He kept no account of them, and they were not recorded by Micajah Staley nor by Miss Becky. The season ran into summer and then into fall. One night he went to the Staley cabin, cut the two old people an armful of wood, and seated himself on the door-steps, where he rested. He was always thankful—and proud, as it seemed—when Miss Becky gave him a cup of coffee, which she was sometimes thoughtful enough to do. He was especially thankful on this particular night.

"You er still layin' off for to strike up wi' Lucindy out thar in the woods, I reckon," said Micajah Staley, smiling grimly. The situation was not without its humorous aspects.

"Oh, dey er comin', Mars Cajy, dey er comin', sho," Free Joe replied. "I boun' you dey'll come; en w'en dey does come, I'll des take en fetch um yer, whar you kin see um wid your own eyes, you en Miss Becky."

"No," said Mr. Staley, with a quick and emphatic gesture of disapproval. "Don't! don't fetch 'em anywheres. Stay right wi' 'em as long as may be."

Free Joe chuckled, and slipped away into the night, while the two old people sat gazing in the fire. Finally Micajah spoke.

"Look at that nigger; look at 'im. He's pine-blank as happy now as a kill-dee by a mill-race. You can't 'faze 'em. I'd in-about give up my t'other hand ef I could stan' flat-footed, an' grin at trouble like that there nigger."

"Niggers is niggers," said Miss Becky, smiling grimly, "an' you can't rub it out; yit I lay I've seed a heap of white people lots meaner'n Free Joe. He grins,—an' that's nigger,—but I've ketched his under jaw a-trimblin' when Lucindy's name uz brung up. An' I tell you," she went on, bridling up a little, and speaking with almost fierce emphasis, "the old Boy's done sharpened his claws for Spite Calderwood. You'll see it."

"Me, Rebecca?" said Mr. Staley, hugging his palsied arm; "me? I hope not."

"Well, you'll know it then," said Miss Becky, laughing heartily at her brother's look of alarm.

The next morning Micajah Staley had occasion to go into the woods after a piece of timber. He saw Free Joe sitting at the foot of the poplar, and the sight vexed him somewhat.

"Git up from there," he cried, "an' go an' arn your livin'. A mighty purty pass it's come to, when great big buck niggers can lie a-snorin' in the woods all day, when t'other folks is got to be up an' a-gwine. Git up from there!"

Receiving no response, Mr. Staley went to Free Joe, and shook him by the shoulder; but the negro made no response. He was dead. His hat was off, his head was bent, and a smile was on his face. It was as if he had bowed and smiled when death stood before him, humble to the last. His clothes were ragged; his hands were rough and callous; his shoes were literally tied together with strings; he was shabby in the extreme. A passer-by, glancing at him, could have no idea that such a humble creature had been summoned as a witness before the Lord God of Hosts.

CHARLES WADDELL CHESNUTT

(1858–1932)

With the local-color dialect story Charles Waddell Chesnutt entered the American literary scene in 1889,—and like Thomas Nelson Page and Joel Chandler Harris he created a benevolent, unctuous old black uncle who told stories to the white folks. But Chesnutt's Uncle Julius, the tale-teller of his first book of stories, *The Conjure Woman* (1899), had objectives that were quite different from those of Page and Harris. Chesnutt—as a black man—used stories of conjuring to enable his white audience to see life on the old plantation as it appeared to the slaves, and the picture he presented was far different from, and less attractive than, the way in which white authors portrayed it.

Chesnutt himself was never a slave. He was born in Cleveland, Ohio, the son of a prosperous farmer. When he was eight the family moved to Fayetteville, North Carolina, where Chesnutt grew up. Formally educated only through grade school, Chesnutt was a voracious reader. He taught school in Fayetteville for nine years, tried journalism, then settled in Cleveland, where he became a skilled court stenographer, read law in the office of a Cleveland attorney, and was admitted to the Ohio bar.

George W. Cable was among the earliest admirers of Chesnutt's writings and he sought to help him get his stories published. Chesnutt's first published story, for *The Atlantic Monthly*, was printed without his race being identified; the editors felt that readers might be offended. During the 1890s he wrote two kinds of stories, the local color dialect pieces collected in *The Conjure Woman* and more direct stories on race relations that were collected as *The Wife of His Youth and Other Stories of the Color Line*, also published in 1899. But the latter stories were not nearly so popular as his dialect tales, and none of his three novels—*The House Behind the Cedars* (1900), *The Marrow of Tradition* (1901), and *The Colonel's Dream* (1905)—was commercially successful. Thereafter, save for a biography of Frederick Douglass and an unpublished novel, Chesnutt wrote little.

MARS JEEMS'S NIGHTMARE

We found old Julius very useful when we moved to our new residence. He had a thorough knowledge of the neighborhood, was familar with the roads and the watercourses, knew the qualities of the various soils and what they would produce, and where the best hunting and fishing were to be had. He was a marvelous hand in the management of horses and dogs, with whose mental processes he manifested a greater familiarity than mere use would seem to account for, though it was doubtless due to the simplicity of a life that had kept him close to nature. Toward my tract of land and the things that were on it—the creeks, the swamps, the hills, the meadows, the stones, the trees—he maintained a peculiar personal attitude, that might be called predial rather than proprietary. He had been accustomed, until long after middle life, to look upon himself as the property of another. When this relation was no longer possible, owing to the war, and to his master's death and the dispersion of the family, he had been unable to break off entirely the mental habits of a lifetime, but had attached himself to the old plantation, of which he seemed to consider himself an appurtenance. We found him useful in many ways and entertaining in others, and my wife and I took quite a fancy to him.

Shortly after we became established in our home on the sand-hills, Julius brought up to the house one day a colored boy of about seventeen, whom he introduced as his grandson, and for whom he solicited employment. I was not favorably impressed by the youth's appearance—quite the contrary, in fact; but mainly to please the old man I hired Tom—his name was Tom—to help about the stables, weed the garden, cut wood and bring water, and in general to make himself useful about the outdoor work of the household.

My first impression of Tom proved to be correct. He turned out to be very trifling, and I was much annoyed by his laziness, his carelessness, and his apparent lack of any sense of responsibility. I kept him longer than I should, on Julius's account, hoping that he might improve; but he seemed to grow worse instead of better, and when I finally reached the limit of my patience, I discharged him.

"I am sorry, Julius," I said to the old man; "I should have liked to oblige you by keeping him; but I can't stand Tom any longer. He is absolutely untrustworthy."

"Yas, suh," replied Julius, with a deep sigh and a long shake of the head, "I knows he ain' much account, en dey ain' much 'pen'ence ter be put on 'im. But I wuz hopin' dat you mought make some 'lowance fuh a' ign'ant young nigger, suh, en gib 'im one mo' chance."

But I had hardened my heart. I had always been too easily imposed upon, and had suffered too much from this weakness. I determined to be firm as a rock in this instance.

"No, Julius," I rejoined decidedly, "it is impossible. I gave him more than a fair trial, and he simply won't do."

When my wife and I set out for our drive in the cool of the evening, —afternoon is "evening" in Southern parlance,—one of the servants put into the rock-away two large earthenware jugs. Our drive was to be down through the swamp to the mineral spring at the foot of the sand-hills beyond. The water of this spring was strongly impregnated with sulphur and iron, and, while not particularly agreeable of smell or taste, was used by us, in moderation, for sanitary reasons.

When we reached the spring, we found a man engaged in cleaning it out. In answer to an inquiry he said that if we would wait five or ten minutes, his task would be finished and the spring in such condition that we could fill our jugs. We might have driven on, and come back by way of the spring, but there was a bad stretch of road beyond, and we concluded to remain where we were until the spring should be ready. We were in a cool and shady place. It was often necessary to wait awhile in North Carolina; and our Northern energy had not been entirely proof against the influences of climate and local custom.

While we sat there, a man came suddenly around a turn of the road ahead of us. I recognized in him a neighbor with whom I had exchanged formal calls. He was driving a horse, apparently a high-spirited creature, possessing, so far as I could see at a glance, the marks of good temper and good breeding; the gentleman, I had heard it suggested, was slightly deficient in both. The horse was rearing and plunging, and the man was beating him furiously with a buggy-whip. When he saw us, he flushed a fiery red, and, as he passed, held the reins with one hand, at some risk to his safety, lifted his hat, and bowed somewhat constrainedly as the horse darted by us, still panting and snorting with fear.

"He looks as though he were ashamed of himself," I observed.

"I'm sure he ought to be," exclaimed my wife indignantly. "I think there is no worse sin and no more disgraceful thing than cruelty."

"I quite agree with you," I assented.

"A man w'at 'buses his hoss is gwine ter be ha'd on de folks w'at wuks fer 'im," remarked Julius. "Ef young Mistah McLean doan min', he'll hab a bad dream one er dese days, des lack 'is grandaddy had way back yander, long yeahs befo' de wah."

"What was it about Mr. McLean's dream, Julius?" I asked. The man had not yet finished cleaning the spring, and we might as well put in time listening to Julius as in any other way. We had found some of his plantation tales quite interesting.

"Mars Jeems McLean," said Julius, "wuz de grandaddy er dis yer gent'eman w'at is des gone by us beatin' his hoss. He had a big plantation en a heap er niggers. Mars Jeems wuz a ha'd man, en monst'us stric' wid his han's. Eber sence he growed up he nebber 'peared ter hab no feelin' fer nobody. W'en his daddy, ole Mars John McLean, died, de plantation en all de niggers fell ter young Mars Jeems. He had be'n bad 'nuff befo', but it wa'n't long atterwa'ds 'tel he got so dey wuz no use in libbin' at all ef you ha' ter lib roun' Mars Jeems. His niggers wuz bleedzd ter slabe fum daylight ter da'k, w'iles yuther folks's did n' hafter wuk 'cep'n' fum sun ter sun; en dey did n' git no mo' ter eat dan dey oughter, en dat de coa'ses' kin'. Dey wa'n't 'lowed ter sing, ner dance, ner play de banjo w'en Mars Jeems wuz roun' de place; fer Mars Jeems say he would n' hab no sech gwines-on —said he bought his han's ter wuk, en not ter play, en w'en night come dey mus' sleep en res', so dey'd be ready ter git up soon in de mawnin' en go ter dey wuk fresh en strong.

"Mars Jeems did n' 'low no co'tin' er juneseyin' roun' his plantation, —said he wanted his niggers ter put dey min's on dey wuk, en not be wastin' dey time wid no sech foolis'ness. En he would n' let his han's git married,—said he wuz n' raisin' niggers, but wuz raisin' cotton. En w'eneber any er de boys en gals 'ud 'mence ter git sweet on one ernudder, he'd sell one er de yuther un 'em, er sen' 'em way down in Robeson County ter his yuther plantation, whar dey could n' nebber see one ernudder.

"Ef any er de niggers eber complained, dey got fo'ty; so co'se dey did n' many un 'em complain. But dey did n' lack it, des de same, en nobody could n' blame 'em, fer dey had a ha'd time. Mars Jeems did n' make no 'lowance fer nachul bawn laz'ness, ner sickness, ner trouble in de min', ner nuffin; he wuz des gwine ter git so much wuk outer eve'y han', er know de reason w'y.

"Dey wuz one time de niggers 'lowed, fer a spell, dat Mars Jeems mought git bettah. He tuk a lackin' ter Mars Marrabo McSwayne's oldes' gal, Miss Libbie, en useter go ober dere eve'y day er eve'y obenin' en folks said dey wuz gwine ter git married sho'. But it 'pears dat Miss Libbie heared 'bout de gwines-on on Mars Jeems's Plantation, en she des 'lowed she could n' trus' herse'f wid no sech a man; dat he mought git so useter 'busing' his niggers dat he'd 'mence ter 'buse his wife atter he got useter habbin' her roun' de house. So she 'clared she wuz n' gwine ter hab nuffin mo' ter do wid young Mars Jeems.

"De niggers wuz all monst'us sorry w'en de match wuz bust' up, fer now Mars Jeems got wusser'n he wuz befo' he sta'ted sweethea'tin'. De time he useter spen' co'tin' Miss Libbie he put in findin' fault wid niggers, en all his bad feelin's 'ca'se Miss Libbie th'owed 'im ober he 'peared ter try ter wuk on de po' niggers.

"W'iles Mars Jeems wuz co'tin' Miss Libbie, two er de han's on de plantation had got ter settin' a heap er sto' by one ernudder. One un 'em wuz name' Solomon, en de yuther wuz a 'oman w'at wukked in de fiel' 'long er 'im—I fe'git dat 'oman's name, but it doan 'mount ter much in de tale nohow. Now, whuther 'ca'se Mars Jeems wuz so tuk up wid his own junesey dat he did n' paid no 'tention fer a w'ile ter w'at wuz gwine on 'twix' Solomon en his junesey, er wuther his own co'tin' made 'im kin' er easy on de co'tin' in de qua'ters, dey ain' no tellin'. But dey's one thing sho', dat w'en Miss Libbie th'owed 'im ober, he foun' out 'bout Solomon en de gal monst'us quick, en gun Solomon fo'ty, en sont de gal down ter de Robeson County plantation, en tol' all de niggers ef he ketch 'em at any mo' sech foolishness, he wuz gwine ter skin 'em alibe en tan dey hides befo' dey ve'y eyes. Co'se he would n' 'a' done it, but he mought 'a' made things wusser 'n dey wuz. So you kin 'magine dey wa'n't much lubmaking' in de qua'ters fer a long time.

"Mars Jeems useter go down ter de yuther plantation sometimes fer a week er mo', en so he had ter hab a oberseah ter look atter his wuk w'iles he 'uz gone. Mars Jeem's oberseah wuz a po' w'ite man name' Nick Johnson, —de niggers called 'im Mars Johnson ter his face, but behin' his back dey useter call 'im Ole Nick, en de name suited 'im ter a T. He wuz wusser'n Mars Jeems ever da'ed ter be. Co'se de darkies did n' lack de way Mars Jeems used 'em, but he wuz de marster, en had a right ter do ez he please'; but dis yer Ole Nick wa'n't nuffin but a po'buckrah, en all de niggers 'spised 'im ez much ez dey hated 'im, fer he did n' own nobody, en wa'n't no bettah 'n a nigger, fer in dem days any 'spectable pusson would ruther be a nigger dan a po' w'ite man.

"Now, atter Solomon's gal had be'n sont away, he kep' feelin' mo' en mo' bad erbout it, 'tel fin'lly he 'lowed he wuz gwine ter see ef dey could n' be sump'n done fer ter git 'er back, en ter make Mars Jeems treat de darkies bettah. So he tuk a peck er co'n out'n de ba'n one night, en went ober ter see old Aun' Peggy, de free-nigger cunjuh 'oman down by de Wim'l'ton Road.

"Aun' Peggy listen' ter 'is tale, en ax' him some queshtuns, en den tol' 'im she'd wuk her roots, en see w'at dey'd say 'bout it, en ter-morrer night he sh'd come back ag'in en fetch ernudder peck er co'n, en den she'd hab sump'n fer ter tell 'im.

"So Solomon went back de nex' night, en sho' 'nuff, Aun' Peggy tol' 'im w'at ter do. She gun 'im some stuff w'at look' lack it be'n made by poundin' up some roots en yarbs wid a pestle in a mo'tar.

"'Dis yer stuff,' sez she, 'is monst'us pow'ful kin' er goopher. You take dis home, en gin it ter de cook, ef you kin trus' her, en tell her fer ter put it in yo' marster's soup de fus' cloudy day he hab okra soup fer dinnah. Min' you follers de d'rections.'

"'It ain' gwineter p'isen 'im, is it?' ax' Solomon, gittin' kin' er skeered; fer Solomon wuz a good man, en did n' want ter do nobody no rale ha'm.

"'Oh, no,' sez old Aun' Peggy, 'it's gwine ter do 'im good, but he'll hab a monst'us bad dream fus'. A mont' fum now you come down heah en lemme know how de goopher is wukkin'. Fer I ain't done much er dis kin' er cunj'in' er late yeahs, en I has ter kinder keep track un it ter see dat it doan 'complish no mo' d'n I 'lows fer it ter do. En I has ter be kinder keerful 'bout cunj'in' w'ite folks; so be sho' en lemme know, w'ateber you do, des w'at is gwine on roun' de plantation.'

"So Solomon say all right, en tuk de goopher mixtry up ter de big house en gun it ter de cook, en tol' her fer ter put it in Mars Jeems's soup de fus' cloudy day she hab okra soup fer dinnah. It happen' dat de ve'y nex' day wuz a cloudy day, en so de cook made okra soup fer Mars Jeems's dinnah, en put de powder Solomon gun her inter de soup, en made de soup rale good, so Mars Jeems eat a whole lot of it en 'peared ter enjoy it.

"De nex' mawnin' Mars Jeems tol' de oberseah he wuz gwine 'way on some bizness, en den he wuz gwine ter his yuther plantation, down in Robeson County, en he did n' 'spec' he'd be back fer a mont' er so.

" 'But,' sezee, 'I wants you ter run dis yer plantation fer all it's wuth. Dese yer niggers is gittin' monst'us triflin' en lazy en keerless, en dey ain' no 'pen'ence ter be put in 'em. I wants dat stop', en w'iles I'm gone erway I wants de 'spenses cut 'way down en a heap mo' wuk done. Fac', I wants dis yer plantation ter make a reco'd dat'll show w'at kinder oberseah you is.'

"Ole Nick did n' said nuffin but 'Yas, suh,'' but de way he kinder grin' ter hisse'f en show' his big yaller teef, en snap' de rawhide he useter kyar roun' wid 'im, made col' chills run up and down de backbone er dem niggers w'at heared Mars Jeems a-talkin'. En dat night dey wuz mo'nin' en groanin' down in de qua'ters, fer de niggers all knowed w'at wuz comin'.

"So, sho' 'nuff, Mars Jeems went erway nex' mawnin', en de trouble begun. Mars Johnson sta'ted off de ve'y fus' day fer ter see w'at he could hab ter show Mars Jeems w'en he come back. He made de tasks bigger en de rashuns littler, en w'en de niggers had wukked all day, he'd fin' sump'n fer 'em ter do roun' de ba'n er som'ers atter da'k, fer ter keep 'em busy a' hour er so befo' dey went ter sleep.

"About th'ee er fo' days atter Mars Jeems went erway, young Mars Dunkin McSwayne rode up ter de big house one day wid a nigger settin' behin' 'im in de buggy, tied ter de seat, en ax' ef Mars Jeems wuz home. Mars Johnson wuz at de house, and he say no.

" 'Well,' sez Mars Dunkin, sezee, 'I fotch dis nigger ober ter Mistah McLean fer ter pay a bet I made wid 'im las' week w'en we wuz playin' kya'ds te'gedder. I bet 'im a nigger man, en heah's one I reckon 'll fill de bill. He wuz tuk up de yuther day fer a stray nigger, en he could n' gib no 'count er hisse'f, en so he wuz sol' at oction, en I bought 'im. He's kinder brash, but I knows yo' powers, Mistah Johnson, en I reckon ef anybody kin make 'im toe de ma'k, you is de man.'

"Mars Johnson grin' one er dem grins w'at show' all his snaggle teef, en make de niggers 'low he look lack de ole debbil, en sezee ter Mars Dunkin:
—

" 'I reckon you kin trus' me, Mistah Dunkin, fer ter tame any nigger wuz eber bawn. De nigger doan lib w'at I can't take down in 'bout fo' days.'

"Well, Ole Nick had 'is han's full longer er dat noo nigger; en w'iles de res' er de darkies wuz sorry fer de po' man, dey 'lowed he kep' Mars Johnson so busy dat dey got along better 'n dey'd 'a' done ef de noo nigger had nebber come.

"De fus' thing dat happen', Mars Johnson sez ter dis yer noo man:—

" 'W'at's yo' name, Sambo?'

" 'My name ain' Sambo,' 'spon' de noo nigger.

" 'Did I ax you w'at yo' name wa'n't?' sez Mars Johnson. 'You wants ter be pa'tic'lar how you talks ter me. Now, w'at is yo' name, en whar did you come fum?'

" 'I dunno my name,' sez de nigger, 'en I doan 'member whar I come fum. My head is all kin' er mix' up.'

" 'Yas," sez Mars Johnson, 'I reckon I'll ha' ter gib you sump'n fer ter cl'ar yo' head. At de same time, it'll l'arn you some manners, en atter dis mebbe you 'll say "suh" w'en you speaks ter me.'

"Well, Mars Johnson haul' off wid his rawhide en hit de noo nigger once. De noo man look' at Mars Johnson fer a minute ez ef he did n' know w'at ter make er dis yer kin' er l'arnin'. But w'en de oberseah raise' his w'ip ter hit him ag'in, de noo nigger des haul' off en made fer Mars Johnson, en ef some er de yuther niggers had n' stop' 'im, it 'peared ez ef he mought 'a' made it wa'm fer Ole Nick dere fer a w'ile. But de oberseah made de yuther niggers he'p tie de noo nigger up, en den gun 'im fo'ty, wid a dozen er so th'owed in fer good measure, fer Ole Nick wuz nebber stingy wid dem kin' er rashuns. De nigger went on at a tarrable rate, des lack a wil' man, but co'se he wuz bleedzd ter take his med'cine, fer he wuz tied up en could n' he'p hisse'f.

"Mars Johnson lock' de noo nigger up in de ba'n, en did n' gib 'im nuffin ter eat fer a day er so, 'tel he got 'im kin'er quiet' down, en den he tu'nt 'im loose en put 'im ter wuk. De nigger 'lowed he wa'n't useter wukkin', en could n' wuk, en Mars Johnson gun 'im anudder fo'ty fer laziness en impidence, en let 'im fas' a day er so mo', en den put 'im ter wuk ag'in. De nigger went ter wuk, but did n' 'pear ter know how ter han'le a hoe. It tuk des 'bout half de oberseah's time lookin' after 'im, en dat po' nigger got mo' lashin's en cussin's en cuffin's dan any fo' yuthers on de plantation. He did n' mix' wid ner talk much ter de res' er de niggers, en could n' 'pear ter git it th'oo his min' dat he wuz a slabe en had ter wuk en min' de w'ite folks, spite er de fac' dat Ole Nick gun 'im a lesson eve'y day. En fin'lly Mars Johnson 'lowed dat he could n' do nuffin wid 'im; dat ef he wuz his nigger, he'd break his sperrit er break 'is neck, one er de yuther. But co'se he wuz only son ober on trial, en ez he did n' gib sat'sfaction, en he had n' heared fum Mars Jeems 'bout w'en he wuz comin' back; en ez he wuz feared he'd git mad some time er 'nuther en kill de nigger befo' he knowed it, he 'lowed he'd better sen' 'im back ter Mars Dunkin.

"Now, Mars Dunkin McSwayne wuz one er dese yer easy-gwine gent'emen w'at did 'n lack ter hab no trouble wid niggers er nobody e'se, en he knowed ef Mars Ole Nick could n' git 'long wid dis nigger, nobody could. So he tuk de nigger ter town dat same day, en sol' 'im ter a trader w'at wuz gittin' up a gang er lackly niggers fer ter ship off on de steamboat ter go down de ribber ter Wim'l'ton en fum dere ter Noo Orleens.

"De nex' day atter de noo man had be'n sont away, Solomon wuz wukkin' in de cotton-fiel', en w'en he got ter de fence nex' ter de woods, at de een' er de row, who sh'd he see on de yuther side but ole Aun' Peggy. She beckon' ter'im,—de oberseah wuz down on de yuther side er de fiel',—en sez she:—

" 'W'y ain' you done come en 'po'ted ter me lack I tol' you?'

" 'W'y, law! Aun' Peggy,' sez Solomon, 'dey ain' nuffin ter 'po't. Mars Jeems went away de day atter we gun 'im de goopher mixtry, en we ain' seed hide ner hair un 'im sence, en co'se we doan know nuffin 'bout w'at 'fec' it had on 'im.'

" 'I doan keer nuffin 'bout yo' Mars Jeems now; w'at I wants ter know is w'at is be'n gwine on 'mongs' de niggers. Has you be'n gittin' 'long any better on de plantation?'

" 'No, Aun' Peggy, we be'n gittin' 'long wusser. Mars Johnson is stric'er 'n he eber wuz befo', en de po' niggers doan ha'dly git time ter draw dey bref, en dey 'lows dey mought des ez well be dead ez alibe.'

" 'Uh huh!' sez Aun' Peggy, sez she, 'I tol' you dat 'uz monst'us pow'ful goopher, en its wuk doan 'pear all at once.'

" 'Long ez we had dat noo nigger heah,' Solomon went on, 'he kep' Mars Johnson busy pa't er de time; but now he's gone erway, I s'pose de res' un us'll ketch it wusser 'n eber.'

" 'W'at's gone wid de noo nigger?' sez Aun' Peggy, rale quick, battin' her eyes en straight'nin' up.

" 'Ole Nick done sont 'im back ter Mars Dunkin, who had fotch 'im heah fer ter pay a gamblin' debt ter Mars Jeems,' sez Solomon, 'en I heahs Mars Dunkin has sol' 'im ter a nigger-trader up in Patesville, w'at's gwine ter ship 'im off wid a gang ter-morrer.'

"Ole Aun' Peggy 'peared ter git rale stirred up w'en Solomon tol' 'er dat, en sez she, shakin' her stick at 'im:—

" 'W'y did n' you come en tell me 'bout dis noo nigger bein' sol' erway? Did n' you promus me, ef I'd gib you dat goopher, you'd come en 'po't ter me 'bout all w'at wuz gwine on on dis plantation? Co'se I could 'a' foun' out fer myse'f, but I 'pended on yo' tellin' me, en now by not doin' it I's feared you gwine spile my cunj'in'. You come down ter my house ter-night en do w'at I tells you, er I'll put a spell on you dat'll make yo' ha'r fall out so you'll be bal', en yo' eyes drap out so you can't see, en yo' teef fall out so you can't eat, en yo' years grow up so you can't heah. W'en you is foolin' wid a cunjuh 'oman lack me, you got ter min' yo' P's en Q's er dey'll be trouble sho' 'nuff.'

"So co'se Solomon went down ter Aun' Peggy's dat night, en she gun 'im a roasted sweet'n' 'tater.

" 'You take dis yer sweet'n' 'tater,' sez she,—'I done goophered it 'speshly fer dat noo nigger, so you better not eat it yo'se'f er you'll wush you had n',—en slip off ter town, en fin' dat strange man, en gib 'im dis yer sweet'n' tater. He mus' eat it befo' mawnin', sho', ef he doan wanter be sol' erway ter Noo Orleens.'

" 'But s'posen de patteroles ketch me, Aun' Peggy, w'at I gwine ter do?' sez Solomon.

" 'De patteroles ain' gwine tech you, but ef you doan fin' dat nigger, *I'm* gwine git you, en you'll fin' me wusser 'n de patteroles. Des hol' on a minute, en I'll sprinkle you wid some er dis mixtry out'n dis yer bottle, so de patteroles can't see you, en you kin rub yo' feet wid some er dis yer grease out'n dis go'd, so you kin run fas', en rub some un it on yo' eyes so you kin see in de da'k; en den you mus' fin' dat noo nigger en gib 'im dis yer 'tater, er you gwine ter hab mo' trouble on yo' han's 'n you eber had befo' in yo' life er eber will hab sence.'

"So Solomon tuk de sweet'n' 'tater en sta'ted up de road fas' ez he could go, en befo' long he retch' town. He went right 'long by de patteroles, en dey did n' 'pear ter notice 'im, en bimeby he foun' whar de strange nigger was kep', en he walked right pas' de gyard at de do' en foun' 'im. De nigger could n' see 'im, ob co'se, en he could n' 'a' seed de nigger in de da'k, ef it had n' be'n fer de stuff Aun' Peggy gun 'im ter rub on 'is eyes. De nigger wuz layin' in a co'nder, 'sleep, en Solomon des slip' up ter 'im, en hilt dat sweet'n' 'tater 'fo' de nigger's nose, en he des nach'ly retch' up wid his han', en tuk de 'tater en eat it in his sleep, widout knowin' it. W'en Solomon seed he'd done eat de 'tater, he went back en tol's Aun' Peggy, en den went home ter his cabin ter sleep, 'way 'long 'bout two o'clock in de mawnin'.

"De nex' day wuz Sunday, en so de niggers had a little time ter deyse'ves. Solomon wuz kinder 'sturb' in his min' thinkin' 'bout his junesey w'at 'uz gone away, en wond'rin' w'at Aun' Peggy had ter do wid dat noo nigger; en he had sa'ntered up in de woods so's ter be by hisse'f a little, en at de same time ter look atter a rabbit-trap he'd sot down in de aidge er de swamp, w'en who sh'd he see stan'in' unnder a tree but a w'ite man.

"Solomon did n' knowed de w'ite man at fus', 'tel de w'ite man spoke up ter 'im.

" 'Is dat you, Solomon?' sezee.

"Den Solomon reco'nized de voice.

" 'Fer de Lawd's sake, Mars Jeems! is dat you?'

" 'Yas, Solomon,' sez his marster, 'dis is me, er w'at's lef' er me.'

"It wa'n't no wonder Solomon had n' knowed Mars Jeems at fus', fer he wuz dress' lack a po' w'ite man, en wuz barefooted, en look' monst'us pale en peaked, ez ef he'd des come th'oo a ha'd spell er sickness.

" 'You er lookin' kinder po'ly, Mars Jeems,' sez Solomon. 'Is you be'n sick, suh?'

" 'No, Solomon,' sez Mars Jeems, shakin' his head, en speakin' sorter slow en sad, 'I ain' be'n sick, but I's had a monst'us bad dream,—fac', a reg'lar, nach'ul nightmare. But tell me how things has be'n gwine on up ter de plantation sence I be'n gone, Solomon.'

"So Solomon up en tol' 'im 'bout de craps, en 'bout de hosses en de mules, en 'bout de cows en de hawgs. En w'en he 'mence' ter tell 'bout de noo nigger, Mars Jeems prick' up 'is yeahs en listen', en eve'y now en den he'd say, 'Uh huh! uh huh!' en nod 'is head. En bimeby, w'en he'd ax' Solomon some mo' queshtuns, he sez, sezee:—

" 'Now, Solomon, I doan want you ter say a wo'd ter nobody 'bout meetin' me heah, but I wants you ter slip up ter de house, en fetch me some clo's en some shoes,—I fergot ter tell you dat a man rob' me back yander on de road en swap clo's wid me widout axin' me whuther er no,—but you neenter say nuffin 'bout dat, nuther. You go en fetch me some clo's heah, so nobody won't see you, en keep yo' mouf shet, en I'll gib you a dollah.'

"Solomon wuz so s'tonish' he lack ter fell ober in his tracks, w'en Mars Jeems promus' ter gib 'im a dollah. Dey su't'nly wuz a change come ober Mars Jeems, w'en he offer' one er his niggers dat much money. Solomon 'mence' ter 'spec' dat Aun' Peggy's cunj'ation had be'n wukkin' monst'us strong.

"Solomon fotch Mars Jeems some clo's en shoes, en dat same eb'nin' Mars Jeems 'peared at de house, en let on lack he des dat minute got home fum Robeson County. Mars Johnson was all ready ter talk ter 'im, but Mars Jeems sont 'im wo'd he wa'n't feelin' ve'y well dat night, en he 'd see 'im ter-morrer.

"So nex' mawnin' atter breakfus' Mars Jeems sont fer de oberseah, en ax' 'im fer ter gib 'count er his styoa'dship. Ole Nick tol' Mars Jeems how much wuk be'n done, en got de books en showed 'im how much money be'n save'. Den Mars Jeems ax' 'im how de darkies be'n behabin', en Mars Johnson say dey be'n behabin' good, most un 'em, en dem w'at did n' behabe good at fus' change dey conduc' atter he got holt un 'em a time er two.

" 'All,' sezee, cep'n' de noo nigger Mistah Dunkin fotch ober heah en lef' on trial, w'iles you wuz gone.'

" 'Oh, yas,' 'lows Mars Jeems, 'tell me all 'bout dat noo nigger. I heared a little 'bout dat quare noo nigger las' night, en it wuz des too redik'lus. Tell me all 'bout dat noo nigger.'

"So seein' Mars Jeems so good-nachu'd 'bout it, Mars Johnson up en tol' 'im how he tied up de noo han' de fus' day en gun 'im fo'ty 'ca'se he would 'n tell 'im 'is name.

" 'Ha, ha, ha!' sez Mars Jeems, laffin' fit ter kill, 'but dat is too funny fer any use. Tell me some mo' 'bout dat noo nigger.'

"So Mars Johnson went on en tol' 'im how he had ter starbe de noo nigger 'fo' he could make 'im take holt er a hoe.

" 'Dat wuz de beatinis' notion fer a nigger,' sez Mars Jeems, 'puttin' on airs, des lack he wuz a w'ite man! En I reckon you did n' do nuffin ter 'im?'

" 'Oh, no, suh,' sez de oberseah, grinnin' lack a chessy-cat, 'I did n' do nuffin but take de hide off'n 'im.'

"Mars Jeems lafft en lafft, 'tel it 'peared lack he wuz des gwine ter bu'st. '*Tell* me some mo' 'bout dat noo nigger, oh, tell me some mo'. Dat noo nigger int'rusts me, he do, en dat is a fac'.'

"Mars Johnson did n' quite un'erstan' w'y Mars Jeems sh'd make sich a great 'miration 'bout de noo nigger, but co'se he want' ter please de gent'eman w'at hi'ed 'im, en so he 'splain' all 'bout how many times he had ter cowhide de noo nigger, en how he made 'im do tasks twicet ez big ez some er de yuther han's, en how he'd chain 'im up in de ba'n at night en feed 'im on co'n-bread en water.

" 'Oh! but you is a monst'us good obserseah; you is de bes' oberseah in dis county, Mistah Johnson,' sez Mars Jeems, w'en de oberseah got th'oo wid his tale; 'en dey ain' nebber be'n no nigger-breaker lack you roun' heah befo'. En you desarbes great credit fer sendin' dat nigger 'way befo' you sp'ilt 'im fer de market. Fac', you is sech a monst'us good obserseah, en you is got dis yer plantation in sech fine shape, dat I reckon I doan need you no mo'. You is got dese yer darkies so well train' dat I 'spec' I kin run 'em myse'f fum dis time on. But I does wush you had 'a' hilt on ter dat noo nigger 'tel I got home, fer I'd 'a' lack er 'a' seed 'im, I su't'nly should.'

"De oberseah wuz so 'stonish' he did n' ha'dly know w'at ter say, but fin'lly he ax' Mars Jeems ef he would n' gib 'im a riccommen' fer ter git ernudder place.

" 'No, suh,' sez Mars Jeems, 'somehow er 'nuther I doan lack yo' looks sence I come back dis time, en I'd much ruther you would n' stay roun' heah. Fac', I's feared ef I'd meet you alone in de woods some time, I mought wanter ha'm you. But layin' dat aside, I be'n lookin' ober dese yer books er yo'n w'at you kep' w'iles I wuz 'way, en fer a yeah er so back, en dere's some figgers w'at ain' des cl'ar ter me. I ain' got no time fer ter talk 'bout 'em now, but I 'spec' befo' I settles wid you fer dis las' mont', you better come up heah ter-morrer, atter I's look' de books en 'counts ober some mo', en den' we 'll straighten ou' business all up.'

"Mars Jeems 'lowed atterwa'ds dat he wuz des shootin' in de da'k w'en he said dat 'bout de books, but howsomeber, Mars Nick Johnson lef' dat naberhood 'twix' de nex' two suns, en nobody roun' dere nebber seed hide ner hair un 'im sence. En all de darkies t'ank de Lawd, en 'lowed it wuz a good riddance er bad rubbage.

"But all dem things I done tol' you ain' nuffin 'side'n de change w'at come ober Mars Jeems fum dat time on. Aun' Peggy's goopher had made a noo man un 'im enti'ely. De nex' day atter he come back, he tol' de han's dey neenter wuk on'y fum sun ter sun, en he cut dey tasks down so dey did n' nobody hab ter stan' ober 'em wid a rawhide er a hick'ry. En he 'lowed ef de niggers want ter hab a dance in de big ba'n any Sad'day night, dey mought hab it. En bimeby, w'en Solomon seed how good Mars Jeems wuz, he ax' 'im ef he would n' please sen' down ter de yuther plantation fer his junesey. Mars Jeems say su't'nly, en gun Solomon a pass en a note ter de oberseah on de yuther plantation, en sont Solonon down ter Robeson County wid a hoss en buggy fer ter fetch his junesey back. W'en de niggers see how fine Mars Jeems gwine treat 'em, dey all tuk ter sweet-hea'tin' en juneseyin' en singin' en dancin', en eight er ten couples got married, en bimeby eve'ybody 'mence' ter say Mars Jeems McLean got a finer plantation, en slicker-lookin' niggers, en dat he 'uz makin' mo' cotton en co'n, dan any yuther gent'eman in de county. En Mars Jeems's own junesey, Miss Libbie, heared 'bout de noo gwines-on on Mars Jeems's plantation, en she change' her min' 'bout Mars Jeems en tuk 'im back ag'in, en 'fo' long dey had a fine weddin', en all de darkies had a big feas' en dey wuz fiddlin' en dancin' en funnin' en frolic'in' fum sundown 'tel mawnin'."

"And they all lived happy ever after," I said, as the old man reached a full stop.

"Yas, suh," he said, interpreting my remarks as a question, "dey did. Solomon useter say," he added, "dat Aun' Peggy's goopher had turnt Mars Jeems ter a nigger, en dat dat noo han' wuz Mars Jeems hisse'f. But co'se Solomon did n' das' ter let on 'bout w'at he 'spicioned, en ole Aun' Peggy would' a' 'nied it ef she had be'n ax', fer she'd 'a' got in trouble sho', ef it 'uz knowed she'd be'n cunj'in' de w'ite folks.

"Dis yer tale goes ter show," concluded Julius sententiously, as the man came up and announced that the spring was ready for us to get water, "dat w'ite folks w'at is so ha'd en stric', en doan make no 'lowance fer po' ign'ant niggers w'at ain' had no chanst ter l'arn, is li'ble ter hab bad dreams, ter say de leas', en dat dem w'at is kin' en good ter po' people is sho' ter prosper en git 'long in de worl'."

"That is a very strange story, Uncle Julius," observed my wife, smiling, "and Solomon's explanation is quite improbable."

"Yes, Julius," said I, "that was powerful goopher. I am glad, too, that you told us the moral of the story; it might have escaped us otherwise. By the way, did you make that up all by yourself?"

The old man's face assumed an injured look, expressive more of sorrow than of anger, and shaking his head he replied:—

"No, suh, I heared dat tale befo' you er Mis' Annie dere wuz bawn, suh. My mammy tol' me dat tale w'en I wa'n't mo' d'n knee-high ter a hoppergrass."

I drove to town next morning, on some business, and did not return until noon; and after dinner I had to visit a neighbour, and did not get back until supper-time. I was smoking a cigar on the back piazza in the early evening, when I saw a familiar figure carrying a bucket of water to the barn. I called my wife.

"My dear," I said severely, "what is that rascal doing here? I thought I discharged him yesterday for good and all."

"Oh, yes," she answered, "I forgot to tell you. He was hanging round the place all the morning, and looking so down in the mouth, that I told him that if he would try to do better, we would give him one more chance. He seems so grateful, and so really in earnest in his promises of amendment, that I'm sure you'll not regret taking him back."

I was seriously enough annoyed to let my cigar go out. I did not share my wife's rose-colored hopes in regard to Tom; but as I did not wish the servants to think there was any conflict of authority in the household, I let the boy stay.

SIDNEY LANIER

(1842–1881)

The 1870s and 1880s were not good years for Southern poetry, which unlike prose fiction was poorly equipped in its language convention to deal with the presentation of locale and character types that were the principal ingredients of the local-color vogue. For the most part, except for dialect verse the prevailing diction of poetry was abstract and ideal, still very much in the tradition of British romantic poetry but without the accompanying vigor that distinguished the best English work.

The one Southern poet who came nearest to breaking out of the old forms and language conventions was Sidney Lanier, and it was his professional concern for, and involvement in, music that led him in the later years of his short life to strive for a poetic diction that stressed the tonal properties of words over their idea content. In poems such as the "Marshes of Glynn" and "Sunrise" Lanier came closer than any of his Southern contemporaries to freeing his verse from dependence upon poetic abstractions; in searching for more words that would convey sounds and moods, he moved toward a more concrete and specific imagery, such as that used by Walt Whitman.

Lanier was born in Macon, Georgia, and graduated from Oglethorpe University. He had hoped to study in Germany, but the war intervened. He enlisted in the Confederate army and was captured in 1864, spending four months as a prisoner at Point Lookout, Maryland, where he contracted the tuberculosis that ravaged his remaining years. After the war he worked at odd jobs, wrote a novel, *Tiger-Lilies* (1867), and after a brief stay in Texas moved to Baltimore where he obtained a position as first flautist of the Peabody Symphony Orchestra. The poverty that dogged him throughout his life was partially alleviated during his last two years when he was appointed lecturer in English literature at Johns Hopkins University.

It was for his Hopkins lectures that he wrote *The Science of English Verse* (1880), an interesting attempt to establish a scientific basis for English versification using musical principles. He had been writing and publishing verse for some time before this work. In 1875 his first real success as a poet came with "Corn." In that year, too, he was selected to write a cantata for the Philadelphia Centennial Exposition of 1876. Most of his best verse was written during his last years, but no book publication of his late poems appeared until the year after his death, in 1882. Lanier also wrote a number of children's books, a travel book, and several volumes of literary criticism.

THAR'S MORE IN THE MAN THAN THAR IS IN THE LAND

I knowed a man, which he lived in Jones,
Which Jones is a county of red hills and stones,
And he lived pretty much by gittin' of loans,
And his mules was nuthin' but skin and bones,
And his hogs was flat as his corn-bread pones,
And he had 'bout a thousand acres o' land.

This man—which his name it was also Jones—
He swore that he'd leave them old red hills and stones,
Fur he couldn't make nuthin' but yallerish cotton,
And little o' *that*, and his fences was rotten,
And what little corn he had, *hit* was boughten
And dinged ef a livin' was in the land.

And the longer he swore the madder he got,
And he riz and he walked to the stable lot,
And he hollered to Tom to come thar and hitch
Fur to emigrate somewhar whar land was rich,
And to quit raisin' cock-burrs, thistles and sich,
And a wastin' ther time on the cussed land.

So him and Tom they hitched up the mules,
Pertestin' that folks was mighty big fools
That 'ud stay in Georgy ther lifetime out,
Jest scratchin' a livin' when all of 'em mought
Git places in Texas whar cotton would sprout
By the time you could plant it in the land.

And he driv by a house whar a man named Brown
Was a livin', not fur from the edge o' town,

And he bantered Brown fur to buy his place,
And said that bein' as money was skace,
And bein' as sheriffs was hard to face,
Two dollars an acres would git the land.

They closed at a dollar and fifty cents,
And Jones he bought him a waggin and tents,
And loaded his corn, and his wimmin, and truck,
And moved to Texas, which it tuck
His entire pile, with the best of luck,
To git thar and git him a little land.

But Brown moved out on the old Jones' farm,
And he rolled up his breeches and bared his arm,
And he picked all the rocks from off'n the groun',
And he rooted it up and he plowed it down,
Then he sowed his corn and his wheat in the land.

Five years glid by, and Brown, one day
(Which he'd got so fat that he wouldn't weigh),
Was a settin' down, sorter lazily,
To the bulliest dinner you ever see,
When one o' the children jumped on his knee
And says, "Yan's Jones, which you bought his land."

And thar was Jones, standin' out at the fence,
And he hadn't no waggin, nor mules, nor tents,
Fur he had left Texas afoot and cum
To Georgy to see if he couldn't git sum
Employment, and he was a lookin' as hum-
Ble as ef he had never owned any land.

But Brown he axed him in, and he sot
Him down to his vittles smokin' hot,
And when he had filled hisself and the floor
Brown looked at him sharp and riz and swore
That, "whether men's land was rich or poor
Thar was more in the *man* than thar was in the *land*."

1882

THE MARSHES OF GLYNN

Glooms of the live-oaks, beautiful-braided and woven
With intricate shades of the vines that myriad-cloven
  Clamber the forks of the multiform boughs,—

THE MARSHES OF GLYNN

Emerald twilights,—
Virginal shy lights,
Wrought of the leaves to allure to the whisper of vows,
When lovers pace timidly down through the green colonnades
Of the dim sweet woods, of the dear dark woods,
Of the heavenly woods and glades,
That run to the radiant marginal sand-beach within
The wide sea-marches of Glynn;—

Beautiful glooms, soft dusks in the noon-day fire,—
Wildwood privacies, closets of lone desire,
Chamber from chamber parted with wavering arras of leaves,—
Cells for the passionate pleasure of prayer to the soul that grieves,
Pure with a sense of the passing of saints' through the wood,
Cool for the dutiful weighing of ill with good;—

O braided dusks of the oak and woven shades of the vine,
While the riotous noon-day sun of the June-day long did shine
Ye held me fast in your heart and I held you fast in mine;
But now when the noon is no more, and riot is rest,
And the sun is a-wait at the ponderous gate of the West,
And the slant yellow beam down the wood-aisle doth seem
Like a lane into heaven that leads from a dream,—
Ay, now, when my soul all day hath drunken the soul of the oak,
And my heart is at ease from men, and the wearisome sound of the stroke
Of the scythe of time and the trowel of trade is low,
And belief overmasters doubt, and I know that I know,
And my spirit is grown to a lordly great compass within,
That the length and the breadth and the sweep of the marshes of Glynn
Will work me no fear like the fear they have wrought me of yore
When length was fatigue, and when breadth was but bitterness sore,
And when terror and shrinking and dreary unnamable pain
Drew over me out of the merciless miles of the plain,—

Oh, now, unafraid, I am fain to face
The vast sweet visage of space.
To the edge of the wood I am drawn, I am drawn,
Where the gray beach glimmering runs, as a belt of the dawn,
For a mete and a mark
To the forest-dark:—
So:
Affable live-oak, leaning low,—
Thus—with your favor—soft, with a reverent hand,
(Not lightly touching your person, Lord of the land!)
Bending your beauty aside, with a step I stand

On the firm-packed sand,
                    Free
By a world of marsh that borders a world of sea.
  Sinuous southward and sinuous northward the shimmering band
  Of the sand-beach fastens the fringe of the marsh to the folds of the land.
Inward and outward to northward and southward the beachlines linger and
        curl
As a silver-wrought garment that clings to and follows the firm sweet limbs
        of a girl.
Vanishing, swerving, evermore curving again into sight,
Softly the sand-beach wavers away to a dim gray looping of light.
And what if behind me to westward the wall of the woods stands high?
The world lies east: how ample, the marsh and the sea and the sky!
A league and a league of marsh-grass, waist-high, broad in the blade,
Green, and all of a height, and unflecked with a light or a shade,
Stretch leisurely off, in a pleasant plain,
To the terminal blue of the main.
Oh, what is abroad in the marsh and the terminal sea?
    Somehow my soul seems suddenly free
From the weighing of fate and the sad discussion of sin,
By the length and the breadth and the sweep of the marshes of Glynn.

Ye marshes, how candid and simple and nothing-withholding and free
Ye publish yourselves to the sky and offer yourselves to the sea!
Tolerant plains, that suffer the sea and the rains and the sun,
Ye spread and span like the catholic man who hath mightily won
God out of knowledge and good out of infinite pain
And sight out of blindness and purity out of a stain.

As the marsh-hen secretly builds on the watery sod,
Behold I will build me a nest on the greatness of God:
I will fly in the greatness of God as the marsh-hen flies
In the freedom that fills all the space 'twixt the marsh and the skies:
By so many roots as the marsh-grass sends in the sod
I will heartily lay me a-hold on the greatness of God:
Oh, like to the greatness of God is the greatness within
The range of the marshes, the liberal marshes of Glynn.

And the sea lends large, as the marsh: lo, out of his plenty the sea
Pours fast: full soon the time of the flood-tide must be:
Look how the grace of the sea doth go
About and about through the intricate channels that flow
      Here and there,
                    Everywhere,
Till his waters have flooded the uttermost creeks and the low-lying lanes,

And the marsh is meshed with a million veins,
That like as with rosy and silvery essences flow
   In the rose-and-silver evening glow.
              Farewell, my lord Sun!
The creeks overflow: a thousand rivulets run
'Twixt the roots of the sod; the blades of the marsh-grass stir;
Passeth a hurrying sound of wings that westward whirr;
Passeth, and all is still; and the currents cease to run;
And the sea and the marsh are one.

How still the plains of the waters be!
The tide is in his ecstasy.
The tide is at his highest height:
         And it is night.

And now from the Vast of the Lord will the waters of sleep
Roll in on the souls of men,
But who will reveal to our waking ken
The forms that swim and the shapes that creep
        Under the waters of sleep?
And I would I could know what swimmeth below when the tide comes in
On the length and the breadth of the marvellous marshes of Glynn.

1882

SUNRISE

In my sleep I was fain of their fellowship, fain
   Of the live-oak, the marsh, and the main.
The little green leaves would not let me alone in my sleep;
Up-breathed from the marshes, a message of range and of sweep,
Interwoven with waftures of wild sea-liberties, drifting,
   Came through the lapped leaves sifting, sifting,
     Came to the gates of sleep.
Then my thoughts, in the dark of the dungeon-keep
Of the Castle of Captives hid in the City of Sleep,
Upstarted, by twos and by threes assembling:
   The gates of sleep fell a-trembling
Like as the lips of a lady that forth falter *yes*,
     Shaken with happiness:
    The gates of sleep stood wide.

I have waked, I have come, my beloved! I might not abide:
I have come ere the dawn, O beloved, my live-oaks, to hide
    In your gospelling glooms,—to be

As a lover in heaven, the marsh my marsh and the sea my sea.

Tell me, sweet burly-bark'd, man-bodied Tree
That mine arms in the dark are embracing, dost know
From what fount are these tears at thy feet which flow?
They rise not from reason, but deeper inconsequent deeps.
        Reason's not one that weeps.
      What logic of greeting lies
Betwixt dear over-beautiful trees and the rain of the eyes?

O cunning green leaves, little masters! like as ye gloss
All the dull-tissued dark with your luminous darks that emboss
The vague blackness of night into pattern and plan,
          So,
  (But would I could know, but would I could know,)
With your question embroid'ring the dark of the question of man,—
So, with your silences purfling this silence of man
While his cry to the dead for some knowledge is under the ban,
          Under the ban,—
      So, ye have wrought me
Designs on the night of our knowledge,—yea, ye have taught me,
          So,
  That haply we know somewhat more than we know.

       Ye lispers, whisperers, singers in storms,
       Ye consciences murmuring faiths under forms,
       Ye ministers meet for each passion that grieves,
       Friendly, sisterly, sweetheart leaves,
Oh, rain me down from your darks that contain me
Wisdoms ye winnow from winds that pain me,—
Sift down tremors of sweet-within-sweet
That advise me of more than they bring,—repeat
Me the woods-smell that swiftly but now brought breath
From the heaven-side bank of the river of death,—
    Teach me the terms of silence,—preach me
      The passion of patience,—sift me,—impeach me,—
        And there, oh there
As ye hang with your myriad palms upturned in the air
        Pray me a myriad prayer.

     My gossip, the owl,—is it thou
That out of the leaves of the low-hanging bough,
    As I pass to the beach, art stirred?
     Dumb woods, have ye uttered a bird?

.   .   .

SUNRISE

Reverend Marsh, low-couched along the sea,
　　Old chemist, rapt in alchemy,
　　　　Distilling silence,—lo,
That which our father-age had died to know—
　　The menstruum that dissolves all matter—thou
Hast found it: for this silence, filling now
The globéd clarity of receiving space,
This solves us all: man, matter, doubt, disgrace,
Death, love, sin, sanity,
Must in yon silence' clear solution lie.
Too clear! That crystal nothing who'll peruse?
The blackest night could bring us brighter news.
Yet precious qualities of silence haunt ˙
Round these vast margins, ministrant.
Oh, if thy soul's at latter gasp for space,
With trying to breathe no bigger than thy race
Just to be fellow'd, when that thou hast found
No man with room, or grace enough of bound
To entertain that New thou tell'st, thou art,—
'Tis here, 'tis here thou canst unhand thy heart
And breathe it free, and breathe it free,
By rangy marsh, in lone sea-liberty.

The tide's at full: the marsh with flooded streams
Glimmers, a limpid labyrinth of dreams.
Each winding creek in grave entrancement lies
A rhapsody of morning-stars. The skies
Shine scant with one forked galaxy,—
The marsh brags ten: looped on his breast they lie.

Oh, what if a sound should be made!
Oh, what if a bound should be laid
To this bow-and-string tension of beauty and silence a-spring,—
To the bend of beauty the bow, or the hold of silence the string!
I fear me, I fear me yon dome of diaphanous gleam
Will break as a bubble o'er-blown in a dream,—
Yon dome of too-tenuous tissues of space and of night,
Over-weighted with stars, over-freighted with light,
Over-sated with beauty and silence, will seem
　　But a bubble that broke in a dream,
If a bound of degree to this grace be laid,
　　Or a sound or a motion made.

But no: it is made: list! somewhere,—mystery, where?
　　　　In the leaves? in the air?

In my heart? is a motion made:
'Tis a motion of dawn, like a flicker of shade on shade.
In the leaves 'tis palpable: low multitudinous stirring
Upwinds through the woods; the little ones, softly conferring,
Have settled my lord's to be looked for; so; they are still;
But the air and my heart and the earth are a-thrill,—
And look where the wild duck sails round the bend of the river,—
    And look where a passionate shiver
    Expectant is bending the blades
Of the marsh-grass in serial shimmers and shades,—
And invisible wings, fast fleeting, fast fleeting,
                Are beating
The dark overhead as my heart beats,—and steady and free
Is the ebb-tide flowing from marsh to sea—
        (Run home, little streams,
        With your lapfulls of stars and dreams),—
And a sailor unseen is hoisting a-peak,
For list, down the inshore curve of the creek
        How merrily flutters the sail,—
And lo, in the East! Will the East unveil?
The East is unveiled, the East hath confessed
A flush: 'tis dead; 'tis alive: 'tis dead, ere the West
Was aware of it: nay, 'tis abiding, 'tis unwithdrawn:
    Have a care, sweet Heaven! 'Tis Dawn.

Now a dream of a flame through that dream of a flush is up rolled:
    To the zenith ascending, a dome of undazzling gold
Is builded, in shape as a bee-hive, from out of the sea:
The hive is of gold undazzling, but oh, the Bee,
    The star-fed Bee, the build-fire Bee,
    Of dazzling gold is the great Sun-Bee
That shall flash from the hive-hole over the sea.

        Yet now the dew-drop, now the morning gray,
        Shall live their little lucid sober day
        Ere with the sun their souls exhale away.
Now in each pettiest personal sphere of dew
The summ'd morn shines complete as in the blue
Big dew-drop of all heaven: with these lit shrines
O'er-silvered to the farthest sea-confines,
The sacramental marsh one pious plain
Of worship lies. Peace to the ante-reign
Of Mary Morning, blissful mother mild,
Minded of nought but peace, and of a child.
Not slower than Majesty moves, for a mean and a measure

SUNRISE

Of motion,—not faster than dateless Olympian leisure
Might pace with unblown ample garments from pleasure to pleasure,—
The wave-serrate sea-rim sinks unjarring, unreeling,
        Forever revealing, revealing, revealing,
Edgewise, bladewise, halfwise, wholewise,—'tis done!
                Good-morrow, lord Sun!
With several voice, with ascription one,
The woods and the marsh and the sea and my soul
Unto thee, whence the glittering stream of all morrows doth roll,
Cry good and past-good and most heavenly morrow, lord Sun.

O Artisan born in the purple,—Workman Heat,—
Parter of passionate atoms that travail to meet
And be mixed in the death-cold oneness,—innermost Guest
At the marriage of elements,—fellow of publicans,—blest
King in the blouse of flame, that loiterest o'er
The idle skies yet laborest fast evermore,—
Thou, in the fine forge-thunder, thou, in the beat
Of the heart of a man, thou Motive,—Laborer Heat:
Yea, Artist, thou, of whose art yon sea's all news,
With his inshore greens and manifold mid-sea blues,
Pearl-glint, shell-tint, ancientest perfectest hues
Ever shaming the maidens,—lily and rose
Confess thee, and each mild flame that glows
In the clarified virginal bosoms of stones that shine,
                It is thine, it is thine:

Thou chemist of storms, whether driving the winds a-swirl
Or a-flicker the subtiler essences polar that whirl
In the magnet earth,—yea, thou with a storm for a heart,
Rent with debate, many-spotted with question, part
From part oft sundered, yet ever a globéd light,
Yet ever the artist, ever more large and bright
Than the eye of a man may avail of:—manifold One,
I must pass from thy face, I must pass from the face of the Sun:
Old Want is awake and agog, every wrinkle a-frown;
The worker must pass to his work in the terrible town:
But I fear not, nay, and I fear not the thing to be done;
    I am strong with the strength of my lord the Sun:
How dark, how dark soever the race that must needs be run,
                I am lit with the Sun.

Oh, never the mast-high run of the seas
        Of traffic shall hide thee,
Never the hell-colored smoke of the factories

Hide thee,
Never the reek of the time's fen-politics
Hide thee,
And ever my heart through the night shall with knowledge abide thee,
And ever by day shall my spirit, as one that hath tried thee,
Labor, at leisure, in art,—till yonder beside thee
My soul shall float, friend Sun,
The day being done.

1882

ALBERY ALLSON WHITMAN

(1851–1902)

The most accomplished black Southern poet of the late decades of the nineteenth century,—an era which we have seen was not auspicious for Southern poetry in general,—was Albery Allson Whitman of Kentucky. Born a slave near Munfordsville in Hart County and orphaned as a young man, Whitman traveled about after the Emancipation Proclamation gained him his freedom; he then attended school at Troy, Ohio, and at Wilberforce University, where he was a protégé of Bishop Daniel A. Payne. Whitman was at one time an official at Wilberforce and, as an Elder of the African Methodist Church, he was well known as an evangelist and poet. However, he wrote at a time when almost the only paying market for black poetry was for dialect poetry in the magazines and, like other blacks who did not write such poetry, his only recourse was to publish his own books and to sell them following readings before church groups. His books include *Essay on the Ten Plagues and Other Miscellaneous Poems* (date unknown), *Leelah Misled* (1873), *Not a Man and Yet a Man* (1877), *Twasinta's Seminoles, or Rape of Florida* (1885), and *An Idyl of the South, An Epic Poem in Two Parts* (1901).

Whitman was a full-blown romantic in his poetics—his work is inspired by Scott, Wordsworth, Bryant, and Byron. His talent was for long poems, which made use of intricate metric and rhyme patterns. At times, he attains a considerable power and eloquence, especially in his evocations of nature and in his assertions of a freedom of spirit amid the injustices of slavery. There is a vitality to his best work that one finds in very little of the poetry of his day. In the several stanzas that follow, from *Twasinta's Seminoles*, Whitman employs a narrative that recounts the resistance of the Seminole Indians of Florida,

whose ranks included many runaway slaves, to their removal westward by the
United States Army during the Presidency of Andrew Jackson.

From TWASINTA'S SEMINOLES

. . .

XI

I never was a slave—a robber took
My substance—what of that? The *law* my rights
And that? I still was free and had my book—
All nature. And I learned from during hights
How silence is majestic, and invites
In admiration far beholding eyes!
And heaven taught me with her starry nights,
How deepest speech unuttered often lies,
And that Jehovah's lessons mostly He implies.

XII

My birth-place where the scrub-wood thicket grows,
My mother bound, and daily toil by dower;
I envy not the halo title throws
Around the birth of any; place and power
May be but empty phantoms of an hour,—
For me, I find a more enduring bliss:
Rejoicing fields, green woods—the stream—the flower,
To me have speech, and born of God are his
Interpreters, proclaiming what true greatness is.

XIII

Where'er I roam, in all the earth abroad,
I find this written in the human chart:
A love Of Nature is the love of God,
And love of man's the religion of the heart.
Man's right to think, in his majestic part
In his Creator's works—to others bless—
This is the point whence god-like actions start,
And open, conscientious manliness
Is the divinest image mortals can possess.

XIV

Almighty fairness smiling heaven portends,
In sympathy the elements have tears;
The meekest flow'rs are their Creator's friends,
The hungry raven He in patience hears;
And e'en the sparrow's wishes reach His ears!
But when He treads the tyrant in His wrath,
And to crush wrong the horn of battle rears,
The pestilence goes forth on him who hath
Transgressed, and empires fall imploring in His path.

1885

KATE CHOPIN

(1851–1904)

Known during her lifetime as a local colorist and, obscurely, as the author of a somewhat indecent novel, Kate O'Flaherty Chopin has emerged as one who, far ahead of her day in the South and in the United States, dealt in her fiction with powerful psychological and sexual emotions with a directness characteristic of the novel as practiced in France but not in the English language.

She was born in St. Louis, Missouri, of French and Irish descent, and in 1870 married Oscar Chopin, a Louisiana businessman. When her husband died, leaving her with six children, she returned to St. Louis in 1882. Late in the 1880s she began writing, and in two collections of short fiction and two novels, *At Fault* (1890) and *The Awakening* (1899), she wrote extensively of life in the Creole regions of Louisiana. Her earlier work, in particular the stories in *Bayou Folk* (1894), is noteworthy for its delineation of locale and character in the Creole country.

Had she left off there, she might have been remembered only as a second-line local color writer; but during the 1890s she deepened her portrayal of character and of the feminine psyche, until the elements of locale became subordinated to the psychology of her characters in ways not characteristic of the local color fiction. When published in 1899, *The Awakening* was labeled as scandalously shocking and offensive. Today Mrs. Chopin's story of a married woman's awakening into the need for sexual fulfillment, and finding it outside of wedlock, appears not so much as indecent or "poison" to public morality, as one contemporary review described it, but as a remarkable psychological portrayal. On a smaller scale, she was similarly iconoclastic in her handling of supposedly "taboo" racial themes of her day.

DÉSIRÉE'S BABY

As the day was pleasant, Madame Valmondé drove over to L'Abri to see Désirée and the baby.

It made her laugh to think of Désirée with a baby. Why it seemed but yesterday that Désirée was little more than a baby herself; when Monsieur in riding through the gateway of Valmondé had found her lying asleep in the shadow of the big stone pillar.

The little one awoke in his arms and began to cry for "Dada." That was as much as she could do or say. Some people thought she might have strayed there of her own accord, for she was of the toddling age. The prevailing belief was that she had been purposely left by a party of Texans, whose canvas-covered wagon, late in the day, had crossed the ferry that Coton Maïs kept, just below the plantation. In time Madame Valmondé abandoned every speculation but the one that Désirée had been sent to her by a beneficent Providence to be the child of her affection, seeing that she was without child of the flesh. For the girl grew to be beautiful and gentle, affectionate and sincere—the idol of Valmondé.

It was no wonder, when she stood one day against the stone pillar in whose shadow she had lain asleep, eighteen years before, that Armand Aubigny riding by and seeing her there, had fallen in love with her. That was the way all the Aubignys fell in love, as if struck by a pistol shot. The wonder was that he had not loved her before; for he had known her since his father brought him home from Paris, a boy of eight, after his mother died there. The passion that awoke in him that day, when he saw her at the gate, swept along like an avalanche, or like a prairie fire, or like anything that drives headlong over all obstacles.

Monsieur Valmondé grew practical and wanted things well considered: that is, the girl's obscure origin. Armand looked into her eyes and did not care. He was reminded that she was nameless. What did it matter about a name when he could give her one of the oldest and proudest in Louisiana? He ordered the *corbeille* from Paris, and contained himself with what patience he could until it arrived; then they were married.

Madame Valmondé had not seen Désirée and the baby for four weeks. When she reached L'Abri she shuddered at the first sight of it, as she always did. It was a sad looking place, which for many years had not known the gentle presence of a mistress, old Monsieur Aubigny having married and buried his wife in France, and she having loved her own land too well ever to leave it. The roof came down steep and black like a cowl, reaching out beyond the wide galleries that encircled the yellow stuccoed house. Big, solemn oaks grew close to it, and their thick-leaved, far-reaching branches shadowed it like a pall. Young Aubigny's rule was a strict one, too, and under it his negroes had forgotten how to be gay, as they had been during the old master's easy-going and indulgent lifetime.

The young mother was recovering slowly, and lay full length, in her soft white muslins and laces, upon a couch. The baby was beside her, upon her arm, where he had fallen asleep, at her breast. The yellow nurse woman sat beside a window fanning herself.

Madame Valmondé bent her portly figure over Désirée and kissed her, holding her an instant tenderly in her arms. Then she turned to the child.

"This is not the baby!" she exclaimed, in startled tones. French was the language spoken at Valmondé in those days.

"I knew you would be astonished," laughed Désirée, "at the way he has grown. The little *cochon de lait!* Look at his legs, mamma, and his hands and finger-nails—real finger-nails. Zandrine had to cut them this morning. Isn't it true, Zandrine?"

The woman bowed her turbaned head majestically, "*Mais si,* madame."

"And the way he cries," went on Désirée, "is deafening. Armand heard him the other day as far away as La Blanche's cabin."

Madame Valmondé had never removed her eyes from the child. She lifted it and walked with it to the window that was lightest. She scanned the baby narrowly, then looked as searchingly at Zandrine, whose face was turned to gaze across the fields.

"Yes, the child has grown, has changed"; said Madame Valmondé, slowly, as she replaced it beside its mother. "What does Armand say?"

Désirée's face became suffused with a glow that was happiness itself.

"Oh, Armand is the proudest father in the parish, I believe, chiefly because it is a boy, to bear his name; though he says not—that he would have loved a girl as well. But I know it isn't true. I know he says that to please me. And mamma," she added, drawing Madame Valmondé's head down to her, and speaking in a whisper, "he hasn't punished one of them—not one of them—since baby is born. Even Négrillon who pretended to have burnt his leg that he might rest from work—he only laughed, and said Négrillon was a great scamp. Oh, mamma, I'm so happy; it frightens me."

What Désirée said was true. Marriage, and later the birth of his son, had softened Armand Aubigny's imperious and exacting nature greatly. This was what made the gentle Désirée so happy, for she loved him desperately. When he frowned she trembled, but loved him. When he smiled, she asked no greater blessing of God. But Armand's dark, handsome face had not often been disfigured by frowns since the day he fell in love with her.

When the baby was about three months old, Désirée awoke one day to the conviction that there was something in the air menacing her peace. It was at first too subtle to grasp. It had only been a disquieting suggestion; an air of mystery among the blacks; unexpected visits from far-off neighbours who could hardly account for their coming. Then a strange, an awful change in her husband's manner, which she dared not ask him to explain. When he spoke to her, it was with averted eyes, from which the old love-light seemed to have gone out. He absented himself from home; and when there, avoided her presence and that of her child, without excuse. And the very spirit of Satan seemed suddenly to take hold of him in his dealings with the slaves. Désirée was miserable enough to die.

She sat in her room, one hot afternoon, in her *peignoir*, listlessly drawing through her fingers the strands of her long, silky brown hair that hung about her shoulders. The baby, half naked, lay asleep upon her own great mahogany bed, that was like a sumptuous throne, with its satin-lined half-canopy. One of La Blanche's little quadroon boys—half naked too—stood fanning the child slowly with a fan of peacock feathers. Désirée's eyes had been fixed absently and sadly upon the baby, while she was striving to penetrate the threatening mist that she felt closing about her. She looked from her child to the boy who stood beside him, and back again; over and over. "Ah!" It was a cry that she could not help; which she was not conscious of having uttered. The blood turned like ice in her veins, and a clammy moisture gathered upon her face.

She tried to speak to the little quadroon boy; but no sound would come, at first. When he heard his name uttered, he looked up, and his mistress was pointing to the door. He laid aside the great, soft fan, and obediently stole away over the polished floor, on his bare tiptoes.

She stayed motionless, with gaze riveted upon her child, and her face the picture of fright.

Presently her husband entered the room, and without noticing her, went to a table and began to search among some papers which covered it.

"Armand," she called to him, in a voice which must have stabbed him, if he was human. But he did not notice. "Armand," she said again. Then she rose and tottered towards him. "Armand," she panted once more, clutching his arm, "look at our child. What does it mean? tell me."

He coldly but gently loosened her fingers from about his arm and thrust the hand away from him. "Tell me what it means!" she cried despairingly.

"It means," he answered lightly, "that the child is not white; it means that you are not white."

A quick conception of all that this accusation meant for her nerved her with unwonted courage to deny it. "It is a lie; it is not true, I am white! Look at my hair, it is brown; and my eyes are gray, Armand, you know they are gray. And my skin is fair," seizing his wrist. "Look at my hand; whiter than yours, Armand," she laughed hysterically.

"As white as La Blanche's," he returned cruelly; and went away leaving her alone with their child.

When she could hold a pen in her hand, she sent a despairing letter to Madame Valmondé.

"My mother, they tell me I am not white. Armand has told me I am not white. For God's sake tell them it is not true. You must know it is not true. I shall die. I must die. I cannot be so unhappy, and live."

The answer that came was as brief:

"My own Désirée: Come home to Valmondé; back to your mother who loves you. Come with your child."

When the letter reached Désirée she went with it to her husband's study, and laid it open upon the desk before which he sat. She was like a stone image: silent, white, motionless after she placed it there.

In silence he ran his cold eyes over the written words. He said nothing. "Shall I go, Armand?" she asked in tones sharp with agonized suspense.

"Yes, go."

"Do you want me to go?"

"Yes, I want you to go."

He thought Almighty God had dealt cruelly and unjustly with him, and felt, somehow, that he was paying Him back in kind when he stabbed thus into his wife's soul. Moreover he no longer loved her, because of the unconscious injury she had brought upon his home and his name.

She turned away like one stunned by a blow, and walked slowly towards the door, hoping he would call her back.

"Good-by, Armand," she moaned.

He did not answer her. That was his last blow at fate.

Désirée went in search of her child. Zandrine was pacing the sombre gallery with it. She took the little one from the nurse's arms with no word of explanation, and descending the steps, walked away, under the live-oak branches.

It was an October afternoon; the sun was just sinking. Out in the still fields the negroes were picking cotton.

Désirée had not changed the thin white garment nor the slippers which she wore. Her hair was uncovered and the sun's rays brought a golden gleam from its brown meshes. She did not take the broad, beaten road which led to the far-off plantation of Valmondé. She walked across a deserted field, where the stubble bruised her tender feet, so delicately shod, and tore her thin gown to shreds.

She disappeared among the reeds and willows that grew thick along the banks of the deep, sluggish bayou; and she did not come back again.

. . .

Some weeks later there was a curious scene enacted at L'Abri. In the centre of the smoothly swept back yard was a great bonfire. Armand Aubigny sat in the wide hallway that commanded a view of the spectacle; and it was he who dealt out to a half dozen negroes the material which kept this fire ablaze.

A graceful cradle of willow, with all its dainty furbishings, was laid upon the pyre, which had already been fed with the richness of a priceless *layette*. Then there were silk gowns, and velvet and satin ones added to these; laces, too, and embroideries; bonnets and gloves; for the *corbeille* had been of rare quality.

The last thing to go was a tiny bundle of letters; innocent little scribblings that Désirée had sent to him during the days of their espousal. There was the remnant of one back in the drawer from which he took them. But it was not Désirée's; it was part of an old letter from his mother to his father. He read it. She was thanking God for the blessing of her husband's love:

"But, above all," she wrote, "night and day, I thank the good God for having so arranged our lives that our dear Armand will never know that his mother, who adores him, belongs to the race that is cursed with the brand of slavery."

PART FOUR

THE SOUTHERN LITERARY RENASCENCE

"Down there," wrote the critic H. L. Mencken about the Southern cultural scene in the late 1910s, "a poet is now almost as rare as an oboe-player, a dry-point etcher or a metaphysician. It is, indeed, amazing to contemplate so vast a vacuity." Taking aim at what he saw as the artistic sterility of the Southern states of the American Union, Mencken depicted the region as "the Sahara of the Bozart"—the desert of the fine arts in America.

Although he exaggerated, there did appear to be substance to Mencken's evaluation. Once the vogue for local color receded in the 1890s and the early 1900s, the literature of the South offered very little writing of noteworthy achievement. During the first two decades of the new century there were no poets of consequence. Only a pair of novelists in Richmond, Virginia,—Ellen Glasgow and James Branch Cabell—were writing fiction that occasioned attention, and both were to do their best work a little later in their careers. In the 1900s and 1910s the South was faring somewhat better economically and commercially than it did in the many decades past, Southern schools and colleges were improving, and the industrial progress that had been so talked about in the 1870s and 1880s, but so little in evidence, had at last begun to make perceptible inroads upon the almost totally agricultural society. Intellectual and cultural life, however, seemed to lag behind in vitality. The literary ferment of the period seemed to center on the Midwest and on Greenwich Village, New York.

Yet within little more than a decade following the end of the First World War, all had changed. The "Sahara of the Bozart" had overnight been transformed into a literary garden. There were new Southern authors by the score, and they were writing works of literature that were read and admired throughout the nation and in Europe.

To demonstrate the extent of the flowering of Southern literature in the decades after World War I, it is enough merely to enumerate the many writers who at once seemed to enter the literary scene. To join Ellen Glasgow and James Branch Cabell in the years between the two wars, there appeared William Faulkner, Thomas Wolfe, John Crowe Ransom, Allen Tate, Robert Penn Warren, T. S. Stribling, Jean Toomer, Katherine Anne Porter, Caroline Gordon, Donald Davidson, Richard Wright, Andrew Lytle, Paul Green, Margaret Mitchell, Stark Young, Lillian Hellman, DuBose Heyward, Erskine Caldwell, Cleanth Brooks, Elizabeth Madox Roberts, Zora Neale Hurston, Evelyn Scott, Jesse Stuart—and in the early 1940s, Eudora Welty, Carson McCullers, Randall Jarrell, James Agee, Lillian Smith, Peter Taylor, and Tennessee Williams. All these men and women, and others besides, produced work that was of interest and importance far beyond the boundaries of their region. All were Southerners. All tended to ground their writings in their regional experience. However much they differed as individual, original artists, their works seemed to share many characteristics, including some that were largely lacking in other American writers of the period: a sense of the past, an uninhibited reliance upon the full resources of language and the old-fashioned moral absolutes that lay behind such language, an attitude toward evil as being present not only in economic or social forces but integral to the "fallen state" of humankind, a rich surface texture of description that would not be confined to the drab hues of the naturalistic novel, an ability to get at the full complexity of a situation rather than seeking to reduce it to its simplified essentials, a suspicion of abstractions, a bias in favor of the individual, the concrete, the unique, even the exaggerated and outlandish in human portraiture. There was, in short, not only a flourishing literary life now going on in and about the Southern states, but it was identifiably different from other American writing in its forms and attitudes.

The writers who created the new Southern literature were born in the later years of the nineteenth century or the early years of the twentieth. They grew up in the South at a time when the region was at last beginning wholeheartedly to enter the modern world. Slavery, the defeat and devastation of the war, the ordeal of Reconstruction, the withering poverty of an agricultural economy, and the threadbare commercial life of a tributary region stripped of its capital and left to fend for itself in a national marketplace controlled by the manufacturing and financial centers of a protectionist Northeast—in the new century the burden of this heritage began to lift. In 1909 Walter Hines Page of North Carolina described three spectres that persisted in the Southern imagination: "the Ghost of the Confederate dead, the Ghost of religious orthodoxy, the Ghost of Negro domination." It was only in the 1900s and 1910s that these began to be exorcised, so that the region no longer confronted every issue and every change in terms of those habitual points of reference.

The hinterlands began to be opened up; railroads and then automobiles began to break up the old isolation of the rural South. As manufacturing increased, towns and cities grew larger. Far more money was spent on public education than ever before, and the South began to develop a few first-rate universities. Such things as public libraries made their appearance. Although the role of the churches continued strong, no longer was Protestant religious orthodoxy the force for conformity that it had been. The coming of World War I sped up the process of change in the South. The war sent hundreds of thousands of young Southerners off to other sections of the country and to Europe; it brought millions of outsiders into the South; it vastly increased manufactures and promoted urbanization; it created a sellers' market for Southern farm products and introduced folding money into the pockets of farmers; it promoted nationalism and downplayed sectionalism.

In almost every phase of its existence the South was undergoing social change, and the young men and women who were soon to become the writers of the Southern Renascence not only felt it but were themselves part of it. When they went off to college, as most of them did, they were confronted with some of the more advanced philosophical, political, economic, social, and aesthetic ideas of the Western World. They were, indeed, the best educated and least provincial of Southern intellectual generations since the great Virginians of the Revolutionary War period, for the wall of sectional self-defense that had blocked the South's access to the intellectual and social developments and forces of the Western World since the rise of the slavery controversy in the 1800s was at last being removed.

Instead of preparing them to return to the towns and cities of the South to become lawyers, doctors, clergymen, businessmen, and planters as their fathers and grandfathers had done, college propelled these young Southerners, who were the region's future writers, to move outward into full engagement with the modern world. Almost all of them left—and if they came back home, as many ultimately did, it was in a different relationship to that home. For no longer were they prepared to accept without question the attitudes, ideas, values, and actions of the older Southern community. They had become dislodged from that community, and they began exploring the meaning of this new perspective in their writings. They were self-conscious in their Southern identity, as their predecessors, for the most part, had not been. No longer could they share in what Robert Penn Warren was later to call "the great alibi"—the belief that the North, the Yankees, the outside world were to blame for everything that was wrong with their situation. Thus when they read pieces critical of their community, such as Mencken's "Sahara of the Bozart" essay, instead of responding with righteous indignation and total rejection they found much to agree with and to applaud. And as writers they were prepared to explore, not topically so much, but in stories, poems, and essays that were concerned about the dimensions of the life they knew, their own relationship to their community and their society.

These new writers were, in short, modern Americans who were Southerners; and because that identity posed complex problems of self-definition and was fraught with incongruity, discrepancies, oppositions and divisions, and loyalties and contradictions that were rooted in the circumstances of their time and place, their writings probed beneath the everyday surfaces to get at the universal human problems of definition and truth that grew out of the experience of a community and society very much in transition and confronted with forces of change and permanence.

The young Southerners did not confront the modern world unprepared. They had the experience of an older South, with its traditional pieties and urgent loyalties, its community expectations, its powerful mythologies and passionate loves and hatreds, its religious assumptions and historical ties. These, too, were part of their way of viewing the world. In the years after World War I, Allen Tate wrote, "the South again knew the world, but it had a memory of another war; with us, entering the world once more meant not only the obliteration of the past but a heightened consciousness of it . . . ." Thus, the writers of the Southern Literary Renascence were accustomed to observing their region and its people *in time*, as they were now and as they had been in the past. The present was focused in a historical perspective by the image of the past that lay behind it—they were moderns and they were traditionalists. They could believe, and also disbelieve, and in their writings they sought to explore and depict what that meant.

Nowhere was the situation of the young Southern writer more sharply visible than in Nashville, Tennessee, where in the early 1920s a small group of teachers and students at Vanderbilt University, with other residents of the city, began meeting weekly to discuss the poems they were writing. Soon they began publication of a little magazine of verse, *The Fugitive*. Their number included Allen Tate, John Crowe Ransom, Donald Davidson, Robert Penn Warren, and Merrill Moore. They were not, at first, self-consciously Southern in their poetry; they equated a consciously Southern literature with the sentimentality of the local color tradition and the United Daughters of the Confederacy school of poetry—and they would have none of that.

By the late years of the decade, however, the leading Fugitive poets were having second thoughts about the advantages of a modernity that appeared to involve chiefly a tawdry commercialism, a thinly disguised materialism, a faddish sophistication that was without justification smugly condescending toward older religious and community values, an absence of any firm foundation of moral and ethical conviction, and a willingness to tolerate disorder, ugliness, self-serving hypocrisy, and ruthless exploitation of nature and people in the name of "progress." It was one thing for them to live in the modern world and to accept its inevitability; it was another to swallow uncritically its slogans and shibboleths and to discard whatever was humane and gentle and comfortable about the older ways.

Thus, in 1930, *I'll Take My Stand: The South and the Agrarian Tradition*, by Twelve Southerners, was published, calling upon Southerners to put aside the uncritical worship of the industrial gospel and to reassert the values and standards of a traditional community of human beings who refused to become ciphers in a vast, dehumanized urban society.

The Agrarian adventure of the Nashville Writers represented, in polemical and programmatical terms, many of the underlying thematic concerns that characterized the writers of the generation of the Southern Renascence. In other than their Agrarian polemics, the individual Agrarians themselves were not concerned with prescribing for the human welfare of the South. Instead, like all good artists, they were involved in portraying human experience, and what they focused upon was the clash of modes of identity in time, which was their birthright and that of their fellow Southern authors. Thus Allen Tate in his "Ode to the Confederate Dead" envisions a modern man at the gate of a Confederate cemetery, pondering his relationship to the dead and the erosion of that relationship in time, and his inability to view the South, the world, and his place in it from the perspective of the dead soldier. Yet he is also unable to settle for an existence in which actions are divorced from conviction, or in which the intellect and the emotions can find no common unity in a human community peopled by men and women who can love and cherish what they are and have been.

This problem and situation are the same in the finest novels about Southern history. In William Faulkner's *Absalom, Absalom!*, the young Quentin Compson explores in love and hate his relationship to his heritage and his modern circumstance. Indeed, it is legitimate to assert that the Quentin of *Absalom, Absalom!* speaks for the Southern writer of Faulkner's time. Moving out of the order and identity of the older Southern community into a twentieth-century world with different, often contradictory values and attitudes, he is forced to define himself—in the process of apprehension and discovery that is artistic creation—in terms of those two kinds of knowledge, that provided by the past and that of the present. He is, Faulkner says, not one but two separate Quentins: the one who is a young man in the twentieth century, preparing to leave for Harvard, the other the "ghost" Quentin who is bound by his past and is an inheritor of a complex set of pieties, loyalties, resentments, and fears that are bequeathed him as his Mississippi birthright.

In the same way, Thomas Wolfe's Eugene Gant, though eager to leave the Southern mountain community of Altamont at the close of *Look Homeward, Angel* and hopeful of discovering fulfillment in the shining city of the North, is not really sure that what he seeks is to be found there. The discovery of his own dislodgement and separation from his past is the culmination of the novel in which the people and place of Wolfe's origins are depicted within a lavish texture of what Wolfe termed "space, color, and time, the weather of his youth," and this texture is painted with both affection and detestation for a Southern community very much caught up in change.

In Robert Penn Warren's *All The King's Men*, Jack Burden, scion of an old, well-to-do Louisiana family, is drawn to the magnetism and pragmatic political effectiveness of a reforming redneck politician, Willie Stark, who knows how to use power in order to get things done in a Southern state in which, until he came along, government had been self-serving and ineffective. But the ultimate result is tragedy for all concerned. A too-easy dependence upon expediency and a willingness to divorce means from ends fatally compromise the ideals that motivate Willie Stark's and Jack Burden's actions.

One could go on to show how the same perception of divided, contradictory modes and values, the clash of past and present, provides the dramatic excitement in the writings of every one of the twentieth-century Southern writers. John Crowe Ransom's "Captain Carpenter" rides out in a knightly quest, only to find that the world will not conform to the traditions of chivalry. The old lady in Ellen Glasgow's *The Deliverance* will not comprehend the changed times of postbellum Virginia. In that best-selling and best-known of popular historical novels, *Gone With the Wind*, Scarlett O'Hara realizes that the aristocratic survivors of war-ravaged Atlanta society continue to behave as if they were ladies and gentlemen, whereas she is convinced that it takes money to be a lady. And one could continue with other examples.

Viewing the attainment of the South's writers over the course of the several decades that constitute the Southern Literary Renascence, we find that what is perhaps most striking about their work is the way in which they have explored the varieties, modes, and meanings of the Southern experience in their time. If the writings of the antebellum South are notable for a failure to be properly grounded in the actualities of Southern life, and if the local color writers of the late nineteenth century tended to seek out the picturesque and quaint and to look only obliquely at the realities of political, economic, and social forces in a region torn with racial conflict and class tensions, the writers of the Renascence confronted their experience directly and boldly. They did not look away from what was untidy or unpleasant.

In the early decades of the century it was Ellen Glasgow of Virginia who led the way for the new breed of Southern writers, seeking resolutely to bring to the life of her community the "blood and irony" that she found largely absent from previous Southern writing. The writers who came into maturity after the First World War not only followed her lead, but sometimes became so involved in portraying some of the more seamy aspects of regional life that she drew back in dismay. The Southerners would not look obliquely at evil, and they portrayed it in Southern garb. They confronted injustice, whether racial or social, directly. They looked behind the arcadian surface of the plantation novel to show the ruthlessness of ambition and the barbarity of the ownership of human beings as property. They did not fail to examine Southern Protestantism and to depict hypocrisy and intolerance if they found them there. They examined the Confederate heritage and found rascality and self-serving motives present alongside valor and heroism. They portrayed life on the land and did not exclude toil and dirt, tenantry and sharecropping from their picture. They showed the rise of the plain folk in the wake of the defeat of the war, but they did not idealize or glamorize the self-made man.

They could do all this and not fret unduly over the way that outside readers might view the South as depicted in their books, because they were detached from their community in a way that earlier generations of Southern authors generally were not. In their writings, they felt no compulsion to present the South in a favorable light, for as writers they were concerned with exploring experience more than with defending their community. "Why do you hate the South?" Faulkner has a Canadian ask Quentin Compson of Mississippi at the conclusion of *Absalom, Absalom!* Quentin's immediate response is that he doesn't. *"I dont hate it* he thought, panting in the cold air, the iron New England dark; *I dont. I dont. I dont hate it! I dont hate it!"* Clearly the young Mississippian both loves and hates his homeland, in a relationship that is too complex to be conveyed by any such abstract word as hate. An antebellum author such as William Gilmore Simms might well have understood how Quentin felt, but as a loyal Southerner he would never have dared to say so in print.

There is both ample love and hate in the work of the modern Southerners, because it is their own personal identity that they are, in effect, exploring. Instead of uncritically accepting the political, social, and religious standards of the community, the Southern writers of the twentieth century have conducted a searching and often agonizing critique of those values within themselves. The art of these writers has been crafted out of a deep sense of familiarity with the complexity of community life, and they have been powerfully drawn toward that life; yet, at the same time, they have experienced a momentous distancing from that community. In the words of William Faulkner

> It is himself that the Southerner is writing about, not about his environment; who has, figuratively speaking, taken the artist in him in one hand and his milieu in the other and thrust the one into the other like a clawing and spitting cat into a croker sack. And he writes.

ELLEN GLASGOW

(1874–1945)

Although Ellen Glasgow's best and most accomplished novels are probably those she wrote in the late 1920s and early 1930s, her most historically important fiction is that of the early 1900s. For it was then that—determined to deal realistically and honestly with the full range of human experience and consciously in revolt from the Thomas Nelson Page plantation tradition of Southern literature—she produced certain pioneer novels of critical realism that broke new ground for Southern literature.

A native of Richmond, Virginia, Ellen Anderson Gholson Glasgow remained a citizen of that city throughout her life. Her childhood, which she described in *The Woman Within* (1954), a memoir released for publication long after her death, was notably unhappy. Not only her family situation but also an introspective, highly sensitive temperament set her apart from everyday social life in a community whose upper social reaches were highly patterned and prescribed. To this was added a growing deafness that, from girlhood on, made it necessary for her to use a hearing aid. Having a strong intellectual bent, she immersed herself in philosophy and economics, and her early thought was deeply influenced by Herbert Spencer and scientific determinism. Her first two novels, published anonymously, were heavily laden with ideas and ideology.

It was with her third novel, *The Voice of the People* (1900), that she turned decisively to the Virginia scene with the intention of furnishing some of the "blood and irony" that she felt were visibly lacking in the Southern literature of her time. There followed a series of novels in which she explored the political, social, and economic life of her community and commonwealth, searching out its history and its political and cultural life. In *The Deliverance* (1904) she depicts the aftermath of the Civil War and the refusal of the South to face up to present realities; her portrait of an aged, blind Virginia gentlewoman whose children have for twenty years kept from her the news that the South has lost the war, and the fact that it is not the family mansion but the tiny overseer's cabin that she now inhabits is symbolic of much that Glasgow thought was awry in her own commonwealth. Her best novel of the period is probably *Virginia* (1913), in which she portrays the plight of a Virginia lady who has been trained to fill the traditional role of the gentlewoman and is confronted with the changed demands of the modern world.

In 1925 she published *Barren Ground*, a study of a farm girl who refuses to bow to her misfortunes and through force of will establishes herself as a prosperous dairy farmer; in her own words, she has "learned to live without love." This novel was her first major critical success. She then wrote what many consider to be her best work, a trio of Richmond comedies of manners, *The Romantic Comedians* (1926), *They Stooped to Folly* (1929), and *The Sheltered Life* (1932), in which she satirized, deftly and tenderly, upper-class society and life of her own day. In particular, *The Sheltered Life* is a beautifully crafted, fully conceived view of folly and innocence. With *Vein of Iron* (1935) she returned to more somber themes. Her last completed novel, *In This Our Life* (1941), is etched in despair.

The following excerpt is from *The Deliverance* (1904); the action centers on the way in which the family of Mrs. Blake have been willing and able to keep from the old woman any knowledge of the changes that have come to her antebellum world.

From THE DELIVERANCE

CHAPTER VI

CARRAWAY PLAYS COURTIER

At twelve o'clock the next day, Carraway, walking in the June brightness along the road to the Blake cottage, came suddenly, at the bend of the old ice-pond, upon Maria Fletcher returning from a morning ride. The glow of summer was in her eyes, and though her face was still pale, she seemed to him a different creature from the grave, repressed girl of the night before. He noticed at once that she sat her horse superbly, and in her long black habit all the sinuous lines of her figure moved in rhythm with the rapid pace.

As she neared him, and apparently before she had noticed his approach, he saw her draw rein quickly, and screened by the overhanging boughs of a blossoming chestnut, send her glance like a hooded falcon across the neighbouring field. Following the aim of her look, he saw Christopher Blake walking idly among the heavy furrows, watching, with the interest of a born agriculturist, the busy transplanting of Fletcher's crop. He still wore his jean clothes, which, hanging loosely upon his impressive figure, blended harmoniously with the dull-purple tones of the upturned soil. Beyond him there was a background of distant wood, still young in leaf, and his bared head, with the strong, sunburned line of his profile, stood out as distinctly as a portrait done in early Roman gold.

That Maria had seen in him some higher possibility than that of a field labourer was soon evident to Carraway, for her horse was still standing on the slight incline, and as he reached her side she turned with a frank question on her lips.

"Is that one of the labourers—the young giant by the fence?"

"Well, I dare say he labours, if that's what you mean. He's young Blake, you know."

"Young Blake?" She bent her brows, and it was clear that the name suggested only a trivial recollection to her mind. "There used to be some Blake children in the old overseer's house—is this one of them?"

"Possibly; they live in the overseer's house."

She leaned over, fastening her heavy gauntlet. "They wouldn't play with me I remember; I couldn't understand why. Once I carried my dolls over to their yard, and the boy set a pack of hounds on me. I screamed so that an old negro ran out and drove them off, and all the time the boy stood by, laughing and calling me names. Is that he, do you think?"

"I dare say. It sounds like him."

"Is he so cruel?" she asked a little wistfully.

"I don't know about that—but he doesn't like your people. Your grandfather had some trouble with him a long time ago."

"And he wanted to punish me—how cowardly."

"It does sound rather savage, but it isn't an ordinary case, you know. He's the kind of person to curse 'root and branch,' from all I hear, in the good old Biblical fashion."

"Oh, well, he's certainly very large, isn't he?"

"He's superb," said Carraway, with conviction.

"At a distance—so is that great pine over there," she lifted her whip and pointed across the field; then as Carraway made no answer, she smiled slightly and rode rapidly toward the Hall.

For a few minutes the lawyer stood where she had left him, watching in puzzled thought her swaying figure on the handsome horse. The girl fretted him, and yet he felt that he liked her almost in spite of himself—liked something fine and fearless he found in her dark eyes; liked, too, even while he sneered, her peculiar grace of manner. There was the making of a woman in her after all, he told himself, as he turned into the sunken road, where he saw Christopher already moving homeward. He had meant to catch up with him and join company on the way, but the young man covered ground so quickly with his great strides that at last Carraway, losing sight of him entirely, resigned himself to going leisurely about his errand.

When, a little later, he opened the unhinged whitewashed gate before the cottage, the place, as he found it, seemed to be tenanted solely by a family of young turkeys scratching beneath the damask rose-bushes in the yard. From a rear chimney a dark streak of smoke was rising, but the front of the house gave no outward sign of life, and as there came no answer to his insistent knocks he at last ventured to open the door and pass into the narrow hall. From the first room on the right a voice spoke at his entrance, and following the sound he found himself face to face with Mrs. Blake in her massive Elizabethan chair.

"There is a stranger in the room," she said rigidly, turning her sightless eyes; "speak at once."

"I beg pardon most humbly for my intrusion," replied Carraway, conscious of stammering like an offending schoolboy, "but as no one answered my knock, I committed the indiscretion of opening a closed door."

Awed as much by the stricken pallor of her appearance as by the inappropriate grandeur of her black brocade and her thread lace cap, he advanced slowly and stood awaiting his dismissal.

"What door?" she demanded sharply, much to his surprise.

"Yours, madam."

"Not answer your knock?" she pursued, with indignation. "So that was the noise I heard, and no wonder that you entered. Why, what is the matter with the place? Where are the servants?"

He humbly replied that he had seen none, to be taken up with her accustomed quickness of touch.

"Seen none! Why, there are three hundred of them, sir. Well, well, this is really too much. I shall put a butler over Boaz this very day."

For an instant Carraway felt strangely tempted to turn and run as fast as he could along the sunken road—remembering, as he struggled with the impulse, that he had once been caught at the age of ten and whipped for stealing apples. Recovering with an effort his sense of dignity, he offered the suggestion that Boaz, instead of being seriously in fault, might merely have been engaged in useful occupations "somewhere at the back."

"What on earth can he have to do at the back, sir?" inquired the irrepressible old lady; "but since you were so kind as to overlook your inhospitable reception, will you not be equally good and tell me your name?"

"I fear it won't enlighten you much," replied the lawyer modestly, "but my name happens to be Guy Carraway."

"Guy—Guy Carraway," repeated Mrs. Blake, as if weighing each separate letter in some remote social scales. "I've known many a Guy in my day —and that part, at least, of your name is quite familiar. There was Guy Nelson, and Guy Blair, and Guy Marshall, the greatest beau of his time—but I don't think I ever had the pleasure of meeting a Carraway before."

"That is more than probable, ma'am, but I have the advantage of you, since, as a child, I was once taken out upon the street corner merely to see you go by on your way to a fancy ball, where you appeared as Diana."

Mrs. Blake yielded gracefully to the skilful thrust.

"Ah, I was Lucy Corbin then," she sighed. "You find few traces of her in me now, sir."

"Unfortunately, your mirror cannot speak for me."

She shook her head.

"You're a flatterer—a sad flatterer, I see," she returned, a little wistfully; "but it does no harm, as I tell my son, to flatter the old. It is well to strew the passage to the grave with flowers."

"How well I remember that day," said Carraway, speaking softly. "There was a crowd about the door, waiting to see you come out, and a carpenter lifted me upon his shoulder. Your hair was as black as night, and there was a circle round your head———"

"A silver fillet," she corrected, with a smile in which there was a gentle archness.

"A fillet, yes; and you carried a bow and a quiver full of arrows. I declare, it seems but yesterday."

"It was more than fifty years ago," murmured the old lady. "Well, well, I've had my day, sir, and it was a merry one. I am almost seventy years old —I'm half dead, and stone blind into the bargain, but I can say to you that this is a cheerful world in spite of the darkness in which I linger on. I'd take it over again and gladly any day—the pleasure and the pain, the light and the darkness. Why, I sometimes think that my present blindness was given me in order that I might view the past more clearly. There's not a ball of my youth, nor a face I knew, nor even a dress I wore, that I don't see more distinctly every day. The present is a very little part of life, sir; it's the past in which we store our treasures."

"You're right, you're right," replied Carraway, drawing his chair nearer the embroidered ottoman and leaning over to stroke the yellow cat; "and I'm glad to hear so cheerful a philosophy from your lips."

"It is based on a cheerful experience—I've been as you see me now only twenty years."

Only twenty years! He looked mutely round the soiled whitewashed walls, where hung a noble gathering of Blake portraits in massive old gilt frames. Among them he saw the remembered face of Lucy Corbin herself, painted under a rose-garland held by smiling Loves.

"Life has its trials, of course," pursued Mrs. Blake, as if speaking to herself. "I can't look out upon the June flowers, you know, and though the pink crape-myrtle at my window is in full bloom I cannot see it."

Following her gesture, Carraway glanced out into the little yard; no myrtle was there, but he remembered vaguely that he had seen one in blossom at the Hall.

"You keep flowers about you, though," he said, alluding to the scattered vases of June roses.

"Not my crape-myrtle. I planted it myself when I first came home with Mr. Blake, and I have never allowed so much as a spray of it to be plucked."

Forgetting his presence, she lapsed for a time into one of the pathetic day-dreams of old age. Then recalling herself suddenly, her tone took on a sprightliness like that of youth.

"It's not often that we have the pleasure of entertaining a stranger in our out-of-the-way house, sir—so may I ask where you are staying—or perhaps you will do us the honour to sleep beneath our roof. It has had the privilege of sheltering General Washington."

"You are very kind," replied Carraway, with a gratitude that was from his heart, "but to tell the truth, I feel that I am sailing under false colours. The real object of my visit is to ask a business interview with your son. I bring what seems to me a very fair offer for the place."

Grasping the carved arms of her chair, Mrs. Blake turned the wonder in her blind eyes upon him.

"An offer for the place! Why, you must be dreaming, sir! A Blake owned it more than a hundred years before the Revolution."

At the instant, understanding broke upon Carraway like a thundercloud, and as he rose from his seat it seemed to him that he had missed by a single step the yawning gulf before him. Blind terror gripped him for the moment, and when his brain steadied he looked up to meet, from the threshold of the adjoining room, the enraged flash of Christopher's eyes. So tempestuous was the glance that Carraway, impulsively falling back, squared himself to receive a physical blow; but the young man, without so much as. the expected oath, came in quietly and took his stand behind the Elizabethan chair.

"Why, what a joke, mother," he said, laughing; "he means the old Weatherby farm, of course. The one I wanted to sell last year, you know."

"I thought you'd sold it to the Weatherby's, Christopher."

"Not a bit of it—they backed out at the last; but don't begin to bother your head about such things; they aren't worth it. And now, sir," he turned upon Carraway, "since your business is with me, perhaps you will have the goodness to step outside."

With the feeling that he was asked out for a beating, Carraway turned for a farewell with Mrs. Blake, but the imperious old lady was not to be so lightly defrauded of a listener.

"Business may come later, my son," she said, detaining them by a gesture of her heavily ringed hand. "After dinner you may take Mr. Carraway with you into the library and discuss your affairs over a bottle of burgundy, as was your grandfather's custom before you; meanwhile, he and I will resume our very pleasant talk which you interrupted. He remembers seeing me in the old days when we were all in the United States, my dear."

Christopher's brow grew black, and he threw a sharp and malignant glance of sullen suspicion at Carraway, who summoned to meet it his most frank and open look.

"I saw your mother in the height of her fame," he said, smiling, "so I may count myself one of her oldest admirers, I believe. You may assure yourself," he added softly, "that I have her welfare very decidedly at heart."

At this Christopher smiled back at him, and there was something of the June brightness in his look.

"Well, take care, sir," he answered, and went out, closing the door carefully behind him, while Carraway applied himself to a determined entertaining of Mrs. Blake.

To accomplish this he found that he had only to leave her free, guiding her thoughts with his lightest touch into newer channels. The talk had grown merrier now, and he soon discovered that she possessed a sharpened wit as well as a ready tongue. From subject to subject she passed with amazing swiftness, bearing down upon her favourite themes with the delightful audacity of the talker who is born, not made. She spoke of her own youth, of historic flirtations in the early twenties, of great *beaux* she had known, and of famous recipes that had been handed down for generations. Everywhere he felt her wonderful keenness of perception—that intuitive understanding of men and manners which had kept her for so long the reigning belle among her younger rivals.

As she went on he found that her world was as different from his own as if she dwelt upon some undiscovered planet—a world peopled with shades and governed by an ideal group of abstract laws. She lived upon lies, he saw, and thrived upon the sweetness she extracted from them. For her the Confederacy had never fallen, the quiet of her dreamland had been disturbed by no invading army, and the three hundred slaves, who had in reality scattered like chaff before the wind, she still saw in her cheerful visions tilling her familiar fields. It was as if she had fallen asleep with the great blow that had wrecked her body, and had dreamed on steadily throughout the years. Of real changes she was as ignorant as a new-born child. Events had shaken the world to its centre, and she, by her obscure hearth had not felt so much as a sympathetic tremor. In her memory there was no Appomattox, news of the death of Lincoln had never reached her ears, and president had peacefully succeeded president in the secure Confederacy in which she lived. Wonderful as it all was, to Carraway the most wonderful thing was the intricate tissue of lies woven around her chair. Lies—lies —there had been nothing but lies spoken within her hearing for twenty years.

JAMES WELDON JOHNSON

(1871–1938)

Had James Weldon Johnson chosen to devote the time and energy to his literary career that he did to his work as a leader in the crusade for the social betterment of black people, he might well have become one of the major writers of his time. Even so, he wrote a novel and a few poems that have still retained their interest for more than a half century.

James Weldon Johnson was born in Jacksonville, Florida, of a middle-class black family and educated at Atlanta University. Returning to Jacksonville to teach, he studied law on his own and became the first black to be admitted to the Florida bar since Reconstruction times. He had begun to write and in collaboration with his brother Rosamund, a talented composer and musician, he became a highly successful song writer in New York. One of their songs, "Under the Bamboo Tree," was internationally popular. From 1909 to 1913 Johnson was a United States Consul in Latin America. In 1912 he published, anonymously, a novel, *The Autobiography of an Ex-Coloured Man.* His first book of poems, *Fifty Years and Other Poems,* appeared in 1917. The year before, Johnson became field secretary of the National Association for the Advancement of Colored People, and thereafter he moved extensively through the South and West helping to organize chapters of the N.A.A.C.P., which had hitherto confined its operations to the North. In 1927 Johnson published *God's Trombones,* a poetic rendition of familiar black sermons, which became his best-known work. He was named professor of creative literature at Fisk University in 1931. His autobiography, *Along This Way,* appeared in 1934, and in 1935 *Saint Peter Relates an Incident: Selected Poems* was published. Johnson was killed in an automobile accident in 1938.

Johnson's early poems were written either in the abstract style of the poetry of ideality popular in the nineteenth century or in Negro dialect, but as he ventured further into black themes his verse gained maturity and technique. Fascinated by the poetry of Walt Whitman he sought, for some time with little success, to break through the language constraints he felt were inhibiting his verse. In 1918, while traveling in the Midwest for the N.A.A.C.P., he attended a meeting at a church and heard a famed evangelist intoning "the rambling Negro sermon that begins with the creation of the world, touches various high spots in the trials and tribulations of the Hebrew children, and ends with the Judgment Day." He had not heard such a sermon in thirty years; "something primordial in me was stirred," he wrote, and he began work on "The Creation." Only now did he realize that the true language for reproducing the experience of black Americans was neither the bloodless abstractions of the poetry of ideality nor the conventions of dialect poetry, which stemmed from the blackface minstrel tradition and was a parody rather than an evocation of the speech of black people. This language was conveyed through "symbols from within rather than by symbols from without . . . a form that is freer and larger than dialect, but which will still hold the racial flavor; a form expressing the imagery, the idioms, the peculiar turns of thought, and the distinctive humor and pathos, too, of the Negro, but which will also be capable of voicing the deepest and highest emotions and aspirations, and allow of the widest range of subjects and the widest scope of treatment." The result was a poem, "The Creation," in which through rhythms, imagery, and idiom he captured the intonations of black speech. Seven years later he resumed work on additional sermons in verse, which with "The Creation" made up *God's Trombones*. Other black writers would extend and explore the colloquial possibilities of such an approach to language. Johnson was content to show the way.

O BLACK AND UNKNOWN BARDS

O black and unknown bards of long ago,
How came your lips to touch the sacred fire?
How, in your darkness, did you come to know
The power and beauty of the minstrel's lyre?
Who first from midst his bonds lifted his eyes?
Who first from out the still watch, lone and long,
Feeling the ancient faith of prophets rise
Within his dark-kept soul, burst into song?

Heart of what slave poured out such melody
As "Steal Away to Jesus"? On its strains
His spirit must have nightly floated free,
Though still about his hands he felt his chains.
Who heard great "Jordan roll"? Whose starward eye
Saw chariot "swing low"? And who was he
That breathed that comforting, melodic sigh,
"Nobody Knows de Trouble I See"?

JAMES WELDON JOHNSON

What merely living clod, what captive thing,
Could up toward God through all its darkness grope,
And find within its deadened heart to sing
These songs of sorrow, love, and faith, and hope?
How did it catch that subtle undertone,
That note in music heard not with the ears?
How sound the elusive reed so seldom blown,
Which stirs the soul or melts the heart to tears?

Not that great German master in his dream
Of harmonies that thundered amongst the stars
At the creation, ever heard a theme
Nobler than "Go Down, Moses." Mark its bars,
How like a mighty trumpet-call they stir
The blood. Such are the notes that men have sung
Going to valorous deeds; such tones there were
That helped make history when Time was young.

There is a wide, wide wonder in it all,
That from degraded rest and servile toil
The fiery spirit of the seer should call
These simple children of the sun and soil.
O black slave singers, gone, forgot, unfamed,
You—you alone, of all the long, long line
Of those who've sung untaught, unknown, unnamed,
Have stretched out upward, seeking the divine.

You sang not deeds of heroes or of kings;
No chant of bloody war, no exulting pæan
Of arms-won triumphs; but your humble strings
You touched in chord with music empyrean.
You sang far better than you knew; the songs
That for your listeners' hungry hearts sufficed
Still live—but more than this to you belongs:
You sang a race from wood and stone to Christ.

1917

THE CREATION

And God stepped out on space,
And He looked around and said,
"I'm lonely—
I'll make me a world."

And far as the eye of God could see

THE CREATION

Darkness covered everything,
Blacker than a hundred midnights
Down in a cypress swamp.

Then God smiled,
And the light broke,
And the darkness rolled up on one side,
And the light stood shining on the other,
And God said, "*That's good!*"

Then God reached out and took the light in His hands,
And God rolled the light around in His hands,
Until He made the sun;
And He set that sun a-blazing in the heavens.
And the light that was left from making the sun
God gathered up in a shining ball
And flung against the darkness,
Spangling the night with the moon and stars.
Then down between
The darkness and the light
He hurled the world;
And God said, "*That's good!*"

Then God himself stepped down—
And the sun was on His right hand,
And the moon was on His left;
The stars were clustered about His head,
And the earth was under His feet.
And God walked, and where He trod
His footsteps hollowed the valleys out
And bulged the mountains up.

Then He stopped and looked and saw
That the earth was hot and barren.
So God stepped over to the edge of the world
And He spat out the seven seas;
He batted His eyes, and the lightnings flashed;
He clapped His hands, and the thunders rolled;
And the waters above the earth came down,
The cooling waters came down.

Then the green grass sprouted,
And the little red flowers blossomed,
The pine-tree pointed his finger to the sky,
And the oak spread out his arms;
The lakes cuddled down in the hollows of the ground,

And the rivers ran down to the sea;
And God smiled again,
And the rainbow appeared,
And curled itself around His shoulder.

Then God raised His arm and He waved His hand
Over the sea and over the land,
And He said, "*Bring forth! Bring forth!*"
And quicker than God could drop His hand,
Fishes and fowls
And beasts and birds
Swam the rivers and the seas,
Roamed the forests and the woods,
And split the air with their wings,
And God said, "*That's good!*"

Then God walked around
And God looked around
On all that He had made.
He looked at His sun,
And He looked at His moon,
And He looked at His little stars;
He looked on His world
With all its living things,
And God said, "*I'm lonely still.*"

Then God sat down
On the side of a hill where He could think;
By a deep, wide river He sat down;
With His head in His hands,
God thought and thought,
Till He thought, "*I'll make me a man!*"

Up from the bed of the river
God scooped the clay;
And by the bank of the river
He kneeled Him down;
And there the great God Almighty,
Who lit the sun and fixed it in the sky,
Who flung the stars to the most far corner of the night,
Who rounded the earth in the middle of His hand—
This Great God,
Like a mammy bending over her baby,
Kneeled down in the dust
Toiling over a lump of clay
Till He shaped it in His own image;

Then into it He blew the breath of life,
And man became a living soul.
Amen. Amen.

1927

JEAN TOOMER

(1894–1967)

Jean Toomer, whose *Cane* (1923) constitutes the first fully mature work of the Southern Literary Renascence of the years after World War I, was born in Washington, D.C., where he grew up in the care of his grandparents. His grandfather, P. B. S. Pinchback, had been lieutenant governor and acting governor of Louisiana during the Reconstruction—the only black man ever to hold the highest political office in a Southern state. Toomer studied at the University of Wisconsin and the City College of New York, and in the early 1920s went to Sparta, Georgia, as a teacher. He had already begun writing poems and stories, but it was from that experience in the segregated South that he drew much of the subject matter and the form for *Cane.* Thereafter he lived in New York, Chicago, and California, and stayed for a time in France where he was strongly influenced by the teachings of the Russian mystic Gurdjieff. He became involved in setting up a Gurdjieff colony in the United States, was married to a white novelist, Margery Latimer, and, following her death in childbirth, then married the daughter of a white stockbroker, Marjorie Cannon. After the early 1930s Toomer published no more artistic work. He became involved with the Society of Friends in Pennsylvania and dropped out of public sight. *Cane* received relatively little notice upon publication in 1923 and was out of print for several decades until its rediscovery. Toomer died in 1967 while working in Bucks County, Pennsylvania. Among his posthumously published works are segments of an autobiography.

During the 1920s, before and after the publication of *Cane,* Toomer was a frequent contributor to the literary magazines of the day and was also a close associate of Hart Crane, Kenneth Burke, Gorham Munson, Paul Rosenfeld, and Waldo Frank. His familiarity with and his involvement in the leading intellectual and artistic currents and developments of the era are evident in the brilliant show of stylistic effects, experimental virtuosity, and psychological and linguistic techniques that gives the stories and poems of *Cane* the form and coherence of a montage of black life in America. In particular the example of James Joyce, as evidenced in Stephen Dedalus of *A Portrait of the Artist as a Young Man,* is made use of in creatively original fashion, as Toomer strives to show the molding influences of race, history, climate, servitude, religious and social belief, and social class in the formation of his protagonists' heritage.

Cane is grouped in three parts. The first is made up of poems and sketches of black life in the rural, segregated South. The second moves northward to show how the urban milieu modifies and shapes the lives of blacks who have left the South to come to the cities of industrial America. The final section, in the form of a long drama, for reading rather than stage presentation, shows a young black man, Kabnis, who has returned to the rural South, where his people once lived, to teach in a college. In his agonizing effort to discover his own individual identity as a man and an artist, Kabnis must confront the social and economic as well as the cultural expectations and compulsions of black existence in a white-dominated society. In its variety, its awareness of social and racial necessity, its multiplicity of technique, and also in its loose, almost fragmented construction, *Cane* both enunciates and exemplifies the problems of definition and identity that confronted its talented author in his own life. For Toomer was almost white in appearance and declared that he was never even quite certain of his black inheritance. In fact, at various times in his life he insisted that he was not black at all. "I am of no particular race," he once wrote. "I am one of the human race, a man at large in the human world, preparing a new race." Yet it was only in the early 1920s, when he accepted for a time his black ties and traveled to the rural South, where most black Americans still lived, that he was able to achieve in artistic form a resolution of such matters. Ultimately, *Cane* is a brilliant affirmation of the Southern black heritage.

GEORGIA DUSK

The sky, lazily disdaining to pursue
    The setting sun, too indolent to hold
    A lengthened tournament for flashing gold,
Passively darkens for night's barbecue,

A feast of moon and men and barking hounds,
    An orgy for some genius of the South
    With blood-hot eyes and cane-lipped scented
        mouth,
Surprised in making folk-songs from soul sounds.

The sawmill blows its whistle, buzz-saws stop,
    And silence breaks the bud of knoll and hill,
    Soft settling pollen where plowed lands fulfill
Their early promise of a bumper crop.

Smoke from the pyramidal sawdust pile

Curls up, blue ghosts of trees, tarrying low
   Where only chips and stumps are left to show
The solid proof of former domicile.

Meanwhile, the men, with vestiges of pomp,
   Race memories of king and caravan,
   High-priests, an ostrich, and a juju-man,
Go singing through the footpaths of the swamp.

Their voices rise . . the pine trees are guitars,
   Strumming, pine-needles fall like sheets of rain . .
   Their voices rise . . the chorus of the cane
Is caroling a vesper to the stars . .

O singers, resinous and soft your songs
   Above the sacred whisper of the pines,
   Give virgin lips to cornfield concubines,
Bring dreams of Christ to dusky cane-lipped throngs.

1923

PORTRAIT IN GEORGIA

Hair—braided chestnut,
   coiled like a lyncher's rope,
Eyes—fagots,
Lips—old scars, or the first red blisters,
Breath—the last sweet scent of cane,
And her slim body, white as the ash
   of black flesh after flame.

1923

FERN

Face flowed into her eyes. Flowed in soft cream foam and plaintive ripples, in such a way that wherever your glance may momentarily have rested, it immediately thereafter wavered in the direction of her eyes. The soft suggestion of down slightly darkened, like the shadow of a bird's wing might, the creamy brown color of her upper lip. Why, after noticing it, you sought her eyes, I cannot tell you. Her nose was aquiline, Semitic. If you have heard a Jewish cantor sing, if he has touched you and made your own sorrow seem trivial when compared with his, you will know my feeling when I follow the curves of her profile, like mobile rivers, to their common delta. They were strange eyes. In this, that they sought nothing—that is, nothing that was obvious and tangible and that one could see, and they gave the impression that nothing was to be denied. When a woman seeks, you will have observed, her eyes deny. Fern's eyes desired nothing that you could give her; there was no reason why they should withhold. Men saw her eyes and fooled themselves. Fern's eyes said to them that she was easy. When she was young, a few men took her, but got no joy from it. And then, once done, they felt bound to her (quite unlike their hit and run with other girls), felt as though it would take them a lifetime to fulfill an obligation which they could find no name for. They became attached to her, and hungered after finding the barest trace of what she might desire. As she grew up, new men who came to town felt as almost everyone did who ever saw her: that they would not be denied. Men were everlastingly bringing her their bodies. Something inside of her got tired of them, I guess, for I am certain that for the life of her she could not tell why or how she began to turn them off. A man in fever is no trifling thing to send away. They began to leave her, baffled and ashamed, yet vowing to themselves that some day they would do some fine thing for her: send her candy every week and not let her know whom it came from, watch out for her wedding-day and give her a magnificent something with no name on it, buy a house and deed it to her, rescue her from some unworthy fellow who had tricked her into marrying him. As you know, men are apt to idolize or fear that which they cannot understand, especially if it be a woman. She did not deny them, yet the fact was that they were denied. A sort of superstition crept into their consciousness of her being somehow above them. Being above them meant that she was not to be approached by anyone. She became a virgin. Now a virgin in a small southern town is by no means the usual thing, if you will believe me. That the sexes were made to mate is the practice of the South. Particularly, black folks were made to mate. And it is black folks whom I have been talking about thus far. What white men thought of Fern I can arrive at only by analogy. They let her alone.

Anyone, of course, could see her, could see her eyes. If you walked up the Dixie Pike most any time of day, you'd be most like to see her resting listless-like on the railing of her porch, back propped against a post, head tilted a little forward because there was a nail in the porch post just where her head came which for some reason or other she never took the trouble to pull out. Her eyes, if it were sunset, rested idly where the sun, molten and glorious, was pouring down between the fringe of pines. Or maybe they gazed at the gray cabin on the knoll from which an evening folk-song was coming. Perhaps they followed a cow that had been turned loose to roam and feed on cotton-stalks and corn leaves. Like as not they'd settle on some vague spot above the horizon, though hardly a trace of wistfulness would come to them. If it were dusk, then they'd wait for the search-light of the evening train which you could see miles up the track before it flared across the Dixie Pike, close to her home. Wherever they looked, you'd follow them and then waver back. Like her face, the whole countryside seemed to flow into her eyes. Flowed into them with the soft listless cadence of Georgia's South. A young Negro, once, was looking at her, spellbound, from the road. A white man passing in a buggy had to flick him with his whip if he was to get by without running him over. I first saw her on her porch. I was passing with a fellow whose crusty numbness (I was from the North and suspected of being prejudiced and stuck-up) was melting as he found me warm. I asked him who she was. "That's Fern," was all that I could get from him. Some folks already thought that I was given to nosing around; I let it go at that, so far as questions were concerned. But at first sight of her I felt as if I heard a Jewish cantor sing. As if his singing rose above the unheard chorus of a folk-song. And I felt bound to her. I too had my dreams: something I would do for her. I have knocked about from town to town too much not to know the futility of mere change of place. Besides, picture if you can, this cream-colored solitary girl sitting at a tenement window looking down on the indifferent throngs of Harlem. Better that she listen to folk-songs at dusk in Georgia, you would say, and so would I. Or, suppose she came up North and married. Even a doctor or a lawyer, say, one who would be sure to get along—that is, make money. You and I know, who have had experience in such things, that love is not a thing like prejudice which can be bettered by changes of town. Could men in Washington, Chicago, or New York, more than the men of Georgia, bring her something left vacant by the bestowal of their bodies? You and I who know men in these cities will have to say, they could not. See her out and out a prostitute along State Street in Chicago. See her move into a southern town where white men are more aggressive. See her become a white man's concubine. . . Something I must do for her. There was myself. What could I do for her? Talk, of course. Push back the fringe of pines upon new horizons. To what purpose? and what for? Her? Myself? Men in her case seem to lose their selfishness. I lost mine before I touched her. I ask you, friend (it makes no difference if you sit in the Pullman or the Jim Crow as the train crosses her road), what thoughts would come to you—that is, after you'd finished with the thoughts that leap into men's minds at the sight of a pretty woman who will not deny them; what thoughts would come to you, had you seen her in a quick flash, keen and intuitively, as she sat there on her porch when your train thundered by? Would you have got off at the next station and come back for her to take her where? Would you have completely forgotten her as soon as you reached Macon, Atlanta, Augusta, Pasadena, Madison, Chicago, Boston, or New Orleans? Would you tell your wife or sweetheart about a girl you saw? Your thoughts can help me, and I would like to know. Something I would do for her. . .

One evening I walked up the Pike on purpose, and stopped to say hello. Some of her family were about, but they moved away to make room for me.

Damn if I knew how to begin. Would you? Mr. and Miss So-and-So, people, the weather, the crops, the new preacher, the frolic, the church benefit,
rabbit and possum hunting, the new soft drink they had at old Pap's store,
the schedule of the trains, what kind of town Macon was, Negro's migration
north, bollweevils, syrup, the Bible—to all these things she gave a yassur or
nassur, without further comment. I began to wonder if perhaps my own
emotional sensibility had played one of its tricks on me. "Lets take a walk,"
I at last ventured. The suggestion, coming after so long an isolation, was
novel enough, I guess, to surprise. But it wasnt that. Something told me that
men before me had said just that as a prelude to the offering of their bodies.
I tried to tell her with my eyes. I think she understood. The thing from her
that made my throat catch, vanished. Its passing left her visible in a way I'd
thought, but never seen. We walked down the Pike with people on all the
porches gaping at us. "Doesnt it make you mad?" She meant the row of
petty gossiping people. She meant the world. Through a canebrake that was
ripe for cutting, the branch was reached. Under a sweet-gum tree, and
where reddish leaves had dammed the creek a little, we sat down. Dusk,
suggesting the almost imperceptible procession of giant trees, settled with a
purple haze about the cane. I felt strange, as I always do in Georgia, particularly at dusk. I felt that things unseen to men were tangibly immediate. It
would not have surprised me had I had visions. People have them in Georgia more often than you would suppose. A black woman once saw the
mother of Christ and drew her in charcoal on the courthouse wall . . . When
one is on the soil of one's ancestors, most anything can come to one . . .
From force of habit, I suppose, I held Fern in my arms—that is, without at
first noticing it. Then my mind came back to her. Her eyes, unusually weird
and open, held me. Held God. He flowed in as I've seen the countryside
flow in. Seen men. I must have done something—what, I dont know, in the
confusion of my emotion. She sprang up. Rushed some distance from me.
Fell to her knees, and began swaying, swaying. Her body was tortured with
something it could not let out. Like boiling sap it flooded arms and fingers
till she shook them as if they burned her. It found her throat, and spattered
inarticulately in plaintive, convulsive sounds, mingled with calls to Christ
Jesus. And then she sang, brokenly. A Jewish cantor singing with a broken
voice. A child's voice, uncertain, or an old man's. Dusk hid her; I could
hear only her song. It seemed to me as though she were pounding her head
in anguish upon the ground. I rushed to her. She fainted in my arms.

There was talk about her fainting with me in the canefield. And I got one
or two ugly looks from town men who'd set themselves up to protect her. In
fact, there was talk of making me leave town. But they never did. They kept
a watch-out for me, though. Shortly after, I came back North. From the
train window I saw her as I crossed her road. Saw her on her porch, head
tilted a little forward where the nail was, eyes vaguely focused on the sunset.

Saw her face flow into them, the countryside and something that I call God, flowing into them . . . Nothing ever really happened. Nothing ever came to Fern, not even I. Something I would do for her. Some fine unnamed thing . . . And, friend, you? She is still living, I have reason to know. Her name, against the chance that you might happen down that way, is Fernie May Rosen.

JOHN CROWE RANSOM

(1888–1974)

John Crowe Ransom not only taught all the other leading Nashville Fugitive poets at Vanderbilt University, but during the early 1920s when *The Fugitive* magazine was being published he was perhaps its most distinguished contributor. An affable man who was, however, possessed of considerable reserve, Ransom wrote almost all his finest poems during the Fugitive years. He set out deliberately to be a "minor" poet—to write well-crafted, finely wrought lyrics of short and medium length, which would match carefully controlled language with and against passionate emotion. The slender volumes of the several versions of his *Selected Poems* contain certain poems that are among the finest lyrics in the English language.

Ransom was born in Pulaski, Tennessee, the son of a Methodist minister, and, following graduation from Vanderbilt in 1909, he spent several years at Oxford University in England as a Rhodes Scholar. He joined the Vanderbilt faculty in 1914 and, except for army service overseas during World War I, taught there for 23 years. Among his pupils at Vanderbilt and later at Kenyon College were Allen Tate, Donald Davidson, Robert Penn Warren, Andrew Lytle, Merrill Moore, Cleanth Brooks, Randall Jarrell, Robert Lowell, and Peter Taylor. His first book of verse, *Poems About God,* appeared in 1919 while he was overseas. It was *Chills and Fever* (1924) that established him as a leading American poet. In 1926 *Two Gentlemen in Bonds* was published. In the middle of the 1920s Ransom, who was always much concerned with philosophy and aesthetics, became involved in a book that, published in 1930 as *God Without Thunder,* criticized the disappearance of mystery in contemporary religion because of the enshrinement of science; in it he called for a return to a God of awe and supernatural mystery. He also entered wholeheartedly into the Agrarian movement, contributing the "Statement of Principles" and the opening essay to the Agrarian symposium *I'll Take My Stand* (1930).

After busying himself with Agrarian polemics in the early 1930s he turned to literary criticism and theory. His move to Kenyon College in 1937 came in part because of his wish to dissociate himself from programmatical social and sectional concerns. At Kenyon he founded the *Kenyon Review,* which became a leading journal of literary criticism. His own felicitously written essays were collected in *The World's Body* (1938), *The New Criticism* (1941), and *Beating the Bushes* (1972). After 1930 he published very little poetry. His *Selected Poems* appeared in 1945, and in revised form in 1963 and 1969.

The imprint of Ransom's powerful personality was strongly felt by his talented pupils. Some later came to disagree with him but always with profound respect and affection. His philosophical dualism, which played so important a role in his aesthetic and critical thought, was extremely influential in the critical thinking of Tate, Warren, and Brooks and lies behind many of the principal assumptions and concerns of the New Criticism of poetry that has been so important in American and English literary thought for several generations.

BELLS FOR JOHN WHITESIDE'S DAUGHTER

There was such speed in her little body,
And such lightness in her footfall,
It is no wonder her brown study
Astonishes us all.

Her wars were bruited in our high window.
We looked among orchard trees and beyond
Where she took arms against her shadow,
Or harried unto the pond

The lazy geese, like a snow cloud
Dripping their snow on the green grass,
Tricking and stopping, sleepy and proud,
Who cried in goose, Alas,

For the tireless heart within the little
Lady with rod that made them rise
From their noon apple-dreams and scuttle
Goose-fashion under the skies!

But now go the bells, and we are ready,
In one house we are sternly stopped
To say we are vexed at her brown study,
Lying so primly propped.

1924

BLUE GIRLS

Twirling your blue skirts, travelling the sward
Under the towers of your seminary,
Go listen to your teachers old and contrary
Without believing a word.

Tie the white fillets then about your hair
And think no more of what will come to pass
Than bluebirds that go walking on the grass
And chattering on the air.

Practise your beauty, blue girls, before it fail;
And I will cry with my loud lips and publish
Beauty which all our power shall never establish,
It is so frail.

For I could tell you a story which is true;
I know a lady with a terrible tongue,
Blear eyes fallen from blue,
All her perfections tarnished—yet it is not long
Since she was lovelier than any of you.

1924

JANET WAKING

Beautifully Janet slept
Till it was deeply morning. She woke then
And thought about her dainty-feathered hen,
To see how it had kept.

One kiss she gave her mother.
Only a small one gave she to her daddy
Who would have kissed each curl of his shining baby;
No kiss at all for her brother.

"Old Chucky, old Chucky!" she cried,
Running across the world upon the grass
To Chucky's house, and listening. But alas,
Her Chucky had died.

It was a transmogrifying bee
Came droning down on Chucky's old bald head

And sat and put the poison. It scarcely bled,
But how exceedingly

And purply did the knot
Swell with the venom and communicate
Its rigor! Now the poor comb stood up straight
But Chucky did not.

So there was Janet
Kneeling on the wet grass, crying her brown hen
(Translated far beyond the daughters of men)
To rise and walk upon it.

And weeping fast as she had breath
Janet implored us, "Wake her from her sleep!"
And would not be instructed in how deep
Was the forgetful kingdom of death.

1925

CONRAD IN TWILIGHT

Conrad, Conrad, aren't you old
To sit so late in your mouldy garden?
And I think Conrad knows it well,
Nursing his knees, too rheumy and cold
To warm the wraith of a Forest of Arden.

Neuralgia in the back of his neck,
His lungs filling with much miasma,
His feet dipping in leafage and muck:
Conrad! you've forgotten asthma.

Conrad's house has thick red walls,
The log on Conrad's hearth is blazing,
Slippers and pipe and tea are served,
Butter and toast are meant for pleasing!
Still Conrad's back is not uncurved
And here's an autumn on him, teasing.

Autumn days in our section
Are the most used-up thing on earth
(Or in the waters under the earth)
Having no more color nor predilection
Than cornstalks too wet for the fire,
A ribbon rotting on the byre,

PHILOMELA

A man's face as weathered as straw
By the summer's flare and winter's flaw.

1924

PHILOMELA

Procne, Philomela, and Itylus,
Your names are liquid, your improbable tale
Is recited in the classic numbers of the nightingale.
Ah, but our numbers are not felicitous,
It goes not liquidly for us.

Perched on a Roman ilex, and duly apostrophized,
The nightingale descanted unto Ovid;
She has even appeared to the Teutons, the swilled and
      gravid;
At Fontainebleau it may be the bird was gallicized;
Never was she baptized.

To England came Philomela with her pain,
Fleeing the hawk her husband; querulous ghost,
She wanders when he sits heavy on his roost,
Utters herself in the original again,
The untranslatable refrain.

Not to these shores she came! this other Thrace,
Environ barbarous to the royal Attic;
How could her delicate dirge run democratic,
Delivered in a cloudless boundless public place
To an inordinate race?

I pernoctated with the Oxford students once,
And in the quadrangles, in the cloisters, on the Cher,
Precociously knocked at antique doors ajar,
Fatuously touched the hems of the hierophants,
Sick of my dissonance.

I went out to Bagley Wood, I climbed the hill;
Even the moon had slanted off in a twinkling,
I heard the sepulchral owl and a few bells tinkling,
There was no more villainous day to unfulfil,
The diuturnity was still.

Up from the darkest wood where Philomela sat,
Her fairy numbers issued. What then ailed me?
My ears are called capacious but they failed me,

Her classics registered a little flat!
I rose, and venomously spat.

Philomela, Philomela, lover of song,
I am in despair if we may make us worthy,
A bantering breed sophistical and swarthy;
Unto more beautiful, persistently more young,
Thy fabulous provinces belong.

1924

CAPTAIN CARPENTER

Captain Carpenter rose up in his prime
Put on his pistols and went riding out
But had got wellnigh nowhere at that time
Till he fell in with ladies in a rout.

It was a pretty lady and all her train
That played with him so sweetly but before
An hour she'd taken a sword with all her main
And twined him of his nose for evermore.

Captain Carpenter mounted up one day
And rode straightway into a stranger rogue
That looked unchristian but be that as may
The Captain did not wait upon prologue.

But drew upon him out of his great heart
The other swung against him with a club
And cracked his two legs at the shinny part
And let him roll and stick like any tub.

Captain Carpenter rode many a time
From male and female took he sundry harms
He met the wife of Satan crying "I'm
The she-wolf bids you shall bear no more arms."

Their strokes and counters whistled in the wind
I wish he had delivered half his blows
But where she should have made off like a hind
The bitch bit off his arms at the elbows.

And Captain Carpenter parted with his ears
To a black devil that used him in this wise
O Jesus ere his threescore and ten years
Another had plucked out his sweet blue eyes.

CAPTAIN CARPENTER

Captain Carpenter got up on his roan
And sallied from the gate in hell's despite
I heard him asking in the grimmest tone
If any enemy yet there was to fight?

"To any adversary it is fame
If he risk to be wounded by my tongue
Or burnt in two beneath my red heart's flame
Such are the perils he is cast among.

"But if he can he has a pretty choice
From an anatomy with little to lose
Whether he cut my tongue and take my voice
Or whether it be my round red heart he choose."

It was the neatest knave that ever was seen
Stepping in perfume from his lady's bower
Who at this word put in his merry mien
And fell on Captain Carpenter like a tower.

I would not knock old fellows in the dust
But there lay Captain Carpenter on his back
His weapons were the old heart in his bust
And a blade shook between rotten teeth alack.

The rogue in scarlet and grey soon knew his mind
He wished to get his trophy and depart
With gentle apology and touch refined
He pierced him and produced the Captain's heart.

God's mercy rest on Captain Carpenter now
I thought him Sirs an honest gentleman
Citizen husband soldier and scholar enow
Let jangling kites eat of him if they can.

But God's deep curses follow after those
That shore him of his goodly nose and ears
His legs and strong arms at the two elbows
And eyes that had not watered seventy years.

The curse of hell upon the sleek upstart
That got the Captain finally on his back
And took the red red vitals of his heart
And made the kites to whet their beaks clack clack.

1924

JOHN CROWE RANSOM

THE EQUILIBRISTS

Full of her long white arms and milky skin
He had a thousand times remembered sin.
Alone in the press of people traveled he,
Minding her jacinth, and myrrh, and ivory.

Mouth he remembered: the quaint orifice
From which came heat that flamed upon the kiss,
Till cold words came down spiral from the head.
Grey doves from the officious tower illsped.

Body: it was a white field ready for love,
On her body's field, with the gaunt tower above,
The lilies grew, beseeching him to take,
If he would pluck and wear them, bruise and break.

Eyes talking: Never mind the cruel words,
Embrace my flowers, but not embrace the swords.
But what they said, the doves came straightway flying
And unsaid: Honor, Honor, they came crying.

Importunate her doves. Too pure, too wise,
Clambering on his shoulder, saying, Arise,
Leave me now, and never let us meet,
Eternal distance now command thy feet.

Predicament indeed, which thus discovers
Honor among thieves, Honor between lovers.
O such a little word is Honor, they feel!
But the grey word is between them cold as steel.

At length I saw these lovers fully were come
Into their torture of equilibrium;
Dreadfully had forsworn each other, and yet
They were bound each to each, and they did not forget.

And rigid as two painful stars, and twirled
About the clustered night their prison world,
They burned with fierce love always to come near,
But honor beat them back and kept them clear.

Ah, the strict lovers, they are ruined now!
I cried in anger. But with puddled brow
Devising for those gibbeted and brave
Came I descanting: Man, what would you have?

For spin your period out, and draw your breath,

ANTIQUE HARVESTERS

A kinder saeculum begins with Death.
Would you ascend to Heaven and bodiless dwell?
Or take your bodies honorless to Hell?

In Heaven you have heard no marriage is,
No white flesh tinder to your lecheries,
Your male and female tissue sweetly shaped
Sublimed away, and furious blood escaped.

Great lovers lie in Hell, the stubborn ones
Infatuate of the flesh upon the bones;
Stuprate, they rend each other when they kiss,
The pieces kiss again, no end to this.

But still I watched them spinning, orbited nice.
Their flames were not more radiant than their ice.
I dug in the quiet earth and wrought the tomb
And made these lines to memorize their doom:—

EPITAPH

Equilibrists lie here; stranger, tread light;
Close, but untouching in each other's sight;
Mouldered the lips and ashy the tall skull.
Let them lie perilous and beautiful.

1924

ANTIQUE HARVESTERS

(SCENE: *Of the Mississippi the bank sinister, and of the Ohio the bank
sinister.*)

Tawny are the leaves turned but they still hold,
And it is harvest; what shall this land produce?
A meager hill of kernels, a runnel of juice;
Declension looks from our land, it is old.
Therefore let us assemble, dry, grey, spare,
And mild as yellow air.

"I hear the croak of a raven's funeral wing."
The young men would be joying in the song
Of passionate birds; their memories are not long.
What is it thus rehearsed in sable? "Nothing."
Trust not but the old endure, and shall be older

JOHN CROWE RANSOM

Than the scornful beholder.

We pluck the spindling ears and gather the corn.
One spot has special yield? "On this spot stood
Heroes and drenched it with their only blood."
And talk meets talk, as echoes from the horn
Of the hunter—echoes are the old men's arts,
Ample are the chambers of their hearts.

Here come the hunters, keepers of a rite;
The horn, the hounds, the lank mares coursing by
Straddled with archetypes of chivalry;
And the fox, lovely ritualist, in flight
Offering his unearthly ghost to quarry;
And the fields, themselves to harry.

Resume, harvesters. The treasure is full bronze
Which you will garner for the Lady, and the moon
Could tinge it no yellower than does this noon;
But grey will quench it shortly—the field, men, stones.
Pluck fast, dreamers; prove as you amble slowly
Not less than men, not wholly.

Bare the arm, dainty youths, bend the knees
Under bronze burdens. And by an autumn tone
As by a grey, as by a green, you will have known
Your famous Lady's image; for so have these;
And if one say that easily will your hands
More prosper in other lands,

Angry as wasp-music be your cry then:
"Forsake the Proud Lady, of the heart of fire,
The look of snow, to the praise of a dwindled choir,
Sons of degenerate specters that were men?
The sons of the fathers shall keep her, worthy of
What these have done in love."

True, it is said of our Lady, she ageth.
But see, if you peep shrewdly, she hath not stooped;
Take no thought of her servitors that have drooped,
For we are nothing; and if one talk of death—
Why, the ribs of the earth subsist frail as a breath
If but God wearieth.

1927

POETS WITHOUT LAURELS

The poets I refer to in the title are the "moderns": those whom a small company of adept readers enjoys, perhaps enormously, but the general public detests; those in whose hands poetry as a living art has lost its public support.

Consequently I do not refer to such poets as Edna St. Vincent Millay and Robert Frost, who are evidently influenced by modernism without caring to "go modern" in the sense of joining the revolution; which is very much as if they had stopped at a mild or parlor variety of socialism, when all about them the brave, or at least the doctrinaire, were marching under the red banner. Probably they are wise in their time; they have laurels deservedly and wear them gracefully. But they do not define the issue which I wish to discuss. And still less do I refer to poets like E. A. Robinson, Sturge Moore, and John Masefield, who are even less modern; though I have no intention of questioning their laurels either. I refer to poets with no laurels.

I do not wish to seem to hold the public responsible for their condition, as if it had suddenly become phlegmatic, cruel, and philistine. The poets have certainly for their part conducted themselves peculiarly. They could not have estranged the public more completely if they had tried; and smart fellows as they are, they know very well what they have been doing, and what they are still stubborn in doing, and what the consequences are.

For they have failed more and more flagrantly, more and more deliberately, to identify themselves with the public interests, as if expressly to renounce the kind affections which poets had courted for centuries. Accordingly, they do not only encounter public indifference, they sometimes encounter active hostility. A Pulitzer committeeman, I hear, says about some modernist poet whose book is up for judgment: "He will never get the award except over my dead body." The violence of the remark seems to exceed the occasion, but it is not exceptional.

Poets used to be bards and patriots, priests and prophets, keepers of the public conscience, and, naturally, men of public importance. Society crowned them with wreaths of laurel, according to the tradition which comes to us from the Greeks and is perpetuated by official custom in England—and in Oklahoma. Generally the favor must have been gratefully received. But modern poets are of another breed. It is as if all at once they had lost their prudence as well as their piety, and formed a compact to unclasp the chaplet from their brows, inflicting upon themselves the humility of delaureation, and retiring from public responsibility and honors. It is this phenomenon which has thrown critical theory into confusion.

Sir Philip Sidney made the orthodox defense of poetry on the ground of the poet's service to patriotism and virtue:

He doth not only show the way, but giveth so sweet a prospect into the way, as will entice any man to enter into it.

And what was the technique of enticement?

With a tale forsooth he cometh unto you, with a tale which holdeth children from play, and old men from the chimney corner.

The poets, therefore, told entrancing tales, which had morals. But the fact was, also, that the poets were not always content to win to virtue by indirection, or enticement, but were prepared to preach with almost no disguise, and to become sententious and repetitious, and the literature which they created is crowded with precise maxims for the moralists. There it stands on the shelves now. Sometimes the so-called poet has been only a moralist with a poetic manner. And all the poets famous in our tradition, or very nearly all, have been poets of a powerful moral cast.

So I shall try a preliminary definition of the poet's traditional function on behalf of society: he proposed to make virtue delicious. He compounded a moral effect with an æsthetic effect. The total effect was not a pure one, but it was rich, and relished highly. The name of the moral effect was goodness; the name of the æsthetic effect was beauty. Perhaps these did not have to coexist, but the planners of society saw to it that they should; they called upon the artists to reinforce morality with charm. The artists obliged.

When they had done so, the public did not think of attempting to distinguish in its experience as reader the glow which was æsthetic from the glow which was moral. Most persons probably could not have done this; many persons cannot do it today. There is yet no general recognition of the possibility that an æsthetic effect may exist by itself, independent of morality or any other useful set of ideas. But the modern poet is intensely concerned with this possibility, and he has disclaimed social responsibility in order to secure this pure æsthetic effect. He cares nothing, professionally, about morals, or God, or native land. He has performed a work of dissociation and purified his art.

There are distinct styles of "modernity," but I think their net results, psychologically, are about the same. I have in mind what might be called the "pure" style and what might be called the "obscure" style.

A good "pure" poem is Wallace Stevens' "Sea Surface Full of Clouds" —famous perhaps, but certainly not well known. I shall have to deal with it summarily. Time and place, "In that November off Tehuantepec." The poem has five uniform stanzas, presenting as many surface effects beheld at breakfast time "after the slopping of the sea by night grew still." The first surface made one think of rosy chocolate and gilt umbrellas; the second, of chophouse chocolate and sham umbrellas; the third, of porcelain chocolate and pied umbrellas; the fourth, of musky chocolate and frail umbrellas; the fifth, of Chinese chocolate and large umbrellas. Nothing could be more discriminating than these details, which induct us respectively into the five fields of observation. The poem has a calculated complexity, and its technical competence is so high that to study it, if you do that sort of thing, is to be happy. That it has not been studied by a multitude of persons is due to a simple consideration which strikes us at once: the poem has no moral, political, religious, or sociological values. It is not about "res publica," the public thing. The subject matter is trifling.

Poetry of this sort, as it was practised by some French poets of the nineteenth century, and as it is practised by many British and American poets now, has been called pure poetry, and the name is accurate. It is nothing but poetry; it is poetry for poetry's sake, and you cannot get a moral out of it. But it was to be expected that it would never win the public at large. The impulse which led readers to the old poetry was at least as much moral as it was æsthetic, while the new poetry cannot count on any customers except those specializing in strict æsthetic effects. But the modern poets intend to rate only as poets, and would probably think it meretricious to solicit patronage by making moral overtures.

As an example of "obscure" poetry, though not the most extreme one, I cite Allen Tate's "Death of Little Boys." Here are some of its verses:

> Then you will touch at the bedside, torn in two,
> Gold curls now deftly intricate with gray
> As the windowpane extends a fear to you
> From one peeled aster drenched with the wind all day. . . .
>
> Till all the guests, come in to look, turn down
> Their palms; and delirium assails the cliff
> Of Norway where you ponder, and your little town
> Reels like a sailor drunk in his rotten skiff.

There is evidently a wide difference between Stevens and Tate, as poets. Tate has an important subject, and his poem is a human document, with a contagious fury about it: Stevens, pursuing purity, does not care to risk such a subject. But Tate, as if conscious that he is close to moralizing and sententiousness, builds up deliberately, I imagine, an effect of obscurity; for example, he does not care to explain the private meaning of his windowpane and his Norwegian cliff; or else, by some feat, he permits these bright features to belong to his total image without permitting them to reveal any precise meaning, either for himself or for his reader. Stevens, however, is objective from begining to end; he completes all his meanings, knowing these will have little or no moral importance.

JOHN CROWE RANSOM

Pure or obscure, the modern poet manages not to slip into the old-fashioned moral-beautiful compound. If pure, he will not consider a subject which lends itself to moralization; that is, a subject of practical interest. It is his chief problem to find then a subject which has any interest at all. If, however, he prefers the other road, he may take the subject nearest his own humanity, a subject perhaps of terrifying import; but in treating it will stop short of all moral or theoretical conclusions, and confuse his detail to the point where it leaves no positive implications.

To be more technical: it is as if the pure poet presented a subject and declined to make any predication about it or even to start predication; and as if the obscure poet presented a subject in order to play with a great deal of important predication without ever completing any.

Personally, I prefer the rich obscure poetry to the thin pure poetry. The deaths of little boys are more exciting than the sea surfaces. It may be that the public preference, however, is otherwise. The public is inclined simply to ignore the pure poetry, because it lacks practical usefulness; but to hate the obscure poetry, because it looks important enough to attend to, and yet never yields up any specific fruit. Society, through its spokesmen the dozens of social-minded critics, who talk about the necessity of "communication," is now raging with indignation, or it may be with scorn, against the obscure poetry which this particular generation of poets has deposited. Nevertheless, both types of poetry, obscure as well as pure, aim at poetic autonomy; that is, speaking roughly, at purity.

Modern poetry in this respect is like modern painting. European painting used to be nearly as social a thing as poetry. It illustrated the sacred themes prescribed by the priests, whether popularly (Raphael) or esoterically and symbolically (Michelangelo); did the portraits of kings and cardinals, and the scenes of battles and great occasions; worked up allegorical and sentimental subjects. But more or less suddenly it asserted its independence. So we find Impressionists, doing the most innocent tricks with landscapes and mere objects; and we find Cézanne, painting so many times and so lovingly his foolish little bowl of fruits. The procedure was a strange one for the moral laity, who could detect nothing of importance there; and indeed nothing of public importance was there, only matters of technical interest to painters, and to persons who found painting sufficient. Later, and today, we find painters taking up the most heroic human material again in the most promising manner, yet arriving at no explicit meaning and, on the whole, simply playing with its powerful symbols. (Not all painters, of course.)

Apostate, illaureate, and doomed to outlawry the modern poets may be. I have the feeling that modernism is an unfortunate road for them to have taken. But it was an inevitable one. It is not hard to defend them from imputations against their honor and their logic. It is probably a question of whether we really know them, and understand their unusual purpose, and the powerful inhibitions they impose upon themselves.

But let us approach the matter from a slightly different angle. Poets have had to become modern because the age is modern. Its modernism envelops them like a sea, or an air. Nothing in their thought can escape it.

Modern poetry is pure poetry. The motive behind it cannot be substantially different from the motive behind the other modern activities, which is certainly the driving force of all our modernism. What is its name? "Purism" would be exact, except that it does not have the zealous and contriving sound we want. "Platonism" would do, provided there were time to come to an agreement about the essential meaning of Plato's act. I think the name "Puritanism" will describe this motive, if I may extend a little a term whose application in history has been mostly religious and moral.

Our period differs outwardly from other periods because it first differs inwardly. Its spiritual temper is puritanical; that is, it craves to perfect the parts of experience separately or in their purity, and is a series of isolated perfections. These have often been brilliant. But perhaps the modern program, on the whole, is not the one under which men maintain their best health and spirits. A little fear to that effect is beginning to cloud the consciousness of the brilliant moderns.

And here I conclude my defense of the modern poet. He is a good workman, and his purpose is really quite orthodox in its modernism. But it is no better.

The development of modern civilization has been a grand progression in which Puritanism has invaded first one field and then another.

The first field perhaps was religion. The religious impulse used to join to itself and dominate and hold together nearly all the fields of human experience; politics, science, art, and even industry, and by all means moral conduct. But Puritanism came in the form of the Protestant Reformation and separated religion from all its partners. Perhaps the most important of these separations was that which lopped off from religion the æsthetic properties which simple-hearted devotees and loving artists had given it. The æsthetic properties constituted the myth, which to the temperamental Protestants became superstition, and the ceremonial, which became idolatry. Under the progressive zeal of the Reformation the being of God has become rarefied in the degree that it has been purified, until we find difficulty in grasping it, and there are people who tell me, just as there are people who tell the reader, that religion as a living force here in the Western world is spent. Theology is purer or more abstract than ever before, but it would seem to belong exclusively to theologians, and it cannot by itself assemble together all those who once delighted in the moral precepts, the music and the pomp, the social communion, and the concrete Godhead, of the synthetic institution which was called religion.

Next, or perhaps at the same time, Puritanism applied itself to morality. Broad as the reach of morality may be, it is distinct enough as an experience to be capable of purification. We may say that its destiny was to become what we know as sociology, a body of positivistic science. It had to be emancipated from its religious overlords, whose authority, after all, was not a moral one. Then it had to be emancipated from the dictates of taste, or æsthetic, and this latter emancipation was the harder, and perhaps the more needless. The Greeks, though they were incipient Puritans, scarcely attempted it. They had a compound phrase meaning "beautiful-good," which even their philosophers used habitually as the name of something elemental and indissoluble. Suspicion was aroused in Greeks by a goodness which could not produce beauty, just as to a man like Spenser the idea of virtue was incomplete until it flowered into poetic form, and just as to the sympathetic French artist our new American liberty was not quite won until identifiable with an able-bodied demi-goddess lifting a torch. The splitting up of the moral-beautiful compound for the sake of the pure moral article is visibly at work in the New Testament, and in the bourgeois cult of plainness in seventeenth-century England, and in the finicky private life of a Puritan moralist like Kant, and today in moral or sociological treatises (and authors) which neither exhibit nor discuss charm. Now, it is true that we moralize with "maximum efficiency" when we do it technically, or abstractly, but when that comes to be the rule we no longer approach a moral discussion with anything but a moral interest. To be moral is no longer to be "decent," and it looks as if moral appeal had become something less wide and less instant than it was.

Then Puritanism worked upon politics. I am not prepared to go deeply into this, but it is evident that purification consisted in taking the state away from the church, from the monarch, from the feudal aristocracy, from any other concrete attachments, in order that it might propel itself by the force of pure statecraft. Progress in this direction meant constitutionalism, parliamentarianism, republicanism. A modern state like ours is transparent in the perfection of its logic. But that does not make it the more realistic. It is obliged to count upon a universal and continuous will on the part of the citizens to accept an abstract formula of political action. But such a will may not be there. The population, not being composed exclusively of politicians, is inclined to delegate statecraft to those who profess it. The old mixed states had a greater variety of loyalties to appeal to.

Puritanism is an ideal which not all persons are strong enough to realize, but only those with great power of concentration. Its best chance of success lies in individual projects. Accordingly, Puritanism fairly came into its own in the vast multitude of private enterprises which go together to make modern science. Galileo and Kepler found science captive to religious dogma. America, the paradise of Puritanism, was not yet in being, but England was; and there presently, while other Puritanisms were going on, Lord Bacon was able to anticipate the complete emancipation of science by virtue of its adoption of the pure experimental method. Now, there have been other incubi besides religion resting upon science at one time or another; and chiefly the tendency of poetry to haunt its deliberations. Poetry is a figurative way of expression, science is a technical or abstract way; but since science employs language, the figurative associations are hard to keep out. In earlier days poetry kept close to science, and it did not seem so strange if Lucretius wanted to set forth the body of accepted science in verse. But poetry now cannot attend science into its technical labyrinth. The result is greater success for scientists, but not necessarily their greater happiness as men; and the general understanding on our part that we will follow science if we are scientists, but otherwise will leave it to the scientists.

It was but one step that Puritanism had to go from there into the world of business, where the material sciences are systematically applied. The rise of the modern business world is a development attendant upon the freedom which it has enjoyed; upon business for business' sake, or pure business, or "laissez faire," with such unconditioned principles as efficiency, technological improvement, and maximum productivity. If I wished to attack the record of business, I should by now have been long anticipated. It is common opinion that business as a self-contained profession has created business men who are defective in their humanity; that the conduct of business has made us callous to personal relations and to social justice; and that many of the occupations which business has devised are, in the absence of æsthetic standards, servile.

All these exclusions and specializations, and many more, have been making modern life what it is. It is significant that every specialization on the list has had to resist the insidious charms of æsthetic experience before its own perfection could arise. (Evidently the æsthetic interest is remarkably catholic among our faculties in its affinities; ready to attach itself easily to almost any sort of moment; a ubiquitous element in experience, it might be thought, which it would be unhealthy to cast out.) But the energy of so deep an impulse as Puritanism had to flow through all the channels, and to come to its last outlet in a pure art, a pure poetry. Those who have not observed the necessity may choose to hold its predestined agents the poets in contempt, or in amazement. The poets are in the spirit of their time. On the one hand, they have been pushed out of their old attachments, whereby they used to make themselves useful to public causes, by the specialists who did not want the respective causes to be branded with amateurism. On the other hand, they are moved by a universal tendency into their own appropriate kind of specialization, which can be, as they have been at pains to show, as formidable as any other.

Considerations of this kind, I feel sure, have been more or less precisely within the intuition of all modern poets, and have motivated their performance. Technically, they are quite capable of writing the old compound poetry, but they cannot bring themselves to do it; or rather, when they have composed it in unguarded moments, as modern poets still sometimes do, they are under the necessity of destroying it immediately. There is no baffling degree of virtuosity in the old lines,

> Roll on, thou deep and dark blue Ocean, roll!
> Ten thousand fleets sweep over thee in vain:
> Man marks the earth with ruin, his control
> Stops with the shore.

The modern poet can accomplish just as elegant a rumination as this; but thinks it would commit him to an anachronism, for this is the style of an older period. In that period, though it was a comparatively late one, and though this poet thought he was in advance of it, the prophets of society were still numbering and tuning their valuable reflections before they saw fit to release them; and morality, philosophy, religion, science, and art could still meet comfortably in one joint expression, though perhaps not with the same distinction they might have gained if they had had their pure and several expressions. A passage of Byron's if sprung upon an unsuspecting modern would be felt immediately as "dating"; it would be felt as something that did very well for those dark ages before the modern mind achieved its own disintegration and perfected its faculties serially.

Even as readers, we must testify readily to the force of this time-principle. We sometimes pore over an old piece of poetry for so long that we fall under its spell and forget that its spirit is not our spirit. But we began to read it in a peculiar manner; by saying to ourselves, This is early Greek epic, This is seventeenth-century English drama. By means of one of the ripest and subtlest powers in us, that is, the historical sense, we made an adaptation of our minds to its mind, and were able to suspend those centuries which had intervened. Those centuries had made our minds much more knowing and at the same time, it is to be feared, much less suggestible. Yet it is not exactly with our own minds that we are reading the old poetry; otherwise we could not read it. For when we come back to our own world there begins to function in us a different style of consciousness altogether. And if we had begun to read a poetry of this old sort by saying, This was written last night by the poet around the corner, we could not have put up with it. If we throw away impatiently a contemporaneous poetry which displays archaisms of diction, what will we do with that which displays archaisms of temper? It looks spurious; for we require our art, and the living artists require it too, to be as contemporaneous as our banking or our locomotion.

What, then, is the matter with a pure poetry? The question is really more theoretical than practical. A school, an age, is involved by such a question, no merely some small poem or poet. And there is nothing the matter with this particular branch of purity which is not the matter with our other mod-

ern activities. All are affected by Puritanism, just as the vegetation is affected, generally and indifferently, by the climate.

It is impossible to answer the question categorically because the items
are intangible. But we find ourselves reasoning about it as well as we can,
which is as follows.

You may dissociate the elements of experience and exploit them separately. But then at the best you go on a schedule of small experiences, taking them in turn, and trusting that when the rotation is complete you will
have missed nothing. And at the worst you will become so absorbed in
some one small experience that you will forget to go on and complete the
schedule; in that case you will have missed something. The theory that
excellence lies in the perfection of the single functions, and that society
should demand that its members be hard specialists, assumes that there is
no particular harm in missing something. But I do not see why. A maniac
with a fixed idea is a variety of specialist, and an absorbing specialty is a
small mania.

As for poetry, it seems to me a pity that its beauty should have to be
cloistered and conventual, if it is "pure," or teasing and evasive, if it is
"obscure." The union of beauty with goodness and truth has been common
enough to be regarded as natural. It is the dissociation which is unnatural
and painful.

But when we talk about simple and compound experiences, we are evidently employing a chemical mode of speech to represent something we
cannot quite make out. Units of consciousness are hard to handle scientifically; it takes more science than we have. Max Eastman thinks the future of
literary criticism is bound up with the future of psychology, and very likely
it is; but it is difficult to share his sanguine expectations of that science. It
cannot become as effective a science as chemistry.

Nevertheless, I shall make a tentative argument from the analogy of
chemistry. Lemonade is only a mechanical mixture, not very interesting to
chemists. Aside from the water, a drop of lemonade contains lemon and
sugar in no standard proportions. If it tastes too sour, add sugar, and if it
tastes too sweet, add lemon. (And do not forget to stir the mixture.) No
matter what the final proportions, you can still detect in the lemonade the
sweet taste and the sour; though this is too abstract a matter to bother
about if the lemonade is satisfactory, for in that case you simply drink it.

Table salt, however, is a true chemical compound; a molecule of it is
NaCl. Understanding this, you do not claim to know the taste either of
sodium or of chlorine when you say you are acquainted with the taste of
salt. Whatever the Na was and however it tasted by itself, it gave up that
identity when it compounded with Cl; and *vice versa*.

NaCl is found in the state of nature, where it is much commoner than
either of its constituents. But suppose the chemists decided to have nothing
to do with NaCl because of its compoundness, and undertook to extract

from it the pure Na and Cl to serve on the table. Suppose they made war on all the natural compounds, broke them down into the hundred or so atomic elements, and asked us to live on these alone. The beneficiaries would regard this service as well-meaning but mistaken.

But we provide the necessities for our minds and affections with more harshness than we dare use on our stomachs and bodies—so inferior in precision is our knowledge of minds to our knowledge of bodies. Poets are now under the influence of a perfectly arbitrary theory which I have called Puritanism. They pursue A, an æsthetic element thought always to have the same taste and to be the one thing desirable for poets. They will not permit the presence near it of M, the moral element, because that will produce the lemonade MA, and they do not approve of lemonade. In lemonade the A gets itself weakened and neutralized by the M.

But it is possible that MA is not a drop of lemonade after all, but a true molecule, into which the separate M and the separate A have disappeared and out of which an entirely new taste is born. The effects which we attribute to a poet like Virgil, or Milton, are on the following order: pious, philosophical, imaginative, sonorous, and the like. But perhaps the effect which we actually receive from the poetry is not that of an aggregate or series or mechanical mixture of distinct properties but only the single effect of a compound. In that event the properties will exist separate only in our minds, by a later act of qualitative analysis, and they will not really be in the poetry in their own identities.

Is the old-fashioned full poetry a mechanical mixture like lemonade or a chemical compound like table salt? That is probably the most important question which the modern critics have opened up to speculation. There are many corollary questions along with it, like these: When does the display of doctrine in poetry incur the charge of didacticism? And must the poet also bear arms—that is, like the economist and the social reformer, view his performance in the light of a utility rather than an end?

Now some poetry, so-called, is not even lemonade, for the ingredients have not been mixed, much less compounded. Lumps of morality and image lie side by side, and are tasted in succession. T. S. Eliot thinks that this has been the character of a great deal of English poetry since the age of Dryden. Such poetry occupies some of the best room in the library, and takes up some of the best time of the earnest student of literature. It is decidedly one of the causes of that revulsion of feeling on the part of the modern poet which drives him away from the poetic tradition.

When our critical theory is complete, perhaps we shall be able to distinguish various combinations of elements passing for poetry; thus, poetry by assemblage, poetry by mixture, and poetry by composition. The last of these sounds the best.

I suggest that critics and philosophers fix their most loving attention upon certain natural compounds in human experience. But I say so diffidently, and not too hopefully. It will take a long time to change the philosophical set which has come over the practice of the poets. The intellectual climate in which they live will have to be altered first.

DONALD DAVIDSON

(1893–1968)

Donald Grady Davidson was born in Campbellsville, Tennessee, and educated at various schools in Tennessee. He entered Vanderbilt University in 1909 for one year, taught school for four years, then returned in 1914 to complete his work at Vanderbilt, graduating in 1916. Davidson began attending informal evening talks at the apartment of Sidney Mttron Hirsch, to which he soon invited John Crowe Ransom. These sessions, which at first concentrated upon philosophical matters, became the nucleus of the Fugitive group.

Davidson entered the army in August 1917. Before leaving for duty in France he was married to Theresa Sherrer. He was in combat on the Western Front, taught in Kentucky Wesleyan College for a year following demobilization, then returned to Vanderbilt to teach and undertake graduate study in 1920. By now the Fugitives were meeting regularly to read and discuss each others' poetry, and when *The Fugitive* magazine was founded in 1922 Davidson published regularly in it, serving as editor in 1923. In 1924 his first book of poems, *An Outland Piper,* was published. He also edited the book page of the *Nashville Tennessean* from 1924 to 1930.

In the middle of the 1920s Davidson began writing the poems that made up *The Tall Men,* his second book of verse, published in 1927; they were based on Tennessee history and life and were strongly critical of modern society and urban ways. It was Davidson who took the lead in organizing the Agrarian symposium, *I'll Take My Stand* (1930), and in the ensuing years he wrote extensively on agrarian and regional topics. In 1938 he published a book of verse, *Lee in the Mountains and Other Poems,* and a collection of polemical essays, *The Attack on Leviathan: Regionalism and Nationalism.* When Ransom left Vanderbilt for Kenyon in 1937 Davidson was the only one of the leading Fugitive-Agrarians left at the school. In the following years he continued to write verse, essays, and textbooks, publishing in 1946 and 1948 a two-volume history of the Tennessee River in the "Rivers of America" series; several books of essays; a volume of verse, *The Long Street* (1961); and, in 1966 after his retirement from Vanderbilt, a volume of collected verse, *Poems: 1922–1961.*

Although in the early and mid-1920s Davidson seemed to be following his close friend Allen Tate in the direction of literary modernism in poetry, with the poems that made up *The Tall Men* he moved decisively into a less tightly constructed and allusive, more hortatory style of verse, based mainly on Southern themes. His whole-souled involvement in the Agrarian cause on a level far more literal and "practical" than that of Ransom and Tate soon took the form of a fierce identification with the South and its political and racial attitudes and institutions. As the Agrarian concerns of the others began to diminish, Davidson felt more and more estranged from his friends. A passionately loyal man, he remained dedicated to the causes he espoused, and the poetry he wrote after the mid-1920s tended to depend for its success upon the degree to which he could objectify his themes in language that did not demand the reader's preconceived social and political attitudes. Such a poem is the beautifully elegiac "Lee in the Mountains," in which the defeated Confederate leader, now directing the education of the youth of the South as president of Washington College in the Shenandoah Valley, expresses his faith in the land and in God's justice and mercy for future generations of his countrymen.

APPLE AND MOLE

For a high heavy time on the long green bough
Hangs the apple of a summer that is shaken
From its flat hot road to its apple-topped hill
With the scraping of a mole that would awaken.

He is under the turf of the long green meadow,
Snuffling under grass and lusty clover
With a sure blunt snout and capable paws
Up the long green slope past the beeches and the haws
For the summer must be shaken and over.

It's a ripe heavy time for an apply to hang.
He is butting out a path, he is shoveling a furrow,
Till the tree will be aquiver feeling mole at the root.
It is tall, it is green, but he will burrow

Till the root will be sapless and the twig will be dry
And the long green bough it will be shaken.
The apple is too old, it has worms at the core,
And the long green summer will be green no more.
The apple will fall and not awaken.

1925

LEE IN THE MOUNTAINS

1865–1870

Walking into the shadows, walking alone
Where the sun falls through the ruined boughs of locusts
Up to the president's office. . . .
      Hearing the voices
Whisper, *Hush, it is General Lee!* And strangely
Hearing my own voice say, *Good morning, boys.*
(Don't get up. You are early. It is long
Before the bell. You will have long to wait
On these cold steps. . . .)
      The young have time to wait.
But soldiers' faces under their tossing flags
Lift no more by any road or field,
And I am spent with old wars and new sorrow.
Walking the rocky path, where steps decay
And the paint cracks and grass eats on the stone.
It is not General Lee, young men. . . .
It is Robert Lee in a dark civilian suit who walks,
An outlaw fumbling for the latch, a voice
Commanding in a dream where no flag flies.

My father's house is taken and his hearth
Left to the candle-drippings where the ashes
Whirl at a chimney-breath on the cold stone.
I can hardly remember my father's look, I cannot
Answer his voice as he calls farewell in the misty
Mounting where riders gather at gates.
He was old then—I was a child—his hand
Held out for mine, some daybreak snatched away,
And he rode out, a broken man. Now let
His lone grave keep, surer than cypress roots,
The vow I made beside him. God too late
Unseals to certain eyes the drift
Of time and the hopes of men and a sacred cause.
The fortune of the Lees goes with the land
Whose sons will keep it still. My mother
Told me much. She sat among the candles,
Fingering the *Memoirs,* now so long unread.
And as my pen moves on across the page
Her voice comes back, a murmuring distillation
Of old Virginia times now faint and gone,
The hurt of all that was and cannot be.

DONALD DAVIDSON

Why did my father write? I know he saw
History clutched as a wraith out of blowing mist
Where tongues are loud, and a glut of little souls
Laps at the too much blood and the burning house.
He would have his say, but I shall not have mine.
What I do is only a son's devoir
To a lost father. Let him only speak.
The rest must pass to men who never knew
(But on a written page) the strike of armies,
And never heard the long Confederate cry
Charge through the muzzling smoke or saw the bright
Eyes of the beardless boys go up to death.
It is Robert Lee who writes with his father's hand—
The rest must go unsaid and the lips be locked.

If all were told, as it cannot be told—
If all the dread opinion of the heart
Now could speak, now in the shame and torment
Lashing the bound and trampled States—

If a word were said, as it cannot be said—

I see clear waters run in Virginia's Valley
And in the house the weeping of young women
Rises no more. The waves of grain begin.
The Shenandoah is golden with new grain.
The Blue Ridge, crowned with a haze of light,
Thunders no more. The horse is at plough. The rifle
Returns to the chimney crotch and the hunter's hand.
And nothing else than this? Was it for this
That on an April day we stacked our arms
Obedient to a soldier's trust? To lie
Ground by heels of little men,
Forever maimed, defeated, lost, impugned?
And was I then betrayed? Did I betray?

If it were said, as still it might be said—
If it were said, and a word should run like fire,
Like living fire into the roots of grass,
The sunken flag would kindle on wild hills,
The brooding hearts would waken, and the dream
Stir like a crippled phantom under the pines,
And this torn earth would quicken into shouting
Beneath the feet of ragged bands—
                                    The pen
Turns to the waiting page, the sword

LEE IN THE MOUNTAINS

Bows to the rust that cankers and the silence.

Among these boys whose eyes lift up to mine
Within gray walls where droning wasps repeat
A hollow reveille, I still must face,
Day after day, the courier with his summons
Once more to surrender, now to surrender all.
Without arms or men I stand, but with knowledge only
I face what long I saw, before others knew,
When Pickett's men streamed back, and I heard the tangled
Cry of the Wilderness wounded, bloody with doom.

The mountains, once I said, in the little room
At Richmond, by the huddled fire, but still
The President shook his head. The mountains wait,
I said, in the long beat and rattle of siege
At cratered Petersburg. Too late
We sought the mountains and those people came.
And Lee is in mountains now, beyond Appomattox,
Listening long for voices that never will speak
Again; hearing the hoofbeats come and go and fade
Without a stop, without a brown hand lifting
The tent-flap, or a bugle call at dawn,
Or ever on the long white road the flag
Of Jackson's quick brigades. I am alone,
Trapped, consenting, taken at last in mountains.

It is not the bugle now, or the long roll beating.
The simple stroke of a chapel bell forbids
The hurtling dream, recalls the lonely mind.
Young men, the God of your fathers is a just
And merciful God Who in this blood once shed
On your green altars measures out all days,
And measures out the grace
Whereby alone we live;
And in His might He waits,
Brooding within the certitude of time,
To bring this lost forsaken valor
And the fierce faith undying
And the love quenchless
To flower among the hills to which we cleave,
To fruit upon the mountains whither we flee,
Never forsaking, never denying
His children and His children's children forever

Unto all generations of the faithful heart.

1938

ALLEN TATE

(1899–1979)

John Orley Allen Tate was born in Winchester, Kentucky. His mother came from a once-prosperous Northern Virginia family and his father was of Kentucky and Tennessee stock. During his childhood he lived in various places in the Upper South and in Ohio and Indiana. He enrolled at Vanderbilt University in 1918 and soon established himself on campus as a formidable literary figure, precociously well read, familiar with the poetry of the French Symbolists—in the words of Ransom, in whose freshman English course Tate was a student, possessed "of a native sense, or at least a very early sense, of being called to the vocation of literature." Donald Davidson invited him to take part in the informal meetings of the group that soon became known as The Fugitives, and Tate functioned as the apostle of literary modernism in the discussions, early espousing the poetics of T. S. Eliot, Ezra Pound, and other leading creative figures of the post-World War I literary scene.

After graduating from Vanderbilt and teaching briefly in Kentucky, Tate went to New York, married Caroline Gordon, and for the next several years supported himself through editorial work and writings for the *New Republic, The Nation,* the *Herald-Tribune*, and other literary periodicals. His mature style as a poet began to emerge in the mid-1920s, and in the years that followed he published much of his best poetry. In the mid-1920s, his interest in the South also asserted itself. In 1928 he published a biography of Stonewall Jackson and his first collection of verse, *Mr. Pope and Other Poems*. He went to Europe on a Guggenheim Fellowship and while in Paris he began exchanging the letters with Donald Davidson, Ransom, and Robert Penn Warren that eventuated in the Agrarian symposium *I'll Take My Stand*.

The Tates came back to the United States in 1930 and moved into a farmhouse near Clarksville, Tennessee. In the 1930s Tate published *Poems: 1928–1931* (1932), *The Mediterranean and Other Poems* (1936), and *Selected Poems* (1937). He also worked on a biography of Robert E. Lee that was never completed, edited the agrarian-distributist symposium *Who Owns America?* (1936) with Herbert Agar, and produced an historical novel, *The Fathers* (1938). During this decade he also wrote a number of his most influential critical essays, collecting them as *Reactionary Essays in Poetry and Ideas* in 1936 and *Reason in Madness* (1941). He taught at Southwestern University, then moved to Greensboro, North Carolina, to join the faculty of the Women's College of the University of North Carolina in 1938, and afterwards taught for several years at Princeton University. In 1943 he was named consultant in poetry at the Library of Congress, and the year following moved to Sewanee, Tennessee, to become editor of the *Sewanee Review*. In 1946 he was divorced from and then remarried Caroline Gordon, and in subsequent years was an editor in New York and visiting professor at the University of Chicago, until he was named professor of English at the University of Minnesota in 1951, where he remained until his retirement in 1968. Tate joined the Roman Catholic Church in 1950. In 1955 he was divorced by Caroline Gordon and married Isabella Gardner, from whom he was divorced in 1966. That same year he married Helen Heinz.

Throughout the 1940s and afterward he added to his essays and his poetry and published new collections of both, including *Poems 1922–1947* (1948), *On the Limits of Poetry: Selected Essays* (1948), *The Forlorn Demon: Didactic and Critical Essays* (1953), *Collected Essays* (1959), *Essays of Four Decades* (1969), *The Swimmers and Other Poems* (1971), *Memoirs and Opinions* (1975), and *Collected Poems 1919–1976* (1977).

The theme that has most preoccupied Tate in his poetry and fiction, and which he has turned to again and again in his criticism, is the erosion of tradition and the accompanying sense of dislocation inherent in modern urban society. His approach, however, has not been from above or outside the problem; he has identified it within his own sensibility and his creative stance has been one of participation rather than aloof admonition. In his best known poem, the "Ode to the Confederate Dead," he depicts a modern Southerner standing outside the gate of a Confederate cemetery, pondering his relationship to the graves of the soldiers and his inability to equate his situation and sensibility with theirs, yet being convinced of the necessity of the engagement in a human community in which passion and judgment, knowledge and belief may be united within an individual's private and public identity. Again and again, Tate returns to this theme. His own lifetime engagement with the South and its tradition afforded him a rich context whereby he could locate and explore the problem.

MR. POPE

When Alexander Pope strolled in the city
Strict was the glint of pearl and gold sedans.
Ladies leaned out more out of fear than pity
For Pope's tight back was rather a goat's than man's.

Often one thinks the urn should have more bones
Than skeletons provide for speedy dust,
The urn gets hollow, cobwebs brittle as stones

Weave to the funeral shell a frivolous rust.

And he who dribbled couplets like a snake
Coiled to a lithe precision in the sun
Is missing. The jar is empty; you may break
It only to find that Mr. Pope is gone.

What requisitions of a verity
Prompted the wit and rage between his teeth
One cannot say. Around a crooked tree
A moral climbs whose name should be a wreath.

1928

ODE TO THE CONFEDERATE DEAD

Row after row with strict impunity
The headstones yield their names to the element,
The wind whirrs without recollection;
In the riven troughs the splayed leaves
Pile up, of nature the casual sacrament
To the seasonal eternity of death;
Then driven by the fierce scrutiny
Of heaven to their election in the vast breath,
They sough the rumour of mortality.

Autumn is desolation in the plot
Of a thousand acres where these memories grow
From the inexhaustible bodies that are not
Dead, but feed the grass row after rich row.
Think of the autumns that have come and gone!—
Ambitious November with the humors of the year,
With a particular zeal for every slab,
Staining the uncomfortable angels that rot
On the slabs, a wing chipped here, an arm there:
The brute curiosity of an angel's stare
Turns you, like them, to stone,
Transforms the heaving air
Till plunged to a heavier world below
You shift your sea-space blindly
Heaving, turning like the blind crab.

Dazed by the wind, only the wind
The leaves flying, plunge

You know who have waited by the wall

ODE TO THE CONFEDERATE DEAD

The twilight certainty of an animal,
Those midnight restitutions of the blood
You know—the immitigable pines, the smoky frieze
Of the sky, the sudden call: you know the rage,
The cold pool left by the mounting flood,
Of muted Zeno and Parmenides.
You who have waited for the angry resolution
Of those desires that should be yours tomorrow,
You know the unimportant shrift of death
And praise the vision
And praise the arrogant circumstance
Of those who fall
Rank upon rank, hurried beyond decision—
Here by the sagging gate, stopped by the wall.

    Seeing, seeing only the leaves
    Flying, plunge and expire

Turn your eyes to the immoderate past,
Turn to the inscrutable infantry rising
Demons out of the earth—they will not last.
Stonewall, Stonewall, and the sunken fields of hemp,
Shiloh, Antietam, Malvern Hill, Bull Run.
Lost in that orient of the thick-and-fast
You will curse the setting sun.

    Cursing only the leaves crying
    Like an old man in a storm

You hear the shout, the crazy hemlocks point
With troubled fingers to the silence which
Smothers you, a mummy, in time.

                The hound bitch
Toothless and dying, in a musty cellar
Hears the wind only.

           Now that the salt of their blood
Stiffens the saltier oblivion of the sea,
Seals the malignant purity of the flood,
What shall we who count our days and bow
Our heads with a commemorial woe
In the ribboned coats of grim felicity,
What shall we say of the bones, unclean,
Whose verdurous anonymity will grow?
The ragged arms, the ragged heads and eyes
Lost in these acres of the insane green?

ALLEN TATE

The gray lean spiders come, they come and go;
In a tangle of willows without light
The singular screech-owl's tight
Invisible lyric seeds the mind
With the furious murmur of their chivalry.

    We shall say only the leaves
    Flying, plunge and expire

We shall say only the leaves whispering
In the improbable mist of nightfall
That flies on multiple wing;
Night is the beginning and the end
And in between the ends of distraction
Waits mute speculation, the patient curse
That stones the eyes, or like the jaguar leaps
For his own image in a jungle pool, his victim.

What shall we say who have knowledge
Carried to the heart? Shall we take the act
To the grave? Shall we, more hopeful, set up the
      grave
In the house? The ravenous grave?

                           Leave now
The shut gate and the decomposing wall:
The gentle serpent, green in the mulberry bush,
Riots with his tongue through the hush—
Sentinel of the grave who counts us all!

                                  1936

THE MEDITERRANEAN

Quem das finem, rex magne, dolorum?

Where we went in the boat was a long bay
A slingshot wide, walled in by towering stone—
Peaked margin of antiquity's delay,
And we went there out of time's monotone:

Where we went in the black hull no light moved
But a gull white-winged along the feckless wave,
The breeze, unseen but fierce as a body loved,
That boat drove onward like a willing slave:

Where we went in the small ship the seaweed
Parted and gave to us the murmuring shore,
And we made feast and in our secret need
Devoured the very plates Aeneas bore:

Where derelict you see through the low twilight
The green coast that you, thunder-tossed, would win,
Drop sail, and hastening to drink all night
Eat dish and bowl to take that sweet land in!

Where we feasted and caroused on the sandless
Pebbles, affecting our day of piracy,
What prophecy of eaten plates could landless
Wanderers fulfil by the ancient sea?

We for that time might taste the famous age
Eternal here yet hidden from our eyes
When lust of power undid its stuffless rage;
They, in a wineskin, bore earth's paradise.

Let us lie down once more by the breathing side
Of Ocean, where our live forefathers sleep
As if the Known Sea still were a month wide—
Atlantis howls but is no longer steep!

What country shall we conquer, what fair land
Unman our conquest and locate our blood?
We've cracked the hemispheres with careless hand!
Now, from the Gates of Hercules we flood

Westward, westward till the barbarous brine
Whelms us to the tired land where tasseling corn,
Fat beans, grapes sweeter than muscadine
Rot on the vine: in that land were we born.

1936

THE PROFESSION OF LETTERS IN THE SOUTH[1]

The profession of letters in France dates, I believe, from the famous manifesto of Du Bellay and the Pléiade in 1549. It is a French habit to assume that France has supported a profession of letters ever since. There is no other country where the writer is so much honored as in France, no other

---

[1] This essay was written for the tenth anniversary of *The Virginia Quarterly Review*, April, 1935. It has been amplified.

people in western culture who understand so well as the French the value of literature to the state. The national respect for letters begins far down in society. In a French village where I was unknown I was able to use a let-ter-of-credit without identification upon my word that I was a man of let-ters. The French have no illusions; we are not asked to believe that all French writers are respectable. The generation of Rimbaud and Verlaine was notoriously dissolute. French letters are a profession, as law, medicine, and the army are professions. Good writers starve and lead sordid lives in France as elsewhere; yet the audience for high literature is larger in France than in any other country, and a sufficient number of the best writers find a public large enough to sustain them as a class.

It goes somewhat differently with us. The American public sees the writer as a business man because it cannot see any other kind of man, and respects him according to his income. And, alas, most writers themselves respect chiefly and fear only their competitors' sales. A big sale is a "success." How could it be otherwise? Our books are sold on a competitive market; it is a book market, but it is a luxury market; and luxury markets must be fiercely competitive. It is not that the natural depravity of the writer as fallen man betrays him into imitating the tone and standards of his market; actually he cannot find a public at all, even for the most lost of lost causes, the *succès d'estime,* unless he is willing to enter the competitive racket of publishing. This racket, our society being what it is, is a purely economic process, and literary opinion is necessarily manufactured for its needs. Its prime need is shoddy goods, because it must have a big, quick turnover. The overhead in the system is so high that the author gets only ten to fifteen percent of the gross. It is the smallest return that any producer gets in our whole economic system. To live even frugally, a novelist, if he does not do odd jobs on the side, must have a sale of about thirty thousand copies every two years. Not only the publisher's but his turnover, too, must be quick. He has his own self-sweat shop. One must agree with Mr. Herbert Read, in the February, 1935, London *Mercury,* that authors under modern capitalism are a sweated class.

We have heard for years, we began hearing it as early as Jeffrey's review of the first "Hyperion," that science is driving poetry to cover. I suppose it is; and we have the weight of Mr. I. A. Richards's arguments to prove it, and Mr. Max Eastman's weight, which is fairly light. Nineteenth-century science produced a race of "problem" critics and novelists. The new "social" point of view has multiplied the race. Literature needs no depth of background or experience to deal with problems; it needs chiefly the statis-tical survey and the conviction that society lives by formula, if not by bread alone. The nineteenth century began this *genre*, which has become the stan-dard mode. I confess that I cannot decide whether "science" or the mass production of books, or the Spirit that made them both, has given us shoddy in literature. We were given, for example, Bennett and Wells; Millay and Masefield. And I surmise that not pure science but shoddy has driven the poets into exile, where, according to Eastman, they are "talking to themselves."

I shall not multiply instances. The trouble ultimately goes back to the beginnings of finance-capitalism and its creature, machine-production. Under feudalism the artist was a member of an organic society. The writer's loss of professional standing, however, set in before the machine, by which I mean the machine age as we know it, appeared. It began with the rise of mercantile aristocracy in the eighteenth century. The total loss of professionalism in letters may be seen in our age—an age that remembers the extinction of aristocracy and witnesses the triumph of a more inimical plutocratic society.

If my history is not wholly incorrect, it must follow that our unlimited pioneering, the pretext of the newness of the country, and our low standards of education, do not explain the decline of the professional author. Pioneering became our way of industrial expansion, a method of production not special to us; we are a new country insofar as our industrialism gave to the latent vices of the European mind a new opportunity; and our standards of education get lower with the increasing amount of money spent upon them. For my purposes, then, it is sufficient that we should look at the history of professionalism in letters in terms of the kinds of rule that European society, which includes American society, has had.

The South once had aristocratic rule; the planter class was about one fifth of the population; but the majority followed its lead. And so, by glancing at the South, we shall see in American history an important phase of the decline of the literary profession. There was, perhaps, in and around Boston, for a brief period, a group of professional writers. But not all of them, not even most of them, made their livings by writing. Even if they had, we should still have to explain why they were second-rate, and why the greatest of the Easterners, Hawthorne, Melville, Dickinson, had nothing to do with them or with the rising plutocracy of the East. But it is a sadder story still in the South. We had no Hawthorne, no Melville, no Emily Dickinson. We had William Gilmore Simms. We made it impossible for Poe to live south of the Potomac. Aristocracy drove him out. Plutocracy, in the East, starved him to death. I prefer the procedure of the South; it knew its own mind, knew what kind of society it wanted. The East, bent upon making money, could tolerate, as it still tolerates, any kind of disorder on the fringe of society as long as the disorder does not interfere with money making. It did not know its own social mind; it was, and still is, plutocracy.

But let us look a little at the backgrounds of Southern literature. I say backgrounds, for the South is an immensely complicated region. It begins in the Northeast with southern Maryland; it ends with eastern Texas; it includes to the north a little of Missouri. But that the people in this vast expanse of country have enough in common to bind them in a single culture cannot be denied. They often deny it themselves—writers who want to have something to jabber about, or other writers who want to offset the commercial handicap of being Southern; or newly rich persons in cities that would rather be like Pittsburgh than like New Orleans. It must be confessed that the Southern tradition has left no cultural landmark so conspicuous that the people may be reminded by it constantly of what they are. We lack a tradition in the arts; more to the point, we lack a literary tradition. We lack even a literature. We have just enough literary remains from the old régime to prove to us that, had a great literature risen, it would have been unique in modern times.

The South was settled by the same European strains as originally settled the North. Yet, in spite of war, reconstruction, and industrialism, the South to this day finds its most perfect contrast in the North. In religious and social feeling I should stake everything on the greater resemblance to France. The South clings blindly to forms of European feeling and conduct that were crushed by the French Revolution and that, in England at any rate, are barely memories. How many Englishmen have told us that we still have the eighteenth-century amiability and consideration of manners, supplanted in their country by middle-class reticence and suspicion? And where, outside the South, is there a society that believes even covertly in the Code of Honor? This is not idle talk; we are assured of it by Professor H. C. Brearley, who, I believe, is one of the most detached students of Southern life. Where else in the modern world is the patriarchal family still innocent of the rise and power of other forms of society? Possibly in France; probably in the peasant countries of the Balkans and of Central Europe. Yet the "orientation"—let us concede the word to the University of North Carolina —the rise of new Southern points of view, even now in the towns, is tied still to the image of the family on the land. Where else does so much of the reality of the ancient land society endure, along with the infatuated avowal of beliefs that are hostile to it? Where in the world today is there a more supine enthusiasm for being amiable to forces undermining the life that supports the amiability? The anomalous structure of the South is, I think, finally witnessed by its religion. Doctor Poteat of South Carolina deplores a fact which he does not question, that only in the South does one find a convinced supernaturalism: it is nearer to Aquinas than to Calvin, Wesley, or Knox. Nor do we doubt that the conflict between modernism and fundamentalism is chiefly the impact of the new middle-class civilization upon the rural society; nor, moreover, should we allow ourselves to forget that philosophers of the State, from Sir Thomas More to John C. Calhoun, were political defenders of the older religious community.

The key to unlock the Southern mind is, fortunately, like Bluebeard's, bloody and perilous; there is not the easy sesamé to the cavern of gaping success. The South has had reverses that permit her people to imagine what they might have been. (And only thus can people discover what they *are*.)

Given the one great fact of the expanding plantation system at the dawn of the last century, which voice should the South have listened to? Jefferson, or Marshall, or Calhoun? I mean, which voice had the deepest moral and spiritual implications for the permanence of Southern civilization?

There was not time to listen to any voice very long. The great Southern ideas were strangled in the cradle, either by the South herself (for example, by too much quick cotton money in the Southwest) or by the Union armies. It is plain to modern historians of culture that peoples do not make, much less buy, a culture overnight; it takes time. Which view would have given the South a unified sense of its own destiny? Our modern "standard of living" is not a point of view, and it is necessary that a people should gather its experience round some seasoned point of view before it may boast a high culture. It must be able to illuminate from a fixed position all its experience; it must bring to full realization the high forms as well as the contradictions and miseries inherent in human society.

The miseries and contradictions bemuse and alarm us now. I hope I shall not be called flint-hearted if I dare to believe that the humanitarian spirit can never remove them. So long as society is committed to a class system —and it will probably never be committed to a classless system—the hard-hearted will keep on believing that the high forms are as necessary to the whole of society as bread to the major fraction to whom it is now denied. If man does not live by bread alone, he lives thinly upon bread and sentiment; for sentiment and bread will nourish him but little unless they partake of the peculiarly elevating virtues of form. I might even quote Shelley, whom it is becoming fashionable again to quote: "Our calculations have outrun conception; we have eaten more than we can digest." I am willing to take the sentence in full literalness, if I may read form for conception, and produced for eaten. For the concrete forms of the social and religious life are the assimilating structure of society.

Where, as in the Old South, there were high forms, but no deep realization of the spirit was achieved, we must ask questions. (The right questions: not why the South refused to believe in Progress, or why it did not experiment with "ideas.") Was the structure of society favorable to a great literature? Suppose it to have been favorable: Was there something wrong with the intellectual life for which the social order cannot be blamed?

The answer is both yes and no to the first question. It is emphatically yes and no to the second. So our answers are confused. At a glance one would expect the rich leisured class, well educated as the Southern aristocracy was —for the South of the fifties had proportionately a larger educated minority than Massachusetts—to devote a great part of its vitality to the arts, the high and conscious arts. As for the arts otherwise, even peasant societies achieve the less conscious variety—manners, ritual, charming domestic architecture.

Assuming, as I do not think I am allowed to assume very confidently, that this society was a good soil for the high arts, there was yet a grave fault in the intellectual life. It was hagridden with politics. We like to think that Archimago sent the nightmare down from the North. He did. But it was partly rooted in the kind of rule that the South had, which was aristocratic rule. All aristocracies are obsessed politically. (Witness *Henry IV*, Parts One and Two; *Henry V*.) The best intellectual energy goes into politics and goes of necessity; aristocracy is class rule; and the class must fight for interest and power. Under the special conditions of the nineteenth century, the South had less excess of vitality for the disinterested arts of literature than it might have had ordinarily. There are no simple answers to the questions that I have asked. The South was a fairly good place for the arts, as good possibly as any other aristocratic country; only its inherent passion for politics was inflamed by the furious contentions that threatened its life. Every gifted person went into politics, not merely the majority.

The furious contentions themselves provided later answers to the problem of the arts in the South. At the end of the century one of the popular answers was that of the distinguished William Peterfield Trent, who laid bare all the Southern defects with the black magic talisman, Slavery. The defects could be whisked away, he argued in his life of Simms, with "essential faith in American democracy." The Northern people, at that time, may be forgiven this faith; it was the stuffed shirt of plutocracy and it was making them money; they had a right to believe in it. I cannot decide between credulity and venality as the reason for its being believed in the South. I am certain that in Trent's case it was credulity. If slavery was the cause of war, then slavery explained the political mania of the Old South; and the political mania stunted the arts. Partly true; partly false. Such an answer is more dangerous than an answer wholly false. In this instance it led the people to believe that their sole obstacle to perfection, slavery, had been removed. There was no need to be critical of anything else, least of all of the society that had come down and removed the blight: a society that by some syllogistic process unknown to me was accepted as perfect by the new Southern Liberals.

But the abolition of slavery did not make for a distinctively Southern literature. We must seek the cause of our limitations elsewhere. It is worth remarking, for the sake of argument, that chattel slavery is not demonstrably a worse form of slavery than any other upon which an aristocracy may base its power and wealth. That *African* chattel slavery was the worst groundwork conceivable for the growth of a great culture of European pattern, is scarcely at this day arguable. Still, as a favorable "cultural situation" it was probably worse than white chattel, agricultural slavery only in degree. The distance between white master and black slave was unalterably greater than that between white master and white serf after the destruction of feudalism. The peasant *is* the soil. The Negro slave was a barrier between the ruling class and the soil. If we look at aristocracies in Europe, say in eighteenth-century England, we find at least genuine social classes, each carrying on a different level of the common culture. But in the Old South, and under the worse form of slavery that afflicts both races today, genuine social classes could not exist. The enormous "difference" of the Negro doomed him from the beginning to an economic status purely: he has had much the same thinning influence upon the class above him as the anonymous city proletariat has had upon the culture of industrial capitalism.

All great cultures have been rooted in peasantries, in free peasantries, I believe, such as the English yeomanry before the fourteenth century: they have been the growth of the soil. What the Southern system might have accomplished we do not know: it would have been, as I have said, something new. Of course, the absence of genuine cultural capitals in the South has been cited as a cause of lassitude in the arts; perhaps it was a cause, as it is today. But it does not wholly explain the vague and feeble literature that was produced. The white man got nothing from the Negro, no profound image of himself in terms of the soil.

I suspect that, in the age of social science, the term *image* is not clear, and this, I suppose, is due to the disappearance, in such an age, of the deep relation between man and a local habitation. An environment is an abstraction, not a place; Natchez is a place but not an environment. The difference will be clear to those who are morally able to see that it exists. The citizen of Natchez lived in a place but he could not deepen his sense of its life through the long series of gradations represented by his dependents, who stood between him and the earth. He instructed his factor to buy good furniture of the Second Empire, and remained a Colonial. But the Negro, who has long been described as a responsibility, got everything from the white man. The history of French culture, I suppose, has been quite different. The high arts have been grafted upon the peasant stock. We could graft no new life upon the Negro; he was too different, too alien.

Doubtless the confirmed if genteel romanticism of the old Southern imaginative literature (I make exception for the political writers of South Carolina—Hammond, Harper, Calhoun: they are classical and realistic) was in the general stream of romanticism; yet the special qualities that it produced, the unreal union of formless revery and correct sentiment, the inflated oratory—even in private correspondence you see it witness a feeble hold upon place and time. The roots were not deep enough in the soil. Professor Trent was right; but he was right for the wrong reason. It was not that slavery was corrupt "morally." Societies can bear an amazing amount of corruption and still produce high cultures. Black slavery could not nurture the white man in his own image.

Although the Southern system, in spite of the Negro, was closer to the soil than the mercantile-manufacturing system of the middle and New England states, its deficiencies in spiritual soil were more serious even than those of the debased feudal society of eighteenth-century rural England. With this society the ante-bellum South had much in common.

The South came from eighteenth-century England, its agricultural half; there were not enough large towns in the South to complete the picture of an England reproduced. The Virginian and the Carolinian, however, imitated the English squire. They held their land, like their British compeer, in absolute, that is to say unfeudal, ownership, as a result of the destruction, first under Henry VIII and then under Cromwell, of the feudal system of land tenure. The landlord might be humane, but he owed no legal obligation to his land (he could wear it out) or to his labor (he could turn it off: called "enclosure" in England, "selling" under Negro slavery). A pure aristocracy, or the benevolent rule of a landed class in the interest of its own wealth and power, had superseded royalty which, in theory at any rate, and often in practice, had tried to balance class interests under protection of the Crown.

It should be borne in mind, against modern egalitarian and Marxian superstition, that royalty and aristocracy are fundamentally opposed systems of rule; that plutocracy, the offspring of democracy, and that Marxism, the child of plutocracy, are essentially of the aristocratic political mode: they all mean class rule. Virginia took the lead in the American revolution, not to set up democracy, as Jefferson tried to believe, but to increase the power of the tobacco-exporting aristocracy. The planters wished to throw off the yoke of the British merchant and to get access to the free world market.

But the Southern man of letters cannot permit himself to look upon the old system from a purely social point of view, or from the economic view: to him it must seem better than the system that destroyed it, better, too, than any system with which the modern planners, Marxian or other color, wish to replace the present order. Yet the very merits of the Old South tend to confuse the issue: its comparative stability, its realistic limitation of the acquisitive impulse, its preference for human relations compared to relations economic, tempt the historian to defend the poor literature simply because he feels that the old society was a better place to live in than the new. It is a great temptation—if you do not read the literature.

There is, I believe, a nice object lesson to be drawn from the changed relation of the English writer to society in the eighteenth century; it is a lesson that bears directly upon the attitude of the Old South towards the profession of letters. In the seventeenth century, in the year 1634, a young, finical man, then in seclusion at Horton after taking his degrees at Cambridge, and still unknown, was invited by the Earl of Bridgewater to write a masque for certain revels to be celebrated at Ludlow Castle. The masque was *Comus*, and the revels were in the feudal tradition. The whole celebration was "at home"; it was a part of the community life, the common people were present, and the poet was a spiritual member of the society gathered there. He might not be a gentleman: had Milton become a member of Egerton's "household" he would have been a sort of upper servant. But he would have been a member of the social and spiritual community.

Now examine the affair of Johnson and the Earl of Chesterfield: it is the eighteenth century. It was conducted in the new "aristocratic" style. For the flattery of a dedication the nobleman was loftily willing to give his patronage, a certain amount of money, to an author who had already completed the work, an author who had faced starvation in isolation from society. There is no great publishing system in question here; there were only booksellers. But there was already the cash nexus between the writer and society. The Earl of Chesterfield was a capitalist, not a feudal noble as Egerton to some extent still was; Chesterfield had lost the community; he required of the arts a compliment to the power of his class.

He was the forerunner of the modern plutocrat who thinks that the arts are thriving so long as he can buy Italian paintings, or so long as he creates "foundations" for the arts, or the sales sheets of the publishers show a large volume of "business." But the plutocrat no less than the artist participates in his society through the cash nexus. I hope I do not convince the reader that this wicked fellow has undertaken a deliberate conspiracy against the artist. The artist as man invariably has the same relation to the society of his time as everybody else has: his misfortune and his great value is his superior awareness of that relation. The "message" of modern art at present is that social man is living, without religion, morality, or art (without the high form that concentrates all three in an organic whole) in a mere system of money references through which neither artist nor plutocrat can perform as an entire person.

Is there anything in common between the Earl of Chesterfield and a dour Scots merchant building a fortune and a place in the society of Richmond, Virginia, in the first third of the nineteenth century? I think that they have something in common. It was not John Allan who drove Poe out of Virginia. The foreigner, trying to better himself, always knows the practical instincts of a society more shrewdly than the society knows them. Allan was, for once, the spokesman of Virginia, of the plantation South. There was no place for Poe in the spiritual community of Virginia; there was no class of professional writers that Poe could join in dedicating their works to the aristocracy under the system of the cash nexus. The promising young men were all in politics bent upon more desperate emergencies. It was obvious, even to John Allan, I suppose, that here was no dabbler who would write pleasant, genteel poems and stories for magazines where other dabbling gentlemen printed their pleasant, genteel stories and poems. Anybody could have looked at Poe and known that he meant business.

And until the desperate men today who mean business can become an independent class, there will be no profession of letters anywhere in America. It remains only to add to the brief history adumbrated in this essay some comment on the present situation of the desperate men of the South in particular. There are too many ladies and gentlemen, too many Congreves whose coxcombry a visit from Voltaire would do a great deal of good. I trust that I do not argue the case too well. Congreve frivolously gave up the honor of his profession when Voltaire asked to see the great dramatist and got the answer that Mr. Congreve was no scribbler but a man of fashion. They were more explicit about those things in those days. I should barely hope that the Southern writer, or the Northern or Western, for that matter, may decide that his gentility, being a quality over which he has no control, may get along as it can. For the genteel tradition has never done anything for letters in the South; yet the Southern writers who are too fastidious to become conscious of their profession have not refused to write best sellers when they could, and to profit by a cash nexus with New York. I would fain believe that matters are otherwise than so: but facts are facts. If there is such a person as a Southern writer, if there could be such a profession as letters in the South, the profession would require the speaking of unpleasant words and the violation of good literary manners.

I wish this were the whole story: only cranks and talents of the quiet, first order maintain themselves against fashion and prosperity. But even these desperate persons must live, and they cannot live in the South without an "independent income." We must respect the source of our income, that is, we ought to; and if we cannot respect it we are likely to fear it. This kind of writer is not luckier than his penniless fellow. (The only man I know who devotes a large income to changing the system that produced it is a New Yorker.) Because there is no city in the South where writers may gather, write, and live, and no Southern publisher to print their books, the Southern writer, of my generation at least, went to New York. There he was influenced not only by the necessity to live but by theories and movements drifting over from Europe.

It was, possibly, a dangerous situation. Mr. John Crowe Ransom has pointed out its implications:

> If modernism is regarded as nothing but a new technique, what was wrong with the old technique? Principally, perhaps, the fact that it was old; for modernism is apt to assume that tradition is not so much a prop which may be leant upon as a dead burden which must be borne. The substance of modernism is not a technique but an attitude. And a dangerous attitude ...
>
> The Southern artists in going modern offer us their impression of a general decay, and that is not a pleasant thing to think about.[2]

The Southern writer was perilously near to losing his identity, becoming

---

[2] "Modern With the Southern Accent," *The Virginia Quarterly Review*, April, 1935.

merely a "modern" writer. He lost the Southern feeling which, in the case of Mr. Young, informs the Southern style: he might retain a Southern subject and write about it as an outsider, with some novelty of technique and in smart, superior detachment. These bad features of the last decade may be deplored, I hope, without asking the Southerner to stay at home and starve. That, it seems to me, is what Mr. Ransom asks the Southern writer to do. It was not an uprooted modern, but the classical Milton who remarked, "Wherever we do well is home": wherever we are allowed best to realize our natures—a realization that, for an artist, presupposes permission to follow his craft—is the proper place to live. The Southern writer should if possible be a Southerner in the South. The sole condition that would make that possible is a profession of letters.

But the arts everywhere spring from a mysterious union of indigenous materials and foreign influences: there is no great art or literature that does not bear the marks of this fusion. So I cannot assume, as Mr. Ransom seems to do, that exposure to the world of modernism (Petrarchism was modernism in the England of 1540) was of itself a demoralizing experience. Isn't it rather that the Southerner before he left home had grown weak in his native allegiance? That his political and social history, and his domestic life, had been severely adulterated no less by his fellow Southerners than by the people in the North to whom he fled? Apart from this menace abroad, who cannot bring himself to wish that Miss Glasgow had studied James and Flaubert in her apprenticeship, and spared herself and us her first three or four novels? Could Mr. Young have written his fiction, to say nothing of his plays and criticism, had he read only Cable and Page? And, lastly, what shall we say of Mr. Ransom's own distinguished and very modern poetry?

Is not Mr. Ransom really deploring the absence, as I deplore it, of a professional spirit and professional opportunities in Southern literature? There is no reason why the Southern writer should not address a large public, but if he does he will learn sooner or later that—but for happy accidents—the market, with what the market implies, dictates the style. To create a profession of literature in the South we should require first an independent machinery of publication. I fall into the mechanical terms. A Southern publishing system would not, I imagine, publish Southern books alone; nor should Southern magazines print only Southern authors. The point of the argument leads to no such comforting simplicity. The literary artist is seldom successful as a colonial; he should be able to enjoy the normal belief that he is at the center of the world. One aid to that feeling would be a congenial medium of communication with his public. Let the world in this fashion sit at his feet; let him not have to seek the world.

The exact degree of immediate satisfaction that Southern publication would bring to its authors I cannot predict. It, too, would be the system of the cash nexus; and the Southern publisher would be a capitalist plutocrat not noticeably different from his colleague in the North. Like his Northern friend he would, for a few years at least, sell the Southern article mostly north of the border. Until he could be backed by a powerful Southern press he would need the support of the New York journals for his authors, if he expected them to be read at home. I suppose the benefits of a Southern system would lie chiefly in this: that the Southern writer would not have to run the New York gauntlet, from which he emerges with a good understanding of what he can and cannot do.

We have exchanged the reasoned indifference of aristocracy for the piratical commercialism of plutocracy. Repudiating the later master, the new profession in the South would have to tell New York, where it had hitherto hawked its wares, that no more wares of the prescribed kind would be produced. For the prescribed ware is the ware that the Southerner also must produce, and it is not heartening to observe that his own Southern public waits for the New York journals to prescribe the kind, before he can get a hearing at home. Can there be a profession of letters in the South? Our best critical writing—and we have critical writing of distinction— can never constitute a Southern criticism so long as it must be trimmed and scattered in Northern magazines, or published in books that will be read as curiously as travel literature, by Northern people alone.

The considerable achievement of Southerners in modern American letters must not beguile us into too much hope for the future. The Southern novelist has left his mark upon the age; but it is of the age. From the peculiarly historical consciousness of the Southern writer has come good work of a special order; but the focus of this consciousness is quite temporary. It has made possible the curious burst of intelligence that we get at a crossing of the ways, not unlike, on an infinitesimal scale, the outburst of poetic genius at the end of the sixteenth century when commercial England had already begun to crush feudal England. The Histories and Tragedies of Shakespeare record the death of the old régime, and Doctor Faustus gives up feudal order for world power.

The prevailing economic passion of the age once more tempts, even commands, the Southern writer to go into politics. Our neo-communism is the new form in which the writer from all sections is to be dominated by capitalism, or "economic society." It is the new political mania. And there is no escape from it. The political mind always finds itself in an emergency. And the emergency, this time real enough, becomes a pretext for ignoring the arts. We live in the sort of age that Abraham Cowley complained of—a good age to write about but a hard age to write in.

THE AGRARIANS

One of the more original and remarkable expressions of the cultural and social attitudes of the writers of the Southern Literary Renascence was the Agrarian symposium *I'll Take My Stand: The South and the Agrarian Tradition*, by Twelve Southerners, published in 1930. Assembled in Nashville during the late 1920s as an outcome of a feeling on the part of Allen Tate, Donald Davidson, and John Crowe Ransom that something should be done to assert the greater attractiveness of the older Southern rural and small town social ordering over the materialistic and mechanistic values and ways of modern urban industrial society, the book constitutes a rare programmatical and topical declaration of attitudes toward Southern history, the Southern community, the good life, and the proper relationship of man in nature and society that underlie the poetry and fiction not only of the Nashville Agrarians themselves but most of their contemporary fellow Southern authors.

The ranks of the Nashville Agrarians included Tate, Davidson, Ransom, Robert Penn Warren, and Andrew Lytle among the Fugitive contingent, as well as the literary scholar John Donald Wade, the historian Frank Owsley, the political economist Herman Clarence Nixon, the poet John Gould Fletcher, the drama critic and novelist Stark Young, the psychologist Lyle Lanier, and a newspaperman, Henry Blue Kline. Although planned during the boom times of the late 1920s, the symposium appeared just as the nation, including the South, was tumbling precipitously into the economic depression of the 1930s. Its assertion of the agrarian social ideal therefore took on a temporary topical relevance—as a seeming alternative to the failure of industrial capitalism —that in the long run distorted its true significance. For the real dynamics of *I'll Take My Stand* (imperfectly understood, it must be admitted, by some of the participants) consisted of a humanistic rebuke to the depersonalization and inhuman fragmentation of our modern industrial business society. *I'll Take My Stand* was not an economic prescription but a prophetic work: it offered a warning to the South and the nation that unchecked, unthinking squandering of our natural environment in the name of Progress plus the relegation of individual human beings to units of production and consumption in a vast commercial system could only lead to disaster. The Agrarians were saying—at a time when few Americans worried about such things—that if the republic was to live up to its ideals and be what it should be, it had better look long and hard at what it was in danger of becoming and devote conscious effort to controlling its own destiny rather than continuing to drift along on the tides of economic materialism. Almost a half-century after its publication, there are essays and passages from *I'll Take My Stand* that address themselves with startling prescience and clarity to many of the problems and issues confronting our society today.

The "Introduction: A Statement of Principles" to *I'll Take My Stand* was written by John Crowe Ransom, circulated among the participants, and revised from their suggestions. Composed in Ransom's archly felicitous prose style, it sets forth the central arguments of the Agrarian symposium in allusive, topical terms and constitutes an apt enunciation of the book's underlying intentions.

From I'LL TAKE MY STAND

From INTRODUCTION: A STATEMENT OF PRINCIPLES

The authors contributing to this book are Southerners, well acquainted with one another and of similar tastes, though not necessarily living in the same physical community, and perhaps only at this moment aware of themselves as a single group of men. By conversation and exchange of letters over a number of years it had developed that they entertained many convictions in common, and it was decided to make a volume in which each one should furnish his views upon a chosen topic. This was the general background. But background and consultation as to the various topics were enough; there was to be no further collaboration. And so no single author is responsible for any view outside his own article. It was through the good fortune of some deeper agreement that the book was expected to achieve its unity. All the articles bear in the same sense upon the book's title-subject: all tend to support a Southern way of life against what may be called the American or prevailing way; and all as much as agree that the best terms in which to represent the distinction are contained in the phrase, Agrarian *versus* Industrial.

. . .

Industrialism is the economic organization of the collective American society. It means the decision of society to invest its economic resources in the applied sciences. But the word science has acquired a certain sanctitude. It is out of order to quarrel with science in the abstract, or even with the applied sciences when their applications are made subject to criticism and intelligence. The capitalization of the applied sciences has now become extravagant and uncritical; it has enslaved our human energies to a degree now clearly felt to be burdensome. The apologists of industrialism do not like to meet this charge directly; so they often take refuge in saying that they are devoted simply to science! They are really devoted to the applied sciences and to practical production. Therefore it is necessary to employ a certain skepticism even at the expense of the Cult of Science, and to say, It is an Americanism, which looks innocent and disinterested, but really is not either.

The contribution that science can make to a labor is to render it easier by the help of a tool or a process, and to assure the laborer of his perfect economic security while he is engaged upon it. Then it can be performed with leisure and enjoyment. But the modern laborer has not exactly received this benefit under the industrial regime. His labor is hard, its tempo is fierce, and his employment is insecure. The first principle of a good labor is that it must be effective, but the second principle is that it must be enjoyed. Labor is one of the largest items in the human career; it is a modest demand to ask that it may partake of happiness.

The regular act of applied science is to introduce into labor a labor-saving device or a machine. Whether this is a benefit depends on how far it is advisable to save the labor. The philosophy of applied science is generally quite sure that the saving of labor is a pure gain, and that the more of it the better. This is to assume that labor is an evil, that only the end of labor or the material product is good. On this assumption labor becomes mercenary and servile, and it is no wonder if many forms of modern labor are accepted without resentment though they are evidently brutalizing. The act of labor as one of the happy functions of human life has been in effect abandoned, and is practiced solely for its rewards.

Even the apologists of industrialism have been obliged to admit that some economic evils follow in the wake of the machines. These are such as overproduction, unemployment, and a growing inequality in the distribution of wealth. But the remedies proposed by the apologists are always homeopathic. They expect the evils to disappear when we have bigger and better machines, and more of them. Their remedial programs, therefore, look forward to more industrialism. Sometimes they see the system righting itself spontaneously and without direction: they are Optimists. Sometimes they rely on the benevolence of capital, or the militancy of labor, to bring about a fairer division of the spoils: they are Coöperationists or Socialists. And sometimes they expect to find super-engineers, in the shape of Boards of Control, who will adapt production to consumption and regulate prices and guarantee business against fluctuations: they are Sovietists. With respect to these last it must be insisted that the true Sovietists or Communists—if the term may be used here in the European sense—are the Industrialists themselves. They would have the government set up an economic super-organization, which in turn would become the government. We therefore look upon the Communist menace as a menace indeed, but not as a Red one; because it is simply according to the blind drift of our industrial development to expect in America at last much the same economic system as that imposed by violence upon Russia in 1917.

Turning to consumption, as the grand end which justifies the evil of modern labor, we find that we have been deceived. We have more time in which to consume, and many more products to be consumed. But the tempo of our labors communicates itself to our satisfactions, and these also become brutal and hurried. The constitution of the natural man probably does not permit him to shorten his labor-time and enlarge his consuming-time indefinitely. He has to pay the penalty in satiety and aimlessness. The modern man has lost his sense of vocation.

Religion can hardly expect to flourish in an industrial society. Religion is our submission to the general intention of a nature that is fairly inscrutable; it is the sense of our rôle as creatures within it. But nature industrialized, transformed into cities and artificial habitations, manufactured into commodities, is no longer nature but a highly simplified picture of nature. We receive the illusion of having power over nature, and lose the sense of nature as something mysterious and contingent. The God of nature under these conditions is merely an amiable expression, a superfluity, and the philosophical understanding ordinarily carried in the religious experience is not there for us to have.

Nor do the arts have a proper life under industrialism, with the general decay of sensibility which attends it. Art depends, in general, like religion, on a right attitude to nature; and in particular on a free and disinterested observation of nature that occurs only in leisure. Neither the creation nor the understanding of works of art is possible in an industrial age except by some local and unlikely suspension of the industrial drive.

The amenities of life also suffer under the curse of a strictly-business or industrial civilization. They consist in such practices as manners, conversation, hospitality, sympathy, family life, romantic love—in the social exchanges which reveal and develop sensibility in human affairs. If religion and the arts are founded on right relations of man-to-nature, these are founded on right relations of man-to-man.

Apologists of industrialism are even inclined to admit that its actual processes may have upon its victims the spiritual effects just described. But they think that all can be made right by extraordinary educational efforts, by all sorts of cultural institutions and endowments. They would cure the poverty of the contemporary spirit by hiring experts to instruct it in spite of itself in the historic culture. But salvation is hardly to be encountered on that road. The trouble with the life-pattern is to be located at its economic base, and we cannot rebuild it by pouring in soft materials from the top. The young men and women in colleges, for example, if they are already placed in a false way of life, cannot make more than an inconsequential acquaintance with the arts and humanities transmitted to them. Or else the understanding of these arts and humanities will but make them the more wretched in their own destitution.

. . .

The tempo of the industrial life is fast, but that is not the worst of it; it is accelerating. The ideal is not merely some set form of industrialism, with so many stable industries, but industrial progress, or an incessant extension of industrialization. It never proposes a specific goal; it initiates the infinite series. We have not merely capitalized certain industries; we have capitalized the laboratories and inventors, and undertaken to employ all the labor-saving devices that come out of them. But a fresh labor-saving device introduced into an industry does not emancipate the laborers in that industry so much as it evicts them. Applied at the expense of agriculture, for example, the new processes have reduced the part of the population supporting itself upon the soil to a smaller and smaller fraction. Of course no single labor-saving process is fatal; it brings on a period of unemployed labor and unemployed capital, but soon a new industry is devised which will put them both to work again, and a new commodity is thrown upon the market. The laborers were sufficiently embarrassed in the meantime, but, according to the theory, they will eventually be taken care of. It is now the public which is embarrassed; it feels obligated to purchase a commodity for which it had expressed no desire, but it is invited to make its budget equal to the strain. All might yet be well, and stability and comfort might again obtain, but for this: partly because of industrial ambitions and partly because the repressed creative impulse must break out somewhere, there will be a stream of further labor-saving devices in all industries, and the cycle will have to be repeated over and over. The result is an increasing disadjustment and instability.

It is an inevitable consequence of industrial progress that production greatly outruns the rate of natural consumption. To overcome the disparity, the producers, disguised as the pure idealists of progress, must coerce and wheedle the public into being loyal and steady consumers, in order to keep the machines running. So the rise of modern advertising—along with its twin, personal salesmanship—is the most significant development of our industrialism. Advertising means to persuade the consumers to want exactly what the applied sciences are able to furnish them. It consults the happiness of the consumer no more than it consulted the happiness of the laborer. It is the great effort of a false economy of life to approve itself. But its task grows more difficult every day.

It is strange, of course, that a majority of men anywhere could ever as with one mind become enamored of industrialism: a system that has so little regard for individual wants. There is evidently a kind of thinking that rejoices in setting up a social objective which has no relation to the individual. Men are prepared to sacrifice their private dignity and happiness to an abstract social ideal, and without asking whether the social ideal produces the welfare of any individual man whatsoever. But this is absurd. The responsibility of men is for their own welfare and that of their neighbors; not for the hypothetical welfare of some fabulous creature called society.

Opposed to the industrial society is the agrarian, which does not stand in particular need of definition. An agrarian society is hardly one that has no use at all for industries, for professional vocations, for scholars and artists, and for the life of cities. Technically, perhaps, an agrarian society is one in which agriculture is the leading vocation, whether for wealth, for pleasure, or for prestige—a form of labor that is pursued with intelligence and leisure, and that becomes the model to which the other forms approach as well as they may. But an agrarian regime will be secured readily enough where the superfluous industries are not allowed to rise against it. The theory of agrarianism is that the culture of the soil is the best and most sensitive of vocations, and that therefore it should have the economic preference and enlist the maximum number of workers.

These principles do not intend to be very specific in proposing any practical measures. How may the little agrarian community resist the Chamber of Commerce of its county seat, which is always trying to import some foreign industry that cannot be assimilated to the life-pattern of the community? Just what must the Southern leaders do to defend the traditional Southern life? How may the Southern and the Western agrarians unite for effective action? Should the agrarian forces try to capture the Democratic party, which historically is so closely affiliated with the defense of individualism, the small community, the state, the South? Or must the agrarians—even the Southern ones—abandon the Democratic party to its fate and try a new one? What legislation could most profitably be championed by the powerful agrarians in the Senate of the United States? What anti-industrial measures might promise to stop the advances of industrialism, or even undo some of them, with the least harm to those concerned? What policy should be pursued by the educators who have tradition at heart? These and many other questions are of the greatest importance, but they cannot be answered here.

For, in conclusion, this much is clear: If a community, or a section, or a race, or an age, is groaning under industrialism, and well aware that it is an evil dispensation, it must find the way to throw it off. To think that this cannot be done is pusillanimous. And if the whole community, section, race, or age thinks it cannot be done, then it has simply lost its political genius and doomed itself to impotence.

WILLIAM FAULKNER

(1897–1962)

Writing in 1953 to a young woman who was his friend, William Faulkner declared of himself and the books he had written that "now I realize for the first time what an amazing gift I had: uneducated in every formal sense, without even very literate, let alone literary, companions, yet to have made the things I made. I don't know where it came from. I don't know why God or gods or whoever it was, selected me to be the vessel. Believe me, this is not humility, false modesty: it is simply amazement. I wonder if you have ever had that thought about the work and the country man whom you know as Bill Faulkner —what little connection there seems to be between them."

William Faulkner was the foremost Southern writer of his century and one of the greatest American literary artists. He was born in New Albany, Mississippi, of a family that earlier had been prominent in the history of his state. The theme of "decline and fall," so pronounced in Faulkner's writings about the Sartoris and Compson families of Yoknapatawpha County, was greatly drawn from his own family's experience. His great-grandfather, Colonel William Clark Falkner, was a Confederate officer, railroad builder, politician, and author of several novels and other books. As the "Old Colonel" he figures in several of Faulkner's books and stories. His grandfather, the "Young Colonel," John Wesley Thompson Falkner, was a businessman, banker, and political figure. Faulkner's father, Murry Falkner, was less successful; at various times he was a railroad conductor, operator of a livery stable, and treasurer of the University of Mississippi. Three years after William Faulkner's birth (he added the "u" to his name when he began writing), the family moved to Oxford, Mississippi, where Faulkner grew up and resided for most of his life.

Faulkner attended high school in Oxford, read widely, and in 1918 enlisted in the Royal Air Force. He underwent cadet training in Canada but the war ended before he actually began flight training. Returning to Oxford he was admitted to the University of Mississippi even though he did not have a high school diploma. For several years he took courses there, yet his real interest was in writing. During the early 1920s he produced a number of poems and worked at various jobs, including university postmaster. In 1924, with the help of his friend and literary mentor Phil Stone, a book of his poems, *The Marble Faun,* was published. In 1925 he went to live in New Orleans, where he wrote newspaper sketches and became friends with the novelist Sherwood Anderson. He wrote his first novel there, *Soldier's Pay,* which was published the following year. Meanwhile he went on a three-month trip to Europe, and after his return wrote another novel, *Mosquitoes* (1927).

With his third novel, originally entitled *Flags in the Dust,* he discovered his true subject matter; the life and milieu of his mythical Yoknapatawpha County, based strongly upon his home territory of Oxford and Jefferson County, Mississippi. Shortened and named *Sartoris,* this work was published in 1929. In the same year *The Sound and the Fury* appeared, the first of his major works of fiction. Meanwhile he married his childhood sweetheart, Estelle Oldham, after her divorce from her first husband. In 1930 he published *As I Lay Dying.* With *Sanctuary* (1931), written first as a shocker then revised, he achieved his first popular success, acquiring a reputation as a writer about violence, decadence, and sadism. In 1932 he wrote *Light in August;* in that year he began the first of what would be frequent periods as a scriptwriter in Hollywood.

During the 1930s and early 1940s he produced numerous short stories for the *Saturday Evening Post* and other magazines as well as a number of novels, including some of his finest: *Pylon* (1935), *Absalom, Absalom!* (1936), *The Unvanquished* (1938), *The Wild Palms* (1939), *The Hamlet* (1940), and *Go Down, Moses* (1942). For most of this time Faulkner was hard pressed for money; his work sold poorly and the necessity of turning out magazine fiction and spending long periods in Hollywood made it increasingly difficult for him to do what he most wanted: to work uninterrupted on novels for sustained periods. Not until 1946, when the critic Malcolm Cowley edited *The Portable Faulkner,* a carefully selected presentation of his work, did he begin to receive the widespread critical attention and an income from his fiction that would enable him to concentrate on his writing. *Intruder in the Dust* (1948) sold well. In 1950 his international fame was evidenced when he was awarded the Nobel Prize for Literature. The novels he wrote during the 1950s, *Requiem for a Nun* (1951), *A Fable* (1955), *The Town* (1957), and *The Mansion* (1959) did not add materially to his fictional achievement. In 1962 he published a comic novel, *The Reivers,* which in important ways represented a return to his old form. He died that July, barely a month after the book appeared.

WILLIAM FAULKNER

Faulkner's enduring fame rests on the series of Yoknapatawpha novels that he published beginning in 1929 and extending through the early 1940s. Drawing imaginatively upon the life he knew best, with creative roots set pervasively in the history of his family and his native locale, he made of his mythical county a cockpit in which the passions, loyalties, aspirations, and accomplishments of the human condition are reenacted, in tragedy and comedy, in fiction that, while often experimental in technique, is traditional in its moral ordering of experience. His work is deeply historical; what men and women have done and been in the past has inescapable significance for the present. From the time when the earliest white settlers appeared in the new country and bartered or otherwise secured the land from its Indian inhabitants, Faulkner's Yoknapatawpha saga chronicles the events of the generations on the land. The rise to prominence of the First Families, the Compsons, Sartorises, and DeSpains who provided the antebellum leadership, as well as the coming of ruthless and ambitious outsiders such as Thomas Sutpen, is linked indissolubly with the heritage of human slavery and the ownership of property. The Civil War and the downfall of the Old Order; the travail of Reconstruction; the rise of the nondescript family of Snopeses, a rapacious, cunning, amoral clan of poor whites, to wealth and power; the failure of the old aristocratic families to provide moral guidance and ethical leadership in changed times and the drift of the later generations into weakness and decay —all are recounted as stages in the endless struggle of a human community to endure and adapt to new demands and opportunities. The plain folk who farm their lands and seek to establish and sustain themselves in good times and bad are not neglected; Faulkner's Southland is by no means composed exclusively of aristocrats, lower-class whites, and blacks on the land.

Among the foremost of Faulkner's concerns throughout his work is the presence of black people in Yoknapatawpha County and the complex heritage of guilt and human definition that this presence has meant for the whites. Unlike those earlier white Southern authors who assumed confidently that they knew and understood black Southerners, Faulkner concentrated upon the difficulty of doing so, dramatizing the struggle of whites to perceive the humanity of blacks and acknowledge the injustice accompanying their failure to do so. In the novelist Ralph Ellison's words, "He has been more willing perhaps than any other artist to start with the stereotype, accept it as true, and then seek out the human truth which it hides. Perhaps his is the example for our [black] writers to follow, for in his work technique has been put once more to the task of creating value."

With Faulkner, technique is seldom or ever an end in itself. No matter how experimentally and innovatively he uses such devices as stream of consciousness, time shifts, montage, and other rhetorical techniques, he always places them in the service of storytelling. His virtuoso use of language and his willingness to construct sentences and paragraphs of astounding and sometimes bewildering complexity are all part of his struggle to represent the full dimensions of experience, to leave nothing out that would authenticate his rendition of human consciousness in time. Like other great innovative literary artists, he has been forced to push beyond the accepted conventions of storytelling to communicate his perceptions of reality, and consequently we have had to learn how to read him. He has drawn upon some of the most advanced and complex psychological and aesthetic insights of his time, making powerful use of the perceptions of other great artists and thinkers, but always for the purpose of telling his stories as accurately and as completely as possible.

The fictional universe he created in his Yoknapatawpha County is based on what he termed the old verities—"love and honor and pity and pride and compassion and sacrifice." Employing the technical resources of a major literary imagination to explore and delineate the meaning of the experience he knew best, he used language to reveal the moral ordering of his little "postage-stamp's worth" of Mississippi soil. As his fellow Southern novelist Robert Penn Warren wrote of him, "James Joyce went forth from Ireland to forge, as he put it, in the works of his hero Stephen Dedalus, the conscience of his race. Faulkner did a more difficult thing. To forge the conscience of his race, he stayed in his native spot and, in his soul, in vice and in virtue, re-enacted the history of that race."

THAT EVENING SUN

I

Monday is no different from any other weekday in Jefferson now. The streets are paved now, and the telephone and electric companies are cutting down more and more of the shade trees—the water oaks, the maples and locusts and elms—to make room for iron poles bearing clusters of bloated and ghostly and bloodless grapes, and we have a city laundry which makes the rounds on Monday morning, gathering the bundles of clothes into bright-colored, specially-made motor cars: the soiled wearing of a whole week now flees apparitionlike behind alert and irritable electric horns, with a long diminishing noise of rubber and asphalt like tearing silk, and even the Negro women who still take in white people's washing after the old custom, fetch and deliver it in automobiles.

But fifteen years ago, on Monday morning the quiet, dusty, shady streets would be full of Negro women with, balanced on their steady, turbaned heads, bundles of clothes tied up in sheets, almost as large as cotton bales, carried so without touch of hand between the kitchen door of the white house and the blackened washpot beside a cabin door in Negro Hollow.

Nancy would set her bundle on the top of her head, then upon the bundle in turn she would set the black straw sailor hat which she wore winter and summer. She was tall, with a high, sad face sunken a little where her teeth were missing. Sometimes we would go a part of the way down the lane and across the pasture with her, to watch the balanced bundle and the hat that never bobbed nor wavered, even when she walked down into the ditch and up the other side and stooped through the fence. She would go down on her hands and knees and crawl through the gap, her head rigid, uptilted, the bundle steady as a rock or a balloon, and rise to her feet again and go on.

Sometimes the husbands of the washing women would fetch and deliver the clothes, but Jesus never did that for Nancy, even before father told him to stay away from our house, even when Dilsey was sick and Nancy would come to cook for us.

And then about half the time we'd have to go down the lane to Nancy's cabin and tell her to come on and cook breakfast. We would stop at the ditch, because father told us to not have anything to do with Jesus—he was a short black man, with a razor scar down his face—and we would throw rocks at Nancy's house until she came to the door, leaning her head around it without any clothes on.

"What yawl mean, chunking my house?" Nancy said. "What you little devils mean?"

"Father says for you to come on and get breakfast," Caddy said. "Father says it's over a half an hour now, and you've got to come this minute."

"I aint studying no breakfast," Nancy said. "I going to get my sleep out."

"I bet you're drunk," Jason said. "Father says you're drunk. Are you drunk, Nancy?"

"Who says I is?" Nancy said. "I got to get my sleep out. I aint studying no breakfast."

So after a while we quit chunking the cabin and went back home. When she finally came, it was too late for me to go to school. So we thought it was whisky until that day they arrested her again and they were taking her to jail and they passed Mr Stovall. He was the cashier in the bank and a deacon in the Baptist church, and Nancy began to say:

"When you going to pay me, white man? When you going to pay me, white man? It's been three times now since you paid me a cent—" Mr Stovall knocked her down, but she kept on saying, "When you going to pay me, white man? It's been three times now since—" until Mr Stovall kicked her in the mouth with his heel and the marshal caught Mr Stovall back, and Nancy lying in the street, laughing. She turned her head and spat out some blood and teeth and said, "It's been three times now since he paid me a cent."

That was how she lost her teeth, and all that day they told about Nancy and Mr Stovall, and all that night the ones that passed the jail could hear Nancy singing and yelling. They could see her hands holding to the window bars, and a lot of them stopped along the fence, listening to her and to the jailer trying to make her stop. She didn't shut up until almost daylight, when the jailer began to hear a bumping and scraping upstairs and he went up there and found Nancy hanging from the window bar. He said that it was cocaine and not whisky, because no nigger would try to commit suicide unless he was full of cocaine, because a nigger full of cocaine wasn't a nigger any longer.

The jailer cut her down and revived her; then he beat her, whipped her. She had hung herself with her dress. She had fixed it all right, but when they arrested her she didn't have on anything except a dress and so she didn't have anything to tie her hands with and she couldn't make her hands let go of the window ledge. So the jailer heard the noise and ran up there and found Nancy hanging from the window, stark naked, her belly already swelling out a little, like a little balloon.

When Dilsey was sick in her cabin and Nancy was cooking for us, we could see her apron swelling out; that was before father told Jesus to stay away from the house. Jesus was in the kitchen, sitting behind the stove, with his razor scar on his black face like a piece of dirty string. He said it was a watermelon that Nancy had under her dress.

"It never come off of your vine, though," Nancy said.

"Off of what vine?" Caddy said.

"I can cut down the vine it did come off of," Jesus said.

"What makes you want to talk like that before these chillen?" Nancy said. "Whyn't you go on to work? You done et. You want Mr Jason to catch you hanging around his kitchen, talking that way before these chillen?"

"Talking what way?" Caddy said. "What vine?"

"I cant hang around white man's kitchen," Jesus said. "But white man can hang around mine. White man can come in my house, but I cant stop him. When white man want to come in my house, I aint got no house. I cant stop him, but he cant kick me outen it. He cant do that."

Dilsey was still sick in her cabin. Father told Jesus to stay off our place. Dilsey was still sick. It was a long time. We were in the library after supper.

"Isn't Nancy through in the kitchen yet?" mother said. "It seems to me that she has had plenty of time to have finished the dishes."

"Let Quentin go and see," father said. "Go and see if Nancy is through, Quentin. Tell her she can go on home."

I went to the kitchen. Nancy was through. The dishes were put away and the fire was out. Nancy was sitting in a chair, close to the cold stove. She looked at me.

"Mother wants to know if you are through," I said.

"Yes," Nancy said. She looked at me. "I done finished." She looked at me.

"What is it?" I said. "What is it?"

"I aint nothing but a nigger," Nancy said. "It aint none of my fault."

She looked at me, sitting in the chair before the cold stove, the sailor hat on her head. I went back to the library. It was the cold stove and all, when you think of a kitchen being warm and busy and cheerful. And with a cold stove and the dishes all put away, and nobody wanting to eat at that hour.

"Is she through?" mother said.

"She's not doing anything. She's through."

"I'll go and see," father said.

"Maybe she's waiting for Jesus to come and take her home," Caddy said.

"Jesus is gone," I said. Nancy told us how one morning she woke up and Jesus was gone.

"He quit me," Nancy said. "Done gone to Memphis, I reckon. Dodging them city *po*-lice for a while, I reckon."

"And a good riddance," father said. "I hope he stays there."

"Nancy's scaired of the dark," Jason said.

"So are you," Caddy said.

"I'm not," Jason said.

"Scairy cat," Caddy said.

"I'm not," Jason said.

"You, Candace!" mother said. Father came back.

"I am going to walk down the lane with Nancy," he said. "She says that Jesus is back."

"Has she seen him?" mother said.

"No. Some Negro sent her word that he was back in town. I wont be long."

"You'll leave me alone, to take Nancy home?" mother said. "Is her safety more precious to you than mine?"

"I wont be long," father said.

"You'll leave these children unprotected, with that Negro about?"

"I'm going too," Caddy said. "Let me go, Father."

"What would he do with them, if he were unfortunate enough to have them?" father said.

"I want to go, too," Jason said.

"Jason!" mother said. She was speaking to father. You could tell that by the way she said the name. Like she believed that all day father had been trying to think of doing the thing she wouldn't like the most, and that she knew all the time that after a while he would think of it. I stayed quiet, because father and I both knew that mother would want him to make me stay with her if she just thought of it in time. So father didn't look at me. I was the oldest. I was nine and Caddy was seven and Jason was five.

"Nonsense," father said. "We wont be long."

Nancy had her hat on. We came to the lane. "Jesus always been good to me," Nancy said. "Whenever he had two dollars, one of them was mine." We walked in the lane. "If I can just get through the lane," Nancy said, "I be all right then."

The lane was always dark. "This is where Jason got scared on Hallowe'en," Caddy said.

"I didn't," Jason said.

"Cant Aunt Rachel do anything with him?" father said. Aunt Rachel was old. She lived in a cabin beyond Nancy's, by herself. She had white hair and she smoked a pipe in the door, all day long; she didn't work any more. They said she was Jesus' mother. Sometimes she said she was and sometimes she said she wasn't any kin to Jesus.

"Yes, you did," Caddy said. "You were scairder than Frony. You were scairder than T.P. even. Scairder than niggers."

"Cant nobody do nothing with him," Nancy said. "He say I done woke up the devil in him and aint but one thing going to lay it down again."

"Well, he's gone now," father said. "There's nothing for you to be afraid of now. And if you'd just let white men alone."

"Let what white men alone?" Caddy said. "How let them alone?"

"He aint gone nowhere," Nancy said. "I can feel him. I can feel him now, in this lane. He hearing us talk, every word, hid somewhere, waiting. I aint seen him, and I aint going to see him again but once more, with that razor in his mouth. That razor on that string down his back, inside his shirt. And then I aint going to be even surprised."

"I wasn't scaired," Jason said.

"If you'd behave yourself, you'd have kept out of this," father said. "But it's all right now. He's probably in St. Louis now. Probably got another wife by now and forgot all about you."

"If he has, I better not find out about it," Nancy said. "I'd stand there right over them, and every time he wropped her, I'd cut that arm off. I'd cut his head off and I'd slit her belly and I'd shove—"

"Hush," father said.

"Slit whose belly, Nancy?" Caddy said.

"I wasn't scaired," Jason said. "I'd walk right down this lane by myself."

"Yah," Caddy said. "You wouldn't dare to put your foot down in it if we were not here too."

II

Dilsey was still sick, so we took Nancy home every night until mother said, "How much longer is this going on? I to be left alone in this big house while you take home a frightened Negro?"

We fixed a pallet in the kitchen for Nancy. One night we waked up, hearing the sound. It was not singing and it was not crying, coming up the dark stairs. There was a light in mother's room and we heard father going down the hall, down the back stairs, and Caddy and I went into the hall. The floor was cold. Our toes curled away from it while we listened to the sound. It was like singing and it wasn't like singing, like the sounds that Negroes make.

Then it stopped and we heard father going down the back stairs, and we went to the head of the stairs. Then the sound began again, in the stairway, not loud, and we could see Nancy's eyes halfway up the stairs, against the wall. They looked like cat's eyes do, like a big cat against the wall, watching us. When we came down the steps to where she was, she quit making the sound again, and we stood there until father came back up from the kitchen, with his pistol in his hand. He went back down with Nancy and they came back with Nancy's pallet.

We spread the pallet in our room. After the light in mother's room went off, we could see Nancy's eyes again. "Nancy," Caddy whispered, "are you asleep, Nancy?"

Nancy whispered something. It was oh or no, I dont know which. Like nobody had made it, like it came from nowhere and went nowhere, until it was like Nancy was not there at all; that I had looked so hard at her eyes on the stairs that they had got printed on my eyeballs, like the sun does when you have closed your eyes and there is no sun. "Jesus," Nancy whispered. "Jesus."

"Was it Jesus?" Caddy said. "Did he try to come into the kitchen?"

"Jesus," Nancy said. Like this: Jeeeeeeeeeeeeeeeesus, until the sound went out, like a match or a candle does.

"It's the other Jesus she means," I said.

"Can you see us, Nancy?" Caddy whispered. "Can you see our eyes too?"

"I aint nothing but a nigger," Nancy said. "God knows, God knows."

"What did you see down there in the kitchen?" Caddy whispered. "What tried to get in?"

"God knows," Nancy said. We could see her eyes. "God knows."

Dilsey got well. She cooked dinner. "You'd better stay in bed a day or two longer," father said.

"What for?" Dilsey said. "If I had been a day later, this place would be to rack and ruin. Get on out of here now, and let me get my kitchen straight again."

Dilsey cooked supper too. And that night, just before dark, Nancy came into the kitchen.

"How do you know he's back?" Dilsey said. "You aint seen him."

"Jesus is a nigger," Jason said.

"I can feel him," Nancy said. "I can feel him laying yonder in the ditch."

"Tonight?" Dilsey said. "Is he there tonight?"

"Dilsey's a nigger too," Jason said.

"You try to eat something," Dilsey said.

"I dont want nothing," Nancy said.

"I aint a nigger," Jason said.

"Drink some coffee," Dilsey said. She poured a cup of coffee for Nancy. "Do you know he's out there tonight? How come you know it's tonight?"

"I know," Nancy said. "He's there, waiting. I know. I done lived with him too long. I know what he is fixing to do fore he know it himself."

"Drink some coffee," Dilsey said. Nancy held the cup to her mouth and blew into the cup. Her mouth pursed out like a spreading adder's, like a rubber mouth, like she had blown all the color out of her lips with blowing the coffee.

"I aint a nigger," Jason said. "Are you a nigger, Nancy?"

"I hellborn, child," Nancy said. "I wont be nothing soon. I going back where I come from soon."

III

She began to drink the coffee. While she was drinking, holding the cup in both hands, she began to make the sound again. She made the sound into the cup and the coffee sploshed out onto her hands and her dress. Her eyes looked at us and she sat there, her elbows on her knees, holding the cup in both hands, looking at us across the wet cup, making the sound. "Look at Nancy," Jason said. "Nancy cant cook for us now. Dilsey's got well now."

"You hush up," Dilsey said. Nancy held the cup in both hands, looking at us, making the sound, like there were two of them: one looking at us and the other making the sound. "Whyn't you let Mr Jason telefoam the marshal?" Dilsey said. Nancy stopped then, holding the cup in her long brown hands. She tried to drink some coffee again, but it sploshed out of the cup, onto her hands and her dress, and she put the cup down. Jason watched her.

"I cant swallow it," Nancy said. "I swallows but it wont go down me."

"You go down to the cabin," Dilsey said. "Frony will fix you a pallet and I'll be there soon."

"Wont no nigger stop him," Nancy said.

"I aint a nigger," Jason said. "Am I, Dilsey?"

"I reckon not," Dilsey said. She looked at Nancy. "I dont reckon so. What you going to do, then?"

Nancy looked at us. Her eyes went fast, like she was afraid there wasn't time to look, without hardly moving at all. She looked at us, at all three of us at one time. "You member that night I stayed in yawls' room?" she said. She told about how we waked up early the next morning, and played. We had to play quiet, on her pallet, until father woke up and it was time to get breakfast. "Go and ask your maw to let me stay here tonight," Nancy said. "I wont need no pallet. We can play some more."

Caddy asked mother. Jason went too. "I cant have Negroes sleeping in the bedrooms," mother said. Jason cried. He cried until mother said he couldn't have any dessert for three days if he didn't stop. Then Jason said he would stop if Dilsey would make a chocolate cake. Father was there.

"Why dont you do something about it?" mother said. "What do we have officers for?"

"Why is Nancy afraid of Jesus?" Caddy said. "Are you afraid of father, mother?"

"What could the officers do?" father said. "If Nancy hasn't seen him, how could the officers find him?"

"Then why is she afraid?" mother said.

"She says he is there. She says she knows he is there tonight."

"Yet we pay taxes," mother said. "I must wait here alone in this big house while you take a Negro woman home."

"You know that I am not lying outside with a razor," father said.

"I'll stop if Dilsey will make a chocolate cake," Jason said. Mother told us to go out and father said he didn't know if Jason would get a chocolate cake or not, but he knew what Jason was going to get in about a minute. We went back to the kitchen and told Nancy.

"Father said for you to go home and lock the door, and you'll be all right," Caddy said. "All right from what, Nancy? Is Jesus mad at you?" Nancy was holding the coffee cup in her hands again, her elbows on her knees and her hands holding the cup between her knees. She was looking into the cup. "What have you done that made Jesus mad?" Caddy said. Nancy let the cup go. It didn't break on the floor, but the coffee spilled out, and Nancy sat there with her hands still making the shape of the cup. She began to make the sound again, not loud. Not singing and not unsinging. We watched her.

"Here," Dilsey said. "You quit that, now. You get aholt of yourself. You wait here. I going to get Versh to walk home with you." Dilsey went out.

We looked at Nancy. Her shoulders kept shaking, but she quit making the sound. We watched her. "What's Jesus going to do to you?" Caddy said. "He went away."

Nancy looked at us. "We had fun that night I stayed in yawls' room, didn't we?"

"I didn't," Jason said. "I didn't have any fun."

"You were asleep in mother's room," Caddy said. "You were not there."

"Let's go down to my house and have some more fun," Nancy said.

"Mother wont let us," I said. "It's too late now."

"Dont bother her," Nancy said. "We can tell her in the morning. She wont mind."

"She wouldn't let us," I said.

"Dont ask her now," Nancy said. "Dont bother her now."

"She didn't say we couldn't go," Caddy said.

"We didn't ask," I said.

"If you go, I'll tell," Jason said.

"We'll have fun," Nancy said. "They won't mind, just to my house. I been working for yawl a long time. They won't mind."

"I'm not afraid to go," Caddy said. "Jason is the one that's afraid. He'll tell."

"I'm not," Jason said.

"Yes, you are," Caddy said. "You'll tell."

"I won't tell," Jason said. "I'm not afraid."

"Jason ain't afraid to go with me," Nancy said. "Is you, Jason?"

"Jason is going to tell," Caddy said. The lane was dark. We passed the pasture gate. "I bet if something was to jump out from behind that gate, Jason would holler."

"I wouldn't," Jason said. We walked down the lane. Nancy was talking loud.

"What are you talking so loud for, Nancy?" Caddy said.

"Who; me?" Nancy said. "Listen at Quentin and Caddy and Jason saying I'm talking loud."

"You talk like there was five of us here," Caddy said. "You talk like father was here too."

"Who; me talking loud, Mr. Jason?" Nancy said.

"Nancy called Jason 'Mister,' " Caddy said.

"Listen how Caddy and Quentin and Jason talk," Nancy said.

"We're not talking loud," Caddy said. "You're the one that's talking like father—"

"Hush," Nancy said; "hush, Mr. Jason."

"Nancy called Jason 'Mister' aguh—"

"Hush," Nancy said. She was talking loud when we crossed the ditch and stooped through the fence where she used to stoop through with the clothes on her head. Then we came to her house. We were going fast then. She opened the door. The smell of the house was like the lamp and the smell of Nancy was like the wick, like they were waiting for one another to begin to smell. She lit the lamp and closed the door and put the bar up. Then she quit talking loud, looking at us.

"What're we going to do?" Caddy said.

"What do yawl want to do?" Nancy said.

"You said we would have some fun," Caddy said.

There was something about Nancy's house; something you could smell besides Nancy and the house. Jason smelled it, even. "I don't want to stay here," he said. "I want to go home."

"Go home, then," Caddy said.

"I don't want to go by myself," Jason said.

"We're going to have some fun," Nancy said.

"How?" Caddy said.

Nancy stood by the door. She was looking at us, only it was like she had emptied her eyes, like she had quit using them. "What do you want to do?" she said.

"Tell us a story," Caddy said. "Can you tell a story?"

"Yes," Nancy said.

"Tell it," Caddy said. We looked at Nancy. "You don't know any stories."

"Yes," Nancy said. "Yes, I do."

She came and sat in a chair before the hearth. There was a little fire there. Nancy built it up, when it was already hot inside. She built a good blaze. She told a story. She talked like her eyes looked, like her eyes watching us and her voice talking to us did not belong to her. Like she was living somewhere else, waiting somewhere else. She was outside the cabin. Her voice was inside and the shape of her, the Nancy that could stoop under a barbed wire fence with a bundle of clothes balanced on her head as though without weight, like a balloon, was there. But that was all. "And so this here queen come walking up to the ditch, where that bad man was hiding. She was walking up to the ditch, and she say, 'If I can just get past this here ditch,' was what she say . . ."

"What ditch?" Caddy said. "A ditch like that one out there? Why did a queen want to go into a ditch?"

"To get to her house," Nancy said. She looked at us. "She had to cross the ditch to get into her house quick and bar the door."

"Why did she want to go home and bar the door?" Caddy said.

IV

Nancy looked at us. She quit talking. She looked at us. Jason's legs stuck straight out of his pants where he sat on Nancy's lap. "I don't think that's a good story," he said. "I want to go home."

"Maybe we had better," Caddy said. She got up from the floor. "I bet they are looking for us right now." She went toward the door.

"No," Nancy said. "Don't open it." She got up quick and passed Caddy. She didn't touch the door, the wooden bar.

"Why not?" Caddy said.

"Come back to the lamp," Nancy said. "We'll have fun. You don't have to go."

"We ought to go," Caddy said. "Unless we have a lot of fun." She and Nancy came back to the fire, the lamp.

"I want to go home," Jason said. "I'm going to tell."

"I know another story," Nancy said. She stood close to the lamp. She looked at Caddy, like when your eyes look up at a stick balanced on your nose. She had to look down to see Caddy, but her eyes looked like that, like when you are balancing a stick.

"I won't listen to it," Jason said. "I'll bang on the floor."

"It's a good one," Nancy said. "It's better than the other one."

"What's it about?" Caddy said. Nancy was standing by the lamp. Her hand was on the lamp, against the light, long and brown.

"Your hand is on that hot globe," Caddy said. "Don't it feel hot to your hand?"

Nancy looked at her hand on the lamp chimney. She took her hand away, slow. She stood there, looking at Caddy, wringing her long hand as though it were tied to her wrist with a string.

"Let's do something else," Caddy said.

"I want to go home," Jason said.

"I got some popcorn," Nancy said. She looked at Caddy and then at Jason and then at me and then at Caddy again. "I got some popcorn."

"I don't like popcorn," Jason said. "I'd rather have candy."

Nancy looked at Jason. "You can hold the popper." She was still wringing her hand; it was long and limp and brown.

"All right," Jason said. "I'll stay a while if I can do that. Caddy can't hold it. I'll want to go home again if Caddy holds the popper."

Nancy built up the fire. "Look at Nancy putting her hands in the fire," Caddy said. "What's the matter with you, Nancy?"

"I got popcorn," Nancy said. "I got some." She took the popper from under the bed. It was broken. Jason began to cry.

"Now we can't have any popcorn," he said.

"We ought to go home, anyway," Caddy said. "Come on, Quentin."

"Wait," Nancy said; "wait. I can fix it. Don't you want to help me fix it?"

"I don't think I want any," Caddy said. "It's too late now."

"You help me, Jason," Nancy said. "Don't you want to help me?"

"No," Jason said. "I want to go home."

"Hush," Nancy said; "hush. Watch. Watch me. I can fix it so Jason can hold it and pop the corn." She got a piece of wire and fixed the popper.

"It won't hold good," Caddy said.

"Yes, it will," Nancy said. "Yawl watch. Yawl help me shell some corn."

The popcorn was under the bed too. We shelled it into the popper and Nancy helped Jason hold the popper over the fire.

"It's not popping," Jason said. "I want to go home."

"You wait," Nancy said. "It'll begin to pop. We'll have fun then." She was sitting close to the fire. The lamp was turned up so high it was beginning to smoke.

"Why don't you turn it down some?" I said.

"It's all right," Nancy said. "I'll clean it. Yawl wait. The popcorn will start in a minute."

"I don't believe it's going to start," Caddy said. "We ought to start home, anyway. They'll be worried."

"No," Nancy said. "It's going to pop. Dilsey will tell um yawl with me. I been working for yawl long time. They won't mind if yawl at my house. You wait, now. It'll start popping any minute now."

Then Jason got some smoke in his eyes and he began to cry. He dropped the popper into the fire. Nancy got a wet rag and wiped Jason's face, but he didn't stop crying.

"Hush," she said. "Hush." But he didn't hush. Caddy took the popper out of the fire.

"It's burned up," she said. "You'll have to get some more popcorn, Nancy."

"Did you put all of it in?" Nancy said.

"Yes," Caddy said. Nancy looked at Caddy. Then she took the popper and opened it and poured the cinders into her apron and began to sort the grains, her hands long and brown, and we watching her.

"Haven't you got any more?" Caddy said.

"Yes," Nancy said; "yes. Look. This here ain't burnt. All we need to do is—"

"I want to go home," Jason said. "I'm going to tell."

"Hush," Caddy said. We all listened. Nancy's head was already turned toward the barred door, her eyes filled with red lamplight. "Somebody is coming," Caddy said.

Then Nancy began to make that sound again, not loud, sitting there above the fire, her long hands dangling between her knees; all of a sudden water began to come out on her face in big drops, running down her face, carrying in each one a little turning ball of firelight like a spark until it dropped off her chin. "She's not crying," I said.

"I ain't crying," Nancy said. Her eyes were closed. "I ain't crying. Who is it?"

"I don't know," Caddy said. She went to the door and looked out. "We've got to go now," she said. "Here comes father."

"I'm going to tell," Jason said. "Yawl made me come."

The water still ran down Nancy's face. She turned in her chair. "Listen. Tell him. Tell him we going to have fun. Tell him I take good care of yawl until in the morning. Tell him to let me come home with yawl and sleep on the floor. Tell him I won't need no pallet. We'll have fun. You member last time how we had so much fun?"

"I didn't have fun," Jason said. "You hurt me. You put smoke in my eyes. I'm going to tell."

V

Father came in. He looked at us. Nancy did not get up.

"Tell him," she said.

"Caddy made us come down here," Jason said. "I didn't want to."

Father came to the fire. Nancy looked up at him. "Can't you go to Aunt Rachel's and stay?" he said. Nancy looked up at father, her hands between her knees. "He's not here," father said. "I would have seen him. There's not a soul in sight."

"He in the ditch," Nancy said. "He waiting in the ditch yonder."

"Nonsense," father said. He looked at Nancy. "Do you know he's there?"

"I got the sign," Nancy said.

"What sign?"

"I got it. It was on the table when I come in. It was a hog-bone, with blood meat still on it, laying by the lamp. He's out there. When yawl walk out that door, I gone."

"Gone where, Nancy?" Caddy said.

"I'm not a tattletale," Jason said.

"Nonsense," father said.

"He out there," Nancy said. "He looking through that window this minute, waiting for yawl to go. Then I gone."

"Nonsense," father said. "Lock up your house and we'll take you on to Aunt Rachel's."

" 'Twont do no good," Nancy said. She didn't look at father now, but he looked down at her, at her long, limp, moving hands. "Putting it off wont do no good."

"Then what do you want to do?" father said.

"I don't know," Nancy said. "I can't do nothing. Just put it off. And that don't do no good. I reckon it belong to me. I reckon what I going to get ain't no more than mine."

"Get what?" Caddy said. "What's yours?"

"Nothing," father said. "You all must get to bed."

"Caddy made me come," Jason said.

"Go on to Aunt Rachel's," father said.

"It won't do no good," Nancy said. She sat before the fire, her elbows on her knees, her long hands between her knees. "When even your own kitchen wouldn't do no good. When even if I was sleeping on the floor in the room with your chillen, and the next morning there I am, and blood—"

"Hush," father said. "Lock the door and put out the lamp and go to bed."

"I scared of the dark," Nancy said. "I scared for it to happen in the dark."

"You mean you're going to sit right here with the lamp lighted?" father said. Then Nancy began to make the sound again, sitting before the fire, her long hands between her knees. "Ah, damnation," father said. "Come along, chillen. It's past bedtime."

"When yawl go home, I gone," Nancy said. She talked quieter now, and her face looked quiet, like her hands. "Anyway, I got my coffin money saved up with Mr. Lovelady." Mr. Lovelady was a short, dirty man who collected the Negro insurance, coming around to the cabins or the kitchens every Saturday morning, to collect fifteen cents. He and his wife lived at the hotel. One morning his wife committed suicide. They had a child, a little girl. He and the child went away. After a week or two he came back alone. We would see him going along the lanes and the back streets on Saturday mornings.

"Nonsense," father said. "You'll be the first thing I'll see in the kitchen tomorrow morning."

"You'll see what you'll see, I reckon," Nancy said. "But it will take the Lord to say what that will be."

VI

We left her sitting before the fire.

"Come and put the bar up," father said. But she didn't move. She didn't look at us again, sitting quietly there between the lamp and the fire. From some distance down the lane we could look back and see her through the open door.

"What, Father?" Caddy said. "What's going to happen?"

"Nothing," father said. Jason was on father's back, so Jason was the tallest of all of us. We went down into the ditch. I looked at it, quiet. I couldn't see much where the moonlight and the shadows tangled.

"If Jesus is hid here, he can see us, cant he?" Caddy said.

"He's not there," father said. "He went away a long time ago."

"You made me come," Jason said, high; against the sky it looked like father had two heads, a little one and a big one. "I didn't want to."

We went up out of the ditch. We could still see Nancy's house and the open door, but we couldn't see Nancy now, sitting before the fire with the door open, because she was tired. "I just done got tired," she said. "I just a nigger. It ain't no fault of mine."

But we could hear her, because she began just after we came up out of the ditch, the sound that was not singing and not unsinging. "Who will do our washing now, Father?" I said.

"I'm not a nigger," Jason said, high and close above father's head.

"You're worse," Caddy said, "you are a tattletale. If something was to jump out, you'd be scairder than a nigger."

"I wouldn't," Jason said.

"You'd cry," Caddy said.

"Caddy," father said.

"I wouldn't!" Jason said.

"Scairy cat," Caddy said.

"Candace!" father said.

WILLIAM FAULKNER

BARN BURNING

The store in which the Justice of the Peace's court was sitting smelled of cheese. The boy, crouched on his nail keg at the back of the crowded room, knew he smelled cheese, and more: from where he sat he could see the ranked shelves close-packed with the solid, squat, dynamic shapes of tin cans whose labels his stomach read, not from the lettering which meant nothing to his mind but from the scarlet devils and the silver curve of fish —this, the cheese which he knew he smelled and the hermetic meat which his intestines believed he smelled coming in intermittent gusts momentary and brief between the other constant one, the smell and sense just a little of fear because mostly of despair and grief, the old fierce pull of blood. He could not see the table where the Justice sat and before which his father and his father's enemy (*our enemy* he thought in that despair; *ourn! mine and hisn both! He's my father!*) stood, but he could hear them, the two of them that is, because his father had said no word yet:

"But what proof have you, Mr. Harris?"

"I told you. The hog got into my corn. I caught it up and sent it back to him. He had no fence that would hold it. I told him so, warned him. The next time I put the hog in my pen. When he came to get it I gave him enough wire to patch up his pen. The next time I put the hog up and kept it. I rode down to his house and saw the wire I gave him still rolled on to the spool in his yard. I told him he could have the hog when he paid me a dollar pound fee. That evening a nigger came with the dollar and got the hog. He was a strange nigger. He said, "He say to tell you wood and hay kin burn." I said, "What?" "That whut he say to tell you," the nigger said. "Wood and hay kin burn." That night my barn burned. I got the stock out but I lost the barn."

"Where is the nigger? Have you got him?"

"He was a strange nigger, I tell you. I don't know what became of him."

"But that's not proof. Don't you see that's not proof?"

"Get that boy up here. He knows." For a moment the boy thought too that the man meant his older brother until Harris said, "Not him. The little one. The boy," and, crouching, small for his age, small and wiry like his father, in patched and faded jeans even too small for him, with straight, uncombed, brown hair and eyes gray and wild as storm scud, he saw the men between himself and the table part and become a lane of grim faces, at the end of which he saw the Justice, a shabby, collarless, graying man in spectacles, beckoning him. He felt no floor under his bare feet; he seemed to walk beneath the palpable weight of the grim turning faces. His father, stiff in his black Sunday coat donned not for the trial but for the moving, did not even look at him. *He aims for me to lie*, he thought, again with that frantic grief and despair. *And I will have to do it.*

"What's your name, boy?" the Justice said.

"Colonel Sartoris Snopes," the boy whispered.

"Hey?" the Justice said. "Talk louder. Colonel Sartoris? I reckon anybody named for Colonel Sartoris in this country can't help but tell the truth, can they?" The boy said nothing. *Enemy! Enemy!* he thought; for a moment he could not even see, could not see that the Justice's face was kindly nor discern that his voice was troubled when he spoke to the man named Harris: "Do you want me to question this boy?" But he could hear, and during those subsequent long seconds while there was absolutely no sound in the crowded little room save that of quiet and intent breathing it was as if he had swung outward at the end of a grape vine, over a ravine, and at the top of the swing had been caught in a prolonged instant of mesmerized gravity, weightless in time.

"Now!" Harris said violently, explosively. "Damnation! Send him out of here!" Now time, the fluid world, rushed beneath him again, the voices coming to him again through the smell of cheese and sealed meat, the fear and despair and the old grief of blood:

"This case is closed. I can't find against you, Snopes, but I can give you advice. Leave this country and don't come back to it."

His father spoke for the first time, his voice cold and harsh, level, without emphasis: "I aim to. I don't figure to stay in a country among people who. . ." he said something unprintable and vile, addressed to no one.

"That'll do," the Justice said. "Take your wagon and get out of this country before dark. Case dismissed."

His father turned, and he followed the stiff black coat, the wiry figure walking a little stiffly from where a Confederate provost's man's musket ball had taken him in the heel on a stolen horse thirty years ago, followed the two backs now, since his older brother had appeared from somewhere in the crowd, no taller than the father but thicker, chewing tobacco steadily, between the two lines of grim-faced men and out of the store and across the worn gallery and down the sagging steps and among the dogs and half-grown boys in the mild May dust, where as he passed a voice hissed:

"Barn Burner!"

Again he could not see, whirling; there was a face in a red haze, moon-like, bigger than the full moon, the owner of it half again his size, he leaping in the red haze toward the face, feeling no blow, feeling no shock when his head struck the earth, scrabbling up and leaping again, feeling no blow this time either and tasting no blood, scrabbling up to see the other boy in full flight and himself already leaping into pursuit as his father's hand jerked him back, the harsh, cold voice speaking above him: "Go get in the wagon."

It stood in a grove of locusts and mulberries across the road. His two hulking sisters in their Sunday dresses and his mother and her sister in calico and sunbonnets were already in it, sitting on and among the sorry residue of the dozen and more movings which even the boy could remember

—the battered stove, the broken beds and chairs, the clock inlaid with mother-of-pearl, which would not run, stopped at some fourteen minutes past two o'clock of a dead and forgotten day and time, which had been his mother's dowry. She was crying, though when she saw him she drew her sleeve across her face and began to descend from the wagon. "Get back," the father said.

"He's hurt. I got to get some water and wash his . . ."

"Get back in the wagon," his father said. He got in too, over the tail-gate. His father mounted to the seat where the older brother already sat and struck the gaunt mules two savage blows with the peeled willow, but without heat. It was not even sadistic; it was exactly that same quality which in later years would cause his descendants to over-run the engine before putting a motor car into motion, striking and reining back in the same movement. The wagon went on, the store with its quiet crowd of grimly watching men dropped behind; a curve in the road hid it. *Forever* he thought. *Maybe he's done satisfied now, now that he has* . . . stopping himself, not to say it aloud even to himself. His mother's hand touched his shoulder.

"Does hit hurt?" she said.

"Naw," he said. "Hit don't hurt. Lemme be."

"Can't you wipe some of the blood off before hit dries?"

"I'll wash to-night," he said. "Lemme be, I tell you."

The wagon went on. He did not know where they were going. None of them ever did or ever asked, because it was always somewhere, always a house of sorts waiting for them a day or two days or even three days away. Likely his father had already arranged to make a crop on another farm before he . . . Again he had to stop himself. He (the father) always did. There was something about his wolflike independence and even courage when the advantage was at least neutral which impressed strangers, as if they got from his latent ravening ferocity not so much a sense of dependability as a feeling that his ferocious conviction in the rightness of his own actions would be of advantage to all whose interest lay with his.

That night they camped, in a grove of oaks and beeches where a spring ran. The nights were still cool and they had a fire against it, of a rail lifted from a nearby fence and cut into lengths—a small fire, neat, niggard almost, a shrewd fire; such fires were his father's habit and custom always, even in freezing weather. Older, the boy might have remarked this and wondered why not a big one; why should not a man who had not only seen the waste and extravagance of war, but who had in his blood an inherent voracious prodigality with material not his own, have burned everything in sight? Then he might have gone a step farther and thought that that was the reason: that niggard blaze was the living fruit of nights passed during those four years in the woods hiding from all men, blue or gray, with his strings of horses (captured horses, he called them). And older still, he might have divined the true reason: that the element of fire spoke to some deep mainspring of his father's being, as the element of steel or of powder spoke to other men, as the one weapon for the preservation of integrity, else breath were not worth the breathing, and hence to be regarded with respect and used with discretion.

But he did not think this now and he had seen those same niggard blazes all his life. He merely ate his supper beside it and was already half asleep over his iron plate when his father called him, and once more he followed the stiff back, the stiff and ruthless limp, up the slope and on to the starlit road where, turning, he could see his father against the stars but without face or depth—a shape black, flat, and bloodless as though cut from tin in the iron folds of the frockcoat which had not been made for him, the voice harsh like tin and without heat like tin:

"You were fixing to tell them. You would have told him." He didn't answer. His father struck him with the flat of his hand on the side of the head, hard but without heat, exactly as he had struck the two mules at the store, exactly as he would strike either of them with any stick in order to kill a horse fly, his voice still without heat or anger: "You're getting to be a man. You got to learn. You got to learn to stick to your own blood or you ain't going to have any blood to stick to you. Do you think either of them, any man there this morning, would? Don't you know all they wanted was a chance to get at me because they knew I had them beat? Eh?" Later, twenty years later, he was to tell himself, "If I had said they wanted only truth, justice, he would have hit me again." But now he said nothing. He was not crying. He just stood there. "Answer me," his father said.

"Yes," he whispered. His father turned.

"Get on to bed. We'll be there tomorrow."

To-morrow they were there. In the early afternoon the wagon stopped before a paintless two-room house identical almost with the dozen others it had stopped before even in the boy's ten years, and again, as on the other dozen occasions, his mother and aunt got down and began to unload the wagon, although his two sisters and his father and brother had not moved.

"Likely hit ain't fitten for hawgs," one of the sisters said.

"Nevertheless, fit it will and you'll hog it and like it," his father said. "Get out of them chairs and help your Ma unload."

The two sisters got down, big, bovine, in a flutter of cheap ribbons; one of them drew from the jumbled wagon bed a battered lantern, the other a worn broom. His father handed the reins to the older son and began to climb stiffly over the wheel. "When they get unloaded, take the team to the barn and feed them." Then he said, and at first the boy thought he was still speaking to his brother: "Come with me."

"Me?" he said.

"Yes," his father said. "You."

"Abner," his mother said. His father paused and looked back—the harsh level stare beneath the shaggy, graying, irascible brows.

"I reckon I'll have a word with the man that aims to begin to-morrow owning me body and soul for the next eight months."

They went back up the road. A week ago—or before last night, that is —he would have asked where they were going, but not now. His father had struck him before last night but never before had he paused afterward to explain why; it was as if the blow and the following calm, outrageous voice still rang, repercussed, divulging nothing to him save the terrible handicap of being young, the light weight of his few years, just heavy enough to prevent his soaring free of the world as it seemed to be ordered but not heavy enough to keep him footed solid in it, to resist it and try to change the course of its events.

Presently he could see the grove of oaks and cedars and the other flowering trees and shrubs where the house would be, though not the house yet. They walked beside a fence massed with honeysuckle and Cherokee roses and came to a gate swinging open between two brick pillars, and now, beyond a sweep of drive, he saw the house for the first time and at that instant he forgot his father and the terror and despair both, and even when he remembered his father again (who had not stopped) the terror and despair did not return. Because, for all the twelve movings, they had sojourned until now in a poor country, a land of small farms and fields and houses, and he had never seen a house like this before. *Hit's big as a courthouse* he thought quietly, with a surge of peace and joy whose reason he could not have thought into words, being too young for that: *They are safe from him. People whose lives are a part of this peace and dignity are beyond his touch, he no more to them than a buzzing wasp: capable of stinging for a little moment but that's all; the spell of this peace and dignity rendering even the barns and stable and cribs which belong to it impervious to the puny flames he might contrive* . . . this, the peace and joy, ebbing for an instant as he looked again at the stiff black back, the stiff and implacable limp of the figure which was not dwarfed by the house, for the reason that it had never looked big anywhere and which now, against the serene columned backdrop, had more than ever that impervious quality of something cut ruthlessly from tin, depthless, as though, sidewise to the sun, it would cast no shadow. Watching him, the boy remarked the absolutely undeviating course which his father held and saw the stiff foot come squarely down in a pile of fresh droppings where a horse had stood in the drive and which his father could have avoided by a simple change of stride. But it ebbed only for a moment, though he could not have thought this into words either, walking on in the spell of the house, which he could even want but without envy, without sorrow, certainly never with that ravening and jealous rage which unknown to him walked in the ironlike black coat before him: *Maybe he will feel it too. Maybe it will even change him now from what maybe he couldn't help but be.*

They crossed the portico. Now he could hear his father's stiff foot as it

came down on the boards with clocklike finality, a sound out of all proportion to the displacement of the body it bore and which was not dwarfed
either by the white door before it, as though it had attained to a sort of
vicious and ravening minimum not to be dwarfed by anything—the flat,
wide, black hat, the formal coat of broadcloth which had once been black
but which had now that friction-glazed greenish cast of the bodies of old
house flies, the lifted sleeve which was too large, the lifted hand like a curled
claw. The door opened so promptly that the boy knew the Negro must have
been watching them all the time, an old man with neat grizzled hair, in a
linen jacket, who stood barring the door with his body, saying, "Wipe yo
foots, white man, fo you come in here. Major ain't home nohow."

"Get out of my way, nigger," his father said, without heat too, flinging
the door back and the Negro also and entering, his hat still on his head.
And now the boy saw the prints of the stiff foot on the doorjamb and saw
them appear on the pale rug behind the machinelike deliberation of the foot
which seemed to bear (or transmit) twice the weight which the body com-
passed. The Negro was shouting, "Miss Lula! Miss Lula!" somewhere
behind them, then the boy, deluged as though by a warm wave by a suave
turn of carpeted stair and a pendant glitter of chandeliers and a mute gleam
of gold frames, heard the swift feet and saw her too, a lady—perhaps he had
never seen her like before either—in a gray, smooth gown with lace at the
throat and an apron tied at the waist and the sleeves turned back, wiping
cake or biscuit dough from her hands with a towel as she came up the hall,
looking not at his father at all but at the tracks on the blond rug with an
expression of incredulous amazement.

"I tried," the Negro cried. "I tole him to . . ."

"Will you please go away?" she said in a shaking voice. "Major de Spain
is not at home. Will you please go away?"

His father had not spoken again. He did not speak again. He did not
even look at her. He just stood stiff in the center of the rug, in his hat, the
shaggy iron-gray brows twitching slightly above the pebble-colored eyes as
he appeared to examine the house with brief deliberation. Then with the
same deliberation he turned; the boy watched him pivot on the good leg
and saw the stiff foot drag round the arc of the turning, leaving a final long
and fading smear. His father never looked at it, he never once looked down
at the rug. The Negro held the door. It closed behind them, upon the hys-
teric and indistinguishable woman-wail. His father stopped at the top of the
steps and scraped his boot clean on the edge of it. At the gate he stopped
again. He stood for a moment, planted stiffly on the stiff foot, looking back
at the house. "Pretty and white, ain't it?" he said. "That's sweat. Nigger
sweat. Maybe it ain't white enough yet to suit him. Maybe he wants to mix
some white sweat with it."

Two hours later the boy was chopping wood behind the house within
which his mother and aunt and the two sisters (the mother and aunt, not the

two girls, he knew that; even at this distance and muffled by walls the flat loud voices of the two girls emanated an incorrigible idle inertia) were setting up the stove to prepare a meal, when he heard the hooves and saw the linen-clad man on a fine sorrel mare, whom he recognized even before he saw the rolled rug in front of the Negro youth following on a fat bay carriage horse—a suffused, angry face vanishing, still at full gallop, beyond the corner of the house where his father and brother were sitting in the two tilted chairs; and a moment later, almost before he could have put the axe down, he heard the hooves again and watched the sorrel mare go back out of the yard, already galloping again. Then his father began to shout one of the sisters' names, who presently emerged backward from the kitchen door dragging the rolled rug along the ground by one end while the other sister walked behind it.

"If you ain't going to tote, go on and set up the wash pot," the first said.

"You, Sarty!" the second shouted. "Set up the wash pot!" His father appeared at the door, framed against that shabbiness, as he had been against that other bland perfection, impervious to either, the mother's anxious face at his shoulder.

"Go on," the father said. "Pick it up." The two sisters stooped, broad, lethargic; stooping, they presented an incredible expanse of pale cloth and a flutter of tawdry ribbons.

"If I thought enough of a rug to have to git hit all the way from France I wouldn't keep hit where folks coming in would have to tromp on hit," the first said. They raised the rug.

"Abner," the mother said. "Let me do it."

"You go back and git dinner," his father said. "I'll tend to this."

From the woodpile through the rest of the afternoon the boy watched them, the rug spread flat in the dust beside the bubbling wash-pot, the two sisters stooping over it with that profound and lethargic reluctance, while the father stood over them in turn, implacable and grim, driving them though never raising his voice again. He could smell the harsh homemade lye they were using; he saw his mother come to the door once and look toward them with an expression not anxious now but very like despair; he saw his father turn, and he fell to with the axe and saw from the corner of his eye his father raise from the ground a flattish fragment of field stone and examine it and return to the pot, and this time his mother actually spoke: "Abner, Abner. Please don't. Please, Abner."

Then he was done too. It was dusk; the whippoorwills had already begun. He could smell coffee from the room where they would presently eat the cold food remaining from the mid-afternoon meal, though when he entered the house he realized they were having coffee again probably because there was a fire on the hearth, before which the rug now lay spread over the backs of the two chairs. The tracks of his father's foot were gone.

Where they had been were now long, water-cloudy scoriations resembling the sporadic course of a lilliputian mowing machine.

It still hung there while they ate the cold food and then went to bed, scattered without order or claim up and down the two rooms, his mother in one bed, where his father would later lie, the older brother in the other, himself, the aunt, and the two sisters on pallets on the floor. But his father was not in bed yet. The last thing the boy remembered was the depthless, harsh silhouette of the hat and coat bending over the rug and it seemed to him that he had not even closed his eyes when the silhouette was standing over him, the fire almost dead behind it, the stiff foot prodding him awake. "Catch up the mule," his father said.

When he returned with the mule his father was standing in the black door, the rolled rug over his shoulder. "Ain't you going to ride?" he said.

"No. Give me your foot."

He bent his knee into his father's hand, the wiry, surprising power flowed smoothly, rising, he rising with it, on to the mule's bare back (they had owned a saddle once; the boy could remember it though not when or where) and with the same effortlessness his father swung the rug up in front of him. Now in the starlight they retraced the afternoon's path, up the dusty road rife with honeysuckle, through the gate and up the black tunnel of the drive to the lightless house, where he sat on the mule and felt the rough warp of the rug drag across his thighs and vanish.

"Don't you want me to help?" he whispered. His father did not answer and now he heard again that stiff foot striking the hollow portico with that wooden and clocklike deliberation, that outrageous overstatement of the weight it carried. The rug, hunched, not flung (the boy could tell that even in the darkness) from his father's shoulder struck the angle of wall and floor with a sound unbelievably loud, thunderous, then the foot again, unhurried and enormous; a light came on in the house and the boy sat, tense, breathing steadily and quietly and just a little fast, though the foot itself did not increase its beat at all, descending the steps now; now the boy could see him.

"Don't you want to ride now?" he whispered. "We kin both ride now," the light within the house altering now, flaring up and sinking. *He's coming down the stairs now,* he thought. He had already ridden the mule up beside the horse block; presently his father was up behind him and he doubled the reins over and slashed the mule across the neck, but before the animal could begin to trot the hard, thin arm came round him, the hard, knotted hand jerking the mule back to a walk.

In the first red rays of the sun they were in the lot, putting plow gear on the mules. This time the sorrel mare was in the lot before he heard it at all, the rider collarless and even bareheaded, trembling, speaking in a shaking voice as the woman in the house had done, his father merely looking up once before stooping again to the hame he was buckling, so that the man on the mare spoke to his stooping back:

"You must realize you have ruined that rug. Wasn't there anybody here, any of your women . . ." he ceased, shaking, the boy watching him, the older brother leaning now in the stable door, chewing, blinking slowly and steadily at nothing apparently. "It cost a hundred dollars. But you never had a hundred dollars. You never will. So I'm going to charge you twenty bushels of corn against your crop. I'll add it in your contract and when you come to the commissary you can sign it. That won't keep Mrs. de Spain quiet but maybe it will teach you to wipe your feet off before you enter her house again."

Then he was gone. The boy looked at his father, who still had not spoken or even looked up again, who was now adjusting the logger-head in the hame.

"Pap," he said. His father looked at him—the inscrutable face, the shaggy brows beneath which the gray eyes glinted coldly. Suddenly the boy went toward him fast, stopping as suddenly. "You done the best you could!" he cried. "If he wanted hit done different why didn't he wait and tell you how? He won't git no twenty bushels! He won't git none! We'll gether hit and hide hit! I kin watch . . ."

"Did you put the cutter back in that straight stock like I told you?"

"No, sir," he said.

"Then go do it."

That was Wednesday. During the rest of that week he worked steadily, at what was within his scope and some which was beyond it, with an industry that did not need to be driven nor even commanded twice; he had this from his mother, with the difference that some at least of what he did he liked to do, such as splitting wood with the half-size axe which his mother and aunt had earned, or saved money somehow, to present him with at Christmas. In company with the two older women (and on one afternoon, even one of the sisters), he built pens for the shoat and the cow which were a part of his father's contract with the landlord, and one afternoon, his father being absent, gone somewhere on one of the mules, he went to the field.

They were running a middle buster now, his brother holding the plow straight while he handled the reins, and walking beside the straining mule, the rich black soil shearing cool and damp against his bare ankles, he thought *Maybe this is the end of it. Maybe even that twenty bushels that seems hard to have to pay for just a rug will be a cheap price for him to stop forever and always from being what he used to be;* thinking, dreaming now, so that his brother had to speak sharply to him to mind the mule: *Maybe he even won't collect the twenty bushels. Maybe it will all add up and balance and vanish—corn, rug, fire; the terror and grief, the being pulled two ways like between two teams of horses—gone, done with for ever and ever.*

Then it was Saturday; he looked up from beneath the mule he was harnessing and saw his father in the black coat and hat. "Not that," his father said. "The wagon gear." And then, two hours later, sitting in the wagon bed behind his father and brother on the seat, the wagon accomplished a final curve, and he saw the weathered paintless store with its tattered tobacco- and patent-medicine posters and the tethered wagons and saddle animals below the gallery. He mounted the gnawed steps behind his father and brother, and there again was the lane of quiet, watching faces for the three of them to walk through. He saw the man in spectacles sitting at the plank table and he did not need to be told this was a Justice of the Peace; he sent one glare of fierce, exultant, partisan defiance at the man in collar and cravat now, whom he had seen but twice before in his life, and that on a galloping horse, who now wore on his face an expression not of rage but of amazed unbelief which the boy could not have known was at the incredible circumstance of being sued by one of his own tenants, and came and stood against his father and cried at the Justice: "He ain't done it! He ain't burnt . . ."

"Go back to the wagon," his father said.

"Burnt?" the Justice said. "Do I understand this rug was burned too?"

"Does anybody here claim it was?" his father said. "Go back to the wagon." But he did not, he merely retreated to the rear of the room, crowded as that other had been, but not to sit down this time, instead, to stand pressing among the motionless bodies, listening to the voices:

"And you claim twenty bushels of corn is too high for the damage you did to the rug?"

"He brought the rug to me and said he wanted the tracks washed out of it. I washed the tracks out and took the rug back to him."

"But you didn't carry the rug back to him in the same condition it was in before you made the tracks on it."

His father did not answer, and now for perhaps half a minute there was no sound at all save that of breathing, the faint, steady suspiration of complete and intent listening.

"You decline to answer that, Mr. Snopes?" Again his father did not answer. "I'm going to find against you, Mr. Snopes. I'm going to find that you were responsible for the injury to Major de Spain's rug and hold you liable for it. But twenty bushels of corn seems a little high for a man in your circumstances to have to pay. Major de Spain claims it cost a hundred dollars. October corn will be worth about fifty cents. I figure that if Major de Spain can stand a ninety-five dollar loss on something he paid cash for, you can stand a five-dollar loss you haven't earned yet. I hold you in damages to Major de Spain to the amount of ten bushels of corn over and above your contract with him, to be paid to him out of your crop at gathering time. Court adjourned."

It had taken no time hardly, the morning was but half begun. He thought they would return home and perhaps back to the field, since they were late, far behind all other farmers. But instead his father passed on behind the wagon, merely indicating with his hand for the older brother to follow with it, and crossed the road toward the blacksmith shop opposite, pressing on after his father, overtaking him, speaking, whispering up at the harsh, calm face beneath the weathered hat: "He won't git no ten bushels neither. He won't git one. We'll . . ." until his father glanced for an instant down at him, the face absolutely calm, the grizzled eyebrows tangled above the cold eyes, the voice almost pleasant, almost gentle:

"You think so? Well, we'll wait till October anyway."

The matter of the wagon—the setting of a spoke or two and the tightening of the tires—did not take long either, the business of the tires accomplished by driving the wagon into the spring branch behind the shop and letting it stand there, the mules nuzzling into the water from time to time, and the boy on the seat with the idle reins, looking up the slope and through the sooty tunnel of the shed where the slow hammer rang and where his father sat on an upended cypress bolt, easily, either talking or listening, still sitting there when the boy brought the dripping wagon up out of the branch and halted it before the door.

"Take them on to the shade and hitch," his father said. He did so and returned. His father and the smith and a third man squatting on his heels inside the door were talking, about crops and animals; the boy, squatting too in the ammoniac dust and hoof-parings and scales of rust, heard his father tell a long and unhurried story out of the time before the birth of the older brother even when he had been a professional horsetrader. And then his father came up beside him where he stood before a tattered last year's circus poster on the other side of the store, gazing rapt and quiet at the scarlet horses, the incredible poisings and convolutions of tulle and tights and the painted leers of comedians, and said, "It's time to eat."

But not at home. Squatting beside his brother against the front wall, he watched his father emerge from the store and produce from a paper sack a segment of cheese and divide it carefully and deliberately into three with his pocket knife and produce crackers from the same sack. They all three squatted on the gallery and ate, slowly, without talking; then in the store again, they drank from a tin dipper tepid water smelling of the cedar bucket and of living beech trees. And still they did not go home. It was a horse lot this time, a tall rail fence upon and along which men stood and sat and out of which one by one horses were led, to be walked and trotted and then cantered back and forth along the road while the slow swapping and buying went on and the sun began to slant westward, they—the three of them —watching and listening, the older brother with his muddy eyes and his steady, inevitable tobacco, the father commenting now and then on certain of the animals, to no one in particular.

It was after sundown when they reached home. They ate supper by lamplight, then, sitting on the doorstep, the boy watched the night fully accomplish, listening to the whippoorwills and the frogs, when he heard his mother's voice: "Abner! No! No! Oh, God. Oh, God. Abner!" and he rose, whirled, and saw the altered light through the door where a candle stub now burned in a bottle neck on the table and his father, still in the hat and coat, at once formal and burlesque as though dressed carefully for some shabby and ceremonial violence, emptying the reservoir of the lamp back into the five-gallon kerosene can from which it had been filled, while the mother tugged at his arm until he shifted the lamp to the other hand and flung her back, not savagely or viciously, just hard, into the wall, her hands flung out against the wall for balance, her mouth open and in her face the same quality of hopeless despair as had been in her voice. Then his father saw him standing in the door.

"Go to the barn and get that can of oil we were oiling the wagon with," he said. The boy did not move. Then he could speak.

"What . . ." he cried. "What are you . . ."

"Go get that oil," his father said. "Go."

Then he was moving, running, outside the house, toward the stable: this the old habit, the old blood which he had not been permitted to choose for himself, which had been bequeathed him willy nilly and which had run for so long (and who knew where, battening on what of outrage and savagery and lust) before it came to him. *I could keep on,* he thought. *I could run on and on and never look back, never need to see his face again. Only I can't. I can't,* the rusted can in his hand now, the liquid sploshing in it as he ran back to the house and into it, into the sound of his mother's weeping in the next room, and handed the can to his father.

"Ain't you going to even send a nigger?" he cried. "At least you sent a nigger before!"

This time his father didn't strike him. The hand came even faster than the blow had, the same hand which had set the can on the table with almost excruciating care flashing from the can toward him too quick for him to follow it, gripping him by the back of his shirt and on to tiptoe before he had seen it quit the can, the face stooping at him in breathless and frozen ferocity, the cold, dead voice speaking over him to the older brother who leaned against the table, chewing with that steady, curious, sidewise motion of cows:

"Empty the can into the big one and go on. I'll catch up with you."

"Better tie him up to the bedpost," the brother said.

"Do like I told you," the father said. Then the boy was moving, his bunched shirt and the hard, bony hand between his shoulder-blades, his toes just touching the floor, across the room and into the other one, past the sisters sitting with spread heavy thighs in the two chairs over the cold hearth, and to where his mother and aunt sat side by side on the bed, the aunt's arms about his mother's shoulders.

"Hold him," the father said. The aunt made a startled movement. "Not

you," the father said. "Lennie. Take hold of him. I want to see you do it."
His mother took him by the wrist. "You'll hold him better than that. If he
gets loose don't you know what he is going to do? He will go up yonder."
He jerked his head toward the road. "Maybe I'd better tie him."

"I'll hold him," his mother whispered.

"See you do then." Then his father was gone, the stiff foot heavy and
measured upon the boards, ceasing at last.

Then he began to struggle. His mother caught him in both arms, he jerking and wrenching at them. He would be stronger in the end, he knew that.
But he had no time to wait for it. "Lemme go!" he cried. "I don't want to
have to hit you!"

"Let him go!" the aunt said. "If he don't go, before God, I am going up
there myself!"

"Don't you see I can't?" his mother cried. "Sarty! Sarty! No! No! Help
me, Lizzie!"

Then he was free. His aunt grasped at him but it was too late. He
whirled, running, his mother stumbled forward on to her knees behind him,
crying to the nearer sister: "Catch him, Net! Catch him!" But that was too
late too, the sister (the sisters were twins, born at the same time, yet either of
them now gave the impression of being, encompassing as much living meat
and volume and weight as any other two of the family) not yet having
begun to rise from the chair, her head, face, alone merely turned, presenting
to him in the flying instant an astonishing expanse of young female features
untroubled by any surprise even, wearing only an expression of bovine
interest. Then he was out of the room, out of the house, in the mild dust of
the starlit road and the heavy rifeness of honeysuckle, the pale ribbon
unspooling with terrific slowness under his running feet, reaching the gate
at last and turning in, running, his heart and lungs drumming, on up the
drive toward the lighted house, the lighted door. He did not knock, he burst
in, sobbing for breath, incapable for the moment of speech; he saw the
astonished face of the Negro in the linen jacket without knowing when the
Negro had appeared.

"De Spain!" he cried, panted. "Where's . . .!" then he saw the white man
too emerging from a white door down the hall. "Barn!" he cried. "Barn!"

"What?" the white man said. "Barn?"

"Yes!" the boy cried. "Barn!"

"Catch him!" the white man shouted.

But it was too late this time too. The Negro grasped his shirt, but the
entire sleeve, rotten with washing, carried away, and he was out that door
too and in the drive again, and had actually never ceased to run even while
he was screaming into the white man's face.

Behind him the white man was shouting, "My horse! Fetch my horse!"
and he thought for an instant of cutting across the park and climbing the
fence into the road, but he did not know the park nor how high the vine-
massed fence might be and he dared not risk it. So he ran on down the

drive, blood and breath roaring; presently he was in the road again though he could not see it. He could not hear either: the galloping mare was almost upon him before he heard her, and even then he held his course, as if the very urgency of his wild grief and need must in a moment more find him wings, waiting until the ultimate instant to hurl himself aside and into the weed-choked roadside ditch as the horse thundered past and on, for an instant in furious silhouette against the stars, the tranquil early summer night sky which, even before the shape of the horse and rider vanished, stained abruptly and violently upward: a long, swirling roar incredible and soundless, blotting the stars, and he springing up and into the road again, running again, knowing it was too late yet still running even after he heard the shot and, an instant later, two shots, pausing now without knowing he had ceased to run, crying "Pap! Pap!", running again before he knew he had begun to run, stumbling, tripping over something and scrabbling up again without ceasing to run, looking backward over his shoulder at the glare as he got up, running on among the invisible trees, panting, sobbing, "Father! Father!"

At midnight he was sitting on the crest of a hill. He did not know it was midnight and he did not know how far he had come. But there was no glare behind him now and he sat now, his back toward what he had called home for four days anyhow, his face toward the dark woods which he would enter when breath was strong again, small, shaking steadily in the chill darkness, hugging himself into the remainder of his thin, rotten shirt, the grief and despair now no longer terror and fear but just grief and despair. *Father. My father*, he thought. "He was brave!" he cried suddenly, aloud but not loud, no more than a whisper: "He was! He was in the war! He was in Colonel Sartoris' cav'ry!" not knowing that his father had gone to that war a private in the fine old European sense, wearing no uniform, admitting the authority of and giving fidelity to no man or army or flag, going to war as Malbrouck himself did: for booty—it meant nothing and less than nothing to him if it were enemy booty or his own.

The slow constellations wheeled on. It would be dawn and then sun-up after a while and he would be hungry. But that would be to-morrow and now he was only cold, and walking would cure that. His breathing was easier now and he decided to get up and go on, and then he found that he had been asleep because he knew it was almost dawn, the night almost over. He could tell that from the whippoorwills. They were everywhere now among the dark trees below him, constant and inflectioned and ceaseless, so that, as the instant for giving over to the day birds drew nearer and nearer, there was no interval at all between them. He got up. He was a little stiff, but walking would cure that too as it would the cold, and soon there would be the sun. He went on down the hill, toward the dark woods within which the liquid silver voices of the birds called unceasing—the rapid and urgent beating of the urgent and quiring heart of the late spring night. He did not look back.

THOMAS WOLFE

(1900–1938)

William Faulkner, in an interview, once declared that of all the writers of his generation in America he admired Thomas Wolfe the most—not so much for his literary craftsmanship but because "he tried his best to get it all said: he was willing to throw away style, coherence, all the rules of preciseness, to try to put all the experience of the human heart on the head of a pin, as it were." In his brief career Wolfe produced two long novels, a cache of manuscript from which two more novels were hewn by his editor, a memoir, several volumes of short fiction, and several early plays. His first novel, *Look Homeward, Angel* (1929), remains his best.

Thomas Wolfe was born in Asheville, North Carolina, the youngest child of a large family. His father was a stone mason from Pennsylvania and his mother a North Carolina mountain woman, who when her youngest son was six purchased a boarding house that she operated until her death. Wolfe was educated in the public schools and at the North State Fitting School, graduated from the University of North Carolina, did advanced work in literature and playwriting at Harvard, and taught at New York University until after publication of his first novel. *Look Homeward, Angel* was a critical and financial success, though it was not at first well received in Asheville. In 1935, Wolfe published *Of Time and the River*. Criticism of the novel and of the role of his first editor, Maxwell Perkins of Charles Scribner's Sons, in its final shaping led Wolfe to seek a new publisher. In 1937 he signed a contract with Harper and Brothers and was at work on a new novel when, while on a tour of the Far West in 1938, he came down with pneumonia, which developed into tuberculosis of the brain. He was operated on at Johns Hopkins Hospital in Baltimore, but died in September.

Working from a mass of manuscripts, some of which had been written in the form of novellas and published as such, his editor, Edward C. Aswell, put together a narrative, *The Web and the Rock*, published in 1939, and another, *You Can't Go Home Again,* in 1940. Unfortunately, it was not made clear that Aswell had shaped the books from material written over the course of ten years, some of it dating back to the *Look Homeward, Angel* manuscript, and had changed names, altered character descriptions to fit, and even inserted transitions of his own so that the two books published as "novels" by Thomas Wolfe were not for the most part given that form or design by their author. Criticisms of Wolfe's formlessness and self-indulgent rhetorical excess —voiced when *Of Time and the River* had appeared —thus seemed only too clearly borne out. A considerably different and more attractive presentation of Wolfe's literary art emerged in 1961 when C. Hugh Holman edited *The Short*

Novels of Thomas Wolfe; here six unitary works were presented as Wolfe had originally written and published them in magazines during his lifetime, before his editors had broken them up and distributed segments in larger narratives.

Look Homeward, Angel is the only one of Wolfe's novels published in approximately the shape he wrote it. *Of Time and the River* had been composed in the first person, but Wolfe's editors at Scribner's changed it into third person utterance. Although the final responsibility was Wolfe's—his contemporaries Faulkner or Ernest Hemingway would scarcely have acquiesced to such tampering—the result was less than fortunate, for what was written as confessional was made to seem as autobiographical boasting behind the facade of supposed third-person "objectivity."

Written in the form of the "Kunstlerroman," in which the growth of the artist to maturity constitutes the heart of the fiction, *Look Homeward, Angel* is a powerfully lyrical chronicle of the autobiographical protagonist's early years, with vivid descriptions of members of his family and detailed presentations of the mountain community about them. Wolfe's artistic perception was always subjective, but in his first novel the "prison walls of self," as he expressed it, had not so formed themselves as to inhibit or restrict a rich, broadly comic view of a strongly delineated family of diverse individuals living in a closely observed, lively Southern community. All Wolfe's work is chronicle in form: it proceeds against a backdrop of unfolding time, with the main characters as well as the narrator always deeply conscious of the passing of the years and the workings of mortality.

In the following excerpt from *Look Homeward, Angel*, W. O. Gant, the hard-drinking, often roisterous father of the protagonist, is visited at his shop by "Queen Elizabeth," the madame of the local house of ill fame, who wishes to purchase a monument to adorn the grave of one of her girls who has recently died. By playing the inherent incongruity in the situation against the pathos of the themes of death and lost youth, Wolfe achieves a broadly comic yet moving portrayal of ordinary human beings caught in time and, as he put it, moving "deathward in a world of seemings."

From LOOK HOMEWARD, ANGEL

Chapter XIX

One afternoon in the young summer, Gant leaned upon the rail, talking to Jannadeau. He was getting on to sixty-five, his erect body had settled, he stooped a little. He spoke of old age often, and he wept in his tirades now because of his stiffened hand. Soaked in pity, he referred to himself as "the poor old cripple who has to provide for them all."

The indolence of age and disintegration was creeping over him. He now rose a full hour later, he came to his shop punctually, but he spent long hours of the day extended on the worn leather couch of his office, or in gossip with Jannadeau, bawdy old Liddell, Cardiac, and Fagg Sluder, who had salted away his fortune in two big buildings on the Square and was at the present moment tilted comfortably in a chair before the fire department, gossiping eagerly with members of the ball club, whose chief support he was. It was after five o'clock, the game was over.

Negro laborers, grisly with a white coating of cement, sloped down past the shop on their way home. The draymen dispersed slowly, a slouchy policeman loafed down the steps of the city hall picking his teeth, and on the market side, from high grilled windows, there came the occasional howls of a drunken negress. Life buzzed slowly like a fly.

The sun had reddened slightly, there was a cool flowing breath from the hills, a freshening relaxation over the tired earth, the hope, the ecstasy of evening in the air. In slow pulses the thick plume of fountain rose, fell upon itself, and slapped the pool in lazy rhythms. A wagon rattled leanly over the big cobbles; beyond the firemen, the grocer Bradly wound up his awning with slow creaking revolutions.

Across the Square, at its other edge, the young virgins of the eastern part of town walked lightly home in chattering groups. They came to town at four o'clock in the afternoon, walked up and down the little avenue several times, entered a shop to purchase small justifications, and finally went into the chief drug store, where the bucks of the town loafed and drawled in lazy alert groups. It was their club, their brasserie, the forum of the sexes. With confident smiles the young men detached themselves from their group and strolled back to booth and table.

"Hey theah! Wheahd you come from?"

"Move ovah theah, lady. I want to tawk to you."

Eyes as blue as Southern skies looked roguishly up to laughing gray ones, the winsome dimples deepened, and the sweetest little tail in dear old Dixie slid gently over on the polished board.

Gant spent delightful hours now in the gossip of dirty old men—their huddled bawdry exploded in cracked high wheezes on the Square. He came home at evening stored with gutter tidings, wetting his thumb and smiling slyly as he questioned Helen hopefully:

"She's no better than a regular little chippie—eh?"

"Ha-ha-ha-ha," she laughed mockingly. "Don't you wish you knew?"

His age bore certain fruits, emoluments of service. When she came home in the evening with one of her friends, she presented the girl with jocose eagerness to his embrace. And, crying out paternally, "Why, bless her heart! Come kiss the old man," he planted bristling mustache kisses on their white throats, their soft lips, grasping the firm meat of one arm tenderly with his good hand and cradling them gently. They shrieked with throaty giggle-twiddles of pleasure because it tuh-tuh-tuh-tuh-*tickled* so.

"Ooh! Mr. Gant! Whah-whah-whah!"

"Your father's such a nice man," they said. "Such lovely manners."

Helen's eyes fed fiercely on them. She laughed with husky-harsh excitement.

"Hah-ha-ha! He likes that, doesn't he? It's too bad, old boy, isn't it? No more monkey business."

He talked with Jannadeau, while his fugitive eyes roved over the east end of the Square. Before the shop the comely matrons of the town came up from the market. From time to time they smiled, seeing him, and he bowed sweepingly. Such lovely manners.

"The King of England," he observed, "is only a figurehead. He doesn't begin to have the power of the President of the United States."

"His power is severely *limited*," said Jannadeau gutturally, "by custom but not by statute. In actua*lity* he is still one of the most powerful monarchs in the world." His thick black fingers probed carefully into the viscera of a watch.

"The late King Edward for all his faults," said Gant, wetting his thumb, "was a smart man. This fellow they've got now is a nonentity and a nincompoop." He grinned faintly, craftily, with pleasure at the big words, glancing slily at the Swiss to see if they had told.

His uneasy eyes followed carefully the stylish carriage of "Queen" Elizabeth's well clad figure as she went down by the shop. She smiled pleasantly, and for a moment turned her candid stare upon smooth marble slabs of death, carved lambs and cherubim. Gant bowed elaborately.

"Good-evening, madam," he said.

She disappeared. In a moment she came back decisively and mounted the broad steps. He watched her approach with quickened pulses. Twelve years.

"How's the madam?" he said gallantly. "Elizabeth, I was just telling Jannadeau you were the most stylish woman in town."

"Well, that's mighty sweet of you, Mr. Gant," she said in her cool poised voice. "You've always got a good word for every one."

She gave a bright pleasant nod to Jannadeau, who swung his huge scowling head ponderously around and muttered at her.

"Why, Elizabeth," said Gant, "you haven't changed an inch in fifteen years. I don't believe you're a day older."

She was thirty-eight and pleasantly aware of it.

"Oh, yes," she said laughing. "You're only saying that to make me feel good. I'm no chicken any more."

She had a pale clear skin, pleasantly freckled, carrot-colored hair, and a thin mouth live with humor. Her figure was trim and strong—no longer young. She had a great deal of energy, distinction, and elegance in her manner.

"How are all the girls, Elizabeth?" he asked kindly.

Her face grew sad. She began to pull her gloves off.

"That's what I came in to see you about," she said. "I lost one of them last week."

"Yes," said Gant gravely, "I was sorry to hear of that."

"She was the best girl I had," said Elizabeth. "I'd have done anything in the world for her. We did everything we could," she added. "I've no regrets on that score. I had a doctor and two trained nurses by her all the time."

She opened her black leather handbag, thrust her gloves into it, and pulling out a small bluebordered handkerchief, began to weep quietly.

"Huh-huh-huh-huh-huh," said Gant, shaking his head. "Too bad, too bad, too bad. Come back to my office," he said. They went back and sat down. Elizabeth dried her eyes.

"What was her name?" he asked.

"We called her Lily—her full name was Lillian Reed."

"Why, I knew that girl," he exclaimed. "I spoke to her not over two weeks ago."

"Yes," said Elizabeth, "she went like that—one hemorrhage right after another, down here." She tapped her abdomen. "Nobody ever knew she was sick until last Wednesday. Friday she was gone." She wept again.

"T-t-t-t-t," he clucked regretfully. "Too bad, too bad. She was pretty as a picture."

"I couldn't have loved her more, Mr. Gant," said Elizabeth, "if she had been my own daughter."

"How old was she?" he asked.

"Twenty two," said Elizabeth, beginning to weep again.

"What a pity! What a pity!" he agreed. "Did she have any people?"

"No one who would do anything for her," Elizabeth said. "Her mother died when she was thirteen—she was born out here on the Beetree Fork —and her father," she added indignantly, "is a mean old bastard who's never done anything for her or any one else. He didn't even come to her funeral."

"He will be punished," said Gant darkly.

"As sure as there's a God in heaven," Elizabeth agreed, "he'll get what's coming to him in hell. The old bastard!" she continued virtuously, "I hope he rots!"

"You can depend upon it," he said grimly. "He will. Ah, Lord." He was silent a moment while he shook his head with slow regret.

"A pity, a pity," he muttered. "So young." He had the moment of triumph all men have when they hear some one has died. A moment, too, of grisly fear. Sixty-four.

"I couldn't have loved her more," said Elizabeth, "if she'd been one of my own. A young girl like that, with all her life before her."

"It's pretty sad when you come to think of it," he said. "By God, it is."

"And she was such a fine girl, Mr. Gant," said Elizabeth, weeping softly. "She had such a bright future before her. She had more opportunities than I ever had, and I suppose you know"—she spoke modestly—"what I've done."

"Why," he exclaimed, startled, "you're a rich woman, Elizabeth —damned if I don't believe you are. You own property all over town."

"I wouldn't say that," she answered, "but I've got enough to live on without ever doing another lick of work. I've had to work hard all my life. From now on I don't intend to turn my hand over."

She regarded him with a shy pleased smile, and touched a coil of her fine hair with a small competent hand. He looked at her attentively, noting with pleasure her firm uncorseted hips, moulded compactly into her tailored suit, and her cocked comely legs tapering to graceful feet, shod in neat little slippers of tan. She was firm, strong, washed, and elegant—a faint scent of lilac hovered over her: he looked at her candid eyes, lucently gray, and saw that she was quite a great lady.

"By God, Elizabeth," he said, "you're a fine-looking woman."

"I've had a good life," she said. "I've taken care of myself."

They had always known each other—since first they met. They had no excuses, no questions, no replies. The world fell away from them. In the silence they heard the pulsing slap of the fountain, the high laughter of bawdry in the Square. He took a book of models from the desk, and began to turn its slick pages. They showed modest blocks of Georgia marble and Vermont granite.

"I don't want any of those," she said impatiently. "I've already made up my mind. I know what I want."

He looked up surprised. "What is it?"

"I want the angel out front."

His face was shocked and unwilling. He gnawed the corner of his thin lip. No one knew how fond he was of the angel. Publicly he called it his White Elephant. He cursed it and said he had been a fool to order it. For six years it had stood on the porch, weathering, in all the wind and the rain. It was now brown and fly-specked. But it had come from Carrara in Italy, and it held a stone lily delicately in one hand. The other hand was lifted in benediction, it was poised clumsily upon the ball of one phthisic foot, and its stupid white face wore a smile of soft stone idiocy.

In his rages, Gant sometimes directed vast climaxes of abuse at the angel. "Fiend out of Hell!" he roared. "You have impoverished me, you have ruined me, you have cursed my declining years, and now you will crush me to death, fearful, awful, and unnatural monster that you are."

But sometimes when he was drunk he fell weeping on his knees before it, called it Cynthia, and entreated its love, forgiveness, and blessing for its sinful but repentant boy. There was laughter from the Square.

"What's the matter?" said Elizabeth. "Don't you want to sell it?"

"It will cost you a good deal, Elizabeth," he said evasively.

"I don't care," she answered, positively. "I've got the money. How much do you want?"

He was silent, thinking for a moment of the place where the angel stood. He knew he had nothing to cover or obliterate that place—it left a barren crater in his heart.

"All right," he said. "You can have it for what I paid for it—$420."

She took a thick sheaf of banknotes from her purse and counted the money out for him. He pushed it back.

"No. Pay me when the job's finished and it has been set up. You want some sort of inscription, don't you?"

"Yes. There's her full name, age, place of birth, and so on," she said, giving him a scrawled envelope. "I want some poetry, too—something that suits a young girl taken off like this."

He pulled his tattered little book of inscriptions from a pigeonhole, and thumbed its pages, reading her a quatrain here and there. To each she shook her head. Finally, he said:

"How's this one, Elizabeth?" He read:

> She went away in beauty's flower,
> Before her youth was spent;
> Ere life and love had lived their hour
> God called her, and she went.
>
> Yet whispers Faith upon the wind:
> No grief to her was given.
> She left *your* love and went to find
> A greater one in heaven.

"Oh, that's lovely—lovely," she said. "I want that one."

"Yes," he agreed, "I think that's the best one."

In the musty cool smell of his little office they got up. Her gallant figure reached his shoulder. She buttoned her kid gloves over the small pink haunch of her palms and glanced about her. His battered sofa filled one wall, the line of his long body was printed in the leather. She looked up at him. His face was sad and grave. They remembered.

"It's been a long time, Elizabeth," he said.

They walked slowly to the front through aisled marbles. Sentinelled just beyond the wooden doors, the angel leered vacantly down. Jannadeau drew his great head turtlewise a little further into the protective hunch of his burly shoulders. They went out on to the porch.

The moon stood already, like its own phantom, in the clear washed skies of evening. A little boy with an empty paper-delivery bag swung lithely by, his freckled nostrils dilating pleasantly with hunger and the fancied smell of supper. He passed, and for a moment, as they stood at the porch edge, all life seemed frozen in a picture: the firemen and Fagg Sluder had seen Gant, whispered, and were now looking toward him; a policeman, at the high side-porch of the Police Court, leaned on the rail and stared; at the near edge of the central grass-plot below the fountain, a farmer bent for water at a bubbling jet, rose dripping, and stared; from the Tax Collector's office, City Hall, upstairs, Yancey, huge, meaty, shirtsleeved, stared. And in that second the slow pulse of the fountain was suspended, life was held, like an arrested gesture, in photographic abeyance, and Gant felt himself alone move deathward in a world of seemings as, in 1910, a man might find himself again in a picture taken on the grounds of the Chicago Fair, when he was thirty and his mustache black, and, noting the bustled ladies and the derbied men fixed in the second's pullulation, remember the dead instant, seek beyond the borders for what was there (he knew); or as a veteran who finds himself upon his elbow near Ulysses Grant, before the march, in pictures of the Civil War, and sees a dead man on a horse; or I should say, like some completed Don, who finds himself again before a tent in Scotland in his youth, and notes a cricket-bat long lost and long forgotten, the face of a poet who has died, and young men and the tutor as they looked that Long Vacation when they read nine hours a day for "Greats."

Where now? Where after? Where then?

ERSKINE CALDWELL

(1902–   )

Although Erskine Caldwell has written and published more than sixty books, his reputation as an important chronicler of Southern ways rests almost exclusively upon a group of novels and stories published during the 1930s about the lower orders of whites in rural Georgia. In particular, *Tobacco Road* (1932), with its comically degenerate Lester family and their squalid, ribald marginal existence in the worn-out, burnt-over lands of sandhill Georgia, has won what appears to be a permanent place in American literature.

Caldwell was the son of a minister of the Associate Reformed Presbyterian Church. He was born in Newnan, Georgia, and moved about several times as his father was called to different churches. In 1919 the elder Caldwell settled at Wrens, Georgia; in and about this town the fictional locale of Caldwell's *Tobacco Road* may be found. He studied at Erskine College, the University of Virginia, and the University of Pennsylvania, then worked on the *Atlanta Journal*. In 1925 Caldwell married Helen Lannegan and moved to Maine, determined to become a professional writer. He supported himself by odd jobs while writing away steadily. It was not until one hundred stories and novelettes had failed to find publication that his first novel, *The Bastard,* was published in 1929. With his fourth novel, *Tobacco Road,* he achieved widespread popular renown, which was enhanced when a Broadway dramatic production based on the novel amassed a record for consecutive performances during the late 1930s and early 1940s. Other books followed, including *God's Little Acre* (1933), *Journeyman* (1935), *Kneel to the Rising Sun* (1935), and *Trouble in July* (1940). Reprinted in paperback and read primarily for their sexual suggestiveness and bawdy comedy, these books sold millions of copies.

Meanwhile Caldwell worked for a time in Hollywood, was divorced, married the photographer Margaret Bourke-White in 1939, traveled abroad before and during the war, was divorced in 1942 and married June Johnson, and in 1957, after another divorce, married his present wife, Virginia Moffett Fletcher. Throughout this period he produced fiction steadily, though he never repeated the commercial triumphs of his early fiction.

Caldwell's comic, sometimes pathetic depictions of the animal-like Lesters and others of the Tobacco Road company were accompanied by a bitter portrayal of the ravages of capitalism and violation of the humanity of poor whites and blacks in the rural South in an economy based on exploitation. He wrote as a Marxist— though not, he declared, as a Communist. It is questionable whether his depiction of squalid circumstances achieves its authenticity through its political indignation, so that his people are seen by readers as victims, or through his adherence to the comic tradition of regarding the lower levels as humorously appalling freaks and grotesques that has been a staple of Southern fiction from William Byrd II's inhabitants of the early eighteenth century Dismal Swamp country onward. For whatever reason, Jeeter and Duke Lester, Sister Bessie May, and their fellow degenerates of *Tobacco Road* seem destined for a lengthy literary survival.

AUGUST AFTERNOON

Vic Glover awoke with the noon-day heat ringing in his ears. He had been asleep for only half an hour, and he was getting ready to turn over and go back to sleep when he opened his eyes for a moment and saw Hubert's wooly black head over the top of his bare toes. He stretched his eyelids and held them open in the glaring light as long as he could.

Hubert was standing in the yard, at the edge of the porch, with a pine cone in his hand.

Vic cursed him.

The colored man once more raked the cone over Vic's bare toes, tickling them on the under-side, and stepped back out of reach.

"What do you mean by standing there tickling me with that dad-burned cone?" Vic shouted at Hubert. "Is that all you can find to do? Why don't you get out in that field and do something to them boll-weevils? They're going to eat up every boll of cotton on the place if you don't stop them."

"I surely hated to wake you up, Mr. Vic," Hubert said, "but there's a white man out here looking for something. He won't say what he's looking for, but he's hanging around waiting for it."

Vic sat up wide awake. He sat up on the quilt and pulled on his shoes without looking into the yard. The white sand in the yard beat the glare of the sun directly into his eyes and he could see nothing beyond the edge of the porch. Hubert threw the pine cone under the porch and stepped aside.

"He must be looking for trouble," Vic said. "When they come around and don't say anything, and just sit and look, it's trouble they're looking for."

"There he is, Mr. Vic," Hubert said, nodding his head across the yard. "There he sits up against that wateroak tree yonder."

Vic looked around for Willie. Willie was sitting on the top step at the other end of the porch, directly in front of the strange white man. She did not look at Vic.

"You ought to have better sense than to wake me up while I'm taking a nap. This is no time of the day to be up in the summertime. I've got to get a little sleep every now and then."

"Boss," Hubert said, "I wouldn't never wake you up at all, not at any time, but Miss Willie just sits there high up on the steps showing her pretty and that white man has been out there whittling on a little stick a long time without saying nothing. I'm scared about something happening when he whittles that little stick clear through, and it's just about whittled down to nothing now. That's why I waked you up, Mr. Vic. Ain't much left of that little whittling-stick."

Vic glanced again at Willie, and from her he turned to stare at the stranger sitting under the wateroak tree in his front yard.

The piece of wood had been shaved down to paper thinness.

"Boss," Hubert said, shifting the weight of his body uneasily, "we ain't aiming to have no trouble today, is we?"

"Which way did he come from?" Vic asked, ignoring the question.

"I never did see him come from nowhere, Mr. Vic. I just looked up, and there he was, sitting against that wateroak out yonder and whittling on that little stick. I reckon I must have been drowsy when he came, because when I opened my eyes, there he was."

Vic slid down over the quilt until his legs were hanging over the edge of the porch. Perspiration began to trickle down his neck as soon as he sat up.

"Ask him what he's after, Hubert."

"We ain't aiming to have no trouble today, is we, Mr. Vic?"

"Ask him what he wants around here, I said."

Hubert went almost halfway to the wateroak tree and stopped.

"Mr. Vic says what can he do for you, white-folks?"

The man said nothing. He did not even glance up from the little stick he was whittling.

Hubert came back to the porch, the whites of his eyes becoming larger with each step.

"What did he say?" Vic asked him.

"He ain't said nothing yet, Mr. Vic. He acts like he don't hear me at all. You'd better go talk to him, Mr. Vic. He won't give me no attention. Appears to me like he's just sitting there and looking at Miss Willie on the high step. Maybe if you was to tell her to go in the house and shut the door, he might be persuaded to give some notice to what we say to him."

"Ain't no sense in sending her in the house," Vic said. "I can make him talk. Hand me that stillyerd."

"Mr. Vic, I'm trying to tell you about Miss Willie. Miss Willie's been sitting there on that high step showing her pretty and he's been looking at her a right long time, Mr. Vic. If you won't object to me saying so, Mr. Vic, I reckon I'd tell Miss Willie to go sit somewhere else, if I was you. Miss Willie ain't got much on today, Mr. Vic. Just only that skimpy outside dress, Mr. Vic. That's what I've been trying to tell you. I walked out there in the yard this while ago to see what he was looking at so much, and when I say Miss Willie ain't got much on today, I mean she's got on just only that skimpy outside dress, Mr. Vic. You can go look yourself and see if I'm lying to you, Mr. Vic."

"Hand me that stillyerd, I said."

Hubert went to the end of the porch and brought the heavy iron cotton-weighing steelyard to Vic. He stepped back out of the way.

"Boss," Hubert said, "we ain't aiming to have no trouble today, is we?"

Vic was getting ready to jump down into the yard when the man under the wateroak reached into his pocket and pulled out another knife. It was about ten or eleven inches long, and both sides of the handle were covered with hairy cowhide. There was a spring-button in one end. The man pushed the button with his thumb, and the blade sprang from the case. He began playing with both knives, throwing them up into the air and catching them on the backs of his hands.

Hubert moved to the other side of Vic.

"Mr. Vic," he said, "I ain't intending to mess in your business none, but it looks to me like you got yourself in for a peck of trouble when you went off and brought Miss Willie back here. It looks to me like she's got up for a city girl, more so than a country girl."

Vic cursed him.

"I'm telling you, Mr. Vic, you ought to marry yourself a wife who hadn't ought to sit on a high step in front of a stranger, not even when she's wearing something more than just only a skimpy outside dress. I walked out there and looked at Miss Willie, and, Mr. Vic, Miss Willie is as bare as a plucked chicken, except for one little place I saw."

"Shut up," Vic said, laying the steelyard down on the quilt beside him.

The man under the wateroak closed the blade of the small penknife and put it into his pocket. The big hairy cowhide knife he flipped into the air and caught it easily on the back of his hand.

"Mr. Vic," Hubert said, "you've been asleep all the time and you don't know like I do. Miss Willie has been sitting there on that high step showing off her pretty a long time now, and he's got his pecker up. I know, Mr. Vic, because I went out there myself and looked."

Vic cursed him.

The man in the yard flipped the knife into the air and caught it behind his back.

"What's your name?" he asked Willie.

"Willie."

He flipped the knife again.

"What's yours?" she asked him, giggling.

"Floyd."

"Where are you from?"

"Carolina."

He flipped it higher than ever, catching it underhanded.

"What are you doing in Georgia?"

"Don't know," he said. "Just looking around."

Willie giggled, smiling at him.

Floyd got up and walked across the yard to the steps and sat down on the bottom one. He put his arms around his knees and looked up at Willie.

"You're not so bad-looking," he said. "I've seen lots worse-looking."

"You're not so bad yourself," Willie giggled, resting her arms on her knees and looking down at him.

"How about a kiss?"

"What would it be to you?"

"Not bad. I reckon I've had lots worse."

"Well, you can't get it sitting down there."

Floyd climbed the steps on his hands and feet and sat down on the next to the top step. He leaned against Willie, putting one arm around her waist and the other under her knees. Willie slid down the step beside him. Floyd pulled her to him, making a sucking-sound with his lips.

"Boss," Hubert said, his lips twitching, "we ain't aiming to have no trouble today, is we?"

Vic cursed him.

Willie and Floyd moved down a step without loosening their embrace.

"Who is that yellow-headed sapsucker, anyhow?" Vic said. "I'll be dad-burned if he ain't got a lot of nerve—coming here and fooling with Willie."

"You wouldn't do nothing to cause trouble, would you, Mr. Vic? I surely don't want to have no trouble today, Mr. Vic."

Vic glanced at the eleven-inch knife Floyd had stuck into the step at his feet. It stood on its tip, twenty-two inches high, while the sun was reflected against the bright blade and made a streak of light on Floyd's pants-leg.

"Go over there and take that knife away from him and bring it to me," Vic said. "Don't be scared of him."

"Mr. Vic, I surely hate to disappoint you, but if you want that white-folk's knife, you'll just have to get it your own self. I don't aim to have myself all carved up with that thing. Mr. Vic, I surely can't accommodate you this time. If you want that white-folk's knife, you'll just be bound to get it your own self, Mr. Vic."

Vic cursed him.

Hubert backed away until he was at the end of the porch. He kept looking behind him all the time, looking to be certain of the exact location of the sycamore stump that was between him and the pine grove on the other side of the cotton field.

Vic called to Hubert and told him to come back. Hubert came slowly around the corner of the porch and stood a few feet from the quilt where Vic was sitting. His lips quivered and the whites of his eyes grew larger. Vic mentioned for him to come closer, but he would not come an inch farther.

"How old are you?" Floyd asked Willie.

"Fifteen."

Floyd jerked the knife out of the wood and thrust it deeper into the same place.

"How old are you?" she asked him.

"About twenty-seven."

"Are you married?"

"Not now," he said. "How long have you been?"

"About three months," Willie said.

"How do you like it?"

"Pretty good so far."

"How about another kiss?"

"You just had one."

"I'd like another one now."

"I ought not to let you kiss me again."

"Why not?"

"Men don't like girls who kiss too much."

"I'm not that kind."

"What kind are you?"

"I'd like to kiss you a lot."

"But after I let you do that, you'd go away."

"No, I won't. I'll stay for something else."

"What?"

"To get the rest of you."

"You might hurt me."

"It won't hurt."

"It might."

"Let's go inside for a drink and I'll show you."

"We'll have to go to the spring for fresh water."

"Where's the spring?"

"Just across the field in the grove."

"All right," Floyd said, standing up. "Let's go."

He bent down and pulled the knife out of the wood. Willie ran down the steps and across the yard. When Floyd saw that she was not going to wait for him, he ran after her, holding the knives in his pocket with one hand. She led him across the cotton field to the spring in the pine grove. Just before they got there, Floyd caught her by the arm and ran beside her the rest of the way.

"Boss," Hubert said, his voice trembling, "we ain't aiming to have no trouble today, is we?"

Vic cursed him.

"I don't want to get messed up with a heap of trouble and maybe get my belly slit open with that big hairy knife. If you ain't got objections, I reckon I'll mosey on home now and cut me a little firewood for the cookstove."

"Come back here!" Vic said. "You stay where you are and stop making moves to go off."

"What is we aiming to do, Mr. Vic?"

Vic eased himself off the porch and walked across the yard to the water-oak. He looked down at the ground where Floyd had been sitting, and then he looked at the porch steps where Willie had been. The noon-day heat beat down through the thin leaves overhead and he could feel his mouth and throat burn with the hot air he breathed.

"Have you got a gun, Hubert?"

"No, sir, boss," Hubert said.

"Why haven't you?" he said. "Right when I need a gun, you haven't got it. Why don't you keep a gun?"

"Mr. Vic, I ain't got no use for a gun. I used to keep one to shoot rabbits and squirrels with, but I got to thinking hard one day, and I traded it off the first chance I got. I reckon it was a good thing I traded, too. If I had kept it, you'd be asking for it like you did just now."

Vic went back to the porch and picked up the steelyard and hammered the porch with it. After he had hit the porch four or five times, he dropped it and started out in the direction of the spring. He walked as far as the edge of the shade and stopped. He stood listening for a while.

Willie and Floyd could be heard down near the spring. Floyd said something to Willie, and Willie laughed loudly. There was silence again for several minutes, and then Willie laughed again. Vic could not tell whether she was crying or laughing. He was getting ready to turn and go back to the porch when he heard her cry out. It sounded like a scream, but it was not exactly like that; it sounded like a shriek, but it wasn't that, either; it sounded more like someone laughing and crying simultaneously in a high-pitched, excited voice.

"Where did Miss Willie come from, Mr. Vic?" Hubert asked. "Where did you bring her from?"

"Down below here a little way," he said.

Hubert listened to the sounds that were coming from the pine grove.

"Boss," he said after a little while, "it appears to me like you didn't go far enough away."

"I went far enough," Vic said. "If I had gone any farther, I'd have been in Florida."

The colored man hunched his shoulders forward several times while he smoothed the white sand with his broad-soled shoes.

"Mr. Vic, if I was you, the next time I'd surely go that far, maybe farther."

"What do you mean, the next time?"

"I was figuring that maybe you wouldn't be keeping her much longer than now, Mr. Vic."

Vic cursed him.

Hubert raised his head several times and attempted to see down into the pine grove over the top of the growing cotton.

"Shut up and mind your own business," Vic said. "I'm going to keep her till the cows come home. Where else do you reckon I'd find a better-looking girl than Willie?"

"Boss, I wasn't thinking of how she looks—I was thinking of how she acts. That white man came here and sat down and it wasn't no time before she had his pecker up."

"She acts that way because she ain't old enough yet to know who to fool with. She'll catch on in time."

Hubert followed Vic across the yard. While Vic went towards the porch, Hubert stopped and leaned against the wateroak where he could almost see over the cotton field into the pine grove. Vic went up on the porch and stretched out on the quilt. He took off his shoes and flung them aside.

"I surely God knowed something was going to happen when he whittled that stick down to nothing," Hubert was saying to himself. "White-folks take a long time to whittle a little piece of wood, but when they whittle it down to nothing, they're going to be up and doing before the time ain't long."

Presently Vic sat upright on the quilt.

"Listen here, Hubert—"

"Yes, sir, boss!"

"You keep your eye on that stillyerd so it will stay right where it is now, and when they come back up the path, you wake me up in a hurry."

"Yes, sir, boss," Hubert said. "Are you aiming to take a little nap now?"

"Yes, I am. And if you don't wake me up when they come back, I'll break your neck for you when I do wake up."

Vic lay down again on the quilt and turned over on his side to shut out the blinding glare of the early afternoon sun that was reflected upon the porch from the hard white sand in the yard.

Hubert scratched his head and sat down against the wateroak, facing the path from the spring. He could hear Vic snoring on the porch above the sounds that came at intervals from the pine grove across the field. He sat staring down the path, drowsy, singing under his breath. It was a long time until sun-down.

KATHERINE ANNE PORTER

(1890–1980)

Katherine Anne Porter, one of the finest practitioners of the art of short fiction of her century, was born in Indian Creek, Texas. She attended school in San Antonio, acted in summer stock, then ran away to join a traveling theater company. She was married in 1906, but left her husband to be a movie actress in Chicago. Later she became a theater critic for newspapers in Denver, Colorado, and Fort Worth, Texas. Porter then worked in New York, spent time in Mexico, lived in various places in the eastern United States, and began publishing short stories. After a stay in Mexico she traveled to Berlin by ship from Vera Cruz, a trip that years later became the setting for her novel *Ship of Fools* (1962). She stayed in Paris for a while, then returned to the United States, and lived in New Orleans and Baton Rouge in Louisiana and in Saratoga Springs, New York. During the war she worked briefly as a scriptwriter in Hollywood, then supported herself through lecturing and teaching at such colleges and universities as Stanford, Michigan, Liège, Virginia, and Washington and Lee. Not until publication of her novel in 1962 did she finally possess sufficient income to give up lecturing, and she settled near Washington, D.C., to devote her time to writing.

Her short fiction was published in book form throughout the 1930s and 1940s. *Flowering Judas and Other Stories* appeared in 1930, followed by

Hacienda (1934), *Noon Wine* (1937), *Pale Horse, Pale Rider: Three Short Novels* (1939), *The Leaning Tower and Other Stories* (1944), and *The Days Before* (1952). Her *Collected Stories,* published in 1966, won both the Pulitzer Prize and the National Book Award.

Her best work, polished and meticulous in craftsmanship, is notable for the nuance with which she achieves psychological characterization. In particular, the Miranda stories—closely autobiographical in nature and based on her childhood in Texas, her Southern family, her Roman Catholic conversion and its history—are so tightly woven and exquisitely wrought that critics have marveled at how much she is able to accomplish in such short compass. Her fictional surfaces are deceptively simple and her use of symbolism so unobtrusive that at first glance her stories may appear almost anecdotal. Intensely feminine in her perception, she is in her best work neither sentimental nor superficial. In Eudora Welty's words, "how calm is the surface, the invisible surface of it all! In a style as invisible as the rhythm of a voice, and as much her own as her own voice, she tells stories of horror and humiliation and in the doing fills her readers with a rising joy."

THE GRAVE

The grandfather, dead for more than thirty years, had been twice disturbed in his long repose by the constancy and possessiveness of his widow. She removed his bones first to Louisiana and then to Texas as if she had set out to find her own burial place, knowing well she would never return to the places she had left. In Texas she set up a small cemetery in a corner of her first farm, and as the family connection grew, and oddments of relations came over from Kentucky to settle, it contained at last about twenty graves. After the grandmother's death, part of her land was to be sold for the benefit of certain of her children, and the cemetery happened to lie in the part set aside for sale. It was necessary to take up the bodies and bury them again in the family plot in the big new public cemetery, where the grandmother had been buried. At last her husband was to lie beside her for eternity, as she had planned.

The family cemetery had been a pleasant small neglected garden of tangled rose bushes and ragged cedar trees and cypress, the simple flat stones rising out of uncropped sweet-smelling wild grass. The graves were lying open and empty one burning day when Miranda and her brother Paul, who often went together to hunt rabbits and doves, propped their twenty-two Winchester rifles carefully against the rail fence, climbed over and explored among the graves. She was nine years old and he was twelve.

They peered into the pits all shaped alike with such purposeful accuracy, and looking at each other with pleased adventurous eyes, they said in solemn tones: "These were graves!" trying by words to shape a special, suitable emotion in their minds, but they felt nothing except an agreeable thrill of wonder: they were seeing a new sight, doing something they had not done before. In them both there was also a small disappointment at the entire commonplaceness of the actual spectacle. Even if it had once contained a coffin for years upon years, when the coffin was gone a grave was just a hole in the ground. Miranda leaped into the pit that had held her grandfather's bones. Scratching around aimlessly and pleasurably as any young animal, she scooped up a lump of earth and weighed it in her palm. It had a pleasantly sweet, corrupt smell, being mixed with cedar needles and small leaves, and as the crumbs fell apart, she saw a silver dove no larger than a hazel nut, with spread wings and a neat fan-shaped tail. The breast had a deep round hollow in it. Turning it up to the fierce sunlight, she saw that the inside of the hollow was cut in little whorls. She scrambled out, over the pile of loose earth that had fallen back into one end of the grave, calling to Paul that she had found something, he must guess what . . . His head appeared smiling over the rim of another grave. He waved a closed hand at her. "I've got something too!" They ran to compare treasures, making a game of it, so many guesses each, all wrong, and a final showdown with opened palms. Paul had found a thin wide gold ring carved with intricate flowers and leaves. Miranda was smitten at sight of the ring and wished to have it. Paul seemed more impressed by the dove. They made a trade, with some little bickering. After he had got the dove in his hand, Paul said, "Don't you know what this is? This is a screw head for a *coffin!* . . . I'll bet nobody else in the world has one like this!"

Miranda glanced at it without covetousness. She had the gold ring on her thumb; it fitted perfectly. "Maybe we ought to go now," she said, "maybe one of the niggers'll see us and tell somebody." They knew the land had been sold, the cemetery was no longer theirs, and they felt like trespassers. They climbed back over the fence, slung their rifles loosely under their arms —they had been shooting at targets with various kinds of firearms since they were seven years old—and set out to look for the rabbits and doves or whatever small game might happen along. On these expeditions Miranda always followed at Paul's heels along the path, obeying instructions about handling her gun when going through fences; learning how to stand it up properly so it would not slip and fire unexpectedly; how to wait her time for a shot and not just bang away in the air without looking, spoiling shots for Paul, who really could hit things if given a chance. Now and then, in her excitement at seeing birds whizz up suddenly before her face, or a rabbit leap across her very toes, she lost her head, and almost without sighting she flung her rifle up and pulled the trigger. She hardly ever hit any sort of mark. She had no proper sense of hunting at all. Her brother would be often completely disgusted with her. "You don't care whether you get your bird or not," he said. "That's no way to hunt." Miranda could not understand his indignation. She had seen him smash his hat and yell with fury when he had missed his aim. "What I like about shooting," said Miranda, with exasperating inconsequence, "is pulling the trigger and hearing the noise."

"Then, by golly," said Paul, "whyn't you go back to the range and shoot at bulls-eyes?"

"I'd just as soon," said Miranda, "only like this, we walk around more."

"Well, you just stay behind and stop spoiling my shots," said Paul, who, when he made a kill, wanted to be certain he had made it. Miranda, who alone brought down a bird once in twenty rounds, always claimed as her own any game they got when they fired at the same moment. It was tiresome and unfair and her brother was sick of it.

"Now, the first dove we see, or the first rabbit, is mine," he told her. "And the next will be yours. Remember that and don't get smarty."

"What about snakes?" asked Miranda idly. "Can I have the first snake?"

Waving her thumb gently and watching her gold ring glitter, Miranda lost interest in shooting. She was wearing her summer roughing outfit: dark blue overalls, a light blue shirt, a hired-man's straw hat, and thick brown sandals. Her brother had the same outfit except his was a sober hickory-nut color. Ordinarily Miranda preferred her overalls to any other dress, though it was making rather a scandal in the countryside, for the year was 1903, and in the back country the law of female decorum had teeth in it. Her father had been criticized for letting his girls dress like boys and go careering around astride barebacked horses. Big sister Maria, the really independent and fearless one, in spite of her rather affected ways, rode at a dead run with only a rope knotted around her horse's nose. It was said the motherless family was running down, with the Grandmother no longer there to hold it together. It was known that she had discriminated against her son Harry in her will, and that he was in straits about money. Some of his old neighbors reflected with vicious satisfaction that now he would probably not be so stiffnecked, nor have any more high-stepping horses either. Miranda knew this, though she could not say how. She had met along the road old women of the kind who smoked corn-cob pipes, who had treated her grandmother with most sincere respect. They slanted their gummy old eyes side-ways at the granddaughter and said, "Ain't you ashamed of yoself, Missy? It's aginst the Scriptures to dress like that. Whut yo Pappy thinkin about?" Miranda, with her powerful social sense, which was like a fine set of antennae radiating from every pore of her skin, would feel ashamed because she knew well it was rude and ill-bred to shock anybody, even bad-tempered old crones, though she had faith in her father's judgment and was perfectly comfortable in the clothes. Her father had said, "They're just what you need, and they'll save your dresses for school . . ." This sounded quite simple and natural to her. She had been brought up in rigorous economy. Wastefulness was vulgar. It was also a sin. These were truths; she had heard them repeated many times and never once disputed.

Now the ring, shining with the serene purity of fine gold on her rather grubby thumb, turned her feelings against her overalls and sockless feet, toes sticking through the thick brown leather straps. She wanted to go back to the farmhouse, take a good cold bath, dust herself with plenty of Maria's violet talcum powder—provided Maria was not present to object, of course —put on the thinnest, most becoming dress she owned, with a big sash, and sit in a wicker chair under the trees . . . These things were not all she wanted, of course; she had vague stirrings of desire for luxury and a grand way of living which could not take precise form in her imagination but were founded on family legend of past wealth and leisure. These immediate comforts were what she could have, and she wanted them at once. She lagged rather far behind Paul, and once she thought of just turning back without a word and going home. She stopped, thinking that Paul would never do that to her, and so she would have to tell him. When a rabbit leaped, she let Paul have it without dispute. He killed it with one shot.

When she came up with him, he was already kneeling, examining the wound, the rabbit trailing from his hands. "Right through the head," he said complacently, as if he had aimed for it. He took out his sharp, competent bowie knife and started to skin the body. He did it very cleanly and quickly. Uncle Jimbilly knew how to prepare the skins so that Miranda always had fur coats for her dolls, for though she never cared much for her dolls she liked seeing them in fur coats. The children knelt facing each other over the dead animal. Miranda watched admiringly while her brother stripped the skin away as if he were taking off a glove. The flayed flesh emerged dark scarlet, sleek, firm; Miranda with thumb and finger felt the long fine muscles with the silvery flat strips binding them to the joints. Brother lifted the oddly bloated belly. "Look," he said, in a low amazed voice. "It was going to have young ones."

Very carefully he slit the thin flesh from the center ribs to the flanks, and a scarlet bag appeared. He slit again and pulled the bag open, and there lay a bundle of tiny rabbits, each wrapped in a thin scarlet veil. The brother pulled these off and there they were, dark gray, their sleek wet down lying in minute even ripples, like a baby's head just washed, their unbelievably small delicate ears folded close, their little blind faces almost featureless.

Miranda said, "Oh, I want to *see*," under her breath. She looked and looked—excited but not frightened, for she was accustomed to the sight of animals killed in hunting—filled with pity and astonishment and a kind of shocked delight in the wonderful little creatures for their own sakes, they were so pretty. She touched one of them ever so carefully, "Ah, there's blood running over them," she said and began to tremble without knowing why. Yet she wanted most deeply to see and to know. Having seen, she felt at once as if she had known all along. The very memory of her former ignorance faded, she had always known just this. No one had ever told her anything outright, she had been rather unobservant of the animal life around her because she was so accustomed to animals. They seemed simply disorderly and unaccountably rude in their habits, but altogether natural and not very interesting. Her brother had spoken as if he had known about everything all along. He may have seen all this before. He had never said a word to her, but she knew now a part at least of what he knew. She understood a little of the secret, formless intuitions in her own mind and body, which had been clearing up, taking form, so gradually and so steadily she had not realized that she was learning what she had to know. Paul said cautiously, as if he were talking about something forbidden: "They were just about ready to be born." His voice dropped on the last word. "I know," said Miranda, "like kittens. I know, like babies." She was quietly and terribly agitated, standing again with her rifle under her arm, looking down at the bloody heap. "I don't want the skin," she said, "I won't have it." Paul buried the young rabbits again in their mother's body, wrapped the skin around her, carried her to a clump of sage bushes, and hid her away. He came out again at once and said to Miranda, with an eager friendliness, a confidential tone quite unusual in him, as if he were taking her into an important secret on equal terms: "Listen now. Now you listen to me, and don't ever forget. Don't you ever tell a living soul that you saw this. Don't tell a soul. Don't tell Dad because I'll get into trouble. He'll say I'm leading you into things you ought not to do. He's always saying that. So now don't you go and forget and blab out sometime the way you're always doing . . . Now, that's a secret. Don't you tell."

Miranda never told, she did not even wish to tell anybody. She thought about the whole worrisome affair with confused unhappiness for a few days. Then it sank quietly into her mind and was heaped over by accumulated thousands of impressions, for nearly twenty years. One day she was picking her path among the puddles and crushed refuse of a market street in a strange city of a strange country, when without warning, plain and clear in its true colors as if she looked through a frame upon a scene that had not stirred nor changed since the moment it happened, the episode of that far-off day leaped from its burial place before her mind's eye. She was so reasonlessly horrified she halted suddenly staring, the scene before her eyes dimmed by the vision back of them. An Indian vendor had held up before her a tray of dyed sugar sweets, in the shapes of all kinds of small creatures: birds, baby chicks, baby rabbits, lambs, baby pigs. They were in gay colors and smelled of vanilla, maybe. . . . It was a very hot day and the smell in the market, with its piles of raw flesh and wilting flowers, was like the mingled sweetness and corruption she had smelled that other day in the empty cemetery at home: the day she had remembered always until now vaguely as the time she and her brother had found treasure in the opened graves. Instantly upon this thought the dreadful vision faded, and she saw clearly her brother, whose childhood face she had forgotten, standing again in the blazing sunshine, again twelve years old, a pleased sober smile in his eyes, turning the silver dove over and over in his hands.

CAROLINE GORDON

(1895–1981)

Caroline Gordon has written historical fiction, delineations of society, psychological characterization, and, sometimes, work of a strongly autobiographical nature. A vigorous adherent of the Jamesian approach to fiction, she has produced literary criticism that has emphasized problems of form and technique, always placing a premium upon fictional craftsmanship.

She was born in 1895, in Todd County, Kentucky. Her father, a Virginian, was a teacher and classical scholar as well as a passionate fisherman and hunter, and is the model for the figure of Aleck Maury who appears in the novel *Aleck Maury, Sportsman* (1934) and various short stories, including "The Last Day in the Field." Educated privately, Caroline Gordon enrolled at Bethany College and graduated in 1916. Afterward she taught high school and did newspaper work. In 1924 she married Allen Tate. Her first novel, *Penhally,* appeared in 1931. Subsequent novels include *None Shall Look Back* (1937), *The Garden of Adonis* (1937), *Green Centuries* (1941), *The Women on the Porch* (1944), *The Strange Children* (1951), *The Malefactors* (1956), and *The Glory of Hera* (1972). Her short fiction has been collected in *The Forest of the South* (1945) and *Old Red and Other Stories* (1963). In 1957 she published a volume of criticism, *How To Read a Novel* (1957).

In the late 1940s she joined the Roman Catholic Church. Her marriage to Allen Tate ended in divorce in 1957. Caroline Gordon has taught and been writer-in-residence at a number of colleges and universities, and since 1973 has been head of the Creative Writing program at the University of Dallas in Irving, Texas.

THE LAST DAY IN THE FIELD

That was the fall when the leaves stayed green so long. We had a drouth in August and the ponds everywhere were dry and the water courses shrunken. Then in September heavy rains came. Things greened up. It looked like winter was never coming.

"You aren't going to hunt this year, Aleck?" Molly said. "Remember how you stayed awake nights last fall with that pain in your leg."

In October light frosts came. In the afternoons when I sat on the back porch going over my fishing tackle I marked their progress on the elderberry bushes that were left standing against the stable fence. The lower, spreading branches had turned yellow and were already sinking to the ground but the leaves in the top clusters still stood up stiff and straight.

"Ah-ha, it'll get you yet!" I said, thinking how frost creeps higher and higher out of the ground each night of fall.

The dogs next door felt it and would thrust their noses through the wire fence scenting the wind from the north. When I walked in the back yard they would bound twice their height and whine, for meat scraps Molly said, but it was because they smelt blood on my old hunting coat.

They were almost matched liver-and-white pointers. The big dog had a beautiful, square muzzle and was deep-chested and rangy. The bitch, Judy, had a smaller head and not so good a muzzle but she was springy-loined too and had one of the merriest tails I've ever watched.

When Joe Thomas, the boy that owned them, came home from the hardware store he would change his clothes and then come down the back way and we would stand there watching the dogs and wondering how they would work. They had just been with a trainer up in Kentucky for three months. Joe said they were keen as mustard. He was going to take them out the first good Saturday and he wanted me to come along.

"I can't make it," I said. "My leg's worse this fall than it was last."

The fifteenth of November was clear and so warm that we sat out on the porch till nine o'clock. It was still warm when we went to bed towards eleven. The change must have come in the middle of the night. I woke once, hearing the clock strike two and felt the air cold on my face and thought before I went back to sleep that the weather had broken at last. When I woke again towards dawn the cold air slapped my face hard. I came wide awake, turned over in bed and looked out of the window. The sun was just coming up behind a wall of purple clouds streaked with amber. As I watched, it burned through and the light everywhere got bright.

There was a scaly bark hickory tree growing on the east side of the house. You could see its upper branches from the bedroom window. The leaves had turned yellow a week ago. But yesterday evening when I walked out there in the yard they had still been flat, with green streaks showing in them. Now they were curled up tight and a lot of leaves had fallen to the ground.

I got out of bed quietly so as not to wake Molly, dressed and went down the back way over to the Thomas house. There was no one stirring but I knew which room Joe's was. The window was open and I could hear him snoring. I went up and stuck my head in.

"Hey," I said, "killing frost!"

He opened his eyes and looked at me and then his eyes went shut. I reached my arm through the window and shook him. "Get up," I said. "We got to start right away."

He was awake now and out on the floor, stretching. I told him to dress and be over at the house as quick as he could. I'd have breakfast ready for us both.

Aunt Martha had a way of leaving fire in the kitchen stove at night. There were red embers there now. I poked the ashes out and piled kindling on top of them. When the flame came up I put some heavier wood on, filled the coffeepot and put some grease on in a skillet. By the time Joe got there I had coffee ready and had stirred up some hoe cakes to go with our fried eggs. Joe had brought a thermos bottle. We put the rest of the coffee in it and I found a ham in the pantry and made some sandwiches.

While I was fixing the lunch Joe went down to the lot to hitch up. He was just driving the buggy out of the stable when I came down the back steps. The dogs knew what was up, all right. They were whining and surging against the fence and Bob, the big dog, thrust his paw through and into the pocket of my hunting coat as I passed. While Joe was snapping on the leashes I got a few handfuls of straw from the rack and put in the foot of the buggy. It was twelve miles where we were going; the dogs would need to ride warm coming back.

Joe said he would drive. We got in the buggy and started out, up Seventh street, on over to College and out through Scufftown. When we got into the nigger section we could see what a killing frost it had been. A light shimmer over all the ground still and the weeds around all the cabins dark and matted the way they are when the frost hits them hard and twists them.

We drove on over the Red River bridge and out into the open country. At Jim Gill's place the cows had come up and were standing there waiting to be milked but nobody was stirring yet from the house. I looked back from the top of the hill and saw that the frost mists still hung heavy in the bottom and thought it was a good sign. A day like this when the earth is warmer than the air currents is good for the hunter. Scent particles are borne on the warm air; and birds will forage far on such a day.

It took us over an hour to get from Gloversville to Spring Creek. Joe wanted to get out as soon as we hit the big bottom there but I held him down and we drove on through and up Rollow's hill to the top of the ridge. We got out there, unhitched Old Dick and turned him into one of Rob Fayerlee's pastures—I thought how surprised Rob would be when he looked out and saw him grazing there—put our guns together and started out, with the dogs still on leash.

It was rough, broken ground, scrub oak with a few gum trees and lots of buckberry bushes. One place a patch of corn ran clear up to the top of the ridge. As we passed along between the rows, I could see the frost glistening on the north side of every stalk. I knew it was going to be a good day.

I walked over to the brow of the hill. From there you could see off over the whole valley—I've hunted over every foot of it in my time—tobacco land, mostly. One or two patches of cowpeas there on the side of the ridge. I thought we might start there and then I knew that wouldn't do. Quail will linger on the roost a cold day and feed in shelter during the morning. It is only in the afternoon that they will work out well into the open.

The dogs' whining made me turn around. Joe had bent down and was about to slip the leashes. "Hey, boy," I said, "wait a minute."

I turned around and looked down the other side of the hill. It looked better that way. The corn land of the bottoms ran high up on to the ridge in several places there and where the corn stopped there were big patches of ironweed and buckberry. I stooped and knocked my pipe out on a stump.

"Let's go that way," I said.

Joe was looking at my old buckhorn whistle that I had slung around my neck. "I forgot to bring mine," he said.

"All right," I said, "I'll handle 'em."

He unfastened their collars and cast off. They broke away, racing for the first hundred yards and barking, then suddenly swerved. The big dog took off to the right along the hillside. The bitch, Judy, skirted a belt of corn along the upper bottomlands. I kept my eye on the big dog. A dog that has bird sense knows cover when he sees it. This big Bob was an independent hunter. I could see him moving fast through the scrub oaks, working his way down towards a patch of ironweed. He caught the first scent traces just on the edge of the weed patch and froze. Judy, meanwhile, had been following the line of the corn field. A hundred yards away she caught sight of Bob's point and backed him.

We went up and flushed the birds. They got up in two bunches. I heard Joe's shot while I was in the act of raising my gun and I saw his bird fall not thirty paces from where I stood. I had covered a middle bird of the larger bunch—that's the one led by the boss cock—the way I usually do. He fell, whirling head over heels, driven a little forward by the impact. A wellcentered shot. I could tell by the way the feathers fluffed as he tumbled.

The dogs were off through the grass. They had retrieved both birds. Joe stuck his in his pocket. He laughed. "I thought there for a minute you were going to let him get away."

I looked at him but I didn't say anything. It's a wonderful thing to be twenty years old.

The majority of the singles had flown straight ahead to settle in the rank grass that jutted out from the bottom land. Judy got down to work at once but the big dog broke off to the left, wanting to get footloose to find another covey. I thought of how Gyges, the best dog I ever had—the best dog any man ever had—used always to want to do the same thing, and I laughed.

"Naw, you won't," I said. "Come back here, you scoundrel, and hunt these singles."

He stopped on the edge of a briar patch, looked at me and heeled up promptly. I clucked him out again. He gave me another look. I thought we were beginning to understand each other better. We got some nice points among those singles and I found him reasonably steady to both wing and shot, needing only a little control.

We followed that valley along the creek bed through two or three more corn fields without finding another covey. Joe was disappointed but I wasn't worrying yet; you always make your bag in the afternoon.

It was twelve o'clock by this time. We turned up the ravine towards Buck Springs. They had cleared out some of the big trees on the sides of the ravine but the spring itself was just the same: the tall sycamore tree and the water pouring in a thin stream over the slick rocks. I unwrapped the sandwiches and the pieces of cake and laid them on a stump. Joe had got the thermos bottle out of his pocket. Something had gone wrong with it and the coffee was stone cold. We were about to drink it that way when Joe saw a good tin can flung down beside the spring. He made a trash fire and we put the coffee in the can and heated it to boiling.

Joe finished his last sandwich and reached for the cake. "Good ham," he said.

"It's John Ferguson's," I said. I was watching the dogs. They were tired, all right. Judy had scooped out a soft place between the roots of the sycamore but the big dog, Bob, lay there with his forepaws stretched out before him, never taking his eyes off our faces. I looked at him and thought how different he was from his mate and like some dogs I had known—and men, too—who lived only for hunting and could never get enough no matter how long the day was. There was something about his head and his markings that reminded me of another dog I used to hunt with a long time ago and I asked the boy who had trained him. He said the old fellow he bought the dogs from had been killed last spring, over in Trigg: Charley Morrison.

Charley Morrison. I remembered how he died. Out hunting by himself and the gun had gone off, accidentally, they said.

Charley had called the dog to him, got blood all over him and sent him home. The dog went; all right, but when they got there Charley was dead. Two years ago that was and now I was hunting the last dogs he'd ever trained. . . .

Joe lifted the thermos bottle. "Another cup?"

I held my cup out and he filled it. The coffee was still good and hot. I lit my pipe and ran my eye over the country in front of us. I always enjoy figuring out which way they'll go. This afternoon with the hot coffee in me and the ache gone from my leg I felt like I could do it. It's not as hard as it looks. A well-organized covey has a range, like chickens. I knew what they'd be doing this time of day: in a thicket, dusting—sometimes they'll get up in grapevine swings. Then after they've fed and rested they'll start out again, working always towards the open.

Joe was stamping out his cigarette. "Let's go."

The dogs were already out of sight but I could see the sedge grass ahead moving and I knew they'd be making for the same thing that took my eye: a spearhead of thicket that ran far out into this open field. We came up over a little rise. There they were. Bob on a point and Judy, the staunch little devil, backing him, not fifty feet from the thicket. I saw it was going to be tough shooting. No way to tell whether the birds were between the dog and the thicket or in the thicket itself. Then I saw that the cover was more open along the side of the thicket and I thought that that was the way they'd go if they were in the thicket. But Joe had already broken away to the left. He got too far to the side. The birds flushed to the right and left him standing, flat-footed, without a shot.

He looked sort of foolish and grinned.

I thought I wouldn't say anything and then found myself speaking:

"Trouble with you, you try to out-think the dog."

There was nothing to do about it now, though, and the chances were that the singles had pitched through the trees below. We went down there. It was hard hunting. The woods were open, the ground heavily carpeted everywhere with leaves. Dead leaves make a tremendous rustle when the dogs surge through them; it takes a good nose to cut scent keenly in such dry, noisy cover. I kept my eye on Bob. He never faltered, getting over the ground in big, springy strides but combing every inch of it. We came to an open place in the woods. Nothing but big hickory trees and bramble thickets overhung with trailing vines. Bob passed the first thicket and came to a beautiful point. We went up. He stood perfectly steady but the bird flushed out fifteen or twenty steps ahead of him. I saw it swing to the right, gaining altitude very quickly, and it came to me how it would be.

I called to Joe: "Don't shoot yet."

He nodded and raised his gun, following the bird with the barrel. It was directly over the treetops when I gave the word and he shot, scoring a clean kill.

He laughed excitedly as he stuck the bird in his pocket. "*Man!* I didn't know you could take that much time!"

We went on through the open woods. I was thinking about a day I'd had years ago, in the woods at Grassdale, with my uncle, James Morris, and his son Julian. Uncle James had given Julian and me hell for missing just such a shot. I can see him now, standing up against a big pine tree, his face red from liquor and his gray hair ruffling in the wind: "*Let him alone. Let him alone!* And establish your lead as he *climbs!*"

Joe was still talking about the shot he'd made. "Lord, I wish I could get another one like that."

"You won't," I said. "We're getting out of the woods now."

We struck a path that led through the woods. My leg was stiff from the hip down and every time I brought it over the pain would start in my knee, zing, and travel up and settle in the small of my back. I walked with my head down, watching the light catch on the ridges of Joe's brown corduroy trousers and then shift and catch again as he moved forwards. Sometimes he would get on ahead and then there would be nothing but the black tree trunks coming up out of the dead leaves that were all over the ground.

Joe was talking about that wild land up on the Cumberland. We could get up there some Saturday on an early train. Have a good day. Might even spend the night. When I didn't answer he turned around. "Man, you're sweating!"

I pulled my handkerchief out and wiped my face. "Hot work," I said.

He had stopped and was looking about him. "Used to be a spring somewhere around here."

He had found the path and was off. I sat down on a stump and mopped my face some more. The sun was halfway down through the trees, the whole west woods ablaze with light. I sat there and thought that in another hour it would be good dark and I wished that the day could go on and not end so soon and yet I didn't see how I could make it much farther with my leg the way it was.

Joe was coming up the path with his folding cup full of water. I hadn't thought I was thirsty but the cold water tasted good. We sat there awhile and smoked. It was Joe said we ought to be starting back, that we must be a good piece from the rig by this time.

We set out, working north through the edge of the woods. It was rough going and I was thinking that it would be all I could do to make it back to the rig when we climbed a fence and came out at one end of a long field. It sloped down to a wooded ravine, broken ground badly gullied and covered with sedge everywhere except where sumac thickets had sprung up—as birdy a place as ever I saw. I looked it over and I knew I'd have to hunt it, leg or no leg, but it would be close work, for me and the dogs too.

I blew them in a bit and we stood there watching them cut up the cover. The sun was down now; there was just enough light left to see the dogs work. The big dog circled the far wall of the basin and came upwind just off the drain, then stiffened to a point. We walked down to it. The birds had obviously run a bit, into the scraggly sumac stalks that bordered the ditch. My mind was so much on the dogs that I forgot Joe. He took one step too many and the fullest blown bevy of the day roared up through the tangle. It had to be fast work. I raised my gun and scored with the only barrel I had time to peg. Joe shouted: I knew he had got one too.

We stood awhile trying to figure out which way the singles had gone. But they had fanned out too quick for us and after beating around the thicket for fifteen minutes or so we gave up and went on.

We came to the rim of the swale, eased over it, crossed the dry creek bed that was drifted thick with leaves and started up the other side. I had blown in the dogs, thinking there was no use for them to run their heads off now we'd started home, but they didn't come. I walked a little way, then I looked back and saw Bob's white shoulders through a tangle of cinnamon vines.

Joe had turned around too. "Look a yonder! They've pinned a single out of that last covey."

"Your shot," I told him.

He shook his head. "No, you take it."

I went back and flushed the bird. It went skimming along the buckberry bushes that covered that side of the swale. In the fading light I could hardly make it out and I shot too quick. It swerved over the thicket and I let go with the second barrel. It staggered, then zoomed up. Up, up, up, over the rim of the hill and above the tallest hickories. I saw it there for a second, its wings black against the gold light, before, wings still spread, it came whirling down, like an autumn leaf, like the leaves that were everywhere about us, all over the ground.

ROBERT PENN WARREN

(1905–)

In 1924, when Robert Penn Warren was still an undergraduate student at Vanderbilt University, Allen Tate declared to Donald Davidson that their young colleague "has more sheer genius than any of us; watch him: his work from now on will have what none of us can achieve—power." Indeed, Warren did have power as a writer and he has been using it prodigally for more than a half-century.

Youngest of the major Fugitive poets, Warren was born in Guthrie, Kentucky, which during his earliest years was a place of considerable unrest and violence resulting from the Black Patch Tobacco War, in which tobacco farmers turned to night-riding to resist the monopolistic practices of the tobacco trust. Throughout his childhood and youth Warren spent his summers at the farm of his grandfather, a Confederate veteran who told him stories of the war and the bushwhacking operations and lawlessness in its aftermath. At Vanderbilt University, he enrolled in John Crowe Ransom's freshman English course and in Donald Davidson's literature class, was invited to join the Fugitives, and soon became convinced that literature was his career. Following graduation, he went on for graduate study at the University of California and at Yale, then to England and spent two years as a Rhodes Scholar at Oxford. He was already publishing poetry, essays, articles, and book reviews in various magazines. His first book, a biography, *John Brown: The Making of a Martyr*, came out in 1929. At Oxford he wrote his essay, "The Briar Patch," for

I'll Take My Stand and began his lifelong involvement in the writing of fiction with a novella based on the Black Patch War, "Prime Leaf." He returned to the United States in 1930 to teach at Southwestern University, then to Vanderbilt for a teaching appointment there, and in 1934 joined his friend Cleanth Brooks at Louisiana State University. With Brooks and Charles W. Pipkin he founded the *Southern Review*, which from 1936 until its wartime demise in 1942 was perhaps the leading literary periodical in America. Throughout this time he was writing poetry. In 1935 came *Thirty-Six Poems*, in 1942 *Eleven Poems on the Same Theme*, and in 1944 *Selected Poems 1923–1943*. Meanwhile, his engagement with fiction continued, and in 1939 he published his first full-length novel, *Night Rider*.

Warren left Louisiana to be professor of English at the University of Minnesota in 1942. The following year he brought out his second novel, *At Heaven's Gate*. He had also begun working on a verse play that turned into a novel and in 1946 was published as *All The King's Men*. Based on a figure much like the late Huey P. Long, governor of Louisiana and United States Senator before his assassination in 1935, *All The King's Men* was not only a critical and popular success, but in the decades since its publication it has won and held international acclaim for its compelling fictional examination of the meanings of public power and private moral responsibility in a democracy.

In 1950 Warren joined the faculty at Yale University, where except for a five-year hiatus he taught until his retirement in 1973. Divorced in 1951 from Emma Brescia, he married the novelist Eleanor Clark in 1952. He has published seven more novels: *World Enough and Time* (1950), *Band of Angels* (1955), *The Cave* (1959), *Wilderness* (1961), *Flood* (1964), *Meet Me in the Green Glen* (1971), and *A Place to Come To* (1977). Always very much concerned with the workings of politics and society, and with the history of the South and the nation, he has written books on *Segregation: The Inner Conflict in the South* (1957), *The Legacy of the Civil War* (1961), *Who Speaks for the Negro?* (1965) and *Democracy and Poetry* (1975). As a literary critic he was editor, with Cleanth Brooks, of the textbook anthology *Understanding Poetry* (1938), a volume that, in giving a practical application of the methods of the New Criticism, has had enormous influence in the teaching of poetry in colleges and universities. Warren acted as editor for other Brooks and Warren textbook anthologies including *Understanding Fiction* (1943), *An Approach to Literature* (1936, with John T. Purser), *Modern Rhetoric* (1949), and *American Literature: The Makers and the Making* (1973, with R. W. B. Lewis). His own books of criticism include *Selected Essays* (1958) and *Homage to Theodore Dreiser* (1972).

Warren's poetry, which along with *All The King's Men* may turn out to be his most lasting achievement as a writer, has changed and developed over the years. His early reputation was as a poet of compressed, intricately wrought lyric poems, of which "Bearded Oaks" is an example. During the late

1930s, however, he began moving toward a longer, more meditative form, with greater personal assertion. During the middle and late 1940s Warren ceased for a time to write much poetry. In 1953, however, he published a long poem in dramatic form, "Brother to Dragons," based on an incident in early Kentucky history, in which the presence of the poet as "R. P. W." functioned as a kind of chorus, conversing with the characters and offering a commentary on the events and their meanings. Perhaps the experience of that role, in which as speaker of the poem he could directly address the reader as "I" and offer personal interpolations on the subject and theme of the poem, helped effect his return to lyric poetry; in any event, beginning with the new poems collected in *Promises: Poems 1954-1956* (1957) Warren moved into a new and sustained involvement with verse. The following years saw publication of *You, Emperors and Others: Poems 1957–1960* (1960), *Selected Poems: New and Old, 1923–1966* (1966), *Incarnations: Poems 1966–1968* (1968), *Audubon: A Vision* (1969), and *Selected Poems: 1923-1975* (1975). With each new volume Warren seemed to deepen his insights and expand the range and variety of his techniques. In particular, the poetry of *Audubon* offered a flowing, freely changing meditative lyricism together with the sharply focused intensification of language that from the early Fugitive days onward has marked Warren's poetry.

BEARDED OAKS

The oaks, how subtle and marine,
Bearded, and all the layered light
Above them swims; and thus the scene,
Recessed, awaits the positive night.

So, waiting, we in the grass now lie
Beneath the languorous tread of light:
The grasses, kelp-like, satisfy
The nameless motions of the air.

Upon the floor of light, and time,
Unmurmuring, of polyp made,
We rest; we are, as light withdraws,
Twin atolls on a shelf of shade.

Ages to our construction went,
Dim architecture, hour by hour:
And violence, forgot now, lent
The present stillness all its power.

The storm of noon above us rolled,
Of light the fury, furious gold,

The long drag troubling us, the depth:
Dark is unrocking, unrippling, still.

Passion and slaughter, ruth, decay
Descend, minutely whispering down,
Silted down swaying streams, to lay
Foundations for our voicelessness.

All our debate is voiceless here,
As all our rage, the rage of stone;
If hope is hopeless, then fearless is fear,
And history is thus undone.

Our feet once wrought the hollow street
With echo when the lamps were dead
At windows, once our headlight glare
Disturbed the doe that, leaping, fled.

I do not love you less that now
The caged heart makes iron stroke,
Or less that all that light once gave
The graduate dark should now revoke.

We live in time so little time
And we learn all so painfully,
That we may spare this hour's term
To practice for eternity.

1944

From PROMISES

VII

SUMMER STORM (CIRCA 1916), AND GOD'S GRACE

Toward sun, the sun flared suddenly red.
　The green of woods was doused to black.
　The cattle bellowed by the haystack.
Redder than ever, red clay was red.
　Up the lane the plowhands came pelting back.

Astride and no saddle, and they didn't care
　If a razor-back mule at a break-tooth trot
　Was not the best comfort a man ever got,
But came huddling on, with jangling gear,

And the hat that jounced off stayed off, like as not.

In that strange light all distance died.
   You know the world's intensity.
   Field-far, you can read the aphid's eye.
The mole, in his sod, can no more hide,
   And weeps beneath the naked sky.

Past silence, sound insinuates
   Past ear into the inner brain.
   The toad's asthmatic breath is pain,
The cutworm's tooth grinds and grates,
   And the root, in earth, screams, screams again,

But no cloud yet. No wind, though you,
   A half a county off, now spy
   The crow that, laboring zenith-high,
Is suddenly, with wings askew,
   Snatched, and tumbled down the sky.

And so you wait. You cannot talk.
   The creek-side willows shudder gray.
   The oak leaves turn the other way,
Gray as fish-belly. Then, with a squawk,
   The henhouse heaves, and dies away,

And darkness rides in on the wind.
   The pitchfork lightning tosses the trees,
   And God gets down on hands and knees
To peer and cackle and commend
   His own sadistic idiocies.

Next morning you stood where the bridge had washed out.
   A drowned cow bobbled down the creek.
   Raw-eyed, men watched. They did not speak.
Till one shrugged, said he guessed he'd make out.
   Then turned, took the woods-path up the creek.

VIII

FOUNDING FATHERS, NINETEENTH-CENTURY STYLE, SOUTHEAST U.S.A.

They were human, they suffered, wore long black coat and gold watch
chain.

They stare from daguerreotype with severe reprehension,
Or from genuine oil, and you'd never guess any pain
In those merciless eyes that now remark our own time's sad declension.

Some composed declarations, remembering Jefferson's language.
Knew pose of the patriot, left hand in crook of the spine or
With finger to table, while the right invokes the Lord's just rage.
There was always a grandpa, or cousin at least, who had been a real Signer.

Some were given to study, read Greek in the forest, and these
Longed for an epic to do their own deeds right honor:
Were Nestor by pigpen, in some tavern brawl played Achilles.
In the ring of Sam Houston they found, when he died, one word
engraved: *Honor*.

Their children were broadcast, like millet seed flung in a wind-flare.
Wives died, were dropped like old shirts in some corner of country.
Said, "Mister," in bed, the child-bride; hadn't known what to find there;
Wept all next morning for shame; took pleasure in silk; wore the keys to
the pantry.

"Will die in these ditches if need be," wrote Bowie, at the Alamo.
And did, he whose left foot, soft-catting, came forward, and breath hissed:
Head back, gray eyes narrow, thumb flat along knife-blade, blade low.
"Great gentleman," said Henry Clay, "and a patriot." Portrait by
Benjamin West.

Or take those, the nameless, of whom no portraits remain,
No locket or seal ring, though somewhere, broken and rusted,
In attic or earth, the long Decherd, stock rotten, has lain;
Or the mold-yellow Bible, God's Word, in which, in their strength,
they also trusted.

Some wrestled the angel, and took a fall by the corncrib.
Fought the brute, stomp-and-gouge, but knew they were doomed
in that glory.

All night, in sweat, groaned; fell at last with spit red and a cracked rib.
How sweet then the tears! Thus gentled, they roved the dark land with
the old story.

Some prospered, had black men and acres, and silver on table,
But remembered the owl call, the smell of burnt bear fat on dusk-air.
Loved family and friends, and stood it as long as able—
"But money and women, too much is ruination, am Arkansas-bound."
So went there.

One of mine was a land shark, or so the book with scant praise
Denominates him. "A man large and shapeless,
Like a sack of potatoes set on a saddle," it says,
"Little learning but shrewd, not well trusted." Rides thus out of history,
neck fat and napeless.

One fought Shiloh and such, got cranky, would fiddle all night.
The boys nagged for Texas. "God damn it, there's nothing, God damn it,
In Texas"—but took wagons, went, and to prove he was right,
Stayed a year and a day—"hell, nothing in Texas"—had proved it,
came back to black vomit,

And died, and they died, and are dead, and now their voices
Come thin, like the last cricket in frost-dark, in grass lost,
With nothing to tell us for our complexity of choices,
But beg us only one word to justify their own old life-cost.

So let us bend ear to them in this hour of lateness,
And what they are trying to say, try to understand,
And try to forgive them their defects, even their greatness,
For we are their children in the light of humanness, and under the shadow
of God's closing hand.

1957

From AUDUBON

V

THE SOUND OF THAT WIND

[A]

He walked in the world. Knew the lust of the eye.

Wrote: "Ever since a Boy I have had an astonishing desire
      to see Much of the World and particularly
      to acquire a true knowledge of the Birds of North America."

AUDUBON

He dreamed of hunting with Boone, from imagination painted his portrait.
He proved that the buzzard does not scent its repast, but sights it.
He looked in the eye of the wounded white-headed eagle.

Wrote: ". . . the Noble Fellow looked at his Ennemies
      with a Contemptible Eye."

At dusk he stood on a bluff, and the bellowing of buffalo
Was like distant ocean. He saw
Bones whiten the plain in the hot daylight.

He saw the Indian, and felt the splendor of God.

Wrote: ". . . for there I see the Man Naked from his
      hand and yet free from acquired Sorrow."

Below the salt, in rich houses, he sat, and knew insult.
In the lobbies and couloirs of greatness he dangled,
And was not unacquainted with contumely.

Wrote: "My lovely Miss Pirrie of Oackley Passed by Me
      this Morning, but did not remember how beautifull
      I had rendered her face once by Painting it
      at her Request with Pastelles."

Wrote: ". . . but thanks to My humble talents I can run
      the gantlet throu this World without her help."

And ran it, and ran undistracted by promise of ease,
Nor even the kind condescension of Daniel Webster.

Wrote: ". . . would give me a fat place was I willing to
      have one; but I love indepenn and piece more
      than humbug and money."

And proved same, but in the end, entered
On honor. Far, over the ocean, in the silken salons,
With hair worn long like a hunter's, eyes shining,
He whistled the bird-calls of his distant forest.

Wrote: ". . . in my sleep I continually dream of birds."

And in the end, entered into his earned house,
And slept in a bed, and with Lucy.

                 But the fiddle
Soon lay on the shelf untouched, the mouthpiece
Of the flute was dry, and his brushes.
                  His mind
Was darkened, and his last joy

Was in the lullaby they sang him, in Spanish, at sunset.

He died, and was mourned, who had loved the world.

Who had written ". . . a world which though wicked enough
               in all conscience is *perhaps* as good
               as worlds unknown."

[B]

So died in his bed, and
Night leaned, and now leans,
Off the Atlantic, and is on schedule.
Grass does not bend beneath that enormous weight
That with no sound sweeps westward. In the Mississippi,
On a mud bank, the wreck of a great tree, left
By flood, lies, the root-system and now-stubbed boughs
Lifting in darkness. It
Is white as bone. That whiteness
Is reflected in dark water, and a star
Thereby.

      Later,
In the shack of a sheep-herder, high above the Bitterroot,
The light goes out. No other
Light is visible

The Northwest Orient plane, New York to Seattle, has passed,
                         winking westward.

[C]

For everything there is a season.

But there is the dream
Of a season past all seasons.

. . .

In such a dream the wild-grape cluster,
High-hung, exposed in the gold light,
Unripening, ripens.

Stained, the lip with wetness gleams.

I see your lip, undrying, gleam in the bright wind.

I cannot hear the sound of that wind.

1969

EVENING HAWK

From plane of light to plane, wings dipping through
Geometries and orchids that the sunset builds,
Out of the peak's black angularity of shadow, riding
The last tumultuous avalanche of
Light above pines and the guttural gorge,
The hawk comes.

        His wing
Scythes down another day, his motion
Is that of the honed steel-edge, we hear
The crashless fall of stalks of Time.

The head of each stalk is heavy with the gold of our error.

Look! look! he is climbing the last light
Who knows neither Time nor error, and under
Whose eye, unforgiving, the world, unforgiven, swings
Into shadow.

        Long now,
The last thrush is still, the last bat
Now cruises in his sharp hieroglyphics. His wisdom
Is ancient, too, and immense. The star
Is steady, like Plato, over the mountain.

If there were no wind we might, we think, hear
The earth grind on its axis, or history
Drip in darkness like a leaking pipe in the cellar.

1975

ANDREW NELSON LYTLE

(1902–   )

Andrew Lytle was born in Murfreesboro, Tennessee, graduated from Vanderbilt University and was briefly a member of the Fugitives, then studied at the Yale School of Drama, and worked in New York as an actor. He came back to Tennessee to manage his father's farm, "Cornsilk," and to write. His essay in the Agrarian symposium *I'll Take My Stand* established the theme and locale of almost all his writing: the rural South, not the South of plantations but of upcountry farms and farmers, and its history and ways. His first book was a biography, *Bedford Forest and His Critter Company* (1931). In 1936 his first novel appeared, *The Long Night.* Lytle taught at Southwestern University in Memphis, the University of the South, the State University of Iowa, and the University of Florida. He was acting editor of the *Sewanee Review* in 1943–1944, served as managing editor in 1947–1948, and in 1961 returned to Sewanee as editor of the magazine and professor of English. He retired in 1973, lived for a while in Kentucky, then returned to Sewanee to live at nearby Monteagle.

In addition to several works of short fiction, Lytle has written four novels, including *At The Moon's Inn* (1941), *A Name for Evil* (1947), and *The Velvet Horn* (1957), and a novella, *Alchemy* (1942). In 1966 a volume of his essays, *The Hero with the Private Parts*, was published. His most recent work is a memoir, *A Wake for the Living: A Family Chronicle* (1975), an anecdotal account of his family from colonial times onward, in which he displays his widely acknowledged mastery of storytelling, including some of the tall-tale variety, together with a stern moral commentary on the erosion of traditional rural values in modern urban society.

From A WAKE FOR THE LIVING

From "SHARDS"

Uncle Tom Lytle set himself up as a lawyer, with political interests. In out-of-the-way boardinghouses and inns he found himself at home. He liked the trades over tobacco and whiskey, as the spittoons rang with juice. And he liked but was not too good at poker. At one time he was to run for governor, but the trades fell through. Uncle Eph was left with five thousand dollars' worth of campaign pictures in his attic, a good price to pay when all you have to do is step out of the door and see your brother in the flesh.

Uncle Tom was a big-boned man and tall and large. He was persuasive before judge and jury. As chancellor he often would argue with the lawyers appearing before him. Once in Grundy County, where everybody was armed, he had a case thrown out of court on a technicality. And nobody bothered him.

In the early days the men in the mountains, as well as elsewhere in the country, generally fought with their fists. Sometimes with knives, but the usual question was, "Fist and skull or stomp and gouge?" The feuds we hear about started in the Civil War. Both sides raided and bushwhacked enemy families and soldiers home on leave. Or just home. This began the shootings and ugly doings.

The railroad at Monteagle separates Marion and Grundy counties. On the tracks once a man was stabbed and brought home to die. The church members gathered and prayed and sang, especially that good old hymn "We Shall Gather at the River." At their urging he forgave his enemy, but he did not promise the kiss of peace. The doctor was slow to arrive. The roads were none too good, sandy and twisting, and made for horse and buggy or just a saddle horse. When he did arrive, he looked at the wound, took a washcloth and cleaned it out. "It's just a flesh wound. You'll be all right in a few days."

"Give me my breeches," the man said, swinging to the side of the bed. "I'll kill the son of a bitch."

This world Uncle Tom was familiar with in his younger days. He didn't seem very fit for domestic life, but he courted Miss Lizzie Robertson. She never loved another so well, but he was slow to come to the point. He would forget to take her to dances, and my father would have to stand in for him. She finally got tired of this and married a Mr. Fox, who conveniently died and left her a small estate. Not too long afterwards she and Uncle Tom were married. And not too long after the hymeneal celebration she wrote a three-dollar check and it bounced. There was some mistake, she knew, for she had just deposited ten thousand dollars. But there was no mistake. Uncle Tom had gambled it away.

She came to Uncle Eph in tears. He promised to speak sternly to his brother, but as she turned away, she said, "Don't be too hard on him, Eph."

Uncle Tom thought it the best of jests. "Who do you love best, Lizzie," he asked, "the quick or the dead?"

I don't know when it was that Mammy married a second time. She and her children would have been nearby Grandma until she did. Grandma's good management was by now a habit at Rose Hill. Her table was as good. The preachers still accepted her Sunday invitations to dinner, to the chagrin of her neighbors. This is the best measure of her food. Kin and connections frequently drove up to spend the day or longer. In the country you made no afternoon town visits.

Cousin Ada Colville from McMinnville, her husband's niece, would spend the day when she came to visit her family on the Franklin Dirt Road. She had married into an old family in McMinnville. Old almost means conservative, for such this town was in morals and money. During the bank holiday under Roosevelt, the Colville bank was the only bank in the United States that didn't close its doors.

Its citizens cut crossties and timber and bought ginseng. "Sang" it is called, an herb with a rare mandrake-looking root worth more than its weight in gold. The Chinese thought, still think, it is a cure-all and in instances can restore potency. A man from the hills would come in with a little sack over his shoulder and drive home with a two-horse wagonload of supplies.

Cousin Ada was a round jolly little matron and gave much pleasure to those about her. On this particular visit Grandma had other guests. Her table groaned, as they used to say. The meat would have been broilers, if

554

ANDREW NELSON LYTLE

they sat down in May, fried chicken if in June, or possibly spring lamb. If in early fall mutton, the old ewe being called upon to do her part. Beef would have been unlikely. Few country houses had icehouses. Even so, if the winter was mild, the ponds would not freeze over and the ice, what there was of it, wouldn't last.

In this predicament people formed beef clubs, and a young heir could not inherit a more valuable gift than his father's membership. The club was composed of twelve men, each of whom, when his turn came, furnished an animal for slaughter. The meat was divided twelve ways each month, so that a member in a year's time ate a whole cow. The butcher got the hide and a dollar.

I doubt if Grandma belonged to such a club, but with the fowl or meat there would have been a two-year-old ham on the sideboard. Ham was a side dish in her house and in most houses of the time, except on Sunday nights. The bread would have been some kind of cornbread or rolls, with plenty of jams and jellies and pickles and citron made of watermelon rind. These condiments were delicacies to me, for there were no artificial aids then. Strawberries can stand very little heat or they lose their fragrancy. Grandma never cooked them on the stove. She put the sugar on the berries in a pan and the pan on the roof and let the sun do it. These skills of hers showed that day, ice cream made of custard and cake with icing so thick it was like soft candy. The dessert, however, was plum pudding. Maybe the weather was frosty and drawing towards Christmas and a two-year-old turkey hen. She had a plain man for guest. When the pudding came in blazing, and the blue flames licked the air, he called out in alarm, "Look thar, Miss Jule, your bread's afare."

It had been noticed that towards the end of the meal Cousin Ada had grown restless in her chair, so Grandma did not linger at table. The guests followed her into the family room.

This was a country house, and although dogs were forbidden the house, they would slip in. Where there are dogs, there are fleas. One of them got on Cousin Ada. The cousin excused herself and went into the parlor. Parlors were usually dark, except on formal occasions such as death, weddings, or courtships reaching serious considerations. Then a fire would be made to blaze and cheer the young couple in their anticipation. It so happened that Uncle Jack had had too much cheer to join his mother's guests and was lying on a sofa in the parlor to recover himself.

Cousin Ada's entrance aroused him somewhat, although in her haste she did not see him. The flea which was making a hop exploration beneath her underskirts absorbed her attention. The flea was active and bit hard. She lifted her skirt and underskirts, no easy matter in those days when skirts reached to the floor. Finally she bent way over and pinched. Well, she had eaten hearty. Either the meat or the plum pudding on top of everything else undid her. It brought Uncle Jack up from the couch. "That's right, Ada. If you cain't ketch him, shoot him."

One day shortly after this, Uncle Jack was in town and his brother Tom had him to the Robertsons' for dinner, thinking no doubt the food would do him good. The Robertson women were painfully shy and all had flashing eyes. As he sat before the fire, old Mrs. Robertson addressed him. She had just had her chimney worked on. "Mr. Lytle," she asked, "do you think my chimney will draw?"

"Draw," he said. "It'll draw your coattails over your head."

Coattails and women's garments were much in his mind. It was ideal love with him as a young man. He saw flesh and spirit as one union, but the Muse who roosts upon the rooftree likes best soft, dulcet tones. And this requires a mellow palate, not a cleft one. No matter how seductive the words, it is hard to raise a mush-mouthed drone to lyrical heights. But Uncle Jack tried. At times he must have thought upon the advantages of a cleft foot.

One night he was courting in a neighbor's house. The weather turned bad and he found himself benighted. Time came to go up into the boys' room and he remembered he had forgotten to put on any socks. He could hear what unkind people would say about the old sock, or sockless but not bootless. He pulled away in the corner and when the boot yielded said to his roommates, "Off come boot, sock, and all."

Luckless as he continued in these affairs, he had visions of maenads and nymphs with gently stroking hands, brought at last to earth in a foot-washing Baptist church house at Christiana. It was rumored that young ladies would minister to the foot-weary and to all sinners. Jack could hardly wait, thinking of those sweet-smelling fingers and the tickling water submerging the foot, the lifting out, the rough caress as the flesh was dried. He was careful this time to wash a foot and put on a fresh sock. Alas, before he could protest, a buxom country girl jerked off the wrong boot. With averted nose and a scowl she passed him by. When the collection pan was passed and the last hymn sung, he went outside, untied the halter, and took a drink.

One wonders if he knew he had become a comic figure. Sober, he was painfully shy and did not go about much among people, not even to his nephew's wedding. He hunted and fished the streams with his companions, shot marbles and drank. One morning his hostess called up the stairwell, "Now, boys, get up. This is Monday. Let's turn over a new leaf."

Uncle Jack leaned up from his feather pillow. "All right," he said. "Turn her over, boys," and he and his companions spooned back into sleep.

It was to be expected that his lovelorn plight and equally bad luck would get about. People began to tease him, and since he was forever hopeful, this was easy sport. In those days there were play party games for entertainment. They were very like children's games: Fox in the Wonder, Goose and the Gander, Musical Chairs, and charades. One game the lights were turned down and you hid. For the finder a kiss. At a particular country house a young woman came up to Uncle Jack and said, "Mr. Lytle, if you hide in the chest, I'll find you."

"I'll shore do it," he said.

Her eyes were mischievous and alluring as she lowered the lid upon him. And then he heard the key turn in the lock. She was being extra careful. The players wandered about, calling and jesting and pretending their parts, when a voice yelled, "Fire."

There can be no more frightening word in a country house. Furniture was moved. People scurried about. Uncle Jack suspected a trick, until the old grandmother raised a quavering voice, "Be sure and save my sewing machine," a fairly new and valuable instrument.

Uncle Jack's shout was muffled but he was heard, "Let the sewing machine rest. Take the chest. Take the chest and set it way out in the yard."

This was coarse humor, but it is a humor common to farming society and to our inheritance from the old country. Malvolio suffered it. It had a quality which the traveling salesman's joke and the general obscenity of so-called humor lacks. The jester in receiving his public embarrassment received it through laughter, kind as well as humiliating. All it hurt was vanity, unless wit is lacking. Such chastisement allows the community to purge itself, to remind itself of our common plight.

At last Fortune perched upon his rooftree. A schoolteacher from Mississippi agreed to marry him. But he must promise to give up drinking. He made the heroic decision, but who can tell what lies in wait to undo us. He had a friend whose wife was ambitious to take all the prizes at the County Fair. She had sewed and baked and jellied and jammed and even tried her hand at making beaten biscuit, when everybody knew that Aunt Susie's Carline got the prize one year and Ada Rohan, Wright Ross's aunt's cook, the next. Nevertheless she took the challenge. It was a bold one, and there is little doubt but what the domestic routine of her household suffered an unusual strain. She did get a ribbon, a red one maybe, I think, for her husband's sorghum molasses.

Uncle Jack helped tote the defeated artifacts down to the spring wagon. The steps were very steep in the woman's pavilion. The lady's ire blinded her vision. She stumbled over a dragging quilt and fell to the bottom of the stairs and lay there. Her husband didn't offer to pick her up. He did say, "Well, now, showed everything you've got and ain't taken a prize yet."

Uncle Jack had no notion of this aspect of marriage. The skies darkened with rain clouds and a chill came into the air. Downcast in mind, he found he had taken a drink. No man can stand on one leg; so he took another. Before the day was out, his girl smelled his breath and gave his ring back. Each time he thought of woman thereafter, her unreasonableness and, he was compelled to acknowledge, her greed, he took another drink.

He decided to go and get his presents back. He hitched up his wagon

—he had only to drive into Bedford County—but he was late coming home. The entire family came out to greet him, hoping the lovers had made it up. He was muddy. It could be seen that the wagon had turned over several times. Upon the wagon bed sat a parrot with ruffled feathers in a muddy cage. Uncle Jack turned his head. "I offered Poll a drink, but she declined. 'One of us better remain sober,' she said."

After this there were for him only the mourning doves, which he shot occasionally for the table. He took a housekeeper. There is not much to go on as to how well she cooked or how tender her care. She must have been a stout woman, for one night in her presence he shot at a clock Mammy had given him. Apparently this didn't impress her. She remarked that she was a good pistol shot herself, which he seems not to have been, as the clock was still running next morning. He brought the pieces to his sister. "Here, Sis Kate, are thirteen superfluous works out of that clock."

His plight found at times the shocking reprieve of delirium tremens. Even this failed to arouse sympathy. One Christmas he and my father, a growing boy, were together in the family room. Two candles burned on the mantel. Uncle Jack looked at them unsteadily and turned to his nephew. "How many candles burning there?"

"One," his nephew said.

There is only one sensible contemplation for the lover perpetually denied: those spirits which giveth the desire but take away the execution. When these fail, the lover wanders out the night, and in a country neighborhood, out of loneliness, calls where his horse takes him. Sometimes a young Fletcher would find Uncle Jack as bedfellow, or he might drop by Squire Fletcher's and engage a serving man of his in conversation. And perhaps in drink.

This man was a Yankee who had stopped by on his way home after the war to remain in the squire's service. Uncle Jack sat up with him in his last illness. The squire came in with a yardstick and began to measure him for his coffin.

"Don't do the work of the worms, Squire," Uncle Jack said. "They'll measure us all without pay."

The squire licked his pencil and wrote down a figure. "I've got a wagon going to town tomorrow," he said.

Between Christmas and New Year's there is a surfeit which dulls the palate and cloys appetite. He must have tried hard to drink this away. Certainly charity had run out on him. His decline must have seemed obvious to many. I found copies of these two notes, both in a very fine hand.

Mr. R. L. Jamison

        Having reliable information that you have charged me with appropriating funds from your cash drawer, I demand that you give over your signature a denial in toto, that the charge may be proven a base fabrication without the least grounds for suspicion.

(Signed) John Lytle,
Christmas Dec. 29, 1876

Mr. John Lytle
Dear Sir

Yours of this date to hand, in reply would say that if you have given the least credence to the report from any circulation that I may have given it, I assure you that I heartily retract all that I may have said and farther state, I believe you have been maliciously misrepresented. Hoping the above may be satisfactory

I am yours as ever
(signed) R. L. Jamison.
Christmas Dec. 29, 1879

The later date must be the right one, or had Uncle Jack along with the clock shot time away?

Matters did not improve for him. Increasingly he became the subject of rough humor. Once somebody put salt in Uncle Jack's jug of whiskey. He flourished his pistol, and everybody fled the house but Grandma. She said, "You may shoot me, but you are not going to run me out of my own house."

He was not, in spite of his sorrows, without friends. I knew one of them, Captain Weaver, conductor on the boat train coming upriver from Hobbs Island, Huntsville's river port. It stopped at Gunter's landing, untrained freight cars and passengers; then waited to reload its downriver traffic. The boat train ran from Guntersville over Sand Mountain to Gadsden, where it turned around to make the return trip. The captain was a little man. One leg was shorter than the other, but he had the merriest eyes and a quick temper. I saw him always with a corncob pipe in his mouth. I wondered if their disabilities did not increase their common sympathies, but then nobody has defined the essential attraction between friends and lovers. This friendship certainly proved lasting. He refused to take up our tickets, my mother being connected and I blood kin to Uncle Jack. There was no embarrassment on the captain's part for his favoritism, even though his courtesy was beyond the call of manners.

It was not his train, but he was not quite sure about this. He knew he was in charge. Once in a dry time, when the river was low and the slough almost dry, the boat had to stop too far from shore and there was delay in landing. It started to rain and, knowing we were aboard, the captain came out in a skiff, with an umbrella which he held over my mother's head until we reached the bank and climbed aboard.

This was the way he ran things. One time the engineer was slow to respond to his signal to start. (The engineer was talking with a member of his family.) Captain Weaver jerked the cord sharply; the engine panted but did not move. In a rage he walked down the platform, onto the cinders, up to the water tank and drew a pistol. "Start this train," he commanded. The words were high; then the engineer leaned out of the cab and bared his breast. "Shoot!" he said. "Shoot."

Happily the boat train got under way, among cinders and smoke but no blood. The captain rarely bluffed, except as a prelude for position. He was a great chicken fighter. This part of Alabama, especially Huntsville, was given to the sport. I'm told people came from as far away as Texas and that bets ran as high as fifty thousand dollars. In his eagerness the captain had been known, no uncommon practice, to jump into the pit and suck the blood which was choking his prone rooster and the rooster would flap and fight again.

My father gave him lumber to build a chicken coop and yard at the edge of the sawmill, which was right across from the depot. He soon began to lose some of his pullets. He rigged up a contraption he thought would stop the thefts. He tied a string to the trigger of a pistol and the other end to the doorknob. The pistol was aimed breast high.

Guntersville was a river town then. It had its special qualities. The streets were red clay and in a rainy season deep and heavy and slick. We lived at first in the West house, on top of a ridge behind the Oliver Day Streets and below to one side was the schoolhouse. It was pretty rough to a boy from Murfreesboro. I can smell now the creosote put down on the floors for protection. The West house was a high perch but not too high for an occasional wildcat to cross the porch at night. Many evenings, sitting on the verandah, my father, just to keep in practice, shot not the hickory nuts but the twigs which bound them to the tree. People in public matters had to help themselves. There was a bucket brigade in case of fire. A fire at night, and pistol shots out of windows, aroused the town. One evening about chicken-stealing time shots were heard from the direction of the depot. People got up from the supper table and ran down to see who the culprit was.

The culprit was a rooster who had gone to roost on the string. The point was got across, however. This kind of familiarity with violence and sudden death is now gone. We understand death in a more abstract way. A secular society accepting matter as the only truth must pretend that death doesn't really exist. Not believing in a hereafter, but fearful, it disguises the end of things. But everybody knows in his backbone that the impersonal must become personal.

There was nothing impersonal about my father. We were not always in residence in Guntersville. A lumberman's life, certainly his kind, was unsettled. My mother preferred Murfreesboro, as do all the Nelsons. When we were there, he boarded at the hotel. If not the only, it was *the* hostelry at

Guntersville, owned and run by Miss Bessie Samuels. She got weary of dealing with the public, longed for a farm, and rented the hotel for a season. My father's room was over that of the new proprietor. He was kept awake one night by a quarrel between man and wife. The next morning the man with some embarrassment apologized. My father said, "I heard it all, and I want you to know I took your wife's part." Afterwards the proprietor began to raise his rent. Very quietly my father went to Miss Bessie and rented the hotel. He got a cantankerous bachelor, Mr. Galbreath (pronounced Gil) to run it.

When the boat train got in in the late afternoon, everybody took hacks and went to the hotel. Frequently they had to stand in line. Mr. Galbreath's meticulous hand moved slowly. His tone of voice in the usual questions was suspicious, as if nobody ought to be away from home. It came a young couple's turn to register. Mr. Galbreath meant to ask, "Do you want one bed?" an irrelevant question, as they were obviously bride and groom. He said, "Do you want to sleep with the woman?" They both blushed to the roots of their hair, but the boy was a man. He blurted out, "Of course I do."

He kept the hotel rooms cold in the winter. To complaints he would reply, "My mother raised five healthy boys. We had no fire in our rooms. We undressed by the baseburner and jumped into bed. It never hurt a one of us."

He kept the eggs under his bed and doled them out on breakfast orders. When people asked for butter, he suggested they try the gravy. My father, the invisible proprietor, would be at meals and overhear the complaints. It was a matter of great humor to him, but not to Miss Bessie. The word got back, and she took over the hotel again.

I was riding with my father out in the country looking for timber. As we passed a sandy-soil farm, a big man with purpose began to run across a field and shout at us. My father always drove fast horses; so we moved out of hearing. He made no comment. Later, as he was going to Murfreesboro for the weekend, this man confronted him at the depot. "Let me put my valise on the train, and I'll talk with you," he said.

He stepped aboard and asked the captain if he had a pistol.

'Two of them," the captain replied.

"I won't need but one."

With this he went back outside and talked to the bully. And right behind him stood Captain Weaver, no pipe in mouth this time, for this was a formal occasion. But he had the other pistol slightly lifted, en garde.

RICHARD WRIGHT

(1908–1960)

In 1940 Richard Wright's *Native Son*, a powerful story of a young black man who is driven to murder and is sentenced to death, laid bare the desperate situation and human degradation of black ghetto life in modern American society. Awkward in structure, flawed in characterization, the book nevertheless was a landmark in writings by and about black Americans, for it revealed the frustration and rage of men and women suffering ruthless economic exploitation and racial injustice, and demonstrated, in the helplessness of the protagonist Bigger Thomas before inhuman social forces and rending poverty and degradation, the guilt of white Americans north and south in countenancing such misery.

Bigger Thomas was not a Southerner, but Richard Wright was. He was born on a farm near Natchez, Mississippi, and early in his childhood moved to Memphis, Tennessee, with his mother. His mother's illness and poverty caused Wright and his brother to be put into an orphanage. Later they lived with his grandmother and aunt, whose fanatical religious beliefs ultimately drove Wright to rebel and run away. For a while he lived and worked in Memphis. In 1927 he went to Chicago, where he began writing and became affiliated with the Communist Party. During the Depression he was director of the Federal Negro Theatre and a member of the Federal Writers Project. His early work was strongly influenced by Communist Party theory and discipline, but later he began to find these unduly restrictive. In 1937 he moved to New York City to become Harlem editor of the *Daily Worker*.

His first book was *Uncle Tom's Children* (1938), a set of short stories about black life in the South in which he concentrated on depicting the wretched plight of sharecroppers and the often brutal repression they encountered. With the triumph of *Native Son* two years later, Wright enjoyed a considerable reputation as the leading black writer of his day. In 1945 he published what many consider his best book, *Black Boy*, an autobiography of his early years. "It needed to be said," his fellow Mississippian William Faulkner wrote to him, "and you said it well."

After the end of World War II Wright moved to France, where he became friends with Jean-Paul Sartre and Albert Camus and was very much involved in existential philosophy. There he wrote three more novels, *The Outsider* (1953), *The Long Dream* (1958), and *Lawd Today* (1963); a volume of short stories, *Eight Men* (1961); and two books about race and society, *Black Power* (1954), and *White Man, Listen!* (1957). Wright was twice married, first to Rose Dhima Meadman in 1940, then to Ellen Poplar in 1941; both of his wives were white. In his later years he was an active anti-Communist and a strong advocate of black solidarity and opposition to colonialism. He died in Paris, under somewhat mysterious circumstances, in 1960.

From beginning to end, Wright's best work is shaped by the urgency of protest. Out of his early experience, and the anger and truculence with which he refused to conform to the subservient role his family and society would have forced upon him, he drew the attitudes that characterize his fiction: rage and frustration at racial injustice and a powerful need to strike out at the forces victimizing black Americans. In Ralph Ellison's words, he "has converted the American Negro impulse toward self-annihilation and 'going-underground' into a will to confront the world, to evaluate his experience honestly and throw his feelings unashamedly into the guilty conscience of America."

BIG BOY LEAVES HOME

Is it true what they say about Dixie?
Does the sun really shine all the time?
Do sweet magnolias blossom at everybody's door?
Do folks keep eating 'possum, till they can't eat no more?
Is it true what they say about Swanee?
Is a dream by that stream so sublime?
Do they laugh, do they love, like they say in ev'ry song? . . .
If it's true, that's where I belong.

Popular Song

I

Yo mama don wear no drawers . . .
Clearly, the voice rose out of the woods, and died away. Like an echo another voice caught it up:
Ah seena when she pulled em off . . .
Another, shrill, cracking, adolescent:
N she washed 'em in alcohol . . .
Then a quartet of voices, blending in harmony, floated high above the tree tops:
N she hung 'em out in the hall . . .
Laughing easily, four black boys came out of the woods into cleared pasture. They walked lollingly in bare feet, beating tangled vines and bushes with long sticks.

"Ah wished Ah knowed some mo lines t tha song."
"Me too."

"Yeah, when yuh gits t where she hangs em out in the hall yuh has t stop."

"Shucks, what goes wid *hall?*"

"*Call.*"

"*Fall.*"

"*Wall.*"

"*Quall.*"

They threw themselves on the grass, laughing.

"Big Boy?"

"Huh?"

"Yuh know one thing?"

"Whut?"

"Yuh sho is crazy!"

"Crazy?"

"Yeah, yuh crazys a bed-bug!"

"Crazy bout whut?"

"Man, whoever hearda *quall?*"

"Yuh said yuh wanted something to go wid *hall*, didnt yuh?"

"Yeah, but whuts a *quall?*"

"Nigger, a *qualls* a quall."

They laughed easily, catching and pulling long green blades of grass with their toes.

"Waal, ef a *qualls* a *quall*, whut IS a *quall?*"

"Oh, Ah know."

"Whut?"

"Tha ol song goes something like this:

> *Yo mama don wear no drawers,*
> *Ah seena when she pulled em off,*
> *N she washed em in alcohol,*
> *N she hung em out in the hall,*
> *N then she put em back on her QUALL!*"

They laughed again. Their shoulders went flat to the earth, their knees propped up, and their faces square to the sun.

"Big Boy, yuhs CRAZY!"

"Don ax me nothin else."

"Nigger, yuhs CRAZY!"

They fell silent, smiling, drooping the lids of their eyes softly against the sunlight.

"Man, don the groun feel warm?"

"Jus lika bed."

"Jeeesus, Ah could stay here ferever."

"Me too."

"Ah kin feel tha ol sun goin all thu me."

"Feels like mah bones is warm."

In the distance a train whistled mournfully.

"There goes number fo!"

"Hittin on all six!"

"Highballin it down the line!"

"Boun fer up Noth, Lawd, boun fer up Noth!"

They began to chant, pounding bare heels in the grass.

> *Dis train boun fo Glory*
> *Dis train, Oh Hallelujah*
> *Dis train boun fo Glory*
> *Dis train, Oh Hallelujah*
> *Dis train boun fo Glory*
> *Ef yuh ride no need fer fret er worry*
> *Dis train, Oh Hallelujah*
> *Dis train . . .*
>
> *Dis train don carry no gambler*
> *Dis train, Oh Hallelujah*
> *Dis train don carry no gambler*
> *Dis train, Oh Hallelujah*
> *Dis train don carry no gambler*
> *No fo day creeper er midnight rambler*
> *Dis train, Oh Hallelujah*
> *Dis train . . .*

When the song ended they burst out laughing, thinking of a train bound for Glory.

"Gee, thas a good ol song!"

"Huuuuummmmmmmmmman . . ."

"Whut?"

"Gee whiiiiiiz . . ."

"Whut?"

"Somebody don let win! Das whut!"

Buck, Bobo and Lester jumped up. Big Boy stayed on the ground, feigning sleep.

"Jeeesus, tha sho stinks!"

"Big Boy!"

Big Boy feigned to snore.

"Big Boy!"

Big Boy stirred as though in sleep.

"Big Boy!"

"Hunh?"

"Yuh rotten inside!"
"Rotten?"
"Lawd, cant yuh smell it?"
"Smell whut?"
"Nigger, yuh mus gotta bad col'"
"Smell whut?"
"NIGGER, YUH BROKE WIN!"
Big Boy laughed and fell back on the grass, closing his eyes.
"The hen whut cackles is the hen whut laid the egg."
"We ain no hens."
"Yuh cackled, didnt yuh?"
The three moved off with noses turned up.
"C mon!"
"Where yuh-all goin?"
"T the creek fer a swim."
"Yeah, les swim."
"Naw buddy naw!" said Big Boy, slapping the air with a scornful palm.
"Aw, c mon! Don be a heel!"
"N git *lynched?* Hell naw!"
"He ain gonna see us."
"How yuh know?"
"Cause he ain."
"Yuh-all go on. Ahma stay right here," said Big Boy.
"Hell, let im stay! C mon, les go," said Buck.
The three walked off, swishing at grass and bushes with sticks. Big Boy looked lazily at their backs.
"Hey!"
Walking on, they glanced over their shoulders.
"Hey, niggers!"
"C mon!"
Big Boy grunted, pick up his stick, pulled to his feet and stumbled off.
"Wait!"
"C mon!"
He ran, caught up with them, leaped upon their backs, bearing them to the ground.
"Quit, Big Boy!"
"Gawddam, nigger!"
"Git t hell offa me!"
Big Boy sprawled in the grass beside them, laughing and pounding his heels in the ground.
"Nigger, whut yuh think we is, hosses?"
"How come yuh awways hoppin on us?"
"Lissen, wes gonna double-team on yuh one of these days n beat yo ol ass good."

Big Boy smiled.

"Sho nough?"

"Yeah, don yuh like it?"

"We gonna beat yuh sos yuh cant walk!"

"N dare yuh t do nothing erbout it!"

Big Boy bared his teeth.

"C mon! Try it now!"

The three circle around him.

"Say, Buck, yuh grab his feets!"

"N yuh git his head, Lester!"

"N Bobo, yuh git berhin n grab his arms!"

Keeping more than arm's length, they circled round and round Big Boy.

"C mon!" said Big Boy, feinting at one and then the other.

Round and round they circled, but could not seem to get any closer. Big Boy stopped and braced his hands on his hips.

"Is all three of yuh-all scareda me?"

"Les git im some other time," said Bobo, grinning.

"Yeah, we kin ketch yuh when yuh ain thinkin," said Lester.

"We kin trick yuh," said Buck.

They laughed and walked together.

Big Boy belched.

"Ahm hongry," he said.

"Me too."

"Ah wished Ah hada big hot pota belly-busters!"

"Cooked wid some good ol salty ribs . . ."

"N some good ol egg cornbread . . ."

"N some buttermilk . . ."

"N some hot peach cobbler swimmin in juice . . ."

"Nigger, hush!"

They began to chant, emphasizing the rhythm by cutting at grass with sticks.

> *Bye n bye*
> *Ah wanna piece of pie*
> *Pies too sweet*
> *Ah wanna piece of meat*
> *Meats too red*

"Waal, wes here now," said Big Boy. "Ef he ketched us even like this thered be trouble, so we just as waal go on in . . ."

"Ahm wid the nex one!"

"Ahl go ef anybody else goes!"

Big Boy looked carefully in all directions. Seing nobody, he began jerking off his overalls.

"LAS ONE INS A OL DEAD DOG!"

"THAS YO MA!"
"THAS YO PA!"
"THAS BOTH YO MA N YO PA!"

They jerked off their clothes and threw them in a pile under a tree. Thirty seconds later they stood, black and naked, on the edge of the hole under a sloping embankment. Gingerly Big Boy touched the water with his foot.

"Man, this waters col," he said.

"Ahm gonna put mah cloes back on," said Bobo, withdrawing his foot.

Big Boy grabbed him about the waist.

"Like hell yuh is!"

"Git outta the way, nigger!" Bobo yelled.

"Throw im in!" said Lester.

"Duck im!"

Bobo crouched, spread his legs, and braced himself against Big Boy's body. Locked in each other's arms, they tussled on the edge of the hole, neither able to throw the other.

"C mon, les me n yuh push em in."

Laughing, Lester and Buck gave the two locked bodies a running push. Big Boy and Bobo splashed, sending up silver spray in the sunlight. When Big Boy's head came up he yelled:

"Yuh bastard!"

"That wuz yo ma yuh pushed!" said Bobo, shaking his head to clear the water from his eyes.

They did a surface dive, came up and struck out across the creek. The muddy water foamed. They swam back, waded into shallow water, breathing heavily and blinking eyes.

"C mon in!"

"Man, the waters fine!"

Lester and Buck hesitated.

"Les wet em," Big Boy whispered to Bobo.

Before Lester and Buck could back away, they were dripping wet from handsful of scooped water.

"Hey, quit!"

"Gawddam, nigger! Tha waters col!"

"C mon in!" called Big Boy.

"We jus as waal go on in now," said Buck.

Ah wanna piece of bread
Breads too brown
Ah wanna go t town
Towns too far
Ah wanna ketch a car
Cars too fas
Ah fall n break mah ass

RICHARD WRIGHT

Ahll understan it better bye n bye . . .

They climbed over a barbed-wire fence and entered a stretch of thick woods. Big Boy was whistling softly, his eyes half-closed.

"LES GIT IM!"

Buck, Lester, and Bobo whirled, grabbed Big Boy about the neck, arms, and legs, bearing him to the ground. He grunted and kicked wildly as he went back into weeds.

"Hol him tight!"

"Git his arms! Git his arms!"

"Set on his legs so he cant kick!"

Big Boy puffed heavily, trying to get loose.

"WE GOT YUH NOW, GAWDDAMMIT, WE GOT YUH NOW!"

"Thas a Gawddam lie!" said Big Boy. He kicked, twisted, and clutched for a hold on one and then the other.

"Say, yuh-all hep me hol his arms!" said Bobo.

"Aw, we got this basterd now!" said Lester.

"Thas a Gawddam lie!" said Big Boy again.

"Say, yuh-all hep me hol his arms!" called Bobo.

Big Boy managed to encircle the neck of Bobo with his left arm. He tightened his elbow scissors-like and hissed through his teeth:

"Yuh got me, ain yuh?"

"Hol im"

"Les beat this bastard's ass!"

"Say, hep me hol his *arms!* Hes got aholda mah *neck!*" cried Bobo.

Big Boy squeezed Bobo's neck and twisted his head to the ground.

"Yuh got me, ain yuh?"

"Quit, Big Boy, yuh chokin me; yuh hurtin mah neck!" cried Bobo.

"Turn me loose!" said Big Boy.

"Ah ain got yuh! Its the others whut got yuh!" pleaded Bobo.

"Tell them others t git t hell offa me or Ahma break yo neck," said Big Boy.

'Ssssay, yyyuh-all gggit ooooffa Bbig Boy. Hhhes got me," gurgled Bobo.

"Cant yuh hol im?"

"Nnaw, hhes ggot mmah nneck . . ."

Big Boy squeezed tighter.

"N Ahma break it too less yuh tell em t git t hell offa me!"

"Ttturn mmmeee llloose," panted Bobo, tears gushing.

"Cant yuh hol im, Bobo?" asked Buck.

"Nnaw, yuh-all tturn im lloose; hhhes got mah nnneck . . ."

"Grab his neck, Bobo . . ."

"Ah cant; yugurgur . . ."

To save Bobo, Lester and Buck got up and ran to a safe distance. Big

Boy released Bobo, who staggered to his feet, slobbering and trying to stretch a crick out of his neck.

"Shucks, nigger, yuh almos broke mah neck," whimpered Bobo.

"Ahm gonna break yo ass nex time," said Big Boy.

"Ef Bobo coulda hel yuh we woulda had yuh," yelled Lester.

"Ah waznt gonna let im do that," said Big Boy.

They walked together again, swishing sticks.

"Yuh see," began Big Boy, "when a ganga guys jump on yuh, all yuh gotta do is just put the heat on one of them n make im tell the others to let up, see?"

"Gee, thas a good idee!"

"Yeah, thas a good idee!"

"But yuh almos broke mah neck, man," said Bobo.

"Ahma smart nigger," said Big Boy, thrusting out his chest.

II

They came to the swimming hole.

"Ah ain goin in," said Bobo.

"Done got scared?" asked Big Boy.

"Naw, Ah ain scared . . ."

"How come yuh ain going in?"

"Yuh know ol man Harvey don erllow no niggers to swim in his hole."

"N jus las year he took a shot at Bob fer swimmin in here," said Lester.

"Shucks, ol man Harvey ain studyin bout us niggers," said Big Boy.

"Hes at home thinkin about his jelly-roll," said Buck.

They laughed.

"Buck, yo mins lowern a snakes belly," said Lester.

"Ol man Harvey too doggone ol t think erbout jelly-roll," said Big Boy.

"Hes dried up: all the saps done lef im," said Bobo.

"C mon, les go!" said Big Boy.

Bobo pointed.

"See tha sign over yonder?"

"Yeah."

"Whut it say?"

"NO TRESPASSIN," read Lester.

"Know whut tha mean?"

"Mean ain no dogs n niggers erllowed," said Buck.

'Look n see ef anybodys comin."

Kneeling, they squinted among the trees.

"Ain nobody."

"C mon, les go."

They waded in slowly, pausing each few steps to catch their breath. A desperate water battle began. Closing eyes and backing away, they shunted water into one another's faces with the flat palms of hands.

"Hey, cut it out!"

"Yeah, Ahm bout drownin!"

They came together in water up to their navels, blowing and blinking. Big Boy ducked, upsetting Bobo.

"Look out, nigger!"

"Don holler so loud!"

"Yeah, they kin hear yo ol big mouth a mile erway."

"This waters too col fer me."

"Thas cause it rained yistiddy."

They swam across and back again.

"Ah wish we hada bigger place to swim in."

"The white folks got plenty swimmin pools n we ain got none."

"Ah useta swim in the ol Missippi when we lived in Vicksburg."

Big Boy put his head under the water and blew his breath. A sound came like that of a hippopotamus.

"C mon, les be hippos.'

Each went to a corner of the creek and put his mouth just below the surface and blew like a hippopotamus. Tiring, they came and sat under the embankment.

"Look like Ah gotta chill."

"Me too."

"Les stay here n dry off."

"Jeeesus, Ahm col!"

They kept still in the sun, suppressing shivers. After some of the water had dried off their bodies they began to talk through clattering teeth.

"Whut would yuh do ef ol man Harveyd come erlong right now?"

"Run like hell."

"Man, Ahd run so fas hed thinka black streaka lightnin shot pass im."

"But spose he hada gun?"

"Aw, nigger, shut up!"

They were silent. They ran their hands over wet, trembling legs, brushing water away. Then their eyes watched the sun sparkling on the restless creek.

Far away a train whistled.

"There goes number seven!"

"Headin fer up Noth!"

"Blazin it down the line!"

"Lawd, Ahm going Noth some day."

"Me too, man."

"They say colored folks up Noth is got ekual rights."

They grew pensive. A black winged butterfly hovered at the water's edge. A bee droned. From somewhere came the sweet scent of honeysuckles.

Dimly they could hear sparrows twittering in the woods. They rolled from side to side, letting sunshine dry their skins and warm their blood. They plucked blades of grass and chewed them.

"Oh!"

They looked up, their lips parting.

"Oh!"

A white woman, poised on the edge of the opposite embankment, stood directly in front of them, her hat in her hand and her hair lit by the sun.

"Its a woman!" whispered Big Boy in an underbreath. "A *white* woman!"

They stared, their hands instinctively covering their groins. Then they scrambled to their feet. The white woman backed slowly out of sight. They stood for a moment looking at one another.

"Les git outta here!" Big Boy whispered.

"Wait till she goes erway."

"Les run, theyll ketch us here naked like this!"

"Mabbe theres a man wid her."

"C mon, les git our cloes," said Big Boy.

They waited a moment longer, listening.

"Whut t hell! Ahma git mah cloes," said Big Boy.

Grabbing at short tufts of grass, he climbed the embankment.

"Don run out there now!"

"C mon back, fool!"

Bobo hesitated. He looked at Big Boy, and then at Buck and Lester.

"Ahm goin wid Big Boy n git mah cloes," he said.

"Don run out there naked like tha, fool!" said Buck. "Yuh don know whos out there!"

Big Boy was climbing over the edge of the embankment.

"C mon," he whispered.

Bobo climbed after. Twenty-five feet away the woman stood. She had one hand over her mouth. Hanging by fingers, Buck and Lester peeped over the edge.

"C mon back; that womans scared," said Lester.

Big Boy stopped, puzzled. He looked at the woman. He looked at the bundle of clothes. Then he looked at Buck and Lester.

"C mon, les git our cloes!"

He made a step.

"Jim!" the woman screamed.

Big Boy stopped and looked around. His hands hung loosely at his sides. The woman, her eyes wide, her hand over her mouth, backed away to the tree where their clothes lay in a heap.

"Big Boy, come back n wait till shes gone!"

Bobo ran to Big Boy's side.

"Les go home! Theyll ketch us here," he urged.

Big Boy's throat felt tight.

"Lady, we wanna git our cloes," he said.

Buck and Lester climbed the embankment and stood indecisively. Big Boy ran toward the tree.

"Jim!" the woman screamed. "Jim! Jim!"

Black and naked, Big Boy stopped three feet from her.

"We wanna git our cloes," he said again, his words coming mechanically. He made a motion.

"You go away! You go away! I tell you, you go away!"

Big Boy stopped again, afraid. Bobo ran and snatched the clothes. Buck and Lester tied to grab theirs out of his hands.

"You go away! You go away! You go away!" the woman screamed.

"Les go!" said Bobo, running toward the woods.

CRACK!

Lester grunted, stiffened, and pitched forward. His forehead struck a toe of the woman's shoes.

Bobo stopped, clutching the clothes. Buck whirled. Big Boy stared at Lester, his lips moving.

"Hes gotta gun; hes gotta gun!" yelled Buck, running wildly.

CRACK!

Buck stopped at the edge of the embankment, his head jerked backward, his body arched stiffly to one side; he toppled headlong, sending up a shower of bright spray to the sunlight. The creek bubbled.

Big Boy and Bobo backed away, their eyes fastened fearfully on a white man who was running toward them. He had a rifle and wore an army officer's uniform. He ran to the woman's side and grabbed her hand.

"You hurt, Bertha, you hurt?"

She stared at him and did not answer.

The man turned quickly. His face was red. He raised the rifle and pointed it a Bobo. Bobo ran back, holding the clothes in front of his chest.

"Don shoot me, Mistah, don shoot me . . ."

Big Boy lunged for the rifle, grabbing the barrel.

"You black sonofabitch!"

Big Boy clung desperately.

"Let go, you black bastard!"

The barrel pointed skyward.

CRACK!

The white man, taller and heavier, flung Big Boy to the ground. Bobo dropped the clothes, ran up, and jumped onto the white man's back.

"You black sonsofbitches!"

The white man released the rifle, jerked Bobo to the ground, and began to batter the naked boy with his fists. Then Big Boy swung, striking the man in the mouth with the barrel. His teeth caved in and he fell, dazed. Bobo was on his feet.

"C mon, Big Boy, les go!"

Breathing hard, the white man got up and faced Big Boy. His lips were trembling, his neck and chin wet with blood. He spoke quietly.

"Give me that gun, boy!"

Big Boy leveled the rifle and backed away.

The white man advanced.

"Boy, I say give me that gun!"

Bobo had the clothes in his arms.

"Run, Big Boy, run!"

The man came at Big Boy.

"Ahll kill yuh; Ahll kill yuh!" said Big Boy.

His fingers fumbled for the trigger.

The man stopped, blinked, spat blood. His eyes were bewildered. His face whitened. Suddenly, he lunged for the rifle, his hands outstretched.

CRACK!

He fell forward on his face.

"Jim!"

Big Boy and Bobo turned in surprise to look at the woman.

"Jim!" she screamed again, and fell weakly at the foot of the tree.

Big Boy dropped the rifle, his eyes wide. He looked around. Bobo was crying and clutching the clothes.

"Big Boy, Big Boy . . ."

Big Boy looked at the rifle, started to pick it up, but didn't. He seemed at a loss. He looked at Lester, then at the white man; his eyes followed a thin stream of blood that seeped to the ground.

"Yoh don killed im," mumbled Bobo.

"Les go home!"

Naked, they turned and ran toward the woods. When they reached the barbed-wire fence they stopped.

"Les git our cloes on," said Big Boy.

They slipped quickly into overalls. Bobo held Lester's and Buck's clothes.

"Whut we gonna do wid these?"

Big Boy stared. His hands twitched.

"Leave em."

They climbed the fence and ran through the woods. Vines and leaves switched their faces. Once Bobo tripped and fell.

"C mon!" said Big Boy.

Bobo started crying, blood streaming from his scratches.

"Ahm scared!"

"C mon! Don cry! We wanna git home fo they ketches us!"

Big Boy grabbed his hand and dragged him along.

"C mon!"

III

They stopped when they got to the end of the woods. They could see the open road leading home, home to ma and pa. But they hung back, afraid. The thick shadows cast from the trees were friendly and sheltering. But the wide glare of sun stretching out over the fields was pitiless. They crouched behind an old log.

"We gotta git home," said Big Boy.

"Theys gonna lynch us," said Bobo, half questioningly.

Big Boy did not answer.

"Theys gonna lynch us," said Bobo again.

Big Boy shuddered.

"Hush!" he said. He did not want to think of it. He could not think of it; there was but one thought, and he clung to that one blindly. He had to get home, home to ma and pa.

Their heads jerked up. Their ears had caught the rhythmic jingle of a wagon. They fell to the ground and clung flat to the side of a log. Over the crest of the hill came the top of a hat. A white face. Then shoulders in a blue shirt. A wagon drawn by two horses pulled into full view.

Big Boy and Bobo held their breath, waiting. Their eyes followed the wagon till it was lost in dust around a bend of the road.

"We gotta git home," said Big Boy.

"Ahm scared," said Bobo.

"C mon! Les keep t the fields."

They ran till they came to the cornfields. Then they went slower, for last year's corn stubbles bruised their feet.

They came in sight of a brickyard.

"Wait a minute," gasped Big Boy.

They stopped.

"Ahm goin on t mah home n yuh better go on t yos."

Bobo's eyes grew round.

"Ahm scared!"

"Yuh better go on!"

"Lemme go wid yuh; theyll ketch me . . ."

"Ef yuh kin git home mabbe yo folks kin hep yuh t git erway."

Big Boy started off. Bobo grabbed him.

"Lemme go wid yuh!"

Big Boy shook free.

"Ef yuh stay here theys gonna lynch yuh!" he yelled, running.

After he had gone about twenty-five yards he turned and looked. Bobo was flying through the woods like the wind.

Big Boy slowed when he came to the railroad. He wondered if he ought to go through the streets or down the track. He decided on the tracks. He could dodge a train better than a mob.

He trotted along the ties, looking ahead and back. His cheek itched and he felt it. His hand came away smeared with blood. He wiped it nervously on his overalls.

When he came to his back fence he heaved himself over. He landed among a flock of startled chickens. A bantam rooster tried to spur him. He slipped and fell in front of the kitchen steps, grunting heavily. The ground was slick with greasy dishwater.

Panting, he stumbled through the doorway.

"Lawd, Big Boy, whuts wrong wid yuh?"

His mother stood gaping in the middle of the floor. Big Boy flopped wordlessly onto a stool, almost toppling over. Pots simmered on the stove. The kitchen smelled of food cooking.

"Whuts the matter, Big Boy?"

Mutely, he looked at her. Then he burst into tears. She came and felt the scratches on his face.

"Whut happened t yuh, Big Boy? Somebody been botherin yuh?"

"They after me, Ma! They after me . . ."

"Who!"

"Ah . . . Ah . . . We . . ."

"Big Boy, whuts wrong wid yuh?"

"He killed Lester n Buck," he muttered simply.

"Killed!"

"Yessum."

"Lester n Buck!"

"Yessum, Ma!"

"How killed?"

"He shot em, Ma!"

"Lawd Gawd in Heaven, have mercy on us all! This is mo trouble, mo trouble," she moaned, wringing her hands.

"N Ah killed im, Ma . . ."

She stared, trying to understand.

"Whut happened, Big Boy?"

"We tried t git our cloes from the tree . . ."

"Whut tree?"

"We wuz swimmin, Ma. N the white woman . . ."

"*White* woman? . . ."

"Yessum. She wuz at the swimmin hole . . ."

"Lawd have mercy! Ah knowed yuh boys wuz gonna keep on til yuh got into somethin like this!"

She ran into the hall.

"Lucy!"

"Mam?"

"C mere!"

"Mam?"

"C mere, Ah say!"

"Wutcha wan, Ma? Ahm sewin."

"Chile, wil yuh c mere like Ah ast yuh?"

Lucy came to the door holding an unfinished apron in her hands. When she saw Big Boy's face she looked wildly at her mother.

"Whuts the matter?"

"Wheres Pa?"

"Hes out front, Ah reckon."

"Git im, quick!"

"Whuts the matter, Ma?"

"Go git yo Pa, Ah say!"

Lucy ran out, the mother sank into a chair, holding a dish rag. Suddenly, she sat up.

"Big Boy, Ah thought yuh wuz at school?"

Big Boy looked at the floor.

"How come yuh didnt go t school?"

"We went t the woods."

She sighed.

"Ah done done all Ah kin fer yuh, Big Boy. Only Gawd kin hep yuh now."

"Ma, don let em git me; don let em git me . . ."

His father came into the doorway. He stared at Big Boy, then at his wife.

"Whuts Big Boy inter now?" he asked sternly.

"Saul, Big Boys done gone n got inter trouble wid the white folks."

The old man's mouth dropped, and he looked from one to the other.

"Saul, we gotta git im erway from here."

"Open yo mouth n talk! Whut yuh been doin?" The old man gripped Big Boy's shoulders and peered at the scratches on his face.

"Me n Lester n Buck n Bobo wuz out on ol man Harveys place swimmin . . ."

"Saul, its a *white* woman!"

Big Boy winced. The old man compressed his lips and stared at his wife. Lucy gaped at her brother as though she had never seen him before.

"Whut happened? Cant yuh-all talk?" the old man thundered with a certain helplessness in his voice.

"We wuz swimmin," Big Boy began, "n then a white woman comes up t the hole. We got up right erway t git our cloes sos we could git erway, n she started screamin. Our cloes wuz right by the tree where she wuz standin, n when we started t git em she jus screamed. We tol her we wanted our cloes . . . Yuh see, Pa, she wuz standin right *by* our cloes; n when we went t git em she jus screamed . . . Bobo got the cloes, n then he shot Lester . . ."

"*Who* shot Lester?"

"The white man."

"Whut white man?"

"Ah dunno, Pa. He wuz a soljer, n he had a rifle."

"A soljer?"

"Yessuh."

"A *soljer?*"

"Yessuh, Pa. A soljer."

The old man frowned.

"N then whut yuh-all do?"

"Waal, Buck said, 'He's gotta gun!' N we started runnin. N then he shot Buck, n he fell in the swimmin hole. We didnt see im no mo . . . He wuz close on us then. He looked at the white woman n then he started t shoot Bobo. Ah grabbed the gun, n we started fightin. Bobo jumped on his back. He started beatin Bobo. Then Ah hit im wid the gun. Then he started at me n Ah shot im. Then we run . . ."

"Who seen?"

"Nobody."

"Wheres Bobo?"

"He went home."

"Anybody run after yuh-all?"

"Nawsuh."

"Yuh see anybody?"

"Nawsuh. Nobody but a white man. But he didnt see us."

"How long fo yuh-all lef the swimmin hole?"

"Little while ergo."

The old man nervously brushed his hand across his eyes and walked to the door. His lips moved, but no words came.

"Saul, whut we gonna do?"

"Lucy," began the old man, "go t Brother Sanders n tell im Ah said c mere; n go t Brother Jenkins n tell im Ah said c mere; n go t Elder Peters n tel im Ah said c mere. N don say nothin t nobody but whut Ah tol yuh. N when yuh git thu come straight back. Now go!"

Lucy dropped her apron across the back of a chair and ran down the steps. The mother bent over, crying and praying. The old man walked slowly over to Big Boy.

"Big Boy?"

Big Boy swallowed.

"Ahm talkin t yuh!"

"Yessuh."

"How come yuh didnt go t school this mawnin?"

"We went t the woods."

"Didnt yo ma send yuh t school?"

"Yessuh."

"How come yuh didnt go?"

"We went t the woods."

"Don yuh know thas wrong?"

"Yessuh."

"How come yuh go?"

Big Boy looked at his fingers, knotted them, and squirmed in his seat.

"AHM TALKIN T YUH!"

His wife straightened up and said reprovingly:

"Saul!"

The old man desisted, yanking nervously at the shoulder straps of his overalls.

"How long wuz the woman there?"

"Not long."

"Wuz she young?"

"Yessuh. Lika gal."

"Did yuh-all say anythin t her?"

"Nawsuh. We jus said we wanted our cloes."

"N whut she say?"

"Nothin, Pa. She jus backed erway t the tree n screamed."

The old man stared, his lips trying to form a question.

"Big Boy, did yuh-all bother her?"

"Nawsuh, Pa. We didnt *touch* her."

"How long fo the white man come up?"

"Right erway."

"Whut he say?"

"Nothin. He jus cussed us."

Abruptly the old man left the kitchen.

"Ma, cant Ah go fo they ketches me?"

"Sauls doin whut he kin."

"Ma, Ma, Ah don wan em t ketch me . . ."

"Sauls doin whut he kin. Nobody but the good Lawd kin hep us now."

The old man came back with a shotgun and leaned it in a corner. Fascinatedly, Big Boy looked at it.

There was a knock at the front door.

"Liza, see whos there."

She went. They were silent, listening. They could hear her talking.

"Whos there?"

"Me."

"Who?"

"Me, Brother Sanders."

"C mon in. Sauls waitin fer yuh."

Sanders paused in the doorway, smiling.

"Yuh sent fer me, Brother Morrison?"

"Brother Sanders, wes in deep trouble here."

Sanders came all the way into the kitchen.

"Yeah?"

"Big Boy done gone n killed a white man."

Sanders stopped short, then came forward, his face thrust out, his mouth open. His lips moved several times before he could speak.

"A *white* man?"

"They gonna kill me; they gonna kill me!" Big Boy cried, running to the old man.

"Saul, cant we git im erway somewhere?"

"Here now, take it easy; take it easy," said Sanders, holding Big Boy's wrists.

"They gonna kill me; they gonna lynch me!"

Big Boy slipped to the floor. They lifted him to a stool. His mother held him closely, pressing his head to her bosom.

"Whut we gonna do?" asked Sanders.

"Ah done sent fer Brother Jenkins n Elder Peters."

Sanders leaned his shoulders against the wall. Then, as the full meaning of it all came to him, he exclaimed:

"Theys gonna git a mob! . . ." His voice broke off and his eyes fell on the shotgun.

Feet came pounding on the steps. They turned toward the door. Lucy ran in crying. Jenkins followed. The old man met him in the middle of the room, taking his hand.

"Wes in bad trouble here, Brother Jenkins. Big Boy's done gone n killed a white man. Yuh-alls gotta hep me . . ."

Jenkins looked hard at Big Boy.

"Elder Peters says hes comin," said Lucy.

"When all this happen?" asked Jenkins.

"Near bout a hour ergo, now," said the old man.

"Whut we gonna do?" asked Jenkins.

"Ah wanna wait till Elder Peters come," said the old man helplessly.

"But we gotta work fas ef we gonna do anythin," said Sanders. "Well git in trouble jus standin here like this."

Big Boy pulled away from his mother.

"Pa, lemme go now! Lemme go now!"

"Be still, Big Boy!"

"Where kin yuh go?"

"Ah could ketch a freight!"

"Thas *sho* death!" said Jenkins. "Theyll be watchin em all!"

"Kin yuh-all hep me wid some money?" the old man asked.

They shook their heads.

"Saul, whut kin we do? Big Boy cant stay here."

There was another knock at the door.

The old man backed stealthily to the shotgun.

"Lucy go!"

Lucy looked at him, hesitating.

"Ah better go," said Jenkins.

It was Elder Peters. He came in hurriedly.

"Good evenin, everybody!"

"How yuh, Elder?"

"Good evenin."

"How yuh today?"

Peters looked around the crowded kitchen.

"Whuts the matter?"

"Elder, wes in deep trouble," began the old man. "Big Boy n some mo boys . . ."

". . . Lester n Buck n Bobo . . ."

". . . wuz over on ol man Harveys place swimmin . . ."

"N he don like us niggers *none*," said Peters emphatically. He widened his legs and put his thumbs in the armholes of his vest.

". . . n some white woman . . ."

"Yeah?" said Peters, coming closer.

". . . comes erlong n the boys tries t git their cloes where they done lef em under a tree. Waal, she started screamin n all, see? Reckon she thought the boys wuz after her. Then a white man in a soljers suit shoots two of em . . ."

". . . Lester n Buck . . ."

"Huummm," said Peters. "Tha wuz ol man Harveys son."

"Harveys son?"

"Yuh mean the one tha wuz in the Army?"

"Yuh mean Jim?"

"Yeh," said Peters. "The papers said he wuz here for a vacation from his regiment. N tha woman the boys saw wuz jus erbout his wife . . ."

They stared at Peters. Now that they knew what white person had been killed, their fears became definite.

"N whut else happened?"

"Big Boy shot the man . . ."

"Harveys *son?*"

"He had t, Elder. He wuz gonna shoot im ef he didnt . . ."

"Lawd!" said Peters. He looked around and put his hat back on.

"How long ergo wuz this?"

"Mighty near an hour, now, Ah reckon."

"Do the white folks know yit?"

"Don know, Elder."

"Yuh-all better git this boy outta here right now," said Peters. "Cause ef yuh don theres gonna be a lynchin . . ."

"Where kin Ah go, Elder?" Big Boy ran up to him.

They crowded around Peters. He stood with his legs wide apart, looking up at the ceiling.

"Mabbe we kin hide im in the church till he kin git erway," said Jenkins.

Peters' lips flexed.

"Naw, Brother, thall never do! Theyll git im there sho. N anyhow, ef they ketch im there itll ruin us all. We gotta git the boy outta town . . ."

Sanders went up to the old man.

"Lissen," he said in a whisper. "Mah son, Will, the one whut drives for the Magnolia Express Company, is taking a truck o goods t Chicawgo in the mawnin. If we kin hide Big Boy somewhere till then, we kin put im on the truck . . ."

"Pa, please, lemme go wid Will when he goes in the mawnin," Big Boy begged.

The old man stared at Sanders.

"Yuh reckon thas safe?"

"Its the only thing yuh *kin* do," said Peters.

"But where we gonna hide im till then?"

"Whut time yo boy leavin out in the mawnin?"

"At six."

They were quiet, thinking. The water kettle on the stove sang.

"Pa, Ah knows where Will passes erlong wid the truck out on Bullards Road. Ah kin hide in one of them ol kilns . . ."

"Where?"

"In one of them kilns we built . . ."

"But theyll git yuh there," wailed the mother.

"But there ain no place else fer im t go."

"Theres some holes big ernough fer me t git in n stay till Will comes erlong," said Big Boy. "Please, Pa, lemme go fo they ketches me . . ."

"Let im go!"

"Please, Pa . . ."

The old man breathed heavily.

"Lucy, git his things!"

"Saul, theyll git im out there!" wailed the mother, grabbing Big Boy.

Peters pulled her way.

"Sister Morrison, ef yuh don let im go n git erway from here hes gonna be caught shos theres a Gawd in Heaven!"

Lucy came running with Big Boy's shoes and pulled them on his feet. The old man thrust a battered hat on his head. The mother went to the stove and dumped the skillet of corn pone into her apron. She wrapped it, and unbuttoning Big Boy's overalls, pushed it into his bosom.

"Heres somethin fer yuh t eat; n pray, Big Boy, cause thas all anybody kin do now . . ."

Big Boy pulled to the door, his mother clinging to him.

"Let im go, Sister Morrison!"

"Run fas, Big Boy!"

Big Boy raced across the yard, scattering the chickens. He paused at the fence and hollered back:

"Tell Bobo where Ahm hidin n tell im t c mon!"

IV

He made for the railroad, running straight toward the sunset. He held his left hand tightly over his heart, holding the hot pone of corn bread there. At times he stumbled over the ties, for his shoes were tight and hurt his feet. His throat burned from thirst; he had had no water since noon.

He veered off the track and trotted over the crest of a hill, following Bullard's Road. His feet slipped and slid in the dust. He kept his eyes straight ahead, fearing every clump of shrubbery, every tree. He wished it were night. If he could only get to the kilns without meeting anyone. Suddenly a thought came to him like a blow. He recalled hearing the old folks tell tales of blood-hounds, and fear made him run slower. None of them had thought of that. Spose blood-houns wuz put on his trail? Lawd! Spose a whole pack of em, foamin n howlin tore im t pieces? He went limp and his feet dragged. Yeah, thas whut they wuz gonna send after im, blood-houns! N then thered be no way fer im to dodge! Why hadnt Pa let im take tha shotgun? He stopped. He oughta go back n git tha shotgun. And then when the mob came he would take some with him.

In the distance he heard the approach of a train. It jarred him back to a sharp sense of danger. He ran again, his big shoes sopping up and down in the dust. He was tired and his lungs were bursting from running. He wet his lips, wanting water. As he turned from the road across a plowed field he heard the train roaring at his heels. He ran faster, gripped in terror.

He was nearly there now. He could see the black clay on the sloping hillside. Once inside a kiln he would be safe. For a little while, at least. He thought of the shotgun again. If he only had something; Someone to talk to . . . Thas right! Bobo! Bobod be wid im. Hed almost fergot Bobo. Bobod bringa gun; he knowed he would. N tergether they could kill the whole mob. Then in the mawning theyd git inter Will's truck n go far erway, t Chicawgo . . .

He slowed to a walk, looking back and ahead. A light wind skipped over the grass. A beetle lit on his cheek and he brushed it off. Behind the dark pines hung a red sun. Two bats flapped against that sun. He shivered, for he was growing cold; the sweat on his body was drying.

He stopped at the foot of the hill, trying to choose between two patches of black kilns high above him. He went to the left, for there lay the ones he, Bobo, Lester, and Buck had dug only last week. He looked around again; the landscape was bare. He climbed the embankment and stood before a row of black pits sinking four and five feet deep into the earth. He went to the largest and peered in. He stiffened when his ears caught the sound of a whir. He ran back a few steps and poised on his toes. Six foot of snake slid out of the pit and went into coil. Big Boy looked around wildly for a stick. He ran down the slope, peering into the grass. He stumbled over a tree limb. He picked it up and tested it by striking it against the ground.

Warily, he crept back up the slope, his stick poised. When about seven feet from the snake he stopped and waved the stick. The coil grew tighter, the whir sounded louder, and a flat head reared to strike. He went to the right, and the flat head followed him, the blue-black tongue darting forth; he went to the left, and the flat head followed him there too.

He stopped, teeth clenched. He had to kill this snake. Jus had t kill im! This wuz the safest pit on the hillside. He waved the stick again, looking at the snake before, thinking of a mob behind. The flat head reared higher. With stick over shoulder, he jumped in, swinging. The stick sang through the air, catching the snake on the side of the head, sweeping him out of coil. There was a brown writhing mass. Then Big Boy was upon him, pounding blows home, one on top of the other. He fought viciously, his eyes red, his teeth bared in a snarl. He beat till the snake lay still; then he stomped it with his heel, grinding its head into the dirt.

He stopped, limp, wet. The corners of his lips were white with spittle. He spat and shuddered.

Cautiously, he went to the hole and peered. He longed for a match. He imagined whole nests of them in there waiting. He put the stick into the hole and waved it around. Stooping, he peered again. It mus be awright. He looked over the hillside, his eyes coming back to the dead snake. Then he got to his knees and backed slowly into the hole.

When inside he felt there must be snakes all about him, ready to strike. It seemed he could see and feel them there, waiting tensely in coil. In the dark he imagined long white fangs ready to sink into his neck, his side, his legs. He wanted to come out, but kept still. Shucks, he told himself, ef there wuz any snakes in here they sho woulda done bit me by now. Some of his fear left, and he relaxed.

With elbows on ground and chin on palms, he settled. The clay was cold to his knees and thighs, but his bosom was kept warm by the hot pone of corn bread. His thirst returned and he longed for a drink. He was hungry, too. But he did not want to eat the corn pone. Naw, not now. Mabbe after erwhile, after Bobo came. Then theyd both eat the corn pone.

The view from his hole was fringed by the long tufts of grass. He could see all the way to Bullard's Road, and even beyond. The wind was blowing, and in the east the first touch of dusk was rising. Every now and then a bird floated past, a spot of wheeling black printed against the sky. Big Boy sighed, shifted his weight, and chewed at a blade of grass. A wasp droned. He heard number nine, far away and mournful.

The train made him remember how they had dug these kilns on long hot summer days, how they had made boilers out of big tin cans, filled them with water, fixed stoppers for steam, cemented them in holes with wet clay, and built fires under them. He recalled how they had danced and yelled when a stopper blew out of a boiler, letting out a big spout of steam and a shrill whistle. There were times when they had the whole hillside blazing and smoking. Yeah, yuh see, Big Boy wuz Casey Jones n wuz speedin it down the gleamin rails of the Southern Pacific. Bobo had number two on the Santa Fe. Buck wuz on the Illinoy Central. Lester the Nickel Plate. Lawd, how they shelved the wood in! The boiling water would almost jar the cans loose from the clay. More and more pine-knots and dry leaves would be piled under the cans. Flames would grow so tall they would have to shield their eyes. Sweat would pour off their faces. Then, suddenly, a peg would shoot high into the air, and

Pssseeeezzzzzzzzzzzzzzzzzzzzzz . . .

Big Boy sighed and stretched out his arm, quenching the flames and scattering the smoke. Why didnt Bobo c mon? He looked over the fields; there was nothing but dying sunlight. His mind drifted back to the kilns. He remembered the day when Buck, jealous of his winning, had tried to smash his kiln. Yeah, that ol sonofabitch! Naw, Lawd! He didnt go t say tha! Whut wuz he thinkin erbout? Cussin the dead! Yeah, po ol Buck wuz dead now. N Lester too. Yeah, it wuz awright fer Buck t smash his kiln. Sho. N he wished he hadnt socked ol Buck so hard tha day. He wuz sorry fer Buck now. N he sho wished he hadnt cussed po ol Bucks ma, neither. Tha wuz sinful! Mabbe Gawd would git im fer tha? But he didnt go t do it! Po Buck! Po Lester! Hed never treat anybody like tha ergin, never . . .

Dusk was slowly deepening. Somewhere, he could not tell exactly where, a cricket took up a fitful song. The air was growing soft and heavy. He looked over the fields, longing for Bobo . . .

He shifted his body to ease the cold damp of the ground, and thought back over the day. Yeah, hed been dam right erbout not wantin t go swimmin. N ef hed followed his right min hed neverve gone n got inter all this trouble. At first hed said naw. But shucks, somehow hed just went on wid the res. Yeah, he shoulda went on t school tha mawnin, like Ma told im t do. But, hell, who wouldnt git tireda school? T hell wid school! Tha wuz the big trouble, awways drivin a guy t school. He wouldnt be in all this trouble now ef it wuznt for that Gawddam school! Impatiently, he took the grass out of his mouth and threw it away, demolishing the little red school house . . .

Yeah, ef they had all kept still n quiet when that ol white woman showed-up, mabbe shedve went on off. But yuh never kin tell erbout these white folks. Mabbe she wouldntve went. Mabbe that white man woulda killed all of em! All *fo* of em! Yeah, yuh never kin tell erbout white folks. Then, ergin, mabbe tha white woman woulda went on off n laffed. Yeah, mabbe tha white man woulda said: *Yuh nigger bastards git t hell outta here! Yuh know Gawddam well yuh don berlong here!* N then they woulda grabbed their cloes n run like all hell . . . He blinked the white man away. Where wuz Bobo? Why didnt he hurry up n c mon?

He jerked another blade and chewed. Yeah, ef pa had only let im have tha shotgun? He could stan off a whole mob wid a shotgun. He looked at the ground as he turned a shotgun over in his hands. Then he leveled it at an advancing white man. *Boooom!* The man curled up. Another came. He reloaded quickly, and let him have what the other had got. He too curled up. Then another came. He got the same medicine. Then the whole mob swirled around him, and he blazed away, getting as many as he could. They closed in; but, by Gawd, he had done his part, hadnt he? N the newspapersd say: NIGGER KILLS DOZEN OF MOB BEFO LYNCHED! Er mabbe theyd say: TRAPPED NIGGER SLAYS TWENTY BEFO KILLED! He smiled a little. Tha wouldnt be so bad, would it? Blinking the newspaper away, he looked over the fields. Where wuz Bobo? Why didnt he hurry up n c mon?

He shifted, trying to get a crick out of his legs. Shucks, he wuz gittin tireda this. N it wuz almos dark now. Yeah, there wuz a little bittie star way over yonder in the eas. Mabbe that white man wuznt dead? Mabbe they wuznt even lookin for im? Mabbe he could go back home now? Naw, better wait erwhile. Thad be bes. But, Lawd, ef he only had some water! He could hardly swallow, his throat was so dry. Gawddam them white folks! Thas all they wuz good fer, t run a nigger down lika rabbit! Yeah, they git yuh in a corner n then they let yuh have it. A thousan of em! He shivered, for the cold of the clay was chilling his bones. Lawd, spose they foun im here in this hole? N wid nobody t hep im? . . . But ain no use in thinkin erbout tha; wait till trouble come fo yuh start fightin it. But ef tha mob came one by one hed wipe em all out. Clean up the whole bunch. He caught one by the neck and choked him long and hard, choked him till his tongue and eyes popped out. Then he jumped upon his chest and stomped him like he had stomped that snake. When he had finished with one, another came. He choked him too. Choked till he sank slowly to the ground, gasping . . .

"Hoalo!"

Big Boy snatched his fingers from the white man's neck and looked over the fields. He saw nobody. Had someone spied him? He was sure that somebody had hollered. His heart pounded. But, shucks, nobody couldnt see im here in this hole . . . But mabbe theyd seen im when he wuz comin n had laid low n wuz now closin in on im! Praps they wuz signalin fer the others? Yeah, they wuz creepin up on im! Mabbe he oughta git up n run . . . Oh! Mabbe tha wuz Bobo! Yeah, Bobo! He oughta clim out n see ef Bobo wuz lookin fer im . . . He stiffened.

"Hoalo!"

"Hoalo!"

"Wheres yuh?"

"Over here on Bullards Road!"

"C mon over!"

"Awright!"

He heard footsteps. Then voices came again, low and far away this time.

"Seen anybody?"

"Naw. Yuh?"

"Naw."

"Yuh reckon they got erway?"

"Ah dunno. Its hard t tell."

"Gawddam them sonofabitchin niggers!"

"We oughta kill ever black bastard in this country!"

"Waal, Jim got two of em, anyhow."

"But Bertha said there wuz *fo*!"

"Where in hell they hidin?"

"She said one of em wuz named Big Boy, or somethin like tha."

"We went t his shack lookin fer im."

"Yeah?"

"But we didnt fin im."

"These niggers stick tergether; they don never tell on each other."

"We looked all, thu the shack n couldnt fin hide ner hair of im. Then we drove the ol woman n man out n set the shack on fire . . ."

"Jeesus! Ah wished Ah coulda been there!"

"Yuh shoulda heard the ol nigger woman howl . . ."

"Hoalo!"

"C mon over!"

Big Boy eased to the edge and peeped. He saw a white man with a gun slung over his shoulder running down the slope. Wuz they gonna search the hill? Lawd, there wuz no way fer im t git erway now; he wuz caught! He shoulda knowed theyd git im here. N he didnt hava thing, notta thing t fight wid. Yeah, soon as the blood-houns came theyd fin im. Lawd, have mercy! Theyd lynch im right here on the hill . . . Theyd git im n tie im t a stake n burn im erlive! Lawd! Nobody but the good Lawd could hep im now, nobody . . .

He heard more feet running. He nestled deeper. His chest ached. Nobody but the good Lawd could hep now. They wuz crowdin all round im n when they hada big crowd theyd close in on im. Then itd be over . . . The good Lawd would have t hep im, cause nobody could hep im now, nobody . . .

And then he went numb when he remembered Bobo. Spose Bobod come now? Hed be caught sho! Both of em would be caught! They'd make Bobo tell where he wuz! Bobo oughta not try to come now. Somebody oughta tell im . . . But there wuz nobody; there wuz no way . . .

He eased slowly back to the opening. There was a large group of men. More were coming. Many had guns. Some had coils of rope slung over shoulders.

"Ah tell yuh they still here, somewhere . . ."

"But we looked all over!"

"What t hell! Wouldnt do t let em git erway!"

"Naw. Ef they git erway notta woman in this town would be safe."

"Say, whuts tha yuh got?"

"Er pillar."

"Fer whut?"

"Feathers, fool!"

"Chris! Thisll be hot ef we kin ketch them niggers!"

"Ol Anderson said he wuz gonna bringa barrela tar!"

"Ah got some gasoline in mah car ef yuh need it."

Big Boy had no feelings now. He was waiting. He did not wonder if they were coming after him. He just waited. He did not wonder about Bobo. He rested his cheek against the cold clay, waiting.

A dog barked. He stiffened. It barked again. He balled himself into a knot at the bottom of the hole, waiting. Then he heard the patter of dog feet.

"Look!"

"Whuts he got?"

"Its a snake!"

"Yeah, the dogs foun a snake!"

"Gee, its a big one!"

"Shucks, Ah wish he could fin one of them sonofabitchin niggers!"

The voices sank to low murmurs. Then he heard number twelve, its bell tolling and whistle crying as it slid along the rails. He flattened himself against the clay. Someone was singing:

"We'll hang ever nigger t a sour apple tree . . ."

When the song ended there was hard laughter. From the other side of the hill he heard the dog barking furiously. He listened. There was more than one dog now. There were many and they were barking their throats out.

"Hush, Ah hear them dogs!"

"When theys barking like tha they foun somethin!"

"Here they come over the hill!"

"WE GOT IM! WE GOT IM!"

There came a roar. Tha mus be Bobo; tha mus be Bobo . . . In spite of his fear, Big Boy looked. The road, and half of the hillside across the road, were covered with men. A few were at the top of the hill, stenciled against the sky. He could see dark forms moving up the slopes. They were yelling.

"By Gawd, we got im!"

"C mon!"

"Where is he?"

"Theyre bringin im over the hill!"

"Ah got a rope fer im!"

"Say, somebody go n git the others!"

"Where is he? Cant we see im, Mister?"

"They say Berthas comin, too."

"Jack! Jack! Don leave me! Ah wanna see im!"

"Theyre bringin im over the hill, sweetheart!"

"AH WANNA BE THE FIRS T PUT A ROPE ON THA BLACK BASTARDS NECK!"

"Les start the fire!"

"Heat the tar!"

"Ah got some chains t chain im."

"Bring im over this way!"

"Chris, Ah wished Ah hada drink . . ."

Big Boy saw men moving over the hill. Among them was a long dark spot. Tha mus be Bobo; tha mus be Bobo theys carryin . . . They'll git im here. He oughta git up n run. He clamped his teeth and ran his hand across his forehead, bringing it away wet. He tried to swallow, but could not; his throat was dry.

They had started the song again:

> *"We'll hang ever nigger t a sour apple tree . . ."*

There were women singing now. Their voices made the song round and full. Song waves rolled over the top of pine trees. The sky sagged low, heavy with clouds. Wind was rising. Sometimes cricket cries cut surprisingly across the mob song. A dog had gone to the utmost top of the hill. At each lull of the song his howl floated full into the night.

Big Boy shrank when he saw the first tall flame light the hillside. Would they see im here? Then he remembered you could not see into the dark if you were standing in the light. As flames leaped higher he saw two men rolling a barrel up the slope.

"Say, gimme a han here, will yuh?"

"Awright, heave!"

"C mon! Straight up! Git t the other end!"

"Ah got the feathers here in this pillar!"

"BRING SOME MO WOOD!"

Big Boy could see the barrel surrounded by flames. The mob fell back, forming a dark circle. Theyd fin im here! He had a wild impulse to climb out and fly across the hills. But his legs would not move. He stared hard, trying to find Bobo. His eyes played over a long dark spot near the fire. Fanned by wind, flames leaped higher. He jumped. That dark spot had moved. Lawd, thas Bobo; thas Bobo . . .

He smelt the scent of tar, faint at first, then stronger. The wind brought it full into his face, then blew it away. His eyes burned and he rubbed them with his knuckles. He sneezed.

"LES GIT SOURVINEERS!"

He saw the mob close in around the fire. Their faces were hard and sharp in the light of the flames. More men and women were coming over the hill. The long dark spot was smudged out.

"Everybody git back!"

"Look! Hes gotta finger!"

"C MON! GIT THE GALS BACK FROM THE FIRE!"

"Hes got one of his ears, see?"

"Whuts the matter!"

"A woman fell out! Fainted, Ah reckon . . ."

The stench of tar permeated the hillside. The sky was black and the wind was blowing hard.

"HURRY UP N BURN THE NIGGER FO IT RAINS!"

Big Boy saw the mob fall back, leaving a small knot of men about the fire. Then, for the first time, he had a full glimpse of Bobo. A black body flashed in the light. Bobo was struggling, twisting; they were binding his arms and legs . . .

When he saw them tilt the barrel he stiffened. A scream quivered. He knew the tar was on Bobo. The mob fell back. He saw a tar-drenched body glistening and turning.

"THE BASTARDS GOT IT!"

There was a sudden quiet. Then he shrank violently as the wind carried, like a flury of snow, a widening spiral of white feathers into the night. The flames leaped tall as the trees. The scream came again. Big Boy trembled and looked. The mob was running down the slopes, leaving the fire clear. The he saw a writhing white mass cradled in yellow flame, and heard screams, one on top of the other, each shriller and shorter than the last. The mob was quiet now, standing still, looking up the slopes at the writhing white mass gradually growing black, growing black in a cradle of yellow flame.

"PO ON MO GAS!"

"Gimme a lif, will yuh!"

Two men were struggling, carrying between them a heavy can. They set it down, tilted it, leaving it so that the gas would trickle down to the hollowed earth around the fire.

Big Boy slid back into the hole, his face buried in clay. He had no feelings now, no fears. He was numb, empty, as though all blood had been drawn from him. Then his muscles flexed taut when he heard a faint patter. A tiny stream of cold water seeped to his knees, making him push back to a drier spot. He looked up; rain was beating in the grass.

"Its rainin!"

"C mon, les git t town!"

". . . don worry, when the fire git thu wid im hell be gone . . ."

"Wait, Charles! Don leave me; its slippery here . . ."

"Ahll take some of yuh ladies back in mah car . . ."

Big Boy heard the dogs barking again, this time closer. Running feet pounded past. Cold water chilled his ankles. He could hear rain-drops steadily hissing.

Now a dog was barking at the mouth of the hole, barking furiously, sensing a presence there. He balled himself into a knot and clung to the bottom, his knees and shins buried in water. The bark came louder. He heard paws scraping and felt the hot scent of dog breath on his face. Green eyes glowed and drew nearer as the barking, muffled by the closeness of the hole, beat upon his eardrums. Backing till his shoulders pressed against the clay, he held his breath. He pushed out his hands, his fingers stiff. The dog yawped louder, advancing, his bark rising sharp and thin. Big Boy rose to his knees, his hands before him. Then he flattened out still more against the bottom, breathing lungsful of hot dog scent, breathing it slowly, hard, but evenly. The dog came closer, bringing hotter dog scent. Big Boy could go back no more. His knees were slipping and slopping in the water. He braced himself, ready. Then, he never exactly knew how—he never knew whether he had lunged or the dog had lunged—they were together, rolling in the water. The green eyes were beneath him, between his legs. Dognails bit into his arms. His knees slipped backward and he landed full on the dog; the dog's breath left in a heavy gasp. Instinctively, he fumbled for the throat as he felt the dog twisting between his knees. The dog snarled, long and low, as though gathering strength. Big Boy's hands traveled swiftly over the dog's back, groping for the throat. He felt dognails again and saw green eyes, but his fingers had found the throat. He choked, feeling his fingers sink; he choked, throwing back his head and stiffening his arms. He felt the dog's body heave, felt dognails digging into his loins. With strength flowing from fear, he closed his fingers, pushing his full weight on the dog's throat. The dog heaved again, and lay still . . . Big Boy heard the sound of his own breathing filling the hole, and heard shouts and footsteps above him going past.

For a long, long time he held the dog, held it long after the last footstep had died out, long after the rain had stopped.

V

Morning found him still on his knees in a puddle of rainwater, staring at the stiff body of a dog. As the air brightened he came to himself slowly. He held still for a long time, as though waking from a dream, as though trying to remember.

The chug of a truck came over the hill. He tried to crawl to the opening. His knees were stiff and a thousand needle-like pains shot from the bottom of his feet to the calves of his legs. Giddiness made his eyes blur. He pulled up and looked. Through brackish light he saw Will's truck standing some twenty-five yards away, the engine running. Will stood on the running board, looking over the slopes of the hill.

Big Boy scuffled out, falling weakly in the wet grass. He tried to call to Will, but his dry throat would make no sound. He tried again.

"Will!"

Will heard, answering:

"Big Boy, c mon!"

He tried to run, and fell. Will came, meeting him in the tall grass.

"C mon," Will said, catching his arm.

They struggled to the truck.

"Hurry up!" said Will, pushing him onto the runningboard.

Will pushed back a square trapdoor which swung above the back of the driver's seat. Big Boy pulled through, landing with a thud on the bottom. On hands and knees he looked around in the semi-darkness.

"Wheres Bobo?"

Big Boy stared.

"Wheres Bobo?"

"They got im."

"When?"

"Las night."

"The mob?"

Big Boy pointed in the direction of a charred sapling on the slope of the opposite hill. Will looked. The trapdoor fell. The engine purred, the gears whined, and the truck lurched forward over the muddy road, sending Big Boy on his side.

For a while he lay as he had fallen, on his side, too weak to move. As he felt the truck swing around a curve he straightened up and rested his back against a stack of wooden boxes. Slowly, he began to make out objects in the darkness. Through two long cracks fell thin blades of daylight. The floor was of smooth steel, and cold to his thighs. Splinters and bits of sawdust danced with the rumble of the truck. Each time they swung around a curve he was pulled over the floor; he grabbed at corners of boxes to steady himself. Once he heard the crow of a rooster. It made him think of home, of ma and pa. He thought he remembered hearing somewhere that the house had burned, but could not remember where . . . It all seemed unreal now.

He was tired. He dozed, swaying with the lurch. Then he jumped awake. The truck was running smoothly, on gravel. Far away he heard two short blasts from the Buckeye Lumber Mill. Unconsciously, the thought sang through his mind: Its six erclock . . .

The trapdoor swung in. Will spoke through a corner of his mouth.

"How yuh comin?"

"Awright."

"How they git Bobo?"

"He wuz comin over the hill."

"What they do?"

"They burnt im . . . Will, Ah wan some water; mah throats like fire . . ."

"Well git some when we pass a fillin station."

Big Boy leaned back and dozed. He jerked awake when the truck stopped. He heard Will git out. He wanted to peep through the trapdoor, but was afraid. For a moment, the wild fear he had known in the hole came back. Spose theyd search n fin im? He quieted when he heard Will's footstep on the runningboard. The trapdoor pushed in. Will's hat came through dripping.

"Take it quick!"

Big Boy grabbed, spilling water into his face. The truck lurched. He drank. Hard cold lumps of brick rolled into his hot stomach. A dull pain made him bend over. His intestines seemed to be drawing into a tight knot. After a bit it eased, and he sat up, breathing softly.

The truck swerved. He blinked his eyes. The blades of daylight had turned brightly golden. The sun had risen.

The truck sped over the asphalt miles, sped northward, jolting him, shaking out of his bosom the crumbs of corn bread, making them dance with the splinters and sawdust in the golden blades of sunshine.

He turned on his side and slept.

EUDORA WELTY

(1909–   )

One of the great writers of her century, Eudora Welty has been the master of the everyday, the ordinary—made extraordinary through her vision of the intense humanity embodied in the lives of her characters. Unlike her fellow Mississippian William Faulkner (perhaps her only peer among the South's writers of her time), she has found her art not in the great tragic struggles of larger-than-life protagonists who confront epic situations in ultimate terms, but in "normal" people: men and women who live lives of daily routine and apparently uneventful circumstance. In *Delta Wedding* a little girl spends a week at a plantation home in the Mississippi Delta, observing the preparations for a wedding in the family. In *The Golden Apples* forty years go by in a Mississippi town; people are born, grow older, are married, die. *Losing Battles* chronicles a day-long rural family reunion. In *The Optimist's Daughter* a middle-aged woman comes home to Mississippi from Chicago for her father's last illness and then stays for several days to sort out things in her parents' home. Violence is downplayed; crises are private; men and women go about the business of being human. Welty's art achieves its triumphs in her insight into her characters' humanity and the delineation of what it means for them.

Eudora Welty was born in Jackson, Mississippi, the daughter of an Ohio-born insurance executive and a West Virginia-born schoolteacher. She attended high school in Jackson, studied for two years at Mississippi State College for Women and then graduated from the University of Wisconsin, and studied advertising for a year at Columbia University. During the 1930s she worked in journalism, traveled about Mississippi as a publicity agent and photographer for the Works Progress Administration, and began writing short stories. Her first book, *A Curtain of Green*, a collection of short stories, appeared in 1941. The following year she published an historical fantasy of early Mississippi, *The Robber Bridegroom*. Another collection, *The Wide Net and Other Stories*, came out in 1943. Her first novel, *Delta Wedding*, was published in 1946, and the cycle of stories entitled *The Golden Apples* in 1949. A comic novella, *The Ponder Heart*, appeared in 1954, and another collection, *The Bride of the Innisfallen and Other Stories*, in 1955. For fifteen years thereafter she published no major work. Finally, in 1970 she brought out her most ambitious novel, *Losing Battles*. It was followed by *One Time, One Place: Mississippi in the Depression, A Snapshot Album* (1971), a remarkable collection of photographs she had taken during the Depression, and *The Optimist's Daughter* (1972). Throughout her career she has written essays, articles, and book reviews, and in 1978 these were collected under the title *The Eye of the Story*.

Most often Eudora Welty's art is comic. She has a connoisseur's eye for the eccentric, the zany, the unexpected, and—particularly in her short fiction—the seemingly grotesque. But her people are almost always active and integral parts of the comings and goings of community life, and she is never content to stay on the immediately comic surface of experience; unerringly she focuses on details of characterization to get at underlying meanings. Paradoxically, she develops the profundities of her storytelling through a concentration on surfaces: in the significance of the rich clusterings of details and minute observation she reveals the truths of her fiction.

WHY I LIVE AT THE P.O.

I was getting along fine with Mama, Papa-Daddy and Uncle Rondo until my sister Stella-Rondo just separated from her husband and came back home again. Mr. Whitaker! Of course I went with Mr. Whitaker first, when he first appeared here in China Grove, taking "Pose Yourself" photos, and Stella-Rondo broke us up. Told him I was one-sided. Bigger on one side than the other, which is a deliberate, calculated falsehood: I'm the same. Stella-Rondo is exactly twelve months to the day younger than I am and for that reason she's spoiled.

She's always had anything in the world she wanted and then she'd throw it away. Papa-Daddy gave her this gorgeous Add-a-Pearl necklace when she was eight years old and she threw it away playing baseball when she was nine, with only two pearls.

So as soon as she got married and moved away from home the first thing she did was separate! From Mr. Whitaker! This photographer with the popeyes she said she trusted. Came home from one of those towns up in Illinois and to our complete surprise brought this child of two.

Mama said she like to made her drop dead for a second. "Here you had this marvelous blonde child and never so much as wrote your mother a word about it," says Mama. "I'm thoroughly ashamed of you." But of course she wasn't.

Stella-Rondo just calmly takes off this *hat*, I wish you could see it. She says, "Why, Mama, Shirley-T.'s adopted, I can prove it."

"How?" says Mama, but all I says was, "H'm!" There I was over the hot stove, trying to stretch two chickens over five people and a completely unexpected child into the bargain, without one moment's notice.

"What do you mean—'H'm!'?" says Stella-Rondo, and Mama says, "I heard that, Sister."

I said that oh, I didn't mean a thing, only that whoever Shirley-T. was, she was the spit-image of Papa-Daddy if he'd cut off his beard, which of course he'd never do in the world. Papa-Daddy's Mama's papa and sulks.

Stella-Rondo got furious! She said, "Sister, I don't need to tell you you got a lot of nerve and always did have and I'll thank you to make no future reference to my adopted child whatsoever."

"Very well," I said. "Very well, very well. Of course I noticed at once she looks like Mr. Whitaker's side too. That frown. She looks like a cross between Mr. Whitaker and Papa-Daddy."

"Well, all I can say is she isn't."

"She looks exactly like Shirley Temple to me," says Mama, but Shirley-T. just ran away from her.

So the first thing Stella-Rondo did at the table was turn Papa-Daddy against me.

"Papa-Daddy," she says. He was trying to cut up his meat. "Papa-Daddy!" I was taken completely by surprise. Papa-Daddy is about a million years old and's got this long-long beard. "Papa-Daddy, Sister says she fails to understand why you don't cut off your beard."

So Papa-Daddy l-a-y-s down his knife and fork! He's real rich. Mama says he is, he says he isn't. So he says, "Have I heard correctly? You don't understand why I don't cut off my beard?"

"Why," I says, "Papa-Daddy, of course I understand, I did not say any such of a thing, the idea!"

He says, "Hussy!"

I says, "Papa-Daddy, you know I wouldn't any more want you to cut off your beard than the man in the moon. It was the farthest thing from my mind! Stella-Rondo sat there and made that up while she was eating breast of chicken."

But he says, "So the postmistress fails to understand why I don't cut off my beard. Which job I got you through my influence with the government. 'Bird's nest'—is that what you call it?"

Not that it isn't the next to smallest P.O. in the entire state of Mississippi.

I says, "Oh, Papa-Daddy," I says, "I didn't say any such of a thing, I never dreamed it was a bird's nest, I have always been grateful though this is the next to smallest P.O. in the state of Mississippi, and I do not enjoy being referred to as a hussy by my own grandfather."

But Stella-Rondo says, "Yes, you did say it too. Anybody in the world could of heard you, that had ears."

"Stop right there," says Mama, looking at *me*.

So I pulled my napkin straight back through the napkin ring and left the table.

As soon as I was out of the room Mama says, "Call her back, or she'll starve to death," but Papa-Daddy says, "This is the beard I started growing on the Coast when I was fifteen years old." He would of gone on till nightfall if Shirley-T. hadn't lost the Milky Way she ate in Cairo.

So Papa-Daddy says, "I am going out and lie in the hammock, and you can all sit here and remember my words: I'll never cut off my beard as long as I live, even one inch, and I don't appreciate it in you at all." Passed right by me in the hall and went straight out and got in the hammock.

It would be a holiday. It wasn't five minutes before Uncle Rondo suddenly appeared in the hall in one of Stella-Rondo's flesh-colored kimonos, all cut on the bias, like something Mr. Whitaker probably thought was gorgeous.

"Uncle Rondo!" I says. "I didn't know who that was! Where are you going?"

"Sister," he says, "get out of my way, I'm poisoned."

"If you're poisoned stay away from Papa-Daddy," I says. "Keep out of the hammock. Papa-Daddy will certainly beat you on the head if you come within forty miles of him. He thinks I deliberately said he ought to cut off his beard after he got me the P.O., and I've told him and told him and told him, and he acts like he just don't hear me. Papa-Daddy must of gone stone deaf."

"He picked a fine day to do it then," says Uncle Rondo, and before you could say "Jack Robinson" flew out in the yard.

What he'd really done, he'd drunk another bottle of that prescription. He does it every single Fourth of July as sure as shooting, and it's horribly expensive. Then he falls over in the hammock and snores. So he insisted on zigzagging right on out to the hammock, looking like a half-wit.

Papa-Daddy woke up with this horrible yell and right there without moving an inch he tried to turn Uncle Rondo against me. I heard every word he said. Oh, he told Uncle Rondo I didn't learn to read till I was eight years old and he didn't see how in the world I ever got the mail put up at the P.O., much less read it all, and he said if Uncle Rondo could only fathom the lengths he had gone to to get me that job! And he said on the other hand he thought Stella-Rondo had a brilliant mind and deserved credit for getting out of town. All the time he was just lying there swinging as pretty as you please and looping out his beard, and poor Uncle Rondo was *pleading* with him to slow down the hammock, it was making him as dizzy as a witch to watch it. But that's what Papa-Daddy likes about a hammock. So Uncle Rondo was too dizzy to get turned against me for the time being. He's Mama's only brother and is a good case of a one-track mind. Ask anybody. A certified pharmacist.

Just then I heard Stella-Rondo raising the upstairs window. While she was married she got this peculiar idea that it's cooler with the windows shut and locked. So she has to raise the window before she can make a soul hear her outdoors.

So she raises the window and says, "*Oh!*" You would have thought she was mortally wounded.

Uncle Rondo and Papa-Daddy didn't even look up, but kept right on with what they were doing. I had to laugh.

I flew up the stairs and threw the door open! I says, "What in the wide world's the matter, Stella-Rondo? You mortally wounded?"

"No," she says, "I am not mortally wounded but I wish you would do me the favor of looking out that window there and telling me what you see."

So I shade my eyes and look out the window.

"I see the front yard," I says.

"Don't you see any human beings?" she says.

"I see Uncle Rondo trying to run Papa-Daddy out of the hammock," I says. "Nothing more. Naturally, it's so suffocating-hot in the house, with all the windows shut and locked, everybody who cares to stay in their right mind will have to go out and get in the hammock before the Fourth of July is over."

"Don't you notice anything different about Uncle Rondo?" asks Stella-Rondo.

"Why, no, except he's got on some terrible-looking flesh-colored contraption I wouldn't be found dead in, is all I can see," I says.

"Never mind, you won't be found dead in it, because it happens to be part of my trousseau, and Mr. Whitaker took several dozen photographs of me in it," says Stella-Rondo. "What on earth could Uncle Rondo *mean* by wearing part of my trousseau out in the broad open daylight without saying so much as 'Kiss my foot,' *knowing* I only got home this morning after my separation and hung my negligee up on the bathroom door, just as nervous as I could be?"

"I'm sure I don't know, and what do you expect me to do about it?" I says. "Jump out the window?"

"No, I expect nothing of the kind. I simply declare that Uncle Rondo looks like a fool in it, that's all," she says. "It makes me sick to my stomach."

"Well, he looks as good as he can," I says. "As good as anybody in reason could." I stood up for Uncle Rondo, please remember. And I said to Stella-Rondo, "I think I would do well not to criticize so freely if I were you and came home with a two-year-old child I had never said a word about, and no explanation whatever about my separation."

"I asked you the instant I entered this house not to refer one more time to my adopted child, and you gave me your word of honor you would not," was all Stella-Rondo would say, and started pulling out every one of her eyebrows with some cheap Kress tweezers.

So I merely slammed the door behind me and went down and made some green-tomato pickle. Somebody had to do it. Of course Mama had turned both the niggers loose; she always said no earthly power could hold one anyway on the Fourth of July, so she wouldn't even try. It turned out that Jaypan fell in the lake and came within a very narrow limit of drowning.

So Mama trots in. Lifts up the lid and says, "H'm! Not very good for your Uncle Rondo in his precarious condition, I must say. Or poor little adopted Shirley-T. Shame on you!"

That made me tired. I says, "Well, Stella-Rondo had better thank her lucky stars it was her instead of me came trotting in with that very peculiar-looking child. Now if it had been me that trotted in from Illinois and brought a peculiar-looking child of two, I shudder to think of the reception I'd of got, much less controlled the diet of an entire family."

"But you must remember, Sister, that you were never married to Mr. Whitaker in the first place and didn't go up to Illinois to live," says Mama, shaking a spoon in my face. "If you had I would of been just as overjoyed to see you and your little adopted girl as I was to see Stella-Rondo, when you wound up with your separation and came on back home."

"You would not," I says.

"Don't contradict me, I would," says Mama.

But I said she couldn't convince me though she talked till she was blue in the face. Then I said, "Besides, you know as well as I do that that child is not adopted."

"She most certainly is adopted," says Mama, stiff as a poker.

I says, "Why, Mama, Stella-Rondo had her just as sure as anything in this world, and just too stuck up to admit it."

"Why, Sister," said Mama. "Here I thought we were going to have a pleasant Fourth of July, and you start right out not believing a word your own baby sister tells you!"

"Just like Cousin Annie Flo. Went to her grave denying the facts of life," I remind Mama.

"I told you if you ever mentioned Annie Flo's name I'd slap your face," says Mama, and slaps my face.

"All right, you wait and see," I says.

"I," says Mama, "*I* prefer to take my children's word for anything when it's humanly possible." You ought to see Mama, she weighs two hundred pounds and has real tiny feet.

Just then something perfectly horrible occurred to me.

"Mama," I says, "can that child talk?" I simply had to whisper! "Mama, I wonder if that child can be—you know—in any way? Do you realize," I says, "that she hasn't spoken one single, solitary word to a human being up to this minute? This is the way she looks," I says, and I looked like this.

Well, Mama and I just stood there and stared at each other. It was horrible!

"I remember well that Joe Whitaker frequently drank like a fish," says Mama. "I believed to my soul he drank *chemicals*." And without another word she marches to the foot of the stairs and calls Stella-Rondo.

"Stella-Rondo? O-o-o-o-o! Stella-Rondo!"

"What?" says Stella-Rondo from upstairs. Not even the grace to get up off the bed.

"Can that child of yours talk?" asks Mama.

Stella-Rondo says, "Can she what?"

"Talk! Talk!" says Mama. "Burdyburdyburdyburdy!"

So Stella-Rondo yells back, "Who says she can't talk?"

"Sister says so," says Mama.

"You didn't have to tell me, I know whose word of honor don't mean a thing in this house," says Stella-Rondo.

And in a minute the loudest Yankee voice I ever heard in my life yells out, "OE'm Pop-OE the Sailor-r-r-r Ma-a-an!" and then somebody jumps up and down in the upstairs hall. In another second the house would of fallen down.

"Not only talks, she can tap-dance!" calls Stella-Rondo. "Which is more than some people I won't name can do."

"Why, the little precious darling thing!" Mama says, so surprised. "Just as smart as she can be!" Starts talking baby talk right there. Then she turns on me. "Sister, you ought to be thoroughly ashamed! Run upstairs this instant and apologize to Stella-Rondo and Shirley-T."

"Apologize for what?" I says. "I merely wondered if the child was normal, that's all. Now that she's proved she is, why, I have nothing further to say."

But Mama just turned on her heel and flew out, furious. She ran right upstairs and hugged the baby. She believed it was adopted. Stella-Rondo hadn't done a thing but turn her against me from upstairs while I stood there helpless over the hot stove. So that made Mama, Papa-Daddy and the baby all on Stella-Rondo's side.

Next, Uncle Rondo.

I must say that Uncle Rondo has been marvelous to me at various times in the past and I was completely unprepared to be made to jump out of my skin, the way it turned out. Once Stella-Rondo did something perfectly horrible to him—broke a chain letter from Flanders Field—and he took the radio back he had given her and gave it to me. Stella-Rondo was furious! For six months we all had to call her Stella instead of Stella-Rondo, or she wouldn't answer. I always thought Uncle Rondo had all the brains of the entire family. Another time he sent me to Mammoth Cave, with all expenses paid.

But this would be the day he was drinking that prescription, the Fourth of July.

So at supper Stella-Rondo speaks up and says she thinks Uncle Rondo ought to try to eat a little something. So finally Uncle Rondo said he would try a little cold biscuits and ketchup, but that was all. So *she* brought it to him.

"Do you think it wise to disport with ketchup in Stella-Rondo's flesh-colored kimono?" I says. Trying to be considerate! If Stella-Rondo couldn't watch out for her trousseau, somebody had to.

"Any objections?" asks Uncle Rondo, just about to pour out all the ketchup.

"Don't mind what she says, Uncle Rondo," says Stella-Rondo. "Sister has been devoting this solid afternoon to sneering out my bedroom window at the way you look."

"What's that?" says Uncle Rondo. Uncle Rondo has got the most terrible temper in the world. Anything is liable to make him tear the house down if it comes at the wrong time.

So Stella-Rondo says, "Sister says, 'Uncle Rondo certainly does look like a fool in that pink kimono!'"

Do you remember who it was really said that?

Uncle Rondo spills out all the ketchup and jumps out of his chair and tears off the kimono and throws it down on the dirty floor and puts his foot on it. It had to be sent all the way to Jackson to the cleaners and re-pleated.

"So that's your opinion of your Uncle Rondo, is it?" he says. "I look like a fool, do I? Well, that's the last straw. A whole day in this house with nothing to do, and then to hear you come out with a remark like that behind my back!"

"I didn't say any such of a thing, Uncle Rondo," I says, "and I'm not saying who did, either. Why, I think you look all right. Just try to take care of yourself and not talk and eat at the same time," I says. "I think you better go lie down."

"Lie down my foot," says Uncle Rondo. I ought to of known by that he was fixing to do something perfectly horrible.

So he didn't do anything that night in the precarious state he was in —just played Casino with Mama and Stella-Rondo and Shirley-T. and gave Shirley-T. a nickel with a head on both sides. It tickled her nearly to death, and she called him "Papa." But at 6:30 A.M. the next morning, he threw a whole five-cent package of some unsold one-inch firecrackers from the store as hard as he could into my bedroom and they every one went off. Not one bad one in the string. Anybody else, there'd be one that wouldn't go off.

Well, I'm just terribly susceptible to noise of any kind, the doctor has always told me I was the most sensitive person he had ever seen in his whole life, and I was simply prostrated. I couldn't eat! People tell me they heard it as far as the cemetery, and old Aunt Jep Patterson, that had been holding her own so good, thought it was Judgment Day and she was going to meet her whole family. It's usually so quiet here.

And I'll tell you it didn't take me any longer than a minute to make up my mind what to do. There I was with the whole entire house on Stella-Rondo's side and turned against me. If I have anything at all I have pride.

So I just decided I'd go straight down to the P.O. There's plenty of room there in the back, I says to myself.

Well! I made no bones about letting the family catch on to what I was up to. I didn't try to conceal it.

The first thing they knew, I marched in where they were all playing Old Maid and pulled the electric oscillating fan out by the plug, and everything got real hot. Next I snatched the pillow I'd done the needlepoint on right off the davenport from behind Papa-Daddy. He went "Ugh!" I beat Stella-Rondo up the stairs and finally found my charm bracelet in her bureau drawer under a picture of Nelson Eddy.

"So that's the way the land lies," says Uncle Rondo. There he was, piecing on the ham. "Well, Sister, I'll be glad to donate my army cot if you got any place to set it up, providing you'll leave right this minute and let me get some peace." Uncle Rondo was in France.

"Thank you kindly for the cot and 'peace' is hardly the word I would select if I had to resort to firecrackers at 6:30 A.M. in a young girl's bedroom," I says back to him. "And as to where I intend to go, you seem to forget my position as postmistress of China Grove, Mississippi," I says. "I've always got the P.O."

Well, that made them all sit up and take notice.

I went out front and started digging up some four-o'clocks to plant around the P. O.

"Ah-ah-ah!" says Mama, raising the window. "Those happen to be my four-o'clocks. Everything planted in that star is mine. I've never known you to make anything grow in your life."

"Very well," I says. "But I take the fern. Even you, Mama, can't stand there and deny that I'm the one watered that fern. And I happen to know where I can send in a box top and get a packet of one thousand mixed seeds, no two the same kind, free."

"Oh, where?" Mama wants to know.

But I says, "Too late. You 'tend to your house, and I'll 'tend to mine. You hear things like that all the time if you know how to listen to the radio. Perfectly marvelous offers. Get anything you want free."

So I hope to tell you I marched in and got that radio, and they could of all bit a nail in two, especially Stella-Rondo, that it used to belong to, and she well knew she couldn't get it back, I'd sue for it like a shot. And I very politely took the sewing-machine motor I helped pay the most on to give Mama for Christmas back in 1929, and a good big calendar, with the first-aid remedies on it. The thermometer and the Hawaiian ukelele certainly were rightfully mine, and I stood on the step-ladder and got all my water-melon-rind preserves and every fruit and vegetable I'd put up, every jar. Then I began to pull the tacks out of the bluebird wall vases on the archway to the dining room.

"Who told you you could have those, Miss Priss?" says Mama, fanning as hard as she could.

"I bought 'em and I'll keep track of 'em," I says. "I'll tack 'em up one on each side the post office window, and you can see 'em when you come to ask me for your mail, if you're so dead to see 'em."

"Not I! I'll never darken the door to that post office again if I live to be a hundred," Mama says. "Ungrateful child! After all the money we spent on you at the Normal."

"Me either," says Stella-Rondo. "You can just let my mail lie there and *rot*, for all I care. I'll never come and relieve you of a single, solitary piece."

"I should worry," I says. "And who you think's going to sit down and write you all those big fat letters and postcards, by the way? Mr. Whitaker? Just because he was the only man ever dropped down in China Grove and you got him—unfairly—is he going to sit down and write you a lengthy cor-respondence after you come home giving no rhyme nor reason whatsoever for your separation and no explanation for the presence of that child? I may not have your brilliant mind, but I fail to see it."

So Mama says, "Sister, I've told you a thousand times that Stella-Rondo simply got homesick, and this child is far too big to be hers," and she says, "Now, why don't you all just sit down and play Casino?"

Then Shirley-T. sticks out her tongue at me in this perfectly horrible way. She has no more manners than the man in the moon. I told her she was going to cross her eyes like that some day and they'd stick.

"It's too late to stop me now," I says. "You should have tried that yester-day. I'm going to the P.O. and the only way you can possibly see me is to visit me there."

So Papa-Daddy says, 'You'll never catch me setting foot in that post office, even if I should take a notion into my head to write a letter some place." He says, "I won't have you reachin' out of that little old window with a pair of shears and cuttin' off any beard of mine. I'm too smart for you!"

"We all are," says Stella-Rondo.

But I said, "If you're so smart, where's Mr. Whitaker?"

So then Uncle Rondo says, "I'll thank you from now on to stop reading all the orders I get on postcards and telling everybody in China Grove what you think is the matter with them," but I says, "I draw my own conclusions and will continue in the future to draw them." I says, "If people want to write their inmost secrets on penny postcards, there's nothing in the wide world you can do about it, Uncle Rondo."

"And if you think we'll ever *write* another postcard you're sadly mistaken," says Mama.

"Cutting off your nose to spite your face then," I says. "But if you're all determined to have no more to do with the U.S. mail, think of this: What will Stella-Rondo do now, if she wants to tell Mr. Whitaker to come after her?"

"Wah!" says Stella-Rondo. I knew she'd cry. She had a conniption fit right there in the kitchen.

"It will be interesting to see how long she holds out," I says. "And now —I am leaving."

"Good-bye," says Uncle Rondo.

"Oh, I declare," says Mama, "to think that a family of mine should quarrel on the Fourth of July, or the day after, over Stella-Rondo leaving old Mr. Whitaker and having the sweetest little adopted child! It looks like we'd all be glad!"

"Wah!" says Stella-Rondo, and has a fresh conniption fit.

"*He* left *her*—you mark my words," I says. "That's Mr. Whitaker. I know Mr. Whitaker. After all, I knew him first. I said from the beginning he'd up and leave her. I foretold every single thing that's happened."

"Where did he go?" asks Mama.

"Probably to the North Pole, if he knows what's good for him," I says.

But Stella-Rondo just bawled and wouldn't say another word. She flew to her room and slammed the door.

"Now look what you've gone and done, Sister," says Mama. "You go apologize."

"I haven't got time, I'm leaving," I says.

"Well, what are you waiting around for?" asks Uncle Rondo.

So I just picked up the kitchen clock and marched off, without saying "Kiss my foot" or anything, and never did tell Stella-Rondo good-bye.

There was a nigger girl going along on a little wagon right in front.

"Nigger girl," I says, "come help me haul these things down the hill, I'm going to live in the post office."

Took her nine trips in her express wagon. Uncle Rondo came out on the porch and threw her a nickel.

And that's the last I've laid eyes on any of my family or my family laid eyes on me for five solid days and nights. Stella-Rondo may be telling the most horrible tales in the world about Mr. Whitaker, but I haven't heard them. As I tell everybody, I draw my own conclusions.

But oh, I like it here. It's ideal, as I've been saying. You see, I've got everything cater-cornered, the way I like it. Hear the radio? All the war news. Radio, sewing machine, book ends, ironing board and that great big piano lamp—peace, that's what I like. Butter-bean vines planted all along the front where the strings are.

Of course, there's not much mail. My family are naturally the main people in China Grove, and if they prefer to vanish from the face of the earth, for all the mail they get or the mail they write, why, I'm not going to open my mouth. Some of the folks here in town are taking up for me and some turned against me. I know which is which. There are always people who will quit buying stamps just to get on the right side of Papa-Daddy.

But here I am, and here I'll stay. I want the world to know I'm happy.

And if Stella-Rondo should come to me this minute, on bended knees, and *attempt* to explain the incidents of her life with Mr. Whitaker, I'd simply put my fingers in both my ears and refuse to listen.

TENNESSEE WILLIAMS

(1911–1983)

Thomas Lanier Williams, considered by many drama critics to be the most powerful and original force in the American theatre since Eugene O'Neill, was born in Columbus, Mississippi. His grandfather was an Episcopal minister and the family lived in the rectory of the church until Williams was 12, when his father, a salesman, was transferred to St. Louis. He began writing poetry during his childhood. After graduating from high school he attended George Washington University for several years, then worked in a shoe factory until his health failed and he went to live with his grandparents in Memphis, Tennessee. He began to write and sell stories, and he returned to college, graduating from the State University of Iowa in 1938. In 1940 a play, *Battle of Angels,* was staged by the Theatre Guild but did not survive beyond its trial run. During World War II Williams worked as a screenwriter in Hollywood. In

1945 his first hit, *The Glass Menagerie,* was produced on Broadway and won the Critics' Circle Award. *A Streetcar Named Desire,* produced in 1947, was a major success. His subsequent plays, which won him several Pulitzer Prizes, include *Summer and Smoke* (1948), *The Rose Tattoo* (1950), *Cat on a Hot Tin Roof* (1955), *Orpheus Descending* (1958), *Suddenly Last Summer* (1958), *Sweet Bird of Youth* (1959), *The Night of the Iguana* (1962) and *The Milk Train Doesn't Stop Here Anymore* (1963). A collection of his shorter plays is *Twenty-Seven Wagons Full of Cotton and Other Plays* (1945). Williams has also published three volumes of short stories; a novel, *The Roman Spring of Mrs. Stone* (1950); and an autobiography, *Memoirs* (1975). In recent years he has lived in New Orleans.

As a dramatist Williams has been fascinated with people caught in change who struggle against social constraint and puritanical repression, which he sees as inflicting upon men and women an unnatural frustration that results in perversion, neurosis, hysteria, and debasement. In his best-known work, *A Streetcar Named Desire,* a woman of a once well-to-do and socially respectable but now decayed Mississippi family, living with her sister and brother-in-law in New Orleans, is driven by sex-frustration and hysteria to cause evil wherever she goes and at the end retreats into psychotic self-delusion and is committed to a mental hospital. In the play there is something of the theme of aristocratic decline-and-fall that William Faulkner has used in such novels as *The Sound and the Fury*; indeed, in certain respects Blanche DuBois might be seen as playing the same role as Mrs. Compson in that novel, though in far more active, flaunting, hysterical fashion. Her decadence, snobbery, and frustrated malaise are contrasted with what is portrayed as the virile, healthy, profane vulgarity of Stanley Kowalski, the Polish artisan who is her brother-in-law. Throughout much of Williams' most successful work a "healthy" primitivism is set against a "decadent" refinement and civilized effeteness in a Gothic clash of violence, perversion, sadism, and shame. Among his Southern contemporaries, Williams' art would seem to be closest to that of Carson McCullers and Truman Capote.

THIS PROPERTY IS CONDEMNED

CHARACTERS
WILLIE, *a young girl.*
TOM, *a boy.*

SCENE: *A railroad embankment on the outskirts of a small Mississippi town on one of those milky white winter mornings peculiar to that part of the country. The air is moist and chill. Behind the low embankment of the tracks is a large yellow frame house which has a look of tragic vacancy. Some of the upper windows are boarded, a portion of the roof has fallen away. The land is utterly flat. In the left background is a billboard that says "GIN WITH JAKE" and there are some telephone poles and a few bare winter trees. The sky is a great milky whiteness: crows occasionally make a sound of roughly torn cloth.*

The girl Willie is advancing precariously along the railroad track, balancing herself with both arms outstretched, one clutching a banana, the other an extraordinarily dilapidated doll with a frowsy blond wig.

She is a remarkable apparition—thin as a beanpole and dressed in outrageous cast-off finery. She wears a long blue velvet party dress with a filthy cream lace collar and sparkling rhinestone beads. On her feet are battered silver kid slippers with large ornamental buckles. Her wrists and her fingers are resplendent with dimestore jewelry. She has applied rouge to her childish face in artless crimson daubs and her lips are made up in a preposterous Cupid's bow. She is about thirteen and there is something ineluctably childlike and innocent in her appearance despite the makeup. She laughs frequently and wildly and with a sort of precocious, tragic abandon.

The boy Tom, slightly older, watches her from below the embankment. He wears corduroy pants, blue shirt and a sweater and carries a kite of red tissue paper with a gaudily ribboned tail.

TOM: Hello. Who are you?

WILLIE: Don't talk to me till I fall off. (*She proceeds dizzily. Tom watches with mute fascination. Her gyrations grow wider and wider. She speaks breathlessly.*) Take my—crazy doll—will you?

TOM: (*scrambling up the bank*) Yeh.

WILLIE: I don't wanta—break her when—I fall! I don't think I can—stay on much—longer—do you?

TOM: Naw.

WILLIE: I'm practically—off—right now! (*Tom offers to assist her.*) No, don't touch me. It's no fair helping. You've got to do it—all—by yourself! God, I'm wobbling! I don't know what's made me so nervous! You see that water-tank way back yonder?

TOM: Yeah?

WILLIE: That's where I—started—from! This is the furthest—I ever gone —without once—falling off. I mean it will be—if I can manage to stick on—to the next—telephone—pole! Oh! Here I go! (*She becomes completely unbalanced and rolls down the bank.*)

TOM: (*standing above her now*) Hurtcha self?

WILLIE: Skinned my knee a little. Glad I didn't put my silk stockings on.

TOM: (*coming down the bank*) Spit on it. That takes the sting away.

Willie: Okay.

Tom: That's animal's medicine, you know. They always lick their wounds.

Willie: I know. The principal damage was done to my bracelet, I guess. I knocked out one of the diamonds. Where did it go?

Tom: You never could find it in all them cinders.

Willie: I don't know. It had a lot of shine.

Tom: It wasn't a genuine diamond.

Willie: How do you know?

Tom: I just imagine it wasn't. Because if it was you wouldn't be walking along a railroad track with a banged-up doll and a piece of rotten banana.

Willie: Oh, I wouldn't be so sure. I might be peculiar or something. You never can tell. What's your name?

Tom: Tom.

Willie: Mine's Willie. We've both got boy's names.

Tom: How did that happen?

Willie: I was expected to be a boy but I wasn't. They had one girl already. Alva. She was my sister. Why ain't you at school?

Tom: I thought it was going to be windy so I could fly my kite.

Willie: What made you think that?

Tom: Because the sky was so white.

Willie: Is that a sign?

Tom: Yeah.

Willie: I know. It looks like everything had been swept off with a broom. Don't it?

Tom: Yeah.

Willie: It's perfectly white. It's white as a clean piece of paper.

Tom: Uh-huh.

Willie: But there isn't a wind.

Tom: Naw.

Willie: It's up too high for us to feel it. It's way, way up in the attic sweeping the dust off the furniture up there!

Tom: Uh-huh. Why ain't you at school?

Willie: I quituated. Two years ago this winter.

Tom: What grade was you in?

Willie: Five A.

Tom: Miss Preston.

Willie: Yep. She used to think my hands was dirty until I explained that it was cinders from falling off the railroad tracks so much.

Tom: She's pretty strict.

Willie: Oh, no, she's just disappointed because she didn't get married. Probably never had an opportunity, poor thing. So she has to teach Five A for the rest of her natural life. They started teaching algebra an' I didn't give a goddam what X stood for so I quit.

TOM: You'll never get an education walking the railroad tracks.

WILLIE: You won't get one flying a red kite neither. Besides . . .

TOM: What?

WILLIE: What a girl needs to get along is social training. I learned all of that
from my sister Alva. She had a wonderful popularity with the railroad
men.

TOM: Train engineers?

WILLIE: Engineers, firemen, conductors. Even the freight sup'rintendent.
We run a boarding-house for railroad men. She was I guess you might
say The Main Attraction. Beautiful? Jesus, she looked like a movie star!

TOM: Your sister?

WILLIE: Yeah. One of 'em used to bring her regular after each run a great
big heart-shaped red-silk box of assorted chocolates and nuts and hard
candies. Marvelous?

TOM: Yeah. (*The cawing of crows sounds through the chilly air.*)

WILLIE: You know where Alva is now?

TOM: Memphis?

WILLIE: Naw.

TOM: New Awleuns?

WILLIE: Naw.

TOM: St. Louis?

WILLIE: You'll never guess.

TOM: Where is she then? (*Willie does not answer at once.*)

WILLIE: (*very solemnly*) She's in the bone-orchard.

TOM: What?

WILLIE: (*violently*) Bone-orchard, cemetery, graveyard! Don't you
understand English?

TOM: Sure. That's pretty tough.

WILLIE: You don't know the half of it, buddy. We used to have some high
old times in that big yellow house.

TOM: I bet you did.

WILLIE: Musical instruments going all of the time.

TOM: Instruments? What kind?

WILLIE: Piano, victrola, Hawaiian steel guitar. Everyone played on
something. But now it's—awful quiet. You don't hear a sound from
there, do you?

TOM: Naw. Is it empty?

WILLIE: Except for me. They got a big sign stuck up.

TOM: What does it say?

WILLIE: (*loudly but with a slight catch*) "THIS PROPERTY IS
CONDEMNED!"

TOM: You ain't still living there?

WILLIE: Uh-huh.

TOM: What happened? Where did everyone go?

WILLIE: Mama run off with a brakeman on the C.& E.I. After that
   everything went to pieces. (*A train whistles far off.*) You hear that whistle?
   That's the Cannonball Express. The fastest thing on wheels between St.
   Louis, New Awleuns an' Memphis. My old man got to drinking.
TOM: Where is he now?
WILLIE: Disappeared. I guess I ought to refer this case to the Bureau of
   Missing Persons. The same as he done with Mama when she
   disappeared. Then there was me and Alva. Till Alva's lungs got affected.
   Did you see Greta Garbo in *Camille*? It played at the Delta Brilliant one
   time las' spring. She had the same what Alva died of. Lung affection.
TOM: Yeah?
WILLIE: Only it was—very beautiful the way she had it. You know. Violins
   playing. And loads and loads of white flowers. All of her lovers come
   back in a beautiful scene!
TOM: Yeah?
WILLIE: But Alva's all disappeared.
TOM: Yeah?
WILLIE: Like rats from a sinking ship! That's how she used to describe it.
   Oh, it—wasn't like death in the movies.
TOM: Naw?
WILLIE: She says, "Where is Albert? Where's Clemence?" None of them
   was around. I used to lie to her, I says, "They send their regards. They're
   coming to see you tomorrow." "Where's Mr. Johnson?" she asked me.
   He was the freight sup'rintendent, the most important character we ever
   had in our rooming-house. "He's been transferred to Grenada," I told
   her. "But wishes to be remembered." She known I was lying.
TOM: Yeah?
WILLIE: "This here is the pay-off!" she says. "They all run out on me like
   rats from a sinking ship!" Except Sidney.
TOM: Who was Sidney?
WILLIE: The one that used to give her the great big enormous red-silk box
   of American Beauty choc'lates.
TOM: Oh.
WILLIE: He remained faithful to her.
TOM: That's good.
WILLIE: But she never did care for Sidney. She said his teeth was decayed
   so he didn't smell good.
TOM: Aw!
WILLIE: It wasn't like death in the movies. When somebody dies in the
   movies they play violins.
TOM: But they didn't for Alva.
WILLIE: Naw. Not even a goddam victrola. They said it didn't agree with
   the hospital regulations. Always singing around the house.
TOM: Who? Alva?

WILLIE: Throwing enormous parties. This was her favorite number. (*She closes her eyes and stretches out her arms in the simulated rapture of the professional blues singer. Her voice is extraordinarily high and pure with a precocious emotional timbre.*)

> You're the only star
> In my blue hea-ven
> And you're shining just
> For me!

This is her clothes I got on. Inherited from her. Everything Alva's is mine. Except her solid gold beads.

TOM: What happened to them?

WILLIE: Them? She never took 'em off.

TOM: Oh!

WILLIE: I've also inherited all of my sister's beaux. Albert and Clemence and even the freight sup'rintendent.

TOM: Yeah?

WILLIE: They all disappeared. Afraid that they might get stuck for expenses I guess. But now they turn up again, all of 'em, like a bunch of bad pennies. They take me out places at night. I've got to be popular now. To parties an' dances an' all of the railroad affairs. Lookit here!

TOM: What?

WILLIE: I can do bumps! (*She stands in front of him and shoves her stomach toward him in a series of spasmodic jerks.*)

TOM: Frank Waters said that . . .

WILLIE: What?

TOM: You know.

WILLIE: Know what?

TOM: You took him inside and danced for him with your clothes off.

WILLIE: Oh. Crazy Doll's hair needs washing. I'm scared to wash it though 'cause her head might come unglued where she had that compound fracture of the skull. I think that most of her brains spilled out. She's been acting silly ever since. Saying an' doing the most outrageous things.

TOM: Why don't you do that for me?

WILLIE: What? Put glue on your compound fracture?

TOM: Naw. What you did for Frank Waters.

WILLIE: Because I was lonesome then an' I'm not lonesome now. You can tell Frank Waters that. Tell him that I've inherited all of my sister's beaux. I go out steady with men in responsible jobs. The sky sure is white. Ain't it? White as a clean piece of paper. In Five A we used to draw pictures. Miss Preston would give us a piece of white foolscap an' tell us to draw what we pleased.

TOM: What did you draw?

WILLIE: I remember I drawn her a picture one time of my old man getting conked with a bottle. She thought it was good, Miss Preston, she said, "Look here. Here's a picture of Charlie Chaplin with his hat on the side of his head!" I said, "Aw, naw, that's not Charlie Chaplin, that's my father, an' that's not his hat, it's a bottle!"

TOM: What did she say?

WILLIE: Oh, well. You can't make a school-teacher laugh.

> You're the only star
> In my blue hea-VEN . . .

The principal used to say there must've been something wrong with my home atmosphere because of the fact that we took in railroad men an' some of 'em slept with my sister.

TOM: Did they?

WILLIE: She was The Main Attraction. The house is sure empty now.

TOM: You ain't still living there, are you?

WILLIE: Sure.

TOM: By yourself?

WILLIE: Uh-huh. I'm not supposed to be but I am. The property is condemned but there's nothing wrong with it. Some county investigator come snooping around yesterday. I recognized her by the shape of her hat. It wasn't exactly what I would call stylish-looking.

TOM: Naw?

WILLIE: It looked like something she took off the lid of the stove. Alva knew lots about style. She had ambitions to be a designer for big wholesale firms in Chicago. She used to submit her pictures. It never worked out.

> You're the only star
> In my blue hea-ven . . .

TOM: What did you do? About the investigators?

WILLIE: Laid low upstairs. Pretended like no one was home.

TOM: Well, how do you manage to keep on eating?

WILLIE: Oh, I don't know. You keep a sharp look-out you see things lying around. This banana, perfectly good, for instance. Thrown in a garbage pail in back of the Blue Bird Café. (*She finishes the banana and tosses away the peel.*)

TOM: (*grinning*) Yeh. Miss Preston for instance.

WILLIE: Naw, not her. She gives you a white piece of paper, says "Draw what you please!" One time I drawn her a picture of—Oh, but I told you that, huh? Will you give Frank Waters a message?

TOM: What?

WILLIE: Tell him the freight sup'rintendent has bought me a pair of kid slippers. Patent. The same as the old ones of Alva's. I'm going to dances with them at Moon Lake Casino. All night I'll be dancing an' come home drunk in the morning! We'll have serenades with all kinds of musical instruments. Trumpets an' trombones. An' Hawaiian steel guitars. Yeh! Yeh! (*She rises excitedly.*) The sky will be white like this.

TOM: (*impressed*) Will it?

WILLIE: Uh-huh. (*She smiles vaguely and turns slowly toward him.*) White—as a clean—piece of paper . . . (*then excitedly*) I'll draw—pictures on it!

TOM: Will you?

WILLIE: Sure!

TOM: Pictures of what?

WILLIE: Me dancing! With the freight sup'rintendent! In a pair of patent kid shoes! Yeh! Yeh! With French heels on them as high as telephone poles! An' they'll play my favorite music!

TOM: Your favorite?

WILLIE: Yeh. The same as Alva's (*breathlessly, passionately*)

You're the only STAR—
In my blue HEA-VEN . . .

I'll—

TOM: What?

WILLIE: I'll—wear a corsage!

TOM: What's that?

WILLIE: Flowers to pin on your dress at a formal affair! Rosebuds! Violets! And lilies-of-the-valley! When you come home it's withered but you stick 'em in a bowl of water to freshen 'em up.

TOM: Uh-huh.

WILLIE: That's what Alva done. (*She pauses, and in the silence the train whistles.*) The Cannonball Express . . .

TOM: You think a lot about Alva. Don't you?

WILLIE: Oh, not so much. Now an' then. It wasn't like death in the movies. Her beaux disappeared. An' they didn't have violins playing. I'm going back now.

TOM: Where to, Willie?

WILLIE: The water-tank.

TOM: Yeah?

WILLIE: An' start all over again. Maybe I'll break some kind of continuous record. Alva did once. At a dance marathon in Mobile. Across the state line. Alabama. You can tell Frank Waters everything that I told you. I don't have time for inexperienced people. I'm going out now with popular railroad men, men with good salaries, too. Don't you believe me?

TOM: No. I think you're drawing an awful lot on your imagination.

WILLIE: Well, if I wanted to I could prove it. But you wouldn't be worth convincing. (*She smooths out Crazy Doll's hair.*) I'm going to live for a long, long time like my sister. An' when my lungs get affected I'm going to die like she did—maybe not like in the movies, with violins playing

—but with my pearl earrings on an' my solid gold beads from Memphis
...

TOM: Yes?

WILLIE: (*examining Crazy Doll very critically*) An' then I guess—

TOM: What?

WILLIE: (*gaily but with a slight catch*) Somebody else will inherit all of my beaux! The sky sure is white.

TOM: It sure is.

WILLIE: White as a clean piece of paper. I'm going back now.

TOM: So long.

WILLIE: Yeh. So long. (*She starts back along the railroad track, weaving grotesquely to keep her balance. She disappears. Tom wets his finger and holds it up to test the wind. Willie is heard singing from a distance.*)

You're the only star
In my blue heaven—

(*There is a brief pause. The stage begins to darken.*)

An' you're shining just—
For me!

CURTAIN

PART FIVE

AFTER THE RENASCENCE

Southern writing in the years following the end of World War II showed few signs of any important diminution of vigor, even though no new towering figures such as William Faulkner appeared. Faulkner himself continued to produce new books regularly until his death in 1963, although none had the importance of the great novels of the 1930s. By contrast, Robert Penn Warren became extremely productive. In 1946 he published *All The King's Men*, one of the great political novels of all time. Thereafter he brought out new fiction with regularity. His poetry, which reached a temporary halt in the late 1940s and early 1950s, gained new vigor with the publication of *Promises: Poems 1954–1956*; he then wrote some of his most exciting and beautiful verse, in a form that was more personal, freer, and less constrained than the work of his earlier years. The other leading Nashville Fugitive poets—in particular John Crowe Ransom and Allen Tate—seemed already to have said most of what they had to say as poets, though Tate produced several parts of a long poem in terza rima, which he later gave up and allowed the published sections to stand as separate poems, and Donald Davidson wrote a great deal of new verse of a high order in the late 1950s and early 1960s. Katherine Anne Porter wrote little other than the short fiction that was her métier, but in 1962 she brought out *Ship of Fools*, a long novel on which she had been at work for many years.

By the time World War II ended, however, there were a host of younger writers on the Southern literary scene. Eudora Welty had published two collections of short stories and a novella during the war years. Now she moved into the longer forms. Between 1946 and 1955 she published two novels, *Delta Wedding* and *The Ponder Heart*; a set of closely related stories, *The Golden Apples*, all of them set in a town of Morgana, Mississippi, over the course of forty years; and a new collection of short stories. *The Golden Apples* was a major work; it was a chronicle of human beings in time and flux, a Southern community whose members grappled with ultimate human problems while going through the day-by-day routine of their lives. After the stories of *The Bride of Innisfallen* in 1955 there was a 14-year period during which Welty published no new books of fiction. Then in 1970 she produced *Losing Battles*, the most ambitious of all her novels thus far, and two years later *The Optimist's Daughter*, a beautifully written, elegiac short novel that represented in many ways a tying together of several themes developed in her previous work. In depth of insight, in range, in richness of characterization and complex vision of human beings caught up in time, her fiction attained a mastery that—once it was fully recognized—seemed unequalled by any of her contemporaries except Faulkner.

Another Southern woman writer, Carson McCullers, did not so develop. Her two novels of the war years, *The Heart Is a Lonely Hunter* and *Reflections in a Golden Eye*, had demonstrated a rare talent for conveying the sense of loneliness and pain of people living in a world of isolation and frustrated love. *The Member of the Wedding*, published in 1946, advanced this talent even

615

further, and because McCullers' latest protagonist, an adolescent girl, seemed more "normal" and less twisted than any of her earlier characters, the novel was even more widely admired than the first two books. Thereafter, however, except for a novella, *The Ballad of the Sad Café*, McCullers published no more fiction until *Clock Without Hands* in 1961, and that novel showed a considerable decline in achievement. As a writer of fiction she seemed essentially to have had only one story to tell.

In the late 1940s and early 1950s an entirely new generation of Southern writers began making their appearance, to join the ranks of somewhat older writers such as Welty, McCullers, the poet Randall Jarrell, James Agee, Peter Taylor, and the playwright-short story writer Tennessee Williams. Agee had been on the literary scene since his first book of poems in the early 1930s; in 1941 he had published his brilliantly unclassifiable *Let Us Now Praise Famous Men*. His talents as a fiction writer finally shone forth in *The Morning Watch* in 1951 and, after his too-early death, *A Death in the Family* in 1957. Williams was 34 years old in 1945 when *The Glass Menagerie* thrust him into the forefront of American dramatists. With *A Streetcar Named Desire* in 1947 he emerged as the leading connoisseur of Southern Gothic on the stage; decayed gentry and coarse plebeians offered sex, violence, perversion, frustration and hysteria in a volatile mixture that enthralled Broadway audiences. Taylor, a Vanderbilt University graduate who had gone to Kenyon College along with Randall Jarrell when John Crowe Ransom moved there, began producing some extraordinarily accomplished short stories in the mid-1940s, and his first book, *A Long Fourth and Other Stories* (1948), established him as one of the more skilled practitioners of fiction in his day. Though he later wrote a short novel and a play, it was in the short story form that he continued to be most effective.

The new generation of writers, however, had grown up in the towns and cities of the South—few were from the rural South—during the decades between the two world wars and their experience was significantly different from the previous generation of the Renascence. Importantly, unlike the writers of Faulkner's generation, they had not known aging but still active Confederate veterans; the Lost Cause was something they read about in books, or heard about from their elders, who remembered it from what they had been told. The South they knew had been industrializing at a great rate for some years; for the most part they had never undergone the rural isolation that their predecessors were born into and had seen disappear around them. The South of their formative years had remained massively segregated, yet there were subtle but important differences in their relationship to it. They had not grown up in the backwash of the vitriolic racism that had accompanied the Populist period, the "Revolt of the Rednecks," and the thoroughgoing disfranchisement and elimination of blacks from participation in Southern politics. Their South was segregated—but there was more good will among their own elders along with a growing uneasiness and embarrassment over the economic victimization, brutality, and violence of racism and the rabble-rousing of the "peckerwood politicians" who capitalized on lower-class white racial prejudice to get and hold office. Moreover, they grew up in a day of mass communications and their attitudes and emotions were nurtured on the same movies, radio programs, magazine articles as their counterparts in other areas of the country, so that however rarely the South's racial customs were challenged in the popular media of the day, they saw the values and beliefs that could accommodate segregation and racial injustice with somewhat different eyes than their elders.

Most importantly of all perhaps, they had the experience of the Great Depression of the early 1930s as part of their heritage. The empty storefronts, the shutdown factories, the unemployment, the business failures, the reversals of fortune that marked those desperate times were part of their experience. When, therefore, the New Deal of President Franklin D. Roosevelt went into action to battle poverty and economic stagnation with a series of bold, imaginative, precedent-breaking public measures, they gave their allegiance to it and to the forces of economic and social reform, equality of opportunity, and governmental intervention to effect needed change that the New Deal set in motion. And although in the 1930s the national Democratic leadership did not overtly challenge Southern racial segregation, this reform was in the air and lay implicitly behind much that was done. Thus when some leading Southern politicians in the late 1930s and early 1940s began drawing back from the national administration because now that the economic emergency was over they recognized the underlying threat to Southern racial arrangements in the Roosevelt policies, the young Southerners who were growing up around them did not follow their elders. For they—not all, of course, but many, including those who would become writers—had been nurtured on the liberal democratic fervor of the New Deal; it was part of their way of viewing their relationship to their community and society. They would not be content with Things As They Are, for they had been taught that they need not be. And when the late 1930s saw the rise of Fascism and Nazism and ultimately a world war for human freedom, far greater and more desperate than that of 1917–1918, they went into it without reservation.

After the war, when the South, while experiencing economic and social change as never before, attempted to continue on as in the past with the old racial arrangements unchanged, these young men and women who were now finished with college and military service and starting out as writers were simply not willing or able to settle back into a fond contemplation of the status quo, whether in racial matters or otherwise. Moreover, they were the heirs to the Southern Literary Renascence, with its searching scrutiny of the institutions, attitudes, and social and moral values of the Southern community. They read "The Bear," *Absalom, Absalom!, Light in August, All The King's Men, Look Homeward, Angel, Native Son, The Fathers*; they were enormously impressed. As writers they saw their experience in important ways through the eyes of Faulkner and his colleagues. And in the change and confusion of the postwar South and nation and world, they began to write their own stories and poems and give their account of what was going on and what it meant. In 1949 Shelby Foote published *Tournament*. In 1951 William Styron published *Lie Down In Darkness*. In 1952 Flannery O'Connor published *Wise Blood*. And there were others: Elizabeth Spencer, Peter Taylor, Truman Capote, George Garrett, Madison Jones, James Dickey, William Humphrey, Peter Feibleman, Max Steele, Calder Willingham, Reynolds Price, Guy Owen, Walker Percy, A. R. Ammons.

For these writers, especially in their earlier work, the shadow of Faulkner and of Thomas Wolfe loomed large, and each in his or her own way had to come to terms with them. Their South wasn't Yoknapatawpha County, even though much of the Faulknerian vision (i.e., the vision of the writers of the Southern Renascence of the 1920s, 1930s, and 1940s) was still very valid indeed. The old themes of dynastic decline and fall, rural versus urban values, the still-palpable heritage of Civil War and Reconstruction, the provincial experience in the metropolis, the close-knit patriarchal (and matriarchal) family in a suddenly mobile society were now significantly modified. Yet at the same time such motifs as the fragmentation of culture, the clash between community identity and individual sensibility, the secularization of modern society and the erosion of religious orthodoxy, the historical sense and community expectation (without specific historical institutions and myths as such), and the continuing and ever more morally apprehended presence of black Southerners within the experience, were not by any means obsolete or irrelevant.

Thus the post-World War II Southern writers had to learn, in the terms and the forms that fitted their own experience, to deal with the life of a South in which much was changed and yet much abided. There is not space here to chronicle how each of them dealt with the problem—how they wrote novels, stories, poems that embodied their own way of looking at their place in time and history. Some have produced work of lasting distinction, and although in the work of each, in however varying degree, the continuity with the great writers of the Renascence has been quite observable, these writers have been able to successfully create fiction and poetry for and of *their* day, yet recognizably rooted in a South that was both changing and holding to its own.

In 1952 a novel appeared that at once won national and international acclaim and that today, more than a quarter-century later, seems securely established as a classic of its kind. Ralph Ellison's *Invisible Man* was indeed epoch making. It drew together, confidently and even magisterially, two central, unreconciled motifs of literature by black Americans. It was on the one hand a novel of protest, one that enunciated, for its own day, the critique of second-class citizenship in a South (and metropolitan North as well) that still discriminated, economically, socially, politically, against black people. And it was also and equally a work of literature that in language, characterization, and form drew authoritatively upon the techniques and insights of fiction as practiced by the great masters of the modern novel such as Faulkner, Hemingway, Joyce, and Andre Malraux. Ellison was able, therefore, to develop the themes of political and social impoverishment without also having to accept cultural and aesthetic impoverishment as part of his formal presentation of human experience. The novel's arrival had not been unheralded: Jean Toomer's *Cane* had anticipated Ellison's achievements of technique three decades earlier. But *Invisible Man* was a full-fledged, formally coherent novel, written in a major key, unfragmented and thoroughly articulated. Although Ellison was an Oklahoman, whose people had emigrated westward on foot in the late nineteenth century, and though Oklahoma might not itself be strictly considered part of the South, the black community there lived under much the same conditions as did blacks of the Deep South and was so closely tied to its Southern origins historically and culturally that it made the geographical exclusion close to meaningless. Ellison went to Tuskegee Institute in the 1930s to study, and it was out of the Southern literary and cultural milieu —especially as exemplified in the fiction of Faulkner, with its rich surfaces, its historical sensibility, its community patterns, and its unwillingness to define its people behavioristically or in economic terms alone—that the artistry of *Invisible Man* spoke.

Meanwhile the South itself was continuing to change—and at a rate that made the developments of the 1930s and 1940s seem slow-paced by comparison. Economically, the region leaped ahead, with its rate of growth far surpassing that of the Northeast and the Midwest. The indices that measured the South's industrial, financial, and business levels against those of the nation as a whole steadily showed a substantial narrowing of the gap, to a point at which by the 1970s there was little significant variation. Industries moved south at a great rate. Southern cities mushroomed; the isolation of the old rural South became a fading memory. Subsistence farming had become agribusiness. The blacks who had furnished the farm labor now lived in the cities. Most striking of all was the stunning change in racial arrangements. Following the 1954 *Brown* v. *Board of Education* decision of the U. S. Supreme Court the leaders of the white South in opposition huffed and puffed mightily; the politicians vowed eternal resistance to integration of school, ballot box, and subdivision. Then, almost overnight, the whole complex structure of racial segregation collapsed. By the mid-1970s the states of the onetime Confederacy were integrated beyond the wildest expectations of anyone, and very much to the envy of the ghetto-blighted cities of the West, Midwest, and Northeast. Thus, during the Bicentennial year a Southern white man running for President of the United States could declare that the Supreme Court desegregation decision of 1954 was the best thing that had ever happened to the South and could be elected President by the votes of black and white Southerners.

The writer of the post-World War II literary generation who has perhaps dealt most directly and even topically with such massive change has been Walker Percy. Although somewhat older than the other Southern writers, Percy did not begin publishing fiction until the 1960s. *Lanterns on the Levee* (1941), the autobiographical memoir by his cousin and adopted father, William Alexander Percy, was an articulate enunciation of the traditional Southern ethos by one who represented much that was best in the gentlemanly leadership of the region. Walker Percy, by contrast, entitled his second novel *The Last Gentleman* and premised it and his other works of fiction on the conviction that the older Southern rural attitudes and patrician virtues—the notion of "role" that Will Percy had automatically assumed—had been rendered totally irrelevant by the vast changes that had occurred since Will Percy's day and his own. In Walker Percy's novels protagonists of patrician origins but vastly different circumstance and outlook seek to find personal and religious meaning for themselves in a modern, eclectic, cosmopolitan, urban society in which the old landmarks are gone. In *The Last Gentleman*, for example, young Bill Barrett, long since moved from his hometown, looks on his old family house as his elderly aunts seated out on the front porch watching a television giveaway program "let out a holler. Bill Cullen had given away a cabin cruiser to a lady from Michigan City, Indiana."

Yet oddly, in his very depiction and dissection of the supposedly transformed and unrecognizable South of the present, in his own language, attitude, social sense, ear for dialect, eye for detail, taste for the ornamental rather than the merely functional, and view of men and women as being importantly the product of the past (their own familial past, not the historical past as such, but nevertheless the *past*), Walker Percy demonstrates the significant survival and even flourishing of much that thematically he declares irrelevant and even absurd. And it will be noted that his protagonists, however catastrophic the events that attend and await them and their societies, always end up living in familiar places and settling in to stay for good.

During the late 1960s and the 1970s three works by Southern authors managed to create a considerable stir among readers and, in two instances, among nationwide television audiences. One was by a white writer, William Styron. Two were by black writers, Ernest J. Gaines and Alec Haley. All three works focused upon the South's history. Each depicted slavery from the viewpoint of the slave. Styron's *Confessions of Nat Turner* became the center of a heated controversy. Gaines' *The Autobiography of Miss Jane Pittman* and Haley's *Roots* described the determined survival and flourishing of black people in the South through decades and even generations of trials and vicissitudes. It is interesting that at a time when the old Southern historical sense had supposedly been all but eroded, it could still provide ample substance for the imaginations of three good literary artists. And it is noteworthy that Gaines and Haley were both intent upon showing the continuity of past and present, the heritage of the past as anchor for human definition in time. Both seemed, in their own way, to be using the regional past for just the virtues that another Southern writer, Robert Penn Warren, once said it offered the writer:

> The past is always a rebuke to the present; it's bound to be, one way or another; it's your great rebuke. It's a better rebuke than any dream of the future. It's a better rebuke because you can see what some of the costs were, what frail virtues were achieved in the past by frail men. And it's there, and you can see it and see what it cost them, and how they had to go at it. . . . The drama of the past that corrects us is the drama of our struggles to be human, or our struggles to define the values of our forebears in the face of their difficulties.

Whether the Southern literary imagination as we have known it is importantly outmoded and fated to lose its recognizable identity remains to be seen. It has undergone significant change; of that there can be no question. And doubtless it will change still more. For if literature grows out of the life and times of a society—as the literature of the twentieth-century South has so abundantly done—then as the Southern community confronts different situations and vastly changed circumstances, its literature must undergo important mutations. Yet to say, as some have said, that either the literature or the region has lost or is swiftly losing its identity is to ignore some striking evidence to the contrary. Those who live in the changing region may perhaps be so conscious of the extent and impact of the change going on around them that they lose sight of what remains constant and abides amid that change. Someone coming from outside its bounds, however, has no doubt that much of the South remains recognizably itself and identifiably different from other places.

Indeed, perhaps it is in changing—and being able to change—that the South has kept its identity. For, as the historian George Brown Tindall reminds us, to change is not necessarily to lose one's identity; to change, sometimes, is to find it. Thus it may be that the Southern literary imagination of today and tomorrow will remain itself because it changes with an ever-changing South.

RANDALL JARRELL

(1914–1965)

"His realm," James Dickey once wrote of Randall Jarrell, "is one of pity and terror, of a kind of non-understanding understanding . . . and above all of helplessness. All his people, the wounded soldiers, the children, the cancer patients, all these are people in predicaments that happen all the time. They are the things that our situation as human beings can't help bringing to bear on us. It is through the kind of compulsion that these things force up in us that Jarrell writes his poems." In the late 1940s and 1950s, during his years as an active poet, critic, and reviewer, Jarrell was a formidable force on the American literary scene—argumentative, combative, dogmatic, intensely excited and excitable about poetry and literature. Very well read and with a discerning intellect, he brought to his verse and criticism a massive array of literary allusions, recondite references, obscure sources, and off-the-beaten-track opinions—but these were placed, as Dickey says, at the service of the commonplace, ordinary, and everyday experience of being human.

Jarrell was born in Nashville, Tennessee, lived during his very early years in California, then returned to Nashville where he grew up and attended the public schools. He graduated from Vanderbilt University, where he studied under John Crowe Ransom and Robert Penn Warren, in 1935. There he became a strong literary presence, brilliant and disputative in argument. In 1938 he received his M.A. degree at Vanderbilt and moved on to Kenyon College with Ransom. He then taught at the University of Texas, where he married Mackie Langham. In 1942 *Blood for a Stranger*, his first book of poems, appeared. That year he enlisted in the Army Air Force and served as an instructor for several years. He used this experience to write a number of poems about men at war, many of which are contained in *Little Friend, Little Friend* (1945). After the war Jarrell taught at Sarah Lawrence College for a year and then accepted appointment at the Women's College of the University of North Carolina, where he taught for the remainder of his life. He also took time out to be consultant in poetry at the Library of Congress and to serve as a visiting professor at Princeton and other places. After being divorced from his first wife, he married Mary von Schrader in 1952. For some years he was a regular poetry reviewer for *The Nation*, and his argumentative, always interesting commentaries on American poetry were widely read. In 1953 he published a collection of his critical writings, *Poetry and the Age*. His new poems appeared successively in *Losses* (1948), *The Seven-League Crutches* (1951), *Selected Poems* (1955), *The Woman at the Washington Zoo* (1960), and *The Lost World* (1965). In 1965, while a patient in the Memorial Hospital at the University of North Carolina, he was struck by an automobile and killed while walking erratically along a highway at night.

Jarrell was a dedicated and inspiring teacher, and a number of his students pursued careers in writing. His death was a shock to the literary world. His friends Robert Lowell and Peter Taylor, who were with him at Kenyon, and Robert Penn Warren assembled a notable collection of critical tributes, *Randall Jarrell, 1914–1965*, published in 1967.

A GIRL IN A LIBRARY

An object among dreams, you sit here with your shoes off
And curl your legs up under you; your eyes
Close for a moment, your face moves toward sleep . . .
You are very human.
     But my mind, gone out in tenderness,
Shrinks from its object with a thoughtful sigh.
This is a waist the spirit breaks its arm on.
The gods themselves, against you, struggle in vain.
This broad low strong-boned brow; these heavy eyes;
These calves, grown muscular with certainties;
This nose, three medium-sized pink strawberries
—But I exaggerate. In a little you will leave:
I'll hear, half squeal, half shriek, your laugh of greeting—
Then, *decrescendo*, bars of that strange speech
In which each sound sets out to seek each other,
Murders its own father, marries its own mother,
And ends as one grand trancendental vowel.
(Yet for all I know, the Egyptian Helen spoke so.)
As I look, the world contracts around you:
I see Brünnhilde had brown braids and glasses
She used for studying; Salome straight brown bangs,
A calf's brown eyes, and sturdy light-brown limbs
Dusted with cinnamon, an apple-dumpling's . . .
Many a beast has gnawn a leg off and got free,
Many a dolphin curved up from Necessity—
The trap has closed about you, and you sleep.
If someone questioned you, *What doest thou here?*
You'd knit your brows like an orangoutang
(But not so sadly; not so thoughtfully)
And answer with a pure heart, guilelessly:
I'm studying. . . .
     If only you were not!
Assignments,
   recipes,
     the *Official Rulebook*
Of Basketball—ah, let them go; you needn't mind.
The soul has no assignments, neither cooks
Nor referees: it wastes its time.
        It wastes its time.
Here in this enclave there are centuries
For you to waste: the short and narrow stream
Of Life meanders into a thousand valleys

Of all that was, or might have been, or is to be.
The books, just leafed through, whisper endlessly . . .
Yet it is hard. One sees in your blurred eyes
The "uneasy half-soul" Kipling saw in dogs'.
One sees it, in the glass, in one's own eyes.
In rooms alone, in galleries, in libraries,
In tears, in searchings of the heart, in staggering joys
We memorize once more our old creation,
Humanity: with what yawns the unwilling
Flesh puts on its spirit, O my sister!

So many dreams! And not one troubles
Your sleep of life? no self stares shadowily
From these worn hexahedrons, beckoning
With false smiles, tears? . . .
                      Meanwhile Tatyana
Larina (gray eyes nickel with the moonlight
That falls through the willows onto Lensky's tomb;
Now young and shy, now old and cold and sure)
Asks, smiling: "But what is she dreaming of, fat thing?"
I answer: She's not fat. She isn't dreaming.
She purrs or laps or runs, all in her sleep;
Believes, awake, that she is beautiful;
She never dreams.
                Those sunrise-colored clouds
Around man's head—that inconceivable enchantment
From which, at sunset, we come back to life
To find our graves dug, families dead, selves dying:
Of all this, Tanya, she is innocent.
For nineteen years she's faced reality:
They look alike already.
                  They say, man wouldn't be
The best thing in this world—and isn't he?—
If he were not too good for it. But she
—She's good enough for it.
                 And yet sometimes
Her sturdy form, in its pink strapless formal,
Is as if bathed in moonlight—modulated
Into a form of joy, a Lydian mode;
This Wooden Mean's a kind, furred animal
That speaks, in the Wild of things, delighting riddles
To the soul that listens, trusting . . .
                   Poor senseless Life:
When, in the last sleep of dawn, the messenger

Comes with his message, you will not awake.
He'll give his feathery whistle, shake you hard,
You'll look with wide eyes at the dewy yard
And dream, with calm slow factuality:
"Today's Commencement. My bachelor's degree
In Home Ec., my doctorate of philosophy
In Phys. Ed.
        [Tanya, they won't even *scan*]
Are waiting for me. . . . ."
             Oh, Tatyana,
The Angel comes: better to squawk like a chicken
Than to say with truth, "But I'm a *good* girl,"
And Meet his Challenge with a last firm strange
Uncomprehending smile; and—then, then!—see
The blind date that has stood you up: your life.
(For all this, if it isn't, perhaps, life,
Has yet, at least, a language of its own
Different from the books'; worse than the books'.)
And yet, the ways we miss our lives are life.
Yet . . . yet . . .
           to have one's life add up to *yet!*

You sigh a shuddering sigh. Tatyana murmurs,
"Don't cry, little peasant"; leaves us with a swift
"Good-bye, good-bye . . . Ah, don't think ill of me . . ."
Your eyes open: you sit here thoughtlessly.

I love you—and yet—and yet—I love you.

Don't cry, little peasant. Sit and dream.
One comes, a finger's width beneath your skin,
To the braided maidens singing as they spin;
There sound the shepherd's pipe, the watchman's rattle
Across the short dark distance of the years.
I am a thought of yours: and yet, you do not think . . .
The firelight of a long, blind, dreaming story
Lingers upon your lips; and I have seen
Firm, fixed forever in your closing eyes,
The Corn King beckoning to his Spring Queen.

1951

RANDALL JARRELL

THE KNIGHT, DEATH, AND THE DEVIL

Cowhorn-crowned, shockheaded, cornshuck-bearded,
Death is a scarecrow—his death's-head a teetotum
That tilts up toward man confidentially
But trimmed with adders; ringlet-maned, rope-bridled,
The mare he rides crops herbs beside a skull.
He holds up, warning, the crossed cones of time:
Here, narrowing into now, the Past and Future
Are quicksand.
                A hoofed pikeman trots behind.
His pike's claw-hammer mocks—in duplicate, inverted—
The pocked, ribbed, soaring crescent of his horn.
A scapegoat aged into a steer; boar-snouted;
His great limp ears stuck sidelong out in air;
A dewlap bunched at his breast; a ram's-horn wound
Beneath each ear; a spur licked up and out
From the hide of his forehead; bat-winged, but in bone;
His eye a ring inside a ring inside a ring
That leers up, joyless, vile, in meek obscenity—
This is the devil. Flesh to flesh, he bleats
The herd back to the pit of being.

In fluted mail; upon his lance the bush
Of that old fox; a sheep-dog bounding at his stirrup,
In its eyes the cast of faithfulness (our help,
Our foolish help); his dun war-horse pacing
Beneath in strength, in ceremonious magnificence;
His castle—some man's castle—set on every crag:
So, companioned so, the knight moves through this world.
The fiend moos in amity, Death mouths, reminding:
He listens in assurance, has no glance
To spare for them, but looks past steadily
At—at—
               a man's look completes itself.

The death of his own flesh, set up outside him;
The flesh of his own soul, set up outside him—
Death and the devil, what are these to him?
His being accuses him—and yet his face is firm
In resolution, in absolute persistence;
The folds of smiling do for steadiness;
The face is its own fate—*a man does what he must*—

And the body underneath it says: *I am.*

1951

CARSON McCULLERS

(1917–1967)

Lula Carson Smith McCullers was born in Columbus, Georgia, and attended public grammar and high school there; she studied music and began writing at an early age, and in 1935 went to New York to study at the Julliard School of Music. Returning shortly afterward to Columbus, she married a soldier, Reeves McCullers, and in Charlotte and Fayetteville, North Carolina, where her husband was working, she wrote the novel that was published in 1940 as *The Heart is a Lonely Hunter*. It was a considerable success and was followed the next year by *Reflections in a Golden Eye*. During the 1940s she lived in New York at the Yaddo Colony and elsewhere. Her marriage ended in divorce, and she began associating with homosexual and lesbian friends. She was remarried to Reeves McCullers after World War II, but the reunion failed. In 1953 Reeves McCullers committed suicide.

In 1946 she published *The Member of the Wedding*, which was later made into a highly successful Broadway play. A novella, *The Ballad of the Sad Cafe*, was published in 1952 with six other short stories. She wrote another play, *The Square Root of Wonderful*, which was produced in 1957 and published in 1958. In 1961 another novel, *Clock Without Hands*, was published.

Much of her adult life was beset with pain and illness. She drank heavily, suffered from various illnesses, some of which have been described as psychosomatic, attempted suicide on one occasion, and was crippled by several strokes, paralysis, and cancer, and died of a massive brain hemorrhage in 1967. However, she was, as her friend Tennessee Williams declared of her, "despite the early onset of her many illnesses, . . . in her spirit, a person of rare and luminous health."

In her fiction, particularly that involving adolescents, she was able as an artist to translate her private pain, misfortune, and sexual ambivalence into metaphor for what she saw as the human condition: lovelessness, a yearning for impossible fulfillment, a sense of brooding, sensuous loneliness. Her forte is the ability to capture the evolution of moods; writing very simply and carefully, using words with a lapidary precision, and with great skill, she conveys the emotions of lonely creatures who inhabit forsaken places. Perhaps her most fully realized work is *The Ballad of the Sad Cafe*, a short work, poignant in its pain and sadness. Although as a writer her range is narrow, it is intense and moving.

A TREE. A ROCK. A CLOUD

It was raining that morning, and still very dark. When the boy reached the streetcar café he had almost finished his route and he went in for a cup of coffee. The place was an all-night café owned by a bitter and stingy man called Leo. After the raw, empty street the café seemed friendly and bright: along the counter there were a couple of soldiers, three spinners from the cotton mill, and in a corner a man who sat hunched over with his nose and half his face down in a beer mug. The boy wore a helmet such as aviators wear. When he went into the café he unbuckled the chin strap and raised the right flap up over his pink little ear; often as he drank his coffee someone would speak to him in a friendly way. But this morning Leo did not look into his face and none of the men were talking. He paid and was leaving the café when a voice called out to him:

'Son! Hey Son!'

He turned back and the man in the corner was crooking his finger and nodding to him. He had brought his face out of the beer mug and he seemed suddenly very happy. The man was long and pale, with a big nose and faded orange hair.

'Hey Son!'

The boy went toward him. He was an undersized boy of about twelve, with one shoulder drawn higher than the other because of the weight of the paper sack. His face was shallow, freckled, and his eyes were round child eyes.

'Yeah Mister?'

The man laid one hand on the paper boy's shoulders, then grasped the boy's chin and turned his face slowly from one side to the other. The boy shrank back uneasily.

'Say! What's the big idea?'

The boy's voice was shrill; inside the café it was suddenly very quiet.

The man said slowly: 'I love you.'

All along the counter the men laughed. The boy, who had scowled and sidled away, did not know what to do. He looked over the counter at Leo, and Leo watched him with a weary, brittle jeer. The boy tried to laugh also. But the man was serious and sad.

'I did not mean to tease you, Son,' he said. 'Sit down and have a beer with me. There is something I have to explain.'

Cautiously, out of the corner of his eye, the paper boy questioned the men along the counter to see what he should do. But they had gone back to their beer or their breakfast and did not notice him. Leo put a cup of coffee on the counter and a little jug of cream.

'He is a minor,' Leo said.

The paper boy slid himself up onto the stool. His ear beneath the upturned flap of the helmet was very small and red. The man was nodding at him soberly. "It is important," he said. Then he reached in his hip pocket and brought out something which he held up in the palm of his hand for the boy to see.

'Look very carefully,' he said.

The boy stared, but there was nothing to look at very carefully. The man held in his big, grimy palm a photograph. It was the face of a woman, but blurred, so that only the hat and the dress she was wearing stood out clearly.

'See?' the man asked.

The boy nodded and the man placed another picture in his palm. The woman was standing on a beach in a bathing suit. The suit made her stomach very big, and that was the main thing you noticed.

'Got a good look?' He leaned over closer and finally asked: 'You ever seen her before?'

The boy sat motionless, staring slantwise at the man. 'Not so I know of.'

'Very well.' The man blew on the photographs and put them back into his pocket. 'That was my wife.'

'Dead?' the boy asked.

Slowly the man shook his head. He pursed his lips as though about to whistle and answered in a long-drawn way: 'Nuuu—' he said. 'I will explain.'

The beer on the counter before the man was in a large brown mug. He did not pick it up to drink. Instead he bent down and, putting his face over the rim, he rested there for a moment. Then with both hands he tilted the mug and sipped.

'Some night you'll go to sleep with your big nose in a mug and drown,' said Leo. 'Prominent transient drowns in beer. That would be a cute death.'

The paper boy tried to signal to Leo. While the man was not looking he screwed up his face and worked his mouth to question soundlessly: 'Drunk?' But Leo only raised his eyebrows and turned away to put some pink strips of bacon on the grill. The man pushed the mug away from him, straightened himself, and folded his loose crooked hands on the counter. His face was sad as he looked at the paper boy. He did not blink, but from time to time the lids closed down with delicate gravity over his pale green eyes. It was nearing dawn and the boy shifted the weight of the paper sack.

'I am talking about love,' the man said. 'With me it is a science.'

The boy half slid down from the stool. But the man raised his forefinger, and there was something about him that held the boy and would not let him go away.

'Twelve years ago I married the woman in the photograph. She was my wife for one year, nine months, three days, and two nights. I loved her. Yes . . .' He tightened his blurred, rambling voice and said again: 'I loved her. I thought also that she loved me. I was a railroad engineer. She had all home comforts and luxuries. It never crept into my brain that she was not satisfied. But do you know what happened?'

'Mgneeow!' said Leo.

The man did not take his eyes from the boy's face. 'She left me. I came in one night and the house was empty and she was gone. She left me.'

'With a fellow?' the boy asked.

Gently the man placed his palm down on the counter. 'Why naturally, Son. A woman does not run off like that alone.'

The café was quiet, the soft rain black and endless in the street outside. Leo pressed down the frying bacon with the prongs of his long fork. 'So you have been chasing the floozie for eleven years. You frazzled old rascal!'

For the first time the man glanced at Leo. 'Please don't be vulgar. Besides, I was not speaking to you.' He turned back to the boy and said in a trusting and secretive undertone: 'Let's not pay any attention to him. O.K.?'

The paper boy nodded doubtfully.

'It was like this,' the man continued. 'I am a person who feels many things. All my life one thing after another has impressed me. Moonlight. The leg of a pretty girl. One thing after another. But the point is that when I had enjoyed anything there was a peculiar sensation as though it was laying around loose in me. Nothing seemed to finish itself up or fit in with the other things. Women? I had my portion of them. The same. Afterwards laying around loose in me. I was a man who had never loved.'

Very slowly he closed his eyelids, and the gesture was like a curtain drawn at the end of a scene in a play. When he spoke again his voice was excited and the words came fast—the lobes of his large, loose ears seemed to tremble.

'Then I met this woman. I was fifty-one years old and she always said she was thirty. I met her at a filling station and we were married within three days. And do you know what it was like? I just can't tell you. All I had ever felt was gathered together around this woman. Nothing lay around loose in me any more but was finished up by her.'

The man stopped suddenly and stroked his long nose. His voice sank down to a steady and reproachful undertone: 'I'm not explaining this right. What happened was this. There were these beautiful feelings and loose little pleasures inside me. And this woman was something like an assembly line for my soul. I run these little pieces of myself through her and I come out complete. Now do you follow me?'

'What was her name?' the boy asked.

'Oh,' he said. 'I called her Dodo. But that is immaterial.'

'Did you try to make her come back?'

The man did not seem to hear. 'Under the circumstances you can imagine how I felt when she left me.'

Leo took the bacon from the grill and folded two strips of it between a bun. He had a gray face, with slitted eyes, and a pinched nose saddled by faint blue shadows. One of the mill workers signaled for more coffee and Leo poured it. He did not give refills on the coffee free. The spinner ate breakfast there every morning, but the better Leo knew his customers the stingier he treated them. He nibbled his own bun as though he grudged it to himself.

'And you never got hold of her again?'

The boy did not know what to think of the man, and his child's face was uncertain with mingled curiosity and doubt. He was new on the paper route; it was still strange to him to be out in the town in the black, queer early morning.

'Yes,' the man said. 'I took a number of steps to get her back. I went around trying to locate her. I went to Tulsa where she had folks. And to Mobile. I went to every town she had ever mentioned to me, and I hunted down every man she had formerly been connected with. Tulsa, Atlanta, Chicago, Cheehaw, Memphis. . . . For the better part of two years I chased around the country trying to lay hold of her.'

'But the pair of them had vanished from the face of the earth!' said Leo.

'Don't listen to him,' the man said confidentially. 'And also just forget those two years. They are not important. What matters is that around the third year a curious thing begun to happen to me.'

'What?' the boy asked.

The man leaned down and tilted his mug to take a sip of beer. But as he hovered over the mug his nostrils fluttered slightly; he sniffed the staleness of the beer and did not drink. 'Love is a curious thing to begin with. At first I thought only of getting her back. It was a kind of mania. But then as time went on I tried to remember her. But do you know what happened?'

'No,' the boy said.

'When I laid myself down on a bed and tried to think about her my mind became a blank. I couldn't see her. I would take out her pictures and look. No good. Nothing doing. A blank. Can you imagine it?'

'Say Mac!' Leo called down the counter. 'Can you imagine this bozo's mind a blank!'

Slowly, as though fanning away flies, the man waved his hand. His green eyes were concentrated and fixed on the shallow little face of the paper boy.

'But a sudden piece of glass on a sidewalk. Or a nickel tune in a music box. A shadow on a wall at night. And I would remember. It might happen in a street and I would cry or bang my head against a lamppost. You follow me?'

'A piece of glass . . .' the boy said.

'Anything. I would walk around and I had no power of how and when to remember her. You think you can put up a kind of shield. But remembering don't come to a man face forward—it corners around sideways. I was at the mercy of everything I saw and heard. Suddenly instead of me combing the countryside to find her she begun to chase me around in my very soul. *She* chasing *me*, mind you! And in my soul.'

The boy asked finally: 'What part of the country were you in then?'

'Ooh,' the man groaned. 'I was a sick mortal. It was like smallpox. I confess, Son, that I boozed. I fornicated. I committed any sin that suddenly appealed to me. I am loath to confess it but I will do so. When I recall that period it is all curdled in my mind, it was so terrible.'

The man leaned his head down and tapped his forehead on the counter. For a few seconds he stayed bowed over in this position, the back of his stringy neck covered with orange furze, his hands with their long warped fingers held palm to palm in an attitude of prayer. Then the man straightened himself; he was smiling and suddenly his face was bright and tremulous and old.

'It was in the fifth year that it happened,' he said. 'And with it I started my science.'

Leo's mouth jerked with a pale, quick grin. 'Well none of we boys are getting any younger,' he said. Then with sudden anger he balled up a dishcloth he was holding and threw it down hard on the floor. 'You draggletailed old Romeo!'

'What happened?' the boy asked.

The old man's voice was high and clear: 'Peace,' he answered.

'Huh?'

'It is hard to explain scientifically, Son,' he said. 'I guess the logical explanation is that she and I had fleed around from each other for so long that finally we just got tangled up together and lay down and quit. Peace. A queer and beautiful blankness. It was spring in Portland and the rain came every afternoon. All evening I just stayed there on my bed in the dark. And that is how the science come to me.'

The windows in the streetcar were pale blue with light. The two soldiers paid for their beers and opened the door—one of the soldiers combed his hair and wiped off his muddy puttees before they went outside. The three mill workers bent silently over their breakfasts. Leo's clock was ticking on the wall.

'It is this. And listen carefully. I meditated on love and reasoned it out. I realized what is wrong with us. Men fall in love for the first time. And what do they fall in love with?'

The boy's soft mouth was partly open and he did not answer.

'A woman,' the old man said. 'Without science, with nothing to go by, they undertake the most dangerous and sacred experience in God's earth. They fall in love with a woman. Is that correct, Son?'

'Yeah,' the boy said faintly.

'They start at the wrong end of love. They begin at the climax. Can you wonder it is so miserable? Do you know how men should love?'

The old man reached over and grasped the boy by the collar of his leather jacket. He gave him a gentle little shake and his green eyes gazed down unblinking and grave.

'Son, do you know how love should be begun?'

The boy sat small and listening and still. Slowly he shook his head. The old man leaned closer and whispered:

'A tree. A rock. A cloud.'

It was still raining outside in the street: a mild, gray, endless rain. The mill whistle blew for the six o'clock shift and the three spinners paid and went away. There was no one in the café but Leo, the old man, and the little paper boy.

'The weather was like this in Portland,' he said. 'At the time my science was begun. I meditated and I started very cautious. I would pick up something from the street and take it home with me. I bought a goldfish and I concentrated on the goldfish and I loved it. I graduated from one thing to another. Day by day I was getting this technique. On the road from Portland to San Diego————'

'Aw shut up!' screamed Leo suddenly. 'Shut up! Shut up!'

The old man still held the collar of the boy's jacket; he was trembling and his face was earnest and bright and wild. 'For six years now I have gone around by myself and built up my science. And now I am a master. Son. I can love anything. No longer do I have to think about it even. I see a street full of people and a beautiful light comes in me. I watch a bird in the sky. Or I meet a traveler on the road. Everything, Son. And anybody. All stranger and all loved! Do you realize what a science like mine can mean?'

The boy held himself stiffly, his hands curled tight around the counter edge. Finally he asked: 'Did you ever really find that lady?'

'What? What say, Son?'

'I mean,' the boy asked timidly. 'Have you fallen in love with a woman again?'

The old man loosened his grasp on the boy's collar. He turned away and for the first time his green eyes had a vague and scattered look. He lifted the mug from the counter, drank down the yellow beer. His head was shaking slowly from side to side. Then finally he answered: 'No, Son. You see that is the last step in my science. I go cautious. And I am not quite ready yet.'

'Well!' said Leo. 'Well well well!'

The old man stood in the open doorway. 'Remember,' he said. Framed there in the gray damp light of the early morning he looked shrunken and seedy and frail. But his smile was bright. 'Remember I love you,' he said with a last nod. And the door closed quietly behind him.

The boy did not speak for a long time. He pulled down the bangs on his forehead and slid his grimy little forefinger around the rim of his empty cup. Then without looking at Leo he finally asked:

'Was he drunk?'

'No,' said Leo shortly.

The boy raised his clear voice higher. 'Then was he a dope fiend?'

'No.'

The boy looked up at Leo, and his flat little face was desperate, his voice urgent and shrill. 'Was he crazy? Do you think he was a lunatic?' The paper boy's voice dropped suddenly with doubt. 'Leo? Or not?'

But Leo would not answer him. Leo had run a night café for fourteen years, and he held himself to be a critic of craziness. There were the town characters and also the transients who roamed in from the night. He knew the manias of all of them. But he did not want to satisfy the questions of the waiting child. He tightened his pale face and was silent.

So the boy pulled down the right flap of his helmet and as he turned to leave he made the only comment that seemed safe to him, the only remark that could not be laughed down and despised:

'He sure has done a lot of traveling.'

JAMES AGEE

(1909–1955)

During his lifetime James Rufus Agee was considered to be a writer of great talent and enormous promise who had never been able to focus his abilities long enough to produce a fully realized work of literary art. It was not until two years after his death, when *A Death in the Family* was published, that it became obvious that here was one of the masters of modern Southern literature. Agee was born in Knoxville, Tennessee, where his mother's family lived; his father's family was from the Tennessee mountains. In 1916, three years after his father's death in an automobile accident, he was entered in St. Andrew's School near Sewanee, Tennessee. In 1925, after returning to Knoxville for a year in school there, he entered Phillips Exeter Academy, where he began displaying a remarkable and precocious talent. Enrolling at Harvard University in 1928, he wrote extensively for the *Harvard Advocate*, became its editor, attracted the attention of important literary figures, and upon graduation in 1932 became a staff writer for *Fortune* magazine in New York. In 1934 his book of poems, *Permit Me Voyage*, appeared.

Although Agee was a valued writer at *Fortune*, with the ability to become immersed in an assigned subject and produce excellent journalism, he was discontented with the kind of work he was doing. Meanwhile, in 1933, he married Olivia Saunders, from whom he was divorced in 1939, when he married Alma Mailman. This marriage, too, ended in divorce in 1944 and was followed by his marriage to Mia Fritsch.

In 1936 Agee was given an assignment to go south with the photographer Walker Evans and produce an article on tenant farmers. He became fascinated by the subject, lived with several families, and grew convinced that the kind of article he was expected to write would violate the human dignity of his subjects. The result was ultimately a remarkable, if somewhat unfocused book, *Let Us Now Praise Famous Men*, which appeared in 1941. Little noticed at the time, it was rediscovered following his death and attracted extensive attention.

During the 1940s he wrote film criticism and reviewed books for *Time* magazine and *The Nation*, wrote other essays, and in the late 1940s and 1950s wrote some film scripts, screenplays, and a television series on Abraham Lincoln for the CBS Omnibus program. He also began working at autobiographical fiction—he started the novel that eventually became *A Death in the Family*, interrupted its writing to produce a short novel, *The Morning Watch* (1947), and returned intermittently to the earlier work. When he died, *A Death in the Family* was close to being finished; his editor, David McDowell, had only to insert a few unplaced segments at what seemed appropriate intervals. The selection given below, though not written for *A Death in the Family*, constitutes an appropriate prologue for it, and was published as such.

In the years since *A Death in the Family* appeared, much of Agee's periodical prose, scripts, and other work has been published in book form. The letters that Agee wrote to an Episcopal minister, Father James Harold Flye, were collected in 1962 and have proved extremely popular.

From A DEATH IN THE FAMILY

Knoxville: Summer 1915

We are talking now of summer evenings in Knoxville, Tennessee in the time that I lived there so successfully disguised to myself as a child. It was a little bit mixed sort of block, fairly solidly lower middle class, with one or two juts apiece on either side of that. The houses corresponded: middle-sized gracefully fretted wood houses built in the late nineties and early nineteen hundreds, with small front and side and more spacious back yards, and trees in the yards, and porches. These were softwooded trees, poplars, tulip trees, cottonwoods. There were fences around one or two of the houses, but mainly the yards ran into each other with only now and then a low hedge that wasn't doing very well. There were few good friends among the grown people, and they were not poor enough for the other sort of intimate acquaintance, but everyone nodded and spoke, and even might talk short times, trivially, and at the two extremes of the general or the particular, and ordinarily next door neighbors talked quite a bit when they happened to run into each other, and never paid calls. The men were mostly small businessmen, one or two very modestly executives, one or two worked with their hands, most of them clerical, and most of them between thirty and forty-five.

But it is of these evenings, I speak.

Supper was at six and was over by half past. There was still daylight, shining softly and with a tarnish, like the lining of a shell; and the carbon lamps lifted at the corners were on in the light, and the locusts were started, and the fire flies were out, and a few frogs were flopping in the dewy grass, by the time the fathers and the children came out. The children ran out first hell bent and yelling those names by which they were known; then the fathers sank out leisurely in crossed suspenders, their collars removed and their necks looking tall and shy. The mothers stayed back in the kitchen washing and drying, putting things away, recrossing their traceless footsteps like the lifetime journeys of bees, measuring out the dry cocoa for breakfast. When they came out they had taken off their aprons and their skirts were dampened and they sat in rockers on their porches quietly.

It is not of the games children play in the evening that I want to speak now, it is of a contemporaneous atmosphere that has little to do with them: that of the fathers of families, each in his space of lawn, his shirt fishlike pale in the unnatural light and his face nearly anonymous, hosing their lawns. The hoses were attached at spiggots that stood out of the brick foundations of the houses. The nozzles were variously set but usually so there was a long sweet stream of spray, the nozzle wet in the hand, the water trickling the right forearm and the peeled-back cuff, and the water whishing out a long loose and low-curved cone, and so gentle a sound. First an insane noise of violence in the nozzle, then the still irregular sound of adjustment, then the smoothing into steadiness and a pitch as accurately tuned to the size and style of stream as any violin. So many qualities of sound out of one hose: so many choral differences out of those several hoses that were in earshot. Out of any one hose, the almost dead silence of the release, and the short still arch of the separate big drops, silent as a held breath, and the only noise the flattering noise on leaves and the slapped grass at the fall of each big drop. That, and the intense hiss with the intense stream; that, and that same intensity not growing less but growing more quiet and delicate with the turn of the nozzle, up to that extreme tender whisper when the water was just a wide bell of film. Chiefly, though, the hoses were set much alike, in a compromise between distance and tenderness of spray, (and quite surely a sense of art behind this compromise, and a quiet deep joy, too real to recognize itself), and the sounds therefore were pitched much alike; pointed by the snorting start of a new hose; decorated by some man playful with the nozzle; left empty, like God by the sparrow's fall, when any single one of them desists: and all, though near alike, of various pitch; and in this unison. These sweet pale streamings in the light lift out their pallors and their voices all together, mothers hushing their children, the hushing unnaturally prolonged, the men gentle and silent and each snail-like withdrawn into the quietude of what he singly is doing, the urination of huge children stood loosely military against an invisible wall, and gentle happy and peaceful, tasting the mean goodness of their living like the last of their suppers in their mouths; while the locusts carry on this noise of hoses on their much higher and sharper key. The noise of the locust is dry, and it seems not to be rasped or vibrated but urged from him as if through a small orifice by a breath that can never give out. Also there is never one locust but an illusion of at least a thousand. The noise of each locust is pitched in some classic locust range out of which none of them varies more than two full tones: and yet you seem to hear each locust discrete from all the rest, and there is a long, slow, pulse in their noise, like the scarcely defined arch of a long and high set bridge. They are all around in every tree, so that the noise seems to come from nowhere and everywhere at once, from the whole shell heaven, shivering in your flesh and teasing your eardrums, the boldest of all the sounds of night. And yet it is habitual to summer nights, and is of the great order of noises, like the noises of the sea and of the blood her precocious grandchild, which you realize you are hearing only when you catch yourself listening. Meantime from low in the dark, just outside the swaying horizons of the hoses, conveying always grass in the damp of dew and its strong green-black smear of smell, the regular yet spaced noises of the crickets, each a sweet cold silver noise threenoted, like the slipping each time of three matched links of a small chain.

But the men by now, one by one, have silenced their hoses and drained and coiled them. Now only two, and now only one, is left, and you see only ghostlike shirt with the sleeve garters, and sober mystery of his mild face like the lifted face of large cattle enquiring of your presence in a pitchdark pool of meadow; and now he too is gone; and it has become that time of evening when people sit on their porches, rocking gently and talking gently and watching the street and the standing up into their sphere of possession of the trees, of birds hung havens, hangars. People go by; things go by. A horse, drawing a buggy, breaking his hollow iron music on the asphalt; a loud auto; a quiet auto; people in pairs, not in a hurry, scuffling, switching their weight of aestival body, talking casually, the taste hovering over them of vanilla, strawberry, pasteboard and starched milk, the image upon them of lovers and horsemen, squared with clowns in hueless amber. A street car raising its iron moan; stopping, belling and starting; stertorous; rousing and raising again its iron increasing moan and swimming its gold windows and straw seats on past and past and past, the bleak spark crackling and cursing above it like a small malignant spirit set to dog its tracks; the iron whine rises on rising speed; still risen, faints; halts; the faint stinging bell; rises again, still fainter; fainting, lifting, lifts, faints forgone: forgotten. Now is the night one blue dew.

Now is the night one blue dew, my father has drained, he has coiled the hose.
Low on the length of lawns, a frailing of fire who breathes.
Content, silver, like peeps of light, each cricket makes his comment over and over in the drowned grass.
A cold toad thumpily flounders.
Within the edges of damp shadows of side yards are hovering children nearly sick with joy of fear, who watch the unguarding of a telephone pole.
Around white carbon corner lamps bugs of all sizes are lifted elliptic, solar systems. Big hardshells bruise themselves, assailant: he is fallen on his back, legs squiggling.
Parents on porches: rock and rock: From damp strings morning glories: hang their ancient faces.
The dry and exalted noise of the locusts from all the air at once enchants my eardrums.

On the rough wet grass of the back yard my father and mother have spread quilts. We all lie there, my mother, my father, my uncle, my aunt, and I too am lying there. First we were sitting up, then one of us lay down, and then we all lay down, on our stomachs, or on our sides, or on our backs, and they have kept on talking. They are not talking much and the talk is quiet, of nothing in particular, of nothing at all in particular, of nothing at all. The stars are wide and alive, they seem each like a smile of great sweetness, and they seem very near. All my people are larger bodies than mine, quiet, with voices gentle and meaningless like the voices of sleeping birds. One is an artist, he is living at home. One is a musician, she is living at home. One is my mother who is good to me. One is my father who is good to me. By some chance, here they are, all on this earth; and who shall ever tell the sorrow of being on this earth, lying, on quilts, on the grass, in a summer evening, among the sounds of the night. May God bless my people, my uncle, my aunt, my mother, my good father, oh, remember them kindly in their time of trouble; and in the hour of their taking away.

After a little I am taken in and put to bed. Sleep, soft smiling, draws me unto her: and those receive me, who quietly treat me, as one familiar and well-beloved in that home: but will not, oh, will not, not now, not ever; but will not ever tell me who I am.

RALPH ELLISON

(1914–   )

Ralph Waldo Ellison was born in Oklahoma City, Oklahoma, the descendant of former slaves who had migrated to the West after the Reconstruction. Ellison attended the public schools of Oklahoma City, where he grew interested in poetry and in music. For three years he studied music at Tuskegee Institute in Alabama, where he also began writing, while reading extensively in modern poetry, fiction, and criticism.

In 1936 he moved to New York and was involved in both literature and politics. He became friends with Langston Hughes and Richard Wright and Wright outlined a course of selected reading for him. Ellison worked for the New York Federal Writers' Project and also began to establish himself as a writer, publishing stories, articles, and essays. Earlier he had begun a novel; now he worked hard to complete it.

In 1952 *Invisible Man* was published. It won critical attention at once and was awarded the National Book Award. However, unlike many other good novels, *Invisible Man* did not experience any decline in critical attention after a few years—its reputation only grew. A nationwide poll of critics in 1960 selected it as the book of its era that was most likely to endure. It has been widely taught in colleges and universities; no survey of the post-World War II American novel can ignore it. Although Ellison has published only a book of critical writings, *Shadow and Act* (1964), and a segment of a new novel in a magazine, in the quarter-century since *Invisible Man* came out, his reputation as a major practitioner of black American fiction has not diminished.

In a very real sense, *Invisible Man* seemed to signal the critical maturity of the black American writer of fiction. For unlike even the fiction of Ellison's great teacher and predecessor, Richard Wright, *Invisible Man* combines the traditional elements of social protest hitherto characteristic of the black novel with the formal expertise, psychological subtlety, and rich stylistic virtuosity of the novel as practiced by Faulkner, Hemingway, and other modern masters. As Ellison has written, "protest is *not* the source of the inadequacy characteristic of most novels by Negroes, but the simple failure of craft, bad writing; the belief that racial suffering, social injustice or ideologies of whatever mammy-made variety, is enough."

In *Invisible Man* the stunning technique and the evocative surfaces of the human experience portrayed intensify protest to the level of art and thus make it compelling in its own right as well as for what it asserts about the society. Ellison has drawn upon a rich tradition of a sense of social complexity and community identity, a pervasive distrust of the falsification of human experience through overreliance upon ideology, an insistence upon rhetorical fullness and sensuous textures, and a strong historical consciousness. All these characteristics of his work demonstrate his strong links to the Southern imagination—white and black.

From INVISIBLE MAN

CHAPTER 1

It goes a long way back, some twenty years. All my life I had been looking for something, and everywhere I turned someone tried to tell me what it was. I accepted their answers too, though they were often in contradiction and even self-contradictory. I was naïve. I was looking for myself and asking everyone except myself questions which I, and only I, could answer. It took me a long time and much painful boomeranging of my expectations to achieve a realization everyone else appears to have been born with: That I am nobody but myself. But first I had to discover that I am an invisible man!

And yet I am no freak of nature, nor of history. I was in the cards, other things having been equal (or unequal) eighty-five years ago. I am not ashamed of my grandparents for having been slaves. I am only ashamed of myself for having at one time been ashamed. About eighty-five years ago they were told that they were free, united with others of our country in everything pertaining to the common good, and, in everything social, separate like the fingers of the hand. And they believed it. They exulted in it. They stayed in their place, worked hard, and brought up my father to do the same. But my grandfather is the one. He was an odd old guy, my grandfather, and I am told I take after him. It was he who caused the trouble. On his deathbed he called my father to him and said, "Son, after I'm gone I want you to keep up the good fight. I never told you, but our life is a war and I have been a traitor all my born days, a spy in the enemy's country ever since I give up my gun back in the Reconstruction. Live with your head in the lion's mouth. I want you to overcome 'em with yeses, undermine 'em with grins, agree 'em to death and destruction, let 'em swoller you till they vomit or bust wide open." They thought the old man had gone out of his mind. He had been the meekest of men. The younger children were rushed from the room, the shades drawn and the flame of the lamp turned so low that it sputtered on the wick like the old man's breathing. "Learn it to the younguns," he whispered fiercely; then he died.

But my folks were more alarmed over his last words than over his dying. It was as though he had not died at all, his words caused so much anxiety. I was warned emphatically to forget what he had said and, indeed, this is the first time it has been mentioned outside the family circle. It had a tremendous effect upon me, however. I could never be sure of what he meant.

Grandfather had been a quiet old man who never made any trouble, yet on his deathbed he had called himself a traitor and a spy, and he had spoken of his meekness as a dangerous activity. It became a constant puzzle which lay unanswered in the back of my mind. And whenever things went well for me I remembered my grandfather and felt guilty and uncomfortable. It was as though I was carrying out his advice in spite of myself. And to make it worse, everyone loved me for it. I was praised by the most lily-white men of the town. I was considered an example of desirable conduct—just as my grandfather had been. And what puzzled me was that the old man had defined it as *treachery*. When I was praised for my conduct I felt a guilt that in some way I was doing something that was really against the wishes of the white folks, that if they had understood they would have desired me to act just the opposite, that I should have been sulky and mean, and that that really would have been what they wanted, even though they were fooled and thought they wanted me to act as I did. It made me afraid that some day they would look upon me as a traitor and I would be lost. Still I was more afraid to act any other way because they didn't like that at all. The old man's words were like a curse. On my graduation day I delivered an oration in which I showed that humility was the secret, indeed, the very essence of progress. (Not that I believed this—how could I, remembering my grandfather?—I only believed that it worked.) It was a great success. Everyone praised me and I was invited to give the speech at a gathering of the town's leading white citizens. It was a triumph for our whole community.

It was in the main ballroom of the leading hotel. When I got there I discovered that it was on the occasion of a smoker, and I was told that since I was to be there anyway I might as well take part in the battle royal to be fought by some of my schoolmates as part of the entertainment. The battle royal came first.

All of the town's big shots were there in their tuxedoes, wolfing down the buffet foods, drinking beer and whiskey and smoking black cigars. It was a large room with a high ceiling. Chairs were arranged in neat rows around three sides of a portable boxing ring. The fourth side was clear, revealing a gleaming space of polished floor. I had some misgivings over the battle royal, by the way. Not from a distaste for fighting, but because I didn't care too much for the other fellows who were to take part. They were tough guys who seemed to have no grandfather's curse worrying their minds. No one could mistake their toughness. And besides, I suspected that fighting a battle royal might detract from the dignity of my speech. In those pre-invisible days I visualized myself as a potential Booker T. Washington. But the other fellows didn't care too much for me either, and there were nine of them. I felt superior to them in my way, and I didn't like the manner in which we were all crowded together into the servants' elevator. Nor did they like my being there. In fact, as the warmly lighted floors flashed past the elevator we had words over the fact that I, by taking part in the fight, had knocked one of their friends out of a night's work.

We were led out of the elevator through a rococo hall into an anteroom and told to get into our fighting togs. Each of us was issued a pair of boxing gloves and ushered out into the big mirrored hall, which we entered looking cautiously about us and whispering, lest we might accidentally be heard above the noise of the room. It was foggy with cigar smoke. And already the whiskey was taking effect. I was shocked to see some of the most important men of the town quite tipsy. They were all there—bankers, lawyers, judges, doctors, fire chiefs, teachers, merchants. Even one of the more fashionable pastors. Something we could not see was going on up front. A clarinet was vibrating sensuously and the men were standing up and moving eagerly forward. We were a small tight group, clustered together, our bare upper bodies touching and shining with anticipatory sweat; while up front the big shots were becoming increasingly excited over something we still could not see. Suddenly, I heard the school superintendent, who had told me to come, yell, "Bring up the shines, gentlemen! Bring up the little shines!"

We were rushed up to the front of the ballroom, where it smelled even more strongly of tobacco and whiskey. Then we were pushed into place. I almost wet my pants. A sea of faces, some hostile, some amused, ringed around us, and in the center, facing us, stood a magnificent blonde—stark naked. There was dead silence. I felt a blast of cold air chill me. I tried to back away, but they were behind me and around me. Some of the boys stood with lowered heads, trembling. I felt a wave of irrational guilt and fear. My teeth chattered, my skin turned to goose flesh, my knees knocked. Yet I was strongly attracted and looked in spite of myself. Had the price of looking been blindness, I would have looked. The hair was yellow like that of a circus kewpie doll, the face heavily powdered and rouged, as though to form an abstract mask, the eyes hollow and smeared a cool blue, the color of a baboon's butt. I felt a desire to spit upon her as my eyes brushed slowly over her body. Her breasts were firm and round as the domes of East Indian temples, and I stood so close as to see the fine skin texture and beads of pearly perspiration glistening like dew around the pink and erected buds of her nipples. I wanted at one and the same time to run from the room, to sink through the floor, or go to her and cover her from my eyes and the eyes of the others with my body; to feel the soft thighs, to caress her and destroy her, to love her and murder her, to hide from her, and yet to stroke where below the small American flag tattooed upon her belly her thighs formed a capital V. I had a notion that of all in the room she saw only me with her impersonal eyes.

And then she began to dance, a slow sensuous movement; the smoke of a hundred cigars clinging to her like the thinnest of veils. She seemed like a fair bird-girl girdled in veils calling to me from the angry surface of some gray and threatening sea. I was transported. Then I became aware of the clarinet playing and the big shots yelling at us. Some threatened us if we looked and others if we did not. On my right I saw one boy faint. And now a man grabbed a silver pitcher from a table and stepped close as he dashed ice water upon him and stood him up and forced two of us to support him as his head hung and moans issued from his thick bluish lips. Another boy began to plead to go home. He was the largest of the group, wearing dark red fighting trunks much too small to conceal the erection which projected from him as though in answer to the insinuating low-registered moaning of the clarinet. He tried to hide himself with his boxing gloves.

And all the while the blonde continued dancing, smiling faintly at the big shots who watched her with fascination, and faintly smiling at our fear. I noticed a certain merchant who followed her hungrily, his lips loose and drooling. He was a large man who wore diamond studs in a shirt front which swelled with the ample paunch underneath, and each time the blonde swayed her undulating hips he ran his hand through the thin hair of his bald head and, with his arms upheld, his posture clumsy like that of an intoxicated panda, wound his belly in a slow and obscene grind. This creature was completely hypnotized. The music had quickened. As the dancer flung herself about with a detached expression on her face, the men began reaching out to touch her. I could see their beefy fingers sink into the soft flesh. Some of the others tried to stop them and she began to move around the floor in graceful circles, as they gave chase, slipping and sliding over the polished floor. It was mad. Chairs went crashing, drinks were spilt, as they ran laughing and howling after her. They caught her just as she reached a door, raised her from the floor, and tossed her as college boys are tossed at a hazing, and above the red, fixed-smiling lips I saw the terror and disgust in her eyes, almost like my own terror and that which I saw in some of the other boys. As I watched, they tossed her twice and her soft breasts seemed to flatten against the air and her legs flung wildly as she spun. Some of the more sober ones helped her to escape. And I started off the floor, heading for the anteroom with the rest of the boys.

Some were still crying and in hysteria. But as we tried to leave we were stopped and ordered to get into the ring. There was nothing to do but what we were told. All ten of us climbed under the ropes and allowed ourselves to be blindfolded with broad bands of white cloth. One of the men seemed to feel a bit sympathetic and tried to cheer us up as we stood with our backs against the ropes. Some of us tried to grin. "See that boy over there?" one of the men said. "I want you to run across at the bell and give it to him right in the belly. If you don't get him, I'm going to get you. I don't like his looks." Each of us was told the same. The blindfolds were put on. Yet even then I had been going over my speech. In my mind each word was as bright as flame. I felt the cloth pressed into place, and frowned so that it would be loosened when I relaxed.

But now I felt a sudden fit of blind terror. I was unused to darkness. It was as though I had suddenly found myself in a dark room filled with poisonous cottonmouths. I could hear the bleary voices yelling insistently for the battle royal to begin.

"Get going in there!"

"Let me at that big nigger!"

I strained to pick up the school superintendent's voice, as though to squeeze some security out of that slightly more familiar sound.

"Let me at those black sonsabitches!" someone yelled.

"No, Jackson, no!" another voice yelled. "Here, somebody, help me hold Jack."

"I want to get at that ginger-colored nigger. Tear him limb from limb," the first voice yelled.

I stood against the ropes trembling. For in those days I was what they called ginger-colored, and he sounded as though he might crunch me between his teeth like a crisp ginger cookie.

Quite a struggle was going on. Chairs were being kicked about and I could hear voices grunting as with a terrific effort. I wanted to see, to see more desperately than ever before. But the blindfold was tight as a thick skin-puckering scab and when I raised my gloved hands to push the layers of white aside a voice yelled, "Oh, no you don't, black bastard! Leave that alone!"

"Ring the bell before Jackson kills him a coon!" someone boomed in the sudden silence. And I heard the bell clang and the sound of the feet scuffling forward.

A glove smacked against my head. I pivoted, striking out stiffly as someone went past, and felt the jar ripple along the length of my arm to my shoulder. Then it seemed as though all nine of the boys had turned upon me at once. Blows pounded me from all sides while I struck out as best I could. So many blows landed upon me that I wondered if I were not the only blindfolded fighter in the ring, or if the man called Jackson hadn't succeeded in getting me after all.

Blindfolded, I could no longer control my motions. I had no dignity. I stumbled about like a baby or a drunken man. The smoke had become thicker and with each new blow it seemed to sear and further restrict my lungs. My saliva became like hot bitter glue. A glove connected with my head, filling my mouth with warm blood. It was everywhere. I could not tell if the moisture I felt upon my body was sweat or blood. A blow landed hard against the nape of my neck. I felt myself going over, my head hitting the floor. Streaks of blue light filled the black world behind the blindfold. I lay prone, pretending that I was knocked out, but felt myself seized by hands and yanked to my feet. "Get going, black boy! Mix it up!" My arms were like lead, my head smarting from blows. I managed to feel my way to the ropes and held on, trying to catch my breath. A glove landed in my mid-section and I went over again, feeling as though the smoke had become a knife jabbed into my guts. Pushed this way and that by the legs milling around me, I finally pulled erect and discovered that I could see the black, sweat-washed forms weaving in the smoky-blue atmosphere like drunken dancers weaving to the rapid drum-like thuds of blows.

Everyone fought hysterically. It was complete anarchy. Everybody fought everybody else. No group fought together for long. Two, three, four, fought one, then turned to fight each other, were themselves attacked. Blows landed below the belt and in the kidney, with the gloves open as well as closed, and with my eye partly opened now there was not so much terror. I moved carefully, avoiding blows, although not too many to attract attention, fighting from group to group. The boys groped about like blind, cautious crabs crouching to protect their mid-sections, their heads pulled in short against their shoulders, their arms stretched nervously before them, with their fists testing the smoke-filled air like the knobbed feelers of hypersensitive snails. In one corner I glimpsed a boy violently punching the air and heard him scream in pain as he smashed his hand against a ring post. For a second I saw him bend over holding his hand, then going down as a blow caught his unprotected head. I played one group against the other, slipping in and throwing a punch then stepping out of range while pushing the others into the melee to take the blows blindly aimed at me. The smoke was agonizing and there were no rounds, no bells at three minute intervals to relieve our exhaustion. The room spun around me, a swirl of lights, smoke, sweating bodies surrounded by tense white faces. I bled from both nose and mouth, the blood spattering upon my chest.

The men kept yelling, "Slug him, black boy! Knock his guts out!"

"Uppercut him! Kill him! Kill that big boy!"

Taking a fake fall, I saw a boy going down heavily beside me as though we were felled by a single blow, saw a sneaker-clad foot shoot into his groin as the two who had knocked him down stumbled upon him. I rolled out of range, feeling a twinge of nausea.

The harder we fought the more threatening the men became. And yet, I had begun to worry about my speech again. How would it go? Would they recognize my ability? What would they give me?

I was fighting automatically when suddenly I noticed that one after another of the boys was leaving the ring. I was surprised, filled with panic, as though I had been left alone with an unknown danger. Then I understood. The boys had arranged it among themselves. It was the custom for the two men left in the ring to slug it out for the winner's prize. I discovered this too late. When the bell sounded two men in tuxedoes leaped into the ring and removed the blindfold. I found myself facing Tatlock, the biggest of the gang. I felt sick at my stomach. Hardly had the bell stopped ringing in my ears than it clanged again and I saw him moving swiftly toward me. Thinking of nothing else to do I hit him smash on the nose. He kept coming, bringing the rank sharp violence of stale sweat. His face was a black blank of a face, only his eyes alive—with hate of me and aglow with a feverish terror from what had happened to us all. I became anxious. I wanted to deliver my speech and he came at me as though he meant to beat it out of me. I smashed him again and again, taking his blows as they came. Then on a sudden impulse I struck him lightly and as we clinched, I whispered, "Fake like I knocked you out, you can have the prize."

"I'll break your behind," he whispered hoarsely.

"For *them?*"

"For *me,* sonofabitch!"

They were yelling for us to break it up and Tatlock spun me half around with a blow, and as a joggled camera sweeps in a reeling scene, I saw the howling red faces crouching tense beneath the cloud of blue-gray smoke. For a moment the world wavered, unraveled, flowed, then my head cleared and Tatlock bounced before me. That fluttering shadow before my eyes was his jabbing left hand. Then falling forward, my head against his damp shoulder, I whispered,

"I'll make it five dollars more."

"Go to hell!"

But his muscles relaxed a trifle beneath my pressure and I breathed, "Seven?"

"Give it to your ma," he said, ripping me beneath the heart.

And while I still held him I butted him and moved away. I felt myself bombarded with punches. I fought back with hopeless desperation. I wanted to deliver my speech more than anything else in the world, because I felt that only these men could judge truly my ability, and now this stupid clown was ruining my chances. I began fighting carefully now, moving in to punch him and out again with my greater speed. A lucky blow to his chin and I had him going too—until I heard a loud voice yell, "I got my money on the big boy."

Hearing this, I almost dropped my guard. I was confused: Should I try to win against the voice out there? Would not this go against my speech, and was not this a moment for humility, for nonresistance? A blow to my head as I danced about sent my right eye popping like a jack-in-the-box and settled my dilemma. The room went red as I fell. It was a dream fall, my body languid and fastidious as to where to land, until the floor became impatient and smashed up to meet me. A moment later I came to. An hypnotic voice said FIVE emphatically. And I lay there, hazily watching a dark red spot of my own blood shaping itself into a butterfly, glistening and soaking into the soiled gray world of the canvas.

When the voice drawled TEN I was lifted up and dragged to a chair. I sat dazed. My eye pained and swelled with each throb of my pounding heart and I wondered if now I would be allowed to speak. I was wringing wet, my mouth still bleeding. We were grouped along the wall now.

The other boys ignored me as they congratulated Tatlock and speculated as to how much they would be paid. One boy whimpered over his smashed hand. Looking up front, I saw attendants in white jackets rolling the portable ring away and placing a small square rug in the vacant space surrounded by chairs. Perhaps, I thought, I will stand on the rug to deliver my speech.

Then the M.C. called to us, "Come on up here boys and get your money."

We ran forward to where the men laughed and talked in their chairs, waiting. Everyone seemed friendly now.

"There it is on the rug," the man said. I saw the rug covered with coins of all dimensions and a few crumpled bills. But what excited me, scattered here and there, were the gold pieces.

"Boys, it's all yours," the man said. "You get all you grab."

"That's right, Sambo," a blond man said, winking at me confidentially.

I trembled with excitement, forgetting my pain, I would get the gold and the bills, I thought. I would use both hands. I would throw my body against the boys nearest me to block them from the gold.

"Get down around the rug now," the man commanded, "and don't anyone touch it until I give the signal."

"This ought to be good," I heard.

As told, we got around the square rug on our knees. Slowly the man raised his freckled hand as we followed it upward with our eyes.

I heard, "These niggers look like they're about to pray!"

Then, "Ready," the man said. "Go!"

I lunged for a yellow coin lying on the blue design of the carpet, touching it and sending a surprised shriek to join those rising around me. I tried frantically to remove my hand but could not let go. A hot, violent force tore through my body, shaking me like a wet rat. The rug was electrified. The hair bristled up on my head as I shook myself free. My muscles jumped, my nerves jangled, writhed. But I saw that this was not stopping the other boys. Laughing in fear and embarrassment, some were holding back and scooping up the coins knocked off by the painful contortions of the others. The men roared above us as we struggled.

"Pick it up, goddamnit, pick it up!" someone called like a bass-voiced parrot. "Go on, get it!"

I crawled rapidly on the floor, picking up the coins, trying to avoid the coppers and to get greenbacks and the gold. Ignoring the shock by laughing, as I brushed the coins off quickly, I discovered that I could contain the electricity—a contradiction, but it works. Then the men began to push us onto the rug. Laughing embarrassedly, we struggled out of their hands and kept after the coins. We were all wet and slippery and hard to hold. Suddenly I saw a boy lifted into the air, glistening with sweat like a circus seal, and dropped, his wet back landing flush upon the charged rug, heard him yell and saw him literally dance upon his back, his elbows beating a frenzied tattoo upon the floor, his muscles twitching like the flesh of a horse stung by many flies. When he finally rolled off, his face was gray and no one stopped him when he ran from the floor amid booming laughter.

"Get the money," the M.C. called. "That's good hard American cash!"

And we snatched and grabbed, snatched and grabbed. I was careful not to come too close to the rug now, and when I felt the hot whiskey breath descend upon me like a cloud of foul air I reached out and grabbed the leg of a chair. It was occupied and I held on desperately.

"Leggo, nigger! Leggo!"

The huge face wavered down to mine as he tried to push me free. But my body was slippery and he was too drunk. It was Mr. Colcord, who owned a chain of movie houses and "entertainment palaces." Each time he grabbed me I slipped out of his hands. It became a real struggle. I feared the rug more than I did the drunk, so I held on, surprising myself for a moment by trying to topple *him* upon the rug. It was such an enormous idea that I found myself actually carrying it out. I tried not to be obvious, yet when I grabbed his leg, trying to tumble him out of the chair, he raised up roaring with laughter, and, looking at me with soberness dead in the eye, kicked me viciously in the chest. The chair leg flew out of my hand and I felt myself going and rolled. It was as though I had rolled through a bed of hot coals. It seemed a whole century would pass before I would roll free, a century in which I was seared and heated to the point of explosion. It'll all be over in a flash, I thought as I rolled clear. It'll all be over in a flash.

But not yet, the men on the other side were waiting, red faces swollen as though from apoplexy as they bent forward in their chairs. Seeing their fingers coming toward me I rolled away as a fumbled football rolls off the receiver's fingertips, back into the coals. That time I luckily sent the rug sliding out of place and heard the coins ringing against the floor and the boys scuffling to pick them up and the M.C. calling, "All right, boys, that's all. Go get dressed and get your money."

I was limp as a dish rag. My back felt as though it had been beaten with wires.

When we had dressed the M.C. came in and gave us each five dollars, except Tatlock, who got ten for being last in the ring. Then he told us to leave. I was not to get a chance to deliver my speech, I thought. I was going out into the dim alley in despair when I was stopped and told to go back. I returned to the ballroom, where the men were pushing back their chairs and gathering in groups to talk.

The M.C. knocked on a table for quiet. "Gentlemen," he said, "we almost forgot an important part of the program. A most serious part, gentlemen. This boy was brought here to deliver a speech which he made at his graduation yesterday ..."

"Bravo!"

"I'm told that he is the smartest boy we've got out there in Greenwood. I'm told that he knows more big words than a pocket-sized dictionary."

Much applause and laughter.

"So now, gentlemen, I want you to give him your attention."

There was still laughter as I faced them, my mouth dry, my eye throbbing. I began slowly, but evidently my throat was tense, because they began shouting, "Louder! Louder!"

"We of the younger generation extol the wisdom of that great leader and educator," I shouted, "who first spoke these flaming words of wisdom: 'A ship lost at sea for many days suddenly sighted a friendly vessel. From the mast of the unfortunate vessel was seen a signal: "Water, water; we die of thirst!" The answer from the friendly vessel came back: "Cast down your bucket where you are." The captain of the distressed vessel, at last heeding the injunction, cast down his bucket, and it came up full of fresh sparkling water from the mouth of the Amazon River.' And like him I say, and in his words, 'To those of my race who depend upon bettering their condition in a foreign land, or who underestimate the importance of cultivating friendly relations with the Southern white man, who is his next-door neighbor, I would say: "Cast down your bucket where you are"—cast it down in making friends in every manly way of the people of all races by whom we are surrounded . . .' "

I spoke automatically and with such fervor that I did not realize that the men were still talking and laughing until my dry mouth, filling up with blood from the cut, almost strangled me. I coughed, wanting to stop and go to one of the tall brass, sand-filled spittoons to relieve myself, but a few of the men, especially the superintendent, were listening and I was afraid. So I gulped it down, blood, saliva and all, and continued. (What powers of endurance I had during those days! What enthusiasm! What a belief in the rightness of things!) I spoke even louder in spite of the pain. But still they talked and still they laughed, as though deaf with cotton in dirty ears. So I spoke with greater emotional emphasis. I closed my ears and swallowed blood until I was nauseated. The speech seemed a hundred times as long as before, but I could not leave out a single word. All had to be said, each memorized nuance considered, rendered. Nor was that all. Whenever I uttered a word of three or more syllables a group of voices would yell for me to repeat it. I used the phrase "social responsibility" and they yelled:

"What's that word you say, boy?"

"Social responsibility," I said.

"What?"

"Social . . ."

"Louder."

". . . responsibility."

"More!"

"Respon—"

"Repeat!"

"—sibility."

The room filled with the uproar of laughter until, no doubt, distracted by having to gulp down my blood, I made a mistake and yelled a phrase I had often seen denounced in newspaper editorials, heard debated in private.

"Social . . ."

"What?" they yelled.

". . . equality—"

The laughter hung smokelike in the sudden stillness. I opened my eyes, puzzled. Sounds of displeasure filled the room. The M.C. rushed forward. They shouted hostile phrases at me. But I did not understand.

A small dry mustached man in the front row blared out, "Say that slowly, son!"

"What, sir?"

"What you just said!"

"Social responsibility, sir," I said.

"You weren't being smart, were you, boy?" he said, not unkindly.

"No, sir!"

"You sure that about 'equality' was a mistake?"

"Oh, yes, sir," I said. "I was swallowing blood."

"Well, you had better speak more slowly so we can understand. We mean to do right by you, but you've got to know your place at all times. All right, now, go on with your speech."

I was afraid. I wanted to leave but I wanted also to speak and I was afraid they'd snatch me down.

"Thank you, sir," I said, beginning where I had left off, and having them ignore me as before.

Yet when I finished there was a thunderous applause. I was surprised to see the superintendent come forth with a package wrapped in white tissue paper, and gesturing for quiet, address the men.

"Gentlemen, you see that I did not overpraise this boy. He makes a good speech and some day he'll lead his people in the proper paths. And I don't have to tell you that that is important in these days and times. This is a good, smart boy, and so to encourage him in the right direction, in the name of the Board of Education I wish to present him a prize in the form of this . . ."

He paused, removing the tissue paper and revealing a gleaming calfskin brief case.

". . . in the form of this first-class article from Shad Whitmore's shop."

"Boy," he said, addressing me, "Take this prize and keep it well. Consider it a badge of office. Prize it. Keep developing as you are and some day it will be filled with important papers that will help shape the destiny of your people."

I was so moved that I could hardly express my thanks. A rope of bloody saliva forming a shape like an undiscovered continent drooled upon the leather and I wiped it quickly away. I felt an importance that I had never dreamed.

"Open it and see what's inside," I was told.

My fingers a-tremble, I complied, smelling the fresh leather and finding an official-looking document inside. It was a scholarship to the state college for Negroes. My eyes filled with tears and I ran awkwardly off the floor.

I was overjoyed; I did not even mind when I discovered that the gold pieces I had scrambled for were brass pocket tokens advertising a certain make of automobile.

When I reached home everyone was excited. Next day the neighbors came to congratulate me. I even felt safe from grandfather, whose deathbed curse usually spoiled my triumphs. I stood beneath his photograph with my brief case in hand and smiled triumphantly into his stolid black peasant's face. It was a face that fascinated me. The eyes seemed to follow everywhere I went.

That night I dreamed I was at a circus with him and that he refused to laugh at the clowns no matter what they did. Then later he told me to open my brief case and read what was inside and I did, finding an official envelope stamped with the state seal; and inside the envelope I found another and another, endlessly, and I thought I would fall of weariness. "Them's years," he said, "Now open that one." And I did and in it I found an engraved document containing a short message in letters of gold. "Read it," my grandfather said. "Out loud!"

"To Whom It May Concern," I intoned. "Keep This Nigger-Boy Running."

I awoke with the old man's laughter ringing in my ears.

(It was a dream I was to remember and dream again for many years after. But at that time I had no insight into its meaning. First I had to attend college.)

PETER TAYLOR

(1917–   )

A master of the contemporary short story, Peter Hillsman Taylor writes deftly and sensitively about "the ramifications of family, the nuances of domestic frictions and affections," to quote Walter Sullivan's summation. Taylor possesses a gentle but often profound insight into the ways people cope with

PETER TAYLOR

time and change; he is at his best in depicting Southern people, often of good family, as they confront the domestic crises and requirements of a traditional society very much caught up in social transition. Although he has written novels and plays, short fiction is his true métier.

Taylor was born in Trenton, Tennessee, in 1917. His family was long prominent in Tennessee public life. He studied at Southwestern College and at Vanderbilt University, and when in 1938 John Crowe Ransom left Vanderbilt for Kenyon College, Taylor followed him there, where he was closely associated with Randall Jarrell and Robert Lowell. He graduated from Kenyon in 1940, studied briefly at Louisiana State University, then entered the Army. In 1943 he married the poet Eleanor Ross. He has since taught at the University of North Carolina at Greensboro, Indiana University, the University of Chicago, Kenyon College, Ohio State University, and Harvard University. In 1967 he became professor of English at the University of Virginia.

Taylor's first book of short stories was *The Long Fourth* (1948). Subsequent books have included *A Woman of Means* (1950), *The Widows of Thornton* (1954), *Tennessee Day in St. Louis* (1957), *Happy Families Are All Alike* (1959), *Miss Leonora When Last Seen* (1963), *A Stand in the Mountains* (1965), *Collected Stories* (1969), *Presences* (1973), *As Darker Grows the Night* (1976), and *In the Miro District and Other Stories* (1977).

THEIR LOSSES

At Grand Junction, the train slowed down for its last stop before getting into the outskirts of Memphis. Just when it had jerked to a standstill, Miss Patty Bean came out of the drawing room. She had not slept there but had hurried into the drawing room the minute she'd waked up to see how her aunt, who was gravely ill and who occupied the room with a trained nurse, had borne the last hours of the trip. Miss Patty had been in there with her aunt for nearly an hour. As she came out the nurse was whispering to her, but Miss Patty pulled the door closed with apparent indifference to what the nurse might be saying. The train, which had rocked mercilessly all night long, now stood motionless. For a moment Miss Patty, clad in a dark dressing gown and with her graying auburn hair contained in a sort of mesh cap, faced the other passengers in the Pullman car with an expression of alarm.

The other passengers, several of whom, already dressed, were standing in the aisle while the porter made up their berths, glanced at Miss Patty, then returned their attention immediately to their luggage or to their morning papers, which had been brought aboard at Corinth. They were mostly businessmen, and the scattering of women appeared to be businesswomen. In the silence and stillness of the train stop, not even those who were traveling together spoke to each other. At least half the berths had already been converted into seats, but the passengers did not look out the windows. They were fifty miles from Memphis, and they knew that nothing outside the windows would interest them until the train slowed down again, for the suburban stop of Buntyn.

After a moment Miss Patty's expression faded from one of absolute alarm to one of suspicion. Then, as though finally gathering her wits, she leaned over abruptly and peered out a window of the first section on her left. What she saw was only a deserted-looking cotton shed and, far beyond it, past winter fields of cotton stalks and dead grass, a two-story clapboard house with a sagging double gallery. The depot and the town were on the other side of the train, but Miss Patty knew this scene and she gave a sigh of relief. "Oh, uh-huh," she muttered to herself. "Grand Junction."

"Yes, sweet old Grand Junction," came a soft whisper.

For an instant Miss Patty could not locate the speaker. Then she became aware of a very tiny lady, dressed in black, seated right beside where she stood; indeed, she was leaning almost directly across the lady's lap. Miss Patty brought herself up straight, throwing her shoulders back and her heavy, square chin into the air, and said, "I was not aware that this section was occupied."

"Why, now, of course you weren't—of course you weren't, my dear," said the tiny lady. She was such an inconspicuous little soul that her presence could not alter the impression that there were only Memphis business-people in the car.

"I didn't know you were there," Miss Patty explained again.

"Why, of course you didn't."

"It was very rude of me," Miss Patty said solemnly, blinking her eyes.

"Oh, no," the tiny lady protested gently.

"Oh, but indeed it was," Miss Patty assured her.

"Why, it was all right."

"I didn't see you there. I beg your pardon."

The tiny lady was smiling up at Miss Patty with eyes that seemed as green as the Pullman upholstery. "I came aboard at Sweetwater during the night," she said. She nodded toward the curtains of Miss Patty's berth, across the aisle. "I guess you were as snug as a bug in a rug when I got on."

Miss Patty lowered her chin and scowled.

"You're traveling with your sick aunt, aren't you?" the lady went on. "I saw you go in there awhile ago, and I inquired of the porter." The smile faded from her eyes but remained on her lips. "You see, I haven't been to bed. I'm bringing my mother to Brownsville for burial." She nodded in the direction of the baggage car ahead.

"I see," Miss Patty replied. She had now fixed this diminutive person with a stare of appraisal. She was someone from her own world. If she heard the name, she would undoubtedly know the family. Without the name, she already *knew* the life history of the lady, and she could almost have guessed the name or made up one that would have done as well. Her impulse was to turn away, but the green eyes of Miss Ellen Watkins prevented her. They were too full of unmistakable sweetness and charity. Miss Patty remained a moment, observing the telltale paraphernalia: the black gloves and purse on the seat beside Miss Ellen; the unobtrusive hat, with its wisp of a veil turned back; the fresh powder on the wrinkled neck.

"I'm Ellen Louise Watkins," the tiny lady said. "I believe you're Miss Bean, from Thornton."

Miss Patty gave a formal little bow—a Watkins from Brownsville, a daughter of the late Judge Davy Watkins. They were kin to the Crocketts. Davy Crockett's blood had come to this end: a whispering old maid in a Pullman car.

"How *is* your aunt this morning?" Miss Ellen whispered, leaning forward.

But Miss Patty had turned her back. She put her head and shoulders inside the curtains of her berth, and as Miss Ellen waited for an answer, all to be seen of Miss Patty was the dark watered silk of her dressing gown, drawn tightly about her narrow hips and falling straight to a hemline just above her very white and very thin and bony ankles.

When Miss Patty pushed herself into the aisle again and faced Miss Ellen, she held, thrown over her arms, a navy-blue dress, various white and pink particulars of underwear, and a pair of extremely long and rumpled silk stockings, and in her hands she had bunched together her black pumps, an ivory comb and brush, and other articles she would need in the dressing room. The train began to move as she spoke. "I believe," she said, as though she were taking an oath, "that there has been no change in my aunt's condition during the night."

Miss Ellen nodded. The display of clothing over Miss Patty's arms brought a smile to her lips, and she was plainly making an effort to keep her eyes off the clothing and on Miss Patty's face. This uninhibited and even unladylike display reminded her of what she had always heard about the Bean family at Thornton. They were eccentric people, and bigoted. But quickly she reproached herself for retaining such gossip in her mind. Some of the Beans used to be in politics, and unfair things are always said about people in public life. Further, Miss Ellen reminded herself, the first instant she had set eyes on Miss Patty, she had *known* the sort of person she was. Even if the porter had not been able to tell her the name, she could almost have guessed it. She knew how Miss Patty would look when she had got into those garments—as though she had dressed in the dark and were proud of it. And there would be a hat—a sort of brown fedora—that she would pull on at the last minute before she got off the train. She had known many a Miss Patty Bean in her time, and their gruffness and their mannish ways didn't frighten her. Indeed, she felt sorry for such women. "Are you going to have breakfast in the diner?" she asked.

"I am," Miss Patty replied.

"Then I'll save you a seat. I'll go ahead and get a table. There's not too much time, Miss Bean."

"As you will, Miss Watkins." Miss Patty turned toward the narrow passage that led to the ladies' dressing room. Suddenly she stopped and backed into Miss Ellen's section. She was making way for the conductor and a passenger who had evidently come aboard at Grand Junction. A porter followed, carrying a large piece of airplane luggage. The Pullman conductor came first, and the passenger, a lady, was addressing him over his shoulder. "But why could not they stop the *Pullman* at the platform, instead of the *coaches?*" It was a remarkably loud voice, and it paused after every word, obviously trying for a humorous effect.

The conductor was smiling grimly. "Here you are, ma'am," he said. "You can sit here till I find space for you—if this lady don't mind. She has the whole section." He indicated Miss Ellen's section and continued down the aisle, followed by the porter, without once looking back.

"But suppose she *does* mind?" the new passenger called after him, and she laughed heartily. Some of the other passengers looked up briefly and smiled. The lady turned to Miss Patty, who was still there holding her possessions: "*Do* you mind?" And then, "Why, Patty Bean! How very nice!"

"It is not my section." Miss Patty thrust herself into the aisle. "It is not my section, Cornelia."

"Then it must be—Why, will wonders never cease? Ellen Louise Watkins!"

Miss Ellen and Miss Patty exchanged surprised glances.

"Why, of course you shall sit here with me," Miss Ellen said. "How good to see you, Cornelia!"

Cornelia Weatherby Werner had already seated herself, facing Miss Ellen. She was a large woman in all her dimensions, but a good-looking woman still. She wore a smart three-cornered hat, which drew attention to her handsome profile, and a cloth coat trimmed with Persian lamb. "I declare it's like old times," she said breathlessly. "Riding the Southern from Grand Junction to Memphis and seeing everybody you know! Nowadays it's mostly *that* sort you see on the Southern." She gestured openly toward the other passengers. "I'll bet you two have been gadding off to Washington. Are you traveling together?"

Miss Ellen and Miss Patty shook their heads.

"Ellen and I are old schoolmates, too, Patty," Cornelia continued. "We were at Ward's together after I was dismissed from Belmont. By the way," she said, smiling roguishly and digging into her purse for cigarettes, "I still have that infernal habit. It's old-fashioned now, but I still call them my coffin nails. Which reminds me—" She hesitated, a package of cigarettes in one hand, a silver lighter in the other. "Oh, do either of you smoke? Well, not before breakfast anyhow. And not on a Pullman, even when the conductor isn't looking, I'll bet. I was saying it reminds me I have just been to

Grand Junction to put my old mother to her last rest." As she lit her cigarette, she watched their faces, eager for the signs of shock.

Miss Ellen gave a sympathetic "Oh." Miss Patty stared.

"You mustn't look so lugubrious," Cornelia went on. "The old dear
hadn't spoken to me in thirty-one years—not since I got married and went
to Memphis. I married a Jew, you know. You've both met Jake? He's a
bank examiner and a good husband. Let's see, Patty, when was it I came
down to Thornton with Jake? During the Depression sometime—but we
saw Ellen only last May."

Miss Ellen leaned forward and stopped her, resting a tiny hand on her
knee. "Cornelia, dear," she whispered, "we're all making sad trips these
days. I'm taking Mother to Brownsville for burial. She died while we were
visiting her invalid cousin at Sweetwater."

Cornelia said nothing. Presently she raised her eyes questioningly to
Miss Patty.

"My aged aunt," Miss Patty said. "She is not dead. She is in the drawing
room with an Irish nurse. I'm bringing her from Washington to spend her
last days at Thornton, where she is greatly loved."

Miss Ellen looked up at Miss Patty and said, "I'm sure she is."

"She is," Miss Patty affirmed. There was a civility in her tone that had
not been there when she had last addressed Miss Ellen, and the two
exchanged a rather long glance.

Cornelia gazed out the window at the passing fields. Her features in
repose looked tired. It was with obvious effort that she faced her two friends
again. Miss Patty was still standing there, with her lips slightly parted, and
Miss Ellen still rested a hand on Cornelia's knee. Cornelia shuddered visibly. She blushed and said, "A rabbit ran over my grave, I guess." Then she
blushed again, but now she had regained her spirit. "Oh, just listen to me."
She smiled, "I've never said the right thing once in my life. Is there a diner?
Can we get any breakfast? You used to get the *best* breakfast on the
Southern."

At the word "breakfast," Miss Patty did an about-face and disappeared
down the passage to the ladies' room. Miss Ellen seized her purse and
gloves. "Of course, my dear," she said. "Come along. We'll all have breakfast together."

There were no other passengers in the diner when Cornelia and Miss
Ellen went in. The steward was eating at a small table at the rear of the car.
Two Negro waiters were standing by the table talking to him, but he
jumped to his feet and came toward the ladies. He stopped at the third table
on the right, as though all the others might be reserved, and after wiping his
mouth with a large white napkin, he asked if there would be anyone else in
their party.

"Why, yes, as a matter of fact," Miss Ellen answered politely, "there will be one other."

"Do you think you can squeeze one more in?" Cornelia asked, narrowing her eyes and laughing. The steward did not reply. He helped them into chairs opposite each other and by the broad window, and darted away to get menus from his desk at the front of the car. A smiling Negro waiter set three goblets upright, filled them with water, and removed a fourth goblet and a setting of silver. "Sometime during the past thirty years," Cornelia remarked when the waiter had gone, "conductors and stewards lost their sense of humor. It makes you thank God for porters and waiters, doesn't it? Next thing you know—Why, merciful heavens, here's Patty already!"

Miss Ellen glanced over her shoulder. There was Miss Patty, looking as though she had dressed in the dark and were proud of it. She was hatless, her hair apparently without benefit of the ivory comb and brush. The steward was leading her toward their table. Without smiling, Cornelia said, "He didn't have to ask her if she were the other member of this party." Miss Ellen raised her eyebrows slightly. "Most passengers don't eat in the diner any more," Cornelia clarified. "They feel they're too near to Memphis to bother." When Miss Patty sat down beside Miss Ellen, Cornelia said, "Gosh a'might, Patty, we left you only two seconds ago and here you are dressed and in your right mind. How do you do it?"

They received their menus, and when they had ordered, Miss Patty smiled airily. "I'm always in my right mind, Cornelia, and I don't reckon I've ever been 'dressed' in my life." As she said "dressed," her eyes traveled from the three-cornered hat to the brocaded bosom of Cornelia's rust-colored dress.

Cornelia looked out the window, silently vowing not to speak again during the meal, or, since speaking was for her the most irresistible of all life's temptations, at least not to let herself speak sharply to either of these crotchety old maids. She sat looking out the window, thanking her stars for the great good luck of being Mrs. Jake Werner, of Memphis, instead of an embittered old maid from Grand Junction.

Miss Ellen was also looking out the window. "Doesn't it look bleak?" she said, referring to the brown-and-gray fields under an overcast sky.

"Oh, doesn't it!" Cornelia agreed at once, revealing that Miss Ellen had guessed her very thoughts.

"It *is* bleak," Miss Patty said. "See how it's washed. This land along here didn't use to look like that." The two others nodded agreement, each remembering how it had used to look. "This used to be fine land," she continued, "but it seems to me that all West Tennessee is washing away. Look at those gullies! And not a piece of brush piled in them." Miss Ellen and Cornelia shook their heads vaguely, they were not really certain why there should be brush in the gullies. Cornelia discovered that a glass of tomato juice had been set before her and she began pouring salt into it. Miss Ellen was eating her oatmeal. Miss Patty took a sip from her first cup of coffee. She had specified that it be brought in a cup instead of a pot. It was black and a little cool, the way she liked it. She peered out the window again and pursued her discourse warmly. "And the towns! Look! We're going through Moscow. It's a shambles. Why, half the square's been torn away, and the rest ought to be. Mind you, we went through La Grange without even noticing it. They used to be good towns, fine towns."

"Lovely towns!" responded Miss Ellen. The thought of the vanishing towns touched her.

"There was something about them," Cornelia said, groping. "An atmosphere, I think."

Miss Patty cleared her throat and defined it: "The atmosphere of a prosperous and civilized existence."

Miss Ellen looked bewildered, and Cornelia frowned thoughtfully and pursed her lips. Presently Cornelia said profoundly, "All the business has gone to Memphis."

"Yes," Miss Patty said. "Indeed it has!"

They were being served their main course now. Cornelia looked at her trout and said to the waiter, "It looks delicious. Did you cook this, boy?"

"No, ma'am," the waiter said cheerfully.

"Well, it looks delicious. The same old Southern Railway cooking."

Miss Patty and Miss Ellen had scrambled eggs and ham. Miss Patty eyed hers critically. "The Southern Railway didn't use to cook eggs this way," she said. 'And it's no improvement."

Miss Ellen leaned forward and bent her neck in order to look directly up into Miss Patty's face. "Why, now, you probably like them country style, with some white showing," she said. "*These* are what my niece calls Toddle House style. They cook them with milk, of course. They're a little like an omelet." The subject held great interest for her, and she was happy to be able to inform Miss Patty. "And you don't break them into such a hot pan. You don't really break them in the pan, that is." Miss Patty was reaching across Miss Ellen's plate for the pepper. Miss Ellen said no more about the eggs. She busied herself with a small silver box of saccharin, prying the lid open with her fingernail. She saw Cornelia looking at the box and said, "It was my grandmother's snuffbox. For years it was just a keepsake, but now I carry my tablets in it."

The old box, which Miss Patty was now examining admiringly, somehow made Cornelia return to the subject they had left off. "In my grandmother's day, there was a lot of life in this section—entertainment and social life. My own mother used to say, 'In Mama's day, there were people in the country; in my day, there were people in town; now there's nobody.' "

Miss Patty gazed at Cornelia with astonishment. "Your mother was a very wise woman, Cornelia," she said.

"That's a moot question," Cornelia answered. Now they were on a subject that she was sure she knew something about, and she threw caution to the wind. She spoke excitedly and seemed to begin every sentence without knowing how it would end. "My mother is dead now, and I don't mean to ever say another word against her, but just because she is dead, I don't intend to start deceiving myself. The fact remains that she was opinionated and narrow and mentally cruel to her children and her husband and was tied to things that were over and done with before she was born. She's dead now, but I shall make no pretense of mourning someone I did not love. We don't mourn people we don't love. It's not honest."

"No, we don't, do we?" Miss Ellen said sympathetically.

"I beg to differ with you," Miss Patty said with the merest suggestion of a smile. She, too, felt on firm ground. She had already mourned the deaths of all her immediate family and of most of her near kin. She addressed her remarks to Miss Ellen. "Mourning is an obligation. We only mourn those with whom we have some real connection, people who have represented something important and fundamental in our lives."

Miss Ellen was determined to find agreement. "Of course, of course —you are speaking of wearing black."

"I am not speaking of the symbol. I am speaking of the mourning itself. I shall mourn the loss of my aunt when she goes, because she is my aunt, because she is the last of my aunts, and particularly because she is an aunt who has maintained a worthwhile position in the world."

Miss Ellen gasped. "Oh, no, Miss Bean! Not because of her position in the world!"

"Don't mistake me, Miss Watkins."

"I beg you to reconsider. Why, why—" she fumbled, and Miss Patty waited. "Now that Mother's gone, I've lost nearly everybody, and it has always been my part and my privilege to look after the sick in our family. My two older brothers never married; they were quiet, simple, home-loving men, who made little stir in the world, content to live there in the house with Mother and Nora and me after Father was gone. And Nora, my only sister, developed melancholia. One morning, she could just not finish lacing her high shoes, and after that she seldom left the house or saw anybody. What I want to say is that we also had a younger brother, who was a distinguished professor at Knoxville, with four beautiful children. You see, I've lost them all, one by one, and it's been no different whether they were distinguished or not. I can't conceive—" She stopped suddenly, in real confusion.

"Don't mistake me," Miss Patty said calmly. "I am speaking of my aunt's moral position in the world."

"Why, of course you are," said Miss Ellen, still out of breath.

"My aunt has been an indomitable character," Miss Patty continued. "Her husband died during his first term in Congress, forty years ago, and she has felt it her duty to remain in Washington ever since. With very slight means, she has maintained herself there in the right manner through all the years, returning to Thornton every summer, enduring the heat and the inconvenience, with no definite place of abode, visiting the kin, subjecting herself to the role of the indigent relation, so that she could afford to return to Washington in the fall. Her passing will be a loss to us all, for through her wit and charm she was an influence on Capitol Hill. In a sense, she represented our district in Washington as none of our elected officials has done since the days of"—bowing her head deferentially toward Miss Ellen—"of David Crockett."

"What a marvelous woman!" exclaimed Miss Ellen.

Cornelia looked at Miss Ellen to see whether she meant Miss Patty's aunt or Miss Patty. She had been marveling privately at Miss Patty's flow of speech, and reflected that she could already see it in print in the county paper's obituary column. "If my mother had been a person of such wit and charm" she said, "I would mourn her, too."

"I never knew your mother," Miss Patty replied, "but from what you say I can easily guess the sort of woman she was. I would mourn her passing if I were in your shoes, Cornelia. She wanted to retain the standards of a past era, a better era for all of *us*. A person can't do that and be a pleasant, charming personality and the darling of a family."

"All I know," said Cornelia, taking the last bite of her trout, "is that my young-ladyhood was a misery under that woman's roof and in that town." She glanced dreamily out the window. The train was speeding through the same sort of country as before, perhaps a little more hilly, a little more eroded. It sped through small towns and past solitary stations where only the tiresome afternoon local stopped—Rossville, Collierville, Bailey, Forest Hill. Cornelia saw a two-story farmhouse that was painted up only to the level of the second story. "That house has been that way as long as I can remember," she said, and smiled. "Why do you suppose they don't make them a ladder, or lean out the upstairs windows?" Then, still looking out at the dismal landscape—the uncultivated land growing up in sweet gum and old field pine, with a gutted mud road crossing and recrossing the railroad track every half mile or so—Cornelia said, "I only got away by the skin of my teeth! I came back from Ward's with a scrapbook full of names, but they were nothing but 'cute Vanderbilt boys.' I would have been stuck in Grand Junction for life, nursing Mama and all the hypochondriac kin, if I hadn't met Jake. I met him in Memphis doing Christmas shopping. He was a bank teller at Union Planters." She laughed heartily for the first time since she had come into the diner. "It was an out-and-out pickup. Jake still tells everybody it was an out-and-out pickup."

"I don't like Memphis," said Miss Patty. "I never have."

"I've never felt that Memphis liked me," said Miss Ellen.

"It's a wretched place!" Cornelia said suddenly. And now she saw that she had unwittingly shocked her two friends. The train had passed through

Germantown; big suburban estates and scattered subdivisions began to appear in the countryside. There was even a bulldozer at work on the horizon, grading the land for new suburban sites. "It's the most completely snobbish place in the world," she went on. "They can't forgive you for being from the country—they hate the country so, and they can't forgive your being a Jew. They dare not. If you're either one of those, it's rough going. If you're both, you're just out! I mean *socially*, of course. Oh, Jake's done *well*, and we have our friends. But as Mama would have said—and, God knows, probably did say about us many a time—*we're* nobody." Then, for no reason at all, she added, "And we don't have any children."

"What a shame," Miss Ellen said, hastening to explain, "that you have no children, I mean. I've always thought that if—"

"Oh, no, Ellen. They might have liked me about the way I liked Mama. I'm glad that when I die, there'll be no question of to mourn or not to mourn."

"In truly happy families, Cornelia, there is no question," Miss Ellen said softly. She stole a glance at Miss Patty. "I'm just certain that Miss Bean had a very congenial and happy family, and that she loved them all dearly, in addition to being naturally proud of the things they stood for."

Miss Patty had produced a wallet from somewhere on her person and was examining her check. She slammed the wallet on the table, turned her head, and glared at the dimunitive Miss Ellen. "How I regarded the members of my family as individuals is neither here nor there, Miss Watkins."

But Miss Ellen raised her rather receding chin and gazed directly up at Miss Patty. "To me, it seems of the greatest consequence." Her voice trembled, yet there was a firmness in it. "I am mourning my mother today. I spent last night remembering every endearing trait she had. Some of them were faults and some were virtues, but they were nonetheless endearing. And so I feel strongly about what you say, Miss Bean. We must love people as people, not for what they are, or were, in the world."

"My people happened to be very much *of* the world, Miss Watkins," said Miss Patty. "Not of *this* world but of *a* world that we have seen disappear. In mourning my family, I mourn that world's disappearance. How could I know whether or not we were really happy? There wasn't ever time for asking that. We were all like Aunt Lottie, in yonder, and there was surely never any love or happiness in the end of it. When I went to Washington last week to fetch Aunt Lottie home, I found her living in a hateful little hole at the Stoneleigh Court. All the furniture from larger apartments she had once had was jammed together in two rooms. The tables were covered with framed photographs of the wives of Presidents, Vice-Presidents, Senators, inscribed to Lottie Hathcock. But there was not a friend in sight. During the five days I was there, not one person called." Miss Patty stood up and waved her check and two one-dollar bills at the waiter.

Miss Ellen sat watching the check and the two bills with a stunned expression. But Cornelia twisted about in her chair excitedly. "Your aunt was Mrs. Hathcock!" she fairly screamed. "Oh, Patty, of course! She was *famous* in her day. And don't you remember? I met her once with you at the Maxwell House, when we were at Belmont. You took me along, and after supper my true love from Vandy turned up in the lobby. You were so furious, and Mrs. Hathcock was so cute about it. She was the cleverest talker I've ever listened to, Patty. She was interested in spiritualism and offered to take us to a séance at Mr. Ben Allen's house."

Miss Patty looked at Cornelia absent-mindedly. Her antagonism toward the two women seemed suddenly to have left her, and she spoke without any restraint at all. "Aunt Lottie has long since become a Roman Catholic. Her will leaves her little pittance of money and her furniture to the Catholic Church, and her religious oil paintings to me. The nurse we brought along has turned out to be an Irish Catholic." She glanced in the direction of their Pullman car and said, "The nurse has conceived the notion that Aunt Lottie is worse this morning, and she wanted to wire ahead for a Memphis priest to meet us at the Union Station. She knows there won't be any priests at Thornton."

Cornelia, carried away by incorrigible gregariousness, began, "Ah, Patty, might I see her? It would be such fun to see her again, just for old times' sake. It might even cheer her a little."

Miss Patty stared at Cornelia in silence. Finally she said, "My aunt is a mental patient. She doesn't even remember me, Cornelia." She snatched a piece of change from the waiter's tray and hurried past the steward and out of the car.

Miss Ellen was almost staggering as she rose from the table. She fumbled in her purse, trying to find the correct change for the waiter. She was shaking her head from side to side, and opening and closing her eyes with the same rhythm.

Cornelia made no move toward rising. "Depend upon *me*," she said. "Did you *know?*"

Miss Ellen only increased the speed of her head-shaking. When she saw Cornelia still sitting there, casually lighting a cigarette, she said, "We're approaching Buntyn. I imagine you're getting off there."

"No, that's the country-club stop. I don't get off at the country-club stop."

"There's not much time," Miss Ellen said.

Presently Cornelia pulled a bill from her purse and summoned the waiter. "Well, Ellen," she said, still not getting up. "I guess there's no way I could be of help to you at the station, is there?"

"No, there's nothing, dear."

In her lethargy Cornelia seemed unable to rise and even unable to tell Miss Ellen to go ahead without her. "I suppose you'll be met by a hearse," she said, "and Patty will be met by an ambulance, and—and I'll be met by Jake." For a moment, she sat behind a cloud of cigarette smoke. There was a puzzled expression in her eyes, and she was laughing quietly at what she had said. It was one of those sentences that Cornelia began without knowing how it would end.

WALKER PERCY

(1916–   )

The literary career of Walker Percy began quite late. He was in his mid-forties when his first novel, *The Moviegoer* (1961), was published, though before then he had written two novels that did not find a publisher. *The Moviegoer* won the National Book Award for 1962 and since then he has had four more novels, a book of essays, and a book of criticism published and is generally considered one of the most original and important fiction writers on the literary scene today.

Percy was born in Birmingham, Alabama. Shortly after his father's death by suicide when Percy was eleven, his cousin William Alexander Percy took him and his two brothers to live at his home in Greenville, Mississippi, and later legally adopted them. Living in Will Percy's house, listening to classical music and talking about literature and ideas with a man who was a well-known minor poet, essayist, outspoken critic of demagoguery, and foe of anti-Negro politicians, he was strongly influenced in the direction of the arts, though some years were to intervene during which he studied medicine. He graduated from Greenville High School a year ahead of his friend Shelby Foote and went on to the University of North Carolina. Percy then enrolled at the Columbia University School of Medicine and graduated with high honors, but during his residency at Bellevue Hospital contracted pulmonary tuberculosis. After several years of illness and slow recovery, during which he began reading widely in philosophy, psychology, and theology, he decided to give up medicine.

In 1946 Percy married Mary Bernice Townsend, became a Roman Catholic, and moved to Covington, Louisiana. He began writing philosophical and critical essays and then concentrated his efforts on the writing of fiction. After *The Moviegoer* he wrote *The Last Gentleman* (1966), *Love in the Ruins* (1971), and *Lancelot* (1977). His essays were collected in 1975 as *The Message in the Bottle*. All four of Percy's published novels center on a man who is unable to accept the behavioristic, biological explanations of science as a sufficient solution to human experience. He is one who is incapable any longer of believing in the old Southern aristocratic ideals of *noblesse oblige* and stoic fortitude (as exemplified in characters resembling Will Percy). This protagonist is in a state of spiritual "sickness" and seeks to know how to cope, not with abstract problems of belief and nonbelief, but with the problem —as the protagonist of Percy's second novel, *The Last Gentleman*, expresses it—of "how to live from one ordinary minute to the next on a Wednesday afternoon." Yet Percy treats just such ultimate problems in his fiction and essays. He is a "philosophical" novelist whose characters and situations are shaped to exemplify and comment upon issues of knowledge, faith, and meaning. In all of them there is the expectation of a "role" on the protagonist's part—an expectation that has been made to seem meaningless by the passage of time and social change.

Although Percy has declared that "the day of Southern regional writing is all gone," his protagonists not only live in the modern South but have a remarkable concern for the traditional preoccupations of Southern fiction: caste and class, the sense of "decline and fall," the individual's private relationship to a known community identity, the weight of the past, the presence of black people and the moral dilemmas attendant on their presence, attachment to place and the assumption that to be out of one's place dictates a redefinition of one's role—and many other themes of this nature. It is not too difficult to see Percy's spiritually disturbed protagonists as the latest exemplars of a long line of estranged Southern fictional wayfarers, including Faulkner's Quentin Compson, Wolfe's Eugene Gant, Warren's Jack Burden, Tate's Lacy Buchan, Styron's Cass Kinsolving, and Katherine Anne Porter's Miranda.

In *The Last Gentleman*, from which the following excerpt is taken, Williston Bibb Barrett, after a long spell in New York during which he has undergone psychoanalysis and has had recurring spells of amnesia and terror, returns south and plans to marry his girlfriend and settle down. Before he can, however, he must go to the western desert in search of his dying friend Jamie and Jamie's physician-brother Sutter Vaught, who Barrett thinks can answer his questions about ultimate meaning. En route he stops in Ithaca, Mississippi, where he grew up, becomes involved in a racial incident, and confronts, for the first time, his memory of the night when his father killed himself.

From THE LAST GENTLEMAN

4.

His friends waited for him but not long enough. By the time he rounded the lower curve of Milliken Bend, having walked the inner shoulder of the levee out of sight of highway and town, the Trav-L-Aire had already lumbered out of the willows and started up the levee—at an angle! The cabin teetered dangerously. He forgot to tell Mona not to do this. He covered his face with his hands: Mona, thinking to spare the G.M.C. the climb straight up, was in a fair way to turn her plumb over. When he looked up, however, the levee was clear.

It was two o'clock. He was hungry. At the levee end of Theard Street he bought a half dozen tamales from a street vendor (but not the same whose cry *Rayed hot!* used to echo up and down the summer night in the 1950's). Now finding a patch of waist-high elephant grass past the towhead and out of sight of anyone standing on the levee behind him, he rolled to and fro and made a hollow which was tilted like a buttercup into the westering sun. It was warm enough to take off his coat and roll up his sleeves. He ate the tamales carefully, taking care not to stain his clothes. The meat was good but his tooth encountered a number-eight shot: rabbit or possibly squirrel. Afterwards he washed his hands in river water, which still thrashed through the lower level of the towhead, and dried them with his handkerchief. Returning to his hollow, he sat cross-legged for a while and watched a tow-boat push a good half acre of sulphur barges up the dead water on the Louisiana side. Then he curled up and, using his coat folded wrong-side-out for a pillow, went to sleep.

Cold and stiffness woke him. It was a moonless overcast night, but he could make out Scorpio writhing dimly over Louisiana, convulsed around great bloody Antares. Buttoning all three buttons of his jacket, he ran along the inner shoulder of the levee, out of sight of town, until he got warm. When he came abreast of the stacks of the gypsum mill, he went quickly over and down into Blanton Street and took the Illinois Central tracks, which went curving away behind the high school. It was pitch dark under the stadium, but his muscles remembered the spacing of the ties. The open rear of the bleachers exhaled a faint odor of cellar earth and urine. At the Chinaman's he took the tangent of Houston Street, which ran through a better Negro neighborhood of neat shotgun cottages and flower gardens, into the heavy humming air and ham-rich smell of the cottonseeed oil mill, and out at De Ridder.

He stood in the inky darkness of the water oaks and looked at his house. It was the same except that the gallery had been closed by glass louvers and a flagpole stuck out of a second-story window. His aunts were sitting on the porch. They had moved out, television and all. He came closer and stood amid the azaleas. They were jolly and fit, were the aunts, and younger than ever. Three were watching "Strike It Rich," two were playing canasta, and one was reading *Race and Reason* and eating Whitman's Sampler. He remembered now that Sophie wrote love letters to Bill Cullen. What a tough hearty crew they were! hearty as muzhiks, and good haters, yet not ill-natured—they'd be honestly and unaffectedly glad to see him walk in, would kiss him and hold him off and make over him—rosy-skinned, easy in their consciences, arteries as supple as a girl's, husbands dead and gone these forty years, pegged out so long ago that he could not remember any-one ever speaking of them; Christian ladies every one, four Protestant, Pres-

byterian, and Scotch-Irish, two Catholic and Creole, but long since reconciled, ecumenized, by bon appétit and laughter and good hearty hatred.

It was here under the water oaks that his father used to stroll of a summer night, hands in his pockets and head down, sauntering along the
sidewalk in his old Princeton style of sauntering, right side turning forward
with right leg. Here under the water oaks or there under the street light, he
would hold parley with passers-by, stranger and friend, white and black,
thief and police. The boy would sit on the front steps, close enough to speak
with his father and close enough too to service the Philco which played its
stack of prewar 78's but always had trouble doing it. The mechanism
creaked and whirred and down came the record plop and round it went for
a spell, hissing under the voyaging needle. From the open window came
Brahms, nearly always Brahms. Up and down the sidewalk went his father,
took his turn under the street light sometimes with a client, sometimes
alone. The clients, black and white and by and large the sorriest of crews
but of course listening now with every eager effort of attention and even of
a special stratospheric understanding. Between records the boy could hear
snatches of talk: "Yassuh, that's the way it is now! I have notice the same
thing myself!"—the father having said something about the cheapness of
good intentions and the rarity of good character—"I'm sho gon' do like you
say"—the passer-by working him of course for the fifty cents or five dollars
or what, but working him as gracefully as anyone ever worked, they as good
at their trade as he at his. The boy listening: what was the dread in his heart
as he heard the colloquy and the beautiful terrible Brahms which went
abroad into the humming summer night and the heavy ham-rich air?

The aunts let out a holler. Bill Cullen had given away a cabin cruiser to a
lady from Michigan City, Indiana.

It was on such an evening—he passed his hand over his eyes and stretching it forth touched the sibilant corky bark of the water oak—that his father
had died. The son watched from the step, old Brahms went abroad, the
father took a stroll and spoke to a stranger of the good life and the loneliness of the galaxies. "Yes suh," said the stranger. "I have heard tell it was
so" (that the closest star was two light years away).

When the man came back the boy asked him:

"Father, why do you walk in the dark when you know they have sworn
to kill you?"

"I'm not afraid, son."

To the west the cars of the white people were nosing up the levee, head-
lights switched first to parking, then out altogether. From the east, beyond
the cottonseed-oil mill, came the sound of Negro laughter.

The man walked until midnight. Once a police car stopped. The policeman spoke to the man.

"You've won," said the youth when the man came back. "I heard the
policeman. They've left town."

"We haven't won, son. We've lost."

"But they're gone, Father."

"Why shouldn't they leave? They've won."

"How have they won, Father?"

"They don't have to stay. Because they found out that we are like them after all and so there was no reason for them to stay."

"How are we like them, Father?"

"Once they were the fornicators and the bribers and the takers of bribes and we were not and that was why they hated us. Now we are like them, so why should they stay? They know they don't have to kill me."

"How do they know that, Father?"

"Because we've lost it all, son."

"Lost what?"

"But there's one thing they don't know."

"What's that, Father?"

"They may have won, but I don't have to choose that."

"Choose what?"

"Choose them."

This time, as he turned to leave, the youth called out to him. "Wait."

"What?"

"Don't leave."

"I'm just going to the corner."

But there was a dread about this night, the night of victory. (Victory is the saddest thing of all, said the father.) The mellowness of Brahms had gone overripe, the victorious serenity of the Great Horn Theme was false, oh fake fake. Underneath, all was unwell.

"Father."

"What?"

"Why do you like to be alone?"

"In the last analysis, you are alone." He turned into the darkness of the oaks.

"Don't leave." The terror of the beautiful victorious music pierced his very soul.

"I'm not leaving, son," said the man and, after taking a turn, came back to the steps. But instead of stopping to sit beside the youth, he went up past him, resting his hand on the other's shoulder so heavily that the boy looked up to see his father's face. But the father went on without saying anything: went into the house, on through the old closed-in dogtrot hall to the back porch, opened the country food press which had been converted to a gun cabinet, took down the double-barrel twelve-gauge Greener, loaded it, went up the back stairs into the attic, and, fitting the muzzle of the Greener into the notch of his breastbone, could still reach both triggers with his thumbs. That was how it had to happen, the sheriff told the youth, that was the only way it could have happened.

The sound came crashing through the music, louder than twenty Philcos, a single sound, yet more prolonged and thunderous than a single shot. The youth turned off the Philco and went upstairs.

"—and Anacin does not upset your stummick," said Bill Cullen.

Again his hand went forth, knowing where it was, though he could not see, and touched the tiny iron horsehead of the hitching post, traced the cold metal down to the place where the oak had grown round it in an elephant lip. His fingertips touched the warm finny whispering bark.

Wait. While his fingers explored the juncture of iron and bark, his eyes narrowed as if he caught a glimmer of light on the cold iron skull. *Wait.* I think he was wrong and that he was looking in the wrong place. No, not he but the times. The times were wrong and one looked in the wrong place. It wasn't even his fault because that was the way he was and the way the times were, and there was no other place a man could look. It was the worst of times, a time of fake beauty and fake victory. *Wait.* He had missed it! It was not in the Brahms that one looked and not in solitariness and not in the old sad poetry but—he wrung out his ear—but here, under your nose, here in the very curiousness and drollness and extraness of the iron and the bark that—he shook his head—that—

The TV studio audience laughed with its quick, obedient, and above all grateful Los Angeles laughter—once we were lonesome back home, the old sad home of our fathers, and here we are together and happy at last.

A Negro came whistling toward him under the street light, a young man his own age. Entering the darkness of the water oaks, the Negro did not at first see him (though it had been his, the Negro's, business, until now, to see him first), then did see him two yards away and stopped for a long half second. They looked at each other. There was nothing to say. Their fathers would have had much to say: "In the end, Sam, it comes down to a question of character." "Yes suh, Lawyer Barrett, you right about that. Like I was saying to my wife only this evening—" But the sons had nothing to say. The engineer looked at the other as the half second wore on. You may be in a fix and I know that but what you don't know and won't believe and must find out for yourself is that I'm in a fix too and you got to get where I am before you even know what I'm talking about and I know that and that's why there is nothing to say now. Meanwhile I wish you well.

It was only then, belatedly, as if it were required of him, that the Negro shuddered and went his way.

As he watched his aunts, a squad car came slowly down De Ridder and stopped not twelve feet beyond the iron horse. A policeman, not Ross or Gover, went up to the porch and spoke to Aunt Sophie. She shook her head four or five times, hand to her throat, and when the policeman left, turned off the television and in her excitement stumbled a little as she told the others. Aunt Bootie forgot the Whitman's Sampler in her lap, stood up and scattered nougats and bird eggs in all directions. No one noticed.

Without taking much care about it, he walked through the azaleas and around to the back screen door, which was locked and which he opened, without knowing that he remembered, by wedging the door back against its hinges so that the bolt could be forced free of its worn wooden mortise, and went straight up the two flights to the attic and straight into the windowless interior room built into the peak of the house. His uplifted hand felt for and found the string. The old clear-glass 25-watt bulb shed a yellow mizzling light, a light of rays, actual striae. The room had not been touched, they were still here; the grandfather's army blanket, Plattsburg issue, the puttees, a belt of webbing, the Kaiser Bill helmets, the five-pound binoculars with an artillery scale etched into one lens. He picked up the Greener, broke the breech and sighted at the yellow bulb. The bore was still speckled with powder grains. And the collapsible boat: an English contraption of silvery zeppelin fabric with varnished spruce spars to spring it into shape. It lay as it had lain ten years ago, half disassembled and hastily packed from a duck hunt he and his father had taken on the White River in the early fifties. Now, as if it were the very night of their return, he knelt absently and repacked the boat, remembering the feel and fit of the spar-ends and the brass sockets and even the goofy English directions: "—Don't be discouraged if spar L does not fit immediately into socket J—patience is required."

After he repacked the boat, he lay on the cot and, propping himself against the wall, drew the hard scratchy army blanket up to his armpits. For two hours he sat so, wakeful and alert, while his eyes followed the yellow drizzle of light into every corner of the attic room.

It was eight o'clock when he went downstairs, English boat slung over one shoulder, artillery binoculars over the other. The aunts had not gotten up. Hearing D'lo shuffling about the kitchen, he took care not to startle her: he slipped out the back door and came in noisily again.

"Law, if it ain't Mr. Billy," said D'lo, rolling her eyes conventionally and noticing the wall clock as she did so. She was no more surprised by the doings of white folks than he was.

D'lo stirred steaming boilers of grits and batter, fist sunk deep into her side, knees driven together by her great weight and bare heels ridden off her old pink mules and onto the floor. It crossed his mind that D'lo had somehow known he was here. He asked her not to tell his aunts.

"I ain't gon' tell them nothing!"

"I'm surprised you're still here."

"Where I'm going!"

"They still fight?"

"Fight! You don't know, fight."

"The police are looking for me."

"Uh-oh," said D'lo. This was serious. Yet he could not have sworn she did not know all about it.

D'lo found him his father's Rolls razor and, while he washed and shaved in the downstairs bathroom, fixed him a big breakfast of grits and sausage and batter cakes. When he left, he gave her twenty dollars.

"I thank you," said D'lo formally and twisted the bill into the stocking roll below her fat old knee, which curved out in six different arcs of rich cinnamon flesh.

A step creaked. "Here *she* come," said D'lo. Sophie was *she*, ole miss, the one who gave the orders.

"I'll be seeing you, D'lo," he said, shouldering the boat.

"All right now, Mist' Billy," she cried politely, socking down the grits spoon on the boiler and curling her lip in a rich and complex acknowledgment of his own queerness and her no more than mild sympathy and of the distance between them, maybe not even sympathy but just a good-humored letting him be. (All right now, you was a good little boy, but don't mess with me too much, go on, get out of my kitchen.)

Ten minutes later he was up and over the levee and down into the willows, where he assembled the boat and the two-bladed paddle. It was a sparkling day. The river was ruffled by glittering steel wavelets like a northern lake. Shoving off and sitting buttoned up kayak style in the aft hole, he went dropping away in the fast water, past the barrow pits and blue holes, and now beginning to paddle, went skimming over the wide river, which seemed to brim and curve up like a watchglass from the great creamy boils that shed tons of cold bottom water, down past old Fort Ste. Marie on the Louisiana side, its ramparts gone back to blackberries and honeysuckle. He knew every tunnel, embrasure, magazine room, and did not bother to look. Two Negroes in a skiff were running a trotline under the caving bank. They watched him a second longer than they might have. Now they were watching him again, under their arms as they handed a line along. He frowned, wondering how he looked in the face, then recollected himself: it was after all an uncommon sight, a man fully dressed in coat and necktie and buttoned up in a tiny waterbug of a boat and at nine o'clock of a Tuesday morning. They could not encompass him; he was beyond their reckoning. But hold on, something new! As he drifted past the fort, he rubbed his eyes. A pennant fluttered from the parapet, the Stars and Bars! And the entire fort was surrounded by a ten-foot-high hurricane fence. But of course! This very month marked the hundredth anniversary of the reduction of the fort by Admiral Foote's gunboats. It was part of the preparation for the Centennial! No doubt they would, at the proper time, imprison the "Confederates" behind the fence.

But as he dropped past the fort, he was surprised to see "sentinels" patrolling the fence and even a few prisoners inside, but as unlikely a lot of Confederates as one could imagine—men and women! the men bearded properly enough, but both sexes blue-jeaned and sweated-shirted and altogether disreputable. And Negroes! And yonder, pacing the parapet—Good Lord!—was Milo Menander, the politician, who was evidently playing the role of Beast Banks, the infamous federal commandant of the infamous federal prison into which the fort was converted after its capture. Capital! And hadn't he got himself up grandly for the occasion: flowing locks, big cigar, hand pressed Napoleonically into his side, a proper villainous-looking old man if ever there was one.

But hold on! Something was wrong. Were they not two years late with their celebration? The fort was captured early in the war, and here it was 19 — What year was this? He wrang out his ear and beat his pockets in vain for his Gulf calendar card. Another slip: if Beast Banks had reduced and occupied the fort, why was the Stars and Bars still flying?

It was past figuring even it he'd a stomach for figuring. Something may be amiss here, but then all was not well with him either. Next he'd be hearing singing ravening particles. Besides, he had other fish to fry and many a mile to travel. British wariness woke in him and, putting his head down, he dropped below the fort as silently as an Englishman slipping past Heligoland.

SHELBY FOOTE

(1916–)

Fiction and history have been kindred passions for Shelby Foote, and each has reinforced the other. He began his literary career as a novelist, moved in his fiction toward his regional past, spent twenty years writing a military history of the Civil War, then returned to fiction with renewed mastery.

A native of Greenville, Mississippi, he came under the influence of William Alexander Percy and grew up with Walker Percy, with whom he attended the University of North Carolina. In 1940 he went on active Army duty in the field artillery. Discharged in 1944 he worked briefly as a newspaperman in New York City, then spent eleven months in the U.S. Marines. His first novel, *Tournament*, begun before the war, was published in 1949. In the next year *Follow Me Down* appeared, and in 1951 *Love in a Dry Season*. This was followed by *Shiloh* (1952), a novel based on a Civil War battle. With *Jordan County*, published in 1954, he essayed a set of related short stories that carried the history of this mythical county back to earliest colonial times. The following story is from that collection.

Also in 1954 he began work on what was originally planned as a one-volume narrative history of the Civil War. As he became immersed in his subject, however, it grew both in range and depth. Volume I of *The Civil War: A*

Narrative appeared in 1958, Volume II in 1963, and the third and final volume not until 1974. Magisterial, profound in its intricate patterning of the major campaigns, personalities, and evolving meanings of the war, it provides a portrait of the four years of conflict that joins the narrative sweep of the novel with the painstaking historical fidelity of minutely researched nonfiction.

Foote returned to fiction in 1978 with *September, September*, a fast-moving story about a kidnapping, with complex racial and social overtones. It is set in Memphis, Tennessee, where he has made his home since the early 1950s. A wartime marriage ended in divorce, and in 1953 he married Gwyn Rainer of Memphis. He is now at work on a fictional trilogy.

THE SACRED MOUND

Province of Mississippi, A.D. 1797
Number 262: CRIMINAL

Against the Indian, Chisahahoma (John Postoak) *of the Choctaws, self-accused of the grisly murders of* Lancelot Fink *and*_____Tyree (*or* Tyree_____) *1796.*
   Master Fiscal Judge, Mr John the Baptist of Elquezable, *Lieutenant Colonel and Governor.*

Scrivener,
Andrew Benito Courbiere.

DECLARATION: HEREIN SWORN & SUBSCRIBED. In the town of Natchez and garrison of St Iago, on the 23d of September, 1797, I, Mr John the Baptist of Elquezable, Lieutenant Colonel of Cavalry and Provisional Governor of this said Province of Mississippi, proceeded to the house Royal of said town (accompanied from the first by Lieutenant Francisco Amangual and Ensign Joseph of Silva, both of the company of my office, as witnesses in the present procedure) where I found the prisoner Chisahahoma, a young man of the color of dusky copper, smallpox pitted, with hair cut straight along his forehead and falling lank to his shoulders at the back, who having been commanded to appear in my presence and in that of the said witnesses, before them had put to him by me the following interrogatories:

Question. What is he called, of what country is he a native, and what religion he professes? Answered that he is called Chisahahoma, that he is a native to a region six sleeps north and also on the river, and that he is a Roman Catholic these nine months since the turning of the year. *Q.* Is he sufficiently acquainted with the Spanish language, or if he needs an interpreter to explain his declaration? Answered that he understood the language after a fashion and that if he doubted any question he would call for the advice of the interpreter. *Q.* If he would promise by our Lord God and the sign of the Cross to speak the truth concerning these interrogations? Answered that he would promise and swear, and did. And spoke as follows, making first the sign of the Cross and kissed his thumbnail:

Lo: truth attend his words, the love of God attend our understanding: all men are brothers. He has long wanted to cleanse his breast of the matter herein related, and has done so twice: first to the priest, as shall be told, then to the sergeant, answering his heart as advised by the priest, and now to myself makes thrice. His people and my people have lived in enmity since the time of the man Soto (so he called him, of glorious memory in the annals of Spain: Hernando de Soto) who came in his forefathers' time, appearing in May two sleeps to the north, he and his men wild-looking and hairy, wearing garments of straw and the skins of animals under their armor; who, having looked on the river, crossed westward and was gone twelve moons, and reappeared (in May again) three sleeps to the south, his face gray and wasted to the bone; and died there, and was buried in the river.

Desecration! his forefathers cried. Pollution!

So they fought: the strangers in armor, man and horse looking out through slits in the steel—of which he says rusty fragments survive in the long-house to commemorate the battle where the Spaniards (he says) wore blisters on their palms with excess of killing—swinging their swords and lances wearily and standing in blood to the rowels of their spurs: and at last retreated, marched away to the south, and were seen no more.

Then all was quiet; the young ones might have believed their fathers dreamed it, except for the rusting bits of armor and the horse skulls raised on poles in the long-house yard. Then came other white men in canoes, wearing not steel but robes of black with ropes about their waists, and bearing their slain god on a cross of sticks, whose blood ran down from a gash in his side: saying, Bow down; worship; your gods are false; This is the true God! and sang strange songs, swinging utensils that sprinkled and smoked, and partook of the wafer and a thin blood-colored liquid hot to the throat; then went away. But the Choctaws kept their gods, saying: How should we forsake the one that made us of spit and straw and a dry handful of dust and sent us here out of Nanih Waiya? How should we exchange Him for one who let himself be stretched on sticks with nails through the palms of his hands and feet, a headdress of thorns, pain in his face, and a spearpoint gash in his side where the life ran out?

Q. Was he here to blaspheme?—for his eyes rolled back showing only the whites and he chanted singsong fashion. Answered nay, he but told it as it was in the dark time; he was the Singer, as all his fathers had been. And continued:

Then came others down the years, also in boats—all came by the river since Soto's time—but bearing neither the arquebus nor the Cross: bringing goods to trade, beads of colored stuff and printed cloth and magic circles no bigger than the inside of a hand, where sunlight flashed and a man could see himself as in unspillable water; for which, all these, the traders sought only the skins of animals in return. Now of all the creatures of the field, only certain ones were worthy of being hunted by a man: the bear, the deer, the broad-wing turkey—the rest were left for boys. Yet the traders prized highest the pelt of a creature not even a boy would hunt: the beaver: and this caused his people to feel a certain contempt. Lo, too, these strangers placed an undue value on women, for they would force or woo a man's wife and lie with her, not asking the husband's permission or agreeing before-hand on a price or an exchange, and though they were liberal with their gifts when the thing was done, there began to be not only contempt but also hard feelings in the breasts of his people.

So much was legend: he but told it as his father before him told it, having it from the father before him, and so on back. Yet what follows, he says, he saw with his own eyes and heard with his ears; God be his witness. And continued, no longer with his eyes rolled, speaking singsong, but as one who saw and heard and now reported (making once more, in attest of truth, the Cross upon his breastbone):

Two summers back, in the late heat of the year, spokesmen arrived from many sleeps to the south, near the great salt river. Three they were, the sons of chiefs, tall men sound of wind and limb, sent forth by their fathers, say-ing: We have a thing to impart. Will our brothers hear? That night they rested and were feasted in the long-house, and runners went out to bring in the chiefs. Next day as the sun went bleeding beyond the river all assembled on the sacred mound, the leaders and the singers (himself being one) and the three came forward, lean with travel, clean-favored and handsome in feathers and paint, upright as became the sons of chiefs, and the tallest spoke. It is transcribed.

—Brothers: peace. We bring a message and a warning. May you hear and heed and so be served. The white ones speak with forked tongues, no matter what crown they claim their great chief wears beyond the sea. We bring a warning of calamity. It will be with you as it was with us, for they will do as they have done. Thus. First they came boasting of their gods and seeking a yellow metal in their various languages: Or, they call it, or Oro. Then, in guile, they exchanged valuables for the worthless pelts of animals, calling us Brother, and we believed and answered likewise, Brother. And they lived among us and shared our pipe and all was well between us. So we thought.

—Then, lo, they began to ask a strange thing of us, seeking to buy the land. Sell us the land, they said: Sell us the land. And we told them, disguis-ing our horror: No man owns the land; take and live on it; it is lent you for your lifetime; are we not brothers? And they appeared satisfied. They put up houses of plank and iron, like their ships, and sent back for their women. Soon they were many; the bear and the deer were gone (—they had seen and known in their hearts, without words; but we, being men with words, were blind) and the white men sent forth laws and set up courts, saying This shalt thou do and This shalt thou not do, and punishment followed hard upon offense, both the whip and the branding iron and often the rope. And we said, Can this be? Are we not brothers, to dwell in one land? And they answered, Yea: but this is Law.

—Nor was it long till the decree came forth, in signs on paper nailed to the walls of houses and even on trees, and the chiefs were called into the courts to hear it read. Go forth, the judges read: Go forth from the land, you and your people, into the north or beyond the river; for this land now is ours. And our fathers spoke, no longer trying to disguise the horror: How can this be? Are we not brothers? How can we leave this land, who were sent here out of Nanih Waiya to dwell in it forever down through time? And they answered, Howsomever.

—So it was and is with us, for our people are collecting their goods and preparing for the journey out. So too will it be with you. And soon; for this was all in our own time, and we are young.

I have spoken, the tallest said, and rejoined the circle. The chiefs sat smoking. Then another of the young men spoke, asking permission to retire to the long-house to sleep, for they had far to go tomorrow. And it was granted; they left, all three; and still the chiefs sat smoking.

The moon rose late, red and full to the rear of where the chiefs sat passing the pipe from hand to hand. But no one spoke, neither the chiefs on the mound nor the people below, their faces back-tilted, looking up. Then one did speak—Loshumitubbe, the oldest chief, with the hawk beak and thin gray hair that his ears showed through, a great killer in his day, and lines in his face like earth where rain has run: saying, Yea, the moon be my witness: we have offended, we have strayed. This is not the cunning of the white man. This is anger from the gods. They want it as it was in the old time.

So saying, he made a quick, downward motion with the pipe; it might have been a hatchet or a knife. Some among them understood, the older chiefs and the singers—he being one—and nodded their heads, saying Yea, or smoked in silence. And down at the base of the mound the people waited, faces pale in the moonlight, looking up. After a term the chiefs spoke in turn, grave-faced, drawing out the words, some for and some against. By morning it was decided; they came down off the mound with their minds made up.

Runners were sent one sleep to the north: five they were, strung out along the river bank, a hard run apart. Three weeks the people waited. It was cold and then it faired, the air hazy, leaves bright red and yellow though not yet brown; it was nearing the time of the corn dance, when a man's heart should rejoice for the fruits of the earth. And the people said to one another behind their hands, Can this thing be? (for such had not been done since far before the time of the man Soto; not even in that hard time, he says, was such a thing considered) but others answered, not behind their hands but openly, proud to have gone back: Yea, can and shall: Loshumitubbe says it.

Then came one running, the nearest of the five posted along the river bank, running with his legs unstrung, and knelt before Loshumitubbe, unable to speak but holding up two fingers. Then he could speak, panting the words between breaths: Two come by water. Trappers, O chief. In buckskin.

Here was a halt, the dinner hour being come. Next morning, again at the house Royal, immediately I, the said Governor, together with the aforesaid witnesses of my company, commanded to appear before me Chisahahoma, whom I found a prisoner in the care of the guard as before and still in bonds, who once more subscribed and swore the oath and resumed as follows, confronting the witnesses and Benito Courbiere, scrivener:

That night in the long-house they played the drum and painted, himself among them. Next morning they waited in the willows down at the river bank, again himself among them. For a long time, nothing. The sun went past the overhead; they waited. Then two together pointed, raising each an arm: Lo: for the trappers were rounding the bend in a canoe. Still they waited, knee-deep in the water, screened by willows, watching. The trappers held near to bank, seeking signs of game—one tall and slim; he sat in the stern, and the other short and fat; he was the older. They wondered if they could catch them, for his people had only dugouts: when suddenly the man in the bow stopped paddling. Lance! he shouted, and pointed directly at the willow clump. So he and his people bent their backs to launch out in pursuit. But the one in the stern changed sides with his paddle and the canoe swung crossways to the current, approaching. A sign from the gods, his people thought; their hearts grew big with elation. And when the two were within arm's length they took them so quickly they had not even time to reach for their rifles. Truly a sign from the gods! his people cried, and some began to leap and scream, squeezing their throats with their hands to make it shriller.

So the two were bound at the water's edge and brought up to the town, walking hunched for their wrists were strapped with rawhide at the crotch, one hand coming through from the rear and one from the front so they cound not stand upright, though the tall one almost could; his arms were long. They were marched the length of the street, the smell of fear coming strong off the short one. Bent forward—his arms were short, his belly large —he turned his head this way and that, watching the gestures of the women hopping alongside, the potbellied children staring round-eyed, and skipped to save his ankles from the dogs; twice he fell and had to be lifted from the dust. The tall one, however, kept his eyes to the front. The dogs did not snap at him, for even bound he was half a head taller than any Indian.

Hi! the women shouted: Hi! A brave! and made gestures of obscenity, fanning their skirts. Hi! Hi!

The chiefs sat in the council room, wearing feathers and paint in gaudy bars, and the two were brought before them. Now they looked at each other, chiefs and trappers, and no one spoke. Then Loshumitubbe made a gesture, the hand palm down, pushing downward, and they were taken to the pit room at the far end of the long-house. It was dark in there, no fire; the only light was what fell through the paling disk of the smoke hole. The cries of the women came shrill through the roof, mixed with the yapping of dogs. The time wore on. From outside, he says, they began to hear the short one weeping, asking questions in his language, but the tall one only cursed him, once then twice, and then ignored him.

So it was: they on the outside, waiting for the moon to fill, knowing; the trappers on the inside, in the pit, waiting but not knowing. Seven suns they were in there, feeding like hogs on broken bits of food flung through the smoke hole—for they remained bound, the rawhide shrinking on their wrists, and had to grovel for it. They fouled themselves and were gut-sick on the scraps, he says, and the stench was so great that the women approaching the hole to taunt them held their noses and made squealing sounds. From outside, listening, his people heard words in the strange language: at first only the short one, calling the other Fink or Lance and sometimes Lancelot: then later, toward the close, the tall one too, calling the short one Tyree, though which of his two names this was no man could say, not even now, for they were Americans, a people whose names are sometimes indistinguishable, the last from the first, since they name not necessarily for the saints. At the end, however, they called to one another not by name but by growls, for the food was scant and hard to find on the dark earth floor; they fought for it like dogs, snapping their teeth, still being bound.

Then, lo, the moon would be full that night. Long before sundown the people were painted and ready, dressed as for the corn dance. The young ones wore only breech clouts and feathers, fierce with red and yellow bars of paint, but the older ones brought out blankets rancid with last year's grease and sweat. The cold had returned; the leaves were brown now, falling, and they crackled underfoot. It was yet above freezing, he says, and there was no wind, but the cold was steady and bitter and sharp and a thick mist came rolling off the river.

The trappers were taken from the pit as soon as the sun was gone. Their clothes were cut from their bodies and they were sluiced with hot water to cleanse them of their filth; they stood in only their boots and bonds, their hands purple and puffy because the rawhide had shrunk on their wrists, their skin first pink from the heat of the water, then pale gray, goose-fleshed.

and their teeth chattered behind their bluing lips. Then was when they saw that the short one was covered with what appeared to be louse bites, small hard red welts like pimples. The time in the pit had changed them indeed, and not only in appearance. For now it was the tall one who kept glancing about, shifting his eyes this way and that, while the short one stood looking down over his belly at his boots; he did not care. Just as the tall one had used up his courage, so had the short one exhausted his cowardice. Then at a signal the guards took told of their arms and they went toward the mound, stepping stiff-kneed. The old men with blankets over their shoulders walked alongside. The young men, wearing only feathers and breech clouts, leaped and shouted, their breaths making steam.

Atop the mound the chiefs were waiting, seated in a half circle with a bonfire burning behind them for light. They faced the stakes. One was a single pole with a rawhide thong up high; the other was two low poles with a third lashed as a crosspiece at the height of a man's waist. Then the trappers were brought. From the flat top of the mound, he says, they could see torches burning in the lower darkness, spangling the earth, countless as stars, for the people had come from three sleeps around; they stood holding torches, looking up to where the bonfire burned against the night. The tall trapper was tied to the single stake, arms overhead, hands crossed so high that only the toes of his boots touched the earth—the tallest man they had ever seen, taller than ever, now, with skin as pale in the firelight as the underbark of sycamores in spring. The short trapper stood between the two low stakes, his wrists lashed to the crossbar on each side of his waist. Both were breathing fast little jets of steam, partly from having climbed the mound but mostly from fear; for now, he says, they knew at least a part of what they had been wondering all that long time in the darkness of the pit.

The moon rose, swollen golden red, and now the dancing began, the young men stepping pigeon-toed, shuffling dust, and Otumatomba the rainmaker stood by the fire with his knife. When the dancing was done he came forward, extending the knife flat on the palms of both hands, and Loshumitubbe touched it. The drums began. Then Otumatomba came slowly toward the short one, who was held by four of the dancers, two at the knees and two at the shoulders, bent backward over the crosspole. He did not struggle or cry out; he looked down his chest, past the jut of his belly, watching the knife. What follows happened so fast, he says, that afterwards looking back it seemed to have been done in the flick of an eye.

Otumatomba placed the point of the knife, then suddenly leaned against the handle and drew it swiftly across, a long deep slash just under the last left rib. So quick the eye could barely follow, his hand went in The knife fell and the hand came out with the heart. It was meaty and red, the size of a fist, with streaks of yellow fat showing through the skin-sack; vessels dangled, collapsed and dripping, except the one at the top, which was dingy white, the thickness of a thumb, leading back through the lips of the gash.

Then (there was no signal, he says; they knew what to do, for Otumatomba had taught them) the men at the shoulders pushed forward, bringing the trapper upright off the bar, and for a moment he stood looking down at his heart, which Otumatomba held in front of his chest for him to see. It did not pulse; it flickered, the skinsack catching highlights from the fire, and it smoked a bit in the night air. That was all. The short one fell, collapsing; he hung with his face just clear of the ground, his wrists still tied to the cross-pole.

Hi! a brave, he heard one say among the chiefs.

But that was all; the rest were quiet as the rainmaker took up the knife again and turned toward the tall one, lashed on tiptoe to the stake. As he drew closer the trapper began to swing from side to side, bound overhead at the wrists and down at the ankles. When Otumatomba was very near, the tall white man began to shout at him in his language: No! No! swinging from side to side and shouting hoarsely, until the rainmaker, with a sudden darting motion like the strike of a snake, shot out one hand and caught hold: whereupon the trapper stopped swinging and shouted still more shrilly, like women in the longhouse at the death of a chief, in the final moment before the cutting began. While Otumatomba sawed with the knife, which seemed duller now and slippery with the blood of the other, the tall one was screaming, hysterical like a woman in labor, repeating a rising note: Ee! Eee! Then he stopped. He stopped quite suddenly. Otumatomba stepped back and tossed the trapper's manhood at his feet. The trapper looked down—more than pain, his face showed grief, bereavement—and now he began to whimper. Blood ran down his thighs, curving over the inward bulge of his knees, and filled his boots. He was a long time dying and he died badly, still crying for mercy when he was far beyond it.

Again the young men danced. The moon sailed higher, silver now, flooding the mound. In the distance the river glided slow, bright silver too, making its two great curves. Then it was over; the dead were left to the bone-pickers. The chiefs rose, filing down the mound, and he heard Loshumitubbe say to one beside him:

This will stop them. This will make an end.

Yea, the other told him. This will stop them.

But some there were—himself among them: so he says—who shook their heads, now it was done and they had seen, asking themselves in their hearts: Were they savages, barbarians, to come to this?

Here was a halt, the hour being noon, and after the midday meal and the siesta we returned to the house Royal: I the Governor, together with the aforesaid witnesses and scrivener: before whom the prisoner Chisahahoma, in care of the guard, swore and subscribed and continued, making an end:

Sudden and terrible then came the curse on his people, the wrath of God. The moon was barely on the wane and they felt pain in their heads, their backs, their loins; their skin was hot and dry to the touch; dark spots appeared on their foreheads and scalps, among the roots of hair. The spots became hard-cored blisters; the burning cooled for a day and then returned, far worse, and the blisters (so he called them: meaning *pustules*) softened and there was a terrible itching. Some scratched so hard with their nails and fishbone combs that their faces and bodies were raw. Many died. First went Otumatomba the rainmaker, then Loshumitubbe chief of chiefs, he who had given the signal; men and women and children, so fast they died the bone-pickers had not time to scaffold them. They lay in the houses and in the street, self-mutilated, begging the god for sudden death, release from the fever and itching.

He himself was sick with the sickest, and thought to have died and wished for it; he too lay and hoped for death, but was spared with only this (passing his hand across his face) to show the journey he had gone. Then he lay recovering, the moon swelling once more toward the full. And he remembered the short trapper, the marks on his face and body when they brought him out of the pit, and he knew.

Then he was up, recovered though still weak, and was called before Issatiwamba, chief of chiefs now Loshumitubbe was dead. He too had been the journey; he too remembered the marks on the short trapper. The people still lay dying, the dead unscaffolded.

O chief, he said, and made his bow, and Issatiwamba said:

I have called; are you not the singer? This is the curse of the white man's god, and you must go a journey.

He left next morning, taking the trappers' canoe. Cold it was, approaching the turning of the year, with ice among the willows and overhead a sky the color of a dove's breast. He wore a bearskin and paddled fast to keep from freezing. The second day he reached the Walnut Hills, where the white man had a town, and went ashore. But there was no house for the white man's god; he was in the canoe, continuing downriver, before sunset. The fifth day he reached this place and came ashore, and here was the house of the white man's god and, lo! the God himself as he had heard it told and sung, outstretched and sagging, nailed to the wall and wearing a crown of thorns and the wound in his side and pain in his face that distorted his mouth so you saw the edges of the teeth. And he stood looking, wrapped in the bearskin.

Then came one in a robe of cloth, a man who spoke with words he could not understand. He made a sign to show he would speak, and the priest beckoned: Come, and he followed to the back of the house and through a door, and—lo again, a thing he had never seen before—here was an Indian wearing trousers and a shirt, one of the flatheads of the South, who acted as interpreter.

The priest listened while he told it as Issatiwamba had instructed. The Indians had killed in the Indian way, incurring the wrath of the white man's god; now was he sent for the white men to kill in the white man's way, thus to appease the god and lay the plague. So he told it, as instructed. The flathead interpreted and when it was done the priest beckoned as before: *Come*, and led the way through another door. He followed, expecting this to be the pit where he would wait. But lo, the priest put food before him: *Eat*, and he ate. Then he followed through yet another door, thinking now surely this would be the pit. But lo again, it was a small room with a cot and blankets, and the priest put his hands together, palm to palm, and laid his cheek against the back of one: *Sleep*. And he slept, still expecting the pit.

When he woke it was morning; he knew not where he was. The pit! he thought. Then he remembered and turned on his side, and the flathead stood in the doorway with a bucket in one hand, steaming, and soap and cloth in the other. First he declined; it was winter, he said, no time to scrape away the crust. But the other said thus it must be, and when he had washed he led him to the room where he had eaten. He ate again, then followed the other still to a third room where the priest was waiting, and there again on the wall the god was hung, this time in ivory with the blood in bright red droplets like fruit of the holly. The three sat at table; the priest talked and the flathead interpreted, and all this time the god watched from the wall. Here began his conversion, he says, making yet again the sign of the Cross upon his person.

He heard of the Trinity, the creation, the Garden, the loss of innocence, and much else which he could not follow. When the priest later questioned him of what he had heard he found that he had not heard aright, for the priest had said there were three gods and one god; did that not make four? And the priest at first was angry: then he smiled. They had best go slow, he said, and began again, telling now of the Man-God, the redeemer, who died on the cross of sticks but would return. There was where he began to understand, for just as the Garden had been like Nanih Waiya, this was like the Corn God, who laid him down to rise again; perhaps they were cousins, the two gods. But the priest said no, not cousins, not cousins at all; and began again, in soft tones and with patience, not in anger. In time they needed the interpreter no more, for he believed and the words came to him; he understood; Christ Jesus had reached him, Whose strength was in His gentleness, Whose beginning was in His end. Winter was past, and spring came on, and summer, and he was shrived and christened. His name was John; John Postoak, for Postoak was the translation of his name.

Then, being converted, he called to mind the instructions of Issatiwamba; a duty was a duty, whether to tribe or to church. So he asked the priest, kneeling at confession: must he go to the authorities? For a time the priest said nothing, sitting in the box with the odor of incense coming off him, the smell of holiness, and he who now was called Postoak watching through the panel. Then he said, calling him now as always My Son, that was a matter to be decided within himself, between his heart and his head. And he said as before, Bless me, father: knowing. And the priest put forth his hand and blessed him, making the sign of the Cross above his head, for the priest knew well what would follow when he went before the authorities and told what he had told the day when the priest first found him in the bearskin, outside the church where Christ hung on the wall.

He went then to the sergeant of the guard, Delgado, and standing there told it in Spanish, what had been done on the mound and how and his share in the thing, and offered himself this second time, as instructed by Issatiwamba, not to lay the plague, however, but rather to lay the guilt in his own breast. Delgado heard him through, listening with outrage in his face, and when it was done gave orders in a voice that rang like brass. Then was he in the pit indeed, with iron at his wrists and ankles. He dwelt in darkness, how many days he knew not; the year moved into September, the hottest weather; and then forth under guard to face ourselves, Governor and witnesses, in the formalities which ensued and here have been transcribed even as he spoke, including whatever barbarisms, all his own. So it was and here he stands, having told it this third time: God be his witness.

Q. If he had anything to add or take from this deposition, it having been read to him. Answered that he has nothing to add or take, and that what he has said is the truth under the obligation of the oath he took at the outset, which he affirms and certifies and says he is twenty-four years old, and he subscribes with me and the witnesses over the citation I certify:

Witnessed:	*he signs this*	John the Baptist
Joseph of Silva	Chisa- -hahoma	of Elquezable
Frsco Amangual	HIS MARK	Lt Col Governor

DISPOSITION: BY THE GOVERNOR. In the said Garrison this September 27th 1797 without delay I, Mr John the Baptist of Elquezable, Lieutenant Colonel of Cavalry of the Royal Army, Provisional Governor of the Province of Mississippi, in view of finding the conclusion of the present proceedings, commanded that the original fifteen useful leaves be directed to the Lord Commanding General, Marshal of the Country, Sir Peter de Narva, that they may serve to inform him in reviewing my disposition (tendered subject to his agreeing in the name of His Most Christian Majesty) to wit:

Free him.

First: in that he has renounced his former worship which led him to participate in these atrocities, and intends now therefore (I am assured by the priest, Friar Joseph Manuel Gaetan) to serve as a missionary among his heathen people. Second: in that we are even now preparing to depart this barbarous land, being under orders to leave it to them of the North. And third, lastly: in that the victims were neither of our Nation nor our Faith.

For which I sign with my present scrivener:

J the B
of El

A Benito
Courbiere.

JAMES DICKEY

(1923–   )

James Dickey's poetry is marked by a highly intense, formal, cadenced language working with and against an impassioned, personal, emotional statement; though his work is seldom in rhyme, it is metrically intricate and compressed, so that far from seeming loose and slack, it moves in sustained bursts of image and meaning. Much of his best verse is drawn directly from his own life: a Southern, urban, middle-class experience, in which the role of the poet is to note and point out the extraordinary, profound dimensions of seemingly commonplace people, events, emotions. Performing tricks with a piece of string, serving as lifeguard at a lake, observing a man at work on a power line—from such beginnings Dickey develops his poems.

A native of Atlanta, Georgia, he enrolled at Clemson University on a football scholarship, then served as a fighter pilot in the Pacific during World War II. He returned to school afterwards, taking his bachelor's and master's degrees at Vanderbilt University. He taught for a while, was called back to active Air Force duty during the Korean War, and then for a time wrote advertising copy in Atlanta. In 1960 his first book of poems, *Into the Stone*, was published. The following year he resigned from the advertising business to make his career as a poet and teacher. He taught at various colleges and universities, served as consultant in poetry at the Library of Congress, and wrote steadily. His books include *Drowning With Others* (1962), *Helmets* (1964), *Buckdancer's Choice* (1966), which won the National Book Award in 1966, and *Poems 1957–1967* (1967). In the late 1960s he drew on his outdoors experience for a novel, *Deliverance*, which when published in 1970 was a best-seller and became a widely popular motion picture. Meanwhile he joined the faculty of the University of South Carolina, where he now teaches. He has since published several volumes of poetry and some literary criticism and self-interviews. His wife Maxine died in 1976, and he married Deborah Dodson in 1977.

JAMES DICKEY

POWER AND LIGHT

. . . only connect . . .
　　　E. M. Forster

I may even be
A man, I tell my wife: all day I climb myself
Bowlegged up those damned poles　　rooster-heeled in all
Kinds of weather　　and what is there when I get
Home? Yes, woman trailing ground-oil
Like a snail, home is where I climb down,
And this is the house I pass through on my way

To power and light.
Going into the basement is slow, but the built-on smell of home
Beneath home gets better with age　　the ground fermenting
And spilling through the barrel-cracks of plaster　　the dark
Lying on the floor, ready for use　　as I crack
The seal on the bottle　　like I tell you it takes
A man to pour whiskey in the dark　　and CLOSE THE DOOR between

The children and me.
The heads of nails drift deeper through their boards
And disappear. Years in the family dark have made me good
At this　　nothing else is so good　　pure fires of the Self
Rise crooning in lively blackness　　and the silence around them,
Like the silence inside a mouth, squirms with colors,
The marvellous worms of the eye float out into the real

World　　sunspots
Dancing as though existence were
One huge closed eye　　and I feel the wires running
Like the life-force along the limed rafters　　and all connections
With poles　　with the tarred naked belly-buckled black
Trees I hook to my heels　　with the shrill phone calls leaping
Long distance　　long distances through my hands　　all connections

Even the one
With my wife, turn good　　turn better than good　　turn good
Not quite, but in the deep sway of underground　　among the roots
That bend like branches　　all things connect　　and stream
Toward light and speech　　tingle　　rock like a powerline in wind,
Like a man working, drunk on pine-moves　　the sun in the socket
Of his shoulder　　and on his neck dancing like dice-dots,

THE STRING

And I laugh
Like my own fate watching over me night and day   at home
Underground   or flung up on towers walking
Over mountains   my charged hair standing on end   crossing
The sickled, slaughtered alleys of timber
Where the lines loop and crackle on their gallows.
Far under the grass of my grave, I drink like a man

The night before
Resurrection Day. My watch glows with the time to rise
And shine. Never think I don't know my profession
Will lift me: why, all over hell the lights burn in your eyes,
People are calling each other   weeping with a hundred thousand
Volts   making deals   pleading   laughing like fate,
Far off, invulnerable   or with the right word pierced

To the heart
By wires I held, shooting off their ghostly mouths,
In my gloves. The house spins   I strap crampons to my shoes
To climb the basement stairs, sinking my heels in the tree-
life of the boards. Thorns! Thorns! I am bursting
Into the kitchen, into the sad way-station
Of my home, holding a double handful of wires

Spitting like sparklers
On the Fourth of July. Woman, I know the secret of sitting
In light   of eating a limp piece of bread   under
The red-veined eyeball of a bulb. It is all in how you are
Grounded. To bread I can see, I say, as it disappears and agrees
With me   the dark is drunk   and I am a man
Who turns on. I am a man.

1967

THE STRING

Except when he enters my son,
The same age as he at his death,
I cannot bring my brother to myself.
I do not have his memory in my life,
Yet he is in my mind and on my hands.
I weave the trivial string upon a light
Dead before I was born.

Mark how the brother must live,
Who comes through the words of my mother.
I have been told he lay

JAMES DICKEY

In his death-bed singing with fever,
Performing with string on his fingers
Incredible feats of construction
There before he was born.

His Jacob's Coffin now
Floats deeply between my fingers.
The strings with my thin bones shake.
My eyes go from me, and down
Through my bound, spread hands
To the dead, from the kin of the dead,
Dead before I was born.

The gaze of genius comes back.
The rose-window of Chartres is in it,
And Diogenes' lines upon sand,
And the sun through the Brooklyn Bridge,
And, caught in a web, the regard
Of a skeletal, blood-sharing child
Dead before I was born.

I believe in my father and mother
Finding no hope in these lines.
Out of grief, I was myself
Conceived, and brought to life
To replace the incredible child
Who built on this string in a fever
Dead before I was born.

A man, I make the same forms
For my son, that my brother made,
Who learnt them going to Heaven:
The coffin of light, the bridge,
The cup and saucer of pure air,
Cradle of Cat, the Foot of a Crow
Dead before I was born.

I raise up the bridge and the tower.
I burn the knit coffin in sunlight
For the child who has woven this city:
Who loved, doing this, to die:
Who thought like a spider, and sang,
And completed the maze of my fingers,
Dead before I was born.

1959

WALKING ON WATER

Feeling it with me
On it, barely float, the narrow plank on the water,
I stepped from the clam-shell beach,
Breaking in nearly down through the sun
Where it lay on the sea,
And poled off, gliding upright
Onto the shining topsoil of the bay.

Later, it came to be said
That I was seen walking on water,
Not moving my legs
Except for the wrong step of sliding:
A child who leaned on a staff,
A curious pilgrim hiking
Between two open blue worlds,

My motion a miracle,
Leaving behind me no footprint,
But only the shimmering place
Of an infinite step upon water
In which sat still and were shining
Many marsh-birds and pelicans.
Alongside my feet, the shark

Lay buried and followed,
His eyes on my childish heels.
Thus, taking all morning to stalk
From one littered beach to another,
I came out on land, and dismounted,
Making marks in the sand with my toes
Which truly had walked there, on water,

With the pelicans beating their shadows
Through the mirror carpet
Down, and the shark pursuing
The boy on the burning deck
Of a bare single ship-wrecked board.
Shoving the plank out to sea, I walked
Inland, on numb sparkling feet,

With the sun on the sea unbroken,
Nor the long quiet step of the miracle
Doing anything behind me but blazing,
With the birds in it nodding their heads,

That must ponder that footstep forever,
Rocking, or until I return
In my ghost, which shall have become, then,

A boy with a staff,
To loose them, beak and feather, from the spell
Laid down by a balancing child,
Unstable, tight-lipped, and amazed,
And, under their place of enthrallment,
A huge, hammer-headed spirit
Shall pass, as if led by the nose into Heaven.

1960

FLANNERY O'CONNOR

(1925–1964)

During her less than forty years of life, much of it while crippled by the disease of the blood vessels that would eventually kill her as it had her father, Flannery O'Connor wrote two novels, two collections of short stories, and a few occasional pieces of nonfiction. Yet her reputation as an important, incisive writer of hauntingly powerful fiction in which Southerners of various kinds are made to play parts in a modern-day drama of salvation seems secure and lasting.

Mary Flannery O'Connor was born in Savannah, Georgia, in 1925. In 1938 the O'Connors moved to Milledgeville, Georgia. Her father died in 1941 of disseminated lupus erythematosis, a disease that attacks the body's connective tissues. In 1942 O'Connor graduated from Peabody High School and entered Georgia State College for Women. There she began writing fiction and drawing cartoons for the college yearbook. After graduation she attended the Writer's Workshop of the State University of Iowa, where she was awarded the Master of Fine Arts degree in 1947. The previous summer her first published short story appeared in *Accent*. For several years she lived in New York City and Connecticut, until in 1950 she suffered her first major attack of lupus and from then on lived with her mother on a farm, "Andalusia," near Milledgeville. *Wise Blood,* her first novel, appeared in 1952, but it was with her first collection of short stories, *A Good Man Is Hard to Find* (1955), that her fiction began to receive widespread recognition. Her second novel, *The Violent Bear It Away,* appeared in 1960. In 1964 her illness, which had for some years forced her to walk with crutches, flared up again and she died in August of that year. Another collection of short stories, *Everything That Rises Must Converge,* was published in 1965. In 1971 the *Complete Stories of Flannery O'Connor* received the National Book Award. A volume of her collected nonfiction, *Mystery and Manners*, was edited in 1969 by Sally and Robert Fitzgerald.

Flannery O'Connor was a Georgian and a Roman Catholic, a combination that she used to create some unusual fiction. Much of her work appears rooted in the great comic tradition of Middle Georgia literature, which goes back to the Old Southwestern humor of A. B. Longstreet and others in the early nineteenth century. There is something of the same delight in the doings of the rural folk, a fine eye for comic detail and exaggeration, a preoccupation with the humor inherent in the country-come-to-town situation, and the use of a narrative viewpoint that portrays rural highjinks from above, often in tones of appalled fascination. Added to this, however—and structuring and informing all her fiction—is an intense moral and theological concern whereby the worldly doings of her characters embody the weakness and sinfulness of unregenerate man and the workings of God's grace. Her emotional affinity is for those primitive fundamentalists who, like Haze Motes in *Wise Blood* and Mason Tarwater in *The Violent Bear It Away*, refuse to settle for the primacy of the things of this world and feel impelled to conduct their lives from the same perspective as the signs posted along the highways on which her unheeding materialists drive: WHERE WILL YOU SPEND ETERNITY? Each of Flannery O'Connor's stories is a carefully wrought commentary on her times, and in her best ones naturalistic surfaces, keen observation, and a shrewd ear for comic dialogue combine with the working out of a problem in moral self-realization to become fiction that, in Robert Fitzgerald's words, "must be called religious but with no false note in our voices, because her writing will make any false note that is applied to it very clear indeed."

THE LIFE YOU SAVE MAY BE YOUR OWN

The old woman and her daughter were sitting on their porch when Mr. Shiftlet came up their road for the first time. The old woman slid to the edge of her chair and leaned forward, shading her eyes from the piercing sunset with her hand. The daughter could not see far in front of her and continued to play with her fingers. Although the old woman lived in this desolate spot with only her daughter and she had never seen Mr. Shiftlet before, she could tell, even from a distance, that he was a tramp and no one to be afraid of. His left coat sleeve was folded up to show there was only half an arm in it and his gaunt figure listed slightly to the side as if the breeze were pushing him. He had on a black town suit and a brown felt hat that was turned up in front and down in the back and he carried a tin tool box by a handle. He came on, at an amble, up her road, his face turned toward the sun which appeared to be balancing itself on the peak of a small mountain.

The old woman didn't change her position until he was almost into her yard; then she rose with one hand fisted on her hip. The daughter, a large girl in a short blue organdy dress, saw him all at once and jumped up and began to stamp and point and make excited speechless sounds.

Mr. Shiftlet stopped just inside the yard and set his box on the ground and tipped his hat at her as if she were not in the least afflicted; then he turned toward the old woman and swung the hat all the way off. He had long black slick hair that hung flat from a part in the middle to beyond the tips of his ears on either side. His face descended in forehead for more than half its length and ended suddenly with his features just balanced over a jutting steel-trap jaw. He seemed to be a young man but he had a look of composed dissatisfaction as if he understood life thoroughly.

"Good evening," the old woman said. She was about the size of a cedar fence post and she had a man's gray hat pulled down low over her head.

The tramp stood looking at her and didn't answer. He turned his back and faced the sunset. He swung both his whole and his short arm up slowly so that they indicated an expanse of sky and his figure formed a crooked cross. The old woman watched him with her arms folded across her chest as if she were the owner of the sun, and the daughter watched, her head thrust forward and her fat helpless hands hanging at the wrists. She had long pink-gold hair and eyes as blue as a peacock's neck.

He held the pose for almost fifty seconds and then he picked up his box and came on to the porch and dropped down on the bottom step. "Lady," he said in a firm nasal voice, "I'd give a fortune to live where I could see me a sun do that every evening."

"Does it every evening," the old woman said and sat back down. The daughter sat down too and watched him with a cautious sly look as if he were a bird that had come up very close. He leaned to one side, rooting in his pants pocket, and in a second he brought out a package of chewing gum and offered her a piece. She took it and unpeeled it and began to chew without taking her eyes off him. He offered the old woman a piece but she only raised her upper lip to indicate she had no teeth.

Mr. Shiftlet's pale sharp glance had already passed over everything in the yard—the pump near the corner of the house and the big fig tree that three or four chickens were preparing to roost in—and had moved to a shed where he saw the square rusted back of an automobile. "You ladies drive?" he asked.

"That car ain't run in fifteen year," the old woman said. "The day my husband died, it quit running."

"Nothing is like it used to be, lady," he said. "The world is almost rotten."

"That's right," the old woman said. "You from around here?"

"Name Tom T. Shiftlet," he murmured, looking at the tires.

"I'm pleased to meet you," the old woman said. "Name Lucynell Crater and daughter Lucynell Crater. What you doing around here, Mr. Shiftlet?"

He judged the car to be about a 1928 or '29 Ford. "Lady," he said, and turned and gave her his full attention, "lemme tell you something. There's one of these doctors in Atlanta that's taken a knife and cut the human heart —the human heart," he repeated, leaning forward, "out of a man's chest and held it in his hand," and he held his hand out, palm up, as if it were slightly weighted with the human heart, "and studied it like it was a day-old chicken, and lady," he said, allowing a long significant pause in which his head slid forward and his clay-colored eyes brightened, "he don't know no more about it than you or me."

"That's right," the old woman said.

"Why, if he was to take that knife and cut into every corner of it, he still wouldn't know no more than you or me. What you want to bet?"

"Nothing," the old woman said wisely. "Where you come from, Mr. Shiftlet?"

He didn't answer. He reached into his pocket and brought out a sack of tobacco and a package of cigarette papers and rolled himself a cigarette, expertly with one hand, and attached it in a hanging position to his upper lip. Then he took a box of wooden matches from his pocket and struck one on his shoe. He held the burning match as if he were studying the mystery of flame while it traveled dangerously toward his skin. The daughter began to make loud noises and to point to his hand and shake her finger at him, but when the flame was just before touching him, he leaned down with his hand cupped over it as if he were going to set fire to his nose and lit the cigarette.

He flipped away the dead match and blew a stream of gray into the evening. A sly look came over his face. "Lady," he said, "nowadays, people'll do anything anyways. I can tell you my name is Tom T. Shiftlet and I come from Tarwater, Tennessee, but you never have seen me before: how you know I ain't lying? How you know my name ain't Aaron Sparks, lady, and I come from Singleberry, Georgia, or how you know it's not George Speeds and I come from Lucy, Alabama, or how you know I ain't Tompson Bright from Toolafalls, Mississippi?"

"I don't know nothing about you," the old woman muttered, irked.

"Lady," he said, "people don't care how they lie. Maybe the best I can tell you is, I'm a man; but listen lady," he said and paused and made his tone more ominous still, "what is a man?"

The old woman began to gum a seed. "What you carry in that tin box, Mr. Shiftlet?" she asked.

"Tools," he said, put back. "I'm a carpenter."

"Well, if you come out here to work, I'll be able to feed you and give you a place to sleep but I can't pay. I'll tell you that before you begin," she said.

There was no answer at once and no particular expression on his face.

He leaned back against the two-by-four that helped support the porch roof. "Lady," he said slowly, "there's some men that some things mean more to them than money." The old woman rocked without comment and the daughter watched the trigger that moved up and down in his neck. He told the old woman then that all most people were interested in was money, but he asked what a man was made for. He asked her if a man was made for money, or what. He asked her what she thought she was made for but she didn't answer, she only sat rocking and wondered if a one-armed man could put a new roof on her garden house. He asked a lot of questions that she didn't answer. He told her that he was twenty-eight years old and had lived a varied life. He had been a gospel singer, a foreman on the railroad, an assistant in an undertaking parlor, and he come over the radio for three months with Uncle Roy and his Red Creek Wranglers. He said he had fought and bled in the Arm Service of his country and visited every foreign land and that everywhere he had seen people that didn't care if they did a thing one way or another. He said he hadn't been raised thataway.

A fat yellow moon appeared in the branches of the fig tree as if it were going to roost there with the chickens. He said that a man had to escape to the country to see the world whole and that he wished he lived in a desolate place like this where he could see the sun go down every evening like God made it to do.

"Are you married or are you single?" the old woman asked.

There was a long silence. "Lady," he asked finally "where would you find you an innocent woman today? I wouldn't have any of this trash I could just pick up."

The daughter was leaning very far down, hanging her head almost between her knees, watching him through a triangular door she had made in her overturned hair; and suddenly fell in a heap on the floor and began to whimper. Mr. Shiftlet straightened her out and helped her get back in the chair.

"Is she your baby girl?" he asked.

"My only," the old woman said, "and she's the sweetest girl in the world. I would give her up for nothing on earth. She's smart too. She can sweep the floor, cook, wash, feed the chickens, and hoe. I wouldn't give her up for a casket of jewels."

"No," he said kindly, "don't ever let any man take her away from you."

"Any man come after her," the old woman said, " 'll have to stay around the place."

Mr. Shiftlet's eye in the darkness was focused on a part of the automobile bumper that glittered in the distance. "Lady," he said, jerking his short arm up as if he could point with it to her house and yard and pump, "there ain't a broken thing on this plantation that I couldn't fix for you, one-arm jackleg or not. I'm a man," he said with a sullen dignity, "even if I ain't a whole one. I got," he said, tapping his knuckles on the floor to emphasize the immensity of what he was going to say, "a moral intelligence!" and his face pierced out of the darkness into a shaft of doorlight and he stared at her as if he were astonished himself at this impossible truth.

The old woman was not impressed with the phrase. "I told you you could hang around and work for food," she said, "if you don't mind sleeping in that car yonder."

"Why listen, lady," he said with a grin of delight, "the monks of old slept in their coffins!"

"They wasn't as advanced as we are," the old woman said.

The next morning he began on the roof of the garden house while Lucynell, the daughter, sat on a rock and watched him work. He had not been around a week before the change he had made in the place was apparent. He had patched the front and back steps, built a new hog pen, restored a fence, and taught Lucynell, who was completely deaf and had never said a word in her life, to say the word "bird." The big rosy-faced girl followed him everywhere, saying "Burrttddt ddbirrrttdt," and clapping her hands. The old woman watched from a distance, secretly pleased. She was ravenous for a son-in-law.

Mr. Shiftlet slept on the hard narrow back seat of the car with his feet out the side window. He had his razor and a can of water on a crate that served him as a bedside table and he put up a piece of mirror against the back glass and kept his coat neatly on a hanger that he hung over one of the windows.

In the evenings he sat on the steps and talked while the old woman and Lucynell rocked violently in their chairs on either side of him. The old woman's three mountains were black against the dark blue sky and were visited off and on by various planets and by the moon after it had left the chickens. Mr. Shiftlet pointed out that the reason he had improved this plantation was because he had taken a personal interest in it. He said he was even going to make the automobile run.

He had raised the hood and studied the mechanism and he said he could tell that the car had been built in the days when cars were really built. You take now, he said, one man puts in one bolt and another man puts in another bolt and another man puts in another bolt so that it's a man for a bolt. That's why you have to pay so much for a car: you're paying all those men. Now if you didn't have to pay but one man, you could get you a cheaper car and one that had had a personal interest taken in it, and it would be a better car. The old woman agreed with him that this was so.

Mr. Shiftlet said that the trouble with the world was that nobody cared, or stopped and took any trouble. He said he never would have been able to teach Lucynell to say a word if he hadn't cared and stopped long enough.

"Teach her to say something else," the old woman said.

"What you want her to say next?" Mr. Shiftlet asked.

The old woman's smile was broad and toothless and suggestive. "Teach her to say 'sugarpie,' " she said.

Mr. Shiftlet already knew what was on her mind.

The next day he began to tinker with the automobile and that evening he told her that if she would buy a fan belt, he would be able to make the car run.

The old woman said she would give him the money. "You see that girl yonder?" she asked, pointing to Lucynell who was sitting on the floor a foot away, watching him, her eyes blue even in the dark. "If it was ever a man wanted to take her away, I would say, 'No man on earth is going to take that sweet girl of mine away from me!' but if he was to say, 'Lady, I don't want to take her away. I want her right here,' I would say, 'Mister, I don't blame you none. I wouldn't pass up a chance to live in a permanent place and get the sweetest girl in the world myself. You ain't no fool,' I would say."

"How old is she?" Mr. Shiftlet asked casually.

"Fifteen, sixteen," the old woman said. The girl was nearly thirty but because of her innocence it was impossible to guess.

"It would be a good idea to paint it too," Mr. Shiftlet remarked. "You don't want it to rust out."

"We'll see about that later," the old woman said.

The next day he walked into town and returned with the parts he needed and a can of gasoline. Late in the afternoon, terrible noises issued from the shed and the old woman rushed out of the house, thinking Lucynell was somewhere having a fit. Lucynell was sitting on a chicken crate, stamping her feet and screaming, "Burrddttt! bddurrddtttt!" but her fuss was drowned out by the car. With a volley of blasts it emerged from the shed, moving in a fierce and stately way. Mr. Shiftlet was in the driver's seat, sitting very erect. He had an expression of serious modesty on his face as if he had just raised the dead.

That night, rocking on the porch, the old woman began her business at once. "You want you an innocent woman, don't you?" she asked sympathetically. "You don't want none of this trash."

"No'm, I don't," Mr. Shiftlet said.

"One that can't talk," she continued, "can't sass you back or use foul language. That's the kind for you to have. Right there," and she pointed to Lucynell sitting cross-legged in her chair, holding both feet in her hands.

"That's right," he admitted. "She wouldn't give me any trouble."

"Saturday," the old woman said, "you and her and me can drive into town and get married."

Mr. Shiftlet eased his position on the steps.

"I can't get married right now," he said. "Everything you want to do takes money and I ain't got any."

"What you need with money?" she asked.

"It takes money," he said. "Some people'll do anything anyhow these days, but the way I think, I wouldn't marry no woman that I couldn't take on a trip like she was somebody. I mean take her to a hotel and treat her. I wouldn't marry the Duchesser Windsor," he said firmly, "unless I could take her to a hotel and giver something good to eat.

"I was raised thataway and there ain't a thing I can do about it. My old mother taught me how to do."

"Lucynell don't even know what a hotel is," the old woman muttered. "Listen here, Mr. Shiftlet," she said sliding forward in her chair, "you'd be getting a permanent house and a deep well and the most innocent girl in the world. You don't need no money. Lemme tell you something; there ain't any place in the world for a poor disabled friendless drifting man."

The ugly words settled in Mr. Shiftlet's head like a group of buzzards in the top of a tree. He didn't answer at once. He rolled himself a cigarette and lit it and then he said in an even voice, "Lady, a man is divided into two parts, body and spirit."

The old woman clamped her gums together.

"A body and a spirit," he repeated. "The body, lady, is like a house: it don't go anywhere; but the spirit, lady, is like a automobile: always on the move, always . . ."

"Listen. Mr. Shiftlet," she said, "my well never goes dry and my house is always warm in the winter and there's no mortgage on a thing about this place. You can go to the courthouse and see for yourself. And yonder under that shed is a fine automobile." She laid the bait carefully. "You can have it painted by Saturday. I'll pay for the paint."

In the darkness, Mr. Shiftlet's smile stretched like a weary snake waking up by a fire. After a second he recalled himself and said, "I'm only saying a man's spirit means more to him than anything else. I would have to take my wife off for the week end without no regards at all for cost. I got to follow where my spirit says to go."

"I'll give you fifteen dollars for a week-end trip," the old woman said in a crabbed voice. "That's the best I can do."

"That wouldn't hardly pay for more than the gas and the hotel," he said. "It wouldn't feed her."

"Seventeen-fifty," the old woman said. "That's all I got so it isn't any use you trying to milk me. You can take a lunch."

Mr. Shiftlet was deeply hurt by the word "milk." He didn't doubt that she had more money sewed up in her mattress but he had already told her he was not interested in her money. "I'll make that do," he said and rose and walked off without treating with her further.

On Saturday the three of them drove into town in the car that the paint had barely dried on and Mr. Shiftlet and Lucynell were married in the Ordinary's office while the old woman witnessed. As they came out of the courthouse, Mr. Shiftlet began twisting his neck in his collar. He looked morose and bitter as if he had been insulted while someone held him. "That didn't satisfy me none," he said. "That was just something a woman in an office did, nothing but paper work and blood tests. What do they know about my blood? If they was to take my heart and cut it out," he said, "they wouldn't know a thing about me. It didn't satisfy me at all."

"It satisfied the law," the old woman said sharply.

"The law," Mr. Shiftlet said and spit. "It's the law that don't satisfy me."

He had painted the car dark green with a yellow band around it just under the windows. The three of them climbed in the front seat and the old woman said, "Don't Lucynell look pretty? Looks like a baby doll." Lucynell was dressed up in a white dress that her mother had uprooted from a trunk and there was a Panama hat on her head with a bunch of red wooden cherries on the brim. Every now and then her placid expression was changed by a sly isolated little thought like a shoot of green in the desert. "You got a prize!" the old woman said.

Mr. Shiftlet didn't even look at her.

They drove back to the house to let the old woman off and pick up the lunch. When they were ready to leave, she stood staring in the window of the car, with her fingers clenched around the glass. Tears began to seep sideways out of her eyes and run along the dirty creases in her face. "I ain't ever been parted with her for two days before," she said.

Mr. Shiftlet started the motor.

"And I wouldn't let no man have her but you because I seen you would do right. Good-by, Sugarbaby," she said, clutching at the sleeve of the white dress. Lucynell looked straight at her and didn't seem to see her there at all. Mr. Shiftlet eased the car forward so that she had to move her hands.

The early afternoon was clear and open and surrounded by pale blue sky. Although the car would go only thirty miles an hour, Mr. Shiftlet imagined a terrific climb and dip and swerve that went entirely to his head so that he forgot his morning bitterness. He had always wanted an automobile but he had never been able to afford one before. He drove very fast because he wanted to make Mobile by nightfall.

Occasionally he stopped his thoughts long enough to look at Lucynell in the seat beside him. She had eaten the lunch as soon as they were out of the yard and now she was pulling the cherries off the hat one by one and throwing them out the window. He became depressed in spite of the car. He had driven about a hundred miles when he decided that she must be hungry again and at the next small town they came to, he stopped in front of an aluminum-painted eating place called The Hot Spot and took her in and ordered her a plate of ham and grits. The ride had made her sleepy and as soon as she got up on the stool, she rested her head on the counter and shut her eyes. There was no one in The Hot Spot but Mr. Shiftlet and the boy behind the counter, a pale youth with a greasy rag hung over his shoulder. Before he could dish up the food, she was snoring gently.

THE LIFE YOU SAVE MAY BE YOUR OWN

"Give it to her when she wakes up," Mr. Shiftlet said. "I'll pay for it now."

The boy bent over her and stared at the long pink-gold hair and the half-shut sleeping eyes. Then he looked up and stared at Mr. Shiftlet. "She looks like an angel of Gawd," he murmured.

"Hitch-hiker," Mr. Shiftlet explained. "I can't wait. I got to make Tuscaloosa."

The boy bent over again and very carefully touched his finger to a strand of the golden hair and Mr. Shiftlet left.

He was more depressed than ever as he drove on by himself. The late afternoon had grown hot and sultry and the country had flattened out. Deep in the sky a storm was preparing very slowly and without thunder as if it meant to drain every drop of air from the earth before it broke. There were times when Mr. Shiftlet preferred not to be alone. He felt too that a man with a car had a responsibility to others and he kept his eye out for a hitchhiker. Occasionally he saw a sign that warned: "Drive carefully. The life you save may be your own."

The narrow road dropped off on either side into dry fields and here and there a shack or a filling station stood in a clearing. The sun began to set directly in front of the automobile. It was a reddening ball that through his windshield was slightly flat on the bottom and top. He saw a boy in overalls and a gray hat standing on the edge of the road and he slowed the car down and stopped in front of him. The boy didn't have his hand raised to thumb the ride, he was only standing there, but he had a small cardboard suitcase and his hat was set on his head in a way to indicate that he had left somewhere for good. "Son," Mr. Shiftlet said, "I see you want a ride."

The boy didn't say he did or he didn't but he opened the door of the car and got in, and Mr. Shiftlet started driving again. The child held the suitcase on his lap and folded his arms on top of it. He turned his head and looked out the window away from Mr. Shiftlet. Mr. Shiftlet felt oppressed. "Son," he said after a minute, "I got the best old mother in the world so I reckon you only got the second best."

The boy gave him a quick dark glance and then turned his face back out the window.

"It's nothing so sweet," Mr. Shiftlet continued, "as a boy's mother. She taught him his first prayers at her knee, she give him love when no other would, she told him what was right and what wasn't, and she seen that he done the right thing. Son," he said, "I never rued a day in my life like the one I rued when I left that old mother of mine."

The boy shifted in his seat but he didn't look at Mr. Shiftlet. He unfolded his arms and put one hand on the door handle.

"My mother was a angel of Gawd," Mr. Shiftlet said in a very strained voice. "He took her from heaven and giver to me and I left her." His eyes were instantly clouded over with a mist of tears. The car was barely moving.

The boy turned angrily in the seat. "You go to the devil!" he cried. "My old woman is a flea bag and yours is a stinking pole cat!" and with that he flung the door open and jumped out with his suitcase into the ditch.

Mr. Shiftlet was so shocked that for about a hundred feet he drove along slowly with the door still open. A cloud the exact color of the boy's hat and shaped like a turnip had descended over the sun, and another, worse looking, crouched behind the car. Mr. Shiftlet felt that the rottenness of the world was about to engulf him. He raised his arm and let it fall again to his breast. "Oh Lord!" he prayed, "Break forth and wash the slime from this earth!"

The turnip continued slowly to descend. After a few minutes there was a guffawing peal of thunder from behind and fantastic raindrops, like tin-can tops, crashed over the rear of Mr. Shiftlet's car. Very quickly he stepped on the gas and with his stump sticking out the window he raced the galloping shower into Mobile.

WILLIAM STYRON

(1925–   )

William Styron is a native of Newport News, Virginia. He was educated in the public schools and, after the death of his mother in 1938, entered Christchurch School in Middlesex County, Virginia. Upon graduation he enrolled at Davidson College, but soon left to enter Marine Corps V-12 training at Duke University. He was commissioned in 1945, shortly before the war ended. After his discharge he resumed his education at Duke, entering the creative writing courses of William Blackburn. When he completed his work at Duke he went to New York City and was an editor at a publishing house for a while. He resumed the study of creative writing at the New School for Social Research, where his teacher was the novelist and publisher Hiram Haydn. Haydn encouraged him to begin the novel that in 1951 was published as *Lie Down In Darkness*.

After a brief tour of Marine duty during the Korean War he went to Europe. In Paris he wrote the novella, *The Long March*, published in 1953, and was a founding editor of the *Paris Review*. When awarded the Prix de Rome by the American Academy of Arts and Sciences he was able to live there, where he met and married Rose Burgunder of Baltimore. Soon after their return to the United States they settled in Roxbury, Connecticut, where Styron still lives.

In 1960 Styron published a new novel, *Set This House on Fire*; unlike his first book it received mixed reviews. During the early 1960s he went to work on a novel about the Nat Turner Slave Insurrection of 1831, which had long fascinated him. Published in 1967, *The Confessions of Nat Turner* was received with considerable critical acclaim, and then became the object of a furious attack by black and New Left critics who accused him of distorting history by making a black slave hero into a neurotic liberal. The controversy became a cause célèbre. Other critics and historians replied to such attacks, notably the Marxist historian Eugene Genovese, who severely criticized Styron's foes and declared the novel a solid contribution to the understanding of the nature of antebellum slavery. In 1973 Styron published a play, *In the Clap Shack*. Since then he has been at work on a novel based upon the experiences of former concentration camp inmates.

When Styron's first novel appeared, reviewers treated it as a work very much in the Faulknerian tradition; indeed, many details of the plot and situation clearly derive from Faulkner. Yet the similarity was essentially superficial, for Styron's mode of Southern tragedy did not importantly involve the dynastic patterns of decline and fall that Faulkner used so well. His protagonists are considerably more private, and their situation is depicted as existential rather than historical. *Set This House on Fire* confirmed the difference; it was not at all in the traditional mode, but rather a sprawling, periodically intense depiction of the anguish of an artist who cannot create. With *The Confessions of Nat Turner* Styron turned to subject matter that had been a staple of the Southern literary imagination for several generations: slavery and racism in the Southern community. However, he handled it from the slave's point of view, with the obvious intention—in part at least—of showing white audiences the outrage of how it was to be treated as subhuman property. The uproar occasioned by its publication was one more indication of the aesthetic dimensions of the almost compulsive fascination with the discrepancy between community ideals and the treatment of black Southerners that has exemplified the moral concern of so much twentieth-century Southern writing.

From THE CONFESSIONS OF NAT TURNER

From III: "STUDY WAR"

The whole day after Moore's encounter on the road with Isham we unloaded wood at various places in Jerusalem. Moore had contracted to "store" at each house we visited and at the courthouse and the jail. This meant no disorderly heap of logs thrown in a hodgepodge behind the kitchen but rather a tidy arrangement of cords which it was Hark's and my duty to stack wherever Marse Jim or Marse Bob wished them stacked. It was monotonous and gut-wrenching labor. This strain, combined with the stifling heat of the town and my continuing fatigue and dizziness, made me stumble often and once I fell sprawling, only to be helped up by Hark, who said: "You jes' take it easy, Nat, and let ole Hark do de work." But I kept up a steady pace, retreating as was my custom into a kind of daydream—a reverie in which the brute toil of the moment was softened and soothed by my mind's murmurous incantation: *Deliver me out of the mire, and let me not sink, let not the deep swallow me up, hear me O Lord, turn unto me according to the multitude of thy tender mercies* ...

At noon Hark and I made our dinner in the shade of one of the wagons, eating cold hoppin' john—mashed cowpeas mixed with rice—and sat list-lessly afterward cooling ourselves while Moore and Wallace went off to visit the town whore—a two-hundred-pound free mulatto woman named Jose-phine. The food revived me slightly but I still felt faint and weird, with the mystery and wonder of my vision in the woods lingering not in my mind alone but as if throughout my entire being, my soul, like the shadow of a cloud that has appeared out of nowhere to smudge the bright face of the day. I shivered, the mystery haunted me as if great fingers the size of pine boughs rested on my back, ever so lightly, and a mood of evil premonition stole over me as we went back to work. I could not shake the feeling off while we sweated through the waning afternoon. That night the languor and illness returned, I ached with fever, and as Hark and I lay asleep beneath one of the wagons, parked in a field smelling of sweet mustard and golden-rod, I had dreams of giant black angels striding amid a spindrift immensity of stars.

Then late in the forenoon of the next day after another hot morning's work, we made our delivery to the market—the last. It was a Saturday, mar-ket day, and as usual the gallery was thronged with Negroes from the coun-try who were generally allowed a few idle hours to fritter away while their masters attended to business in the town. After we unloaded the last logs Moore and Wallace went off on some errand and Hark and I retired—he with his pine-strip banjo, I with my Bible—to a shady corner of the gallery where I could meditate on a certain passage in Job which had attracted my curiosity. Hark strummed softly, humming a tune. Quite a few of the Negroes loitering about I had become acquainted with by now, largely because of these market days. Daniel, Joe, Jack, Henry, Cromwell, Marcus Aurelius, Nelson, half a dozen more—they had arrived with their masters from all over the county, had helped load or unload their owners' produce, and now stood about with nothing to do but ogle the passing bottoms or breasts of the Negro girls of the town, jabbering the while loudly about poontang and pussy, goosing each other and scuffling around in the dust. One or two succeeded with the girls and stole off with them into a field of alfalfa. Others played mumbletypeg with rusty stolen jackknives, or simply drowsed in the sunlight, waking now and then to exchange their sorry belongings: a straw hat bartered for a homemade jew's-harp, a lucky hair-ball from a cow's belly for a big of pilfered snuff. I looked at them briefly, then returned to Job's racking, imponderable vision. But I found it difficult to concentrate, for although I had recovered somewhat from my fever I could not dislodge the sensation that I had somehow been utterly changed and now dwelt at a distance from myself, in a new world apart. It was noon and Hark offered me a biscuit from a panful he had spirited out of the kitchen of one of Moore's customers, but I had no stomach for food. Even here in town the air was hazy, smelling of far-off fires.

Suddenly I became aware of a commotion—laughter and shouts from a cluster of white men behind the blacksmith's stable perhaps fifty yards away across the road. The bare earthen plot at the rear of the stable was the Saturday gathering place for the poor whites of the county just as the market gallery had become the social focus for the Negroes. These white idlers were the rogues and dregs of the community: penniless drunks and cripples, scroungers, handymen, ex-overseers, vagabonds from North Carolina, hare-lipped roustabouts, squatters on pineland barrens, incorrigible loafers, cretins, rapscallions, and dimwits of every description, they made my present owner by comparison appear to possess the wisdom and dignity of King Solomon. There by the stable each Saturday with straws hats and cheap denim overalls they gathered in a shiftless mob, cadging from each other quarterplugs of chewing tobacco or snorts of rotgut brandy, palavering endlessly (like the Negroes) about pussy and cooze, scheming out ways to make a dishonest half-dollar, tormenting stray cats and dogs, and allowing the slaves from their market promontory a bracing glimpse of white men worse off—in certain important respects at least—than themselves. Now when I looked up to find the source of the disturbance among them I saw that they had assembled in a rough circle. In the midst of the circle, perched upon a horse, was the squat, hunched form of Nathaniel Francis, roaring drunk, his round face besotted with swollen pleasure as he gazed down at something taking place on the ground. I was only mildly curious, thinking at first that it was a white man's wrestling match or drunken fist fight: hardly a Saturday passed without one or the other. But through the baggy pants' legs of one of the bystanders I saw what appeared to be two Negroes moving about, engaged in doing what I could not tell. Cackles of glee went up from the crowd, wild hoots and cries. They seemed to be egging the Negroes on, and Francis drunk in the saddle caused the horse to stamp and prance at the space within the encircling mob, raising an umbrella of dust. Hark had risen to his feet to gawk and I told him that he had better go find out what was happening; he moved slowly off.

After a minute or so Hark came back to the gallery, and the sheepish half-smile on his face—I will never forget that expression, its mixed quality of humor and gentle bewilderment—filled me with a sad foreboding, as if I had known, sensed what he was going to say the instant before his mouth opened to say it.

"Ole Francis he puttin' on a show fo' dem white trash," he proclaimed, loud enough for most all of the other Negroes to hear. "He drunker dan a scritch owl and he makin' dem two niggers Will and Sam fight each other. Don't neither of 'em want to fight but ev'y time one of 'em draw back an' *don't* whop de other, ole Francis he give dat nigger a stroke wid his whip. So dem niggers dey *got* to fight and Sam he done raised a bleedin' whelp on Will's face and Will I do believe he done broke off one of Sam's front teeth. Hit sho is some kind of cock fight."

At this, all the Negroes within hearing began to laugh—there was indeed something oddly comical about Hark's *way* of describing things—but at the same time my heart seemed to shrivel and die within me. That was *all*. All! Of the indignities and wrongs that a Negro might endure—blistering toil and deprivation, slights and slurs and insults, beatings, chains, exile from beloved kin—none seemed more loathsome, at that minute, than this: that he be pitted in brutal combat against his own kind for the obscene amusement of human beings of any description—but especially those so mean and reptilian in spirit, so worthless, so likewise despised in the scheme of things and saved from the final morass only by the hairline advantage of a lighter skin. Not since the day years before when I was first sold had I felt such rage, intolerable rage, rage that echoed a memory of Isham's fury as he howled at Moore, rage that was a culmination of all the raw buried anguish and frustration growing inside me since the faraway dusk of childhood, on a murmuring veranda, when I first understood that I was a slave and a slave forever. My heart, as I say, shrank inside me, died, disappeared, and rage like a newborn child exploded there to fill the void: it was at this instant that I knew beyond doubt or danger that—whatever the place, whatever the appointed time, whoever the gentle young girl now serenely plucking blossoms within a bower or the mistress knitting in the coolness of a country parlor or the innocent lad seated contemplating the cobwebbed walls of an outhouse in a summery field—the whole world of white flesh would someday founder and split apart upon my retribution, would perish by my design and at my hands. My stomach heaved and I restrained the urge to vomit on the boards where I sat.

But now the commotion across the road dwindled, the shouts fell away, and the circle of white men broke up as they turned their attention to other pleasures. Aslant to one side in the saddle, Francis rode off at a lurching pace down the street, exhausted by his sport, smiling a smile of gratification and conquest. And at this moment I saw Will and Sam—battered-looking, bruised, and dusty—cross the road together, weaving toward the market. Will was muttering to himself as he stroked a swollen jaw and Sam shivered while he walked, trembling in pain, misery, and in the throes of grievous shame and abasement—a short, wiry little mulatto neither too old yet nor too calloused by suffering to be prevented from sobbing bitterly like a child as he wiped the blood away from a jagged cut across his lips. Still unperceiving of anything at all, still witlessly amused by Hark's account of the fray, the Negroes on the gallery watched Sam and Will approach and kept laughing. It was then that I rose to face them.

"My brothers!" I cried. "Stop yo' laughin' and listen to me! Leave off from the laughin', brothers, and listen to a minister of the Holy Word!" A hush fell over the Negroes and they stirred restlessly, turned toward me, puzzlement and wonder in their eyes. "Come closer!" I commanded them. "This here is no time for laughin'! This is a time for weepin', for *lamentation!* For rage! You is *men*, brothers, *men* not beasts of the field! You ain't no four-legged dogs! You is *men*, I say! Where oh where, my brothers, is yo' pride?"

Slowly, one by one, the Negroes drew near, among them Will and Sam, who climbed up from the road and stood gazing at me as they mopped their faces with gray slimy wads of waste cotton. Still other shuffled closer —young men mostly, along with a few older slaves; they scratched themselves out of nervousness, some eyes darted furtively across the road. But all were silent now, and with a delicious chill I could feel the way in which they had responded to the fury in my words, like blades of sawgrass bending to a sudden wind. And I began to realize, far back in the remotest corner of my mind, that I had commenced the first sermon I had ever preached. They became still. Brooding, motionless, the Negroes gazed at me with watchful and reflective concern, some of them hardly drawing a breath. My language was theirs, I spoke it as if it were a second tongue. My rage had captured them utterly, and I felt a thrill of power course out from myself to wrap them round, binding us for this moment as one.

"My bothers," I said in a gentler tone, "many of you has been to church with yo' mastahs and mist'esses at the Whitehead church or up Shiloh way or down at Nebo or Mount Moriah. Most of you hasn't got no religion. That's awright. White man's religion don't teach nothin' to black folk except to obey ole mastah and live humble—walk light and talk small. That's awright. But them of you that recollects they Bible teachin' knows about Israel in Egypt an' the peoples that was kept in bondage. Them peoples was Jewish peoples an' they had names just like us black folk—like you right there, Nathan, an' you, Joe—Joe is a Jewish name—an' you there, Daniel. Them Jews was just like the black folk. They had to sweat they fool asses off fo' ole Pharaoh. That white man had them Jews haulin' wood an' pullin' rock and thrashin' corn an' makin' bricks until they was near 'bout dead an' didn't git ary penny for none of it neither, like ev'y livin' mothah's son of us, them Jews was in *bondage.* They didn't have enough to eat neither, just some miser'ble cornmeal with weevils in it an' sour milk an' a little fatback that done got so high it would turn a buzzard's stomach. Drought an' hunger run throughout the land, just like now. Oh, my brothers, that was a sad time in Egypt fo' them Jews! It was a time fo' weepin' an' lamentation, a time of toil an' hunger, a time of *pain!* Pharaoh he whupped them Jews until they had red whelps on 'em from head to toe an' ev'y night they went to bed cryin', 'Lord, Lord, when is you goin' to make that white man set us free?' "

There was a stirring among the Negroes and I heard a voice in the midst of them say "Yes, yes," faint and plaintive, and still another voice: "Mm-huh, dat's *right!*" I stretched out an arm slowly, as if to embrace them, and some of the crowd moved nearer still.

"Look aroun' you, brothers," I said, "what does you see? What does you see in the air? What does you see blowin' in the air?" The Negroes turned their faces toward the town, raised their eyes skyward: there in amber translucent haze the smoke from the distant fires swam through the streets, touching the gallery, even as I spoke, with its acrid and apple-sweet taste of scorched timber, its faint smell of corruption.

"That there is the smoke of *pestilence*, brothers," I went on, "the smoke of pestilence an' death. The same smoke that hanged over the Jews in bondage down there in Egypt land. The same smoke of pestilence an' death that hanged over them Jews in Egypt hangs over all black folk, all men whose skin is black, yo' skin and mine. An' we got a tougher row to to hoe even than them Jews. Joseph he was at least a man, not no four-legged dog. My brothers, laughter is good, laughter is bread and salt and buttermilk and a balm for pain. But they is a time for ev'ything. They is a time for weepin' too. A time for rage! And in bondage black folk like you an' me must weep in they rage. *Leave off* from such dumb laughter like just now!" I cried, my voice rising. "When a white man he lift a hand against one of us'ns we must not laugh but rage and weep! 'By the rivers of Babylon, there we sat down, yea, we wept when we remembered Zion!' That's right!" ("Mm-huh, dat's right!" came the voice again, joined by another.) " 'We hanged our harps upon the willows, for they that carried us away captive required of us a song. How shall we sing the Lord's song in a strange land?' *That's right!*" I said, the words bitter on my tongue. "White man make you sing an' dance, make you shuffle, do the buck-an'-wing, play 'Ole Zip Coon' on the banjo and the fiddle. 'They that carried us away captive required of us a song.' Yes! Leave off from that singin', leave off from that banjo, leave off from that buck-an-wing! They is a time for ev'ything. This is no time fo' singin', fo' laughter. Look aroun' you, my brothers, look into each other's eyes! You jest seen a white man pit brother 'gainst brother! Ain't none of you no four-legged beasts what can be whupped an' hurt like some flea-bit cur dog. You is men! You is *men*, my dear brothers, look at yo'selves, look to yo' *pride!*"

As I spoke, I saw two older black men at the rear of the crowd mutter to each other and shake their heads. Glances of puzzlement and worry crossed their faces and they sidled off, disappeared. The others still listened, intent, brooding, nearly motionless. I heard a soft sigh and a gentle "Amen." I raised my arms to either side of me and extended my hands, palms outward, as if in benediction. I felt the sweat pouring from my face.

"In the visions of the night, brother," I continued, "God spoke to Jacob an' He said, 'I am God, the God of thy father: fear not to go down into Egypt, for I will there make of thee a great nation.' An' Jacob went down into Egypt an' the peoples of Israel multipled an' Moses was born. Moses he was born in the bulrushers an' he delivered the Jews out of Egypt an' into the Promised Land. Well, there they had a powerful lot of troubles too. But in the Promised Land them Jewish peoples they could stand up an' live like *men*. They become a great nation. No more fatback, no more pint of salt, no more peck of corn fo' them Jews; no more overseers, no more auction blocks; no more horn blow at sunrise fo' them mothahs' sons. They had chicken with pot likker an' spoonbread an' sweet cider to drink in the shade. They done got paid an honest dollar. Them Jews become *men*. But oh, my brothers, black folk ain't never goin' to be led from bondage without they has *pride!* Black folk ain't goin' to be free, they ain't goin' to have no spoonbread an' sweet cider less'n they studies to love they own *selves*. Only then will the first be last, and the last first. Black folk ain't never goin' to be no great nation until they studies to love they own black skin an' the beauty of that skin an' the beauty of them black hands that toils so hard and black feet that trods so weary on God's earth. And when white men in they hate an' wrath an' meanness fetches blood from that beautiful black skin then, oh *then*, my brothers, it is time not fo' laughing but fo' weeping an' rage an' lamentation! *Pride!*" I cried after a pause, and let my arms descend. "Pride, pride, *everlasting* pride, pride will make you free!"

I ceased speaking and gazed at the rapt black faces. Then I finished slowly and in a soft voice: "Arise, shine; for thy light is come, an' the glory of the Lord is risen upon thee. Amen."

The Negroes were silent. Far off in Jerusalem, through the hot afternoon, a church bell let fall a single chime, striking the half-hour. Then the Negroes one by one straggled away across the gallery, some with troubled looks, some stupid and uncomprehending, some fearful. Others drew toward me, radiant; and Henry, who was deaf, who had read my lips, came up close to me and silently clasped my arm. I heard Nelson say, "You done spoke de truth," and he too drew near, and I felt their warmth and their brotherhood and hope and knew then what Jesus must have known when upon the shores of Galilee he said: "*Follow me, and I will make you fishers of men.*"

ERNEST J. GAINES

(1933–   )

The Autobiography of Miss Jane Pittman, published in 1971, and its subsequent reenactment as a powerful television drama, brought Ernest Gaines the public recognition as a craftsman of fiction about black Southerners in their time and place that had already been accorded him by critics. These critics had identified in his work a profound feeling for the texture of everyday black experience, together with a growing mastery of the sophisticated techniques of the art of fiction as developed by the Russians, Hemingway, and Faulkner, and such black authors as Ralph Ellison and James Baldwin.

Gaines was born in Oscar, Louisiana, and worked in the fields as a boy. Interested in literature while quite young, he began to read extensively as a teenager in Vallejo, California, where he moved in 1948 to live with his mother and stepfather. When he was 16 he wrote a novel. After attending junior college in Vallejo he served in the Army for two years and then enrolled at San Francisco State College. Upon graduation he received a creative writing fellowship for graduate study at Stanford. There he reworked the novel he had written at 16, which in 1964 was published under the title *Catherine Carmier*. In 1967 he brought out a second novel, *Of Love and Dust*, and in 1968 a collection of short stories, *Bloodline*. In 1978 came another novel, *In My Father's House*.

The Autobiography of Miss Jane Pittman is, like his other work, drawn from the life of blacks in the rural South. Using his aunt Augusteen Jefferson as a model, he recounts the story of a woman who not only endures through decades of misfortune and injustice but in her bravery and independence achieves a triumph of human spirit. In her Gaines has created a fictional heroine of major proportions to join the ranks of the great characters of Southern literature.

JUST LIKE A TREE

> *I shall not;*
>> *I shall not be moved.*
> *I shall not;*
>> *I shall not be moved.*
> *Just like a tree that's*
> *planted 'side the water.*
>> *Oh, I shall not be moved.*
> *I made my home in glory;*
>> *I shall not be moved.*

JUST LIKE A TREE

Made my home in glory;
I shall not be moved.
Just like a tree that's
planted 'side the water.
Oh, I shall not be moved.

From an old Negro spiritual

CHUCKKIE

Pa hit him on the back and he jeck in them chains like he pulling, but ever'body in the wagon know he ain't, and Pa hit him on the back again. He jeck again like he pulling, but even Big Red know he ain't doing a thing.

"That's why I'm go'n get a horse," Pa say. "He'll kill that other mule. Get up there, Mr. Bascom."

"Oh, let him alone," Gran'mon say. "How would you like it if you was pulling a wagon in all that mud?"

Pa don't answer Gran'mon; he just hit Mr. Bascom on the back again.

"That's right, kill him," Gran'mon say. "See where you get mo' money to buy another one."

"Get up there, Mr. Bascom," Pa say.

"You hear me talking to you, Emile?" Gran'mon say. "You want me hit you with something?"

"Ma, he ain't pulling," Pa say.

"Leave him alone," Gran'mon say.

Pa shake the lines little bit, but Mr. Bascom don't even feel it, and you can see he letting Big Red do all the pulling again. Pa say something kind o' low to hisself, and I can't make out what it is.

I low' my head little bit, 'cause that wind and fine rain was hitting me in the face, and I can feel Mama pressing close to me to keep me warm. She sitting on one side o' me and Pa sitting on the other side o' me, and Gran'mon in the back o' me in her setting chair. Pa didn't want bring the setting chair, telling Gran'mon there was two boards in that wagon already and she could sit on one of 'em all by herself if she wanted to, but Gran'mon say she was taking her setting chair with her if Pa liked it or not. She say she didn't ride in no wagon on nobody board, and if Pa liked it or not, that setting chair was going.

"Let her take her setting chair," Mama say. "What's wrong with taking her setting chair."

"Ehhh, Lord," Pa say, and picked up the setting chair and took it out to the wagon. "I guess I'll have to bring it back in the house, too, when we come back from there."

Gran'mon went and clambed in the wagon and moved her setting chair back little bit and sat down and folded her arms, waiting for us to get in, too. I got in and knelt down 'side her, but Mama told me to come up there and sit on the board 'side her and Pa so I could stay warm. Soon 's I sat down, Pa hit Mr. Bascom on the back, saying what a trifling thing Mr. Bascom was, and soon 's he got some mo' money he was getting rid o' Mr. Bascom and getting him a horse.

I raise my head to look see how far we is.

"That's it, yonder," I say.

"Stop pointing," Mama say, "and keep you hand in your pocket."

"Where?" Gran'mon say, back there in her setting chair.

" 'Cross the ditch, yonder," I say.

"Can't see a thing for this rain," Gran'mon say.

"Can't hardly see it," I say. "But you can see the light little bit. That chinaball tree standing in the way."

"Poor soul," Gran'mon say. "Poor soul."

I know Gran'mon was go'n say "poor soul, poor soul," 'cause she had been saying "poor soul, poor soul," ever since she heard Aunt Fe was go'n leave from back there.

EMILE

Darn can crop to finish getting in and only a mule and a half to do it. If I had my way I'd take that shotgun and a load o' buckshots and—but what's the use.

"Get up, Mr. Bascom—please," I say to that little dried-up, long-eared, tobacco-color thing. "Please, come up. Do your share for God sake—if you don't mind. I know it's hard pulling in all that mud, but if you don't do your share, then Big Red'll have to do his and yours, too. So, please, if it ain't asking you too much to—"

"Oh, Emile, shut up," Leola say.

"I can't hit him," I say, "or Mama back there'll hit me. So I have to talk to him. Please, Mr. Bascom, if you don't mind it. For my sake. No, not for mine; for God sake. No, not even for His'n; for Big Red sake. A fellow mule just like yourself is. Please, come up."

"Now, you hear that boy blaspheming God right in front o' me there," Mama say. "Ehhh, Lord—just keep it up. All this bad weather there like this whole world coming apart—a clap o' thunder come there and knock the fool out you. Just keep it up."

Maybe she right, and I stop. I look at Mr. Bascom there doing nothing, and I just give up. That mule know long 's Mama's alive he go'n do just what he what to do. He know when Papa was dying he told Mama to look after him, and he know no matter what he do, no matter what he don't do, Mama ain't go'n never let me do him anything. Sometimes I even feel mama care mo' for Mr. Bascom 'an she care for me her own son.

We come up to the gate and I pull back on the lines.

"Whoa up, Big Red," I say. "You don't have to stop, Mr. Bascom. You never started."

I can feel mama looking at me back there in that setting chair, but she don't say nothing.

"Here," I say to Chuckkie.

He take the lines and I jump down on the ground to open the old beat-up gate. I see Etienne's horse in the yard, and I see Chris new red tractor 'side the house, shining in the rain. When Mama die, I say to myself, Mr. Bascom, you going. Ever'body getting tractors and horses and I'm still stuck with you. You going, brother.

"Can you make it through?" I ask Chuckkie. "That gate ain't too wide."

"I can do it," he say.

"Be sure to make Mr. Bascom pull," I say.

"Emile, you better get back up here and drive 'em through," Leola say. "Chuckkie might break up that wagon."

"No, let him stay down there and give orders," Mama say, back there in that setting chair.

"He can do it." I say. "Come on, Chuckkie boy."

"Come up, here, mule," Chuckkie say.

And soon 's he say that, Big Red make a lunge for the yard, and Mr. Bascom don't even move, and 'fore I can bat my eyes I hear *pow-pow; sagg-sagg; pow-pow*. But above all that noise, Leola up there screaming her head off. And Mama—not a word; just sitting in that chair, looking at me with her arms still folded.

"Pull Big Red," I say. "Pull Big Red, Chuckkie."

Poor little Chuckkie up there pulling so hard till one of his little arms straight out in back; and Big Red throwing his shoulders and ever'thing else in it, and Mr. Bascom just walking there just 's loose and free, like he's suppose to be there just for his good looks. I move out the way just in time to let the wagon go by me, pulling half o' the fence in the yard behind it. I glance up again, and there's Leola still hollering and trying to jump out, but Mama not saying a word—just sitting there in that setting chair with her arms still folded.

"Whoa," I hear little Chuckkie saying. "Whoa up, now."

Somebody open the door and a bunch o' people come out on the gallery.

"What the world—?" Etienne say. "Thought the whole place was coming to pieces there."

"Chuckkie had a little trouble coming in the yard," I say.

"Goodness," Etienne say. "Anybody hurt?"

Mama just sit there about ten seconds, then she say something to herself and start clambing out the wagon.

"Let me help you there, Aunt Lou," Etienne say, coming down the steps.

"I can make it," Mama say. When she get on the ground she look up at Chuckkie. "Hand me my chair there, boy."

Poor little Chuckkie, up there with the lines in one hand, get the chair and hold it to the side, and Etienne catch it just 'fore it hit the ground. Mama start looking at me again, and it look like for at least a' hour she stand there looking at nobody but me. Then she say, "Ehhh, Lord," like that again, and go inside with Leola and the rest o' the people.

I look back at half o' the fence laying there in the yard, and I jump back on the wagon and guide the mules to the side o' the house. After unhitching 'em and tying 'em to the wheels, I look at Chris pretty red tractor again, and me and Chuckkie go inside: I make sure he kick all that mud off his shoes 'fore he go in the house.

LEOLA

Sitting over there by that fireplace, trying to look joyful when ever'body there know she ain't. But she trying, you know; smiling and bowing when people say something to her. How can she be joyful, I ask you; how can she be? Poor thing, she been here all her life—or the most of it, let's say. 'Fore they moved in this house, they lived in one back in the woods 'bout a mile from here. But for the past twenty-five or thirty years, she been right in this one house. I know ever since I been big enough to know people I been seeing her right here.

Aunt Fe, Aunt Fe, Aunt Fe, Aunt Fe; the name's been 'mongst us just like us own family name. Just like the name o' God. Like the name of town —the city. Aunt Fe, Aunt Fe, Aunt Fe, Aunt Fe.

Poor old thing; how many times I done come here and washed clothes for her when she couldn't do it herself. How many times I done hoed in that garden, ironed her clothes, wrung a chicken neck for her. You count the days in the year and you'll be pretty close. And I didn't mind it a bit. No, I didn't mind it a bit. She there trying to pay me. Proud—Lord, talking 'bout pride. "Here." "No, Aunt Fe; no." "Here, here; you got a child there, you can use it." "No, Aunt Fe. No. No. What would Mama think if she knowed I took money from you? Aunt Fe, Mama would never forgive me. No. I love doing these thing for you. I just wish I could do more."

And there, now, trying to make 'tend she don't mind leaving. Ehhh, Lord.

I hear a bunch o' rattling round in the kitchen and I go back there. I see Louise stirring this big pot o' eggnog.

"Louise," I say.

"Leola," she say.

We look at each other and she stir the eggnog again. She know what I'm go'n say next, and she can't even look in my face.

"Louise, I wish there was some other way."

"There's no other way," she say.

"Louise, moving her from here's like moving a tree you been used to in your front yard all your life."

"What else can I do?"

"Oh, Louise, Louise."

"Nothing else but that."

"Louise, what people go'n do without her here?"

She stir the eggnog and don't answer.

"Louise, us'll take her in with us."

"You all no kin to Auntie. She go with me."

"And us'll never see her again."

She stir the eggnog. Her husband come back in the kitchen and kiss her on the back o' the neck and then look at me and grin. Right from the start I can see I ain't go'n like that nigger.

"Almost ready, honey?" he say.

"Almost."

He go to the safe and get one o' them bottles of whiskey he got in there and come back to the stove.

"No," Louise say. "Everybody don't like whiskey in it. Add the whiskey after you've poured it up."

"Okay, hon."

He kiss her on the back o' the neck again. Still don't like that nigger. Something 'bout him ain't right.

"You one o' the family?" he say.

"Same as one," I say. "And you?"

He don't like the way I say it, and I don't care if he like it or not. He look at me there a second, and then he kiss her on the ear.

"Un-unnn," she say, stirring the pot.

"I love your ear, baby," he say.

"Go in the front room and talk with the people," she say.

He kiss her on the other ear. A nigger do all that front o' public got something to hid. He leave the kitchen. I look at Louise.

"Ain't nothing else I can do," she say.

"You sure, Louise? You positive?"

"I'm positive," she say.

The front door open and Emile and Chuckkie come in. A minute later Washington and Adrieu come in, too. Adrieu come back in the kitchen, and I can see she been crying. Aunt Fe is her godmother, you know.

"How you feel, Adrieu?"

"That weather out there," she say.

"Y'all walked?"

"Yes."

"Us here in the wagon. Y'all can go back with us."

"Y'all the one tore the fence down?" she ask.

"Yes, I guess so. That brother-in-law o' yours in there letting Chuckkie drive that wagon."

"Well, I don't guess it'll matter too much. Nobody go'n be here, anyhow."

And she start crying again. I take her in my arms and pat her on the shoulder, and I look at Louise stirring the eggnog.

"What I'm go'n do and my nan-nane gone? I love her so much."

"Ever'body love her."

"Since my mama died, she been like my mama."

"Shh," I say. "Don't let her hear you. Make her grieve. You don't want her grieving, now, do you?"

She sniffs there 'gainst my dress few times.

"Oh, Lord," she say. "Lord, have mercy."

"Shhh," I say. "Shhh. That's what life's 'bout."

"That ain't what life's 'bout," she say. "It ain't fair. This been her home all her life. These the people she know. She don't know them people she going to. It ain't fair."

"Shhh, Adrieu," I say. "Now, you saying things that ain't your business."

She cry there some mo'.

"Oh, Lord, Lord," she say.

Louise turn from the stove.

"About ready now," she say, going to the middle door. "James, tell everybody to come back and get some."

JAMES

Let me go on back here and show these country niggers how to have a good time. All they know is talk, talk, talk. Talk so much they make me buggy round here. Damn this weather—wind, rain. Must be a million cracks in this old house.

I go to that old beat-up safe in that corner and get that fifth of Mr. Harper (in the South now; got to say Mister), give the seal one swipe, the stopper one jerk, and head back to that old wood stove. (Man, like, these cats are primitive—goodness. You know what I mean? I mean like wood stoves. Don't mention TV, man, these cats here never heard of that.) I start to dump Mr. Harper in the pot and Baby catches my hand again and say not all of them like it. You ever heard of anything like that? I mean a stud's going to drink eggnog, and he's not going to put whiskey in it. I mean he's going to drink it straight. I mean, you ever heard anything like that? Well, I wasn't pressing none of them on Mr. Harper. I mean, me and Mr. Harper get along too well together for me to go around there pressing.

I hold my cup there and let Baby pour a few drops of this egg stuff in it;

then I jerk my cup back and let Mr. Harper run a while. Couple of these cats come over (some of them aren't so lame) and set their cups, and I let Mr. Harper run for them. Then this cat says he's got 'nough. I let Mr. Harper run for this other stud, and pretty soon he says, "Hold it. Good." Country cat, you know. "Hold it. Good." Real country cat. So I raise the cup to see what Mr. Harper's doing. He's just right. I raise the cup again. Just right, Mr. Harper; just right.

I go to the door with Mr. Harper under my arm and the cup in my hand and I look into the front room where they all are. I mean, there's about ninety-nine of them in there. Ole ones, young ones, little ones, big ones, yellow ones, black ones, brown ones—you name them, brother, and they were there. And what for? Brother, I'll tell you what for. Just because me and Baby are taking this old chick out of these sticks. Well, I'll tell you where I'd be at this moment if I was one of them. With that weather out there like it is, I'd be under about five blankets with some little warm belly pressing against mine. Brother, you can bet your hat I wouldn't be here. Man, listen to that thing out there. You can hear that rain beating on that old house like grains of rice; and that wind coming through them cracks like it does in those old Charlie Chaplin movies. Man, like you know—like *whooo-ee; whooo-ee.* Man, you talking about some weird cats.

I can feel Mr. Harper starting to massage my wig and I bat my eyes twice and look at the old girl over there. She's still sitting in that funny-looking little old rocking chair, and not saying a word to anybody. Just sitting there looking into the fireplace at them two pieces of wood that aren't giving out enough heat to warm a baby, let alone ninety-nine grown people. I mean, you know, like that sleet's falling out there like all get-up-and-go, and them two pieces of wood are lying there just as dead as the rest of these way-out cats.

One of the old cats—I don't know which one he is—Mose, Sam, or something like that—leans over and pokes in the fire a minute; then a little blaze shoots up, and he raises up, too, looking as satisfied as if he'd just sent a rocket into orbit. I mean, these cats are like that. They do these little bitty things, and they feel like they've really done something. Well, back in these sticks, I guess there just isn't nothing big to do.

I feel Mr. Harper touching my skull now—and I notice this little chick passing by me with these two cups of eggnog. She goes over to the fireplace and gives one to each of these old chicks. The one sitting in that setting chair she brought with her from God knows where, and the other cup to the old chick that Baby and I are going to haul from here sometime tomorrow morning. Wait, man, I mean like, you ever heard of anybody going to somebody else's house with a chair? I mean, wouldn't you call that an insult at the basest point? I mean, now, like tell me what you think of that? I mean —dig—here I am at my pad, and in you come with your own stool. I mean, now, like man, you know. I mean that's an insult at the basest point. I mean, you know . . . you know, like way out . . .

Mr. Harper, what you trying to do, boy—I mean, *sir*. (Got to watch myself, I'm in the South. Got to keep watching myself.)

This stud touches me on the shoulder and raise his cup and say, "How 'bout a taste?" I know what the stud's talking about, so I let Mr. Harper run for him. But soon 's I let a drop get in, the stud say, " 'Nough." I mean I let about two drops get in, and already the stud's got enough. Man, I mean, like you know. I mean these studs are 'way out. I mean like 'way back there.

This stud takes a swig of his eggnog and say, "Ahhh." I mean this real down-home way of saying "Ahhhh." I mean, man, like these studs—I notice this little chick passing by me again, and this time she's crying. I mean weeping, you know. And just because this old ninety-nine-year-old chick's packing up and leaving. I mean, you ever heard of anything like that? I mean, here she is pretty as the day is long and crying because Baby and I are hauling this old chick away. Well, I'd like to make her cry. And I can assure you, brother, it wouldn't be from leaving her.

I turn and look at Baby over there by the stove, pouring eggnog in all these cups. I mean, there're about twenty of these cats lined up there. And I bet you not half of them will take Mr. Harper along. Some way-out cats, man. Some way-out cats.

I go up to Baby and kiss her on the back of the neck and give her a little pat where she likes for me to pat her when we're in the bed. She say "Uh-uh," but I know she likes it anyhow.

BEN O

I back under the bed and touch the slop jar, and I pull back my leg and back somewhere else, and then I get me a good sight on it. I spin my aggie couple times and sight again and then I shoot. I hit it right square in the middle and it go flying over the fireplace. I crawl over there to get it and I see 'em all over there drinking they eggnog and they didn't even offer me and Chuckkie none. I find my marble on the bricks, and I go back and tell Chuckkie they over there drinking eggnog.

"You want some?" I say.

"I want shoot marble," Chuckkie say. "Yo' shot. Shoot up."

"I want some eggnog," I say.

"Shoot up, Ben O," he say. "I'm getting cold staying in one place so long. You feel that draft?"

"Coming from that crack under that bed," I say.

"Where?" Chuckkie say, looking for the crack.

"Over by that bedpost over there," I say.

"This sure's a beat-up old house," Chuckkie say.

"I want me some eggnog," I say.

"Well, you ain't getting none," Gran'mon say, from the fireplace. "It ain't good for you."

"I can drink eggnog," I say. "How come it ain't good for me? It ain't nothing but eggs and milk. I eat chicken, don't I? I eat beef, don't I?"

Gran'mon don't say nothing.

"I want me some eggnog," I say.

Gran'mon still don't say no more. Nobody else don't say nothing, neither.

"I want me some eggnog," I say.

"You go'n get a eggnog," Gran'mon say. "Just keep that noise up."

"I want me some eggnog," I say; "and I 'tend to get me some eggnog tonight."

Next thing I know, Gran'mon done picked up a chip out o' that corner and done sailed it back there where me and Chuckkie is. I duck just in time, and the chip catch old Chuckkie side the head.

"Hey, who that hitting me?" Chuckkie say.

"Move, and you won't get hit," Gran'mon say.

I laughed at old Chuckkie over there holding his head, and next thing I know here's Chuckkie done haul back there and hit me in my side. I jump up from there and give him two just to show him how it feel, and he jump up and hit me again. Then we grab each other and start tussling on the floor.

"You, Ben O," I hear Gran'mon saying. "You, Ben O, cut that out. Y'all cut that out."

But we don't stop, 'cause neither one o' us want be first. Then I feel somebody pulling us apart.

"What I ought to do is whip both o' you," Mrs. Leola say. "Is that what y'all want?"

"No'm," I say.

"Then shake hand."

Me and Chuckkie shake hand.

"Kiss," Mrs. Leola say.

"No, ma'am," I say. "I ain't kissing no boy. I ain't that crazy."

"Kiss him, Chuckkie," she say.

Old Chuckkie kiss me on the jaw.

"Now, kiss him, Ben O."

"I ain't kissing no Chuckkie," I say. "No'm. Uh-uh. You kiss girls."

And the next thing I know, Mama done tipped up back o' me and done whop me on the leg with Daddy belt.

"Kiss Chuckkie," she say.

Chuckkie turn his jaw to me and I kiss him. I almost wipe my mouth. I even feel like spitting.

"Now, come back here and get you some eggnog," Mama say.

"That's right, spoil 'em," Gran'mon say. "Next thing you know, they be drinking from bottles."

"Little eggnog won't hurt 'em, Mama," Mama say.

"That's right, never listen," Gran'mon say. "It's you go'n suffer for it. I be dead and gone, me."

AUNT CLO

Be just like wrapping a chain round a tree and jecking and jecking, and then shifting the chain little bit and jecking and jecking some in that direction, and then shifting it some mo' and jecking and jecking in that direction. Jecking and jecking till you get it loose, and then pulling with all your might. Still it might not be loose enough and you have to back the tractor up some and fix the chain round the tree again and start jecking all over. Jeck, jeck, jeck. Then you hear the roots crying, and then you keep on jecking, and then it give, and you jeck some mo', and then it falls. And not till then that you see what you done done. Not till then you see the big hole in the ground and piece of the taproot still way down in it—a piece you won't never get out no matter if you dig till doomsday. Yes, you got the tree —least got it down on the ground, but did you get the taproot? No. No, sir, you didn't get the taproot. You stand there and look down in this hole at it and you grab yo' axe and jump down in it and start chopping at the taproot, but do you get the taproot? No. You don't get the taproot, sir. You never get the taproot. But, sir, I tell you what you do get. You get a big hole in the ground, sir; and you get another big hole in the air where the lovely branches been all these years. Yes, sir, that's what you get. The holes, sir, the holes. Two holes, sir, you can't never fill no matter how hard you try.

So you wrap yo' chain round yo' tree again, sir, and you start dragging it. But the dragging ain't so easy, sir, 'cause she's a heavy old tree—been there a long time, you know—heavy. And you make yo' tractor strain, sir, and the elements work 'gainst you, too, sir, 'cause she part o' the elements, they on her side, too, 'cause she part o' the elements, and the elements, they part o' her. So the elements, they do they little share to discourage you—yes, sir, they does. But you will not let the elements stop you. No, sir, you show the elements that they just elements, and man is stronger than elements, and you jeck and jeck on the chain, and soon she start to moving with you, sir, but if you look over yo' shoulder one second you see her leaving a trail—a trail, sir, that can be seen for miles and miles away. You see her trying to hook her little fine branches in different little cracks, in between pickets, round hills o' grass, round anything they might brush 'gainst. But you is a determined man, sir, and you jeck and you jeck, and she keep on grabbing and trying to hold, but you stronger, sir—course you the strongest—and you finally get her out on the pave road. But what you don't notice, sir, is just 'fore she get on the pave road she leave couple her little branches to remind the people that it ain't her that want to leave, but you, sir, that think she ought to. So you just drag her and drag her, sir, and the folks that live in the houses 'side the pave road, they come out on they gallery and look at her go by, and then they go back in they house and sit by the fire and forget her. So you just go on, sir, and you just go and you go—and for how many days? I don't know. I don't have the least idea. The North to me, sir, is like the elements. It mystify me. But never mind, you finally get there, and then you try to find a place to set her. You look in this corner and you look in that corner, but no corner is good. She kind o' stand in the way no matter where you set her. So finally, sir, you say, "I just stand her up here a little while and see, and if it don't work out, if she keep getting in the way, I guess we'll just have to take her to the dump."

CHRIS

Just like him, though, standing up there telling them lies when everybody else feeling sad. I don't know what you do without people like him. And, yet, you see him there, he sad just like the rest. But he just got to be funny. Crying on the inside, but still got to be funny.

He didn't steal it, though; didn't steal it a bit. His grandpa was just like him. Mat? Mat Jefferson? Just like that. Mat could make you die laughing. 'Member once at a wake. Who was dead? Yes—Robert Lewis. Robert Lewis laying up in his coffin dead as a door nail. Everybody sad and droopy. Mat look at that and start his lying. Soon, half o' the place laughing. Funniest wake I ever went to, and yet—

Just like now. Look at 'em. Look at 'em laughing. Ten minutes ago you would 'a' thought you was at a funeral. But look at 'em now. Look at her there in that little old chair. How long she had it? Fifty years—a hundred? It ain't a chair no mo', it's little bit o' her. Just like her arm, just like her leg.

You know, I couldn't believe it. I couldn't. Emile passed the house there the other day, right after the bombing, and I was in my yard digging a water drain to let the water run out in the ditch. Emile, he stopped the wagon there 'fore the door. Little Chuckkie, he in there with him with that little rain cap buckled up over his head. I go out to the gate and I say, "Emile, it's the truth?"

"The truth," he say. And just like that he say it. "The truth."

I look at him there, and he looking up the road to keep from looking back at me. You know, they been pretty close to Aunt Fe ever since they was children coming up. His own mon, Aunt Lou, and Aunt Fe, they been like sisters, there, together.

Me and him, we talk there little while 'bout the cane cutting, then he say he got to get on to the back. He shake the lines and drive on.

Inside me, my heart feel like it done swole up ten times the size it ought to be. Water come in my eyes, and I got to 'mit I cried right there. Yes sir, I cried right there by that front gate.

Louise come in the room and whisper something to Leola, and they go back in the kitchen. I can hear 'em moving things round back there, still getting things together they go'n be taking along. If they offer me anything, I'd like that big iron pot out there in the back yard. Good for boiling water when you killing hog, you know.

You can feel the sadness in the room again. Louise brought it in when she come in and whispered to Leola. Only, she didn't take it out when her and Leola left. Every pan they move, every pot they unhook keep telling you she leaving, she leaving.

Etienne turn over one o' them logs to make the fire pick up some, and I see that boy, Lionel, spreading out his hands over the fire. Watch out, I think to myself, here come another lie. People, he just getting started.

ANNE-MARIE DUVALL

"You're not going?"

"I'm not going," he says, turning over the log with the poker. "And if you were in your right mind, you wouldn't go, either."

"You just don't understand, do you?"

"Oh, I understand. She cooked for your daddy. She nursed you when your mama died."

"And I'm trying to pay her back with a seventy-nine cents scarf. Is that too much?"

He is silent, leaning against the mantel, looking down at the fire. The fire throws strange shadows across the big, old room. Father looks down at me from against the wall. His eyes do not say go nor stay. But I know what he would do.

"Please go with me, Edward."

"You're wasting your breath."

I look at him a long time, then I get the small package from the coffee table.

"You're still going?"

"I am going."

"Don't call for me if you get bogged down anywhere back there."

I look at him and go out to the garage. The sky is black. The clouds are moving fast and low. A fine drizzle is falling, and the wind coming from the swamps blows in my face. I cannot recall a worse night in all my life.

I hurry into the car and drive out of the yard. The house stands big and black in back of me. Am I angry with Edward? No, I'm not angry with Edward. He's right. I should not go out into this kind of weather. But what he does not understand is I must. Father definitely would have gone if he were alive. Grandfather definitely would have gone, also. And, therefore, I must. Why? I cannot answer why. Only, I must go.

As soon as I turn down that old muddy road, I begin to pray. Don't let me go into that ditch, I pray. Don't let me go into that ditch. Please, don't let me go into that ditch.

The lights play on the big old tree along the road. Here and there the lights hit a sagging picket fence. But I know I haven't even started yet. She lives far back into the fields. Why? God, why does she have to live so far back? Why couldn't she have lived closer to the front? But the answer to that is as hard for me as is the answer to everything else. It was ordained before I—before father—was born—that she should live back there. So why should I try to understand it now?

The car slides towards the ditch, and I stop it dead and turn the wheel, and then come back into the road again. Thanks, father. I know you're with me. Because it was you who said that I must look after her, didn't you? No, you did not say it directly, father. You said it only with a glance. As grandfather must have said it to you, and as his father must have said it to him.

But now that she's gone, father, now what? I know. I know. Aunt Lou, Aunt Clo, and the rest.

The lights shine on the dead, wet grass along the road. There's an old pecan tree, looking dead and all alone. I wish I was a little nigger gal so I could pick pecans and eat them under the big old dead tree.

The car hits a rut, but bounces right out of it. I am frightened for a moment, but then I feel better. The windshield wipers are working well, slapping the water away as fast as it hits the glass. If I make the next half mile all right, the rest of the way will be good. It's not much over a mile now.

That was too bad about the bombing—killing that woman and her two children. That poor woman; poor children. What is the answer? What will happen? What do they want? Do they know what they want? Do they really know what they want? Are they positively sure? Have they any idea? Money to buy a car, is that it? If that is all, I pity them. Oh, how I pity them.

Not much farther. Just around that bend and—there's a water hole. Now what?

I stop the car and just stare out at the water a minute; then I get out to see how deep it is. The cold wind shoots through my body like needles. Lightning comes from towards the swamps and lights up the place. For a split second the night is as bright as day. The next second it is blacker than it has ever been.

I look at the water, and I can see that it's too deep for the car to pass through. I must turn back or I must walk the rest of the way. I stand there a while wondering what to do. Is it worth it all? Can't I simply send the gift by someone tomorrow morning? But will there be someone tomorrow morning? Suppose she leaves without getting it, then what? What then? Father would never forgive me. Neither would grandfather or great-grandfather, either. No, they wouldn't.

The lightning flashes again and I look across the field, and I can see the tree in the yard a quarter of a mile away. I have but one choice: I must walk. I get the package out of the car and stuff it in my coat and start out.

I don't make any progress at first, but then I become a little warmer and I find I like walking. The lightning flashes just in time to show up a puddle of water, and I go around it. But there's no light to show up the second puddle, and I fall flat on my face. For a moment I'm completely blind, then I get slowly to my feet and check the package. It's dry, not harmed. I wash the mud off my raincoat, wash my hands, and I start out again.

The house appears in front of me, and as I come into the yard, I can hear the people laughing and talking. Sometimes I think niggers can laugh and joke even if they see somebody beaten to death. I go up on the porch and knock and an old one opens the door for me. I swear, when he sees me he looks as if he's seen a ghost. His mouth drops open, his eyes bulge—I swear.

I go into the old crowded and smelly room, and every one of them looks at me the same way the first one did. All the joking and laughing has ceased. You would think I was the devil in person.

"Done, Lord," I hear her saying over by the fireplace. They move to the side and I can see her sitting in that little rocking chair I bet you she's had since the beginning of time. "Done, Master," she says. "Child, what you doing in weather like this? Y'all move; let her get to that fire. Y'all move. Move, now. Let her warm herself."

They start scattering everywhere.

"I'm not cold, Aunt Fe," I say. "I just brought you something —something small—because you're leaving us. I'm going right back."

"Done, Master," she says. Fussing over me just like she's done all her life. "Done, Master. Child, you ain't got no business in a place like this. Get close to this fire. Get here. Done, Master."

I move closer, and the fire does feel warm and good.

"Done, Lord," she says.

I take out the package and pass it to her. The other niggers gather around with all kinds of smiles on their faces. Just think of it—a white lady coming through all of this for one old darky. It is all right for them to come from all over the plantation, from all over the area, in all kinds of weather: this is to be expected of them. But a white lady, a white lady. They must think we white people don't have their kind of feelings.

She unwraps the package, her bony little fingers working slowly and deliberately. When she sees the scarf—the seventy-nine-cents scarf—she brings it to her mouth and kisses it.

"Y'all look," she says. "Y'all look. Ain't it the prettiest little scarf y'all ever did see? Y'all look."

They move around her and look at the scarf. Some of them touch it.

"I go'n put it on right now," she says. "I go'n put it on right now, my lady."

She unfolds it and ties it round her head and looks up at everybody and smiles.

"Thank you, my lady," she says. "Thank you, ma'am, from the bottom of my heart."

"Oh, Aunt Fe," I say, kneeling down beside her. "Oh, Aunt Fe."

But I think about the other niggers there looking down at me, and I get up. But I look into that wrinkled old face again, and I must go back down again. And I lay my head in that bony old lap, and I cry and I cry—I don't know how long. And I feel those old fingers, like death itself, passing over my hair and my neck. I don't know long I kneel there crying and when I stop, I get out of there as fast as I can.

ETIENNE

The boy come in, and soon, right off, they get quiet, blaming the boy. If people could look little farther than the tip of they nose—No, they blame the boy. Not that they ain't behind the boy, what he doing, but they blame him for what she must do. What they don't know is that the boy didn't start it, and the people that bombed the house didn't start it, neither. It started a million years ago. It started when one man envied another man for having a penny mo' 'an he had, and then the man married a woman to help him work the field so he could get much 's the other man, but when the other man saw the man had married a woman to get much 's him, he, himself, he married a woman, too, so he could still have mo'. Then they start having children—not from love; but so the children could help 'em work so they could have mo'. But even with the children one man still had a penny mo' 'an the other, so the other man went and bought him a ox, and the other man did the same—to keep ahead of the other man. And soon the other man had bought him a slave to work the ox so he could get ahead of the other man. But the other man went out and bought him two slaves so he could stay ahead of the other man, and the other man went out and bought him three slaves. And soon they had a thousand slaves apiece, but they still wasn't satisfied. And one day the slaves all rose and kill the masters, but the masters (knowing slaves was men just like they was, and kind o' expected they might do this) organized theyself a good police force, and the police force, they come out and killed the two thousand slaves.

So it's not this boy you see standing here 'fore you, 'cause it happened a million years ago. And this boy here's just doing something the slaves done a million years ago. Just that this boy here ain't doing it they way. 'Stead of raising arms 'gainst the masters, he bow his head.

No, I say; don't blame the boy 'cause she must go. 'Cause when she's dead, and that won't be long after they get her up there, this boy's work will still be going on. She's not the only one that's go'n die from this boy's work. Many mo' of 'em go'n die 'fore it's over with. The whole place—everything. A big wind is rising, and when a big wind rise, the sea stirs, and the drop o' water you see laying on top the sea this day won't be there tomorrow. 'Cause that's what wind do, and that's what life is. She ain't nothing but one little drop o' water laying on top the sea, and what this boy's doing is called the wind . . . and she must be moved. No, don't blame the boy. Go out and blame the wind. No, don't blame him, 'cause tomorrow, what he's doing today, somebody go'n say he ain't done a thing. 'Cause tomorrow will be his time to be turned over just like it's hers today. And after that, be somebody else time to turn over. And it keep going like that till it ain't nothing left to turn—and nobody left to turn it.

"Sure, they bombed the house," he say; "because they want us to stop. But if we stopped today, then what good would we have done? What good? Those who have already died for the cause would have just died in vain."

"Maybe if they had bombed your house you wouldn't be so set on keeping this up."

"If they had killed my mother and my brothers and sisters, I'd press just that much harder. I can see you all point. I can see it very well. But I can't agree with you. You blame me for their being bombed. You blame me for Aunt Fe's leaving. They died for you and for your children. And I love Aunt Fe as much as anybody in here does. Nobody in here loves her more than I do. Not one of you." He looks at her. "Don't you believe me, Aunt Fe?"

She nods—that little white scarf still tied round her head.

"How many times have I eaten in your kitchen, Aunt Fe? A thousand times? How many times have I eaten tea cakes and drank milk on the back steps, Aunt Fe? A thousand times? How many times have I sat at this same fireplace with you, just the two of us, Aunt Fe? Another thousand times —two thousand times? How many times have I chopped wood for you, chopped grass for you, ran to the store for you? Five thousand times? How many times have we walked to church together, Aunt Fe? Gone fishing at the river together—how many times? I've spent as much time in this house as I've spent in my own. I know every crack in the wall. I know every corner. With my eyes shut, I can go anywhere in here without bumping into anything. How many of you can do that? Not many of you." He looks at her. "Aunt Fe?"

She looks at him.

"Do you think I love you, Aunt Fe?"

She nods.

"I love you, Aunt Fe, much as I do my own parents. I'm going to miss you much as I'd miss my own mother if she were to leave me now. I'm going to miss you, Aunt Fe, but I'm not going to stop what I've started. You told me a story once, Aunt Fe, about my great-grandpa. Remember? Remember how he died?"

She looks in the fire and nods.

"Remember how they lynched him—chopped him into pieces?"

She nods.

"Just the two of us were sitting here beside the fire when you told me that. I was so angry I felt like killing. But it was you who told me get killing out of my mind. It was you who told me I would only bring harm to myself and sadness to the others if I killed. Do you remember that, Aunt Fe?"

She nods, still looking in the fire.

"You were right. We cannot raise our arms. Because it would mean death for ourselves, as well as for the others. But we will do something —and that's what we will do." He looks at the people standing round him. 'And if they were to bomb my own mother's house tomorrow, I would still go on."

"I'm not saying for you not to go on," Louise says. "That's up to you. I'm just taking Auntie from here before hers is the next house they bomb."

The boy look at Louise, and then at Aunt Fe. He go up to the chair where she sitting.

"Good-bye, Aunt Fe," he say, picking up her hand. The hand done shriveled up to almost nothing. Look like nothing but loose skin's covering the bones. "I'll miss you," he say.

"Good-bye Emmanuel," she say. She look at him a long time. "God be with you."

He stand there holding the hand a while longer, then he nods his head, and leaves the house. The people stir round little bit, but nobody say anything.

AUNT LOU

They tell her good-bye, and half of 'em leave the house crying, or want cry, but she just sit there 'side the fireplace like she don't mind going at all. When Leola ask me if I'm ready to go, I tell her I'm staying right there till Fe leave that house. I tell her I ain't moving one step till she go out that door. I been knowing her for the past fifty some years now, and I ain't 'bout to leave her on her last night here.

That boy, Chuckkie, want stay with me, but I make him go. He follow his mon and paw out the house and soon I hear that wagon turning round. I hear Emile saying something to Mr. Bascom even 'fore that wagon get out the yard. I tell myself, well, Mr. Bascom, you sure go'n catch it, and me not there to take up for you—and I get up from my chair and go to the door.

"Emile?" I call.

"Whoa," he say.

"You leave that mule 'lone, you hear me?"

"I ain't done Mr. Bascom a thing, Mama," he say.

"Well, you just mind you don't," I say. "I'll sure find out."

"Yes'm," he say. "Come up here, Mr. Bascom."

"Now, you hear that boy. Emile?" I say.

"I'm sorry, Mama," he say. "I didn't mean no harm."

They go out in the road, and I go back to the fireplace and sit down again. Louise stir round in the kitchen a few minutes, then she come in the front where we at. Everybody else gone. That husband o' hers, there, got drunk long 'fore midnight, and Emile and them had to put him to bed in the other room.

She come there and stand by the fire.

"I'm dead on my feet," she say.

"Why don't you go to bed," I say. "I'm go'n be here."

"You all won't need anything?"

"They got wood in that corner?"

"Plenty."

"Then we won't need a thing."

She stand there and warm, and then she say good night and go round other side.

"Well, Fe?" I say.

"I ain't leaving here tomorrow, Lou," she say.

" 'Course you is," I say. "Up there ain't that bad."

She shake her head. "No, I ain't going nowhere."

I look at her over in her chair, but I don't say nothing. The fire pops in the fireplace, and I look at the fire again. It's a good little fire—not too big, not too little. Just 'nough there to keep the place warm.

"You want sing, Lou?" she say, after a while. "I feel like singing my 'termination song."

"Sure," I say.

She start singing in that little light voice she got there, and I join with her. We sing two choruses, and then she stop.

"My 'termination for Heaven," she say. "Now—now—"

"What's the matter, Fe?" I say.

"Nothing," she say. "I want get in my bed. My gown hanging over there."

I get the gown for her and bring it back to the firehalf. She get out of her dress slowly, like she don't even have 'nough strength to do it. I help her on with her gown, and she kneel down there 'side the bed and say her prayers. I sit in my chair and look at the fire again.

She pray there a long time—half out loud, half to herself. I look at her kneeling down there, little like a little old girl. I see her making some kind o' jecking motion there, but I feel she crying 'cause this her last night here, and 'cause she got to go and leave ever'thing behind. I look at the fire.

She pray there ever so long, and then she start to get up. But she can't make it by herself. I go to help her, and when I put my hand on her shoulder, she say, "Lou? Lou?"

I say, "What's the matter, Fe?"

"Lou?" she say. "Lou?"

I feel her shaking in my hand with all her might. Shaking, shaking, shaking—like a person with the chill. Then I hear her take a long breath, longest I ever heard anybody take before. Then she ease back on the bed —calm, calm, calm.

"Sleep on, Fe," I tell her. "When you get up there, tell 'em all I ain't far behind."

1968

A. R. AMMONS

(1926–   )

Archie Randolph Ammons, a native of Columbus County, North Carolina, was in his middle forties before he began to receive much critical attention or recognition, but within the last few years he has come to be recognized as possessing one of the most versatile and sustained talents for lyric poetry of his time. His specialties, as William Harmon has written, are "the epigram, the middle-sized nature lyric, and the lengthy and rather casual verse-essay or verse-diary." He has drawn upon his rural North Carolina origins as well as his experience as teacher and businessman to produce poems that combine lyric intensity with a pragmatic, deceptively casual openness of form.

Born in 1926, he was graduated from Wake Forest University in 1949, then worked at various jobs in North Carolina and New Jersey, served as principal of an elementary school in coastal North Carolina, was an executive in a glass manufacturing company, and in 1964 became an instructor at Cornell University where he is now Goldwin Smith Professor of the Humanities.

His first book, *Ommateum* (1955), was scarcely noticed. After a nine-year wait, he brought out *Expressions of Sea Level* (1964), and has produced a book almost every year since. His *Collected Poems 1951–1971* received the National Book Award for 1973. Among other books are *Tape for the Turn of the Year* (1965), *Sphere: The Form of a Motion* (1974), *Diversifications* (1975), and *The Snow Poems* (1977).

A. R. AMMONS

HIPPIE HOP

I have no program for
saving this world or scuttling
the next: I know no political,
sexual, racial cures: I make
analogies, my bucketful of
flowers: I give flowers to people
of all policies, sexes, and races
including the vicious, the
uncertain, and the white.

1971

GLASS

The song
sparrow puts all his
saying
into one
repeated song:
what

variations, subtleties
he manages,
to encompass denser
meanings, I'm
too coarse
to catch: it's

one song, an over-reach
from which
all possibilities,
like filaments,
depend:
killing,

nesting, dying,
sun or cloud,
figure up
and become
song—simple, hard:
removed.

1963

COON SONG

I got one good look
    in the raccoon's eyes
        when he fell from the tree
came to his feet
    and perfectly still
        seized the baying hounds
in his dull fierce stare,
    in that recognition all
        decision lost,
choice irrelevant, before the
    battle fell
        and the unwinding
of his little knot of time began:

        Dostoevsky would think
it important if the coon
    could choose to
        be back up the tree:
or if he could choose to be
    wagging by a swamp pond,
        dabbling at scuttling
crawdads: the coon may have
    dreamed in fact of curling
        into the holed-out gall
of a fallen oak some squirrel
    had once brought
        high into the air
clean leaves to: but

        reality can go to hell
is what the coon's eyes said to me:
    and said how simple
        the solution to my
problem is: it needs only
    not to be: I thought the raccoon
        felt no anger,
saw none; cared nothing for cowardice,
    bravery; was in fact
        bored at
knowing what would ensue:
    the unwinding, the whirling growls,
        exposed tenders,
the wet teeth—a problem to be

solved, the taut-coiled vigor
of the hunt
ready to snap loose:

you want to know what happened,
you want to hear me describe it,
to placate the hound's-mouth
slobbering in your own heart:
I will not tell you: actually the coon
possessing secret knowledge
pawed dust on the dogs
and they disappeared, yapping into
nothingness, and the coon went
down to the pond
and washed his face and hands and beheld
the world: maybe he didn't:
I am no slave that I
should entertain you, say what you want
to hear, let you wallow in
your silt: one two three four five:
one two three four five six seven eight nine ten:

(all this time I've been
counting spaces
while you were thinking of something else)
mess in your own sloppy silt:
the hounds disappeared
yelping (the way you would at extinction)
into—the order
breaks up here—immortality:
I know that's where you think the brave
little victims should go:
I do not care what
you think: I do not care what you think:
I do not care what you
think: one two three four five
six seven eight nine ten: here we go
round the here-we-go-round, the
here-we-go-round, the here-we-
go-round: coon will end in disorder at the
teeth of hounds: the situation
will get him:
spheres roll, cubes stay put: now there
one two three four five
are two philosophies:

COON SONG

here we go round the mouth-wet of hounds:

    what I choose
    is youse:
    baby

1964

CREDITS

INDEX
OF AUTHORS
AND TITLES

INDEX OF AUTHORS AND TITLES